TEN DAYS TO
DESTINY

TEN DAYS TO
DESTINY

The Secret Story of the Hess Peace Initiative and British Efforts to Strike a Deal with Hitler

John Costello

William Morrow and Company, Inc.
New York

First published in 1991 in Great Britain by Bantam

Library of Congress Cataloging-in-Publication Data

Costello, John.
    Ten days to destiny / by John Costello.
      p. cm.
    ISBN 0-688-08662-4
    1. World War, 1939–1945—Diplomatic history. 2. Hess, Rudolf,
1894–1987. 3. Great Britain—Foreign relations—Germany.
4. Germany—Foreign relations—Great Britain. 5. World War,
1939–1945—Peace. 6. World War, 1939–1945—Propaganda.
7. Propaganda, British. I. Title. II. Title: 10 days to destiny.
D750.C67   1991
940.53′2—dc20   91-3372
                                                         CIP

Printed in the United States of America

First U.S. Edition

1 2 3 4 5 6 7 8 9 10

*For my parents and all the others who
fought in World War II and never knew*

CONTENTS

LIST OF MAPS

ACKNOWLEDGEMENTS

"Piecing together the diverse historical record on which this book is based would not have been possible without the help and knowledgeable cooperation of archivists, historians, interviewees, researchers and friends on both sides of the Atlantic.

My gratitude is extended to the staffs of the following institutions: the National Archives in Washington, notably Robert Wolfe, Edward Reese, Terri Hamnet, John Butler, Sally Marks, Kathy Nicastro, Dane Hartgrove – but especially to the inestimable John Taylor. To Robert Parkes of the Franklin D. Roosevelt Library, Hyde Park, I also owe a special thanks, along with the keepers of the manuscript sections of the Hoover Institution at Stanford, the Houghton Library at Harvard, the Stirling Library at Yale and the Georgetown University Library in Washington D.C. Paul Marsden at the National Archives of Canada gave assistance and advice beyond the call of duty. My thanks too to the patient staff of the New York Public Library, the Butler Library at Columbia University, the British Library and the Library of Congress. Dr Andrew Macdonald of the Public Record Office and the staff of the reprographic unit at Kew facilitated the researching and copying of many thousands of pages of British wartime records. Katherine Bligh at the House of Lords Records Office is an expert guide to the riches of the Beaverbrook Collection. At Cambridge the archivists of Churchill College, Trinity College and the University Library provided invaluable assistance. My thanks are also due to the staff of the Manuscripts Division of the Bodleian Library in Oxford and to the Borthwick Institute at Garrowby for access to the papers of

Lord Halifax. The staff of the Archives Nationales and the Records Department of the Ministère des Affaires Etrangères provided assistance in France. In Germany I should like to acknowledge the help given my researches by Dr. Ruth Keipert of the Archives Section of the Auswärtiges Amt in Bonn and by the staff of the Bundesarchiv in Coblenz and the Institut für Zeitgeschichte in Munich. In Stockholm the Riksarkivet permitted me to see their subterranean stack rooms and the revelatory documents in the Swedish Foreign Ministry Archive.

The K.G.B. in Moscow approved unprecedented access to the Soviet archive material provided exclusively through author Oleg Prelin, to whom I am indebted for making available to me documentation he researched in the N.K.V.D. records. The staff of the W. Averell Harriman Institute for Advanced Study of the Soviet Union, Columbia University, New York, particularly Andrea J. Zweibel, were most helpful in assisting with translations and access to their extensive holding of Russian material.

Weaving together this re-interpretation of the most crucial months of the Second World War has involved the specialized knowledge, advice and cooperation of scores of people since I first began following the paper trail in 1982. Major contributions have been made by Robert T. Crowley, the Washington intelligence authority and author, who originally brought the case of the American code clerk to my attention. The late Tyler Kent submitted to lengthy interrogations. I owe a considerable debt to Bruce Lee, whose editorial expertise gave a new dimension to the book. Sadly, Dagmar Henne did not live to see the completion of a project that she encouraged during the years when she was my agent and friend in Germany.

Special thanks are due to James M. Landis, Jean Berknkopf and Susan Leon at William Morrow, my American publishers, and to Mark Barty-King and the production team at Bantam Press in London, who, with Olivier Orban and Anthony Rowley in Paris, have guided this project to international fruition.

The interpretation of the historical records is the sole responsibility of the author, but *Ten Days* draws upon the published and unpublished work of many World War II scholars. A special contribution resulted from correspondence and many hours of discussion with Ulrich Schlie, whose invaluable guidance and critical comments draw on his own extensive researches. Among other members of the academic community who have generously given advice, interviews and guidance are Professor Wilhelm Carlgren; Professor James Barros; Dr. Martin Gilbert; Professor Warren Kimball; Professor Norman Stone; Professor Macgregor Knox; M. R. D. Foot; Dr. Donald Detwiler; Dr. Rheiner Pommerin; Dr. David Carlton; Professor John Burdick; Dr. David Reynolds; Dr.

Richard Griffiths; Professor Trumbell Higgins; Professor Gabriel Gorodetsky and Professor Robin Winks.

Interviews, advice and help had been generously given over the years by other authors, researchers and wartime veterans. In particular I should like to single out for thanks Rupert Allason (Nigel West), Felicity Ashbee, Andrew Barros, Andrew Boyle, Cecil Bryant, Lindsay Charlton, Robert Cecil, Dr. William Corson, Kenneth de Courcy, David Twiston Davies, Kenneth Duke, St Dudley Forwood, Robert Harris, James Hanning, Charles Higham, Duff Hart Davis, Irene Danischewsky, Karel Hille, Lord Home of the Hirsel, Anthony Howard, David Irving, General Sir Ian Jacob, David Kahn, Dr. Georg Knuppfer, David Koskoff, Nicholas Lawford, H.E. Lief Leiflander, Andrew Lownie, Joan Miller, Anthony Masters, Vernon Newton, Colonel Hayden Peake, Walter Pforzheimer, Colonel T. A. Robertson, Andrew Roberts, Sir Frank Roberts, Lord Sherfield, James Rusbridger, Richard Norton Taylor, Dr. Hugh Thomas, Jasper Wight, Mark Weber, Sir Dick White, and Squadron Leader R. G. Woodward.

Logistical support, friendship and encouragement has made this project possible and I extend my thanks to John Alston, Sharon and Stak Avialotis, Robert Entwhistle, Patricia Greenwood, John Hawkins, Kenneth Nichols, David Kagan, Harald Ketzer, Matthew Anderson, Laurence Pratt, Chauncey Smith, Milo O'Sullivan, Hans Zellweger. Chris Hatzissavas of Platinum Travel arranged my international peregrinations. Thanks are also due to my personal bankers, Sandra Carlson in New York and Bill White in London, who kept the currency flowing, and to Adeline Ciego's housekeeping skills. To Julia Wight and Robin Wight I owe my continued gratitude for their generous hospitality and friendship.

London
New York

March 1991

PREFACE

"On 10 May 1941 Rudolf Hess arrived in Scotland bearing – as secret files recently declassified in the United States and the Soviet Union now reveal – an authoritative peace offer and an invitation to support Germany's crusade against the Soviet Union. For fifty years the real object of the Deputy Führer's mission has been shrouded in speculation. On Churchill's orders Hess was discredited as a madman and the real object of his mission entombed in official secrecy.

"Give us the tools and we will finish the job," Churchill had appealed to President Roosevelt. For a year his stirring rhetoric had inspired Britain to defy invasion, but until U.S. soldiers, sailors and airmen were fighting at their side, the Prime Minister and his military chiefs conceded that there was not the slightest prospect of Britain defeating Germany. The military arithmetic in the spring of 1941 was grim. British forces were losing badly on battlefields in Greece and North Africa and in the U-boat war on North Atlantic. If it had become widely known that Hitler was still prepared to let Britain keep her independence and her Empire in return for formal recognition of Germany's *de facto* control of continental Europe, Churchill's authority could have been undermined after surviving an unprecedented no-confidence motion in the House of Commons.

Now the documentary records have come to light that put a new interpretation on the history of World War II. They reveal how leading members of Britain's ruling establishment tried to negotiate peace at the time of the Fall of France. If Hess had been credited as a serious peace emissary in 1941, Churchill had good reason to fear that the "generous" terms he offered would have revived the peace lobby in Parliament and his administration.

The key to understanding what brought Hitler's "winged Parsifal" to Britain in 1941 – and the subsequent British efforts to distort and bury the Hess mission – is to be found in the long-concealed British peace initiatives of the summer of 1940. These show that, despite his own claim to the contrary, Churchill had to bluff and bully a divided and uneasy War Cabinet into rejecting Hitler's tempting peace overtures at the time of the Fall of France. It was a supreme gamble. History has shown that his colleagues were right to be sceptical about the Prime Minister's assurances that Britain had only to carry on the struggle for three months before Roosevelt came to Britain's aid and saved her from going down to certain military defeat. It was more than a year and a half before the Japanese attack on Pearl Harbor brought the United States into the war, enabling a relieved Churchill to proclaim that "we had won after all."

Newly declassified records show how close Britain came to the brink of making peace with Germany in June 1940. If the British had joined the French in accepting Hitler's reasonable terms – as diplomatic logic and military circumstance argued in the wake of Dunkirk – Churchill's administration would have fallen and the Second World War would never have become a global conflict. There was no guarantee that Hitler would adhere to his promises any more than that Britain or her Empire would be saved from precipitous decline and dissolution. Nor is there any certainty that the compromise peace to save the Empire that it now appears was sought by the Foreign Secretary Lord Halifax and his deputy R. A. Butler would in the end have spared the holocaust of the ten million lives that were sacrificed to rid the world of the Nazi tyranny.

What is certain and remarkable is that Churchill in 1940 dictated the course of history by emotion and intrigue rather than with military and political logic. That he succeeded does not diminish his personal achievement, any more than it tarnishes the imperishable glory of Britain's "finest hour." His defiant refusal to negotiate with Hitler was condemned by some British ministers as irrational bravado and lacking in common sense. But Churchill had the rare genius of being able to fulfil his own prophecies. His supreme gamble with Britain's destiny eventually triumphed through a combination of his own dogged courage, good luck and the intervention of the Japanese. Churchill may emerge from the historical record as far more Machiavellian than he portrayed himself or than his biographers have painted him, but no less great.

Churchill's capacity for ruthless intrigue can now be seen to be an important dimension in the diplomatic blackmail and political manipulation in London, Paris, Rome, Berlin and Washington which are the untold story of the climactic summer months of 1940. The fate of Britain and France – and ultimately of western democracy itself – hung on the "walk with destiny" that he began on 10 May 1940. That Friday was the first of ten fateful days during the next three months that determined the ultimate outcome of World War II – and whose fall-out resulted in the Hess mission exactly a year later.

"Historians relate, not so much what is done as what they would have believed," Benjamin Franklin observed two hundred years ago. Now that my own generation has the opportunity for unprecedented access to a far more extensive documentary record of World War II than previous historians, it is to be hoped that this account will inspire others to re-examine the accepted version of this century's pivotal global conflict. In addition to reminding us that "those who cannot remember the past are condemned to repeat it," the American philosopher George Santayana also observed that "history is always written wrong, that is why it is always necessary to rewrite it."

Note. Emphases in quotations added by author unless otherwise indicated.

TEN DAYS TO
DESTINY

Chapter 1

"Gute Nacht, Herr Hess"

"I feel that we are fighting for life and survival from day to day and hour to hour," Prime Minister Winston Churchill declared in the House of Commons on 7 May 1941.[1]

"Members are a bit defeatist," observed Harold Nicolson. He was in the House that afternoon and found it rather like "a hen-coop of wet hens." For the first time since becoming Prime Minister a year before, during the dark days of Dunkirk, Churchill faced parliamentary criticism of his leadership of the war. After a bitter winter when German bombers had systematically blitzed Britain's cities, government censorship had not been able to soften the news that the military forces of the British Empire appeared to be losing the war. Earlier desert victories over the Italian forces in North Africa had dissolved into defeat. General Erwin Rommel's Afrika Corps had steamrollered past the besieged fortress of Tobruk to threaten Egypt and the vital Suez Canal. In April the Wehrmacht had come to Mussolini's aid and had driven the British Army off mainland Greece on to the island of Crete. German support had enabled Italy to intensify the aerial siege of Malta, the Royal Navy's strategic naval base at the centre of the Mediterranean. On the other side of the world, Japan's aggression menaced Britain's weakly protected Empire in the Far East.[2]

The immediate peril to Britain's survival was the rising toll of merchant ship losses in the Battle of the Atlantic. U-boats ranged unchecked against the convoys in "wolf-packs" that were remorselessly gnawing through the seaborne lifeline to the "Arsenal of Democracy" in the United States. President Franklin Roosevelt's

1

Lend-Lease bill to "eliminate the dollar sign" and allow Britain unlimited credit for war supplies had only just squeaked through isolationist opposition in Congress. British hopes that this would bring U.S. Navy help in defeating the U-boats were still unfulfilled. Roosevelt simply could not risk getting too far ahead of American public opinion, which was still strongly against getting directly involved in the war.

"This sudden darkening of the landscape after we had been cheered by a long succession of victories over the Italians is particularly painful," the Prime Minister told Members of Parliament. Lloyd George had criticized Churchill's prescription for defeating Germany as being based on "fatuous" assumptions. Churchill scathingly described the former Prime Minister's contribution as "the sort of speech with which, I imagine, the illustrious and venerable Marshal Pétain might well have enlivened the closing days of Monsieur Reynaud's Cabinet." Hitler, he predicted, was now so bloated by conquest that, "like Napoleon before him," he would make the strategic blunder of attacking Russia. This gave Churchill hope that Britain could survive until America eventually joined the common struggle against the Axis powers. "When I look back on the perils which we have been over, upon the great mountain of waves on which the gallant ship has been driven," Churchill concluded, "I feel sure we have no need to fear the tempest. Let it roar and let it rage. We shall come through."[3]

The Prime Minister's stirring words rallied the House of Commons to an overwhelming show of support. Only three votes were cast against the 447 government majority. As Churchill left the chamber, the spontaneous waving of order papers showed the extent of his popular support. "Winston cheers them up," Harold Nicolson observed philosophically, reflecting that yesterday's wet hens today "all strutted like bantams."[4]

Three days later a direct hit from a German bomb destroyed the House of Commons chamber and shattered the mood of parliamentary confidence. The night of 10 May 1941 brought the most massive air-raid the Luftwaffe had ever mounted. The two thousand lives lost and the damage done to London's historic heart were a dramatic reminder that the strategic odds were lengthening. The raid resurrected the grim question of just how much longer Britain could continue her lone struggle without the direct military intervention of the United States.

Only hours before the Luftwaffe struck its symbolic blow against the forum of democracy where Churchill had rallied the nation to continue fighting overwhelming military odds after the Fall of France in 1940, an emissary from Germany had parachuted on to British soil with an astonishing offer of a negotiated peace. His unarmed Messerschmitt Me 110 fighter had taken off from

2

Augsburg in the heart of Germany six hours before the waves of bombers rumbled into the night skies with their cargoes of destruction. Were these seemingly connected events of 10 May 1941 Adolf Hitler's final bid to wrest a negotiated peace with Britain, or were they just a remarkable historical accident?

The search for the answer to one of the greatest enigmas of World War II has intrigued historians and fascinated writers for nearly fifty years. Taking up the quest has involved following the documentary paper trail through top secret government files and private diaries on both sides of the Atlantic and in the Soviet Union. New documentation from the American and British intelligence records, corroborated by unprecedented access to the Hess files in the K.G.B. archive, argues that the events leading up to 10 May 1941 were not disconnected accidents of history. Hitler, it now appears, chose this moment of crisis to cudgel the British while at the same time offering an olive branch.

"Raid 42"
10 May 1941

Shortly after seven o'clock in the evening on 10 May, the teleprinters sprang into life in the Control Rooms of the Royal Air Force fighter airfields that ringed Britain. THERE IS REASON TO BELIEVE KG 100'S TARGET TONIGHT WILL BE LONDON was the urgent message giving the destination of the crack German pathfinder squadron, whose incendiaries would light the initial fires to guide in the Luftwaffe bomber fleets.[5]

Intercepted radio signals had pinpointed the Luftwaffe's target. Hours in advance of the attack the Germans had begun tuning up the invisible radio beacons that guided the waves of enemy bombers across the Channel and North Sea. One apparently undetected *Knickebein* transmitter did not start fingering the night sky over the British capital until after 10 p.m. Until it swung south to lock in with the others, the Stollberg transmitter in the heart of Germany had been laying down an invisible north-westerly track over the North Sea. Its beam crossed the English coast south of the border town of Berwick-on-Tweed to pass directly over Dungavel hillside south-east of Glasgow. Riding along that beam until the coast of northern England appeared on the horizon was a Messerschmitt Me 110, the twin-engine German fighter that was one of the fastest planes of its time.[6]

The pilot's long flight across the North Sea was aided by the calm weather in the lee of a ridge of high pressure that trailed behind the frontal ridge of clouds south of Norway. The sun was sinking low over the misty coastline when he swung the fighter round to the south over the sea 200 miles due east of the lonely St. Abb's Head promontory on Scotland's east coast. It began piling on speed as it dived from 18,000 feet towards Holy Island and the outlying sandspits of the Farne Islands, the navigational marker that warned the incoming pilot that he was approaching the final and most dangerous stage of his mission. His plane was challenging the most advanced aerial defence system of its time.

Early warning had proved to be a crucial factor in deciding the outcome of the Battle of Britain in the summer of 1940. Although Fighter Command was outnumbered two-to-one by German aircraft, Britain's radar detection had enabled it to concentrate its limited tactical reserves to defeat the Luftwaffe. The lofty towers of the Chain Home radar stations fed their information by telephone to Fighter Command Headquarters in Stanmore, north of London. In the subterranean Filter Room under Bentley Priory, safe from a direct hit, the information was evaluated and correlated with visual sightings from the network of Royal Observer Corps posts that dotted strategic hilltops throughout the British Isles.

"I was lucky that a veil of mist lay over England," the German pilot later recalled. But neither the welcoming mist nor the Me 110's more than 300 m.p.h. speed could hide the German fighter from Britain's extensive radar net. The sudden appearance of this particular intruder on her plot is still fresh in the memory of Felicity Ashby, one of the Women's Auxiliary Air Force "tellers" on duty that evening in the Stanmore Filter Room, whose duty it was to "tell" the range, course and speed of an incoming raider to the Operations Room.[7]

One reason why she remembers so clearly what happened is that "Nothing was going on in that particular part of the North Sea." Another is that she was working with a nervous new W.A.A.F. who was on the receiving end of the telephone line to the Otter Cops Moss Chain Home High radar station, on the Northumberland fells twenty-nine miles north of Newcastle. "We knew that Otter Cops Moss always made mistakes, so that nobody in the Filter Room took its report seriously until it was confirmed," Felicity Ashby said. Confirmation came from the Chain Home Low station at Bamburgh Head shortly after ten, followed by reports from three other stations. Only then did the Filter Room decide they could safely "tell" the intruder on to the Ops Room, where it was given the designation "Raid 42." W.A.A.F. plotters moved a black enemy raid "42" marker on to a giant grid-map of the eastern approaches to Britain.[8]

"Raid 42 was very far out and it was *plotted absolutely consistently* in from the North Sea," Felicity Ashby insisted, recalling its "very unusual track." It appeared to be the latest in a succession of diversionary raids intended to draw attention away from the massive attack that she had been warned would be heading for London in little more than an hour. At the extreme range of the contact, she reckons that it must have been tracked for at least ten minutes before it was confirmed, and that there was therefore a good fifteen minutes in which to warn the sector station to intercept before Raid 42 crossed the coast. As laid down by an April 1941 R.A.F. operational directive, it fell to 13 Fighter Group command to coordinate the interception and shooting down of all intruders that penetrated the northernmost skies of England and both Scottish coasts.[9]

The nerve-centre of 13 Group was at R.A.F. Turnhouse, west of Edinburgh, and the station commander who played a central role in the drama was Wing Commander the Duke of Hamilton and Brandon. "I was then in command of a Fighter Sector," the Duke himself wrote, establishing that he was the man on the spot with the responsibility for responding to Raid 42.[10]

The thirty-seven-year-old Douglas Douglas-Hamilton was amongst the most blue-blooded officers in the R.A.F. Educated at Eton and Balliol College, Oxford, the golden-haired former amateur boxing champion of Scotland had founded the Glasgow air force auxiliary. He had made world headlines in 1933 as leader of the British expedition that made the first flight over Mount Everest. As the Marquess of Clydesdale he had been one of the youngest Conservative M.P.s. When his father died in 1940 he became the premier Scottish Duke, whose hereditary duties included those of Keeper of the Royal Palace of Holyroodhouse and Lord Steward of His Majesty's Household. Called to active service the year before, he was now in command of the R.A.F. station charged with the defence of Scotland and northern England.[11]

"I was in the Operations Room when a lone bandit appeared on the Filter Board out to sea at approximately 22.00 hours" was how Hamilton recalled Raid 42 from notes he made at the time. "*Normal action* had been taken to intercept and shoot down the enemy aircraft," he stated in his official report dated 11 May 1941. "Spitfires at Drem were brought to readiness," according to the Duke's unofficial recollection, "but it was *a section of Hurricanes* from Aclington or Bulmer which were dispatched to intercept, and went very wide of the mark."[12]

Investigation of all the relevant and now declassified Operational Record Books of the R.A.F. fighter squadrons and stations in 13 Group does not support Hamilton's account. Far from showing that "normal action" was taken against Raid 42, the actual logs reveal an extraordinary dilatoriness and lack of response. There is no trace of the "section of Hurricanes" that Hamilton claims were sent up to intercept the Messerschmitt. The records show that during

5

the hour that Raid 42 was in the airspace under 13 Group's control there were only two fighters actually scrambled, in addition to a pair of Hurricanes which were already aloft on a routine patrol. Since the radar warning did not make clear how many enemy aircraft composed the raid, this response appears abnormally puny, especially in the light of Fighter Command "Instruction 17," issued to 13 Group in March 1941, which ordered that on nights when there was a full moon and good visibility, enemy attacks on Glasgow and Newcastle should be countered by defensive "single-engine fighter" patrols.[13]

There is no evidence that fighter patrols *were* sent up that night to guard either city even after the incoming raid had been detected. The planes the Duke claims "went very wide of the mark" were two Hurricanes on a routine coast "dusk patrol" over St. Abb's Head. But the Hurricane did not have the flat-out speed to catch a Me 110, and the patrol did not even sight the intruder. R.A.F. logs confirm that 13 Group at Turnhouse had received the original radar plot and relayed it to the "R" Sector Controller at R.A.F. Usworth. "R" Sector had Spitfires of 72 Squadron ready to scramble at R.A.F. Ouston and Aclington, and they did have the speed and disposition to catch a Me 110. But their logs show that only a single fighter was sent up *after* the raider was already inland and flying fast past their noses. This surprising failure to respond to the radar plot indicating a raider heading for the industrial ports of Tyneside has always puzzled Cecil Bryant, who was on duty that evening in the "R" Sector control room at Usworth.[14]

As a twenty-year-old Radio Telephone Operator who had honed his skills during the Battle of Britain, his task was to provide the link by radio between the Sector Controller, who sat behind him, and the fighters scrambled to intercept enemy aircraft. When Raid 42 appeared on the Usworth plot, shortly after ten, Bryant had a clear view of the plot and of the Army major in the next booth, who was in charge of all the anti-aircraft batteries in the sector. It struck him as unusual that after Raid 42 had been put on the plot there was a delay of more than a quarter of an hour before his controller took any action. "I clearly remember hearing a message stating that *this aircraft was not to be attacked*," Bryant declared, recalling that "the Army major next to me was also given orders not to use ack-ack fire against it."[15]

Suspiciously the R.A.F. Usworth records for May 1941 are missing. The log for neighbouring R.A.F. Aclington shows that it was not until 10.20 – almost a quarter of an hour after the radar plot had been received – that a lone Spitfire was sent up. The pilot, Flight Sergeant Pocock, confirmed that he never even caught sight of the German raider. He was still getting airborne at 10.23, when the Royal Observer Corps post at Embleton, twelve miles up the coast, reported an enemy aircraft passing inland at high speed. Pocock himself admits that he had been scrambled far too late to have any chance of giving chase to the incoming raid.[16]

"The raid was going at a considerable speed," the R.A.F. station log concedes, "the plots jumped too far ahead of him and he was unable to catch it." The Messerschmitt pilot recorded that he saw "a Spitfire in pursuit which I outdistanced" as he sped over the coast, "somewhat south of a small town whose inhabitants must have been terrified when the full throttle of my 2,000 horsepower engines roared at 750 k.p.h. just over their houses and quiet street."[17]

The German plane was so low at 10.25 p.m. that George W. Green, in the Observer Corps post on the border hilltop of Chatton, identified its unmistakable two-engine, twin-rudder silhouette as it raced by at an altitude of fifty feet. Green would later receive the British Empire Medal, but Turnhouse Control rejected his report of a fighter. They put down Raid 42 on their plot as a Dornier 17 bomber. Nor did 13 Group H.Q. revise their misidentification ten minutes later when they received two more Me 110 sightings from the R.O.C. posts at Jedburgh and Ashkirk.[18]

The "hoots of derision that greeted this identification in the Operations Room" were noted by the Duke of Hamilton. Their scorn reflected the R.A.F.'s professional contempt for the Observer Corps amateurs who, according to the Duke, could not know that "an Me 110 was a twin-engine fighter without the endurance to make the return trip to Germany." Their misidentification went unchallenged as the raider flew over the wild border hills and forests where there were no Observer Corps posts. Only when, according to Hamilton, "it reappeared, having climbed again to about four thousand feet, over the county of Ayr," did Turnhouse Control take any further action. "A Defiant was scrambled from Prestwick" and, the Duke stated, was soon *hot on the tail* as the Me 110 spent the next half-hour flying back and forth south of Glasgow.[19]

The R.A.F. records show, however, that there were no Defiant fighters based at Prestwick. But the Operational Record Book of 141 Squadron at Ayr notes that one of their Defiants scrambled at 10.35. Flown by Pilot Officer Cuddie, with Sergeant Hodge as turret gunner, it landed exactly an hour later. Its flight log makes no mention of even spotting the Me 110, let alone of being in "hot pursuit," stating only that this Defiant "attempted to intercept, but failed to do so." It would have been impossible for the lumbering two-seater with its ungainly machine-gun to have been "hot on the tail" of an Me 110, because its top speed was a good fifty miles an hour slower. The Spitfires at Prestwick *did* have the speed to intercept the German fighter – but the station record shows that not one was ordered to scramble. They remained grounded for the night on "normal routine."[20]

It has never been explained why Turnhouse Control decided to send up only one obsolescent interceptor during the whole half-hour that Raid 42 was in the sector south of Glasgow. The shipyards and factories of Clydebank were favourite enemy targets and were ringed by heavy anti-aircraft batteries and nearby fighter bases. In addition to the Spitfires at Prestwick and the Defiants at Ayr, 13 Group could have brought in Hurricanes from Drem or Turnhouse which were less than a dozen minutes' flying time away. While standard R.A.F. operational procedures in 1941 cautioned controllers against scrambling too many planes into a night-time interception, it was not yet dark in these northerly latitudes when the raider appeared in that sector. Moreover, Fighter Command's Instruction 17 specifically laid down that Glasgow must be defended from enemy raids by independent fighter patrols. Since Turnhouse insisted that Raid 42 was a bomber, their failure to respond with the full resources at their command becomes still more surprising.

That was the conclusion reached that night by Major Graham Donald, a World War I Army officer who was then Assistant Group Officer of 34 Glasgow Royal Observer Corps. The city had suffered badly in the Blitz, and as the director of a machine-tool firm he was understandably concerned to protect his factory. When Raid 42 appeared on the plot at Temperance House headquarters he calculated that the German plane was moving at nearly 300 m.p.h., a speed impossible for the Dornier bomber insisted on by Turnhouse Control. He therefore warned the posts under his control to keep a special lookout. Sure enough at 10.45 the observer post at Motherwell reported picking up the characteristic sound-bearing of a twin-engine fighter shortly before the Defiant from Ayr drowned out the faster-moving contact. Major Donald immediately relayed the sightings, together with his calculations, to Turnhouse, with the request that Raid 42 be reclassified as an Me 110.[21]

"It was given to us as a Dornier 215. No mention was made of a Messerschmitt," Major Donald recalled, observing sourly that his request was "not accepted" by the R.A.F. Turnhouse again slapped Glasgow Centre down when it relayed two more visual sightings of an Me 110, reported at 10.55 p.m. from West Kilbride as the German fighter headed out over the Firth of Clyde, twenty-five miles south-west of Glasgow.[22]

"I did not have to look at the map, for I had memorized the most important details," the Me 110 pilot later wrote of his unchallenged aerial dash across Scotland. "At about twenty minutes to eleven I found myself over Dungavel, the estate of the Duke of Hamilton, my unsuspecting host-to-be. But in order to rule out any error, I flew a few minutes farther to the West coast." Overshooting the coast to jettison his empty and potentially explosive "extra petrol tank" into the Firth of Clyde appears to have disrupted his navigational memory map, since he swung back inland, and made the fatal error of not checking the map on his kneepad before heading north-west. So convinced was he that he "recognized the railroad tracks which made a bend near Dungavel" that he did not realize until too late that he was following the wrong lines. More than ten miles too far west of his intended destination, and with daylight and fuel both running out, he vainly flew back and forth looking for Dungavel House and its landing strip.[23]

Shortly after eleven Major Donald relayed to Turnhouse that Eaglesham Moor R.O.C. post, eight miles south of Glasgow, had reported an Me 110 flying an erratic course "as if looking for something." The German had obviously flown a loop to the coast and was now zigzagging back eastwards, south of the suburbs of Glasgow. The pilot, as Hamilton later acknowledged, was "trying to find the Dungavel landing ground" the Duke had laid out on his country estate.[24]

But even if he had found the airstrip, he could not, according to Hamilton, have landed safely, since the Dungavel runway was "virtually on the side of a hill, and although all right for light aircraft and gliding, was quite unsuitable to accommodate an Me 110." This was no longer of concern to the hopelessly lost German pilot, who now had no option but to save himself by bailing out. This was a decision *in extremis*, because he had never thought to practise making a parachute jump. Nor had he practised the difficult manoeuvre of bailing out of a fast-moving aircraft, as his account – which approaches farce – makes very plain. As soon as he jettisoned the canopy he found himself screwed by the slipstream against his seat-back. Attempting a reverse roll that he hoped would drop him from the cockpit caused a black-out. He regained consciousness only just in time to struggle free at the top of the stall before the plane plunged to earth.[25]

"At 23.07 hours, news was received in the Operations Room that the enemy aircraft had crashed in flames," Hamilton wrote, adding "we thought that the Defiant had shot it down." Only later was the Duke "disappointed" to learn the truth. While admitting his Operation Room's "mistake" in dismissing five successive reports of an Me 110, Hamilton's official report implies that the German raider only just escaped being shot down. "A Defiant fighter *in hot pursuit* was approximately four miles away," it states: "It was with disappointment that the Wing Commander learnt that its guns had not been fired." Yet the R.A.F. operational records do not bear out the Duke's assertion of a "hot pursuit." Nor do they provide any evidence at all for his claim that "*fighter squadrons . . . were*

9

sent out to intercept the machine as soon as it was detected." Nor is there anything in any of the squadron flight records to support his statement that *"the patrols missed him narrowly at certain points."*[26]

The declassified R.A.F. records do not show that "normal action" was taken against the Me 110. Quite the reverse. This becomes evident from the log entries before and after Raid 42, which show 13 Group reacting normally to the penetration of its airspace by enemy raiders.[27]

"Almost at the same time a report was received that a big Blitz had started in London," Hamilton wrote by way of justification in his personal account, adding that it was "unlikely that the Turnhouse sector would be bothered by any more action that night." So he left the control room for the Commander's quarters shortly after receiving the Observer Corps report from Eaglesham Moor: "Plane has come down out of control and crashed in flames." All that the Duke of Hamilton admitted knowing when he retired for the night was that the pilot had survived.[28]

"I was rather scared when I saw a parachute dropping from the sky," David Maclean told newspaper reporters next day. He was the ploughman at Flors Farm. He said he had seized a pitchfork and run out of his cottage in his underclothes. The plane had crashed 200 yards away, and he was running towards it when the pilot, who was lying on his back struggling with his parachute, called out in good English that he had broken his ankle. Maclean helped him to his feet and took the limping German to his home. When Lieutenant Clarke, commander of the local Renfrewshire Home Guard Unit at Giffnock, arrived shortly afterwards he found him in an easy chair, sipping a glass of water and passing round snapshots of his wife and small son. He gave his name as Captain Horn. The "Dad's Army" contingent then escorted their prisoner to the Giffnock Scout Hall that served as the 3rd Battalion's Headquarters. At 12.29 a.m. Lieutenant Clarke telephoned Paisley, the headquarters of the nearest regular Army unit, to report the capture of a German prisoner. The sleepy night-duty officer of the 14th Battalion of the Argyll and Sutherland Highlanders suggested that the Home Guard should lock up their prisoner overnight in the local police cell. When the prisoner insisted that he had a "message for the Duke of Hamilton," Clarke decided it was "imperative that he should be interrogated at once . . ." He reported that it took repeated phone calls before the officer at Paisley agreed to send a military escort to relieve the Home Guard of their unusual captive.[29]

"If they cannot catch a Me 110 with a Defiant, I am now going to pick up the bits in a Vauxhall," Major Donald told his staff as, accompanied by an off-duty R.A.F. officer from Ayr, he drove off to Eaglesham at high speed, ignoring Glasgow's red traffic lights. It came as no surprise to him to find that the crumpled remains were indisputably those of a Messerschmitt Me 110. Only a few gallons of petrol remained in its undamaged wing tanks, but his biggest surprise was that the fighter carried neither bomb racks nor ammunition, and its gun barrels were still packed with shipping grease. Baffled as to why a German fighter pilot should set out on a one-way suicide mission over hostile territory in an unarmed plane, he drove to Giffnock.[30]

At the Scout Hall he came face to face with the tall, smartly uniformed German officer, who attempted to prove his identity by producing a postmarked envelope addressed to "Hauptmann Alfred Horn, München 9" and then announced that he "had a secret message for the Duke of Hamilton." To confirm this story he produced his map with a red ring around Dungavel House, where he said he hoped to find the Duke. Major Donald decided that Captain Horn could be "no ordinary pilot," and watching him labour suspiciously long writing out his signature, it struck him that his sardonic expression and black bushy eyebrows were familiar to him from photographs of the Nazi leaders. He began to question him more closely. His real identity became apparent from the sour look, "like a maiden aunt," he gave when Donald asked if he enjoyed Munich's renowned Löwenbrau beer. The Major knew there were two teetotallers in the Nazi hierarchy – Hitler and his deputy Rudolf Hess. And Horn was obviously not the Führer.[31]

"I shall see that your message is conveyed to the Duke," Major Donald assured the prisoner. "I shall also tell him, on my authority, that your true name is Rudolf Hess." The prisoner "jumped about fifteen inches and laughed an exceedingly forced laugh." Donald was now so convinced of the prisoner's identity that he could not resist sharing his sensational discovery with the Home Guard company in the Scout Hall. His revelation was "greeted with hoots of derision."[32]

"Gute Nacht, Herr Hess," Major Donald said as he left the Scout Hall, urging the local police officer and Home Guard to "take very special care of our very special prize." Clarke was inclined to agree, and when the Army escort finally arrived, shortly after 2 a.m., he decided the prisoner should have "an extra measure of courtesy" and be driven in a private car rather than the Army lorry sent to transport him to Maryhill Barracks on the outskirts of Glasgow.[33]

Certain from the German's appearance and reactions that he must be the Deputy Führer, Major Donald drove as fast as he could back to Temperance House. After convincing the duty controller that his identification was correct, he put a telephone call through to the commander of R.A.F. Turnhouse. His report, filed two days later, states that Major Donald was told that the Duke of Hamilton was unavailable. He therefore advised the duty controller that "the plane *was* a Me 110 (stripped), that the pilot came over meaning

11

to surrender." He said the prisoner not only claimed to know the Duke personally, but said he had an urgent message that he would give to no one but Hamilton. He also told the duty controller that "if the name Alfred Horn meant nothing to the Duke, he could say on my authority that the pilot's real name was Rudolf Hess." The R.A.F. officer reacted with dismissive laughter. "I did my best to convince him that I was in dead earnest," Donald wrote, adding that he insisted "that the Duke *should be notified* at the earliest possible moment."[34]

Despite his initial scepticism, the duty controller did telephone through to the commanding officer's quarters. "I thought that another enemy raid had started" was the Duke of Hamilton's reaction on hearing his subordinate, who "demanded that I should return to the Operations Room immediately"; the duty controller said "he *could not divulge* the reason, but . . . I should come at once." Hamilton "crawled out of bed," dressed and went round to the Operations Room, where he was "confronted with the news that the pilot of the Me 110 had asked to see me personally by name, and had given his name as Oberleutnant Alfred Horn."[35]

"There was no precedent for this at all," the Duke wrote; "nothing in King's Regulations to meet the circumstances." He said he first checked a list he had kept from his visit to the 1936 Olympic Games in Berlin, which "noted the names of various German Air Force Officers I had met." When he "went through this list and Horn's name did not appear," he decided the interrogation could wait until the following morning, although R.A.F. standing orders required the immediate interrogation of downed enemy pilots for useful intelligence.[36]

The Duke's version clashes directly with that of Major Donald, who insisted he had informed the Turnhouse duty controller that the German's real name was Hess. If the name of Hitler's deputy did not crop up, why should the Turnhouse duty controller have thought it essential to rouse the Wing Commander from his bed in the middle of the night? Why did he then insist the Duke should return immediately to the Control Room to discuss a matter too secret to entrust to the telephone?

And why did the Duke decide to do nothing until the following morning? In such unusual circumstances it might be expected that he would have immediately consulted his superiors at the Air Ministry. He records only that he went back to bed after making "arrangements to leave for Glasgow early on 11th with the Intelligence Officer whose duty it was to interrogate the German pilot." An Army report later censured the Turnhouse Wing Commander for failing to respond to repeated requests to send over an interviewing officer that night. The prisoner was not only a high-ranking enemy officer but had been mistakenly reported as so badly injured that he might not survive the night. These points emerge from the report of Captain Anthony White, the Night Duty officer at Clyde Army Headquarters, who had concluded that the prisoner's claim that he had "come over to see the Duke of Hamilton" made him a "profitable subject for immediate interrogation."[37]

"The R.A.F. Intelligence Officer at Turnhouse appeared to be in no hurry to interview the prisoner," complained Colonel Firebrace, the Glasgow Area military commander, who did not mince his words. "If it is true that the R.A.F. authorities were informed before 0100 on the 11th that an important prisoner was anxious to make a statement to them, their laxity was most unfortunate," he charged. *"It can only be assumed that the decision to do nothing until the next morning was taken by the Duke of Hamilton."*[38]

Unanswered Questions

The very curious behaviour of the Duke of Hamilton revealed by the official record suggests that, like the fighters under his command, his own reactions that night were very far from normal. One section of the War Office Hess file is still secret. Does it reveal that the Duke's reluctance to confront Rudolf Hess that night might have had less to do with King's Regulations than with the predicament in which he found himself after his command's failure to shoot down Hess's Messerschmitt? When it was revealed in the press on 15 May that Hitler's deputy had risked his life to fly to Scotland to see the Duke, the Wing Commander posted an order at Turnhouse forbidding the communication of "any service information" to unauthorized persons.[39]

The suspicious sequence of events surrounding Hess's arrival were reason enough to make the Duke uneasy. But thirty years later he offered another explanation when he revealed to his son that a month earlier the British secret service had tried to enlist him as a catspaw for a peace initiative involving Albrecht Haushofer, an allegedly homosexual German friend of the Duke's who was also an associate of Hess. This extraordinary plot was apparently so deeply hatched that not even the Prime Minister knew of it. Hamilton always denied that he knew Hess or even recognized him. But the documentary evidence shows that he had not only met Hess but knew of his friend Haushofer's close links with the Nazi Party chief.

Wartime censorship precluded any public investigation of the failure of the R.A.F. fighter squadrons under Hamilton's command to shoot down Hess's plane. A reassuring press agency story that bullet holes had been discovered in the tail of the Me 110 wreckage seemed to show just how lucky Hess had been to escape his pursuers. But the "bullet holes," as any visitor to the R.A.F. Museum at Hendon in north London can see, were made by rivets popping out in the crash. To preserve the face-saving fiction, Churchill banned the public display of the wreckage at an R.A.F. fund-raising exhibition in Whitehall, only two days after the Air Ministry had announced that Hess's plane would be put on show on Horseguards Parade. So the Secretary of State for Air could not be challenged on 22 May when he claimed that "All the usual action was taken to intercept this aircraft, and in fact had he not bailed out Hess was in imminent danger of being shot down."[40]

Rumours immediately began circulating in R.A.F. messes about the enigmatic role played by the Duke of Hamilton. "We all knew the Duke had been part of the pro-German set before the war, so when we heard that Hess had been trying to reach him, we all said 'Well, there you are!'," remembered Felicity Ashby, the W.A.A.F. at Fighter Command Headquarters. Squadron Leader R. G. Woodman, who found himself posted to 13 Group shortly after the Hess flight, heard the same rumours circulating in the mess at R.A.F. Ayr. Woodman, who later retraced Hess's flight across the North Sea in a Mosquito, began immediately after the war to collect eye-witness accounts from R.A.F. and Luftwaffe veterans. After fifty years of single-handed investigation, he still cannot explain why Hess was allowed to fly with impunity for over an hour in airspace controlled by 13 Group, unless, as he put it, the "door was left open" for Hess to slip through. This was the claim made by a "highly reputable observer" in the May 1943 edition of *The American Mercury*. Alongside an article by Winston Churchill, this New York literary quarterly published "The Inside Story of the Hess Flight."[41]

"Far from being a surprise, the arrival of Hess was expected by a limited number of Britishers and the outlines of his mission were known in advance," the readers of *The American Mercury* were told. The claim that "the Nazi leader actually had an R.A.F. escort" is perhaps too fanciful a description of 13 Group's failure to shoot down the Me 110, but the unnamed writer appears to have had access to R.A.F. sources disclosing the early detection of the incoming flight at extreme radar range off the Scottish coast, the initial scepticism at Fighter Command H.Q., the intruder's failure to identify itself and how the radar plot moved so fast that the mystery plane was identified as a fighter way beyond its cruising range. Still more intriguing, the article also cites the alleged instructions issued by Fighter Command not to shoot the intruder down, which, it asserted, R.A.F. "personnel still discuss with varying degrees of puzzlement." The article concluded that the British secret services had lured Hess to Scotland after discovering a peace feeler "not directed to the British government but to a group of influential Britishers, among them the Duke of Hamilton, who belonged to the since discredited Anglo-German Fellowship Association."The message "never reached its destination, but was intercepted by the Secret Service," who then exploited it during "four months of intricate negotiations." Using the names and handwriting of the Duke and his associates, they lured Hess into making his flight, which he undertook, the article states, "not only with Adolf Hitler's blessing, but upon his explicit orders."[42]

Fantastic as these claims appear, many of the details in the article, including the "months of intricate negotiations" and diplomatic manoeuvring through Swiss intermediaries, mesh with the evidence uncovered in once top-secret British, American and Soviet files. Corroboration can also be found in the private correspondence and diaries of the Germans who were involved in the secret peace soundings. Information in these records and German Foreign Ministry files points to the same conclusion: that Hess had the idea for his dramatic personal peace bid in the autumn of 1940, but its discovery by the British secret services enabled them to play him into a trap, using as bait the Duke of Hamilton and British diplomats who were known by Berlin to be sympathetic to a peace deal. The most sensational assertion made in the *American Mercury* was that Hess flew to Scotland "to reach an understanding with Great Britain which would leave Germany free to concentrate everything against Russia."

In recent years all discussion of the Hess affair has been waylaid by the tangential controversy over whether the German who parachuted to Scotland really was Rudolf Hess. Now it is clear that the key to the truth behind the Hess mission is the official silence imposed to conceal the glaring inconsistencies between the Duke of Hamilton's version of the events and the R.A.F. records. That the British government continues to surround the Hess affair with a granite wall of official secrecy is evident from the number of relevant documents that are still classified. The decision to bury the story for ever was taken soon after it made headlines around the world in 1941. Parliament was misled and Churchill, reversing a decision to make a full statement, refused all public comment, prompting President Roosevelt to complain: "I wonder what is really behind this story?"[43]

New Answers

The document that finally provided the key to unlocking the answers to Roosevelt's question came to light in November 1989. It surfaced among the millions of files in the National Archives building whose massive neoclassical colonnades bestride Pennsylvania and Constitution Avenues in Washington D.C.

Every day a hushed line of high-school students files past the row of bombproof, nitrogen-filled glass cases displaying the Declaration of Independence and the Constitution of the United States. Few of the young Americans who make the pilgrimage to this central shrine of their history realize that the building above them houses one of the richest and most accessible archives in the world. Among the most intriguing of the World War II records are the Intelligence Records of the U.S. Army, which are still being declassified. The high acidity of wartime paper and years of poor storage at Fort Meade, the National Security Agency's closely guarded Maryland headquarters, have left many of these formerly top-secret World War II intelligence records – unlike the well-preserved 1776 Constitution – in poor condition. Hours of laborious conservation work are necessary before the brown and crumbling papers can be released for examination by researchers. But amidst the case files relating to long-forgotten investigations of Japanese, German and Soviet spies, the ever-growing index includes such tantalizing references as "Adolf Hitler," "Göring," "von Ribbentrop," and "Eva Braun." It was the file marked "Rudolf Hess" that opened up new leads in the paper trail and a fresh reassessment of the events of 10 May 1941.[44]

Corroboration of the evidence that Hess made his flight to enlist Britain's aid for Hitler's crusade against Russia in the "top secret" U.S. Military Intelligence report came a year later from a surprising source: the K.G.B. archives. As this book was going to press, a Soviet official arrived at my New York apartment on the eve of Thanksgiving Day 1990 to deliver a sealed blue packet that had arrived by diplomatic bag from Moscow. This unprecedented response was the result of a *pro-forma* request filed as a matter of routine six months earlier with little expectation of a reply.

The packet from K.G.B. Headquarters contained the first photocopies of N.K.V.D. cryptograms ever declassified, in addition to reports made for Stalin about Hess that have never been available to western historians. Apart from their intrinsic historic value, the Soviet intelligence reports included a duplicate version of the U.S. Army Intelligence report on Hess supplied by Churchill's aide that had been declassified a year earlier in Washington. It had been passed to Soviet intelligence in London by the head of the Czech Military Intelligence mission who, it now turns out, was a source for the N.K.V.D. The K.G.B. "Hess" File 20566 – codenamed "Black Bertha" – also contains two separate reports received from Soviet agents with British intelligence sources that assert that Hess was indeed lured to Britain as the result of an MI6 plot.

16

Until the British government reverses current policy and releases the relevant section of its historic intelligence service archives, it may be impossible to determine whether the clandestine contacts with Germany that evidently played a part in bringing Hess to Scotland on the night of 14 May were a secret service triumph or part of a sinister peace plot that ran out of control. What is now indisputable is that the Hess mission was very far from being the "brainstorm" of Hitler's deluded deputy that it is *still* being portrayed as by distinguished British historians. The documentary evidence that has now come to light shows that it was the outcome of an interlocking sequence of secret British and German peace manoeuvres that can be tracked right back to the summer of 1940. The missing pieces of this jigsaw puzzle are now falling into place to show that:

- Contrary to his own account, Churchill actively conspired to seize power on 9 May 1940 and succeeded with the aid of a skilfully executed bluff.

- Chamberlain conspired with Churchill to ensure that he became Prime Minister because he knew that Lord Halifax, the Conservative Party's choice, had indicated his willingness to negotiate a peace with Hitler.

- Leading members of Churchill's first War Cabinet saw him as a convenient stop-gap Prime Minster, to be ousted and replaced as soon as Hitler offered a peace deal that would preserve the Empire.

- Hitler's order halting the Panzer advance on Dunkirk was a carefully timed stratagem to persuade the British and French governments to seek a compromise peace.

- A majority of the War Cabinet had decided to trade off Gibraltar and Malta in return for keeping control of the Empire.

- An alarmed President Roosevelt secretly sought Canadian help to stop the British accepting a "soft peace" deal with Hitler.

- French leaders believed on 24 May 1940 that Britain would not fight on but accept a joint peace deal brokered by Mussolini at the end of May 1940.

- Churchill – and Britain – survived only because the Prime Minister resorted to ruthless Machiavellian intrigue and a high-stakes bluff to stop a wobbly Foreign Secretary talking the War Cabinet into a peace deal engineered by R. A. Butler. When France fell, Lord Halifax's Under Secretary actually passed a message to Berlin that "common sense and not bravado" dictated that Britain should negotiate, not fight Hitler.

- The arrest of an American Embassy cipher clerk as a German spy was a "sting" operation orchestrated by MI5 to enable Churchill to force through a draconian law against Fifth Columnists that he used to threaten the parliamentary peace plotters.

- Tyler Kent, the cipher clerk who was tried and convicted in 1940 under the Official Secrets Act, became Churchill's "political hostage" against Roosevelt. The F.B.I. later uncovered evidence that he was a Soviet agent.

- Two days after Churchill had promised "we shall never surrender" Lord Halifax and R. A. Butler signalled to Berlin via Sweden that a British peace proposal would be made after the French armistice on 18 June 1940.

- MI5 reports released inadvertently by the United States reveal that secret British Cabinet records supplied to Ambassador Joseph Kennedy were reaching Berlin.

- Ambassador Kennedy had been in clandestine contact with Hitler's emissaries trying to stop the war while the British government suspected him of illegally profiting from Treasury information to make a killing in international stock and securities dealings.

- The British attempted to compromise Kennedy and force his recall by leaking to the State Department that he might have been the German agent in his Embassy whose codename was "The Doctor."

- Churchill deliberately arranged for his cables to be sent to Roosevelt by insecure American codes to make Hitler aware of their close secret relationship.

- The Duke of Windsor and other members of the Royal Family encouraged German expectations that peace would eventually be negotiable.

- Churchill's decision to order the Royal Navy to sink the French fleet at Oran in July 1940 was a political, not a military necessity, because Roosevelt needed a demonstration of Britain's resolve to continue the fight against Germany.

- F.B.I. wiretaps of the German Consul General in San Francisco revealed that the anti-Churchill faction in the British government continued off-shore peace plotting in the autumn of 1940, when they enlisted the aid of Cardinal Spellman and General Motors Vice-president James D. Mooney.

- The British Minister in Switzerland followed Butler's unofficial instructions to contact German intermediaries, and the Foreign Office had to order him to halt negotiations.

- Hess's plan to fly to Scotland took shape in the final days of the battle for France and was encouraged in September 1940 by his discovery that Britain continued putting out peace feelers via Switzerland and Spain.

- MI5 intercepted Hess's first peace initiative and then turned it into a "double-cross" operation to snare Hess into a trap baited by the Duke of Hamilton and the British Ambassadors in Switzerland and Madrid.

- The Prime Minister did not know of the MI5 operation against Hess, because he was opposed to giving Hitler any hope that Britain might negotiate terms.

- Hess's dramatic arrival left Churchill with no choice but to bury the affair in distortion and official silence in order to protect not only the Duke of Hamilton but senior Tory colleagues who even in 1941 remained convinced that an honourable peace could be struck with Hitler.

For more than fifty years the cloak of British secrecy has clouded and distorted the record. The official histories carefully masked the roles played by the key players in the year-long effort to strike a deal with Hitler behind Churchill's back. Just how close this peace plotting came to succeeding has been concealed to protect the reputations of the British politicians and diplomats who had believed that Hitler was less of a menace to the Empire than Stalin. After 1945, when the opening of the concentration camps had exposed the true horror of the Nazi regime, the reputations of senior ministers were at stake. Churchill also had his own reasons for burying his wartime quarrels with other leading members of the Conservative Party. He did not want any scandal to sully the glory of his leadership during the Battle of Britain and the "white glow, overpowering and sublime, which ran through our Island from end to end." Britain's "Finest Hour" and Churchill's own role in forging it were enshrined as one of the most illustrious chapters in British history. His visionary courage had created, by words rather than military substance, the British people's belief that, against the overwhelming odds, they could defy Hitler in 1940.

"Churchill's contribution was to fling a Union Jack over five tanks and get people to behave as though they were fifteen" was the tribute paid by Aneurin Bevan, one of Churchill's parliamentary sparring partners. Myth-making was still the order of the day after World War II. Britain's military and economic strength was exhausted and her only real claim to world power status was the moral claim to have saved the world from Nazi tyranny by defying Hitler in 1940. As her influence waned and her global empire was divested, the national myth developed into a reassuring national panacea. Churchill himself was not above bending the facts to enhance the legend of sublime national unity during the nation's darkest hour.[45]

"Future generations may deem it noteworthy that the supreme question of whether we should fight on alone never found a place upon the War Cabinet agenda," Churchill declared in his war memoirs. "Never," he assured the readers of his Nobel-prize-winning history of the Second World War, "*was the possibility of a compromise peace ever even mentioned in our most private conclaves.*" While history vindicated Churchill's defiance of overwhelming military odds, the historical record shows how much he had to adjust the facts to conceal the reality of the Cabinet's division over whether to fight on or make peace with Hitler in the summer of 1940.

The patriotic edifice of Britain's body politic was neither as solid nor as sublime as stirring postwar histories make out. The cracks in the edifice of national unity that opened up in 1940 also explain why Hess set off on his peace mission in 1941. Not until 7 December 1941, the day the United States entered the war, could Churchill finally be confident that he had won. The "possibility of a compromise peace" was not only mooted in private Tory conclaves and whispered in parliamentary lobbies but was openly discussed in the War Cabinet. It is one of history's remarkable coincidences that Hess set off for Britain one year to the very day after Churchill became Premier on 10 May 1940. This was the first of the days of crisis during that summer when the fate of Britain and western democracy hung in the balance.[46]

Chapter 2

"Walking with Destiny"

DAY 1
"Your Hour Has Now Come"
A.M., 10 May 1940

"Les Allemands!" the maid shrieked. It was 5.25 a.m. in Brussels on 10 May 1940. American journalist Claire Boothe Luce and *Time Magazine* owner Henry Luce awoke in the top-floor guest suite of the American Embassy in the heart of the Belgian capital. "Wake up! The Germans are coming again!"[1]

The scream of a low-flying plane rent the dawn. The heavy crump of bursting bombs shook the Luces as they rushed to the window. "The house across the street collapsed," Claire Boothe Luce wrote, finding it surprising that only after the attack did the air-raid sirens begin to wail. In the Embassy below, the Ambassador frantically tried to get a transatlantic call put through to the State Department. Four hours earlier John Cudahy had telephoned the President to report that the Belgian Cabinet "believed the German troops would march before dawn." It was a few minutes shy of midnight Washington time when Cudahy got through to Secretary of State Cordell Hull, who could hear the roar of planes and wailing sirens as the anxious Ambassador reported that the invasion of Belgium appeared to have begun. Telephones began ringing in the Chevvy Chase homes of senior State Department officials and in the European legations of Connecticut Avenue's Embassy Row. The news that the Germans had launched their long-awaited attack on the West brought the impact of war home for the first time to official Washington.[2]

"It was more like the ball that Becky Sharp gave in Brussels the night before Waterloo, according to *Vanity Fair*," wrote Assistant Secretary of State Adolf Berle of the large dinner party of

Washington socialites that evening. He was summoned to take a telephone call from the Secretary of State, who told him that German planes were flying over Holland and the Luxembourg government had already fled to France. When he returned briefly to the dinner table the word had already circulated. Berle observed that "The Belgian Ambassador who has a son and a son in law at the front merely lifted an eyebrow and continued to suavely flirt with the ladies."[3]

The State Department officials excused themselves from the table and slipped away to gather, still in their dinner jackets, at the Old Executive Office Building on Pennsylvania Avenue. Many would spend a hectic night rushing between the wire service tickers and the second-floor office of the Secretary of State. Hull and his staff spent much time trying to get priority calls to their European embassies through on the hopelessly jammed transatlantic telephone lines. While he waited for the operators to raise the Paris and Hague embassies, Hull telephoned the White House next door to update the President. When he got through to the Ambassador in London, Joseph P. Kennedy's sleepy reaction provided the only comic relief in a night of serious drama. Although London was only a few hundred miles from the front, the news of the war was taking longer to circulate there than in Washington, nearly four thousand miles away. Kennedy was dumbstruck when Hull told him. "His mind is as blank as uninked paper," Hull announced in his broadest Tennessee drawl, raising a dry laugh from his assembled staff as he slammed the receiver down.[4]

"The war has now begun in earnest," observed Assistant Secretary of State James Pierrepoint Moffat. His words were to be echoed later that morning when President Roosevelt, taut and weary from loss of sleep, addressed his regular Friday press conference. He expressed his "full sympathy" with the "flaming protest" of Queen Wilhelmina at the brutal Nazi violation of the Netherlands' neutrality. The Americans, he said, were "shocked and angered" by the "tragic news" from Europe.[5]

The French Prime Minister, Paul Reynaud, was incensed that he received the news of the German attack not from French High Command but from the Belgian Ambassador in Paris, who telephoned him shortly after 4 a.m. to appeal for help. Although the French H.Q. had received warning at half-past one that morning that the German forces were moving west, it was the Belgian Military Attaché who first alerted General Maurice Gamelin that the attack was under way. The Commander-in-Chief had still not received an official report when he was telephoned by his deputy, General Alphonse Georges, to know whether it was France or Belgium that was under attack. "Since it is the Belgians who are calling us," Gamelin decided, "do you see how it can be anything else?"[6]

22

The Germans wasted no time in trying to portray their invasion as self-defence. Eighty "drowsy, unshaven, breakfastless" news-papermen were summoned to the Foreign Ministry on Berlin's Wilhelmstrasse at 5 a.m. and addressed by Ribbentrop himself. "An attack on the German Ruhr area through Belgium and Holland" by the British and French, the Foreign Minister declared, was in the process of being forestalled by the Wehrmacht, whose advance into Luxembourg, Holland and Belgium was, he claimed, essential "to ensure the neutrality of these countries with all the Reich's military means of power."[7]

Parisians were being roused by the wail of sirens from their slumber at about the same time that morning. "Awakened by air raid about 5 a.m.," Oliver Harvey, Minister at the British Embassy, noted in his diary. He was surprised that it was another three hours before a telephone call from the Embassy belatedly reported that "Germany had invaded Holland and Belgium." The news of the German attack circulated in London that morning with the same official lethargy. The civil servants on night duty in the Whitehall ministries hesitated to disturb their political masters before dawn for anything less than the crack of doomsday.[8]

"I was wakened up at 6 o'clock by a message from the Foreign Office to say the Germans had invaded Holland" was how the For-eign Secretary received the news. Lord Halifax prosaically records that within minutes the Dutch Foreign Minister arrived at the door of his suite at the Dorchester Hotel. "We had a cup of tea together while he gave me a formal Netherlands appeal for help."[9]

"The morning of 10th May dawned and with it came tremendous events," wrote Churchill, his majestic account making no mention that his early-morning nerves needed steadying with anything so mundane as a cup of tea. At six o'clock, clad in silk pyjamas, Churchill, who as First Lord of the Admiralty was also chairman of the Cabinet's Military Co-ordination Committee, was putting a call through to the French Ambassador in London. Could Monsieur Corbin, he demanded, inform him whether the French government would move into Belgium? On the information so far received in London the attack "was on Holland alone." Twenty minutes later the Ambassador telephoned that since Belgium was also now under attack "the whole plan for the advance of the Allied forces into the Low Countries had been set in motion."[10]

"When the news came that the enemy was advancing along the whole front, I could have wept for joy; they'd fallen into the trap!" was how Hitler would recall his euphoria that morning. The Führer had spent a sleepless night poring over the maps of the Allied positions along the western frontiers as his command train steamed through the darkness. It had pulled out from Berlin shortly after nine o'clock, when the code word DANZIG began the final countdown to Hitler's bold military gamble, which marked the end of the 250-day-long "Sitzkrieg." The first rays of dawn were cracking the eastern skies over the forested slopes of the German Ardennes as the Führer's command train pulled into its camouflaged siding at *Felsennest* (crags nest), his headquarters bunker deep in the forests near Bruly le Pêche. An hour after dawn came the news that the Eban Emael fort guarding the Meuse bridges east of Liège had fallen. Hitler was delighted, and his nervousness evaporated. The immense fortress had been built as the lynchpin of Belgium's defence in the expectation that it would hold up a German attack for at least a week.[11]

"Your hour has now come and the battle that begins today is to decide the fate of the German nation for the next thousand years" was the rousing message sent out by Führer headquarters. Hitler then went outside to gloat with mounting satisfaction as the steel vanguard of tanks forged westwards through the narrow forest roads that France's military strategists had written off as "impenetrable" to armoured movement. There were now three widely separate columns, totalling more than fifteen hundred tanks, grinding their way towards France's heavily fortified frontier ninety miles to the west under the protective umbrella of Luftwaffe fighters. The French were still unaware of the German Panzer columns snaking through the Ardennes. This force packed such heavy firepower that Hitler was supremely confident that it could easily punch its way through the static French defence lines and any force that Allied Commander-in-Chief General Maurice Gamelin could muster against it.[12]

"Gamelin is saved. Now he has the battle he waited for and for which he never ceased to prepare and hope," Paul Reynaud observed sourly to the Secretary of the War Committee. Paul Baudouin had arrived at 7.30 a.m. at the French Premier's apartment, a stone's throw from the National Assembly, France's parliament building. Reynaud was a dapper little man with the quick punctilious mind of a lawyer. As he finished dressing, he glanced at the appeals for help received from the governments of Holland and Belgium. Then he spent several minutes studying the large map of the Republic's north-eastern frontiers. Pinned to a wall tapestry, it had taken over the first-floor salon overlooking the tranquil Place du Palais Bourbon. General Gamelin's overstaffed headquarters at Vincennes outside Paris had just sent out confirmation of the order that would send Allied forces advancing, according to the predetermined plan, into Belgium. Supremely confident that the Germans, by attacking Belgium as predicted, were marching into the trap that the Allied armies had spent months preparing, Gamelin insisted that the direction of the attack had not taken him by surprise. Not only had it been anticipated, but since preparations for it were complete he had restored regular army leave three days before. Reynaud, who nursed a deep distrust of Gamelin, turned from the map and remarked to Baudouin that he hoped the Commander-in-Chief knew what he was doing. Despite all the assurances, Reynaud was anxious that the Germans would attack the French First Army during its move north, when it would be at its most vulnerable.[13]

"I am disturbed," Reynaud said. "We shall see what Gamelin is worth." He had good cause to be nervous. He made it no secret that he considered the Commander-in-Chief a "nerveless philosopher" who lacked the qualities of action and vision to lead France's armies in this hour of national peril. The previous afternoon the crisis-prone Third Republic had been plunged once again into political turmoil when Reynaud's efforts to dismiss Gamelin had been thwarted by his foe Edouard Daladier, the Minister of National Defence, whom Reynaud had displaced as premier seven weeks earlier.[14]

"Mickey Mouse" was how his enemies disparagingly referred to Reynaud. He did not lack for opponents, because he had the combative self-assertiveness of a man of small physical stature impatient to scale the loftiest pinnacle of political power. Mentally agile, Reynaud had never concealed that he set out to "master, not to charm." Intensely patriotic, he had angered the reactionary French military establishment before becoming premier by championing the visionary Colonel Charles de Gaulle's theories of armoured warfare. Like Churchill, whom he worshipped, Reynaud had for years been the voice crying in the wilderness warning of the growing threat of Nazi militarism. But in contrast to Churchill, whose adventurism often made him his own worst enemy, Reynaud's Achilles' heel was a woman. His political career was held hostage by his mistress, Madame Hélène de Portes. What this haughty Parisienne lacked in *bien soignée*, she more than made up by her opinionated efforts to dominate not only her lover but also his ministerial colleagues. Characterized as "far more like Diana clinging to her charger than Venus clutching her prey," Madame de Portes had ruthlessly deployed the poison of secret slander against Daladier. When her campaign of calumny helped bring him down, she earned the undying enmity of the deposed premier and his own intimate, the Marquise de Crussol.[15]

Even without the burden of a mistress who nagged him constantly by telephone, Reynaud's hold on the premiership was precarious. As a conservative spokesman for the fragmented right-wing groups, he lacked a strong power base in the left-leaning Chamber of Deputies. This put him at a disadvantage in his attempts to impose his authority on Daladier, whose continued presence as Minister of National Defence in the French Cabinet Council was insisted on by the powerful Radical Party as the price for their continued support of the coalition government.

Reynaud was determined to inject new vigour into the war effort. One of his first acts on becoming premier was to rectify Daladier's hesitation by signing a joint declaration with Britain that neither country would negotiate a separate peace with Germany. His other objective was to revive declining army morale by replacing the Commander-in-Chief. When his proposal that Gamelin should resign to be replaced by either General Georges or Weygand was again resisted by Daladier, he resigned his entire Cabinet on 9 May. France technically had no government when the Germans attacked the next morning, but the President of the Republic insisted that the military emergency required the "un-resignation" of the Prime Minister.[16]

Hitler had therefore saved not only General Gamelin but also Reynaud, whose supporters regarded him as a Gallic Churchill. He now prepared to make the best of a difficult situation and live up to his other nickname of the "fighting cock." On paper he had every reason to feel confident that the massive Allied ground forces under Gamelin's command could resist the German attack. After nine months' digging-in during the "Phoney War" the 144 French, British, Dutch and Belgian divisions amounted to a formidable force.

The Allied right flank was securely hinged on to the Maginot Line. As impressive as the Great Wall of China when seen on maps at Vincennes, this awesome defence line, named after the French Defence Minister who initiated its construction, extended 87 miles from the Swiss frontier of France to the Belgian border. Bristling with armoured mortar emplacements, machine-gun embrasures and bunkers, supported by subterranean barracks and serviced with ammunition by an underground railway, the Maginot Line had been conceived as a great immovable "shield" that would protect the vitals of France. It was intended to free the huge French army to wield its mighty "sword" on the plains of Flanders, the traditional invasion route taken by the Kaiser's armies, which had very nearly smashed through to Paris during World War I.

A static "Maginot mentality" had infected Gamelin and the French generals. Their arthritic strategy resisted Colonel Charles de Gaulle's proposal for two divisions of tanks to constitute an effective "sword" that could be wielded from behind the protective Maginot "shield." The military atrophy of the French General Staff was exacerbated by the Belgian government's adamant insistence on observing strict neutrality. King Leopold of the Belgians declined to permit a single Allied soldier to violate his country's neutral soil until the first German soldier crossed the Meuse, when the British and French would advance north to defend Belgium as well as France. So when the Germans attacked that Friday, the nearest Allied troops were an average of fifty miles and more than two days' march from the Belgian front line. The logistics of moving twenty-two divisions of the French First Army, supported by the nine British Expeditionary Force divisions, into Belgium under heavy air attack, to try to stabilize a rapidly collapsing Belgian front, gave the Allied military planners nightmares.[17]

German military intelligence anticipated the serious tactical and strategic flaws in the Maginot Line and the Allies' plan to send their armies into Belgium in the event of a German invasion. Hitler had argued, bullied and finally ordered his military staff to abandon their preference for a dusted-off version of Germany's 1914 "Schlieffen Plan," and it had taken many revisions before the strategists of the German Army High Command O.K.H. (Oberkommando des Heeres) had come up with the Operation Yellow (*Fall Gelb*) plan that Hitler considered combined the daring and imagination of a scheme for which he would claim credit. Its strategy was essentially that of the matador. German Army Group B was to launch a strike into Holland while simultaneously thrusting into central Belgium north of Liège. This was the matador's cape that would bring British and French armies advancing into Belgium with all the blind inertia of a charging bull. The main weight of the German Panzer divisions concentrated into Army Group A would push through the Ardennes Forest, break through the French defences north of the Maginot Line and slice through with a fast dash to the channel coast. With their supply and communications lines cut off, the Allied armies in Belgium would then be caught between the closing jaws of the giant military vice of the two German armies.

Hitler brushed aside the caution of his generals, who worried about whether such a daring breakthrough could be achieved, since traditional military strategy dictated that an attacking force needed a two-to-one superiority to break through a strong defence such as the Maginot Line. The answer was the heavy concentration of armoured columns supported by close air support and motorized infantry. The so-called Blitzkrieg tactics that the German strategists had developed from the tank-warfare theories of Britain's military theorist Basil Liddell Hart had proved remarkably effective against Poland. They were about to be put to the test again when the German Army High Command O.K.H. sent the 8 May order to the commanders of the 138 German divisions poised along a 250-mile front: "YELLOW, 10 May 1940, 05.35."[18]

When it came to countering the audacious Blitzkrieg strategy, during the critical first day of the German attack, the Allied command lacked the flexibility and vision to be able to mount an effective response. Allied strategic decision-making was exercised through Anglo-French committees under a Supreme War Council that met alternately in London and Paris. This top-heavy bureaucracy made it impossible for the Allies to adjust their military decision-making to the speed and fluidity of armoured warfare. This was to become apparent within a few hours of the Germans launching their attack, when the Air and War Ministers, Sir Samuel Hoare and Oliver Stanley, arrived at the Admiralty shortly after 6 a.m. to discuss the news from France.

Churchill, "far from being shaken by failure or disaster," according to Hoare, was "smoking his large cigar and eating fried eggs and bacon, as if he had just returned from an early morning ride." In the historic Upper War Room of the Admiralty the Chiefs of Staff awaited him to chair the Military Co-ordination Committee. But they could do little more than take note of the latest appeals for help from the Belgian and Dutch governments. General Sir Edmund Ironside, the mastiff-like Chief of the Imperial General Staff, reported that the British and French armies had been ordered to begin their northward march into Belgium, and the Committee approved the decision to send two additional R.A.F. fighter squadrons to France.[19]

"We sat for half an hour listening to rumours that were coming in," Ironside wrote in a diary that crackles with the frustration of a professional soldier trying to run the war by means of committees dominated by politicians. As the war bureaucracy ground on that Friday morning in London, mounting panic set in across the Channel in Holland. At first light German parachutists had begun dropping down among the blazing tulip fields around Amsterdam. The Hague, Leiden and Rotterdam were all targets for fierce enemy attack as the Luftwaffe rained bombs down on Schiphol Airport on the outskirts of Amsterdam. Less than two hours' flying time from London for an enemy bomber, Britain's War Cabinet met at 10 Downing Street at 8 a.m, still astonishingly unaware of what was actually happening at the battle front.[20]

"The troops were not at the highest state of readiness," Churchill reported of the British Expeditionary Force, "but they would certainly be on their way quickly." Seemingly oblivious to the urgent demands of the hour, he then insisted on demonstrating his latest technical gadget. Promising that it "wouldn't take a minute," according to Ironside, he proceeded to explain the intricate workings of a proximity-fuse anti-aircraft shell. "We are impossible," Ironside complained as they wasted valuable time before Churchill moved on to explain what was actually being done to further the war. This included Operation Royal Marine, his long-delayed scheme for floating mines down the Rhine, for which, the First Lord declared, "steps were in motion." He also announced that naval demolition parties were already on their way to disable Dutch port facilities, and British troops in the West Indies had been sent by warship to forestall a German takeover of the oil facilities on the Dutch Caribbean islands of Aruba and Curaçao.[21]

Yet when it came to dispatching British aircraft to attack German industrial targets in the Ruhr, the War Cabinet once again bogged down in cavilling hesitation. The R.A.F. was told that it could only send its heavy bombers to attack targets west of the Rhine "in order to impede the advance of German armies." Bombing of the German steelworks in the Ruhr or of railway marshalling yards was still not permitted. The War Cabinet meekly agreed with Chamberlain's belief that it was "preferable not to begin bombing operations" until they had "definite news" that German attacks "would cause civilian casualties." The Prime Minister's reluctance to prosecute the war ruthlessly and vigorously had mired the British government for weeks in a political wrangle every bit as paralysing as that which beset the French Prime Minister.[22]

"Neville still reigns, but only just," was the assessment of Henry "Chips" Channon, M.P., who had since 1938 been Parliamentary Private Secretary to R. A. ("Rab") Butler, the Under Secretary of State for Foreign Affairs. Channon had arrived at his office that morning to find Whitehall in a state of confusion. This he attributed to the "Mandarins," the permanent officials who "seemed more downhearted that the invasion of the Low Countries has probably saved Chamberlain than cast down by the invasion itself." As a staunch supporter of the Prime Minister he believed that "Neville was saved," because "his policy had been vindicated swiftly and surely within twenty-four hours." But his confidence proved hopelessly misplaced. In a matter of hours his adored Neville announced his intention to resign and his particular bête noire Churchill became Prime Minister, even though, as Churchill himself later conceded, the irony was that the military disaster in Norway that played such a large part in lofting him into power had been largely of his own making.[23]

"Playing Tin Soldiers"
January–May 1940

The Allied adventure in Norway had its roots in Chamberlain's reluctance to fall in with French plans for a Scandinavian operation during Finland's "Winter War" with the Soviet Union. This had infuriated the then Premier, Daladier, who was under domestic political pressure to send Allied support to the Finns in their gallant struggle against the invading Red Army. While the British sympathized with the struggle waged by Finland, their refusal to commit troops or ships to an Allied expeditionary force was a simple matter of logistics. Churchill had believed in March that the French proposal would prove an "unprofitable diversion" of resources from the war with Germany. He argued instead for an Allied intervention limited to mining the coastal waters of Norway to disrupt Germany's Swedish iron-ore supplies, which were transported overland by rail to Narvik and then shipped south down through the Norwegian Leads when winter ice closed the Baltic.[24]

Negotiations on settling the three-month-old war were successfully concluded in Moscow on 13 March 1940 before the Allies' Swedish expeditionary force had even been mobilized. A day earlier, however, Churchill had persuaded the British War Cabinet to go ahead with a more limited operation to capture Narvik as part of his plan for cutting off the Germans from their ore supplies. Fearing that such an aggressive move would "completely alienate the sympathies of Norway and Sweden," the Prime Minister persuaded the War Cabinet to put the Narvik operation on hold. Churchill, complaining about the "fiasco in Scandinavia," proceeded to lobby the French for a revised scheme to mine the Norwegian Leads without a landing.

In the end it was not pressure from France but a Swedish intelligence report that Germany was about to seize Norwegian airfields that persuaded Chamberlain to change his mind and give his approval to Churchill's mining operation. Reynaud had just succeeded Daladier as France's Premier. Aware that his political opponent's failure to act in the Finnish crisis had accelerated his fall from power, Reynaud was looking for some demonstrative action and so was persuaded to approve Churchill's scheme for floating mines down the Rhine from Strasbourg. The Supreme War Council meeting at 10 Downing Street on 28 March authorized the launching of these two mining operations to begin simultaneously on 5 April.

A mood of springtime optimism that these Allied initiatives would break the paralysis of the Phoney War prevailed in London and Paris despite the rumours of an imminent German attack on Belgium. The French government had resolved its crisis and Chamberlain had responded to press and parliamentary criticism of his lacklustre leadership by reshuffling his Cabinet on 3 April. But this did not still the criticisms of some Conservative backbenchers, elder statesmen and peers who were furious that Chamberlain had appointed the unrepentant appeaser Sir Samuel Hoare to the Air Ministry. Led by the influential Lord Salisbury, they constituted themselves into a "Watching Committee of the Government" to review strategy and to demand "a proper War Cabinet." Chamberlain, his confidence restored by his reshuffle, had no intention of stepping down, and as a rebuke to the incipient Tory rebels he gave a bombastic speech on 2 April to the Conservative Party Council in which he declared "Hitler has missed the bus."[25]

Chamberlain might have been wiser than to tempt fate again after claiming two years earlier that "peace in our time" was guaranteed by the scrap of paper he had signed with Hitler at Munich. The Germans were moving fast. A convoy of troopships escorted by a powerful force of warships sailed a week later to carry out "Weserübung," the operation for invading Denmark and Norway. Churchill had announced to the War Cabinet on 8 April that the minefields for "Operation Wilfred" had been laid in Vest Fjord. The next day, as the Supreme Allied War Council met in London, the Germans completed their lightning takeover of Denmark, occupied Oslo and installed the puppet government of the Norwegian Fascist leader Vidkund Quisling. The same day German forces landed at Trondheim and Narvik without any interference from the Royal Navy. It was a spectacular demonstration that it was the Allies, not Hitler, who had "missed the bus."[26]

The Supreme War Council responded to the German invasion by deciding to order "strong forces" to Norway. A French Alpine Division and two British battalions were detailed to sail within forty-eight hours. But their destination became a matter for fierce debate. Churchill wanted to go ahead with his earlier plan to capture the port of Narvik in the far north, while the Secretary of War argued that a strategically more important target was Trondheim, the ancient capital in central Norway. Conceived in indecision and planned in a muddle, when it was eventually launched the Norwegian campaign turned into a disaster.[27]

"You cannot make war by referring everything to Committees and sitting and wobbling and havering," General Ironside lamented, exasperated that Churchill's Co-ordination Committee had "usurped the functions of the General Staff." The first Narvik troop convoy was ready to put to sea when, in the small hours of 14 April, Churchill told Ironside that Trondheim must also be captured to inspire the Norwegians to go on fighting. He demanded that the Narvik force be split in two. Ironside warned the First Lord that such a disruption would put both operations at risk. Churchill was adamant. He left Ironside to make "improvised decisions" for mounting a pincer movement by two forces, one landed at Namsos and the other at Adalsnes, north and south of the Trondheim Fjord.

As Churchill had been warned, the communications problems of the divided command quickly became insurmountable. At Narvik, Admiral of the Fleet the Earl of Cork and Orrery and Major General Macksey were plagued by command problems even before the landings began on 15 April. Nor did fortune smile on the troops who were landed at Namsos and Adalsnes. Progress towards Trondheim was agonizingly slow under constant bombing in the inhospitable

31

terrain. Fresh German troops were rushed up on the railway line from Oslo. But Churchill continued to "paint a rosy picture," forgetting "all the administrative snags." The First Lord sent a battleship to join the Narvik force, when snowshoes would have provided more assistance to British troops ashore. After a week's hard fighting, very little progress had been made towards capturing the port of Narvik.[28]

"Too many damned strategists who all have a finger in the pie, all amateurs who change from minute to minute and are either very optimistic or very pessimistic," Ironside snapped on 23 April. He was now engulfed by talk about "desperate situations" and "evacuation" as it became obvious at the 26 April War Cabinet, even to Churchill, that the Trondheim expedition would have to be abandoned and the French alpine troops transferred north to reinforce the Narvik operation. "Political effect disastrous," Ironside predicted after the decision had been taken without calling a Supreme War Council. The French General Staff were "flabbergasted," and alarmed that the Swedes might capitulate to German demands. As King Haakon, along with Norway's ministers and nine millions in gold, embarked on a British warship for evacuation to Tromsö in the far north, Churchill brushed off his responsibility for the debacle at Trondheim. He blamed the generals for their bad advice and sought the Prime Minister's authority to preside at the meetings of the Chiefs of Staff. Ironside saw that his only hope was that Churchill would tire of "playing tin soldiers on a map" and let the Chiefs of Staff get on with their job.[29]

The growing press and parliamentary clamour against Chamberlain was encouraged by Lord Salisbury and his "Watching Committee," who chivvied senior members of the government throughout the Norwegian campaign. The younger Tory backbench rebels Harold Macmillan and Harold Nicolson began calling for Chamberlain to resign, making common cause with opposition Labour and Liberal Party groups. Even senior Tories had come to resent the iron grip imposed by Chamberlain's henchmen on his two-hundred-seat majority; a special target for their hostility was the Conservative Chief Whip, Captain David Margesson. The leader of these dissidents was Leo Amery, a respected former First Lord of the Admiralty and Secretary of State for the Colonies who had remained out of office because of his outspoken opposition to appeasement. Amery's seniority among Conservatives made him an effective spokesman for the Watching Committee as Chamberlain's political stock crashed during the stalling Norwegian campaign. But as late as the third week in April the Tory rebels could not reach a consensus over who should take over as Prime Minister. Meetings with the two obvious candidates, Winston Churchill and the Foreign Secretary, Lord Halifax, had failed to produce a preference. Finding themselves "rather at sixes and sevens as between Halifax and Winston," they decided on 1 May to call for a national government "without bothering about personalities." Amery declared that he was for change and then change again until the right man emerged, quoting the muleteer's maxim, "always swap mokes crossing a river till you find one that won't founder."[30]

The danger was that Hitler might not be willing to permit the luxury of time to find the right mule. David Lloyd George made known his doubts whether a new war leader would emerge if Chamberlain was unseated, but the canny World War I premier was influenced by his growing anticipation that, despite being in his seventies, he himself might be the elder statesman called on in the last resort to lead the country. He cryptically told Amery that he would not agree to join a National Government "until really wanted." The Liberal leader Sir Archibald Sinclair proved more amenable, but he pointed out to Amery that the Tories must "make up their minds as to Halifax or Winston." The press baron Lord Beaverbrook was still unshakably resolved that Chamberlain could only be removed by a "palace revolution" within the War Cabinet. The Labour Party was the single largest group in opposition to the Tories in Parliament, but its leader, Clement Attlee, had already declined an offer from Chamberlain to join a National Government. He wanted to hold his party aloof from the fray until a parliamentary showdown was in sight. The faltering Norwegian campaign provided the catalyst that united the rebel Tories, Labour and Liberal MPs to force the resignation of the Chamberlain government.[31]

"A Westminster War"
3–9 May 1940

The mounting torrent of press and parliamentary criticism of the Norway debacle mysteriously slid off Churchill like water off a duck's back and diluted the faltering authority of the Prime Minister. The First Lord's larger-than-life image as the only man of action in the government appeared to absolve him. "Winston, to whom as much blame should attach as any other single individual, will ride triumphantly forward on the wave of undeserving national popularity," predicted John Colville, one of Chamberlain's private secretaries. "One of Hitler's cleverest moves has been to make Winston Public Enemy Number One, because this fact has helped to make him Public Hero Number One at home and in the U.S.A."[32]

The poker-faced Foreign Secretary Lord Halifax was unusually forthright over the great efforts being made to attribute the Norwegian failure to "timid colleagues restraining the bold, courageous and dashing Winston." As an insider he knew that "the exact opposite would be at least as near the truth." But truth was disregarded as the public and parliamentary mud-slinging campaign grew more bitter.[33]

"A Westminster war added to a German one is really too much," huffed Chips Channon. "It is terrible that the P.M. and Halifax should have to suffer this additional strain when all their energies are needed to win the war," he complained as the Chief Whip forecast the greatest political crisis since 1931. On 3 May the Prime Minister's statement on the withdrawal from Trondheim sought to oil troubled waters by assuring the House that in Norway "the balance of the advantage rested with us." Far from calming the tempest, his deceptive statement roused a fresh storm of parliamentary fury. "The House knows very well that it was a major defeat," Harold Nicolson declared. Some M.P.s were "so distressed" that they began canvassing Lloyd George as a possible Prime Minister, because they felt that "Churchill is undermined by the Conservative caucus," and "Halifax is believed (with some justice) to be a tired man."[34]

"There is considerable political clamour, but I doubt whether this, at present at all events, will amount to much," Halifax himself observed with all the Olympian detachment of a member of the Lords. "I do wish, though, that the P.M. would pull in Labour," he wrote, in the belief that Chamberlain would have to adopt this strategy if he were to survive. The Prime Minister faced a two-day emergency adjournment debate called by Labour for 7 and 8 May to discuss the Norway expedition. On the eve of the political showdown, Halifax took the highly unusual step of sounding out Herbert Morrison, Attlee's front-bench colleague, on the possibility of Labour joining a coalition. It remained an "open question," he reported that evening to the Prime Minister. On the afternoon of 7 May the full force of parliamentary dissatisfaction with Chamberlain hit him squarely when he entered the House.[35]

"Missed the bus?" cried Opposition M.P.s sarcastically. "Missed the bus!" Outside, the London skies that Tuesday were a cloudless blue, but political storm clouds had been gathering in the packed and sultry Chamber. Foreign ambassadors, members of the public and the press jammed the galleries. Mrs. Chamberlain sat alone in the Speaker's Gallery dressed as for a funeral; only a bunch of violets pinned to her coat relieved her sombre black attire. Channon thought she "looked infinitely sad as she peered down into the mad arena where the lions were out for her husband's blood." Contrary to expectations, there were many hours of speechmaking before a single drop of political blood was spilt.[36]

The Prime Minister opened the debate on which his future depended with "a dull exposition of the whole business." "The flop might have been heard in Birmingham," Amery observed. Attlee, responding for the Opposition, criticized the government's failure in Norway and dismal conduct of the war in an intentionally low-key attack calculated to avoid rousing the Tories to the defence of their embattled leader. Only in the closing moments of his speech did he express the country's general dissatisfaction by asserting that "to win the war we want different people at the helm from those who led us into it."[37]

"Wars are not won on masterly evacuations," declared the Liberal leader Sir Archibald Sinclair. His speech heaped scorn on Chamberlain's claim that the withdrawal of British forces from Trondheim had been a "masterly success." Not until Sir Roger Keyes caught the Speaker's eye did the political lightning bolts begin to crack round the Chamber. The hero of the World War I raid on Zeebrugge rose to speak in the full-dress uniform of an Admiral of the Fleet, complete with six rows of medals. His broadsides against the naval conduct of the Norwegian campaign brought the first thunderclap in the storm that broke over the government front bench. By the time Amery delivered his condemnation, the passions of the House were aflame. Taking his cue from the baying "Hear, hears" of approval, he concluded with a direct attack on the Prime Minister, quoting "with reluctance" Oliver Cromwell's historic injunction to the Long Parliament. "You have sat too long for any good you have been doing," Amery reiterated, gazing down on Chamberlain from the backbenches. "Depart, I say, and let us have done with you. In the name of God go!"[38]

"These were terrible words coming from a friend and fellow colleague of many years," wrote Churchill, himself no mean performer when it came to parliamentary denunciation. Amery's attack did not so much stab his leader in the back as lance the abscess of resentment against Chamberlain that had been festering for months. It set the stage for Labour members to urge that Attlee should call for a division after the debate was adjourned for the night. This had the effect of transforming the second day into a motion of no confidence in the government, as the Tory rebels decided that night to combine forces with the Liberals and vote in defiance of the three-line whip. On the morning of 8 May, the Labour M.P.s, scenting blood, outvoted Attlee, who reluctantly agreed that the Opposition should call for a division.[39]

When Herbert Morrison reopened the debate that afternoon by calling for a vote of censure on the government, Chamberlain's anger got the better of his normally ice-cold judgement, and he jumped to his feet to interrupt, "showing his teeth like a rat in a corner," according to Hugh Dalton, who was sitting a few feet

35

away on the opposition front bench. "I accept the challenge," the Prime Minister declared, with ill-restrained venom. "I ask my friends, and I still have some friends in the House, to support the Government tonight in the lobby."[40]

The taunt was an invitation that no opposition M.P. could resist. It also challenged the rebel Conservatives to register their disgruntlement, and their determination to defy the whip only increased in the course of the evening as the Prime Minister's Parliamentary Private Secretary Lord Dunglass (who would himself become Prime Minister later as Sir Alec Douglas-Home) did his best to bargain with the rebels, promising that if they supported the government Chamberlain would sacrifice the two most unpopular former appeasers in Cabinet: Samuel Hoare, the Secretary of State for Air, and Sir John Simon, the Chancellor of the Exchequer.

The Tory rebels told Chamberlain's emissary that "Things have gone too far." Back in the Chamber the same message was being rammed home on the government front bench.

Lloyd George, rising to the occasion, gave a vivid demonstration that old age had not diminished his ability to spellbind the House. Chamberlain, he scornfully said, had called for sacrifice. Arms flailing, he declared in a Welsh lilt burning with anger: "I solemnly say that the Prime Minister should give an example of sacrifice because there is nothing which can contribute more to victory in this war than that he should sacrifice the seal of office."

The Opposition roared out "Hear, hear, hear," and Chamberlain sat through the noisy tempest in silent fury, his clenched hands frozen beside him. Churchill sprang to his Prime Minister's defence, reminding honourable members that he took his "full share of the burden" for decisions taken at the Admiralty. In a deadly intervention directed at absolving his old friend, Lloyd George scored another direct hit on the Prime Minister by advising that the First Lord of the Admiralty "must not allow himself to be converted into an air-raid shelter to keep the splinters from hitting his colleagues."[41]

After the Chamber had subsided, it fell to Churchill to wind up for the government. That afternoon, when Tory rebel Harold Macmillan had met him in the smoking room, he had wished him luck but said he hoped he would not make his speech too convincing. "Why not?" Churchill asked. "Because," Macmillan replied, "we must have a new Prime Minister, and it must be you." To which the First Lord responded gruffly that he "had signed on for the voyage and would stick to the ship."[42]

Churchill wound up the debate with "a slashing vigorous speech," according to Chips Channon, who nevertheless was convinced that Churchill relished the irony of having to speak for a cause in which he did not really believe. Heckled throughout by Labour members, he did not attempt to excuse or dwell on the military failures or to discuss the question of who bore the blame. Instead he sought to justify the execution and objectives of the Norwegian operations. Peppering his defence of the government with sardonic invective against the Germans which raised Conservative cheers, he ended with an eloquent appeal for unity: "I say let pre-war feuds die: let personal quarrels be forgotten, and let us keep our hatreds for the common enemy."[43]

Whatever his underlying motives, Churchill's masterly speech unleashed the passions of M.P.s on both sides of the House but left him unscathed as the members crowded into the lobbies. Loyal Conservatives jeered "Quislings" and "Rats" at the Tory rebels who defied the three-line whip to file into the "No" lobby with Labour and Liberal M.P.s. "Yes-men," they hurled back at the government supporters passing through the "Aye" lobby. When the Speaker announced the tellers' call of 281 for the "Ayes" and 200 for the "Noes" pandemonium broke out in the Chamber. There were cries of "Resign" from the Opposition. The Tory rebels, led by Harold Macmillan, joined in singing *Rule Britannia*. Chamberlain's supporters tried to drown them with cheers for the victor.

The Prime Minister might have won the division, but his bowled-over appearance as the figures were announced was a visible confirmation that he realized his victory was a hollow one. The government's 213 majority had plummeted to 81. Eight Tory rebels had voted with the Opposition and a further 60 abstained. "Neville may survive, but not for long," Channon reflected. But what he termed the "fatal division" left him wondering "shall I too crash when the Chamberlain edifice crumbles?"[44]

Churchill, asked immediately after the debate for his opinion on whether the government would survive, ventured that he was "doubtful." The Prime Minister nevertheless hurried off to Buckingham Palace to reassure the King that all would be well. Smilingly, Chamberlain explained that he had not yet come to offer his resignation; he hoped to be able to reconstruct his Cabinet on the basis of a national coalition.[45]

Winston or Halifax?
9 May 1940

The morning newspaper headlines on Thursday, 9 May, left no doubt in the public's mind that the Tory rebels had stabbed their own Prime Minister in the back. Lord Salisbury, visibly "distressed," spoke to a 9.30 a.m. meeting of the Watching Committee. The consensus was that a national coalition government was "essential," and since Labour would not enter any coalition containing Chamberlain, Hoare or Simon, Amery said, "they must go." Lord Salisbury agreed to convey this "immediately" to Lord Halifax and to suggest that Chamberlain should consider it his "patriotic duty" to step down at once and call on "either Halifax or Winston to form a real War Cabinet."[46]

Churchill was of course not unaware that he was the favoured candidate of most of the younger rebels in his party, but he was not the Conservative Party's heir apparent; too many members of the Establishment regarded him as a brilliant but unpredictable maverick. His strongest card was his immense popularity amongst the ordinary voters. As the only politician of national stature who had continuously and consistently warned of the dangers posed by Hitler, he would easily have run away with the popular vote if Prime Ministers were elected by the people. But, under the constitutional rules that bound the Conservative Party until the 1960s, the outgoing Tory Prime Minister had the exclusive right of advising the monarch on the choice of his successor. Many Establishment Tories had not forgotten or forgiven the bitterness with which Churchill had assailed the government over appeasement or the relentless parliamentary warfare he had waged in the inter-war years against his own party's bills to reform the government of India. The union men on the Labour benches also remembered how as Home Secretary Churchill had sent troops against striking Tonypandy miners during the South Wales labour dispute of 1912. Despite his brilliant speech, the Norway debacle had also resurrected memories of the disastrous Dardanelles campaign that had forced him to resign from the Admiralty in the First World War.

"Had it not been for your years of exile & repeated warnings re. the German peril, Norway might well have ruined you," Clementine Churchill noted in a perceptive marginal comment on the original manuscript of her husband's memoir. Nor were Churchill's foes to be found only among his political opponents. Even members of his harassed staff at the Admiralty privately regarded the First Lord as a "menace" because of his constant interference in operational matters. "The danger to my mind," Captain Ralph Edwards, the Deputy Director of Operations, confided to his diary, was a government headed by "that arch-idiot Winston." Echoes of that same distrust and apprehension of Churchill's dominant personality were shared in the upper reaches of the Foreign Office. "Winston useless," wrote the Permanent Secretary, Sir Alexander Cadogan, reflecting on the political crisis. "N. C[hamberlain] is the best PM in sight. The only alternative is H[alifax] and that would be the end of that."[47]

These were the factors that Churchill had to weigh that morning with Eden in his spacious bathroom at Admiralty House. While the First Lord shaved, they plotted his strategy for winning the premiership in spite of the Whitehall and parliamentary odds heavily stacked against him. If Churchill was to succeed, he had to play a close hand of political poker, appearing to support the Prime Minister and at the same time relying on his public popularity and the backing of the handful of Tory rebels to raise the stakes. Chamberlain had to acknowledge that no candidate he advised the King to send for could succeed unless Churchill was willing to serve under him, which made it impossible for that candidate to be anyone but himself.

Eden, as a junior member of the Chamberlain government, had to remain outwardly loyal. So Churchill relied on his devoted parliamentary aide Brendan Bracken and the gregarious Robert Boothby. That Thursday, as Churchill attended a War Cabinet meeting and pressed on with the Narvik operation, his small band of parliamentary supporters fanned out to lobby their fellow M.P.s in the Palace of Westminster and the clubs of St. James's and Pall Mall, reinforcing the belief of Conservative Party men that the Prime Minister could not long survive. At the same time they had to indirectly promote Churchill's candidacy by casting doubt on the suggestion that Halifax, his main rival, could make an effective Prime Minister in the House of Lords. But Chamberlain was fighting back.

"The Old Man was telephoning personally from 8 a.m. onwards, trying to conciliate opponents of yesterday," Labour front-bencher Hugh Dalton observed sourly. "He seems determined to stick on – like a dirty old piece of chewing gum on the leg of a chair." Rumours reached the rebel Conservatives that Chamberlain was sounding out Labour leaders and seeking to split their own ranks by offering a Cabinet post to Amery and junior ministerial jobs to some of the backbench rebels.[48]

Rumours were being spread by Chamberlain supporters that Labour would refuse to serve under Churchill because of Tonypandy. Others maintained that if Chamberlain was forced to resign, he intended to hang on to his control of the party by splitting the power of his principal contenders and remaining in the Cabinet as premier in all but name. This depended on two factors: Halifax's willingness to become Prime Minister in the Lords and Churchill's agreeing to be War Minister in the Commons, with Chamberlain as Chancellor of the Exchequer and party leader. This was the scheme that appears to have been in the Prime Minister's mind when he told Halifax at 10 a.m. on Thursday morning that he "thought that it was clearly Winston or myself, and appeared to suggest that if it were myself he might continue to serve in the Government."[49]

"I put all the arguments that I could think of against myself, laying considerable emphasis on the difficult position of a Prime Minister unable to make contact with the centre of gravity in the

House of Commons." Chamberlain may have been dismayed, but he continued to press this scheme as the best solution to the government's crisis. Halifax's diary shows that his reluctance to serve as Prime Minister was not so rock hard that he was not prepared to reconsider: "If it failed," he reflected, "we should all, no doubt, have to boil our broth again." What is clear from Halifax's long diary entry for 9 May is that Chamberlain *never* unconditionally offered the Foreign Secretary the chance to become Prime Minister *in his own right*. This could explain why he wrote that "the evident drift of his mind left me with a bad stomach ache."[50]

The Foreign Secretary's reluctance to succeed to the highest office of state would be convincing if he had not already known he was the front runner in the race. Two days earlier his Under Secretary, Rab Butler, had come to talk to him about that very issue. He had been sent by Chamberlain's Parliamentary Private Secretary Dunglass to "persuade him to become Prime Minister." Before Halifax went to Downing Street that Thursday morning, Butler had also written to tell him that key members of the Labour leadership he had canvassed had all agreed "there was no other choice but you." This letter stated that "Churchill must stick to the war" and emphasized that Labour had *"no objection* in the Lords difficulty." Halifax was therefore well aware *before* he met with Chamberlain that he was the favoured son, not only of the Conservatives, but also of the leading opposition members. Did Halifax's rejection of Chamberlain's offer have more to do with the strings attached than with his too-much-protested reluctance to accept the premiership?[52]

It would have been surprisingly out of character if Lord Halifax's stomach spasm was caused by fear of responsibility. After six years as Viceroy of India, the pinnacle of authority in the Empire, Halifax had held the highest offices of state for nearly a decade. He was not only accustomed to exercising authority; it had been bred into the marrow of his gaunt six-foot-four frame. A fine horseman, despite a withered left hand, he liked to portray himself as the bucolic fox-hunting squire of Garrowby Hall, his beloved Yorkshire estate. But Halifax was by profession a *grand seigneur* of Conservative politics, cast in the true-blue mould of Victorian England's ruling classes. Heir to a viscountcy, he had progressed from Eton and an effortlessly brilliant Oxford academic career, crowned by an All Souls fellowship, to a career of public service which began when he entered Parliament in 1907 as Conservative member for the Yorkshire seat of Ripon.

Since boyhood, Frederick Lindley Edward Wood had been destined to join Britain's ruling elite, and he had been conscientiously grooming himself to rule with the same attention to outward appearance that he insisted on for the immaculate hunters in his stables.

Halifax's career makes it probable that the spasms that gripped him when Chamberlain asked him to consider becoming Prime Minister were triggered not by feelings of personal inadequacy but by sickness that he was not being offered the pinnacle of political power for which he had been preparing himself. The extremely subtle and devious intellect that had earned Halifax the soubriquet of "The Holy Fox" caught only too well the drift of Chamberlain's no less cunning mind. The Foreign Secretary was a "cool, passionless, unemotional man" who had built his career on his intellectual capacity for "assimilating information and analysing it." He would have understood perfectly well that Chamberlain intended him to be a figurehead Prime Minister in the Lords and in a power-sharing triumvirate which would put him very much at a disadvantage. For five years Halifax had dutifully shouldered the burden of appeasement and carried it through in the teeth of Foreign Office opposition. After such loyal service, Chamberlain's denial of real power was enough to give any politician of Halifax's stature a belly-ache.[52]

Halifax did not want to play Herbert Asquith to Churchill's Lloyd George and repeat the 1916 power struggle that had quickly cost Asquith his premiership. In comparison with Asquith, he would be at a double disadvantage, since in the Lords "I should have no access to the House of Commons," he repeated for emphasis. "The inevitable result would be that being outside both these points of vital contact I should speedily become a *more or less honorary Prime Minister*, living in a kind of twilight just outside the things that really mattered."[53]

Confronted with the prideful reluctance of the Foreign Secretary to fall in with his stratagem, Chamberlain proposed they discuss the matter with Churchill later in the afternoon. They then both went off to a 12 o'clock War Cabinet meeting in the Prime Minister's Room in the House of Commons. The battle over the succession was temporarily set aside to discuss the real war priorities in Norway, and for aircraft production and civilian defence. Halifax reported that at 2 a.m. that morning the American Ambassador had relayed a warning received by Washington that Germany had presented an ultimatum to Holland. He dismissed it loftily, saying that the Foreign Office could find no confirmation for it.

Over lunch, closeted with Eden and Sir Kingsley Wood, the Lord Privy Seal, the strategy that preoccupied Churchill was dealing with Halifax, not Hitler. Eden noted in his diary that "Kingsley thought that W. should succeed and urged that if asked he should make plain his willingness." Eden would later write that Kingsley Wood had "shocked" them both by alerting Churchill to the fact that Chamberlain wanted Halifax to become Prime Minister. "Don't agree, and don't say anything," Kingsley Wood advised Churchill, laying down how he was to conduct himself at the afternoon meeting with Halifax and Chamberlain. Eden's surprise was not that Halifax was Downing Street's heir apparent, but that the Lord Privy Seal should have broken ranks to deliver the warning. Kingsley Wood, one of Chamberlain's closest political allies, was considered so sycophantic by the Foreign Office that Cadogan referred to him as "a chicken-hearted little mutton-head." But the Lord Privy Seal obviously gave Churchill good reason to take his advice seriously. Churchill's own record omits any mention of the lunch, but his account of the afternoon meeting confirms that he followed the advice Kingsley Wood had given.[54]

"I have had many important interviews in my public life, and this was certainly the most important," Churchill wrote. "Usually I talk a great deal, but on this occasion I was silent." Chamberlain's diary records only that he "understood" that since the Labour Party preferred Halifax, he "*had him in mind*," but that the Foreign Secretary "decided that after careful reflection he would find it too difficult being in the Lords." It was Halifax who kept the most detailed contemporary record of one of the most critical cabals in modern British history, from which Churchill, who supposedly had entered as underdog, emerged as Prime-Minister-in-Waiting.[55]

"At 4.30 I went across to No. 10 and the PM, Winston, David Margesson and I sat down to it," Halifax wrote, noting how Chamberlain's parliamentary henchman remained silent as "The PM re-capitulated the position and said he had made up his mind that he must go, and that it must be Winston or me. He would serve under either." The final decision depended on whether Labour would "on principle be prepared to join the government (a) under the present Prime Minister, or (b) under other leadership." The Chief Whip then stressed that "unity was essential and that he thought it was impossible to attain under the PM," but he "*did not at that moment pronounce very definitely between Winston* and myself." Halifax adds: "my stomach ache continued." When he responded, it was to agree "that for the reasons given the PM must probably go, but that I had no doubt at all in my own mind that for me to take it would create a quite impossible position."[56]

Churchill's more colourful account puts a very different construction on what was said. His attribution of this crucial meeting to the following day gives reason to doubt the accuracy of his assertion that Chamberlain made his preference for Halifax clear at the outset by expressing his concern that Churchill's "heated controversy with the Labour Party" in the debate "might be an obstacle to my obtaining their adherence at this juncture." Churchill writes that he "remained silent" during the "long pause" before Halifax announced that he "felt that his position as a Peer out of the House of Commons, would make it very difficult for him to discharge the duties of Prime Minister in a war like this." After Halifax had explained his reservations, Churchill said, "it was clear that the duty would fall upon me." Only then did he speak. He guardedly agreed with Halifax's rationale and promised that he "would not attempt to influence the Opposition parties until he had the King's commission to form a government."[57]

Churchill's account does not mention that Chamberlain also made clear his willingness to "serve under either" – the inference being that this was making a condition rather than volunteering a concession. Nor does he record that Chamberlain said that if Halifax was chosen, "Winston would be running defence." The prospect of being an "honorary Prime Minister . . . living in a twilight world just outside the things that really mattered," gave him spasms. Further corroboration that Halifax really *did* want to be Prime Minister, but did not want the honorary post he was offered, comes from the account he gave to Alexander Cadogan at the Foreign Office immediately after the meeting. "It would be a hopeless position," Halifax declared. "If I was *not in charge* of the war [operations] and if I didn't lead in the house, *I should be a cipher.*"[58]

Only after Halifax had declined to serve under such restraints did Churchill seize the opportunity that Kingsley Wood had suggested would be his if he acted out the script he was given. Halifax noted in his diary: "Winston, with suitable expressions of regard and humility, said he could not but feel the force of what I had said. PM reluctantly, and Winston evidently with much less reluctance, finished by accepting my view."[59]

Only after Halifax had ruled himself out of the running did Margesson concede that he had "found a growing feeling in the Labour Party on the point of the House of Lords." According to Halifax, the cabal ended on a somewhat inconclusive note. "So there we left it for the moment," he wrote, "Winston and I having a cup of tea in the garden while the PM kept some other appointment before we all saw Attlee and Greenwood together at 6.15."[60]

The consultation with the Labour leaders, which Churchill, surprisingly, also omits from his own account, determined the outcome of the government crisis. Evidently Chamberlain still sustained some hope that he could charm them into joining his Cabinet so that he could remain Prime Minister. "It was incredible," Attlee later told his biographer. "He seemed to have no idea that he was finished. He seemed to think he could carry on." Attlee was amazed when Chamberlain asked the Labour leaders to serve under him in a National Government. That Churchill intervened with his own ardent invitation was more understandable to Attlee. "Winston had Norway on his back," he observed, recalling that Churchill "was quite sincere" because he "cared more about getting a government that could win the war than about who was to be prime minister." Halifax recorded that the Labour leaders "were a bit evasive, but eventually said they did not think they could get their Party to serve under the PM." Churchill's eloquent testimonies to Chamberlain's efficiency, charm and dispatch were cut short by Greenwood. "This is not a time for oratory," interjected the deputy Labour leader. "The truth of the matter is that there is not one on our side who trusts the Prime Minister."[61]

"Our Party won't have you and I think the country won't have you either," Attlee told Chamberlain. Confronted with the reality that he had no choice but to resign, the Prime Minister remained silent. "Until that moment he thought he could hang on," Attlee suggested, recalling how Chamberlain had then asked whether Labour would join a Cabinet formed by another Conservative leader? Attlee replied that this was possible, but he would have to consult his colleagues. "It was finally left that they should consult their Executive tomorrow on the two points, would the Labour Party join in principle (a) under Neville, (b) under someone else," Halifax records. "They were to telephone tomorrow afternoon 'yes' or 'no' to both." The succession was still unresolved when the meeting broke up. Parliament had already recessed for the Whitsun holiday, and some in Chamberlain's private office were hoping that the week-long holiday might act as a political restorative for the Prime Minister.[62]

"Mr. C. might serve as Minister without Portfolio and right hand man in a Government headed by Winston or Halifax" was how John Colville summed up informed Downing Street opinion that Thursday evening. So despite Churchill's later assurance that he was a shoe-in to the premiership, contemporary records suggest that the final outcome of the power struggle was still in the balance. Even Churchill's parliamentary champion Bob Boothby, who reported that night that "Opinion is hardening against Halifax as Prime Minister," and "you are the inevitable Prime Minister," admitted after the war that he had been wildly optimistic. "The King, the Prime Minister, and a great majority of the Conservative Party wanted Halifax," he wrote in his memoirs. Looking back, he recalled that on Thursday evening he had learned that Attlee and Greenwood "would have settled for Halifax." Dalton had told Butler that "my own view, which I thought was shared by a number of others, was that *it should be Hfax*," and that a prime minister in the Lords would have "some advantages in relieving the strain on him." Dalton confirmed that Attlee "agrees with my preference for Halifax over Churchill, but we both think that either would be tolerable." That was the proposal that they decided to put the next day to the Executive Committee of the Labour Party at its Bournemouth conference.[63]

It had taken Hitler's attack on Poland to get Churchill back into the government, and now the Führer once again played an unwitting hand in making the First Lord Prime Minister. When the Blitzkrieg attack on Holland and Belgium began next day, the leadership struggle came to a head after Chamberlain attempted to turn the military crisis into a lifeboat to save his premiership.

"Winston and His Rabble"
P.M., 10 May 1940

"Imagine the drama of the situation," U.S. Ambassador Joseph P. Kennedy cabled to Washington at 9.40 a.m. that Friday morning. "Here was Churchill realizing his life's ambition to become Prime Minister, spending the night arranging his Cabinet, arranging to announce it at six o'clock tonight, and Hitler invades Holland." Kennedy reported being shown a letter from Chamberlain "to a friend of mine written within the last hour," in which the Prime Minister stated that although he had "agreed to a reorganization plan with Winston and Halifax last night," Hitler's attack had "changed the entire situation" and Chamberlain therefore did not believe that "now was the time for the reorganization" of the Cabinet. "I propose to remain," Chamberlain declared. "The next three or four days' battle will determine the fate of civilization for the next hundred years."[64]

The Prime Minister launched his desperate move to save his administration by sending his Parliamentary Secretary Lord Dunglass to Lord Salisbury's house off Piccadilly, where the Tory rebels were in conclave. When they insisted that the reconstruction of the government must go ahead regardless, the Prime Minister's emissary argued that the "actual danger of the moment" made it impossible for the government to fall. To carry the government through "these first anxious hours," Dunglass proposed a "triumvirate of Chamberlain, Churchill and Halifax." This proved unacceptable to the rebels, who wanted Parliament recalled and Chamberlain out of the Cabinet.[65]

An emergency meeting of the Labour Party National Executive Committee at 10.30 decided not to ask for a recall of Parliament, for fear that the Chamberlain cheer-leaders would rally round and rehabilitate him. Then Chamberlain telephoned from Downing Street to tell Attlee that the German attack had changed the whole situation: Chamberlain felt he should remain in office for the time being. "Not at all," replied the Labour leader, urging him to give way to his successor as soon as possible. "This old man is incorrigibly [a] limpet and is always trying new tricks to keep himself on the rock," Dalton snorted.[66]

Sir Kingsley Wood arrived at the Admiralty shortly after ten to tell Churchill that Chamberlain felt that "the great battle which had broken upon us made it necessary for him to remain at his post." He said he had advised the Prime Minister that "on the contrary, the new crisis made it all the more necessary to have a National Government which alone could confront it." Kingsley Wood said that Chamberlain had "accepted this view."[67]

After a meeting with a haggard minister of the Dutch government, who had just flown from Amsterdam, the First Lord rushed off to the second Cabinet meeting of the day at 11.30 a.m. In the ante-room the Chancellor of the Exchequer, Sir John Simon, criticized Churchill for continuing to press for changes in the Cabinet at a time of great crisis. "Personally, I think if there are to be changes, the sooner the better," Lord Hankey, the Minister without Portfolio, interjected. The political crisis was ignored as the Cabinet concluded that they could not yet order the R.A.F. to bomb the Ruhr and that the Whitsun Bank Holiday should not be cancelled. The Prime Minister and his wife then went off to lunch at the Dorchester with the Halifaxes.[68]

"All quite pleasant and easy," the Foreign Secretary reported in his diary adding that Chamberlain "had the feeling that Winston did not approve of the delay, and left me guessing as to what he was about to do." But Amery's diary clearly shows that Churchill *already knew* the outcome and was proceeding with steps to form the nucleus of his Cabinet. He noted that he "went round after lunch to the Admiralty to see Winston," who, having pledged him to "strictest secrecy," confided that "he meant to keep Neville in the Government as leader of the largest Party." This came as a shock to Amery, who later regretted that he did not "expostulate." He also learned that Churchill intended to "keep defence in his own hands." Then they discussed Amery's possible role in the new administration before he went off to break the unwelcome news about Chamberlain to the Tory rebels. If Churchill was confidently working on a Cabinet that already included Chamberlain more than two hours before the Prime Minister announced his formal decision to resign, it can only indicate that their deal must have been struck before lunch.[69]

Chamberlain was in the Cabinet Room chairing the third session of the day at 4.45 p.m. when the Prime Minister's secretary telephoned the Bournemouth hotel where the Labour executive were meeting to know whether they had their answers to the two questions. Attlee came to the phone and said "No," Labour would not agree to serve under Chamberlain, but "Yes," they would join a government "under a new Prime Minister." The note was taken into the Cabinet Room and handed to Chamberlain, who completed the agenda with a discussion about steps to counter an invasion of Britain by German parachutists before making his eagerly awaited announcement.[70]

"The Labour Party," the Prime Minister said quietly, "are prepared to take their share of responsibility as a full partner in a new Government, under a new Prime Minister, which would command the confidence of the nation." Accordingly he had "come to the conclusion that the right course was that he should at once tender his resignation to the King." In keeping with tradition he did not say who he was going to recommend to the King. Within half an hour his car was speeding through the tall gates of Buckingham Palace.[71]

"I accepted his resignation & told him how grossly unfairly I thought he had been treated & that I was terribly sorry that all this controversy had happened," George VI wrote in his diary. The "informal talk over his successor" which followed appears to have strained constitutional precedent, because the King, not the Prime Minister, "suggested that Halifax" should be called to the Palace. When Chamberlain explained that the Foreign Secretary was "not enthusiastic" because he was in the Lords, the "disappointed" monarch insisted that Halifax was "the obvious man," proposing that the Halifax peerage "should be placed in abeyance for the time being."[72]

The King's diary leaves no doubt about his conviction that Chamberlain was making a terrible error in recommending Churchill. George VI's official biographer described the King as "bitterly opposed" to Chamberlain's recommendation of Churchill. He had expected the Prime Minister to recommend him to send for Lord Halifax. He expressed his displeasure with a royal snub: although Queen Mary and Queen Elizabeth both wrote solicitous expressions of personal regret at the Premier's resignation, the King refrained from sending any written consolation. According to Mrs. Chamberlain, this caused her husband a deep hurt.[73]

George VI's displeasure was not surprising. Churchill had taken his brother Edward's side during the 1936 abdication crisis. Halifax was also a trusted courtier, confidant and frequent dinner companion at Buckingham Palace, where his wife Dorothy was a lady-in-waiting to the Queen. On sunny days the Foreign Secretary exercised the rare privilege of walking through the Palace grounds on his way to Whitehall from his suite at the Dorchester Hotel and would invariably – perhaps by design – encounter the King for a chat. It is therefore understandable that George VI should have

47

tried to press Chamberlain on Halifax's behalf by offering to put Halifax's title in abeyance.[74]

"I would rather have Halifax succeed me than Winston," Chamberlain is on record as writing. Yet what emerges from his meeting at the Palace is that the King was the only one to propose how the Prime Minister might remove the principal obstacle that the Foreign Secretary gave for declining the premiership. That his peerage was seemingly not a problem to Chamberlain or the Labour leaders suggests that Halifax was acceptable to them as Prime Minister only *if* he was impotent of real parliamentary authority in the upper chamber. If Chamberlain really had intended Halifax to be his successor, it was in his power to remove the obstacle. That the King appears to have volunteered to put the peerage in abeyance suggests that he was made aware, through Halifax or Lady Halifax, of the terms under which the Foreign Secretary was prepared to accept his commission to form a government.[75]

Whether Lord Halifax would have accepted the King's commission *if* he had been guaranteed a parliamentary bill to put his peerage in abeyance can only remain a matter of speculation. But without Halifax's refusal to be a figurehead premier, the nation would never have got the leader it needed in its hour of greatest peril. To believe that, as his friend and biographer Lord Birkenhead states, Halifax "had no illusions whatever as to his suitability for the role which a Prime Minister would have to play at this desperate moment in history" belies the facts, though it is difficult to fault Lord Birkenhead's assessment that the Foreign Secretary's qualities were "in many ways the exact opposite of those required in the fighting leader of a forlorn cause." Churchill was soon to discover just how forlorn his Foreign Secretary considered Britain's cause to be. According to hints by Sir Kingsley Wood, Chamberlain harboured doubts about Halifax's will to fight. (See Appendix 1.)[76]

Churchill was aware from the outset of his premiership that he was going to have to depend on his predecessor to overcome Halifax's defeatism. His first act on returning from Buckingham Palace that evening was to write to Chamberlain, telling him that "I am in your hands" and thanking him for "promising to stand by me & to aid the country at this extremely grievous and formidable moment." Evidence that he had already made a firm alliance with Chamberlain never to surrender to Hitler is provided by Churchill's letter to Mrs. Chamberlain on the day her husband died six months later. "I felt when I served under him that *he would never give in* & I knew that when our positions were reversed that *I could count upon his aid & unflinching crusade*," he wrote. "Neville shared your sense of comradeship & *felt secure in the knowledge that you too would never give in*," Chamberlain's widow replied.[77]

Chamberlain's commitment to the new premier was apparent in

the grim determination to help Churchill wage war to the hilt that was the theme of his valedictory broadcast from Downing Street that Friday evening. Warning that the hour would come when Britain would be "put to the test," he concluded with a call for unity and "unshakable courage" to defeat Germany, even going so far as to describe Hitler as a "wild beast which has sprung upon us from his lair." Halifax felt this went beyond diplomatically prudent language.[78]

"Grovel, grovel, grovel, first to the Indians, then to the Germans, now to the Russians – nothing but grovel" was how Churchill later rebuked Lord Halifax's persistent inclination to compromise and appease. Although this scathing assault was not made until 1947, when Halifax criticized Churchill's famous "iron curtain" speech at Fulton, Missouri, its vehemence is significant, because Chamberlain's decision to back Churchill on 10 May 1940 against the wishes of the Conservative Party, his Downing Street staff and the King did much to atone for the disaster he had brought on the world at Munich in 1938. That evening at Buckingham Palace he courted the King's displeasure by leaving George VI with no option but to set aside his personal preference for Halifax and send for Churchill.[79]

"I suppose you don't know why I have sent for you?" the King asked the First Lord of the Admiralty when he arrived at the Palace shortly after 7 p.m. "Sir, I simply couldn't imagine why," Churchill replied. "I want to ask you to form a Government." Britain's new Prime Minister gave the traditional kiss to the monarch's hand and promised to let him have the names of his five War Cabinet members by midnight. After the war Churchill struck an upbeat note when recalling the "profound sense of relief" that came over him when he finally retired at 3 a.m. after the climactic day. "At last I had the authority to give directions over the whole scene. I felt as if I were walking with destiny, and that all my past life had been but a preparation for this hour and for this trial."[80]

For all his prescience, Churchill could not anticipate that some of the sharpest rigours of the trial he was about to face would come not from Hitler but from within the British governing Establishment. He might have had some inkling of the disaffection that would shortly break out in his own government's ranks had he dropped into the Under Secretary's room at the Foreign Office on his way back from the Palace. There he would have found a disgruntled gathering of Halifax's lieutenants. They were joined by Lord Dunglass and John Colville, who had come over to "explain the position" to Rab Butler and Chips Channon. Champagne flowed, not to celebrate Churchill's victory, but to deplore the Foreign Secretary's defeat. The brimming glasses were raised to Chamberlain with the Jacobite rebel toast to the "King over the Water."[81]

The "good clean tradition of English politics," Butler lamented, "had been sold to the greatest adventurer of modern political history." He said he had tried "earnestly and long to persuade Halifax to accept the Premiership" but the "sudden coup of Winston and his rabble was a serious disaster." He blamed Chamberlain, who had "weakly surrendered to a half-breed American whose main support was that of inefficient but talkative people of similar type."[82]

The coming weeks were to prove Butler wrong. Churchill's mixed ancestry made him less prone to compromise with Hitler than the pure-bred English Under Secretary and his master Lord Halifax were, and less defeatist than the American Ambassador in London, who telephoned to offer his breezy congratulations. Joseph P. Kennedy reminded the new Prime Minister of the role he himself had played in the chain of events that had brought him to Downing Street by obtaining Roosevelt's approval for the First Lord's scheme to mine the Norwegian Leads. "Hence Norway, hence Prime Minister," Kennedy said laughingly. Whether Churchill found the gibe amusing is not recorded. But he did not like or trust Kennedy, who had been characterized as pro-German by certain sections of the British press. The feeling of antagonism between the two men, though each was careful to conceal it in official encounters, was mutual.[83]

"Maybe I do him an injustice," Kennedy noted in his diary, "but I just don't trust him. He always impressed me that he was willing to blow up the American Embassy and say it was the Germans if it would get the United States in." The Ambassador had never concealed that he regarded Churchill as an inveterate warmonger or that he believed the Allies would never be able to defeat the Germans without American help. The launching of the Blitzkrieg on the West had only sharpened Kennedy's belief that military disaster loomed over the Allies in France. He was equally convinced that the new Prime Minister would be more determined than ever to drag the United States into the war, warning Roosevelt that Churchill had been in contact with pro-war groups in the United States, "notably certain Jewish leaders." Two months earlier Kennedy, a former movie mogul, had scripted a Hollywood-style scenario for the closing scene when Churchill finally succeeded in getting the United States to declare war on Hitler. "He'll reach for that brandy," Kennedy predicted, "charge his glass, lift his hand on high and say 'I have discharged my duty. Victory is ours! This is our crowning achievement. God save the King.'"[84]

"So we had won after all" was how Churchill would actually describe that final climacteric eighteen months later, on 7 December 1941. On the evening of 10 May 1940, Britain's new Prime Minister had many reasons to doubt whether the nation whose burdens he had just shouldered had enough military strength, treasure, or reserves of national will to carry on the struggle until the United States joined the fight. But he knew that the vital task of rallying the nation for the fight against Hitler was one that he could accomplish.

The task Churchill faced was Herculean. As he drove back from the Palace that evening, his sombre silence impressed Commander "Tommie" Thompson, his private detective. As the car swung into the courtyard of Admiralty House, he congratulated the new Prime Minister and wished him luck in his enormous task. Churchill's eyes became moist.

"God knows how great it is," he exclaimed. "I hope that it is not too late. I am very much afraid that it is. We can only do our best."[85]

Chapter 3

"This Game of Peace Feelers"

"Weaker Vessels"

"It's all a great tragedy, isn't it?" Lord Halifax gloomily told Rab Butler four days after Churchill had become Prime Minister.

"That is because you did not take the premiership yourself," his Under Secretary of State responded.

"You know my reasons," Halifax said; "it's no use discussing that – but the gangsters will shortly be in complete control."[1]

This revealing exchange indicates the depth of the resentment the Foreign Secretary and his deputy harboured against the new Prime Minister. Two days earlier the King had offered Halifax his commiserations as they took one of their strolls through the gardens of Buckingham Palace. He said how disappointed he was not to have him as his premier, because he was "apprehensive of Winston's administrative methods." Halifax had also indicated his concern by turning down Churchill's request that he lead for the government in the House of Lords. "I have seldom met anybody with stranger gaps of knowledge, or whose mind worked in greater jerks," he observed in his diary. "Will it be possible to make it work in orderly fashion? On this much depends." Late-evening meetings of the War Cabinet had made the Foreign Secretary "uneasy as to Winston's methods." He found the new regime "quite intolerable," he noted in his diary, but decided to "acquiesce during these two or three days; after that I shall tell him that if he wants midnight meetings, he can have them without me." Churchill's emotive manner was an irritant to Halifax, and "certainly we shall not have gained much on intellect," he grumbled after the first full meeting of the new Cabinet, disparaging the Labour Party leaders Attlee and Greenwood.[2]

Churchill headed the War Cabinet and the Defence Committee, but the Lord President's Committee under Chamberlain actually ran the civil side of the war. So the old guard of Chamberlain and Halifax dominated Churchill's first wartime administration, much to the concern of his allies in Parliament and the press, who had clamoured for a clean sweep of all the discredited "Men of Munich." Leo Amery, who had hoped for a senior ministerial post, was given the consolation prize of the India Office, and Anthony Eden became Minister for War but not a member of the five-man inner War Cabinet. Despite Churchill's promise that Lord Salisbury's "young men wouldn't be forgotten," only Boothby received a junior secretaryship at the Ministry of Food.[3]

Churchill, wrote Boothby, "showed no undue gratitude to those of us who had put him there." But he acknowledged that, to survive, the new Prime Minister had to ally himself with the forces that had so long and so bitterly opposed him. "To a large extent I am in your hands – and I feel no fear of that," Churchill had written to Chamberlain on the Friday night after returning from Buckingham Palace. It was not just a magnanimous gesture. As a Prime Minister without a party, the irony was that his administration's survival – and Britain's too – now depended on his keeping the support of the old guard who had appeased Hitler. "Glamour Boys have got all the jobs," one Tory elder statesman told Baldwin. In his opinion, "the Tories don't trust Winston," and as a result a "short-lived government" was his prediction. "After the first clash of war is over, it may be that a sounder Govt. may emerge," J. C. C. Davidson wrote, advising the former Prime Minister that the Conservatives should begin the search for a new leader. Even Chamberlain hedged his bets. The day after his resignation, he wrote to his sister Ida that he would live on at 10 Downing Street, only moving next door to No. 11 after a month, "if the Government still stands." He knew that the Conservative loyalists in the House of Commons resented the manner in which Churchill's "gangsters" had hijacked the premiership from Lord Halifax. They intended to keep the new "Glamour Boys" in check through the mechanism of the Conservative backbenchers' powerful "1922 Committee."[4]

"If intrigue or attacks on the Government grow to any great extent," Rab Butler assured his sacked friend Sam Hoare, "all we have to do is to pull the string of the toy dog of the 1922 Committee and make it bark." Churchill would be brought to heel when "After a few staccato utterances it becomes clear that the Government depends upon the Tory squires for its majority." Because the Tory squires distrusted Churchill, he could not drop their champion, Lord Halifax. Halifax's deputy, R. A. Butler, who had sparred with Churchill over India and Munich and who was regarded by younger Foreign Office secretaries as "a public danger, flabby in person and morally and mentally as well," himself expected to be kicked out. He was "down and depressed" until the Prime Minister summoned him to Downing Street. "I wish you to go on with your delicate manner of answering Parliamentary Questions without giving anything away," Churchill told him, leaving him in no doubt about who he had to thank for his political survival. "Halifax asked for you," the Prime Minister said pointedly. "He seems to get on with you."[5]

"Rab was of course very, very weak," explained Roger Makins, now Lord Sherfield, using the contemporary political term "extreme wet" to characterize Butler as an appeaser who continued to work for a negotiated peace with Hitler. As one of the younger Foreign Office professionals, Makins found Butler, with whom he worked day-to-day closely, "very elusive to deal with because you never quite knew what he was thinking." Sir Frank Roberts, another wartime official in the Central Department, described Butler, in the oblique language of a diplomat trained to avoid direct criticism of his political masters, as "One of the 'weaker vessels'."[6]

"Too Late to Stop the War"
September–December 1939

When it came to dealing with Hitler, Sir Frank Roberts was a hardliner. The quicksilver intelligence that took him to the top of the British diplomatic profession as a postwar ambassador to the U.S.S.R. and Germany is evident in the boldly dismissive advice that appears in the thick dossier of German peace feelers that flooded into the Foreign Office during the period of the Phoney War. He had been assigned to deal with Birger Dahlerus, the Swedish businessman and friend of Göring whose August 1939 meetings with Chamberlain and Halifax failed to avert war. It nonetheless came as a surprise to Roberts on 4 September, the day after war was declared, to be woken at 2 a.m. by a telephone operator announcing a call from Karinhall, Göring's palatial hunting lodge.[7]

"We can still save the peace if we can stop the war. I have the Reich Marshal at my side, will you tell the Prime Minister that Göring is still prepared to intervene?" Dahlerus announced. He said that Göring had a plane standing by to fly him to London to personally start the peace negotiations. "It was an extraordinary situation, almost comic," Roberts said, recalling that he was more uncertain as to how the call got through than about how he should exercise his responsibility. "I took it upon myself to say no," he recounted, chuckling at how Göring must have reacted to his dismissal of Dahlerus: "I'm sorry, it's too late to stop the war, I'm in bed, good night!"[8]

"Göring may have wanted to disengage before a general war broke out," Roberts said, "but we knew that war was just what Hitler wanted." The problem for the Central Department of the Foreign Office was that Dahlerus persisted with his efforts. On the way to Oslo next day Dahlerus flew from Berlin to Stockholm to assure the British Minister there that Göring "genuinely regretted the outbreak of war and, short of actual disloyalty to Hitler, he would like to see a truce negotiated." The Foreign Secretary did not follow the Central Department's advice and reject this first peace feeler outright. The message relayed from Lord Halifax invited the Swede to obtain detailed terms. Encouraged, Göring took his intermediary to see Hitler on 26 September. "If the British actually wanted peace," Hitler declared, "they could have it in two weeks without losing face," on condition that Germany received "an entirely free hand in Poland." The possibility was discussed of a secret meeting between Dahlerus and a high-ranking British emissary in the Netherlands or Sweden, and Dahlerus promised to leave for London next day to "put out feelers in the direction indicated."[9]

There was a simultaneous move afoot in Britain to call for negotiations. The success of Blitzkrieg warfare demonstrated by the swift dismemberment of Poland had panicked many politicians, including Lloyd George, who was convinced that the Allied powers lacked both the political resolve and the military resources to defeat Germany. On 20 September the First World War leader told a gathering of concerned M.P.s that the time had come for the government to take stock of its military capacity. If the chances of an Allied victory were assessed at less than 50–50, he said, "we should certainly make peace at the earliest opportunity, possibly with Roosevelt's assistance." This statement fuelled the growing Peace Aims Group in Parliament, led by Liberal pacifists, who now joined forces with the neo-pacifists in the Independent Labour Party. Within three days, "Stop the War" letters began pouring into Downing Street.[10]

"If I were in Hitler's shoes, I think I should let the present menacing go on for several weeks and then put out a reasonable offer," Chamberlain fretted, although he was "certain we ought to reject it." The vociferous campaign for a negotiated peace heartened the American Ambassador, who had already warned the President that he had yet to find any U.S. military expert who believed that "England has a Chinaman's chance." Concerned at what he described as "the growing Jewish influence in the press and in Washington demanding the continuance of the war," Kennedy proposed "that the President can get himself in a spot where he can save the world." Roosevelt, who took the view that Kennedy "has been an appeaser and always will be an appeaser," rejected his ambassador's call to intervene.[11]

"If Germany or Italy made a good peace offer tomorrow, Joe would start working on his friend, the Queen, and from there on down to get everybody to accept it," the President told Treasury Secretary Morgenthau, describing Kennedy as a "pain in the neck." He saw to it that word of his Ambassador's defeatism reached the British Embassy in Washington. Chamberlain duly summoned Kennedy to Downing Street and told him that "any peace offer of the kind that Germany was likely to put forward would be immediately rejected."[12]

Despite the rebuff from both London and Washington, Kennedy continued to push his unofficial "peace offensive" by meeting Halifax on 25 September to suggest that Chamberlain should drop "perpetual reference to the elimination of Hitler" as a precondition for opening peace negotiations. Scornful of Chamberlain's refusal to negotiate with Hitler, Kennedy discounted as dangerously unrealistic the belief that Britain's blockade would bring about the overthrow of the Nazi regime.[13]

Hitler was also preparing to publicly call an end to the war. Within forty-eight hours of the capitulation of Warsaw on 27 September, Berlin Radio officially announced the ending of the war as the Red Army moved into Poland's eastern territories, according to the protocols of the Nazi-Soviet Pact. The Nazi Foreign Minister Joachim Ribbentrop travelled to Moscow to issue a joint statement with the Soviet Foreign Minister: they had "created a secure foundation for European peace" and it was now "in the true interests of all people to put an end to the war between the Reich and Britain and France."[14]

"What we ought to do is just to throw back the peace offers and continue the blockade" was Chamberlain's reaction to the flurry of semi-official peace feelers. Although he did not believe that "holocausts are required," he was unshaken in his conviction that tightening the economic screws would result in a German government that could be trusted to negotiate. On 3 October he told the House of Commons that, while the British government was still open to a sincere German peace overture, he was not prepared to negotiate with Hitler. Lloyd George denounced the Prime Minister's position as unrealistic and dangerously adamant. Next day Halifax assured Kennedy that proposals of "real substance" would be "seriously considered and the United States consulted." The Foreign Secretary evidently did not agree with the hard line advocated by the First Lord of the Admiralty, because he expressed concern about "talk of Churchill supplanting Chamberlain." Halifax found the Ambassador "anxious to lay the groundwork" with Washington for a serious consideration of peace terms. "It would be a calamity," Kennedy told him, "if England felt she could accept them but would not because the United States would tell her that she could not."[15]

Kennedy's assurances reinforced the Foreign Secretary's decision two days later to lay before the Cabinet the peace proposals brought by Dahlerus. Halifax explained that Göring and Hitler had agreed to a preliminary meeting of intermediaries "in some neutral country," and urged that they "should not be rejected out of hand because we should not absolutely shut the door." Churchill's reaction was predictably hostile; he warned the Cabinet that "these German peace feelers might not be sincere and their real object might be to spread division and doubt among us." Chamberlain, who was not prepared to countenance any dealings with Hitler, agreed, but he took it as a positive sign that Dahlerus had hinted that Göring might displace Hitler, "who might eventually assume a presidential role." This illusion should have been dispelled next day, when a triumphant Hitler bombastically called for peace at a cheering session of the Reichstag in the Kroll Opera House in Berlin.[16]

"At no time and in no place have I acted contrary to British interests," the Führer declared, appealing for "Germany and England to come to an understanding." He called for an international conference to consider peace and disarmament. "Let those who consider war to be the better solution reject my outstretched hand," he declared. "If Messrs Churchill and followers should prevail, then this statement will have been my last."[17]

A flat rejection of Hitler's call for peace came from Paris within twenty-four hours, but the British government's delay in turning the proposal down sent a conflicting signal to Berlin. Hitler had made a "clever speech," according to Chamberlain, who admitted being "more afraid of a peace offer than of an air raid," because of U.S. press reports that Hitler had made an "attractive series of proposals." Although he never seriously considered Hitler's terms, the Prime Minister erred by delaying his rejection so as not to send a message to the Americans that the British government was intransigent.[18]

The Foreign Secretary's unwillingness to slam the door on Dahlerus's peace feeler had also given Hitler reason to believe that his peace offer was being seriously considered. Halifax's reputation as a pious high churchman made him the target of injunctions from bishops and clergy to do his duty as a Christian by saving thousands of human lives. Letters arrived by the bagful from members of Lord Buxton's Peace Aims Group and from clergymen all over the country, and thousands more poured in in support of Lloyd George's call for a negotiated peace. Many British citizens' fears for a repetition of the horror and slaughter of four years of trench warfare were greater than their fear of Hitler and the Nazis. Newspaper magnate Lord Rothermere wrote encouragingly to Lloyd George: "You are a grand old war-horse to go ahead with your present policy and you will win hands down."[19]

The Germans cannot have been unaware of the growing desire amongst many sections of the British community for a negotiated peace. Four days after Hitler's Reichstag speech Dahlerus flew into London for further consultations at the Foreign Office. As if on cue, that same morning the Führer had reiterated his "readiness for peace" by declaring that Germany "has no cause for war against the Western Powers." But Hitler was not taking any chances. The same day he called a meeting of his military chiefs to brief them secretly that if England and France "are not willing to make an end of the war, I am determined to act vigorously and aggressively without delay." He then issued his "Directive No. 6," which called for the defeat of the French Army and the occupation of "Holland, Belgium and northern France as a base for conducting a promising air and sea war against England."[20]

"We used Dahlerus to try to make clear to Hitler, through Göring, that we were going to fight": Sir Frank Roberts insists that this was the Foreign Office position. The declassification records show that the Foreign Secretary and his deputy Butler did not rebuff Dahlerus, but asked him to clarify Göring's terms. According to Ambassador Kennedy, Halifax believed that it was most significant that the "most recent peace overtures emanated from Göring rather than Hitler." Although Hitler might not be supplanted soon, Halifax assured Kennedy that he took it as a positive sign that the French too had received another overture from Berlin. Göring played the game on 12 October by having Dahlerus cable a list of specific armistice terms, including acknowledgement of Germany's right to determine Poland's fate and the return of former German colonial territories in Africa. "If his Majesty's Government were not prepared to negotiate with the existing regime in Germany," the telegram advised, "the proposals fell to the ground."[21]

This was the final straw for Chamberlain. He refused to countenance any dealing with Hitler, even if satisfactory guarantees were received that German troops would be withdrawn from Prague and Warsaw. "The Prime Minister is much more bellicose than that," Butler regretfully assured Harold Nicolson on 12 October as they walked down Whitehall to hear the Prime Minister, who that afternoon told the House of Commons that he rejected Hitler's offer of peace as "vague and uncertain." The terms were unacceptable because they contained "no suggestion for righting the wrongs done to Czechoslovakia and Poland." Britain could not rely on the promises "of the present German government." Hitler, Chamberlain made clear, was the principal obstacle to negotiations, because Britain had "no quarrel with the German people except that they allow themselves to be governed by a Nazi government."[22]

Disregarding reality, Göring angrily called Chamberlain's rejection a "declaration of war" in a message relayed to London from Dahlerus, who was in the Hague, anticipating that the British would take up his offer of preliminary secret peace meetings. This was a relief to Foreign Office officials like Roberts, who took a "rather poorer view of Dahlerus" than did Halifax and Butler. But the subsequent twenty-eight entries in the Foreign Secretary's "Peace File" show that they continued to keep the door open to Dahlerus, no doubt sharing the belief of Sir Nevile Henderson, another appeaser, who had been British Ambassador in Berlin, that Göring was the one Nazi leader they could "do business with."[23]

Apparently to "do business" with Göring, Butler made a trip to Switzerland two weeks later that was so secret that Sir Frank Roberts never knew anything about it. The U.S. State Department files contain a report of the Under Secretary's mission to Lausanne for a meeting with "a German representative, Hohenloe [sic] by name" with whom he had "discussed the substitution of Göring for Hitler." Prince Max Egon zu von Hohenlohe-Langenburg was a wealthy Sudeten landowner whose friendship with Göring and Liechtenstein passport made him a convenient intermediary through whom to open up contact with Butler. Another contact in the secret channel of communications that existed between the Under Secretary of State and Berlin was Dr. Carl J. Burckhardt, the Swiss head of the International Red Cross, who had had extensive dealings with Butler in his former capacity as League of Nations Commissioner in Danzig. Burckhardt would also have had an opportunity to confer with Butler in December, when Halifax's deputy, two weeks after his meeting with Hohenlohe, travelled to Switzerland for the final sessions of the League of Nations, where the Soviet Union was expelled for seizing Polish territory.[24]

While all mention of Butler's dealings with Göring's intermediaries has been expunged from the declassified Foreign Office files, they do show that Dahlerus was not the only peace intermediary received by Halifax during the Phoney War. On 17 October a so-called British oil promoter named Rickett arrived with the news that he and a "prominent Wall Street operator" named Smith had seen Mussolini in Rome before meeting Göring in Berlin. Smith, better known as "Sell-em Ben," from his legendary manipulation of the stock market in the thirties, was reported by the State Department to be part of a "Nazi plot" intended to enlist the sympathy of neutrals on the basis of alleged differences between Hitler and

Göring. Another was American oil-broker William R. Davis, who met Roosevelt in the White House on 12 October to offer himself as a peace emissary. The President "squarely hit the roof" when he received a personal message from Göring urging him to support the German peace initiative after Davis had misrepresented Roosevelt's willingness to mediate.[25]

The President had already rejected direct appeals from King Leopold of the Belgians to act as mediator in a European settlement. He was only too well aware that this would lend credence to Hitler's peace offensive and embarrass the Allies. That was why the State Department alerted the Foreign Office that James D. Mooney, a Vice-President of the General Motors Corporation, was "involved in the same business." Mooney's unpublished account of his missions reveals that he was a longer-lived player than Dahlerus in the German "peace game." As GM overseas operations director, Mooney's responsibility for the Adam Opel car factory in Germany had brought him into contact with the banker Dr. Wolthart, who acted as an adviser to Göring. At Wolthart's request, Mooney had a three-hour give-and-take with the Nazi leader like "average burghers in a *Bierstube*." Finally the corpulent Göring came round from his side of the huge office desk and grabbed hold of the American's arm. "Now, Mooney," Göring said, shaking a pudgy finger with a huge emerald ring in the American's face, "I am asking you, for our government, to go over to the British and find out what this war is all about." He offered vague concessions on Czechoslovakia and Poland and promised that if necessary he would "even go himself" to England.[26]

Fired up with these assurances, Mooney arrived in London on 26 October, and Kennedy promised to arrange a meeting with Lord Halifax "right away." The younger brother of Sir Robert Vansittart, the Foreign Secretary's Chief Diplomatic Adviser, was also a Vice President of General Motors' British subsidiary, Vauxhall Motors. He advised that "Mr. Mooney was being used by Göring, but that he was personally honest." Vansittart was one of the hardest of the Foreign Office hardliners, but on Halifax's instructions he urged Mooney to "send word back to Berlin" that Göring's message was "being considered seriously" by the British government. The Foreign Office stalled Mooney's meeting with Halifax until after the U.S. Congress voted to amend the Neutrality Act to allow the United States to supply arms and equipment to the Allies on a cash-and-carry basis.[27]

"I don't want your soldiers," Chamberlain assured the American Ambassador on 3 November. "This is an economic war. We need your resources but not your men," he told Kennedy, while expressing his gratitude for Roosevelt's support. Rejecting the offer to mediate made by Queen Wilhelmina of the Netherlands and

King Leopold of the Belgians on 7 November, he told Kennedy "the German people have still not suffered enough to become disgusted with their leadership," but he remained confident that Britain's blockade would bring about an "internal break-up" in Germany by spring.[28]

The American Ambassador continued to be highly critical of the British government's unrealistic expectation that Hitler would be overthrown. His pessimistic assessment arrived in Washington shortly after "Sell-em Ben" Smith had finally managed to foist himself on the President. Smith's assertion that "a substantial section of British big business was working for an early peace" was the subject of a 9 November cable from the British Ambassador in Washington. So when the Foreign Secretary finally received Mooney next day he stressed Britain's reluctance to embark on any negotiation with Hitler or Ribbentrop. The "official" message given to him next day by Vansittart was that "no progress could be made until somehow or other there was a government in Germany with whom the British could deal, which, at present, is not the case."[29]

Convinced that he was acting "as a sort of catalytic agent," Mooney set out for Berlin on 11 November, which, he noted, happened to be Armistice Day. On the boat train from London to Dover he melodramatically flushed down the lavatory the scraps of the paper from which he had memorized the British government's "vitally important" message. The ferry dodged an abortive attack by a German bomber but Mooney reached Berlin safely next day, only to discover that Wolthart was in Rome. Declining to meet Göring, he hurried on to Italy, where he was told that his contact was in Madrid. It took him two more weeks to track down the elusive German banker at the Madrid Ritz Hotel on Sunday, 10 December. Mooney told Wolthart that the British "were very willing to talk peace if the Germans were willing to save the British government's face by a realignment of their own government." "It's too late," Mooney was told, leading him to conclude that "something had happened in Germany."[30]

Mooney never learned why Berlin lost enthusiasm for his first attempt at peace, but it seems that a searing attack on Hitler broadcast by Churchill on 19 November derailed his mission. Hitler and Hitlerism were denounced as a "monstrous apparition" by Churchill, who appealed directly to the German people, the "millions who stand aloof from this monstrous mass of seething criminality and corruption represented by the Nazi Party machine." This public blasting of the Nazis was immediately defused by Rab Butler, who assured the Italian Ambassador, Giuseppe Bastianini, that "Churchill's speech was in conflict with the Government's views not only in the present instance." When asked to clarify whether the British were still insisting on the evacuation of German troops from Poland as a precondition for opening peace negotiations, Butler denied "in the most categorical manner that this was the intention of his Government." The Italian Ambassador reported that despite "scepticism about the practical feasibility of a peaceful solution at the present time – neither the Foreign Secretary nor the Prime Minister excluded such an eventuality *a priori*." Butler's language may have been elliptical, but his meaning was plain enough, as the Ambassador's report – which was relayed to Berlin – makes very clear.[31]

"I am sure that Rab was operating largely on his own, he was a very elusive character" was the opinion of Lord Sherfield, who was acting at the time as "a sort of speech writer" for Halifax. Sherfield knew Halifax "very well because of the All Souls Mafia," but he was not sure of the precise nature of the Foreign Secretary's relationship with his deputy. He agreed that Butler's conduct was often "feline," but "Halifax did not confide in me on any of this."[32]

As Halifax's dutiful deputy for two years, Butler is not likely to have "acted on his own" without some sign of approval; his remarks to Bastianini contradicted the government's public declaration that it would not negotiate with Hitler, and he could have guessed that the Italian government would pass them straight on to Berlin, where they were interpreted to mean that, despite Chamberlain's rebuff and Churchill's speech, some members of the British government were receptive to peace feelers. Following Mooney's abortive mission to London, Göring saw Dahlerus twice during December, and simultaneously encouraged Baron Bonde, another Swedish businessman, to take a peace memorandum personally to Lord Halifax. Göring was "absolutely loyal to Hitler until the moment comes when he has to lock him up," Bonde told Halifax, who was delighted to learn that "Göring definitely had it in mind to get rid of Hitler." But he declined to give the official "gesture" Bonde said was necessary for "the first step." Dahlerus received a similar response ten days later when he arrived at the Foreign Office just before Christmas to find out what guarantees the British government could give Göring.[33]

Göring's bluff had been called. So, despite Butler's intervention, the semi-official German peace effort had, by the end of 1939, run aground on Chamberlain's flinty refusal to negotiate while Hitler was in power. By the beginning of 1940 Hitler had decided that he was not going to get peace on his terms, so he pressed ahead with the military solution embodied in Directive No. 6, convinced that nothing short of knocking France out of the war would persuade the British to sue for peace.

"Will o'the Wisps"
January–March 1940

The effective end of the "official" German peace offensive did not stop advocates of a negotiated settlement from continuing to lobby the Foreign Secretary. Halifax had been receptive to appeals from fellow peers who had been campaigning for peace since war broke out. The most persistent were the pacifists led by Lord Noel Buxton and a motley group of right-wing peers including the Dukes of Buccleuch and Wellington, who with the Lords Semphill and Lytton believed that Britain should be fighting the Bolshevik menace, not Hitler. The eccentric Marquess of Tavistock, heir to the Duke of Bedford and one of Britain's greatest real-estate fortunes, embarked on independent discussions with the secretary of the German legation in Dublin. He personally delivered what he claimed was an officially sanctioned memorandum of German peace terms to the Foreign Secretary on 23 January 1940. "Halifax was said to have been quite impressed with their fairness but doubtful as to whether Hitler could be trusted to put them into effect," Ambassador Kennedy reported. The Foreign Secretary was more circumspect: he saw "almost insuperable barriers to any progress along these lines." When the sensational news of Tavistock's mission was leaked to the press, he insisted that he had received Halifax's authority to travel to Dublin to clarify his terms, a claim that was quickly denied by Whitehall. Tavistock became an object of ridicule for his pro-Nazi statements.[34]

"Believe me, I do not want to continue this war a moment longer than it seems absolutely necessary," Halifax had told the Bishop of Oslo, spokesman of the World Council of Churches, on 13 December. "But we cannot stop it without having tried to obtain what we started it for." The Foreign Secretary was peculiarly vulnerable to pressure from churchmen because he made a point of parading his own piety by his oft-stated belief that in the final analysis it was the "spiritual side that counts." He answered the Bishop's charges that Britain's refusal to negotiate a quick peace was not only un-Christian but futile and potentially destructive of human life in a high-minded speech he made as Chancellor of Oxford University in February 1940.[35]

Lord Halifax firmly rejected the churchmen's pressure to negotiate as a "one-sided and mistaken interpretation of Our Lord's teaching." The use of force, he contended, could be justified from a moral Christian standpoint when it had the redeeming value of resisting the destructive forces of evil. This begged the question of whose spiritual criteria were to determine government policy, since his public statements were inconsistent with his continuing search for an avenue to negotiate with Hitler. As a fellow member of All Souls observed, "Edward has no sense of Original Sin;" Halifax was dangerously prey to his own high-mindedness and his conviction that he was superior to lesser mortals in politics. The ease with which he manipulated Christian moral tenets to rationalize the practical necessities of his *Realpolitik* made him by inclination a compromiser.[36]

As Viceroy, Halifax had justified his courageous decision to outrage the British Indian civil service by meeting Gandhi with the same lawyerly detachment he later applied to the appeasing of Hitler at Munich. The outbreak of war should have demonstrated just how futile it was to try to appease the Nazis, but the "welcome" sign that Halifax put out to the intermediaries bearing German peace feelers suggests that he believed it was only a matter of time before Hitler responded by behaving with the supreme rationality of a Fellow of All Souls. He had so completely misread the nature of the Nazi leaders that he declared after their meeting in 1938 that Hitler struck him as "very sincere." He had also compared Göring to "the head-gamekeeper at Chatsworth" after shooting boars with the Reich's First Huntsman. The biggest mistake Halifax made was to treat the Nazi leaders like surly employees on his country estate. But they were not amenable to appeals to reason from an English squire, nor were Hitler and Göring going to be cowed into respectful submission by Britain's Phoney War blockade.[37]

"Halifax listened to them all," Lord Sherfield said, "because he felt it was his duty to leave no stone unturned, no avenue unexplored when it came to finding a way to end the war." Yet the accounts of Dahlerus, the Marquess of Tavistock and James D. Mooney suggest that Halifax may have gone further than simply keeping his door open to German peace feelers. The declassified records lead to the conclusion that Halifax and his deputy Butler really were very weak vessels and did not share the Prime Minister's conviction that negotiations should wait until the exigencies of the economic blockade had brought the ouster of Hitler.[38]

Ironically, it was not the blockade but Hitler's Directive No. 6 for a massive simultaneous assault on Holland, Belgium and France that galvanized those generals and bureaucrats opposed to the Nazis. Incredibly, after months of false rumours of a Göring-inspired revolt, Halifax and the Foreign Office discounted the reports of a potential coup brewing in Berlin which began reaching London via the Vatican early in December. British willingness to believe in a German officers' plot had been eroded the previous month when the Germans kidnapped two MI6 officers at the Dutch border town of Venlo. The Foreign Secretary's initial scepticism was to change only after he learned what Pope Pius XII confided to the British delegate to the Holy See on 12 January 1940.[39]

"I had an audience with him," Sir Francis D'Arcy Osborne reported in a "secret and confidential" letter, and the Pontiff revealed that he was "speaking for certain German army chiefs, whose names he knew but would prefer not to give." They had warned that a "Grand German offensive" was being prepared for the coming month. "If the German generals could be assured of a peace with Great Britain," Pius XII said, "it need never be delivered." All that was required of the British government was to give an assurance of generous terms to a new interim German military government that would overthrow Hitler and negotiate an end to the war on the basis of the restoration of Poland and Czechoslovakia, but would make "no concessions over the existing Anschluss with Austria." Stressing that he "did not wish in the slightest degree to endorse or recommend" the peace feeler, Pius XII said he guaranteed the "good faith of the intermediary" but could not do so for the principals. He "begged" the British government to keep the matter "an absolute secret" because he feared that the "lives of the unnamed German generals would be forfeit."[40]

"I might mention this at Cabinet tomorrow," the Foreign Secretary noted on Osborne's letter after reading it on 16 January. As a High Church man who regularly attended Sunday Mass at the Grosvenor Chapel, Halifax could hardly fail to respond to the risk the Pope ran by breaking the precedent of centuries to act in a conspiracy to overthrow a foreign government. He instructed Osborne to find out more. While acknowledging the Pontiff's concern for security, he advised that any guarantees would require informing the French Prime Minister. Authentication by the Pope in a month-long secret exchange with the Vatican still did not convince the hardliners in the Foreign Office that the German generals really were plotting to overthrow Hitler. (See Appendix 2.) Sir Frank Roberts minuted on 13 February that he saw no reason to revise his scepticism about "the various feelers." Vansittart, drawing on his own private channels of communication in Germany, concurred. "It seems highly unlikely that the Generals will do anything until they are convinced by military defeats that Hitlerism is too great a liability for the future of Germany & the Reichswehr," he wrote, advising Halifax: "There is always too much 'jam tomorrow' about them." The Prime Minister was also unconvinced by the Pope's intervention and drafted an uncompromising response for him, stating that Britain "will do nothing without France," and that "a definite programme must be laid down and vouched for authoritatively."[41]

When the Foreign Secretary replied via Osborne on 18 February,

65

it is significant that he went further than the Prime Minister and the Foreign Office hardliners. He told the British Minister to the Holy See to inform the Pope that although the French would have to be involved, the British *were* prepared to entertain discussions provided they received definite proposals. That Halifax took the Pope's approach seriously is clear from the confidential discussion he had the following day with his Cabinet colleague Sir Maurice Hankey, when "we discussed the possibility of making a preliminary peace to be followed by a more considered and wider peace later." It was also a curious coincidence that Lady Dorothy Halifax set off at the same time for Rome, escorting their son Richard to an internship at the British Embassy. She also had an audience with the Pope on 16 February, accompanied by Osborne, after which the Pontiff drew the diplomat aside to assure him that he had just received confirmation that the German generals were serious about ousting Hitler.[42]

"If they want a change of government, why don't they get on with it?" was Osborne's report after forwarding to the Pontiff the conditions outlined in Halifax's letter which arrived in the diplomatic bag on 26 February. More than a month passed before he was again summoned by the Pope, who told him that he "feared that any prospects of favourable developments from approaches made through himself were vitiated by the fact that other similar approaches had reached H.M.G."[43]

Declassified Foreign Office files confirm that peace feelers, "having a family resemblance and probably having the same origin as those which have been reaching us from the Pope," had been received from a number of sources. "It is just as well that the Pope should realize what we are up against in this game of peace feelers," Roberts had minuted on the Vatican file docket. His reference makes it clear that the Foreign Office did not take the "game" very seriously. Lord Halifax, however, did. He ignored the advice of his officials that there were "no good Germans" and encouraged James Lonsdale Bryans, an amateur British diplomat who in January and February 1940 opened up another line to the underground opposition to Hitler. (See Appendix 3).[44]

The Vatican and Lonsdale Bryans's initiatives failed to break through to a Foreign Office accustomed to react with suspicion and indifference to the "will o'the wisps" with which they had been bombarded by Göring. The high hopes of the German opposition had also been wrecked by the 9 February announcement from Washington that Assistant Secretary of State Sumner Welles was to make a "fact-finding mission" of the European capitals to weigh the possibilities for a negotiated peace.

"Just Window Dressing"
March–May 1940

The Foreign Office reacted with angry apprehension to what appeared to be a Presidential *volte-face*. Vansittart immediately urged the Foreign Secretary to "warn President Roosevelt off any undesirable grass, before we have to receive the grass snake, Mr. Welles." The fear prevailing now in Whitehall was that the President was trying to boost his image in order to run for a third term by working for a negotiated peace, because "unless he quickly stops this was the U.S. will be called upon to rescue Great Britain and France from bankruptcy or defeat or both."[45]

Roosevelt, whose motives were far less hostile than the alarmed officials of the Foreign Office supposed, jauntily dismissed his chances of mediating a European peace as "one in a thousand," since he lacked the skills and talents of "the Holy Ghost and Jack Dempsey." Although he had repeatedly refused to countenance Ambassador Kennedy's appeals to intervene, by the first week in January 1940, as the State Department examined the possibility of calling a conference of neutral nations, Roosevelt had broached a fact-finding mission to Sumner Welles, telling the Assistant Secretary of State that his "obligation to the American people made it imperative for him to leave no stone unturned." Roosevelt confided to his trusted aide Breckinridge Long that the fact-finding mission was simply a delaying tactic that had been prompted by "an impulse" that a German offensive was in the offing. "If Welles' visit would delay that offensive or possibly prevent it," he said, "it would be a great deal." Even a week "would mean a lot" in terms of additional supplies reaching the Allies. The President explained the Welles mission as "just window dressing," in order to "get the low-down on Hitler and get Mussolini's point of view."[46]

James D. Mooney credited himself with changing the President's mind, because at their White House discussions on 22 December and 29 January Roosevelt hinted that "he would be willing to play the role of moderator in any peace discussions" and suggested the General Motors executive should use his forthcoming business trip to Germany as cover for an unofficial mission "to get the real feel of what Hitler and the other statesmen had on their minds." After a frosty briefing with State Department officials, Mooney sailed for Italy aboard the *Conte di Savoia*. When he learned that Sumner Welles was following hard on his heels, he assumed that an official peace mission had been set in motion by the "professional jealousy" in the State Department, because he had already received authority to cable his reports back to Washington in the naval cipher, so that they would not be read by the State officials.[47]

"Mr. Sumner Welles's mission is to check up on the reports

of the diplomatists and Mr. Mooney will be checking up on Mr. Sumner Welles," Vansittart decided after receiving a report from his brother, whom Mooney had summoned to meet him in Rome to discuss General Motors business. Halifax allowed his distaste for Americans to show in his marginal comment: "They are strange people and pursue strange methods!"[47]

What was billed in the press as "Roosevelt's peace mission" sailed from New York for Italy on 17 February in a blaze of publicity. Myron Taylor, the President's newly appointed personal emissary to the Vatican, was also aboard the Italian liner. So too was Axel Wenner-Gren, the Swedish business magnate who founded the Electrolux appliance empire. As a friend of Göring, his unofficial role, according to Jay Pierrepoint Moffat, the career diplomat detailed to the Welles mission, was "would-be go-between from Berlin to London and back."[49]

A week later, when Welles landed at Naples accompanied by a growing media circus, Roosevelt's "unofficial envoy" Mooney was already quietly established in the plush splendour of Berlin's Adlon Hotel. He vainly began cabling Welles and the American Chargé d'Affaires in Berlin to propose that they should join forces so as "not to cross wires." But Mooney was left on his own to make contact with German officials with the aid of Dr. Wolthart and the pro-German journalist Louis P. Lochner of Associated Press.[50]

"Unfortunately for the interest of peace," Hitler told Mooney after solicitously praising Roosevelt's initiative, "England refuses to admit that Germany herself is also a reality as a world power." Britain and France could have peace if they demonstrated their "respect" for Germany by agreeing to peace and returning her former colonies. The same theme was echoed by Ribbentrop and Göring, who asked Mooney to urge Roosevelt to assume his "moderator" role because Germany did not want to smash Britain, whose Empire performed "a most useful service to the entire civilized world." Mooney dutifully reported back to Roosevelt all the platitudes delivered to him by the Nazi leaders in reports so long that they tied up naval cryptographers for days.[51]

Meanwhile in Rome on 26 May Welles had met Mussolini, who spoke "with the greatest bitterness" about Britain's embargo of Italy's seaborne trade with Germany. The Italian dictator staked his claim to Gibraltar, Malta and Suez by insisting that "true peace" would not be possible without satisfaction of Italian demands for "free egress from, and access to the Mediterranean."[52]

Welles and Moffat stopped off, *en route* to Germany by train, in Zürich. They heard from John Cudahy, the American Ambassador in Brussels, his own plan for achieving a negotiated peace. Moffat also met, on 29 February, an emissary of the German opposition who told him that "the Army did not want to move until it had received solemn guarantees from Britain and France that Germany (as opposed to Hitler) would get generous peace terms."[53]

The reception that Welles and Moffat received from the Nazi leadership when they reached Berlin on 1 March 1940 quickly killed any hopes the Americans might have had for meaningful peace talks. Ribbentrop, who received them "glacially, and without a semblance of a smile or a word of greeting," launched into a two-hour harangue laying out Germany's claim to a "Monroe Doctrine of Europe." Welles found him "very stupid" and "saturated with hate for England." The next morning Hitler greeted the envoys "very pleasantly, but with great formality." With a "decidedly *gemütlich* look," he delivered "exactly the same historical survey" of Germany's position and willingness to negotiate peace as Ribbentrop. "The German people today are united as one man, and I have the support of every German," Hitler declared. "I can see no hope for the establishment of any lasting peace until the will of England and France to destroy Germany is itself destroyed."

The same bombastic message was delivered next day by Rudolf Hess. He read from a typewritten text, giving Welles the "unmistakable appearance of being devoid of all but a very low order of intelligence." Hess was so obviously parroting Ribbentrop that Welles did not waste any time with the Party Chief. He set off on the hour-and-a-half drive to Karinhall, where Göring received them in his bulging white uniform dripping with decorations, and with jewel-encrusted hands "shaped like the digging-paws of a badger." Göring nonetheless "spoke with greater frankness" about Hitler's reluctance to begin a war that might destroy the British Empire.[54]

When Roosevelt's envoys left Berlin for Paris on 4 March they had already come to the conclusion that Hitler could not be overthrown and that he commanded the military and public support to make good his threat to sacrifice two million men if Britain and France did not agree to his terms. Nothing they learned from the French officials during their brief stop-over in Paris changed Welles's opinion that both sides had dug in too deeply to make any concessions.

Ambassador Kennedy, who had himself returned to London only four days earlier after extended sick leave in the United States, was on hand at Hendon airfield when the Welles mission flew in on 10 March. He told Welles of Chamberlain's anxiety that he was coming to try to persuade the British government to negotiate with Hitler. It was evident that Kennedy hoped this was their purpose, since he pointed out with satisfaction how an anti-war candidate had won a quarter of the votes in a recent parliamentary by-election. The English upper classes, he told Welles and Moffat, were becoming more worried that a two-year war could bankrupt the country. Welles had to disappoint the Ambassador by assuring him that on Roosevelt's instruction he had "no suggestions nor proposals to offer." This was the message Welles gave that afternoon to Halifax.[55]

"I expected to find a very stiff, unsympathetic creature and was favourably disappointed," the Foreign Secretary wrote, recording that he had explained that negotiations with Hitler were out of the question, since "no lasting peace could be made in Europe so long as the Nazi regime dominated and controlled Germany." The message was repeated by Chamberlain, who, his "dark and piercing eyes" gleaming, spoke "with white hot anger" of his betrayal at Munich. But the impression the envoys received from senior British politicians was not unanimous. "Do not believe them when they tell you the British people want this war," Lloyd George told Welles. "I know them and I know they do not – they want security, and if they can obtain it on the terms I have mentioned, they will demand peace." He dismissed Chamberlain as a "third rate incompetent;" Halifax was "a good man, but not strong enough to be a real leader;" and neither Daladier nor Reynaud was "big enough" to lead the Allied war effort to victory.[56]

It was Churchill who struck Welles as the most powerful potential British leader, although his first impression was less than favourable. The First Lord received them at the Admiralty at five o'clock in the afternoon, "smoking a 24-inch cigar and drinking a whisky and soda." He was obviously somewhat the worse for wear, having "consumed a good many whiskeys," and mischievously proffered the decanter to the teetotaller Kennedy. But liquor had not impaired his host's ability to deliver an hour-and-fifty-minute long "cascade of oratory, brilliant and always effective, interlarded with considerable wit." He denounced the Nazi government as a "monster born of hatred and fear," and declared with great emphasis: "we will win the war and that is the only hope of civilization."[57]

"Churchill was one of the most fascinating personalities he had ever met," Welles later told the U.S. Military Attaché in London. But while Churchill was determined to see England fight to the last breath to destroy Nazism, Welles found Chamberlain and Halifax far less viscerally committed to the war when Kennedy tried to get the Prime Minister to see that he was taking an "untenable" position by refusing to negotiate with Hitler, prompting an angry exchange. It was, Welles reported to Roosevelt, the "hen-and-egg" predicament of the British government: Chamberlain had not wanted to get into the war, but now could see no way out.[58]

At a dinner given by the Prime Minister at 10 Downing Street, Hoare admitted to Kennedy that "the PM does not want to fight a minute longer than he has to." Gesturing towards Churchill he sniped that "he would be willing to fight for a hundred years." This remark prompted the American Ambassador to goad Churchill by joking that he had asked the Secretary of State to declare publicly that if the liner *Manhattan*, on which he had just crossed the Atlantic, had blown up, it would not cause the United States to declare war.[59]

"I thought that would give me some protection against Churchill's placing a bomb on the ship," the Ambassador cracked, in a heavy-handed allusion to the myth that Churchill had arranged for the torpedoing of the *Lusitania* in 1916 to inflame American public opinion against Germany. "Not I," Churchill growled. "I am certain that the United States will come in later anyway." No one, he added, understood the determination of the ordinary Britisher better than he. "His back is up. He will stand for no pulling of punches," Churchill declared. "He's tough."

"Well, if you can show me one Englishman that's tougher than you are, Winston," Kennedy shot back, "I'll eat my hat."[60]

This verbal sparring match brought the evening to an end. As the Ambassador drove with Welles back to the Dorchester Hotel, Kennedy grumbled that the evening's conversation had shown that there was "no sense of the shambles that are to come," expressing his main anxiety, that Chamberlain and Halifax might be replaced by Churchill, who hated the Germans and would never compromise with Hitler.[61]

The divisions in the British War Cabinet surfaced the following evening at a dinner given by the Foreign Secretary. Halifax leaned across the table and "confidentially" told Welles that Chamberlain's "harrowing human experience" at Munich had "necessarily affected" his view of the present German government. This the American envoy took to be a hint that, unlike the Prime Minister, the Foreign Secretary would be prepared to talk terms with Hitler. Halifax's suggestion of willingness to compromise was in marked contrast to the show of belligerence the British service chiefs put on to impress the Americans, blazing away at the Nazis for the duration of the dinner. Sir John Anderson, the Minister for Civilian Defence, who had not joined the chorus, took Welles by the arm as he left and assured him: "Please do not for one moment believe that *most of us* agree with the opinions you have heard expressed tonight."[62]

The message that not everyone in the British government was a hardliner over negotiating with Hitler came most strongly from Rab Butler. At a dinner he gave in Moffat's honour, the Under Secretary of State assured his American guest that Halifax "alone could prevail against useless and unwarranted punishment of the German people, though it would probably be at the cost of his career." Butler implied he was only waiting for the right moment to persuade his master to put his career on the line by calling for negotiations with Hitler. "Butler has a quick and interesting mind,"

Moffat observed. "He is clever, quick and intensely ambitious. He is not afraid of expressing his own views, even when they are not orthodox."[63]

Two days later Moffat discovered just how strongly Butler still believed in the need to appease Hitler after a telephone invitation from the Under Secretary "to continue our conversation of the night before last." Butler insisted on strolling out of earshot of his officials through a sun-dappled St. James's Park, where he explained that despite the "fiendish manifestations" of Nazism it was his personal belief that "you cannot destroy an idea and you cannot wipe out great emotional surges." Hitler's rise to power he regarded as a "revolt against vested interest," a political manifestation of a "redistribution of wealth" which he said would "soon reach England." Assuring Moffat that "younger forces in England" were willing to recognize that Germany must be given outlets for its trade and energy, he said he did not foresee "impossible hurdles" in reaching an agreement "fairly readily" with Fascist Italy. What England had then to decide was whether Hitler's "peace offensive" was genuine. He told Moffat that he "might be talking too much – he probably was – but he was reaching the conviction that *Germany would be sincere*, but that no one in England or France at present would believe it." Churchill and Eden "were completely intransigent," he said; "at present they play a very dominant role; but there were *more constructive forces* in existence." The intention behind Butler's suggestion is clear from his own diary entry, which reveals that he had raised the peace issue that very day with the Foreign Secretary: "I said I would not exclude a truce if Mussolini, the Pope and Roosevelt would come in, to which Halifax replied 'You are very bold, what a challenging statement, but *I agree with you.*'"[64]

Moffat's diary shows that Butler paid only lip-service to Chamberlain's insistence that the "easiest way to play the game was to help an overturn within Germany," because he did not believe that this was likely to happen now. He therefore wanted Welles to be told that his mission should be to bring the United States "further into the diplomatic picture." With his broad hints about "constructive forces" willing to break the deadlock, Butler intended to send a strong signal to the State Department that Roosevelt's intervention would give Halifax the chance to put his "career on the line" and press the British government to negotiate with Hitler.[65]

If Roosevelt had intervened, his call for peace negotiations that Butler was evidently anticipating would have been met with fierce resistance from Churchill in the Cabinet and from the hardliners in the Foreign Office. Vansittart appears to have picked up some of the straws that were blowing in the tail-wind of Welles's visit and moved swiftly to squash the idea. "If President Roosevelt were to come out with something on the lines that Mr. Sumner Welles clearly indicated as being in his own mind i.e. a peace with Hitler still in control," he urged the Foreign Secretary that the Prime Minister should, "in the friendliest but firmest fashion," tell the President in advance "that such an idea would have no chance whatever of being accepted." Whatever Halifax had told Butler in private, he was not yet prepared to risk his career, however "right" he believed his Under Secretary to be on the matter of negotiating with Hitler. He complied with Vansittart's suggestion, endorsing his minute that a telegram would be dispatched to the British Ambassador in Washington "in this sense."[66]

Butler's attempted "end-run" at jump-starting the peace process did not have a chance of succeeding, because the Welles mission was nothing more than "window dressing." Although Butler was a "protégé of the Prime Minister" Moffat evidently did not take too seriously the Under Secretary's feline intervention, with his opaque hints of "constructive forces" waiting in the wings to negotiate. If Welles and Moffat had ever, at Kennedy's urging, entertained the faintest hopes that Britain could be persuaded to negotiate, they were dispelled when they met Reynaud in Paris on 19 March. He had seen Churchill two days earlier and confirmed that he "could conceive of no possibility other than a war to the finish – whether that resulted in utter chaos and destruction or not."[67]

When Roosevelt's envoys arrived in Rome two days later, it was to news that Hitler had summoned Mussolini to an 18 March meeting at the Brenner Pass on the Austro-Italian frontier. The British seizure of thirteen Italian ships as they sailed from Rotterdam a week earlier with cargoes of German coal had precipitated a crisis. When Mussolini protested that the blockade was making him "the laughing stock of Europe," Halifax had persuaded the Cabinet to cave in and release the ships, to "avoid getting into a serious dispute with Italy on 'sanctions' lines." Halifax's appeasement of Mussolini came too late. Hitler had seized the initiative in the crisis by ordering Ribbentrop to Rome. "In a few months the French Army will be destroyed and the only British remaining on the continent will be prisoners of war," the German Foreign Minister promised the Duce, offering to ship coal supplies overland. He also delivered a letter from Hitler reminding Mussolini that his obligations under their Axis Pact would require him to confront "those same adversaries" by promising that at "the appropriate moment" Italy was to enter the war.[68]

"The minute hand is pointing to one minute before midnight," Mussolini announced with belligerent bluster at the start of his second meeting with Welles at the Palazzo Venezia on 16 March. Sensing that the Brenner meeting might foreshadow Italy's entry into the war, Welles obtained the President's permission to let

Mussolini know that the "door was still open" to peace negotiations. This message was relayed to Mussolini by Count Ciano, the Italian Foreign Minister who was doing his best to talk his master out of making any irrevocable commitments to Hitler. The next day, as the trains carrying the two dictators rolled into a snow-covered railway siding at the Brenner Pass, Welles arrived by Packard limousine at the Vatican to hear from the Pope that "he had been informed that 'technical' obstacles existed" which made the undertaking of the German offensive "unlikely for at least a month." As they spoke of peace, Hitler announced his "irrevocable decision" to launch a massive offensive in the West, flattering Mussolini into believing he was relying on him to provide "one last push" that "would cause the scales to tip irrevocably in favour of Germany and Italy." The Italian dictator gave Hitler his personal pledge that he would join the war "as soon as Germany thrust forward decisively."[69]

The irrevocable nature of Mussolini's personal commitment to war was carefully concealed from Roosevelt's envoys when Ciano met them for lunch two days later at Rome's fashionable Golf Club restaurant. The previous evening Welles had applauded Beniamino Gigli in a glittering gala performance of Verdi's *Un ballo in maschera*. He little suspected the operatic duplicity of the Italian Foreign Minister's categorical assurance that there was "absolutely no change in Italy's nonbelligerent attitude." Although Ciano knew he now had little hope of reversing Mussolini's pledge to Hitler, he continued to promise "to do everything in his power to keep Italy from getting into the war."[70]

Welles wrapped up his mission the next day by denying a *New York Times* headline that he had presented the Pope's eleven-point peace plan to Hitler. Rumours had still not been laid to rest when the American envoys arrived back in Washington a week later to find the State Department in a turmoil. A week earlier the Navy Department had delivered a grim strategic assessment that "the possibility of a defeat of the Franco-British alliance must now be squarely reckoned with." The chances of the Allies avoiding a military catastrophe if Italy joined Germany in attacking France were now considered so slender that the State Department immediately began recasting its policy. Welles and Moffat did their best to redress the prevailing pessimism by proposing American coal and economic aid to keep Mussolini from tipping the balance against the Allies by joining Hitler. The Germans' lightning invasion of Denmark and Norway in the following week was taken by many State Department officials as confirmation of the accuracy of the Navy's pessimistic strategic estimate.[71]

"That is the way to win wars. Whoever gets there first is right," Mussolini crowed with delight on 9 April as he read Hitler's letter informing him that German troops were moving into Denmark and

Norway. He promised the German Ambassador that he would immediately order the press "to applaud without reservation Germany's action" as he issued his directive calling for Italy's armed forces to prepare for a "parallel" war with the Reich's. Rather than comply with Hitler's request to send Italian divisions to the Upper Rhine to help crack the French Maginot Line, Mussolini, with a jackal's cunning, intended that Italy would seize her share of the spoils of the European war once it became clear that France was defeated. "It is a question of retarding as much as possible, consistent with honour and dignity, our entry into the war," he told Ciano, and called on his military to "prepare ourselves so that our intervention is decisive." The populace, he declared, "is a whore who goes after the conquering male." King Victor Emmanuel II, Marshal Pietro Badoglio and the Italian military chiefs were less enthusiastic about their military resources. At a chiefs-of-staff meeting on 6 May Badoglio deliberately inflated the intelligence reports of British forces in North Africa to try to dissuade the Duce from adding an attack in Libya to his "parallel war" plans. On 10 May Mussolini reached new heights of impatience as he read Hitler's personal letter announcing that Germany had "crossed the Rubicon" by attacking the Belgians, Dutch and French. But instead of announcing that Italy would now join in, he ordered a national poster campaign against the British.[72]

It was three more days before even Mussolini's closest aides discovered that their leader had finally set the timetable for Italy's entry into the war when German forces stormed across the Meuse on 13 May and the great battle that doomed France began.

Chapter 4

"We Have Lost the Battle!"
13–17 May 1940

DAY 2
"Blood, Toil, Tears and Sweat"
13 May

"On the Maginot Line, we shall defend the sacred soil of the nation" was the Order of the Day issued to France's Second Army during the closing hour of 12 May. That Sunday evening urgent intelligence reports began arriving at General Gamelin's headquarters outside Paris warning that German armoured and motorized divisions were emerging from the Belgian Ardennes at the northern hinge of the Maginot Line.[1]

All through the weekend, as the Allied military leadership focused on the battles raging in Holland and Belgium, German armoured columns had pushed stealthily through the Ardennes Forest like a giant toasting fork through a sixty-mile-wide slice of bread. During the final hours of darkness of 13 May the motorized infantry divisions that were tips of its three prongs began emerging from the rolling woodlands into the buttercup-filled meadows along the eastern bank of the River Meuse. Sporadic shelling from the French fortifications on the far bank punctuated the night with gun flashes along the front. The French Second Army garrisoning the fortifications at Sedan could hear the rumble of approaching German tanks as General Heinz Guderian's XIX Panzer Corps, the southernmost prong of the trident, moved towards the river. Sixty miles farther down the Meuse, the bursts of star rockets sent up by the French Ninth Army lit up the river. General Erwin Rommel's motorized infantry brigades, the spearhead of General Hermann Hoth's XV Panzer Corps, the northernmost barb of the German attack, rolled up on the east bank opposite the fortress town of Dinant. Midway between the two at Monthermé, the centre barb of General Rheinhardt's XLI Panzer Corps began massing opposite the row of reinforced concrete pillboxes lining the west bank of the Meuse.

Dawn over these three predetermined German crossing points brought a tremendous eruption of artillery and mortar fire that churned up the Meuse into a maelstrom. Stuka dive-bombers in forty-strong waves hurtled vertically down to plant their 550-lb. bombs with unnerving accuracy on the fortifications and gun emplacements. Junker and Dornier bombers swarmed high overhead, plastering the French defences with high explosive which gave an earthquake-like ferocity to the Wehrmacht's Blitzkrieg.

"We stand and watch what is happening as if hypnotized; down below all hell is let loose," was how Sergeant Prümers described the spectacle as he waited with the 1st Panzer Division across the Meuse at Sedan and watched the black flocks of Stukas screaming down like birds of prey. His men were brimming with confidence at three o'clock that Monday afternoon, when the waves of Stukas shifted their attacks inland and the signal came to begin the crossing. The first wave of German troops paddled their frail boats into water churning with a furious hail of bullets. For the next three hours, wave upon wave of assault troops and engineer companies braved the murderous fire to make the sixty-yard river crossing in inflatable boats. Under murderous mortar and machine-gun fire, they slithered ashore like reptiles to hurl their stick-grenades into the front-line pillboxes and gun emplacements. Fierce hand-to-hand battles raged throughout the afternoon. As the sun started to go down, white flags of surrender began popping up from the French lines. The waiting German divisions on the far bank cheered lustily when the first Swastika went up over the shattered remains of a captured strong-point at dusk.[2]

The first waves of the German troops had only just begun to claw their way to a precarious toehold at Sedan and Dinant that Monday afternoon when Winston Churchill arrived at the House of Commons to make his first speech as Prime Minister. Recalled by telegram from their Whitsun recess, the Members of Parliament crowded in to await the crucial vote of confidence in the new coalition government. Churchill was cheered only by the Labour backbenchers; the Tories reserved their clamour and waving of order papers for Chamberlain in a spontaneous display of loyalty to the fallen Prime Minister, an acknowledgement that he was still undisputed leader of their party.[3]

"I have nothing to offer you but blood, toil, tears and sweat" was to be the centrepiece of the speech Churchill had prepared. He had delivered the same stark appeal to the ministers he invited to join his coalition government. He wanted them to be under no illusion: together they and the country faced a Herculean task.

He had to take control of a rapidly deteriorating military situation in France and Norway; and the survival of his administration, and of the nation, depended on how quickly and effectively he took up the reins of military and political power. In an unprecedented move he had made himself overlord of Britain's military destiny by subsuming into the premiership the title of Minister of Defence; the deliberately small secretariat he established under General Hastings Ismay was intended to cut through paralysing committees. "It was accepted because everyone realized how near death and destruction we stood," Churchill later wrote, but his absorption of personal power worried Halifax and the other carry-overs from the previous administration. There was, however, a general recognition that, if Britain was to survive, the country desperately needed a war leader who could galvanize and inspire the nation in its hour of crisis. Churchill, driven by a powerful sense of personal destiny and fired by the adrenalin of war – to which he was no stranger – exuded inspiration and the confidence that fate had prepared him for this supreme mission of his life.[4]

"Blood, toil, tears and sweat" was all that Churchill could offer to his Cabinet colleagues, Members of Parliament and the people of Britain on 13 May 1940. Yet implicit in his appeal was the promise of survival and ultimate victory that he made the fulcrum of his first speech as Prime Minister. Berlin Radio had warned that Churchill would call for a "war of annihilation." And that was the message he delivered at the dispatch box that Monday afternoon.[5]

In a brief speech that set the uncompromising tone of his administration, Churchill excused his brevity and lack of ceremony by underlining the urgency of the crisis, making a frank appeal for the confidence of the House and for national unity, because they were now locked "in the preliminary stage of one of the greatest battles of history." He promised that his government would "wage war, by land, by sea and by air, with all our might . . . against a monstrous tyranny, never surpassed in the dark, lamentable catalogue of human crime." Churchill's mastery of language gave his rhetoric a rhythm and passion that roused the fighting instincts of members in the Chamber that afternoon, made the collective pulse of the nation beat faster, and offered the hope of ultimate salvation. "It is victory, victory at all costs," the Prime Minister concluded, "victory in spite of all terror, victory, however long and hard the road may be; for without victory, there is no survival."[6]

"The new P.M. spoke well, even dramatically, in support of the new all-Party government, but he was not well received" conceded Chips Channon, the inveterate Chamberlain supporter whose silence, like that of many of his fellow Tories, denied the Prime Minister his deserved triumph in the House that Monday. But the call to arms moved Lloyd George to ecstatic congratulation.

By 381 to 0, the House voted its approval for the new coalition government.[7]

"Good luck, Winnie, God bless you," a small crowd of well-wishers called as the Prime Minister's car drove through the arch of Admiralty House. Churchill was visibly moved. "Poor people. They trust me, and I can give them nothing but disaster for quite a long time," he told his military aide General Ismay. But as the *New York Times* observed, Britain's new leader had already achieved a psychological impact. "New ideals, new personalities will now have their chance," its leader declared next day. "Above all the spectacle of Mr. Churchill as Prime Minister should put a new heart into the British people. He can give them the rallying cry and the thrilling leadership which they deserve."[8]

The ominous military reports reviewed at the first full meeting of the new War Cabinet that evening offered precious little opportunity for Churchill to demonstrate "thrilling leadership." The only encouraging news came from Norway, where the French Alpine troops had that day landed at a fishing village eight miles down the Narvik Fjord. News of the battle raging in the Low Countries was grim.

"Very precarious" was how General Ironside summed up the desperate situation in Holland. Fresh waves of German airborne troops had landed in Rotterdam, and the Belgian forces were in retreat from the city of Liège. The first phase of the British and French troop movement into Belgium would be completed the following morning, but the "whole front showed strong German mechanized forces advancing in a number of directions." Ironside expressed concern that the lines of communication of the British Expeditionary Force would be threatened if the Panzer divisions succeeded in advancing westward across the Meuse.[9]

Churchill did not yet believe that that was the German intention. The situation was still so confused that he himself was uncertain whether the "great land attack" was really under way. Could it not be that the Germans were simply moving their forces up to make contact with the Allied front line? Ironside countered that the very scale of the enemy commitment of air and mechanized forces was confirmation enough that Hitler's long-expected spring offensive was already rolling forward to crash through the defences of France. This gave urgency to Churchill's request for Cabinet approval of "a personal message to President Roosevelt, informing him of the seriousness of the situation." He believed such an appeal might help persuade the United States government to release aircraft for the defence of France from their own military arsenal.[10]

"Things look pretty black. Holland cracking and Belgium not too good" was Cadogan's summary of the situation Churchill confronted. "Awful discussion about bombing the Ruhr," he recorded, reflecting the bitterness of the argument over whether to bomb Germany's major industrial area. Once again Chamberlain argued against any precipitate action, for fear of provoking retaliation on the poorly defended British aircraft factories, which were working round the clock to turn out the Spitfires and Hurricanes so desperately needed to defend the skies of Britain and France. Sir Archibald Sinclair, the Secretary of State for Air, agreed with Chamberlain. He warned that "only 39 squadrons" were currently operational with the R.A.F., far short of the sixty that the air staff believed necessary for the "adequate defence of this country."[11]

The War Cabinet also considered reports that both Italy and Spain were coming under German pressure to join in against the Allies. What the British Ambassador in Rome did not yet know was that the Duce had that very day informed his Foreign Minister that the Allies had "lost the war," and he had therefore decided to "attack France and England by sea and air." When Mussolini learned that Hitler had begun his great offensive against France that morning he told Ciano that Italy would go to war in "ten to fourteen days." 13 May was therefore a climactic day not just for Churchill, France and Britain, but also for Italy. It ended with the Germans poised on the brink of a major breakthrough in France. The Swastika flew over the Gothic town hall at Liège and fluttered over the front line of the French fortifications at three key crossing points along the Meuse front.[12]

"Panic Brooked No Delay"
14 May

The advanced forces of Rommel and Guderian had won a precarious toehold at Dinant and Sedan. Shortly after midnight, to General Guderian's relief, the first mechanized units began rolling over the pontoon bridges under sporadic French counter-fire. "Our front has been pushed in at Sedan," General Alphonse Georges declared at a midnight emergency meeting of his staff in the salon at Les Bondons, the villa that served as his headquarters at La Ferté. The commander of all the French armies at the North-east Front suddenly turned a deathly shade as he read a report brought in by dispatch rider. He fell into an armchair with a sob. General Georges was the first senior commander to grasp the magnitude of the disaster that stalked France's armies that night. Yet it remained a matter of honour for him to keep the news from reaching General Gamelin at his headquarters a hundred miles away at Vincennes. The French Prime Minister knew even less. Reynaud had spent the day trying to find out the news from Gamelin's headquarters. It was six o'clock in the evening before he learned that the situation on the Meuse front had changed for the worse. By the early hours of 14 May, the first German tanks had arrived at the outskirts of Sedan.[13]

If the French forces at Sedan and Dinant had launched a coordinated and determined counterattack that night, they would have had a good chance of driving the German bridgehead into the river. But as the hours passed in fatal inactivity for France, the growing wedge of enemy tanks began to take up positions in support of the advanced infantry units. Daylight brought the Stukas back in force to batter the rear of the French line and thwart any counterattack as the Panzer divisions continued to rumble across pontoon bridges unopposed. As the French High Command struggled to regroup their field commanders for a major counterattack, remorseless Stuka bombing blasted the morale of the French armies along the Meuse.

"Much worse, commanders at all levels pretended they had received orders to withdraw, but were quite unable to show them or even say exactly how or where the orders had come from," wrote General Edouard Ruby. "Panic brooked no delay, command posts emptied like magic." The escalating collapse on the Meuse front did not percolate through to Paris, let alone London, until Tuesday evening.[14]

When Churchill met the War Cabinet at 11.30 a.m. on 14 May, the latest news from France gave no cause for alarm, but by the late afternoon alarming reports started trickling into Paris. The piecemeal news of the disaster overtaking the defenders along the Meuse front was like a tremor that built itself into an earthquake for the French government.[15]

"We felt that the situation had suddenly become very tragic," Paul Baudouin, the French Under Secretary of State, recorded after the six o'clock War Council, at which Gamelin had announced that there was "very bad" news from the Meuse front. German fighters had machine-gunned refugees fleeing from the Ardennes battlefield. Railway lines essential to moving military supplies and reinforcements to the Meuse front had been bombed and cut. Secret measures were being put in hand to evacuate children from Paris. At seven o'clock the Council was in a state of crisis when the Prime Minister suspended the meeting to receive the British and American Ambassadors, who told him that reports from Rome the previous evening indicated that Italy's entry into the war "seemed very probable."[16]

"Germany intends to deliver a mortal blow to Paris," the French Prime Minister warned Churchill in a dramatic telephone call to London that evening. He appealed for ten additional R.A.F. fighter squadrons to be sent "at once, if possible today," because "the

German Army has broken through our fortified line south of Sedan."
France's Second and Ninth Armies "could not resist the combined
attacks of heavy tanks and bomber squadrons" without the British
fighters. "I am confident," Reynaud told Churchill, "that in this
crisis English help will not fail us."[17]

The French Prime Minister's urgent appeal was immediately put
before a hastily convened 7 p.m. meeting of the War Cabinet.
The British Chiefs of Staff did not understand the reason for
such panic, believing, as Churchill did, that there was only a
relatively small penetration of the French front line by German
tanks, which "could not be decisive against a large army unless
heavily reinforced from the rear." Six British fighter squadrons
were already operating with the B.E.F. in the general area, so he
proposed "that we should hesitate before we denuded still further
the heart of the Empire." Air Marshal Sir Cyril Newall, the Chief
of the Air Staff, strongly concurred, arguing that "these squadrons
would never return to this country once they were established on
the other side of the Channel." So the War Cabinet decided that
the situation was still "too obscure" to justify the risk in meeting
the French Prime Minister's demands. "No time is being lost,"
Churchill reassuringly cabled Reynaud, "in studying what we can
do to meet the situation."[18]

"Smashed Up Like Matchwood"
15 May

At 7 a.m. the next morning Churchill was roused from his sleep by
a telephone call from the French Prime Minister, "evidently under
stress."

"We have been defeated. We are beaten. We have lost the battle,"
Reynaud declared, insisting that the Sedan front had collapsed and
the Germans were "pouring through in great numbers with tanks
and armoured cars."

"The road to Paris is open. We are defeated," Reynaud repeated,
with such finality that an alarmed Churchill promised to "come
over and have a talk." This did little to compose the French
Premier, who was to receive a fresh blow at ten that Wednesday
with the news that all "eight or nine divisions" defending the
Meuse "were in full retreat." Deprived of adequate information
and reluctant to telephone Gamelin directly for fear of reopening
his row with Daladier, he telephoned to ask the War Minister what
counter-measures the commander-in-chief was taking. Stunned by
Daladier's reply that there was nothing to be done, Reynaud turned
to Baudouin in utter exasperation. "Ah! if the Marshal were only

here he would be able to influence Gamelin," he said. But Marshal Pétain, whose implacable will had saved France in 1916 by resisting the German attack at Verdun, was far from the battle, in Madrid as France's ambassador. What Reynaud did not tell Baudouin was that he had already issued instructions for Pétain's recall.[19]

At the Wednesday morning War Cabinet meeting Churchill related his dramatic conversation with the French Premier. He was confused, because after the panic-stricken call from Reynaud he had been surprised to hear a "calm" General Georges whom he had telephoned for assurances that the gap in the French lines had been "plugged" and the military situation was now "fairly satisfactory." Determined to do everything he could to help France in her hour of need, he worried that he "could not denude England of her essential defences."[20]

The Prime Minister therefore decided to tell Reynaud that "no further fighter squadrons, for the present, should be sent to France." The War Cabinet, however, considered the military situation to be sufficiently serious to justify the risk entailed in raiding the Ruhr. The news that a hundred heavy bombers, targeted on the German industrial heartland, would be dispatched by the R.A.F. that night was expected to rally the French government. To counter the latest reports from Rome, indicating that Italy might join the war by attacking France in the south sooner rather than later, Churchill dispatched a personal letter to Mussolini appealing that their two countries "should not be divided by bloodshed."[21]

Alarmed by reports from Holland of the havoc wrought by Fifth Columnists aiding the German parachute troops, Churchill was influenced by a five-page report on the "Fifth Column Menace" written at the behest of Lord Halifax by Sir Nevile Bland, the British Minister just back from the Netherlands. Bland's hair-raising evacuation from Holland by Royal Navy destroyer on 14 May coloured the alarmist account he drafted that day of the "frightful dangers" facing the nation from the "enemy in our midst." According to Bland, undercover German agents ranged from a female parachutist who had once been a domestic servant to suicide killer gangs of teenage youths, "sodden with Hitler's ideas," and Nazi sympathizers inside the Dutch government who provided lists of pro-Allied officials who were "shot on sight" by the arriving German paratroops.[22]

The "Fifth Column Menace" was largely the invention of Dutch and French journalists seeking scapegoats to explain the terrifying success of the German Blitzkrieg. But Bland's report made a deep impression on Churchill, who asked the War Cabinet that morning to agree to a "very large round up of enemy aliens and suspect persons" in Britain. Sir John Anderson, the Minister for Home Security, was "opposed to premature action" and tried to forestall

Churchill by setting up a committee to study how aliens, British fascists and communists could be interned without "overtaxing government machinery or the liberty of citizens." This did little to reassure the Prime Minister, who wanted to have "these persons . . . behind barbed wire."[23]

Churchill then read the text of his personal message to President Roosevelt informing him of the "seriousness of the situation." In his first communication to the White House since becoming Prime Minister, he warned that the scene had "darkened swiftly," with Luxembourg, Holland and Belgium "smashed up like matchwood." Trying to strike a note of urgency without sounding too desperate, Churchill's cable assured Roosevelt that Britain "was not afraid" to "continue the war alone," if it came to "a completely subjugated and Nazified Europe," which he warned could be established "with astonishing swiftness." He called on the President to proclaim "non-belligerency" so that the United States could help with "everything short of actually engaging armed forces." Attached to his appeal for help was a "wish list" of American war equipment most urgently needed by the Allies, with top priority to a request for "the loan of 40 or 50 of your older destroyers." In addition he asked for "several hundred of the latest types of aircraft" and supplies of ammunition and anti-aircraft batteries. Nor were Churchill's strategic concerns only focused on the European war theatre. "I am looking to you to keep the Japanese dog quiet in the Pacific," he told Roosevelt, offering the U.S. Navy the facilities of the naval fortress of Singapore.[24]

Roosevelt was alive to the probability that Japan would be encouraged to take advantage of the German onslaught in Europe to step up aggression in the Far East. The deteriorating military position in France was being brought dramatically home to the President by telephone calls from an "almost hysterical" American Ambassador in Paris, William C. Bullitt. The assessment of Assistant Secretary Berle in his Wednesday position paper was that "the Germans, shortly to be reinforced by the Italians, will defeat the French army completely, and will be in a position to smash up England pretty thoroughly."[25]

The steadily expanding armoured wedges that had been driven by the Wehrmacht into the French lines at Sedan and Dinant had by now begun their break-out. Their relentless hammer-blows, reinforced by continuous air bombardment, opened up the first ominous crack in General Huntziger's Second Army defending Sedan, even as the line held by General Corap's Ninth Army at Dinant had sheared apart shortly after dawn that Wednesday. The Panzer divisions thrust cleanly through, slicing apart the 2nd French Armoured Division, whose tanks Gamelin had counted on to lead the counterattack. By late afternoon the Ninth Army, which had been "in critical condition" only hours before, was on the verge of a rout.

"The disorder of the Army is beyond description. Its troops are falling back on all sides," Lieutenant-Colonel Guillaut that evening warned a still remarkably complacent Gamelin. "The Army General Staff has lost its head. It no longer even knows where its divisions are. The situation is worse than we could have imagined." His eyes at last opened to impending catastrophe, Gamelin telephoned Daladier. The French Minister for War happened to be in conference with the American Ambassador, who was appalled by what he overheard.[26]

"No, what you tell me is not possible!" Daladier insisted, refusing to believe his Commander-in-Chief. "We must attack soon!" he shouted down the line. Gamelin told him there were "no more reserves." "Then it means the end of the French Army," Daladier exclaimed, to Bullitt's alarm. Hurrying back to his Embassy, the Ambassador cabled Washington that the military situation was sliding rapidly away from the French High Command. For once the excitable Bullitt was not exaggerating the magnitude of the crisis overtaking the French government.[27]

"Aucune!"
16 May

In the early hours of Thursday morning alarming reports were received at Vincennes that the German tanks had already reached Laon, less than eighty miles north-east of the French capital. With no adequate reserves to stop them, the road to Paris was open. This was the nightmare that Reynaud had foreseen six days earlier. Just before 1 a.m. on Thursday, 16 May, he convened an emergency council meeting at the Ministry of the Interior. It was not a productive meeting. Daladier had "broken down," and the elderly Military Governor of Paris, who was "in a state of collapse," advised that the Government should evacuate the capital without delay.[28]

When the British Chiefs of Staff calmly made their reports that morning to the 10.30 a.m. War Cabinet, they had only just received the first reports of the massive German breakthrough on the Meuse front. Gamelin had followed up with an urgent appeal for the ten R.A.F. fighter squadrons without which, he warned, "the battle would be lost." Churchill decided it was now "right to send further fighters to France." Within the hour the Cabinet would approve the immediate dispatch of four fighter squadrons. The others were to be held in reserve against the developing situation. "It would be a short-sighted policy to squander bit by bit and day by day, the fighter squadrons, which are in effect our Maginot Line," Churchill wrote to Reynaud, explaining why he could not meet the full French demands.[29]

The War Cabinet noted Roosevelt's "further exceedingly strong message to Signor Mussolini," but of more immediate concern was the report from the British Purchasing Mission in the United States dashing hopes of obtaining more fighters from the U.S. Army. The American planes were "obsolete and unsuitable for European conditions."[30]

"The blackest days I have ever lived through," observed Cadogan of Thursday's Cabinet, "at which we received blacker and blacker news from France." The Luftwaffe reportedly "dominated the battle-field," and General Gort now expressed his concern that the German armoured vehicles were driving a deep wedge into the French forces along the Meuse south of the Dyle front in Belgium held by his British Expeditionary Force. Reports that the French had already started to withdraw alarmed General Dill, the Army Chief of Staff. He urged the War Cabinet that Gort should be instructed to begin to pull back the B.E.F. before they were cut off if the German breakthrough accelerated its advance.[31]

"This infuriated Winston, who said we couldn't agree to that, which would jeopardize our whole army," Cadogan recorded, noting how Churchill "sprang up and said he would go to France – it was ridiculous to think that France could be conquered by 120 tanks." The Prime Minister announced he would "leave after lunch," after asking Chamberlain to "mind the shop."

The twin-engined Flamingo transport plane carrying the British Prime Minister and his entourage was bumping through rain clouds over the Channel when the French Prime Minister Reynaud entered a packed Chamber of Deputies at three o'clock on that Thursday afternoon. Wild rumours had been sweeping Paris since dawn that the Germans would arrive in the city by nightfall. The government was widely believed to be abandoning the capital – a rumour that gained credence from the columns of smoke spiralling above the Quai d'Orsay as officials burned bundles of secret documents. Reynaud, now recovered from his earlier panic, appealed to all Frenchmen for calm and national resolution.

"We shall fight before Paris; we shall fight in Paris if need be!" Reynaud declared in the Assemblée Nationale. He accompanied his public display of fighting spirit with a personal pledge that he would take "revolutionary steps" to defend the national honour, promising to "change both methods and men" charged with the defence of France.[32]

When Churchill arrived at the British Embassy at five after driving in from Le Bourget airport First Secretary Oliver Harvey found him "full of fire and fury, saying the French were lily-livered."

Half an hour later, trailed by a bevy of anxious British officials, the Prime Minister strode impatiently past the uniformed lackeys up the sweeping marble staircase of the Quai d'Orsay. The frock-coated *huissier* with his heavy silver chain of office self-importantly led the British party into a magnificent pilastered conference chamber where the French leaders hovered nervously. The dusty Second Empire grandeur of this mirror-and-gilt salon was a fitting stage-set for the drama that unfolded. Its tall windows were tightly closed, but the acrid smoke rising up from the blazing bonfires in the courtyard had seeped in, adding a battlefield stench to the charged atmosphere. Intermittent thuds as Foreign Ministry officials hurled heavy bundles of documents from the upper floors echoed through the Grand Salon like the footsteps of approaching doom.[33]

"Utter dejection was written on every face," Churchill recalled, noting how everyone remained standing. Reynaud spoke first, inviting Gamelin to explain the seriousness of the military situation. The General, a short moustachioed man with button eyes, was dwarfed by the six-foot map of northern France that rested on a student's easel at the centre of the salon. A long black line had been drawn representing the Allied front line into which extended a "small but sinister red bulge at Sedan." The British Prime Minister, who had expressed initial surprise at the gravity of the military situation, was left in doubt as the French Commander-in-Chief delivered a precise and polished lecture. "His ladylike hand marked here and there on the map the positions of our broken units and of our reserves on the move," Baudouin observed. "He explained, but made no suggestions. He had no views on the future; there was not one word of tomorrow, or even of hope."[34]

"The mistake, the unpardonable mistake was to send so many men to Belgium," Daladier could be heard complaining as he sat glumly in a corner, "like a schoolboy in disgrace." Reynaud, sensing that Churchill might not yet have taken in the magnitude of the military disaster facing France, took over the map and in two sentences put their predicament in its truly awful perspective.[35]

"The hard point of the German lance has gone through our troops as through a sand hill," he said, pointing to the red bulge. "I assure you that in this bulge there is at stake not only the fate of France, but also that of the British Empire." A long silence followed, during which Churchill puffed deliberately and noisily on his cigar. Finally he turned to General Gamelin.

"Where is the strategic reserve?" he demanded of the French Commander-in-Chief, deliberately repeating his question in schoolboy French. *"Où est la masse de manœuvre?"*

"Aucune!" Gamelin responded with a shrug. "None."

"There was another long pause," Churchill recorded in his memoirs. "Outside in the garden of the Quai d'Orsay clouds of smoke arose from large bonfires, and I saw from the window venerable officials pushing wheel-barrows of archives on to them. Already therefore the evacuation of Paris was being prepared."[36]

The British Prime Minister was "dumbfounded." It had never for one moment occurred to him that the commanders of an army defending five hundred miles of French frontier could have been so remiss. It took him several seconds to grasp that France did not have a strategic reserve force available to plug any gaps the enemy made in the Maginot Line. Gamelin attempted to justify his position, launching into a staff-college lecture on classic military strategy. It was clear that the French High Command were now looking to the British to provide their strategic reinforcement. Gamelin said that what he needed was more British fighter aircraft to provide the air coverage for his armies and stop the German Panzers.

"No," Churchill interrupted again, "it is the business of the artillery to stop the tanks. The business of the fighters is to cleanse the skies," he said, breaking into French, *"nettoyer le ciel"* over the battle. The desperate military situation confronting the Allies was forcibly brought home to the Prime Minister as recrimination and arguments broke out among the milling French generals.[37]

On his return to the Embassy that evening, he sent instructions to Downing Street to call an emergency War Cabinet to consider his appeal for six additional R.A.F. squadrons. "It was a rending decision either way," he wrote. He knew that his request would leave Britain with only twenty-five fighter squadrons for her own defence while the Air Staff advised that the minimum requirement was sixty. When he telegraphed the French request to the War Cabinet, he cautioned: "It would not be good historically if their requests were denied and their ruin resulted."[38]

"Han," the Hindustani for "Yes," the agreed code-word announcing the War Cabinet's approval, was flashed from London to the British Embassy in Paris shortly after 10.30 p.m. What this abbreviated confirmation did not reveal was that the Air Staff had decided that the six additional squadrons Churchill requested could not be accommodated at the R.A.F. bases in France, since their forward airstrips were already being evacuated. The War Cabinet had therefore agreed to a compromise whereby the Hurricanes would operate over the French battlefield from bases in southern England – three squadrons in the morning and three in the afternoon.

Churchill did not fully appreciate this when he rushed off to Reynaud's apartment to assure him that the fighters that would turn the battle around were on their way. The French Premier appeared in a dressing gown, looking like "some small broken piece of machinery." Despite the lateness of the hour he agreed to summon Daladier. When the War Minister arrived, the British Prime Minister ("crowned like a volcano by the smoke of his cigars," according to Baudouin, who was also present) launched into a vintage Churchillian exhortation to fight on and never surrender which lasted until one in the morning. "Even if France was invaded and vanquished England would go on fighting until the United States came to her aid," Churchill declared, describing a truly "apocalyptic vision" in which he saw himself "in the heart of Canada directing, over an England razed to the ground by high-explosive bombs, over a France whose ruins were already cold, the air war of the New World against the Old dominated by Germany."[39]

"Such a Nightmare"
17 May

The Prime Minister's satisfaction that his night-time performance had rallied the French government was evident next morning to Oliver Harvey. He had slept over at the British Embassy in the bedroom next to Churchill's, and was woken "with his singing and splashing in his bath while he was getting up to catch his aeroplane at six." But by the time he arrived back in England the Prime Minister was having doubts about whether the French could survive the onslaught. "Winston is depressed," his private secretary Colville noted when he met him at Hendon airfield. "He says the French are crumpling up as completely as did the Poles, and that our forces in Belgium will inevitably have to withdraw in order to maintain their contact with the French."[40]

The Prime Minister took care not to convey his pessimism to the War Cabinet when he reported on his trip to Paris. He assured his colleagues that Reynaud was now in "better heart." The German advance had slowed down, he said, now that General Georges "was dealing calmly with the situation." He had made it clear to the French leaders that "unless they made a supreme effort, we would not feel justified in accepting the grave risk to this country which would be entailed by the dispatch of more fighters to France." But his visit to Paris had alerted him to the disaster that would engulf the B.E.F. if the German advance could not be halted. He now conceded that General Gort's plan for the orderly withdrawal of the Force in stages should be put into effect without delay, although he insisted that "we ought not to yield an inch of ground without fighting."[41]

Ironside felt that Churchill was "more like an old boar in a corner than anything else," but Chamberlain chose this moment of high drama to praise the Prime Minister for his "courageous leadership." The Foreign Secretary reported that Mussolini "had very nearly reached the point of bringing Italy into the war." The War Cabinet accepted that it was now a question of when, rather than if, Italy entered the war. The Chiefs of Staff were instructed to put into effect the preparatory plans for war in the Mediterranean. Since the burden would fall principally on the Royal Navy, it came as a bitter disappointment for Churchill to have to tell his colleagues that Roosevelt had refused his appeal for fifty old American destroyers.[42]

"As you know a step of that kind could not be taken except with the specific authorization of Congress," the President said in a cable which explained that he "was not certain that it would be wise for that suggestion to be made to the Congress at this time." He did reply more positively to Churchill's other requests, but he turned down the invitation to send ships of the U.S. Pacific Fleet to Singapore, signing off with "The Best of Luck."[43]

The Prime Minister knew that Britain was not going to survive on such a thin diet of vague promises and good wishes from the United States. But, as Ambassador Kennedy hastened to assure Churchill shortly after the Cabinet meeting, that was all Roosevelt could provide at present. "Never did I think that I could endure such a nightmare," Cadogan wrote, reflecting Kennedy's pessimism that the United States could do nothing to affect the outcome of the Battle of France. It was a nightmare that threatened to become a dreadful reality for the citizens of Paris that Friday morning.[44]

In the pre-dawn stillness the distant rumble of bombing and artillery fire could be heard all over the city. Then at mid-morning came the news that the German armoured columns had slowed their southward advance and appeared to be swinging north-west away from Paris towards the Channel ports. The population of the French capital heaved a collective sigh of relief. The respite may have been temporary, but stock prices on the Paris Bourse jumped on news that the German Panzer divisions had turned away from the city and were heading for the Channel because Hitler was "going to England first."[45]

"The military situation appears to be no worse, possibly because the German armoured divisions have to regroup and revictual," Baudouin noted in his diary, which provides the only surviving record of the French War Council. "Further to the north, our armies in Belgium have begun their retreat," he added, noting that the Prime Minister had told him that because of the gravity of the military situation he had recalled Marshal Pétain from Spain. Then Reynaud headed for an afternoon conference with the President of the Republic to pave the way for his intended move to sack Daladier and assume the post of Minister of National Defence himself.[46]

The decision to slow down the German advance had been taken by the Führer himself. Hitler had convinced himself that the Panzer columns were moving too fast for the infantry columns to catch up, leaving their lengthening flanks vulnerable to counterattack. This was not the opinion of the O.K.H. generals directing the campaign. "Our breakthrough wedge is developing in a positively classic manner," General Halder commented approvingly: "West of the Meuse our advance is sweeping on, smashing tank counterattacks in its path. Superb marching performance of the infantry." The front-line commanders were even more enthusiastic about pushing ahead. "We had broken through the Maginot Line," Rommel wrote jubilantly that day when he saw the "way to the west was open." Leading his armoured column in a headlong rush, on Friday he had advanced an incredible fifty miles that had taken him as far as Avesnes. For casualties of forty men and a single officer the 7th Panzer Division had captured a hundred thousand enemy prisoners and a hundred French tanks.[47]

"The morning picture clearly indicates that the enemy has not taken any serious steps to close the breakthrough gap," Halder recorded in his journal back at O.K.H. headquarters. He concluded from the reports that the "enemy is not strong enough to attack us." Hitler did not agree. "Apparently little mutual understanding," Halder noted of their noon meeting. "The Führer insists that the main threat is from the south – I see no threat at present." That afternoon Hitler left the Felsennest bunkers to see the situation for himself at the Army Group B headquarters in Bastogne.[48]

Field Marshal General Gerd von Rundstedt was a meticulous Prussian who had been a World War I staff officer. The previous day he had ordered his forces to consolidate by delaying their crossing of the River Oise until 18 May. His "mark time" order had infuriated Guderian, who saw it as dangerous interference with the freedom of action of a field commander. He was right. During the enforced halt on 17 May Colonel de Gaulle had carried out orders to make a counterattack with French armoured forces. His 4th French Armoured Division, a hastily assembled scratch force of three battalions of tanks, managed initially to push ten miles north-west of Laon into the German front line at Montcornet on the Serre. Lacking any infantry support, de Gaulle was forced by heavy German resistance and dive-bomber attacks to withdraw his tanks by nightfall. The counterattack was brushed off by Guderian as a pinprick, and he did not even report to Army Group B headquarters when that afternoon he received authority to carry out "reconnaissance in force", an order that permitted him to get his Panzers rolling forward again by turning a blind eye to von Rundstedt's first halt order.[49]

"A Tight Fix"
18 May

"Frightened by his own success, he is afraid to take any chances and so would rather pull the reins on us," was Halder's comment on Hitler's "unaccountable worrying." By Saturday morning the Führer was throwing a tantrum. "He rages and screams that we are on the best way to ruin the whole campaign and that we are leading up to a defeat." Halder and von Brauchitsch did their best to calm Hitler's nerves. His confidence was partly restored by the news that Antwerp had fallen and that the British and French forces were in full retreat from Belgium.[50]

"Every hour is precious," Halder argued, urging Hitler that the French line must be smashed before it was consolidated. Distrustful of the Prussian generals, the former corporal would listen only to his instinct. "He won't have any part of continuing the operation in a westward direction, let alone to the south-west," Halder noted angrily after the Führer handed down a directive that required improvising for "a north-western drive." Hitler did not relent until news came that afternoon that Brussels had fallen. After being assured that the infantry were catching up and that "our tanks are now in line and ready to attack," Hitler finally agreed to resume the advance, "but in an atmosphere of bad feeling."[51]

"The tortoise is thrusting his head very far beyond his carapace," was Churchill's hopeful conclusion as news reached London that the Panzers were rolling forward again towards the Channel coast. His optimistic assessment was sharply at odds with the mounting pessimism of the Chief of the Imperial General Staff.[52]

"We have lived in a fool's paradise, largely depending upon the strength of the French Army," General Ironside reflected, noting that their ally "has crashed or very nearly crashed." In his diary he concluded that there was no doubt that the battle for France was all but lost, and Britain and her Empire were approaching "a turning point in history," when they would soon be confronted by a "completely Nazified Europe." The defeatism Ironside expressed in private was not yet reflected in his official comments to the War Cabinet. At the Saturday morning meeting he appeared to share Churchill's optimism when reporting that the French had "consolidated" their position and the B.E.F. and the French had successfully withdrawn from Belgium to their second defensive position, from Cambrai to the Deule Canal.[53]

When the War Cabinet met for a second session that Saturday afternoon to consider a report drawn up by Chamberlain anticipating the collapse of France, the military assessment of the Joint Planning Committee was not yet ready, but the civilian assessment was chilling enough. It dealt with the situation faced by the British government in the event of a "breakdown of resistance in France, and in particular the question of the evacuation of the B.E.F. and the Defence of these Islands." Britain, the report concluded, could only "continue our resistance single-handed in this country *until the United States of America could be induced to come to our help.*"[54]

"In these circumstances it would be imperative," Chamberlain declared, "that we should abandon our present rather easy-going methods and resort to a form of government which would approach the totalitarian." Gold, arms, equipment, aircraft and machine tools would be removed from France and the French fleet and merchant ships would be sailed to British ports. France's factories and oil reserves would be destroyed and her harbours blocked. Even then the situation would be "so menacing" that the government would have to "take complete power over property, business and labour." In view of the deteriorating military situation, Chamberlain suggested that the Prime Minister should pave the way for an assumption of these powers in a broadcast. "We were in a tight fix and . . . no personal considerations must be allowed to stand in the way of measures necessary for victory" was the message Chamberlain wanted Churchill to convey: the "situation might deteriorate and, if so, further sacrifices would be called for."[55]

The Home Secretary's memorandum on "Invasion of Great Britain: Possible Co-operation of a Fifth Column" took an opposing view of the seriousness of the crisis. Sir John Anderson said he was reluctant to impose another burden on the police, who were already having to screen 100,000 refugees on their way from Belgium. He did not propose any action against British Fascists, "in the absence of evidence which indicated that the organization as such was engaged in disloyal activities." Anderson's soft approach did not please the Prime Minister, who had already minuted to his intelligence aide, Major Desmond Morton, his dissatisfaction with the Ministry's failure to intern the leaders of what he described as "very considerable numbers" of Fascists and Communists. He wanted to "stiffen up the measures already taken" and instructed the Home Secretary to resubmit within a week his plans for firmer action against German sympathizers and Fifth Columnists.[56]

"One must always be prepared," Churchill minuted to General Ismay that evening, "for the fact that the French may be offered very advantageous terms of peace, and the whole weight might be thrown against us." After receiving word that the French line had "started to suppurate again" he suggested recalling one of the Guards divisions from France.[57]

The worsening military situation cast a pall over the meeting of the French War Cabinet that Saturday afternoon. The city of St. Quentin had fallen that morning. By midday German tanks had overrun Le Catelet, taking the entire headquarters staff of the Ninth Army prisoner. "Complete disintegration," reported one of General Gamelin's liaison officers. "Out of 70,000 men and numerous officers, no single unit is commanded, however small . . ." The roads south were clogged with fleeing civilians mingling with deserting soldiers. French writer and aviator Saint-Exupéry observed the tragic rout of the Ninth Army at first hand. "Somewhere in the north of France a boot had scattered an ant-hill, and the ants were on the march," he wrote. "Laboriously. Without panic. Without hope. Without despair. On the march as if duty bound."[58]

"Our front had been broken from Sedan to Dinant; Corap's Army had faded away" was Reynaud's memory of that terrible weekend. "The Allied Armies in Belgium were in full retreat and threatened with encirclement; the onrush of the German Army, with Panzers and Stukas in the van, was invading France." Facing an "overwhelming disaster," he made Marshal Pétain his Deputy Premier, claiming that the eighty-four-year-old hero of Verdun was "the only one with the requisite authority over our army and those of our Allies to restore the situation in so far as it was capable of being restored." After the Saturday War Council meeting, Reynaud set out by car with Pétain to visit the La Ferté army headquarters. The Prime Minister's recharged sense of purpose and confidence was quickly punctured by the latest military reports.[59]

"It is a difficult situation," General Georges explained, with sorrowful eyes, as his grey-gloved hand swept agilely but without purpose over the maps he rolled up and down, each showing more alarmingly than its predecessor the worsening predicament of the French armies being pushed further west by the alarming red bulge that had been driven across northern France by ten Panzer divisions. Reynaud, confronted by the rising tide of military disaster, went before the microphones that evening to foreshadow the changes he was about to make in the war leadership of France and to rally the nation.

"Marshal Pétain is at my side," Reynaud declared. "He will stay there until victory." With the venerated Marshal in his government and General Maxime Weygand on his way back from Syria to take command of the army, "surrounded with the halo of Foch's glory," the embattled Prime Minister hoped to restore public confidence. He was convinced that, despite their age, these two military heroes could "solve the question of morale which was gravely impaired both in the army and the country."[60]

"Blank Panic"
19 May

"The breakthrough is proceeding in a satisfactory manner," General Halder noted after the Sunday morning's staff conference at Felsennest. "Our big tank drive in the direction of Arras (starting 0700) consequently will squarely hit the bulk of the retreating enemy." It would be a "big battle lasting several days," he expected, but the German forces had a "psychological edge" and a "tremendously effective air force" in their favour. Halder's confidence was not misplaced. At dawn the 150 tanks of the 4th Armoured Division plunged northwards towards the Serre river bridges. This shattered de Gaulle's hope of cutting off the onward march of Guderian's Panzers, and he withdrew his armoured division to Laon, under heavy attack from Stukas and artillery fire. That afternoon Rommel's advance forces began overrunning the front lines of the First World War trenches on the Somme that had resisted four years of German attacks. The capture of Cambrai forced the Panzer crews to halt from sheer exhaustion and the need to regroup. Here they paused while their fuel and supply lines caught up with them. To the north two more Panzer divisions were driving into General Blanchard's retreating First Army, which still sheltered the British Expeditionary Force from direct attack. But they soon came under fire. The fall of St. Quentin on the southernmost wing opened up a narrow corridor for the ten German armoured divisions concentrated there to push for the coast sixty miles away.[61]

"You will not be surprised if I cannot answer for victory, nor even give you hope of victory," Weygand cautioned Reynaud when he agreed to take over supreme command at six o'clock that Sunday afternoon. That morning the seventy-five-year-old general had flown in from Tunis and immediately hurried off to the headquarters of Gamelin and Georges. "The position is grave," he concluded, "but one must not despair."[62]

"News pretty bad – Germans now driving N.W. to cut through to Channel ports between us and the French," Cadogan recorded after the 10 a.m. War Cabinet meeting. He echoed General Ironside's warning of the threat now facing the British Expeditionary Force: "The immediate danger was the risk that the Germans would succeed in establishing themselves across the British lines of communication between Amiens and Abbeville."[63]

If the B.E.F. was cut off, the only way of supplying it would be through the Channel ports. This had been anticipated by the Germans, who had already begun heavy bombing raids on Dunkirk, Boulogne and Calais. Ironside insisted that it was of the "utmost importance to prevent the B.E.F. and the Belgian Army on its left from being cut off from the main French armies." Churchill, however, according to Halifax, gave an "optimistic diagnosis." But the predicament of the British Expeditionary Force was considered serious enough for Ironside to dispatch his deputy, General Sir John Dill, to General Georges's headquarters.[64]

The rapid German advance had prompted Mussolini to respond to Churchill's appeal for Italy to stay neutral with a vainglorious declaration that "the same sense of honour and respect for engagements assumed" that had prompted the British to declare war on Germany would now guide Italian policy. The Prime Minister interpreted this as confirmation of "Mussolini's intention to enter the war at his most favourable opportunity." There were also disturbing reports from Madrid that General Franco was coming under pressure from the Germans to invade Gibraltar. It was therefore decided to evacuate civilians from the Rock as a "precautionary measure."[65]

The Foreign Secretary, not yet convinced that war with Italy was inevitable, called for a further attempt to "avoid or at least postpone" it by offering to relax the Royal Navy's rigorous searches of Italian ships entering and leaving the Mediterranean. He believed that buying off the Italians "during the next critical weeks might be well worth while." His diary entry that night anticipated that "if Hitler gets Paris we shall be immediately confronted with menacing peace terms, supported by the blackmailing Mussolini."[66]

Lord Halifax was inclined to resort to appeasement because he knew that Britain's ability to continue the war would largely depend on the support obtained from the United States. But the latest news from Washington gave no cause for relief, since Mussolini had flatly rejected President Roosevelt's appeal. The previous evening the British Ambassador had met the President to impress on him the powerful naval threat that would face the United States in the Atlantic if Britain and France collapsed for lack of American support. After returning from the White House, Lord Lothian had cabled that while Roosevelt had been sympathetic he had given no indication that "showed that he recognized our pressing need for immediate aircraft supplies." The President's failure to respond to Churchill's suggestion that he should authorize the U.S. Army to release aircraft which would be replaced by British planes already ordered was galling to the Prime Minister, who declared that he proposed to send another telegram "at once making clear our immediate needs."[67]

After the crisis-filled Cabinet meeting, Churchill and his wife motored down to their country retreat at Chartwell to take advantage of the "heavenly weather." In the tranquillity of the lush Kent countryside the Prime Minister sought inspiration for his evening broadcast to the nation. His hopes for a few hours of relief were dashed just after lunch when a call came through from Anthony Eden that the War Office had received an alarming telephone request from General Gort. The French army on his right flank had "melted away" and he required permission to retreat to Dunkirk and "fight it out with his back to the sea."[68]

Churchill hurried back to London for an emergency War Cabinet meeting at 4.30 p.m. to decided what Gort should do. General Ironside said he had already informed Gort that his proposal "could not be accepted at all." The Prime Minister concurred. Retreating to Dunkirk, he declared, would put the British Expeditionary Force in a "bomb-trap, and its total loss would only be a matter of time." Gort had not yet received orders from the French, but Dill was that afternoon reviewing the situation with General Georges. The only military strategy that made sense to the Prime Minister was for Gort "at all costs" to move southward towards Amiens. By "attacking all enemy forces encountered" he could join up with the main French Army.[69]

The Prime Minister detailed Ironside to fly over to France that night to convey personally to Gort the War Cabinet orders not to retreat. That evening the Defence Committee confirmed the decision after hearing General Dill's first-hand report that the French were "entirely opposed to any suggestion that the British Expeditionary Force should take independent action by withdrawing to Boulogne." Churchill then went down to the underground Cabinet Room at Storeys Gate to address the nation.[70]

"I speak to you for the first time as Prime Minister," Churchill began, "in a solemn hour for the life of our country, of our Empire, of our Allies, and above all, of the cause of Freedom." Making no attempt to "disguise the gravity of the hour," he contended that it would be "still more foolish to lose heart." He looked forward "with confidence" to the situation in France being stabilized, though he warned that "the battle for our Island – for all that Britain is, and Britain means" was not far off. Britain and France were united, he said, in their determination to rescue the "bludgeoned races" from "the foulest and most soul-destroying tyranny." An all-out effort was needed to save the nations of Europe, on which a "long night of barbarism will descend, unbroken even by a star of hope, unless we conquer, as conquer we must, as conquer we will."[71]

"Arm yourself, ye men of valour, and be in readiness for the conflict" was the biblical injunction with which Churchill concluded what one British newspaper described as a speech of "imperishable resolve." His broadcast moved the masses and even drew congratulations from his old adversary, former Prime Minister Stanley Baldwin, but apparently failed to stir the ruling classes, according to a well-informed *Daily Mail* journalist in Paris. Wilson Broadbent told Oliver Harvey of "defeatism in London among the richer classes," adding that the capital was reacting "badly," although "the provinces and the North were very sound and would fight."[72]

Following the broadcast, Churchill took a decision that was to have a far-reaching impact on Britain's ability to survive and continue the fight independently of the fate of France. In a minute dictated shortly before midnight he ordered that no more fighters were to leave the country, "whatever the need in France." If it became necessary to evacuate the B.E.F., the fighters would be needed for a "very strong covering operation." Despite his talk in the War Cabinet about the Channel ports becoming bomb-traps he instructed the Chiefs of Staff that contingency plans "should be studied today."[73]

It was in anticipation that Britain might soon find herself confronting a Nazi-dominated Europe that Churchill put the finishing touches late that Sunday night to another telegram to Roosevelt. This appealed for him to release "the largest possible number of Curtiss P.40 fighters" in course of delivery to the U.S. Army. "The Battle in France is full of danger to both sides," Churchill told Roosevelt, assuring him that "whatever happens" he intended "to fight to the end in this Island," though he warned that he could not bind his successors. "If members of the present Administration were finished and others came in to parley amid the ruins," he hinted darkly, "you must not be blind to the fact that the sole remaining bargaining counter with Germany would be the Fleet, and if this country was left by the United States to its fate, no one would have the right to blame those then responsible if they made the best terms they could for the surviving inhabitants." While "there is happily no need at present to dwell upon such nightmares," he assured the President, he "bluntly" made him aware that Britain's ultimate bargaining chip was her powerful fleet. This was "rather like blackmail and not very good blackmail at that," a Foreign Office minute cautioned, conceding, however, that the Prime Minister "might continue to play on the idea" raised by Lord Lothian, despite the obvious risks.[74]

What Lord Lothian's earlier cable had not revealed was the degree to which the President was still taking his cue from the State Department. Officials in the Old Executive Office Building were already alarmed by reports of the "blank panic" overtaking the British as well as the French government. "Churchill talking about moving the Empire to Canada; Reynaud going completely off the line; and Bullitt shrieking over the telephone every half hour" was how Adolf Berle summed up the situation. Although not as sympathetic to the British as some of his colleagues, this Assistant Secretary of State did believe that the United States "was just waking up to the fact that an Allied defeat threatened us, and now that the defeat seems possible they are beginning to get frightened." The President had acknowledged it too. He had made a "bully speech" two days earlier calling for "preparedness in the air" by asking Congress to fund 50,000 planes, with an additional 50,000 a year. But Roosevelt had to move very cautiously in earmarking any arms for the Allies because of the Secretary of State's concern that "the country was not coming forward in any unified support of the President."[75]

One reason for the growing pessimism in Washington was the continuing stream of defeatist reports from Ambassador Kennedy in London. Just before the military crisis in France deepened that weekend, Kennedy had cabled the Secretary of State that he had warned Churchill that Roosevelt "would not leave the United States holding the bag for a war in *which the Allies expected to lose.*" The Prime Minister knew all about the baleful influence of Kennedy. That Sunday night he authorized MI5 to execute a long-planned operation that would help pull the carpet from under the defeatist American Ambassador.[76]

Chapter 5

"Bloody Yankees"

DAY 3
20 May 1940

"Here's a telegram for those bloody Yankees," Churchill told his private secretary shortly after midnight. "Send it off tonight." The cable's thinly veiled blackmail that if American help was delayed Churchill might be replaced as Prime Minister disturbed Colville; "Considering the soothing words he always uses to Americans, and in particular to the President, I was somewhat taken aback."[1]

Evidence has come to light that the Prime Minister's menacing tone was not simply the result of the worsening military situation in France or pique at the "bloody Yankees" turning a deaf ear to his earlier appeal for aircraft and destroyers. The cable dispatched to the White House via the American Embassy that Sunday night can now be seen as part of a carefully timed MI5 operation to which Churchill may have alluded when he told his son Randolph the previous day: "I shall drag the United States in." He did not expand on just how he was going to do this, but it seems that the first step was the arrest of the member of Kennedy's Embassy staff responsible for encoding Churchill's cable. The confidential files of the U.S. Embassy reveal how Britain's security service had swung into action that night with an undercover "sting" operation to damage the credibility of the defeatist American Ambassador.[2]

The U.S. records show that at 11.30 a.m. on Saturday, 18 May 1940, the First Secretary of the American Embassy received a telephone call from Captain Guy Liddell of the "Military Intelligence Section of Scotland Yard" – an official euphemism for MI5. Liddell, who was head of the Counter-Espionage Section, asked Herschel

100

V. Johnson, as a matter of urgency, to see an assistant at three that afternoon "on a delicate matter."[3]

The gaunt-looking officer with penetrating dark eyes and the genial manner of a family doctor who was ushered into Johnson's office that afternoon was head of MI5's special counter-subversion section. An expert amateur naturalist whose pockets were often home to small reptiles, Captain Maxwell Knight was also a dabbler in black magic and a furtive homosexual who ran a stable of female undercover agents attracted by his secretive and enigmatic persona. One of the most adept spymasters in the British secret service, Knight had succeeded in planting and running agents inside the Communist Party, the British Union of Fascists and right-wing organizations that MI5 suspected of Fifth Column activity. One of his current operations, he revealed in his confidential briefing of Johnson, involved the "activities of Tyler Kent." Knight explained how this employee of the U.S. Embassy had become mixed up in a circle with connections to both the Germans and the Russians. The details given of MI5 undercover operations that had revealed his activities were considered so sensitive that even forty years later the report Johnson made to the State Department was reclassified at the request of the British government. Fortunately for history, this was *after* the report had been released to the National Archives in Washington and copied.[4]

Kent's post of code clerk gave him access to some of the most secret reports and documents in the London Embassy. The verbatim records of that Saturday afternoon briefing by Captain Knight provide a first-hand view of the extent of the MI5 surveillance operation on the American Embassy that the British government refuses to make public. The file shows that the code clerk had been under observation since he arrived in England in October 1939. This interest in him resulted from his meeting at the Cumberland Hotel in London with a "naturalized Swede of German extraction named Ludwig Ernst Matthias," who, according to a tip-off from the Stockholm police, was an undercover Gestapo agent.[5]

Johnson was understandably shocked and disturbed, since Kent was "one of the most confidential employees of the Embassy." Why, the First Secretary demanded, had the British held back for eight months from telling Ambassador Kennedy that there was a putative spy in his Embassy?

"I immediately told Captain Knight that in my opinion it was most regrettable that Scotland Yard had not informed us of these circumstances at the time," Johnson stated in his report, protesting that "we would never have kept the man in the Code Room if there had been the slightest ground for suspicion against him." Knight could only offer his awkward apologies and the unconvincing excuse that until recently MI5 had never been able to confirm its suspicions. It would soon become obvious to Kennedy that the British security service had good reason for not alerting him about Kent: it provided an opportunity to put a close watch on the Embassy and its Ambassador's extra-curricular activities.

Surveillance of the Embassy and the errant code clerk, as the U.S. report reveals, had been very extensive indeed. Frequent references to "absolutely reliable sources" about Kent's activities were a tell-tale allusion to phone-tapping and a network of undercover MI5 agents who had discovered that information from the U.S. Embassy had been leaking via the "pro-German" cipher clerk to a "Fifth Column" organization. This was the "Right Club," founded in 1939 by Captain Archibald Maule Ramsay, a Conservative Member of Parliament whom Knight described as "a member of one of the best known and most prominent families in the British Isles." The Right Club, MI5 had established, was "definitely a Fifth Column Organization which under the cloak of anti-Jewish propaganda conducts pro-German activities, has contacts in British Government offices and also in several foreign embassies." Diplomatic bags of legations sympathetic to the Third Reich had been used by Kent's friend Anna Wolkoff, who Knight said was "Ramsay's principal agent," to send confidential U.S. telegrams and communicate "with countries abroad and even with Germany."

Anna de Wolkoff, as she styled herself, was the daughter of a former admiral in the Russian Imperial Navy who had sought refuge from the Bolshevik Revolution with his family. A thirty-eight-year-old spinster with a "very attractive and interesting personality," Wolkoff had, according to Knight, "close friends and acquaintances in the highest stretches of British society." Scotland Yard's suspicions about Kent had been confirmed "at the end of February 1940," when an "absolutely reliable source reported that he was regarded as an important contact" by Wolkoff. She considered the American code clerk "pro-German" and believed he had supplied her with "interesting diplomatic information of a confidential nature," including "confidential interviews that had taken place between Ambassador Kennedy and Lord Halifax." On 22 April he had shown her a copy of an MI5 report on radio apparatus sent through the Embassy by the Earl of Cottenham, "an agent of Military Intelligence." Knight also alleged to Johnson that Kent had been using the U.S. diplomatic bag to communicate with contacts in America. This Johnson decided was probably "not true," since all outgoing material was carefully vetted by an embassy officer.

The First Secretary, who had had many years of dealing with MI5, was inclined to believe Knight when he said that Kent had passed to Wolkoff the details of a report that Kennedy had "recently written to President Roosevelt." This, Knight explained with sardonic relish, stated that conditions were so bad in Britain

102

that "serious internal trouble might be expected at any time." The same report contained Kennedy's "libellous and derogatory remarks about Mr. Churchill's behavior at this meeting." Knight also disclosed that Wolkoff's phone calls had been tapped when she spoke to Kent at the Embassy in Russian. This was worrying to the First Secretary, who became even more alarmed when he heard that Wolkoff had given the Right Club's "most incriminating papers" to Kent to keep in embassy safes.

An investigation failed to turn up any stolen papers in the Embassy, but Johnson was seriously worried by the implications of Knight's announcement that MI5 planned to have Wolkoff arrested on the following Monday morning. This would raise the question of conspiracy charges against Kent, who was technically immune from arrest because of his diplomatic status. Johnson was fully alive to the ramifications of the affair and agreed on the need for swift and secret action, promising to consult with his Ambassador in the strictest of confidence so as not to arouse either Kent's suspicions or give him the opportunity to warn "other persons implicated."

Immediately after Knight left the Embassy late that Saturday afternoon, the First Secretary telephoned Kennedy at the seventy-room mansion near Windsor he had recently rented from the Dodge family so as to be safe from the German bombs which he feared would soon be pulverizing London. On the open telephone line Johnson was prudent. He merely gave the Ambassador "some indication of the seriousness of the affair," not mentioning any names or the circumstances. He then telephoned the Foreign Office legal adviser for assurances that there was no lawful impediment to searching Kent's flat "if the Ambassador approved." Next day, Sunday, Johnson motored down to Windsor and gave the Ambassador a full briefing. From Windsor he then telephoned Cadogan at the Foreign Office to let him know officially that the "Ambassador waived any immunity for Kent and would report the matter to the Secretary of State for confirmation and approval."

After the First Secretary returned to London that evening, Knight went to his apartment to alert him to the following day's police operation. At Kennedy's request, Knight agreed that Franklin Gowen, the Embassy's Second Secretary and Security Officer, would accompany the raid on Kent's London flat. The private diary of General Sir Vernon Kell, the Director-General of MI5, reveals that on 16 May he and Knight had met the Metropolitan Police Commissioner, whose Special Branch officers would conduct the operation. Since the Prime Minister had pressed the Home Secretary the day before to begin the rounding up of British Fascists and Fifth Columnists, there is good reason to believe that it was he who ordered that the trap that MI5 sprang to arrest the U.S. Embassy cipher clerk should be snapped shut to provide "proof" of a serious

Fifth Column plot and to put the American Ambassador on notice that MI5 had been monitoring his own activities.[6]

Further evidence that Kent was only one part of a complex manoeuvre orchestrated by MI5 on Churchill's instructions appears in his curious decision to recall his "bloody Yankees" telegram only a matter of an hour after it had been dispatched by messenger to the American Embassy. Colville records that he was "somewhat annoyed to be woken up at 2.30 a.m. and told that the P.M. wanted it back to review what he had said." This he found very odd because not only had a carbon copy been kept, but after the original telegram had been reclaimed it was later redispatched by the Prime Minister, who, to Colville's surprise, had "made no alteration after all."[7]

The Embassy reports confirm that the telegram had arrived at the Chancery at 1.30 a.m. in a sealed envelope addressed to Herschel V. Johnson. Kent, who happened to be one of the code clerks on duty that night, had opened it, although he had no authority to do so, when the call came from the Admiralty that a messenger was coming round to collect the telegram, because the Prime Minister "wished to have it back by six in the morning."

That Churchill's telegram was sent back to the Embassy later that morning for transmission to Roosevelt "quite unaltered" suggests that its recall was a stratagem to catch Kent red-handed. It could also have been that Churchill wanted the President to receive his "blackmailing" cable after the raid on Kent's flat the following morning. Either way, the curious events of the early hours of 20 May are another indication that the arrest of Tyler Kent was a classic case of the old Indian maxim: "Catch a monkey to scare a tiger." Kent was the monkey, and the tiger to be scared was Kennedy.[8]

When the MI5 plan swung into operation early that Monday morning, Cadogan was walking through Buckingham Palace gardens in the company of Lord and Lady Halifax. The Foreign Secretary, he noted, had reacted "with a pained look" when Cadogan remarked that the "one bright spot" was that there were so many Germans and Italians in Madrid that there was a "good chance of S[am] H[oare] being murdered." His sentiments were only reinforced when he met the formidable Lady Maude Hoare waiting for her husband, who was at the Foreign Office for final briefing before taking over as British Ambassador in Madrid. In response to his solicitous concern for the difficulties she would face in a new country, Lady Maude snapped that it "may be easier than having to adapt oneself to living in an old country under new conditions." Cadogan was affronted: "The rats leaving the ship. The quicker we get them out of the country the better," he confided to his diary. "I'd sooner send them to a penal settlement." He believed that Hoare would be the "Quisling of England when Germany conquers us and I am dead."[9]

The Prime Minister came straight to the War Cabinet from a gloomy meeting with the Chiefs of Staff Committee. There were now real doubts whether General Gort would have time to withdraw the retreating B.E.F. to join up with the French, who were supposed to be pushing northwards across the River Somme. As a "precautionary measure" Churchill had decreed that morning that the Admiralty "should assemble a large number of vessels in readiness to proceed to the ports and inlets on the French coast." A further sign of the seriousness of the military situation was a Chiefs of Staff memorandum on the "Air Defence of Britain." Churchill finally advised that "we had reached the limit of air assistance which we could send to France, and that we could not consider despatching further resources permanently to France, thus denuding defences at home."[10]

This decision was a victory for the chief of Fighter Command, who had stubbornly resisted the Prime Minister's repeated efforts to meet French pleas for more fighters. While it earned Air Vice-Marshal Sir Hugh Dowding the enmity of the Prime Minister, the decision was to have far-reaching consequences for the R.A.F. during the Battle of Britain. Conserving fighters, stepping up production and squadron training now assumed an urgent priority. Arthur Purvis, Chairman of the Anglo-French Purchasing Board in the United States, had cabled from Washington that the U.S. Army would reject requests to make any of their operational aircraft available for transfer to Britain. The only hope of getting the fighters released was a strong direct appeal to Roosevelt by the Prime Minister. As the War Cabinet debated how long the United States would hold back the urgently needed planes and destroyers, only Churchill knew that the additional leverage he needed would be provided as a consequence of Special Branch raids that had been taking place that morning.

At 9.30 a.m. a black car had drawn up outside 18 Roland Gardens, a four-storey red-brick house overlooking a quiet tree-lined Kensington square. Captain Knight, accompanied by Inspector Pearson and two Special Branch detectives in plain clothes, hurried down the steps to the basement flat, where they arrested Anna Wolkoff.

At 11.15 a.m. the same car drove up to the American Embassy in Grosvenor Square and picked up Franklin Gowen. The Second Secretary explained that he had been instructed that if Tyler Kent invoked his diplomatic immunity he would be told to "take that up with the Ambassador." In less than five minutes the police car was pulling across Oxford Street. A few hundred yards north of

Selfridge's department store, the driver stopped outside the iron railings of 47 Gloucester Place.[11]

Inspector Pearson got out and rang the doorbell. When a young woman appeared, he asked if Mr. Kent was in. The maid said she would have to speak to Mrs. Welby, the landlady. As she started downstairs, followed by one of the Special Branch officers, Pearson and Knight charged upstairs, obviously well aware of where Kent was located. The bemused American diplomat followed them to the second-floor landing, where they were confronted by a stout lady glaring at them from an open door. Mrs. Welby's protests were silenced by the search warrant and the flashing of Metropolitan Police identification cards.

When asked if Mr. Kent was in, she pointed to a door on the same landing. With practised authority Inspector Pearson rapped at the door and simultaneously tried the handle. It was locked.

"Don't come in!" a man's voice shouted. When the Inspector knocked again he got the same answer – only louder. Pearson, a burly man, did not wait for a third rejection. He put his shoulder to the door and heaved his full weight behind it. To the crunch of splintering wood he crashed through the door, followed by the others. Inside they found a man in his late twenties standing beside the bed in a pair of pyjama trousers. In response to Captain Knight's question he identified himself as Tyler Kent. Producing the warrant, Inspector Pearson announced that he had the full authority of the law to make a thorough search of the premises. Kent made no protest until one of the policeman headed for the closed door leading off the bedroom.

"You can't go there," Kent yelled at him, "there is a lady!" Ignoring this injunction the police officer opened the door and discovered a dark-haired and thoroughly frightened woman of about thirty doing her best to preserve her dignity in a man's striped pyjama jacket. Identifying herself as Irene, she claimed, despite her somewhat inappropriate attire, that she was on her way to Kew Gardens and had dropped by to ask Tyler to join her for a picnic.[12]

Knight, who did not seem in the least surprised by the discovery of the woman, wanted to know if Kent had in his possession "in the house or elsewhere any documents pertaining to the American government." "I have nothing belonging to the American government," Kent replied. "I don't know what you mean." Knight was easily able to demonstrate that he was lying when the Special Branch officers found a leather suitcase in the clothes cupboard. It contained "a large quantity of secret documents belonging to the American government," including hundreds of cipher cables stamped Secret and Confidential. They also discovered a red leather ledger secured by a brass lock. All these papers, together with visiting cards, letters, a box of sticky-backs printed with anti-war slogans and a £50 British banknote, were stuffed into two suitcases.[13]

Inspector Pearson then informed Kent that it was his duty to inform him that he was under arrest. He was not obliged to say anything, but whatever he did say would be taken down and might be used in evidence against him. The American made no response to the standard police caution and did not protest at being taken into custody. He remained silent, apart from reassurances to Irene that everything would be all right and that she was not to worry. As the police fanned out to make a systematic search of every apartment in Mrs. Welby's lodging house, Kent and his girlfriend were allowed to dress under supervision. The woman was then told by Knight to leave. This surprised Gowen, but it was explained that she was no danger because "it was a real case of infatuation." Knight said, with obvious relish, that she was "frightened lest her liaison with Kent become known to her husband." He explained that her phone had been tapped and that MI5 had her "under constant observation."

Kent was then escorted downstairs and bundled into the police car. The suitcases full of seized documents were loaded into a taxi which then carried Knight and Gowen for the short trip back across Oxford Street to the American Embassy in Grosvenor Square.

Gowen's report of the arrest made for the State Department reveals that he was puzzled by a number of aspects. Knight had run through a list of names and asked if Kent knew any of them and whether he thought they were "loyal to Great Britain." Before answering, the code clerk had turned to the Second Secretary and asked: "Do you think I should answer there [sic] questions?" Gowen advised him to "answer everything." When he ignored the advice and continued to be coolly evasive, Kent's sang-froid aroused Gowen's suspicions. He could not explain why the police raid "did not seem to upset Kent very much." The code clerk had seemed "not overly concerned" about his fate. Gowen speculated that he might have been "showing off" or perhaps he expected to be rescued from any serious trouble by "powerful and prominent friends who are involved in his activities."

"What was I supposed to do, fall on my knees and beg for mercy" was Kent's reaction when he was shown Gowen's report more than forty years later. "I have a lot of self-control under any circumstances. Of course I realized what the score was when I saw Gowen." Kent's embittered scorn was his standard reaction to the events that had overtaken him that Monday morning and earned him a footnote in the history books. For decades after the war he had been pursued by journalists and historians in search of the true story of a handsome, blue-eyed twenty-nine-year-old Ivy-Leaguer branded the "American Embassy Spy." Neither his notoriety nor the passing years had treated Kent well. Dissatisfied with his role as a bit-player in the history of World War II, Kent in his seventies was a pot-bellied asthmatic interested only in nourishing the myth that he was the innocent martyr to the Machiavellian scheming of Winston Churchill and Franklin D. Roosevelt. Reclusive and distrustful, it took more than a year of correspondence through intermediaries to persuade Kent that the declassified F.B.I. and State Department files warranted a meeting on neutral ground to discuss his contribution to history.[14]

"I Was Never a Spy"

When Kent arrived at the Phoenix airport terminal on 10 April 1982, he might have passed at a distance for Colonel Sanders with his white goatee and bolo tie. But his sneering high-pitched voice, yellowing panama hat and rumpled seersucker suit would not have made him a popular pitch-man for Kentucky Fried Chicken.

Kent wore his air of genteel impoverishment with obvious discomfort. When he married Clara Hyatt Hodgson in 1946 after she divorced a former diplomatic colleague, he benefited from her inheritance of the "Carter's Little Liver Pills" fortune. For over a quarter of a century his wife's money funded a comfortable lifestyle, including a succession of yachts and farms, in addition to the purchase of a small-town Florida newspaper in the early sixties. Unwise investments of what remained of his wife's inheritance in Mexico shortly before the collapse of the peso in the seventies decimated their remaining resources. By 1982 Kent and his wife were reduced to living in a mobile home in a Texas trailer park. He nevertheless still self-consciously insisted on ordering champagne with his meals and drank with his little finger extended in the affected manner of a high-born Victorian matron.

Kent spared no effort to impress with his erudition. His allusions to Latin texts added a bizarre embellishment to his frequent condemnation of the "liberal-Jewish-influence," over which he chuckled with a malign satisfaction. His snobbishness and aloofness suggested that in his early years he had been too much deferred to by household servants and a doting mother from a blue-blood Virginia family. A distant cousin of the World War II U.S. Army hero General George Patton, Tyler Gatewood had been born in 1911 when his father, William P. Kent, was serving as U.S. Consul at Newchang, Manchuria. Because of his father's postings he was educated at a succession of renowned international schools; Rogivue in Switzerland, then Campbell College, Belfast, had been followed by spells among the sons of the East-Coast "Wasps" at

Kent and St. Albans prep schools in the United States. After a period at Princeton University, he finally took his A.B. equivalent at the Sorbonne in Paris. He then attended the University of Madrid and George Washington University, where he studied history and economics.[15]

Kent's facility for languages, especially Russian, prompted him in 1934 to try to follow in his father's footsteps by entering the U.S. Diplomatic Service. His mother's relations in the Virginia State Assembly pulled political strings, and so did his father, who was a friend of the Secretary of State. But despite Cordell Hull's opinion that Tyler Kent was a "young man of brilliance and promise," the stiff-shirts of the State Department found the over-educated and arrogant Kent Jr. an unsuitable candidate for the U.S. Foreign Service. Later in 1934, however, when Roosevelt appointed William C. Bullitt American Ambassador to the newly established U.S. legation in the Soviet Union, Hull pressed him to take the Russian-speaking Kent to Moscow as a junior member of the embassy staff. Bullitt found Kent "brilliant but neurotic." But Hull prevailed upon him to give the son of his friend, whom he had known as a toddler, a break as a code and cipher clerk.[16]

The State Department officials' rejection of Kent, who considered himself well-qualified for a diplomatic career, had left him embittered, and he was resentful at having to accept a lowly position. But, as he explained, jobs were scarce at the height of the Depression, and his family was far from wealthy. So he joined Bullitt's staff as an adventure, expecting that the assignment might count towards a second try at the coveted Foreign Service commission. Delphically expelling his breath whenever he was confronted with evidence from his extensive F.B.I. file that he was not a martyr but a spy, Kent nevertheless showed a weasel-like interest in evidence that confirmed his long-held conviction that his arrest and imprisonment had been a plot engineered by MI5. But, as the State Department records show, he was himself largely to blame for his own downfall.

"I suppose my opinions were not sufficiently 'liberal' for Bullitt and Roosevelt," Kent said archly. He put this down to his anti-Communism, which he claimed he had picked up at Madrid University. There, he said, it dawned on him that there must be a Jewish conspiracy behind the Russian Revolution and the threat posed to the world by the Bolshevik menace. The State Department confidential personnel files reveal a less political reason why he was repeatedly refused by the Foreign Service. Kent was a philanderer who had blotted his career at the outset by flaunting his affair with a married woman aboard the liner carrying Bullitt and his team to Europe in the spring of 1934. He would have been sent back home, it turns out, but for the respect that Bullitt felt for

Assistant Secretary of State Walton Moore, who happened to be a close friend of the Kent family. Even after a strong reprimand, Kent was involved again within a few months in another "rumpus" with a Soviet staffer at the Embassy. Once more Bullitt decided to keep Kent on his staff, because "his work has greatly improved." But he reported that he would have to keep a close watch on his opinionated twenty-four-year-old staffer.[17]

The surviving records from Kent's four years in Moscow indicate that his high opinion of himself repeatedly led to further clashes with authority. He cavalierly put in annual claims for more pay and allowances which were repeatedly turned down by Washington. Even by Moscow standards he was soon living beyond his meagre clerk's salary and setting up house with a group of other young embassy clerks. He purchased Bullitt's spiffy Essex Roadster and later bought a Soviet-made Ford for $450. The cars, he explained, were needed by him and his friends to drive their Russian girlfriends to a dacha they rented in the countryside on the outskirts of Moscow.

In his seventies Kent still considered himself a "ladies' man," chortling whenever he found references in the F.B.I. files to his long succession of mistresses. They included an actress at the Bolshoi and a long-term Russian mistress, Tatiana Alexandrovna Ilovaiskaya, to whose apartment at Number 11 Priatnitskaya 53 Kent was a frequent visitor. "Tanya," as Kent affectionately called her, was the daughter of a Moscow University professor. He would repeatedly deny when interrogated by the F.B.I. that she was a Soviet undercover agent. But he did admit that she had no difficulty obtaining exit permits for taking holiday trips around Europe that were normally denied to Soviet citizens. He also recalled in an off-handed fashion that Tanya had "sounded him out" in 1936 as to whether he would "like to improve his status and living conditions" by working for the N.K.V.D., as Stalin's secret police were then known. But Kent claimed that he had never made it a secret that he was "anti-Soviet."[18]

Nonetheless it was obvious from the files that the F.B.I. were extremely interested that Tanya had helped the poorly paid American Embassy clerks to supplement their income on the illegal black market. By pooling their resources they bought furs and jewelry from Ilovaiskaia and her friends which they carried back under cover of their diplomatic passports whenever one of the group returned on leave to the United States. The smuggling ring, which could not have gone unnoticed by the N.K.V.D., went undetected until Kent's arrest in 1940 prompted the State Department to call in the F.B.I. to make a full investigation of the goings-on at the Moscow Embassy. Kent's criminal activity was therefore not a factor in a further rejection of his attempt to get commissioned in the U.S.

Foreign Service in 1938 during a trip home for dental treatment. Returning to Russia with few career prospects, he began looking for a job in Moscow as a journalist with the International News service. He then tried unsuccessfully to get transferred to the U.S. Embassy in Berlin, but was posted to London on 19 September 1939.[19]

On 8 October the alleged Gestapo agent Matthias led the British secret service to the Cumberland Hotel in London when he arrived to claim his mysterious package from Kent. It is a curious coincidence that the 5 October diary entry of MI5 chief General Kell contains a cryptic reference "Winston sent for me to evolve a scheme." Even if Kent was not already the "monkey" in the "scheme" Churchill hatched with MI5 to scare Ambassador Kennedy, he became the object of intense surveillance. MI5 reports that surfaced in the National Archives show that the British secret service had good reason in the autumn of 1939 to take very seriously indeed the fact that an official of the American Embassy might be in contact with a Gestapo agent. A tip-off received from "a German operating in Berlin" a few months earlier had alerted MI5 to the fact that Kennedy's confidential reports to Roosevelt were reaching the office of Nazi Party chief Rudolf Hess.[20]

The "Watchers," as the MI5 surveillance teams are called, were rewarded a few weeks later when Kent made contact with the exiled Russian community in London. In 1939 the British security service paid close attention to "white" émigré circles because, despite the Nazi-Soviet Pact, many of the Russian exiles regarded Hitler as their best hope for smashing Bolshevism and restoring the Tsar. Ever since the Red Army had driven the White Russians into exile after the bitterly fought civil war ended in 1920, émigré communities all over Europe had been targeted by Soviet penetration agents. A special objective was the Russian Red Cross, one of the principal charitable and social organizations among the Tsarist refugees.[21]

Like so many of the twists in the strange saga of Tyler Kent, his explanation of how he became involved with Russian émigrés in London is enigmatic. He said it was only by chance that, "out of the blue," he was telephoned at the Embassy shortly after his arrival by a Mrs. Betty Straker, who told him that before her marriage to an Englishman she had known his mother as a girl in Virginia. She was an active member of the London branch of the Russian Red Cross executive committee, and Kent said it was through Mrs. Straker that he met two women of Russian birth who were to play major roles in his life. One was his lover Irene, whom he met at a New Year's Party; the other was Anna Wolkoff, the daughter of Admiral Nicholas Wolkoff, the former Tsarist naval attaché, to whom he had been introduced by Mrs. Straker early in February 1940.[22]

"Anna was a smart woman, fun to talk to, but plain as hell," Kent recalled, vigorously rejecting the suggestion made in several published accounts that Wolkoff was his paramour. He dismissed her as a "well-filled," dark-haired woman some nine years older than he was whom he did not find in any way sexually attractive. But he did agree that he got along famously with her and with her father. This was not simply because he spoke Russian fluently, but because he shared their fanatical anti-semitism. The Wolkoffs' familial hatred of the Jews was regarded as excessive even in the White Russian community, to whom it was an article of faith to believe that Jewish influences had directed the Bolsheviks. Wolkoff, who had been aide de camp to the Tsar, had lost the vast wealth of the family estates in Central Russia. He held a deep grudge against the Jews for the Revolution, which had cost him his inheritance and obliged him to make his living running the "Russian Tea Rooms." Wolkoff admired Hitler and was quite open in his approval of the Nazis' persecution of the Jews. He was repeatedly warned by his friends to be more guarded or else he would be arrested. The Admiral ignored the advice, probably feeling he was safe because he and his wife were working part-time for the government as monitors of mail in Russian that was going overseas. The Censor's Office happened to be housed in quarters adjacent to MI5's temporary wartime headquarters in Wormwood Scrubs prison in west London.[23]

"All Russians in London were tremendously right-wing, and so they had every right to be, considering the atrocities the Bolsheviks had committed," said Joan Miller, "but Anna Wolkoff really went over the top." Miller was a well-bred Englishwoman who had "always wanted to be an actress," an ambition quite unacceptable to her upper-middle-class parents. She got her chance to act, as an undercover agent, when Captain Knight recruited her, along with two other women of impeccably loyal backgrounds. Putting up a convincing performance in the role of a disgruntled secretary at the War Office with strong right-wing sympathies, Miller succeeded in gaining the Wolkoffs' confidence by frequenting the Admiral's restaurant. His daughter, according to Miller, was known as "Julius Streicher." Even as an MI5 agent having to play along with it, she found it difficult to stomach Anna's poisonous anti-semitism. "I didn't want to get involved in it," she said, recalling the long hours she had to spend listening to Anna's harangues in the Russian Tea Rooms, "but there was a war on and I'd volunteered for this job."[24]

The Russian Tea Rooms, which had little in common with their glamorous namesake in New York, were a utilitarian café at 57 Harrington Road, near South Kensington underground station. "Rather a modest, dingy little place, more of an oil-cloth café than a luxury restaurant" was how Kent recalled it. As a connoisseur of Beluga, which he bought by the can in Moscow, he doubted whether it deserved its reputation for having the best caviar in London. He said he had only ever dined there three times at the most with Anna and her father, whom he remembered as a "Russian of the old school." Joan Miller described it as "the sort of café you could visit unescorted without jeopardizing your reputation."[25]

Now a fashionable Kensington hairdressing salon, during the exceptionally bitter winter of 1939–40 the Russian Tea Rooms offered an open fire, fiery vodka, and highly calorific *blinis* and *riaptchiki* that made it a popular gathering place for the Russian émigré community. The Admiral would treat pretty women to extra ladles of steaming dark borscht and sour cream. Miller recalled how he would often come over and sit with her and chat. "He used to tap me on the knee seductively," she laughed, recalling how she had invented a pre-war romance with a German Luftwaffe officer to lend credibility to her cover story. With the assistance of two other MI5 agents, Marjorie Mackie and Helene de Muncke, who had also established themselves as sympathetic confidantes of the Wolkoffs, she soon found herself a trusted member of Anna's circle of amateur pro-Hitler conspirators. This led to an invitation to the meetings of the Right Club which took place in Anna's small flat above the restaurant.

Just how Anna Wolkoff became involved with the Right Club is not clear. It was probably through the social connections she made while a dressmaker, much sought-after by London society. (One of her many distinguished clients had been Wallis Simpson before her romance with the Duke of Windsor became public.) In 1939 Wolkoff's pro-Hitler enthusiasms had been fired up when she had travelled to Germany, where she met the Sudeten leader Karl Frank and other prominent Nazis, including, she would later claim, Rudolf Hess himself. The outbreak of war sent the dressmaking business into a decline, but Anna found her experience with titled clients useful as she found a new outlet for her anti-semitism as the self-styled aide de camp to Captain Ramsay, the founder of the Right Club.[26]

Archibald Maule Ramsay was every inch the six-foot Guards Captain, with ramrod bearing, chiselled nose and clipped moustache. Known to his many military friends as "Jock," he hailed from a distinguished line of Scottish soldiers whose ancestral home was Kellie Castle near Arbroath. After schooling at Eton and Sandhurst he joined the Coldstream Guards, serving on the Western Front in World War I. In 1916 he was badly wounded and invalided out of the army three years later. In 1931 he became Conservative M.P. for the Scottish constituency of Peebles. After briefly serving on the Potato Marketing Board, he found his real vocation during the Spanish Civil War as chairman of the pro-Franco United Christian Front.

In the course of Ramsay's public-speaking crusade to rally

Christian society against the "Godless Comintern," his antipathy to Jews and Bolsheviks turned him into a fanatic. Reading Hitler's *Mein Kampf* and the scurrilous anti-semitic tract *The Protocols of the Learned Elders of Zion* opened his eyes – so he claimed – to the sinister conspiracy of global Jewry, which he blamed for all major revolutions, from the dethroning of Britain's Charles I to the French Revolution and the Spanish Civil War. Campaigning against "this terrible menace of Jew-directed Bolshevism," Ramsay toured the Rotary Clubs of Great Britain delivering his set-piece tirade "Red Wings Over Europe." He introduced Blasphemy Bills in Parliament and mobilized right-wing political colleagues for the coming showdown with Communism, Jews and Freemasons. He became a prominent member of the Imperial Fascist League and in May 1939 founded the Right Club "to oppose and expose the activities of Organized Jewry." Two months before war broke out he went to see Chamberlain, warning him of the subversion that was "overthrowing his peace policy and himself and precipitating the war."[27]

"Our hope was to avert war, which was considered to be mainly the work of Jewish intrigue centred in New York," declared Ramsay. When, despite his best efforts, war did break out, he decided that the Right Club should close down to let the younger members join the forces. But he urged those who stayed at home to "continue the fight against the internal enemy, no less formidable than the Axis Powers and in a way more dangerous." When the other pro-German lobbies, including the Anglo-German Fellowship and the Link, closed down, the Right Club became a semi-secret organization. Ramsay found himself in the uncomfortable position of sharing Hitler's attitudes towards the Jews while at the same time claiming to be fiercely patriotic in his efforts to bring about a negotiated peace.[28]

Ramsay had failed to persuade his friend Chamberlain that "pro-Jewish warmongers" such as Churchill were the real menace to Britain and the Empire. But the Right Club's brand of genteel fascism appealed to the chauvinism and endemic fear of communism of Britain's class-conscious upper-crust. Ramsay's Etonian army and city friends found it appealing to be asked to join a "Club," rather than a vulgar political party. He also gave his word as an officer and gentleman that members' names would never be divulged. Secrecy, Ramsay claimed, was essential to protect his respectable members from smear attacks by Jewish elements. This may explain why he had no difficulty recruiting a dozen parliamentary colleagues, a platoon of Scottish landowners and a regiment of respectable Conservative ladies of the flowered-hat tendency who were the mainstay of Tory summer fêtes. The Right Club made it respectable for the "closet fascists" of the Tory

Party to exercise their anti-semitism when they would never have admitted to sympathizing with the vulgar Jew-baiting Blackshirts of Sir Oswald Mosley's British Union of Fascists. That Ramsay's Club numbered two hundred by the time war broke out was an indication of the underlying anti-semitism in the ranks of the British ruling classes.

The aura of secrecy surrounding the Right Club itself provided a certain social cachet. There were rumours that the Duke of Wellington had chaired some of its meetings; Ramsay would himself assert that the "publication of the names would have been of great assistance to me in every way." But the privacy demanded by his elite members was such that even Ramsay's friend Admiral Sir Barry Domville, the founder of the unashamedly pro-Nazi "Link," did not know of the Club's existence until he learned of it when they were incarcerated together in Brixton Prison for the duration.[29]

Secrecy became paramount for Ramsay after the outbreak of the war when the Right Club was supposed to dissolve itself to avoid police attention. He continued, however, with the Club's efforts to promulgate his campaign against the Jews and Churchill. Membership was supposedly closed, but Lady Mary Ramsay continued vetting and signing up new members who passed muster at the tea session she held at her grand Kensington home at 24 Onslow Square, a block away from the Russian Tea Rooms. They included Joan Miller, who received a silver badge portraying a Christian eagle grappling with a snake symbolic of the twin perils of Communism and Judaism, engraved with the motto "Perish Judah."

Joan Miller reported to MI5 on the activities of the Right Club, whose nerve centre of supposedly subversive operations was Anna Wolkoff's basement flat in Roland Gardens, a short walk from the Russian Tea Rooms and the Ramsays' house in Onslow Square. Anna acted as Ramsay's principal lieutenant in the campaign to deface government posters while fly-posting lamp-posts, telephone kiosks and pillarboxes with such anti-war slogans as "War Destroys Workers" and "Land of Dope and Jewry." Anna managed these forays into the blackout with the passion of a guerrilla commander, issuing instruction leaflets to Right Club members advising them to operate in pairs and take turns "sticking and watching." Incongruously Wolkoff herself proudly wore the uniform of the Auxiliary Fire Service on these outings and when organizing Right Club members to jeer from the darkness in cinemas whenever Churchill appeared in the newsreels.[30]

For all Wolkoff's fanatical enthusiasm, her amateurish activities hardly constituted a subversive threat to Britain's war effort. But MI5 wanted to discover who the Club's members in high places were. Yet despite the six months' infiltration and tapping of Ramsay's and Wolkoff's telephone lines, by the spring of 1940

Knight had still not succeeded in his goal of obtaining the Right Club membership list. According to Joan Miller this was her principal mission after getting herself admitted to the Club. But it was only after Tyler Kent arrived on the scene and made contact with Ramsay that the MI5 operation against the Club assumed a new and altogether more sinister dimension.

"A fine specimen of an English gentleman – not too heavy on the intellect" was how Kent sarcastically recalled Captain Ramsay. He portrayed him as "the sort of British politician you might expect to hail from a backwoods constituency in Scotland." Ramsay was "by definition a gentleman, but his driving force was anti-semitism," according to a Russian émigré, Dr. Georg Knupffer, whom Ramsay had tried to recruit after a two-hour lecture on the Jewish question in the House of Commons tea-room. The Tory M.P. found the American code clerk a more willing disciple. Kent explained that it was at the beginning of March, shortly after he met the Wolkoffs, that Anna had taken him to Onslow Square. "He and I saw pretty much eye to eye on the Jews," Kent recalled, agreeing that the war with Hitler should be brought to an end if Europe was to be saved from Bolshevism. As they saw it, the "warmonger" Churchill, egged on by Jewish interests in New York, was the biggest threat to the possibility of a negotiated peace.[31]

Kent believed he had hard evidence in the telegrams Roosevelt exchanged with Churchill. That his President should be in secret communication with the First Lord of the Admiralty was, Kent believed, a *prima facie* confirmation of a conspiracy. He thought these exchanges were an unconstitutional effort by the President to stoke the Allied war against Hitler and manoeuvre the United States into the fight against the Nazis. Since these messages frequently arrived by Admiralty messenger late in the evening, when Kent was on night duty in the Code Room, it was a simple matter for him to make copies of them. The lax security enabled him to smuggle the papers out of the Embassy front door. From his reading of the American newspapers, Kent also knew about the opposition the President faced from the isolationist lobby led by Charles Lindbergh. This made his growing hoard of secret cables a potentially explosive political bomb.

"I could not have sent them back to the Senators in Washington by the diplomatic bag because all letters had to be approved by an Embassy staffer," Kent said, explaining why he never got any documents to the anti-Roosevelt isolationists of the America First Committee. Nor could he risk sending them by mail, since he knew from Admiral Wolkoff that the British Censor checked every letter that went out of the country. It was therefore only after his meeting with Ramsay, he said, that an alternative way of achieving his goal of exposing the Roosevelt-Churchill war-conspiracy began to take shape. After Wolkoff visited his flat before Easter, in the second week of March, he showed her some of the cables he had removed from the Embassy, including the "Naval Person" to President telegrams and MI5 exchanges on radio equipment and Communist subversives. The intelligence data, he learned by enquiring at the Embassy, was shared with the British secret service under "an executive agreement dating back to 1919."[32]

Wolkoff was impressed and excited. Convinced that her American friend had stumbled on proof of Churchill's warmongering, she rushed off to tell Ramsay. The Captain came around to the first-floor flat at 47 Gloucester Place and was staggered to find that Kent's secret cables revealed how he had been "misinformed and ignorant" of the true extent of "the Jewish International intrigues to bring about total war." It was not simply the "questions of propriety" arising from the Churchill exchanges that Ramsay believed demonstrated a conspiracy against his friend Chamberlain. The cables from the White House to Ambassador Biddle in Warsaw and Bullitt in Paris in 1939 seemed to show that Roosevelt had connived in giving unconstitutional assurances of American support to Paris and Warsaw. These had been instrumental in effecting the Allied guarantee of Polish sovereignty that Ramsay believed was the root cause of the war.[33]

Kent said he told the Conservative M.P. that "these were being shown in confidence," adding that he "did not want to have any trouble with the Embassy." But there was no discussion of the propriety of what they intended to do with U.S. Government secrets. "The question of legality did not occur to me at all," Kent admitted. "I was never a spy," he insisted, because they "came to an understanding" that Ramsay would make use of the documents only to expose the Churchill-Roosevelt conspiracy in Parliament. Shortly afterwards Kent was invited to become a member of the Right Club, not just an ordinary member, but with the title of "steward." He claimed never to have attended any formal meetings, but he was flattered. It appealed to the snob in him to be assured by Ramsay that he was now an official of an important organization and that "there were a lot of pretty highly-placed English people in the Club."[34]

So when Anna Wolkoff called at Gloucester Place on 13 April to "borrow" the Churchill cables of 29 January and 28 February, Kent assumed that Ramsay needed them to support the question he intended raising in the Commons. The telegrams dealt with relatively insignificant matters such as the special dispensation given to American merchant ships to avoid the British blockade. Since Kent had already agreed with Ramsay that he might need these particular cables as "evidence of the facts" of the secret trans-Atlantic conspiracy, he raised no objection to Anna borrowing them "overnight."[35]

Wolkoff, however, had an agenda of her own. She drove to Penywern Road in Earls Court to seek out Nicolas Smirnoff, a former employee of the Tsarist embassy, who eked out a living taking portraits for the Russian exile community in London. She asked him to make copies of the documents. As he had no darkroom set up, Smirnoff testified that he told her to come back that evening, when he made her three glass negatives of documents he was told had been obtained "from a diplomat."

"Anna was a great chatterbox and not a sophisticated conspirator at all," according to Georg Knupffer who soon learned from Admiral Wolkoff of her great secret. "She told me that Tyler Kent was supplying her with information from the American Embassy files long before she was arrested." Kent also allowed Wolkoff to make a pencil copy of the 16 May Churchill telegram appealing for destroyers. A copy of this cable was found in the possession of Christobel Nicholson, another Right Club member who was the wife of retired Admiral Wilmot Nicholson. Ramsay received no copies, either pencil or photographic, before leaving London on 10 May for a fortnight's holiday in Scotland, "intending to resume my investigations on my return." Knupffer said that after seeing the Churchill-Roosevelt cables, Ramsay contacted Buckingham Palace. As a member of the Sovereign's Scottish Bodyguard he knew George VI personally, but he failed to get an audience. When he tried to make an appointment with Chamberlain he was told the Prime Minister was too busy to see him – it was during the crisis-filled week that led to his resignation.[36]

The King and the Prime Minister would have been alerted against meeting Ramsay. As secret MI5 files reveal, two weeks before Churchill became Prime Minister the Right Club became the centrepiece of an elaborate trap sprung by the Secret Service to expose a supposedly dangerous Fifth Column conspiracy. This "plot" depended on setting up Wolkoff, because, as Kent, with some justification, asserted, he and Ramsay were never guilty of conspiring to help the Germans: their targets were Churchill and the White House.

"We were not at all the bunch of terrible German spies," Kent insisted, "but a group of naive people trying to put the skids under Roosevelt and Churchill." The transcript of his secret trial contains evidence that supports Kent's contention that he was framed by the British security service to provide the "proof" of a Fifth Column plot. Anti-semitism was not then in itself an offence under British law, and Kent always claimed that the only crime of which he was guilty was the trivial one of stealing documents – against which he would have pleaded diplomatic immunity. But Kent and Wolkoff were also charged with offences under Britain's notorious Official Secrets Act, whose "catch-all" sections had been hastily framed by a panicky Parliament during a German spy scare in 1911.[37]

The record as it has now become available has all the ingredients of a classic "sting" operation organized by the British secret service. The contortions that Knight and his undercover agents had to resort to in order to persuade Wolkoff to make contact with the Germans, as the trial record reveals, involved a plot worthy of the Marx Brothers. The prosecution's efforts to make Kent out to be the centre of a deadly Fifth Column conspiracy included elaborate court-room antics to impress the six-man wartime jury, whom he characterized as "bemused cockney shopkeepers." Malcolm Muggeridge, who attended the *in camera* hearings in his capacity as an observer for MI6, recalled how the trial had the elements of a farce: the Old Bailey windows papered over for security, and MI5 undercover agents using false names popping up and down to give damning testimony in between the frequent adjournments for German air-raids.[38]

Over forty years later the British government prevented the publication in Britain of Joan Miller's account of the role she and her two MI5 undercover colleagues played in "stitching up" Kent and Wolkoff. Although Miller did not give evidence in the trial, the testimony of her fellow agents reveals how they repeatedly had to egg Wolkoff on to communicate with the Germans. She was not only a hopeless conspirator, but also an inept spy. She had to be directed by an MI5 agent, Marjorie Mackie, into writing an amateurishly coded letter to William Joyce (Lord Haw Haw) at "Rundefunk Haus, Berlin." Miller admitted she had "quite untruthfully" told Wolkoff that Helene de Muncke, another of Knight's agents, had a friend in the Romanian Embassy who could arrange for the letter to leave the country in the diplomatic bag. It was de Muncke who testified that she duped Wolkoff into typing a follow-up message and drawing the Right Club emblem of a snake and eagle on the envelope. This, Anna gleefully announced, "would be like a bombshell" for Lord Haw Haw.[39]

Since de Muncke then passed both of Wolkoff's communications to William Joyce to her chief, Captain Knight, it was MI5 who actually arranged for them to reach Berlin. Major T. A. Robertson, one of MI5's most adept counter-intelligence officers, made a rare court appearance to testify that the crude code in Wolkoff's letter had been broken to reveal that she had betrayed such deadly secrets as "Churchill not popular" and "Ironside believed very anti-Jewish, not so anti-German." Wolkoff had also been coached by Mackie that good spies needed to know whether their reports had been received. So her letter to Berlin said she would listen for the code-word "Carlyle" to signify he had received her message. A B.B.C.

119

official duly came forward in court to testify that Lord Haw Haw's adenoidal voice had been heard on Germany's "New Broadcasting Station" uttering the words: "Who is their Carlyle?"[40]

None of Wolkoff's activities as Lord Haw Haw's self-appointed listening post were known to Kent. But the week before their arrest, he admitted, he had met her Italian friend, "Mr. Macaroni," at a "social" dinner at L'Escargot, a fashionable Soho restaurant. The mysterious foreigner was Colonel the Duca Antonio del Monte, the Assistant Military Attaché at the Italian Embassy. At the trial the MI5 agent de Muncke testified that on the evening of 16 May she had volunteered to deliver a thick envelope from Wolkoff to del Monte's letterbox at 67 Cadogan Square. Wolkoff, she testified, had told her that this letter contained "plans for the invasion of Norway."

A word-for-word translation of President Roosevelt's cable of 16 May declining Churchill's request for the "loan of forty or fifty of our older destroyers" was found among the most secret section of the captured Berlin Foreign Ministry documents. It had been passed to Berlin by the Italians "from an unimpeachable source" on 23 May 1940. There was no evidence in the German records to show who the "unimpeachable source" was, but the cable was almost certainly the one abstracted from the U.S. Embassy by Kent, because a copy was found in his possession. His fellow Right Club member Christobel Nicholson, whom he admitted he knew, had also made a pencil copy from the handwritten copy shown her by Wolkoff. Nicholson, who was arrested on the same day as Kent and Wolkoff, was also charged with offences under the Official Secrets Act. At her trial in November 1940 she was acquitted on all counts, but was immediately re-arrested as she left the court and detained for two years without trial as a suspected German sympathizer.[41]

Roosevelt's message to Churchill rejecting his pleas for destroyers was to have been a crucial piece of evidence in the MI5 case. But it was never used against Kent. The question why the 16 May cable was not made the centrepiece of the charges brought against Kent and Wolkoff is crucial. The reason and the answer to the real significance of the Kent affair is revealed by the "secret and confidential" report sent to the U.S. State Department on 28 May 1940 by the First Secretary of the U.S. Embassy in London. Not surprisingly, this was one of the files that the State Department reclassified in 1982 at the request of G[reat] Br[itain] Intel[ligence].[42]

"Engaged in Espionage for the Russian Government"

Herschel V. Johnson's report on the Kent affair discloses that Joseph P. Kennedy was not in a good humour on 20 May when he was confronted by Captain Knight while the errant code clerk waited down the corridor in Room 119 of the Embassy under the guard of two British police officers. The First Secretary records that the angry Ambassador "spoke strongly" and demanded to know why Scotland Yard had waited so long before disclosing its suspicions about Kent. His vehement protest that this decision was a "mistake" – at least as far as the Americans were concerned – was confirmed when Knight opened the leather suitcase taken from Kent's cupboard to reveal a spies' ransom in top secret cables. The Ambassador was shocked to discover that they included many of his most confidential reports to the President predicting that Britain would be defeated by Germany. It was at that moment, according to Johnson, that they were struck with the full realization of the damage that Kent had inflicted. Until then they had not had "any idea of the extent to which he had abstracted copies of the Embassy's highly confidential material."[43]

In the scuffed leather suitcase were nearly two thousand copies of the Embassy's most secret telegrams. Some dated back to early 1938. It was evident that Kent had spent long hours methodically sifting through and cataloguing his hoard. Many documents were sorted into twenty-five country folders labelled Czechoslovakia, Poland, Russia, Germany, France, Balkan States. The carbons of Kennedy's most confidential reports to the White House were separated out in a folder he had marked "For the Ambassador's File." There were other files for the War Cabinet, Chamberlain, Halifax and Jews. Some included interpretative notes in Kent's handwriting. There was also a sheaf of MI5 reports exchanged on Communist subversives and other matters and a "Churchill" folder with copies of the "Naval Person" cables – including a pencilled copy of the "bloody Yankees" telegram that had arrived and been recalled from the Embassy the night before. The discovery of the three glass negatives raised the alarming prospect that Kent had been disseminating photocopies of top-secret American diplomatic traffic.

The haul of confidential documents was so extensive that Johnson and Kennedy found it "difficult to conjecture why Kent had taken it." They concluded that he must have "simply gathered up a bunch of papers and intended to go through them at his leisure in order to pick out what served his purposes." The question they could not answer – and on which Kent remained suspiciously evasive – was what his purpose really was. The discovery of two brand-new duplicate keys to the Index Bureau and the Code Room suggested that he had even taken steps to ensure his access to the Embassy's most secure files on a long-term basis.[44]

It was Captain Knight who drew the Ambassador's attention to letters addressed to Kent on House of Commons notepaper from Captain Ramsay. While containing "nothing incriminating" these letters from the leader of the pro-German Right Club suggested to Johnson that the code clerk was part of a spy ring of Nazi sympathizers. Suspicion was increased by the red leather padlocked ledger. Kent was brought in and asked for the key. He said he did not have one and did not know what the book contained. With a scrupulousness intended to impress the Ambassador, Knight asked Kennedy's permission to have the lock broken open. Technically the seized material was in the possession of an employee of the U.S. Embassy whose immunity from seizure was guaranteed by his diplomatic passport, but the Ambassador nodded his assent. Inspector Pearson snapped the lock with a steel tool he produced from his pocket. The ledger recorded the handwritten names and membership dues paid by two hundred members of the Right Club, many of whom, Knight assured Kennedy with a knowing look, were under police surveillance.

"Don't you think it strange that a Member of Parliament should come to you, a minor official of the Embassy, and give you a locked book to take care of for him?" Knight demanded of Kent. He responded obtusely that he "didn't know" what was in the book or why Ramsay had come to his bed-sit "about three weeks ago," and left the padlocked red ledger.

"I am quite sure Ramsay told me," Kent admitted forty-two years later. "I think he had a suspicion that Scotland Yard might break into his house, but it would have been quite unusual for them to burst into the apartment of someone who had a diplomatic passport." Ramsay, he believed, had entrusted the Right Club ledger to him in the belief that his diplomatic immunity would protect the "assurances of privacy" given to the members. "I deposited the Red Book of names of the Right Club members at Mr. Kent's flat for the period of my absence from London only," Ramsay himself wrote, explaining that he "had heard of several persons who had their papers (dealing with the same sort of subjects as mine) ransacked by persons in their absence."[45]

The names in the Right Club ledger, according to Knight, were demonstrable proof of Scotland Yard's long-held belief that Kent was involved in a "gang of spies." The planted damage to the Embassy's reputation was bad enough, but the havoc the code clerk had wrought to United States diplomatic security appalled the Ambassador and his First Secretary. To their dismay they found "true readings of telegrams to the Department in the Embassy's most confidential codes and about the most secret subjects." Many of these had been coded and simultaneously copied by Kent himself. His security clearance gave him access to the code books and the Embassy's most secret "Strip Ciphers," which were used to encode confidential communications. Simply having to break this news to the State Department was a major blow to Kennedy's reputation, since as Ambassador he was nominally responsible for embassy security. He was furious – and made no effort to conceal his bitter hostility as he indignantly confronted the code clerk.

"Kennedy was annoyed and angry and kept asking me 'Why did you do it?'" Kent recalled. "Justifiably he was annoyed that some subordinate was doing things which were not exactly kosher." The transcript of the interrogation in the Ambassador's office recounts how Kennedy berated Kent about the "serious situation that you have got your country involved in." Kent had let down his family, his country and especially the Embassy. "What do you think you were doing with our codes and telegrams?" Kennedy demanded. The only response Kent gave to the barrage was that he found the cables "interesting historical documents" which he said he took "only for my own information." Kent did not deny his close association with Anna Wolkoff and Captain Ramsay, because they "had sort of common views, to a certain extent."[46]

"I am going to speak now extremely bluntly," Knight announced. "I am afraid I must take the view that you are either a fool or a rogue, because you cannot possibly be in any position except that of a man who has either been made use of or who knows these people." In Wolkoff's case, he was confident he could "prove that she has a channel of communication with Germany." Adopting a prosecutorial tone the MI5 officer told Kent "You would be a very silly man if you did not realize that certain conclusions might be drawn from that situation." Wolkoff had told her contacts in the Right Club about interviews the Ambassador had had with Lord Halifax about the German landings in Norway. How, he asked pointedly, could she possibly have known what was said if Kent had not told her of the Ambassador's report cabled to Washington over dinner the night before in the Russian Tea Rooms? Kent did not remember the dinner. Nor would he admit to passing on to Wolkoff information in the MI5 letters relating to the purchase of "technical radio apparatus" from the United States.

"You don't expect me to believe for a minute that you had them for your own entertainment," Kennedy interjected, his temper breaking through.

"I didn't say entertainment, I said interest," Kent fired back.

"If you were English you would be in a very difficult position," Knight told him. "You don't impress me by your cocky manner." Then, trying a fresh tack, Knight pointed out that Kent's diplomatic passport would have made it possible for him to smuggle out the documents. He asked whether Kent "considered . . . Anna Wolkoff was a loyal British subject." Kent replied that this was a "matter of opinion," insisting that until that afternoon he had "absolutely no knowledge" that Wolkoff was secretly communicating with the Germans.[47]

The transcript of Knight's first interrogation reveals that Kent sensed that Scotland Yard's case against him was purely circumstantial and that he was protected from the British police by the cloak of diplomatic immunity. Forty-two years later, Kent agreed that during the questioning in front of Kennedy he had little fear that he faced anything more unpleasant than dismissal and being sent home to the United States.

"I was certainly not chewing my fingernails at that point, because I didn't know about the Official Secrets Act then," Kent said. "At the time it did not occur to me that I could be charged with a criminal offence in a British court." It was only when his confrontation with Knight ended that Kennedy gave an ominous sign to the code clerk that he was ready to "throw him to the wolves." This came when the Ambassador asked Knight whether, if Wolkoff was "more or less a spy" and if the United States government waived his diplomatic rights, this would make Kent "part and parcel of that." The British secret service officer told Kennedy: "Subject to the production of evidence under the law, yes."

To Kent's alarm, the Ambassador then agreed that he should be removed from the Embassy into police custody, with no reference to waiving his diplomatic immunity. Kent was hustled out of the Embassy and driven away under guard to the cells of Cannon Row Police Station for further interrogation. But, as Scotland Yard reported to the Embassy next day, he "proved to be very stubborn under questioning." Kent said Knight was a "smart man," who later sent a stool-pigeon to try to pump him for information while he was in Brixton Prison for two months before he was charged. He said he gave nothing away because there was nothing he could reveal, since he was not a spy.[48]

Kent's F.B.I. file obtained under the Freedom of Information Act throws into considerable doubt his claim that he was never involved in espionage. Its "Internal Security R" classification indicates the Bureau's postwar belief that he was a spy for the Russians. The case was circumstantial but appeared convincing to J. Edgar Hoover after he received the report of the F.B.I. Special Agent who was "assigned in an undercover capacity at the American Embassy in Moscow." According to Hoover's "personal and confidential" report for the President, the "checking on Embassy staffs and operations" in the Moscow Embassy was the most alarming; the Director told Roosevelt it painted "such a surprising picture" that he wanted to bring it to the personal attention of the President.[49]

At Moscow the F.B.I. discovered not only shocking lapses of security in the code room, but a complete failure to keep confidential documents and cables from the prying eyes of the Russian hired help. Most serious of all was the rampant "sexual perversion" that must have raised the blood-pressure of the fastidious Hoover. The homosexual ring revolving around the Ambassador's male secretary would also have offered the Soviets the opportunity to extract by blackmail what the secret police did not learn from the ring of prostitutes who had snared Kent and the heterosexual staffers.

Tatiana Ilovaiskaya, Kent's former mistress, was revealed as the leading Soviet secret agent in a "regular Embassy ring with headquarters in the Nosion hotel." Ilovaiskaya and the other women catered "only to the men from the various Embassies and legations" and each one reported "regularly to the G.P.U." After Kent left his "paramour," she moved into a country dacha with the American Vice Consul. "Buba," as she now called herself, had a "special driver's licence issued to her by the G.P.U." She was "a well dressed woman who appears to have all reasonable luxuries" and the right to travel "throughout Europe." This, as the F.B.I. noted, was "a distinction unusual among Soviet citizens," providing strong corroboration for "reliable sources in the Embassy" who believed that Ilovaiskaya was working for the G.P.U. as an "agent of that organization." (See Appendix 4.)

When confronted with the possibility that he had fallen into a classic "honey-trap," Kent laughingly dismissed the idea that Tanya was a Soviet agent as "absolute garbage." He said he was simply "playing ball" because it was "common knowledge at the Embassy that all Soviets were regularly questioned by the G.P.U." His response betrayed incredible naivety or cunning complicity. His file reveals that the F.B.I. reopened his case record four years later, when it was redesignated to reflect suspicions of Kent's Russian connection. Significantly, this was after Kent's imprisonment for stealing Churchill-Roosevelt cables became a *cause célèbre* in 1944 amid sensational rumours in the isolationist press that Kent had evidence that Roosevelt had conspired with Churchill to get the United States into the war. Questions were asked in Congress, and for a time Kent in his prison cell on the Isle of Wight threatened to intrude into Roosevelt's fourth-term election campaign. The potentially explosive issue was not defused until Kennedy, at the President's request, asserted in a press statement that Kent had been spying for the Germans.[50]

But in 1945, when Kent returned to New York after his early release from prison, he did not deliver the sensational revelations that had been expected. "Kent Arrives, Gets Chance To Tell All – And Then Doesn't" was the *New York Post*'s unusually sober headline. Kent continued to maintain public silence while titillating revisionist historians to keep interest in his alleged injustice alive. Not until John F. Kennedy was elected President sixteen years later did Kent resurface to grab the headlines again. He was then proprietor of a strident Florida weekly "hate-sheet" that touted his anti-semitic, anti-Black and anti-Liberal views. When the *Miami Herald* exposed him in an article in which the President's father called him a traitor and a spy, Kent launched a string of libel suits. He had won minor actions against newspapers that had carried the *Herald* story on the grounds that he had never been found guilty of spying against the United States. So he might well have succeeded in settling old scores with the Kennedy family, had not Joseph P. Kennedy been incapacitated by a stroke in 1962.[51]

The F.B.I. had concluded twenty years earlier, after reviewing their investigation of the Moscow Embassy in April 1944, that it "would appear that Kent has been actively engaged in espionage for the Russian government." When he read the report, Hoover ordered that the Bureau were "to keep after this in view of reported activities of Kent." The thick dossier of files on him was the result of a nine-year effort to prove Kent was a Soviet agent. The F.B.I. assiduously interviewed witnesses and excavated his past in an attempt to build a strong enough case to take Kent before a Grand Jury. Their investigation turned up suspicious leads in addition to his involvement with Ilovaiskaya that suggested that Kent had "cleverly concealed" any sympathies behind a mask of "rabidly anti-Soviet feelings." During close interrogation in September 1951 Kent was unable to offer satisfactory explanations for a number of incidents, including his attempted recruitment by an N.K.V.D. agent named Calligos in Moscow's Metropol Hotel. There were many instances where the F.B.I. doubted that Kent was telling the truth when he "emphatically denied ever having been in the pay of the Soviets."[52]

The Kent case investigatory files were therefore redesignated "Espionage R" in 1953, when the F.B.I. decided there was "nothing which was good and clear cut in the question of whether Kent might have been working for the Russians." Since he was now "the husband of a rich woman," Hoover's staff, concluding that it was "unlikely" he was still engaged in Communist activities, advised the Justice Department to drop efforts to bring him before a Grand Jury. But this was not the end of the F.B.I.'s involvement. Kent said that as late as 1972 he was re-interviewed by a State Department security official about his Soviet contacts at the Moscow Embassy. In December 1982, after Kent's interview by B.B.C. television, Nigel West, a British writer with good contacts among the intelligence community, revealed in *The Times* that MI5, like the F.B.I., had reclassified Kent as a Soviet case. Kent dismissed the allegation as another British smear. Yet despite his earlier litigiousness, he took no steps to write to protest or to instigate a suit for libel before he died of cancer in 1988.[53]

If Kent had all along been working for the Russians under cover of being a Jew-hating anti-communist, it would explain one of the central enigmas of the affair: why he never made any attempt to pass on to any American journalists any of the explosive information he had collected. The address list seized at his London apartment contained the names of half a dozen reporters who would have seized on a sensational story that could have threatened Roosevelt's presidential re-election campaign. While it was very much in Hitler's interest to remove Roosevelt, it was certainly not in Stalin's. Not only had Roosevelt restored diplomatic relations with the Soviet Union, but the Russian dictator knew as well as Churchill did that United States support was essential to keep the British in the fight. If England made peace with the Germans, the way would be cleared for Hitler to turn the Wehrmacht east to attack Russia.[54]

Inquiries via K.G.B. sources in Moscow have so far failed to turn up Kent's name on the computerized name-index of archival case files. That he was not apparently an active N.K.V.D. agent does not necessarily rule out Kent's recruitment by Soviet military intelligence, the G.P.U. If the MI5 and F.B.I. assumptions about Kent being a Soviet agent were correct, then Stalin was the silent conspirator and ultimate beneficiary on 20 May when Kennedy picked up the scrambler telephone to break the news to the White House.

Chapter 6

Codename "The Doctor"

"I telephoned the President in Washington saying that our most secret code was no good, any place" was how Kennedy broke the shocking news that one of his Embassy's code clerks was a spy. "I told Mr. Roosevelt that the Germans and Italians, and presumably the Japanese, had possessed the full picture of the problems and decisions and everything else sent in and out of the White House and the State Department."[1]

Four years later, when the former Ambassador was speaking to journalists, he added all the drama that is missing from the "secret and personal" cable he sent on 20 May 1940 to the Secretary of State reporting that two days earlier the British had informed him that Tyler Kent was "closely associated with a gang of spies working in the interests of Germany and Russia." Kennedy claimed that he was the one who had "caused his private quarters to be searched." The investigation had produced "confidential Embassy material including true readings of messages in the most confidential code" as well as "evidence of his personal associations with the spy group." Kennedy excused himself for not informing the State Department in advance on the grounds that he "wished to leave no possible loophole for Kent's being forewarned." He also told the Secretary of State that he had "indicated to the police that I waive any immunity for Kent regarding such proceedings as may be necessary to develop the facts."[2]

Even as the Ambassador's report was being drafted, Franklin Gowen, acting under instructions from Captain Knight, fielded incoming telephone calls for Kent, who was detained at Cannon

128

Street Police Station. Kent's incarceration was premature. The actual message stripping him of his diplomatic immunity did not reach London until well after midnight.[3]

The Secretary of State had been less concerned with the *ex post facto* waiving of Kent's diplomatic immunity than with the security of the Department's worldwide communications. His dismissal cable had been preceded an hour earlier by one from Washington wanting to know urgently if "strip cipher system has been compromised." Kennedy replied that since "true readings of the strip cipher were found among the papers in Kent's possession," it was "impossible to say now that the strip cipher system has not, repeat not, been compromised." Four years later, Kennedy summarized the disaster thus: "That night America's diplomatic blackout started all over the world." "The Germans didn't need any secret service in Europe," he declared, because Kent had been supplying them with "copies of our Embassy's secret cables to the President and the State Department ever since October 1939."[4]

There was real cause for alarm that afternoon in the Old Executive Office building in Washington; the compromising of the State Department's strip cipher system was a major setback. At the very time when the German Blitzkrieg was rolling at full tilt across Western Europe, the United States was deprived of secure channels of communication to monitor the crisis until replacement cipher books and strips could be sent out. The magnitude of the problem became very clear to Kennedy that evening when he received a cable instructing him to keep Washington abreast of developments in the Kent case "in any code you still consider confidential." (See Appendix 5.)[5]

It is now possible to see why it was eight months before the U.S. Embassy was warned by the British that its trusted code clerk was removing true readings of cables enciphered in the State Department's most secure codes. Once MI5 discovered that Kent was taking the Embassy cables, months before February, when Wolkoff began boasting about it to Knight's undercover agents in the Russian Tea Rooms, an irresistible opportunity presented itself for British intelligence and cryptographers. It would have been a simple matter for specialists in breaking and entering to make discreet and regular "visits" to Kent's bed-sit whenever he was on night duty in the Code Room. An inspection of 47 Gloucester Place reveals that his first-floor room could easily have been broken into from the roof of the one-storey house in Montagu Mews at the rear. Former MI5 officers have confirmed that such operations were routine; even in the 1960s their speciality was "bugging and burglarizing their way around London." In wartime, the restraint on such operations, as one retired security service officer confirmed, was even more relaxed. From the cables in Kent's

129

flat the teams of cryptanalysts at the Government Code and Cipher School at Bletchley Park would have been able to read every secret cable going into and out of the U.S. Embassy in Grosvenor Square like an open book.[6]

Ambassador Kennedy's innate Irish suspicion of the English would certainly not have discounted this probability. Nor could he have failed to appreciate just how serious an impact Kent's activity had for him personally, as well as for the security of American diplomacy. The British cryptanalysts had the great advantage that not only were most of the transatlantic cables routed to Europe via England, but the traffic to every U.S. Ambassador on the Continent passed through the London Embassy. Kennedy would therefore have realized that the British could have been eavesdropping on the defeatist and often highly derogatory telegrams he had been sending to Washington from the time that Kent arrived in London.

"A Very Foul Specimen of Double-crosser & Defeatist"

Since the day war broke out, when he had ridiculed the British Cabinet and the British Army's willingness to fight, Kennedy had been a Cassandra whose telegrams to Washington harped on the theme that the United States must not be "left holding the bag for a war in which the Allies expected to be beaten." He had repeatedly tried to sour the President against Churchill, whom he called "a fine two-handed drinker." Roosevelt had not only ignored Kennedy's efforts but, to the Ambassador's intense irritation, in October 1939 opened up a private channel of communication through the U.S. Embassy with Churchill when he was still First Lord of the Admiralty. From March 1940, when Kennedy returned to London after three months' sick leave, he made no secret of his discontent at being increasingly shut out by the President, grumbling that his job "could be done just as well by a $50-a-month clerk."[7]

Kennedy had left Washington soon afterwards under a cloud because he had been as bluntly outspoken in person as in his cables. Interior Secretary Harold Ickes recorded a confrontation with Bullitt in his office on 10 March 1940. In blithe disregard for the journalists present, Kennedy announced that "Germany would win, that everything in France and England would go to hell, and that his one interest was in saving his money for his children." Bullitt attempted to remonstrate with Kennedy when he began badmouthing Roosevelt. The Ambassador shouted that "he would say what he Goddamned liked before whom he Goddamned pleased!" That, at least, was the sense of his words, but, as Ickes put it, "Joe's language is very lurid when it is unrestrained, as it was on this occasion."[8]

Kennedy's April and May cables were those of a "prophet of pure defeatism," according to one senior member of the Foreign Office, who especially resented Kennedy's "considerable influence" on certain sections of the Tory Party. When the disgruntled Ambassador's worst fears were realized and Churchill succeeded Chamberlain, he found himself shut out of the cosy relationship he had enjoyed with the Prime Minister's office. From being an "honorary member of the Cabinet," he became an outsider. Churchill maintained a façade of politeness towards him, but it was apparent to even the most junior members of the Embassy that Britain's new administration was intent on politely cold-shouldering the American Ambassador. Kennedy had by now also grown resentful of the pressure being put on him by the State Department to be more positive about the Allies. He had already decided that the President was wrong in his determination to back Britain and France in the belief that Germany could be defeated by proxy if the Allies were supplied with American military weaponry and supplies.[9]

The jaundiced views of the American Ambassador were well known to the British government officials. The Foreign Office maintained a dossier known to the staff of the American Department as the "Kennediana" file which collected the negative reports of officials who picked up gossip on the diplomatic circuit and in the London clubs. It also included the persistent rumours of his illicit dealing on the stock market and shady financial activities. One of the first reports in the "Kennediana" file reveals that the Ambassador's defeatism owed much to his son John F. Kennedy – the future President – who encouraged his father's belief that the British would be "badly thrashed in this war." It was John Kennedy who had "recently returned from Germany very impressed by what he saw and whose views on the subject Mr. Kennedy telegraphed to the State Department." The unnamed person who passed the word along to the Foreign Office appears to have been the Marquess of Hartington, who later married Kathleen Kennedy.[10]

"Mr. Kennedy is an ambitious man who I am sure is always thinking of his future or relinquishing his present post and concerned to make sure he is not tarred with the pro-British brush," cautioned American Department counsellor John Balfour. "He is also an Irish American and as such, naturally predisposed to twist the lion's tail, the more so when the animal appears to be in 'one hell of a jam'." Others in the Foreign Office worried that the "*défaitiste*" Ambassador was engaged not simply in "twisting the lion's tail" but something more sinister. "The amount of indirect evidence we have fully entitles us, I think, to regard his repeated assertions that England cannot win the war as a definite campaign," Victor Perowne of the American Department minuted in January 1940. The Ambassador was now reported as telling American journalists that "the British were whopped" and "didn't stand an earthly chance of winning." According to the Foreign Office informant, Jack Kennedy "was also abounding in the same sense." Perowne believed that "Mr. Kennedy is not the sort of man to go on talking in the sort of way that has been reported to us without an object." There was discussion whether Kennedy could be curbed by dropping official hints to Johnson, his pro-British First Secretary, who was the senior career diplomat at the U.S. Embassy. Apprehension that such a move would backfire persuaded Cadogan and Halifax to agree with the Prime Minister that only Lord Lothian should be informed and asked "whether he couldn't try a twist in the proper quarter."[11]

The Ambassador's "wheeler-dealer" business image led to some dark suspicions of his motives. His reputation as the banker-turned-stock-manipulator who had moved out before the Great Crash to multiply his fortune in R.K.O. movies and liquor franchises encouraged American Department officials at the Foreign Office to take seriously persistent rumours that Kennedy was manipulating the stock market through intermediaries. "I wish I could resist the feeling that Mr. Kennedy is thinking all the time about (1) his own financial position (2) his political future," minuted David Scott, one of the few officials in the American Department who was prepared to give the Ambassador the benefit of the doubt.[12]

The "Kennediana" file reveals that the strongest hint came from the former Swedish Minister in London, who alerted the Foreign Office in September 1939 that Kennedy was "not a very desirable type of individual." He said he had heard "'funny stories' about him and his dealing in the city." Baron Erik Palmestierna's inference, "though this was not explicitly stated, was that Mr. Kennedy's stock exchange activities, whatever they may be, are capable of being interpreted as affording evidence of anti-British proclivities on his part, as well as, of course, of a desire to make money without being too scrupulous as to the methods employed."[13]

Was there any foundation to the rumour? "Baron P. ought to know!" was the cryptic note added to the Palmestierna report in an unidentified hand. "This is gossip, but gossip which very probably has more than a grain of truth in it" was Balfour's comment. The same story had come to the ears of an American journalist in London during 1940. This source told Yale Law School graduate David Koskoff, who spent more than a decade researching for his detailed work on Joseph Kennedy, that MI5 had discovered the Ambassador was playing the market during the Munich crisis when they started "'bugging' Embassy telephones, including Kennedy's." The story achieved wide credence among the American journalists in London, most of whom were hostile to the Ambassador's defeatist position. The phone-tapping rumours have since been confirmed by the Kent case MI5 reports.[14]

"Joe Kennedy was operating the stock market seven ways till Wednesday" was how one journalist put it. The Ambassador certainly enjoyed privileged access to the Treasury's detailed plans for liquidating Britain's vast holdings of American securities to raise cash for buying war supplies. Kennedy therefore had a unique opportunity for insider trading on an unparalleled scale, and he was never one to pass up the opportunity to make a buck. He had played "bull markets" through a collaborative pool by artificially inflating stock prices, cashing in on the huge profits at the top of the market and then racking up a further killing by short-selling in a sliding "bear market."[15]

The extent to which Kennedy was playing the market "seven ways to Wednesday" during his tenure as Ambassador in London on his way to the $400 million fortune he eventually amassed can only be a matter of conjecture. But in addition to the rumours reaching the ears of Foreign Office officials and American journalists, there are documented two corroborative clues in the paper trail.

The first is a letter from Kennedy of 11 April 1940 telling the President that it was "indefensible for the U.S. to continue to take large quantities of gold from England and France before arranging to take over British investments in the U.S." Was Kennedy anxious for the Allies to liquidate all their securities, so that he and his friends could make a killing before the share prices plummeted in the wake of the anticipated German attack? The second piece of evidence is that a year after Kennedy had returned from London he telephoned the State Department to check up on the rules governing the private financial transactions of U.S. diplomats while serving overseas. Whether it was a pricking conscience or concern about possible transgressions that triggered this belated inquiry from the former Ambassador is not clear. But the Chief of the Foreign Service Division answered with an unambiguous letter that set out the strict prohibitions: an Act of Congress passed in 1915 made it illegal for ambassadors to transact private business and services for which fees are received "to, from, or within the country . . . to which he . . . is accredited."[16]

"Mr. Kennedy is a very foul specimen of double-crosser & defeatist," Lord Vansittart observed in January 1940. "He thinks of nothing but his own pocket. I hope that this war will at least see the elimination of this type." While it can be argued that this blistering assessment simply reflected the strong undercurrent of animosity and distrust in the Foreign Office towards the American Ambassador, the Chief Diplomatic Adviser had extensive sources in business circles in both Britain and Germany.[17]

Vansittart had good reason for his belief that the American Ambassador had been trying to double-cross Britain ever since 1938. Ten days after Chamberlain returned from Munich having struck the infamous deal with Hitler, Kennedy held a frank conversation with the German Ambassador in London. The captured Third Reich Foreign Ministry records reveal that he unilaterally proposed a German–American trade treaty despite the "marked reserve" shown by Secretary Hull when he floated the idea at him. Kennedy assured Ambassador Herbert von Dirksen that the average American looked on Germany more favourably than the average Englishman did. He also told him that "very strong anti-Semitic tendencies existed in the United States and that a large portion of the population has an understanding of the German attitude toward the Jews." Those Americans who were sympathetic to the Reich, he said, were not getting through to the President, so he proposed making a two-week visit "to acquaint himself with the institutions of the new Germany." Kennedy's intention of making himself Roosevelt's intermediary with Hitler collapsed when he did not receive the invitation he asked for. The German Ambassador in Washington squashed the visit by reporting that the American Ambassador in London had totally misread "the hostile and negative attitude toward Germany" of Roosevelt and most of his Cabinet.[18]

Records have now come to light which show that Kennedy did not abandon his self-appointed mission. Six months later, on 25 April 1939, James D. Mooney of General Motors arrived in London hot-foot from Germany. In Berlin, Göring's adviser, Dr. Wolthart of the Reich Economic Ministry, had arranged a meeting for him with Dr. Emil Puhl, the head of the Reichsbank. Four days later Mooney paid what he described as a "courtesy call" on his old friend at the American Embassy. As his unpublished memoir reveals, his real purpose in seeing Kennedy was to convey to him the results of his earlier discussions with the Nazi financial chiefs, who had proposed that the Führer should be bought off in return for a massive Anglo–American gold loan that would enable Germany to restore "normal trading relations." Mooney told the Ambassador that such a financial inducement could persuade Hitler not just to make peace concessions that would end the Polish crisis, but also to agree to general disarmament.[19]

Without referring to Washington, Kennedy took the bait and offered to act as intermediary. He advised Mooney to go back to Berlin and tell his Nazi banker friends that he personally would "certainly like to have a talk with them quietly and privately." The General Motors executive flew to Berlin next day and carried a note from the Hotel Adlon to the Reichsbank telling Puhl that Kennedy had actually agreed to a secret meeting. On 3 May Mooney telephoned Kennedy that he had arranged a meeting with Dr. Wolthart in Paris two days hence. Mooney suggested that Kennedy could come "unobserved" to his apartment at the Ritz Hotel.[20]

It was only at this point that the Ambassador wondered whether he should "put the matter up to the White House," although Mooney warned him that everything had been set up with the Germans. He suggested telling the President only if he was "a good enough salesman to get approval on it, otherwise he would be taking a rather long chance." Kennedy for once appeared to be getting cold feet. Instead of tackling Roosevelt directly, he cabled the State Department and asked in roundabout fashion if there were "any objections" to his going to Paris for dinner with James D. Mooney and "a personal friend of Hitler who has topside influence in the Krupps." Hull's suspicions were aroused immediately and he sent back instructions telling the Ambassador in unequivocal terms "you will not undertake this trip at the moment" because it would be "impossible to prevent your trip to Paris and the names of the persons you will see from being given a great deal of publicity."[21]

Next day in Brussels Mooney received a telephone call from an embarrassed Kennedy informing him that the meeting was off. To try and find a way out of "an awkward situation," the General Motors executive chartered a plane and flew off to London, carrying with him a handwritten summary of the German government's proposal for "Limitation of Armaments" and "Non Aggression Pacts." This set out the terms of the proposed deal that required a "contribution by England and the United States [of a] Gold Loan of $500,000,000 to $1,000,000,000 (via Bank of International Settlements) to provide [a] gold reserve so that orthodox money and price practices can be set up." After reading the paper Kennedy became so enthusiastic that he exclaimed "What a wonderful speech could be built up from those points back home!" He promised to telephone the President to persuade him that he should go to the meeting in Paris after all. But Roosevelt was implacably opposed. Next day Mooney found the Ambassador despondent and complaining he had been "up half the night" trying to get his phone call to the White House "only to be refused for the second time."[22]

Mooney now proposed that they should bypass the President and State Department by arranging that Dr. Wolthart should fly to London the following week for a secret meeting, so that Kennedy would not need to seek Washington's approval. The meeting took place at the Berkeley Hotel at 11 a.m. on Tuesday, 9 May. Mooney performed the introductions and recorded that Kennedy and Wolthart spent two hours discussing the billion-dollar gold loan plan and the international situation. "Each man made an excellent impression on the other," he noted. "It was heartening to sit there and witness

135

the exertion of real effort to reach something constructive." But their hopes that this secret and unauthorized initiative would be the first stage in a constructive settlement with Hitler were killed next day by the sensational headlines in the British press.[23]

"GOERING'S MYSTERY MAN IS HERE" proclaimed the *Daily Mail*, blowing Dr. Wolthart's cover. The Nazi banker managed to fly out of London just before the reporters could catch up with him and discover just who he had come to see. Mooney, who was already en route to Paris when he read the news, suspected that the British secret service had deliberately leaked Wolthart's name to the press. Two weeks later a story about Ambassador Kennedy's "intimate conversations with the Germanophile clique" appeared in *The Week*, a left-wing newsletter edited by Claud Cockburn, who was known for the accuracy of his insider leaks. The story was then picked up by the *New York Post*, which repeated the assertion in *The Week* that Kennedy "goes so far as to insinuate that the democratic party of the United States is a Jewish production, but that Roosevelt will fall in 1940." With the heat being turned up on Kennedy and the State Department now aware that their Ambassador in London had disobeyed the instruction not to see the Nazi banker, the Ambassador dropped his secret bid to solve the Polish crisis by buying off Hitler with a billion-dollar gold loan.[24]

Just how much the British learned of Kennedy's role in the affair cannot be established as long as the MI5 archives remain secret. But a tantalizing snapshot of what those records might contain has surfaced in the Confidential Correspondence Files of the U.S. Embassy in London.

On 7 February 1940, a month before Kennedy's return to London from sick leave, MI5 dropped a bombshell on Herschel V. Johnson, who was Chargé d'Affaires during the Ambassador's absence. Late that Thursday afternoon a courier arrived with a personal and confidential communication stamped "Secret." The First Secretary could only have been filled with alarm as he read through the three-page letter from Guy Liddell, Director of B Division, the Counter-Espionage section of the security service. It warned him that a German "informant whose statements have in other respects proved to be accurate" had told his British contact that "just prior to the war and possibly still, the German Secret Service has been receiving from an American embassy reports, at times two a day," which "contained practically everything from Ambassador Kennedy's despatches to President Roosevelt, including reports of his interviews with British statesmen and officials."[25]

According to MI5's information, "the source from which the German Secret Service got these documents is not definitely known, but is someone who is referred to as 'Doctor'." Their informant thought "the Doctor" might be an employee of the

American Embassy in Berlin. The letter cautioned Johnson, for reasons he was not slow to appreciate, that the information was "extremely delicate" and stressed the need for the State Department to "take every possible step to safeguard our informant."

First thing next morning a worried First Secretary called Liddell to Grosvenor Square to discuss "just what some of the statements mean." He said it was essential to know "what time gap there was between the date of delivery of these papers to the German secret service and the date of the despatches themselves." If the reports were "what might be called 'hot,' it could not possibly have been through anyone in the American Embassy in Berlin, as none of the ambassador's telegrams was ever repeated to Berlin." Nor, "with very few exceptions," had Kennedy ever sent "copies of his confidential telegrams in code or clear to other missions in Europe." Johnson explained that the number of people outside the Code Room who had "legitimate access to these telegrams was extremely limited." It seemed to him that, "if the basic fact is true, then somebody either in the Embassy [in London] or in the State department is involved."[26]

In a "Personal and strictly confidential" report sent by secure diplomatic bag to James C. Dunn of the State Department European Section, Johnson said he had urged Liddell to give him "more specific data." But Liddell claimed to know nothing more than he had put in the letter, as "the matter had been passed on to him from another source" – probably MI6 – with instructions to pass it on. Liddell did not himself "feel sure that Berlin was the place where the information was actually handed to the German Secret Service agent." Johnson, who for many years had been MI5's trusted channel of communication in the U.S. Embassy and knew Liddell well, told Washington that he did not believe the matter would have been brought to his attention "if the British Secret Service did not have substantial evidence to back it up."[27]

Getting MI5 to produce any more specific information about "the Doctor" proved very difficult. The following Wednesday, 14 February, Johnson reported a lengthy discussion with "a man of Liddell's organization." The unnamed MI5 counter-espionage officer disclosed that it was only "incidentally" that this matter had come to light; the German informant had revealed that Kennedy's dispatches and State Department telegrams were reaching Berlin while "conveying other very important information." Johnson was assured again that the British believed the information about the American leak was accurate. "We base it on the fact that the very important information he gave us, after a minute and careful investigation extending over three months, was found to be completely accurate," the MI5 officer said. The need to check it out was the reason given for Johnson's not having been informed about "the Doctor" earlier.[28]

When Johnson pressed the MI5 officer, he learned to his surprise that the British informant "is actually in the German Secret Service." He was told that the source was "in touch with a man named Jahnke, who is in the Abteilung Pfeffer of Hess's office." Johnson reported to the State Department after this meeting that he was "not quite sure that the British have told us all they know," although they had confirmed that they had not been in contact with their informant in the German secret service since the war had started. MI5 had suggested that the State Department should begin their investigation at their Berlin Embassy and had "particularly requested that no instructions be sent to Germany on this subject by telegraph."[29]

Whatever else might be leaking out through tapped cables, Johnson was certain that Berlin was not the source through which the Germans could have obtained Kennedy's reports, since "all of the important conversations with British officials and statesmen which were carried on here in London by this Embassy were sent by telegraph to the Department and were not repeated to other missions, nor were copies in code, with very few exceptions, forwarded by pouch." The only other American document in the files relating to the "Doctor" mystery is a letter Johnson wrote three weeks later asking if the State Department investigation had made any progress. "I don't think the possibility, however remote it may seem, that the leakage occurred along the line of wire can be ignored," he told Dunn on 4 April. Johnson advised, therefore, that the inquiry should concentrate on those who would have had access to the Kennedy telegrams at both ends of the Atlantic.[30]

It is also interesting to find that on 18 March Cadogan sent out an alert to government departments dealing with the American Embassy, which were instructed to "give oral warning" to their staff members "that the Embassy's reports of these conversations may become available to the Germans." It is not clear whether this warning was a result of concern that "the Doctor" might begin dictating again now that Ambassador Kennedy was back from his three-month leave, or of the fact that MI5 had by then reported Tyler Kent's activities to the Foreign Office. What is certain is that "the Doctor" could not have been Kent, who was still at the Moscow Embassy at the time the British received the tip-off from their informant in the "German secret service." Neither does it appear likely that MI5 were delivering a "Valentine" to the U.S. Embassy on 14 February as a roundabout way of drawing attention to the activities of the errant code clerk. Nor was "the Doctor" fabricated by the British secret service as part of a plot to put the skids under Ambassador Kennedy. This was confirmed personally by Sir

Dick White, the former director of both MI5 and MI6, who in 1940 worked for Liddell in the Counter-Espionage Section and therefore knew about both the Kent and "Doctor" cases. They were, he said, quite separate. He confirmed that the "Doctor" story came from a reliable informant, but the strictures of the Official Secrets Act prevented him from naming either the German or "the Doctor."[31]

It is conceivable that the Germans could have obtained diplomatic reports by intercepting the cable lines and breaking the State Department ciphers: their signals intelligence (SIGINT) agencies had extensive decryption and translation facilities. But if "the Doctor" was the codename for a SIGINT source there is no reason why his reports should have been passed to Hess's intelligence section at Nazi Party Headquarters to be translated. All the evidence points to "the Doctor" being a HUMINT (human intelligence) source – an agent whose channel of communication was to Hess's intelligence office.[32]

Liddell identified Kurt Jahnke as the German recipient of "the Doctor's" reports, and told Johnson that according to MI5 records "Jahnke was a German agent in Mexico during the World War, working under Ekhardt." This is confirmed by F.B.I. files obtained under the Freedom of Information Act, which describe Jahnke as one of the masterminds behind the celebrated "Tom River" sabotage ring that in 1916 succeeded in causing the devastating explosion of ammunition barges in New Jersey. Jahnke was a Prussian who capitalized on his exploits with German military intelligence in World War I by founding a remarkably successful private intelligence network, called the Jahnke Büro, which Walter Schellenberg, in his postwar interrogation, described as a "semi-official espionage service working in conjunction with certain branches of the German Intelligence Services." Although he always distrusted Jahnke, Schellenberg, who ran the foreign section of Heydrich's Sicherheitsdienst or SD, made use of him until he came under suspicion after Hess's flight to Scotland.[33]

Schellenberg explained this was because of "the suspicion that attached to his liaison officer S.S. Oberst von Pfeffer." This was Franz Felix Pfeffer von Salomon, a former S.A. leader who was the link between Hess's private intelligence office and that of S.S. chief Himmler. Until the autumn of 1941, Jahnke, who lived in some style in a Berlin villa, operated out of an office at party headquarters. It was his secretary Markus, Schellenberg said, who "dealt with all his office work and was also drawn in to deal with the V-men" – the German agents. Hess had intervened to get Markus, originally with the Abwehr, released from military call-up. But he was eventually sent to the western front, where he crossed the lines to the British in 1944 and was later involved in working for MI6 in postwar Germany.[34]

MI5's claim that their "informant" was in "constant touch" with Admiral Canaris, the head of the Abwehr, is a further clue that Markus was their source "in the German Secret Service." Since he was fluent in English, he probably translated the "Doctor's" dispatches for Jahnke, who had made contact with MI6 shortly before the war. According to Schellenberg's debriefing, Ribbentrop became suspicious of Jahnke when he "tried to avert war and had used every conceivable means *to bring an English intelligence man to Hitler through Hess.*"[35]

If Jahnke, or Markus, or both are the most likely candidates for MI6 informant, who are the potential nominees for "the Doctor"? The evidence, as Johnson implied in his report, pointed to an American who had access to Kennedy's dispatches and was somewhere "along the line of wire." This ruled out the Embassy in Berlin as the source of the leak; and if the spy were a State Department employee, the channel by which the information reached Berlin from Washington would have been the German Embassy, thence via the diplomatic bag or cable to the headquarters of the Abwehr – but not to Hess's private intelligence office. Another factor that argues against the leak being in Washington is the long delays involved in 1939 surface communications. The MI5 report that Kennedy's dispatches were reaching Berlin "sometimes twice a day" is further reason to conclude, as Johnson apparently did, that the source who was feeding Kennedy's dispatches to the Germans must have been in the U.S. Embassy in London.[36]

Another pointer to the obvious suspect is the fact that "the Doctor" – according to MI5 – had been feeding only Ambassador Kennedy's dispatches to the Germans. If the spy had been a code clerk, the presumption must be that, like Kent, he would have been collecting and passing on a wide variety of secret telegrams to Berlin; but "the Doctor" appears to have passed on only Kennedy's reports to Washington.

Just why a German agent with access to every cable passing between Washington and Western Europe should single out Kennedy's dispatches is one of the most significant aspects of the "Doctor" affair. It suggests that the source was not only at the London Embassy but inside Kennedy's office – either that, or the British secret service set out deliberately to frame Kennedy. The Germans, who knew from Mooney and von Dirksen that the American Ambassador was sympathetic, could have had no reason to undermine him. Senior MI5 officers have confirmed that "the Doctor" was not a British plot – and their sending confidential Cabinet deliberations to Berlin to spike the American Ambassador just does not make sense.

The record shows that throughout the summer, as Hitler stoked the flames of the Polish crisis with his demands on the Danzig corridor, Kennedy steadily back-tracked on his earlier bullish support for the guarantees Britain and France had given Poland. A week before war broke out, his calls for more appeasement culminated in his cable to Roosevelt relaying Chamberlain's request for him to ask the Poles to soften their stand against Hitler's demands. "As things stand now that is the place to apply pressure," Kennedy urged. "The British are in no position to press the Poles strongly, but if anything is to be accomplished action must be taken at once, as the Prime Minister feels the blow is fairly near." His barrage of personal phone calls to the State Department was ignored. Neither Hull nor Roosevelt had any wish to be trapped by their panicking Ambassador into a "second Munich." As Pierrepoint Moffat put it, "I fear they have caught Kennedy in this net, but the fish are too wary this side of the Atlantic." Kennedy was instructed to "put some iron up Chamberlain's backside." To which he responded tartly that the British "did not have enough iron with which to fight."[37]

Kennedy had therefore gone way beyond his ambassadorial remit in acting independently of Washington in a personal effort to avert war with Germany. On the day war broke out he was in a state of "unrelieved despair," his voice choking with emotion when he telephoned to tell Roosevelt "It's the end of the world, the end of everything." Kennedy was by no means the only businessman who feared that armed conflict would prove a disaster for capitalism which, by squandering treasure and resources, would only open up the flood-gates to the bolshevization of Europe. His friend Montague Norman, the dour Governor of the Bank of England, had confided to him that "Britain as we have known her was through." Lord Halifax was another who had told the Ambassador of his fears that the war "will mean Bolshevism all over Europe."[38]

At the root of Kennedy's defeatism was the misconception, sown by Charles Lindbergh and fed by his two elder sons after their visits to Germany, that Hitler's military might, especially the Luftwaffe, was so great as to be overwhelming. While neither the Ambassador nor his sons, Joe Jr. and Jack, approved of the Nazi regime, they were certainly taken in – as many were – by the propaganda façade of German power. Charles Hillman, an American journalist who was in London with Kennedy, summed up the Ambassador as "a professing Catholic who loathed Hitler and Hitlerism, though perhaps not quite as much as he loathed Bolshevism." As a self-made man whose wits and determination had enabled him to escape from the impoverished back streets of Boston to fortune and power, he was insecure about his wealth and haunted by the prospect of impoverishment. His blinkered vision flawed his judgement as Ambassador and left him quite unable to comprehend the real issues at stake in Britain's belated decision in 1939 to stand up to

Hitler over Poland. By temperament a financial hustler, he "saw the world through the bars of a dollar mark." According to his Military Attaché, Colonel Raymond E. Lee, "Kennedy has the speculator's smartness, but also has his sharpshooting and facile insensitivity to the great forces which are now playing like lightning over the map of the world."[39]

"Kennedy's Real Ambition Is the White House"

Kennedy's "blindness for intangibles," admitted his long-time friend James M. Landis, the ghost-writer of his unpublished autobiography, reinforced his sympathy for the isolationist sentiments of the American heartland. He also saw that finding a way to appease Hitler was a stepping stone towards laying claim to political power.[40]

This was the conclusion drawn by officials in the Foreign Office, who decided that "Kennedy's real ambition is the White House." When his ambassadorship was announced in 1937 Kennedy was immediately heralded as the "Crown Prince of the Roosevelt Regime" by the *New York Daily News*, which labelled him "FDR's personal selection as his successor to White House honors in 1940." In 1939, with Roosevelt's second term approaching its final year, Kennedy actively encouraged speculation in the American press with the jaunty denials of an undeclared but confident candidate. The enormous popularity that attached to Chamberlain after Munich may have encouraged the Ambassador's belief that if he too could cast himself as the "Saviour of Peace" it would start his presidential bandwagon rolling towards the White House.[41]

In pursuit of an independent European peace initiative Kennedy had unilaterally approached the German Ambassador in London and held secret talks with Göring's economic adviser on a billion-dollar scheme to buy peace with Hitler. Mooney, who had sold him the idea, had already discovered that British bankers in the City would support the plan. At the same time as Kennedy's political aspirations began to stir, his previously warm relationship with the President, who had sent him to the plum posting at the Court of St. James, had been steadily souring. In the summer of 1939 he was snubbed when he was not invited to join the welcoming ceremony for King George VI, who was making the first visit to the United States by a reigning British sovereign. The Ambassador felt himself increasingly shut out and thought Roosevelt relied too heavily on the misguided bullish advice that his crony Bill Bullitt constantly telephoned from the Paris embassy. Kennedy complained to the President in July 1939 that he was being used as a "glorified errand boy." Roosevelt quickly wrote back to reassure the ruffled Ambassador that he counted on his friend "doing a good job there."[42]

For all the President's glad-handing and his belief in personal political loyalty inculcated by a father who had captained the democratic wards of East Boston, Kennedy was fearful and festering in the summer of 1939. The Polish crisis, which Hitler brought to the boil during that sweltering summer, could well have persuaded an overheated and frustrated Ambassador to attempt a desperate secret initiative to get through to Berlin to save the peace. His headstrong temperament and his dislike of stuck-up British society might well have precipitated a blundering indiscretion.

Did Ambassador Kennedy, in a bid to establish his credentials as a peacemaker, relay to the Germans inside information on the positions taken by the British and American governments? This is a hypothesis, but it does not appear so far-fetched in the light of the information that has come to light about "the Doctor." The final answers may not be found until the British release their intelligence archives, or until the still secret Nazi intelligence files are returned to the Germans. But, as in a classic detective trail, the clues for motive, access and opportunity lead inevitably to Kennedy – or possibly his aide Edward Moore – as the prime suspects.

It seems unlikely that Kennedy himself would have risked establishing direct contact with a German agent, but he would have had fewer qualms about entrusting this mission to his faithful confidential aide. The white-haired "Eddie" Moore had been a secretary of four Boston mayors – and was no stranger to the intrigues of the Irish mafia – and had joined the young Kennedy when he was playing the real-estate market. Moore served devotedly for forty years – and the family paid him the compliment of naming their third son Edward after him; he was so self-effacing that he was sometimes referred to as Kennedy's valet. But this belied his real role as principal lieutenant, side-kick, bag-man and fixer for Kennedy in his rise from stock-market manipulator to Hollywood banker and movie mogul. Such was Moore's dog-like dedication to Kennedy that it is inconceivable that he could ever have been "the Doctor" on his own. If, on the other hand, Kennedy was in independent communication with the Germans during the summer of 1939, then the faithful Moore must either have been privy to it or acted as the intermediary.[43]

Moore's role as a trusted courier and contact might explain the real reason behind the Ambassador's unscheduled three-day private trip to Paris on 1–3 April 1939. His official reason, cabled to the State Department, was that his "associate Eddie Moore for 25 years" was ill. But Kennedy's sudden need to visit Moore is unusual because he turns out to have been suffering from nothing more life-threatening than a bout of influenza.[44]

Personal devotion may have been the excuse he gave the State Department, but Kennedy, it turns out, might have had another reason, connected with the return to Europe of his friend James D. Mooney. The General Motors European Vice-President had landed at Southampton three days earlier. Mooney's diary shows that he then left for Berlin on 31 March, the *very day* the Ambassador cabled the State Department for permission to make his errand of mercy to Paris. Such a coincidence appears too fortuitous not to be suspicious. Then within two weeks Kennedy was being slapped down by the Secretary of State for proposing to include in his speech accepting the freedom of the City of Edinburgh on 21 April an endorsement of Roosevelt's appeal to Hitler and Mussolini to join the United States in a global non-aggression pact. This was rejected, with the President's approval, because of State Department fears that any such remarks by an ambassador were inappropriate – especially the day after Hitler's birthday speech. "All international affairs omitted," Kennedy replied by cable to Washington, adding sarcastically that he would speak instead about "flowers, birds, and trees," even though he ran the risk of the Edinburgh citizens making him "Queen of the May."[45]

It was another interesting coincidence that within a week of the Ambassador's intended public declaration in favour of peace Mooney was back in London touting the Wolthart peace plan which Kennedy backed with such enthusiasm. Nor was his April visit to Paris the only private trip Kennedy made to France during the summer crisis of 1939 – during the very same months when "the Doctor" happened to be relaying the Ambassador's Washington reports to Berlin. Kennedy was in Paris again on 21 July, just before his four-week family holiday at the Ranguin estate five miles from Cannes. If Kennedy or Moore had indeed opened a secret channel of communication with the Germans, then France offered the best opportunity to use it without the risk of being caught by British surveillance.[46]

There exists what could be another piece of the "Doctor" puzzle in the Personnel Files of the State Department under Moore's name. On 23 May 1940, in what could only be a direct response to Tyler Kent's arrest, Kennedy cabled the State Department for authorization for his private secretary to return to the United States. The telegram also announced Moore's intention of resigning from the Foreign Service after his leave was up. Five days later Moore and his wife, together with Rosemary, the Kennedys' retarded daughter, left Southampton by air for Lisbon to catch the transatlantic Pan Am Clipper.[47]

The abrupt departure of the faithful Eddie Moore, who had been his right-hand aide for twenty-five unbroken years, suggests that Kennedy must have had a very urgent reason for wanting him out

on behalf of the President. The copied cables in his file packed enough political dynamite to have derailed Roosevelt's chances of re-election. The President's secret exchanges with Churchill, though not nearly such sensational evidence of chicanery as Kent believed, would undoubtedly have made headlines in Republican hands. And there were plenty of Roosevelt-haters who would have made explosive political capital out of them, including the emotive Louisiana minister Gerald L. K. Smith and Charles Lindbergh, the spokesman of the America First Campaign.

The Ambassador's political ambitions must also have been charged by the increasingly hostile attacks being made on him publicly in Britain. No sooner had he returned to London in March 1940 than he was greeted by a scabrous personal attack from the prominent Conservative weekly *The Spectator*, which can have left him in no doubt that he was regarded as potentially the most dangerous Fifth Columnist in the country. Tory M.P. and columnist Harold Nicolson had said as much when he derided Kennedy's "little raft of appeasement" that kept afloat "the bankers and the isolationists . . . the shiver sisters of Mayfair and the wobble-boys of Whitehall . . . the Peace Pledge Union, the Christian Pacifists, the followers of Dr. Buchman, the friends of Herr von Ribbentrop, the *Nürnbergers*, the *Munichois*, Lord Tavistock and the *disjecta membra* of former pro-Nazi organizations."[54]

The American records do not show whether Kennedy's First Secretary ever told him of the MI5 reports on "the Doctor." But as the alarming news of the leaks was given while the Ambassador was out of the country, Johnson may have regarded this as a significant indicator of British suspicion.

Johnson was an old Foreign Service hand who could not have failed to resent the Ambassador's high-handed and undiplomatic way of conducting business. Kennedy's reports were often misleading in that they were one-sided expressions of his own viewpoint intended to influence Washington rather than to give an accurate analysis of the situation in Britain. As Kennedy's Chargé, Johnson had been discreetly trying to redress the balance. An Anglophile (in contrast to the Anglophobe Kennedy), Johnson was a punctilious, correct and respectful diplomat. The absence of any State Department investigatory records suggests that the First Secretary did not tell his Ambassador but maintained a quiet reserve after being warned about "the Doctor."[55]

The arrest of Tyler Kent was yet another blow to the professional status of the London Legation, and the ramifications of the affair further damaged Kennedy's standing in both London and Washington. The Ambassador's surveillance by MI5, with references to phone tapping and monitoring of Embassy employees, must have been extremely discomfiting for him. The incarcerated code clerk was also a useful pawn in the Prime Minister's larger strategy to neutralize the Cassandra Kennedy and to win from the United States more commitment to Britain's support. This is evident because, when the Home Office took out a deportation order against Kent, it signalled to the White House that Churchill was holding a political hostage for Roosevelt. If the code clerk was sent back to be tried in open court in the United States, his revelations about the President's secret cables would give the isolationists ammunition to sink the President's chances of a third term in the White House. Roosevelt's political future therefore depended on Kent being tried in secret and imprisoned in Britain. The political damage that the Kent affair could inflict on the President was starkly apparent to the aide who had played a key role in his previous campaigns. "It is a terrible blow – almost a major catastrophe. It is appalling!" concluded Breckinridge Long as he read the "catalogues of the papers" going right back to 1938 that the code clerk had stolen: "No doubt the Germans will publish another White Book which will have as its purpose the defeat of Roosevelt and the election of the ticket which opposed him and presumably in sympathy with Hitler – an appeasement ticket – an administration to succeed ours which will play ball with Germany or surrender America." The State Department cables also show how strongly Roosevelt reacted to contain the Kent affair. He was especially worried about the threat to his political fortunes posed by the leak of his secret exchanges with Churchill, and it was for this reason that the President's 16 May cable rejecting the loan of destroyers was *not* included in the charges brought against Kent and Wolkoff. When Scotland Yard asked the Embassy for access to the original of this telegram they were refused. Pleas were made that the "entire case" against Kent, Wolkoff, Ramsay and Nicholson depended on inspection of this document by the Public Prosecutor, and assurances were given that the trial would be held *in camera*, with "every human precaution . . . to prevent any leakage." But Ambassador Kennedy was instructed three times to inform the British government that the "Department cannot repeat cannot agree." He accordingly refused to release for inspection either the typewritten original or the pencil copy found on Kent.[56]

The copy discovered in the raid on the Nicholson home was worthless as evidence unless the original could be brought into court. So the Official Secrets charges brought against Kent and Wolkoff in August had to be based on the two Churchill messages and the MI5 report that had originated from British sources. This was insisted upon by the State Department out of White House concern that if there were any leaks they must not directly implicate the President. This refusal to let the President's message be used in Kent's trial underscored his value as a political hostage. At the same time the Prime Minister was very well aware that his own future and Britain's very survival might depend on Roosevelt's re-election to the White House. This could explain why Kent and Wolkoff were not brought to trial for five months, until Ambassador Kennedy had safely departed British shores, a week before the presidential poll in the United States.[57]

Blackmail may be the ugly term for the stratagem effected by Churchill with Kent's arrest. But it has now become clear that Kent was a silent, but far from insignificant, pawn on the political chessboard as the Prime Minister stepped up his appeals to Roosevelt for military support to continue the war against Hitler. The President can have been under no illusion that, if Churchill were toppled and peace was made with the Germans, Kent would be swiftly deported to the United States to blow up his presidential campaign.

All through the summer of momentous crises when Britain struggled for her very survival, the American code clerk languished in Brixton Prison, a political grenade with its safety pin pulled and the firing level held in Churchill's knowing grip. If Kent ended up therefore playing a far more significant role in ensuring that the United States *did* get dragged into the war, his arrest also provided Churchill with the legal authority to strike out against the members of the British establishment who were hoping to make a deal with Hitler.

Chapter 7

"The Edge of a Great Disaster"

"Nobody to Stop Them"
21 May 1940

"I saw Winston, who persists in thinking that the situation is no worse," General Ironside noted after the Tuesday morning meeting of the Chiefs of Staff. On his way back to England from General Gort's headquarters, Ironside had himself been blown out of his bed at the Hotel Excelsior in Calais by a near miss during a heavy German bombing raid. The previous morning, General Guderian's Panzer divisions, after brushing aside British Territorial Army units, had arrived at the gates of Amiens. By Monday afternoon his leading tanks were rolling on across the flat Picardy plain past Abbeville. Nightfall found them at Noyelles on the Channel coast forty miles south of Boulogne at the mouth of the River Somme.[1]

"Today's battles have brought us complete success," Guderian triumphantly signalled to his forces that night. "Along the whole front the enemy is in retreat in a manner that at times approaches a rout." The wedge had been driven between the British and the French Seventh Army by "a gigantic impersonal war machine, run as coolly and efficiently, say, as our automobile industry in Detroit," reported American journalist William Shirer, who was following in the wake of the German forces. In the bunkers of Felsennest Hitler was overjoyed as General Halder laid before him the O.K.H. plans for the final envelopment of the Allied armies in Northern France. This was to be followed by a bold southward drive by the armoured divisions down the French Channel coast to the Bay of Biscay.[2]

"Nobody to stop them and they are supposed to be going to Boulogne" was Ironside's unhappy assessment of the enemy's next

150

objective. "How can one think the thing is not serious?" He had returned convinced that the French Army was too shattered by the ferocity of the Germans' initial breakthrough to regroup in time to block their advance to the Channel coast. General Weygand's first full day commanding the Allied armies could not have been a bigger disaster. On Tuesday morning the spry septuagenarian, who had served as chief of staff to Marshal Ferdinand Foch when he led the Allied armies to victory in 1918, set off for the Belgian headquarters at Ypres. His flight took him over the enemy lines, dodging anti-aircraft fire and Messerschmitt attacks.[3]

Churchill in London remained cheerfully confident. At the Tuesday morning War Cabinet he dwelt on the "overwhelming" superiority of Allied forces that were now being galvanized into action by General Weygand to cut the German lines. Enemy tanks had been reported heading up the coast that morning towards Boulogne, but the Prime Minister predicted that "the situation was more favourable than certain of the obvious symptoms would indicate." He did not mention the "obvious symptoms" of demoralization that had alarmed Ironside the day before at the headquarters of France's First Army, where he found Billotte and Blanchard "in a state of complete depression," with "no thought of a plan" and "ready to be slaughtered." The six-foot-four British general was so incensed by their negativism that he grabbed Billotte by the tunic buttons and shook him. "You must make a plan," he bellowed. "Attack at once to the south with all your forces on Amiens." This verbal and physical assault so startled the short French general that he clicked to attention and meekly agreed to make "an immediate plan of attack."[4]

Rather than provoke an open clash with Churchill in the War Cabinet, the Chief of the Imperial General Staff kept to himself the full extent of his reservations about French willingness and ability to mount an effective counterattack. He said he had found the French commander Billotte in a "state of indecision but had galvanized him into giving orders for a counterattack." He also reported giving Gort the War Cabinet's directive to prepare for an attack southward to cut the German lines south of Arras in conjunction with the French.[5]

Churchill's confidence that the plan would work therefore prevailed. Even the normally gloomy Cadogan was persuaded that there was now a ray of hope, and if Weygand "could get a grip we may yet do something." Reports from Rome suggested that Mussolini might still be induced to think again before plunging into the war. But while the War Cabinet debated Churchill's proposal that Britain's policemen should now be armed to deal with anticipated enemy paratroop raids, the Germans were having their first serious clash with troops of the British Expeditionary Force in Picardy.[6]

151

In response to the instructions brought from London by Ironside, General Gort had ordered an attempt to break through the German lines south of Arras. But with only eight divisions to hold a fifty-mile front, he was understandably reluctant to siphon off too much of the British Expeditionary Force for a concentrated attack towards the Somme. He therefore assigned a tank brigade and two infantry divisions under Major-General Harold Franklyn to launch a southward thrust towards the German lines on 21 May. The attack by the so-called "Frankforce" went ahead as planned – even though Gort was warned by Blanchard that French forces would not be able to coordinate their northward drive for at least another day. The attack by two British battalions, supported by sixteen British tanks and lightly armoured French units, was nevertheless pushed forward with such vigour that it caused the Army Group A headquarters to flinch. "For a short time," General von Rundstedt would later admit, "it was feared that our armoured divisions would be cut off before the infantry divisions could come up to support them." But by nightfall the attack had been halted.[7]

The stalling of the Allied thrust towards Arras that afternoon persuaded Gort that the orders he had received from the War Cabinet were totally unrealistic. He regarded it as only a matter of time before the British Expeditionary Force would have to seriously consider falling back on the Channel ports. The failure of communications that delayed Gort's arrival for the Allied war conference at Ypres that afternoon aroused French suspicions that the B.E.F. command were already secretly intending to withdraw. But it is doubtful if Gort's presence could have altered King Leopold's repeated refusals to agree to Weygand's plan, which called for the Belgian Army to retreat to the River Yser. This withdrawal was essential to shorten the Allied line and release two divisions of British troops for the counter-offensive.

General Gort arrived at the conference an hour after the French commander-in-chief had departed, and it was left to Billotte to expound to the sceptical British general Weygand's ambitious plan for a massive attack south of Arras on 23 May to pincer off the corridor through which the Panzers were funnelling. Gort reluctantly agreed to participate in this plan. But whatever slim chances it had of succeeding received a further setback that evening when General Billotte's staff car crashed into a truck and he was mortally injured.[8]

"We are either on the edge of a great disaster or a great victory! Important to remember both possibilities are there," Oliver Harvey commented after sitting in the French Senate that afternoon to hear Premier Reynaud announce, in an impassioned speech, that *"La patrie est en danger."* The brutal frankness with which he proceeded to detail the loss of French towns in the military disaster brought gasps from many senators. In this "tragic hour" he announced his renewed confidence that the country's fortunes were in firm hands. He could now rely for guidance on Marshal Pétain, "the man who knows how a French victory can come out of a cataclysm," and on Weygand, "Foch's man who halted the German onslaught when the front was broken in 1918." It might need a miracle to save France, but Reynaud declared he had faith in that miracle, because he believed in France.[9]

That night German bombers raided Paris again – this time dropping leaflets urging the French to make peace and abandon their British allies. In London communication problems were causing the Prime Minister renewed concern. On Tuesday afternoon he had received what appeared to be encouraging news from General Dill in France. He then telegraphed to tell Reynaud that the French Army should waste no time before making a concerted counterattack "to drive in upon the flanks" of the main body. When no response had been received by early evening, he stood impatiently over his private secretary, Colville, who repeatedly tried to get a call through to Paris. "In all the history of war, I have never seen such mismanagement," the Prime Minister snapped. Later that evening Colville observed that he had never seen Churchill "so depressed." The Prime Minister sensed that Reynaud's failure to respond was cause for alarm. He decided to make another trip to Paris to stiffen the French resolve next morning.[10]

Before retiring that night, well after midnight, Churchill took a decision about the United States that indicated a marked shift in his strategy for dealing with Roosevelt. A month earlier, as First Lord of the Admiralty, he had initiated a proposal to share British sonar research into "Asdic" submarine detection, radio direction finding, and magnetic mines in return for the assistance of American research laboratories in microwave radar and the highly accurate U.S. Army gyro-stabilized Norden bombsight. That Tuesday Churchill had received a reminder from the new First Lord, A. V. Alexander, suggesting that now was the time to "do everything we can to show good-will towards the United States" by making "an unrestricted offer to pool technical information." Churchill scrawled his dissent on the First Lord's note, in red ink: he "did not think a wholesale offer of military secrets will count for much at the moment."[11]

Considering the urgency of Churchill's pleas for destroyers, his decision to wait for a riper moment to strike a bargain over technical information risked upsetting the Americans at a crucial juncture and might have been foolhardy *if* the Prime Minister had not been holding the American code clerk as a hostage to Roosevelt's political fortunes. The arrest of Tyler Kent enabled Churchill to take a much tougher line with the President; instead

153

of pleading for United States aid, he was going to frighten the Americans into realizing that it was in their own best interests to keep Britain afloat.

The officials in the State Department in Washington that Tuesday were already "working on the assumption that Britain would be defeated." Even strongly pro-British State Department officials were shaking their heads. "The news from the front looks increasingly bad so that we may have to face the possibility that there may be a complete German victory as opposed to a negotiated peace," Pierrepoint Moffat reflected: "What this would mean in relation to the British fleet is the crux of the problem for ourselves." The British Ambassador in Washington was also striking an uncharacteristic note of doom. Dining that evening with Assistant Secretary of State Breckinridge Long, Lord Lothian had predicted that if the Germans got a toehold in Britain "his government would surrender the British fleet" rather than see the populace suffer excruciating punishment. The Ambassador was "very frankly gloomy about the whole situation and permitted the inference that he expected England to be defeated." Long concluded that Churchill had instructed the British Ambassador "to scare the American people with the idea that Germany was going to get the British fleet and consequently the United States ought to get into the war right away to prevent it."[12]

Five days earlier the British Ambassador in Paris had delivered the same warning to Bullitt, who had alerted the President that one of "the ultimate consequences of absolute defeat" was that "the British navy would be against us." The State Department, however, tended to discount Bullitt's increasingly hysterical cables. Breckinridge Long complained that in his panic to destroy the Embassy's secret papers, their Ambassador to France had consigned to the flames not only his State Department code books but also the naval coding machines that were awaiting couriers to take them to other European capitals. This left the Paris Embassy with no secure means of communicating with Washington. "Bullitt must have had a real holiday when he started that fire," Long commented sourly.[13]

The arrest of Tyler Kent caused a big headache for Long and the State Department, while at the same time allowing Churchill to play hardball with the White House. It was also an invaluable weapon for the Prime Minister when it came to dealing with his opponents in the Conservative Party. The night before he left for Paris, he dictated a minute to Chamberlain, who would be chairing the War Cabinet next day when the MI5 report on the Kent affair was to be discussed. Churchill had no doubt that the evidence of a dangerous Fifth Column plot was now so manifest that the time had come for rounding up all aliens, British Fascists and German sympathizers.

154

"Subversive Activities in London"
22 May

Shortly after dawn on Wednesday Churchill set out for Paris in a downpour – the first rain to hit England for months. He was accompanied by General Ismay, his military aide. While their plane was flying over the Channel, the French Prime Minister received a briefing from his commander-in-chief. General Weygand had returned that morning invigorated by his eventful twelve-hour journey back from Ypres, which had taken him from Dunkirk to Dover by torpedo boat and then on to Cherbourg, from where he was driven directly to Paris for his conference with Reynaud at 9.30 a.m.

"So many mistakes have been made that they give me confidence. I believe that in future we shall make less and that we shall be able to avoid final disaster if we take measures against panic and if the army does its duty," Weygand told Reynaud. Outlining his plan to thwart a German encirclement of the forty-five Allied divisions fighting north of the Somme, he said he was counting on the southward thrust of the British Expeditionary Force, which "was in a good state, for up to the present it has hardly been in action." He had already issued orders to Allied armies to move south in step with a northward thrust by the French forces south of the Somme. These would constitute a giant pincer which, Weygand predicted, would cut the German armoured forces off from their infantry reinforcements. "It is all-important to effect this junction," Weygand said. "It will either give us the victory or it will save our honour." He then drove off to Vincennes to prepare for his meeting with the British.[14]

Fortified by a working lunch washed down by the finest French wines and cognac, Churchill was in a mood to believe that Weygand could bring off a military turnabout that would rank with his former commander Foch's 1916 "Miracle of the Marne." Even General Ismay was pleasantly surprised. "Weygand," he commented in his diary, "gave the appearance of being a fighter – resolute, decisive and amazingly active, in spite of his wizened face and advanced years."[15]

Churchill too was reassured by Weygand's drive and determination. Lest the French be in any doubt about Britain's total commitment, he announced that the two Guards battalions just landed at Boulogne were "the last units of the active Army still in England." He completely agreed with Weygand "that the restoring of communications between the armies in the north and the main force in the south, through Arras, was essential." But with the British Expeditionary Force down to four days of food supply, he said it was "absolutely vital" for Gort to preserve his line of

155

communication to the Channel ports during the southward thrust. So when Weygand asked for backing "up to the hilt" from the R.A.F fighters and bombers, the British Prime Minister said he would have their full support in the air.[16]

Churchill was still more heartened to hear, he thought, that the French were to attack *"certainly tomorrow,* with about eight divisions." That, at least, was his interpretation when he "dictated a résumé of the decision and showed it to Weygand who agreed." The General would later deny that he had approved the use of this draft phrase. Churchill, however, was so convinced that a concrete plan had been established that he immediately telegraphed a summary of it to General Gort's Premesques headquarters. The British Expeditionary Force, he instructed, would join the French First Army in an "attack south-west towards Bapaume and Cambrai at the earliest moment . . . with the Belgian Cavalry Corps on the right." Gort's forces were to advance to "join hands" with the French Army attacking northwards towards Amiens.[17]

"Best wishes in the battle" was Churchill's conclusion to his telegram, and he left Vincennes that afternoon full of confidence that Weygand and his plan could reverse the tide of twelve days of uninterrupted German advance. "The only complaint that I have got to make about you," he joked with Weygand as he bade him farewell, "is that you are a little too young."[18]

The Prime Minister's spirits received a further boost when he arrived back in London shortly before seven. He was informed that a new Defence of the Realm Regulation 18B(1A) had been agreed and already promulgated. This cleared the way to moving against alleged Fifth Columnists. The final barrier, the legal restraints that the Home Secretary had complained prevented action against right-wing subversives "in the absence of evidence which indicated that the organization as such was engaged in disloyal activities," had been removed. The Confidential Annexe to the item headed in the War Cabinet Conclusions "Subversive Activities in London" reveals that it was the MI5 report on the arrest of Kent and Wolkoff that was used as the pretext for this substantive change in the law.[19]

"A . . . Bill for taking complete power to do anything required with persons, or property," noted Lord Halifax, had been quickly agreed by the War Cabinet. It had completed all its parliamentary stages by the afternoon, receiving the Royal Assent at six o'clock. With the stage set for action, Chamberlain, who had discussed tactics in a midnight phone call with Churchill, then produced the report on the alleged Kent-Wolkoff spy ring.[20]

The MI5 memorandum that Chamberlain used to impress on the War Cabinet that this plot was an example of the dangerous Fifth Column menace was not even included in the Confidential Annexe;

156

it remains to this day a classified British government secret. But many of the details it contained emerge in the report that Captain Maxwell Knight had used to shock the American Ambassador two days earlier.

"Captain Maule Ramsay MP, who was the principal organizer of the 'Right Club,' had been engaged in treasonable practices," Chamberlain told the War Cabinet. He had operated "in conjunction with an employee (a United States citizen by the name of Tyler Kent) at the United States Embassy." The Home Secretary, not wishing to be left behind in his outrage lest he be thought soft, said he too had been given a full report on Anna Wolkoff, who had "been in relations" with the code clerk at the U.S. Embassy. "It appeared also that Captain Ramsay was in relations with this woman," Anderson said, adding "and also with Sir Oswald Mosley, though as regards the latter not in connection with this woman." Just how the British Fascist leader Mosley was "in relations" with Ramsay was never made clear. It was later vehemently denied by the indignant ex-Guards Captain that there was any connection between the Right Club and Mosley's organization.[21]

The Home Secretary proposed to consult with law officers on how to deal with Ramsay and the members of the Right Club, which he called "a semi secret society, mainly anti-Semitic in its objects, and only pro-Nazi in a secondary degree." Chamberlain took a tougher line. He said that this was a "most serious matter," because the MI5 report showed that "under guise of anti-Semitic propaganda, this body has been carrying on pro-German activities and secret subversive work, with the object of disorganizing the Home Front and hindering the prosecution of the war." Furthermore MI5 had discovered that Wolkoff "had a means of communicating with Germany." The Service Chiefs, who had been pressing for a stiffening of the law, wanted immediate action against the Right Club. Ramsay was not only an M.P., with parliamentary privileges, but because of his sympathies with Hitler's racial policies represented a possibly dangerous subversive element in Parliament. It was quickly agreed that "action should be taken" against other members of the Right Club.

When the War Cabinet turned to the next item on the agenda, dealing with Ramsay and any other German sympathizers became a relatively simple matter. Under the heading "Aliens and the Fifth Column" the Home Secretary raised the issue of organizations such as the British Union of Fascists. Its leader, Sir Oswald Mosley, was a renegade member of the British ruling class and a former Labour Cabinet minister who had created his Black-shirts in imitation of Mussolini, from whom he had clandestinely received funds. But though he applauded Hitler's anti-semitism and thought, like Ramsay, that it was wrong-headed for Britain

157

to have declared war on Germany, he claimed to be fiercely patriotic.[22]

MI5, the Home Secretary told the Cabinet, "had been unable to produce any evidence on which action could be based showing that either the leaders of the Organization or the Organization itself had anything to do with what might be called Fifth Column Activities." Regulation 18B, as it had originally been framed on 1 September 1939, gave the Home Secretary a pre-emptive authority to order the detention of Mosley, Ramsay and any other Hitler sympathizer "with a view to preventing him acting in a matter prejudicial to the public safety or the Defence of the Realm." But strong objections in the House of Commons to what was "tantamount to an open warrant which could be used against any person" had persuaded the government to soften the Regulation by requiring the committing of a "prejudicial act" before a detention warrant was issued. The Cabinet therefore agreed to the Home Secretary's form of words, which would enable him to deal with "any person known to be an active member of an Organization having hostile associations or subject to foreign control," and directed him to take action "as soon as this Regulation had been made."[23]

By Wednesday evening, when Churchill returned from Paris, the Home Secretary had legal authority to detain any members of an organization that in his view was either subject to foreign influence or whose leaders "have or have had associations with" enemy governments or "sympathize with" the "system of government" of enemy powers. "Sympathize" was the catch-all word that permitted the government to detain without trial, indefinitely, members not only of Fascist organizations but of any group that the Home Secretary judged sympathetic to the Germans – including those who advocated negotiations with Hitler.[24]

Acting under the new Regulation 18B, Special Branch squads began their swoops next day at the British Union of Fascists headquarters in Great Smith Street, where Alexander Frances-Hawkings, the party's Director General, and Raven Thompson, editor of its newspaper, *Action*, were arrested. Mosley was picked up at his flat in Dolphin Square – ironically, the same mansion block that housed Captain Knight's secret MI5 counter-subversion unit headquarters. One of the first non-fascists to be taken into custody was Captain Ramsay. He found policemen waiting on the doorstep of his Onslow Square home that Friday morning when he arrived back from his two-week trip to his Scottish estate. Some fifty-nine people, including ten women, were arrested over the next forty-eight hours in the first wave of detentions in the Metropolitan Police area under the new order. Three weeks later, on 14 June, the second wave of arrests began when the Home Office gave every police force in Britain the authority to detain "active members"

158

of organizations sympathetic to Germany "who may be engaged in specially mischievous activities." Among the new haul of detainees were Mosley's wife, Lady Diana, Sir Barry Domville, the founder of the pro-German Link, the brothers of William Joyce (Lord Haw Haw), the former British heavyweight boxing champion Joe Beckett and his wife, half a dozen policemen and the borough surveyor of Guildford. By the end of August over fifteen hundred people had been detained under the 18B Regulation.[25]

"It looks to me as if the country forces were overdoing it," observed an assistant commissioner at Scotland Yard. Thereafter the rate of detentions fell, and detainees began to be released as their cases were reviewed by the Home Office Committee. One detainee whose appeal was rejected was Captain Ramsay. Prominent in the "Particulars" listed by the Home Secretary for locking up the Conservative M.P. was that he "frequently expressed *sympathy* with the policy and aims of the German Government: and at times expressed his desire to co-operate with the German Government in the conquest and subsequent government of Great Britain." Ramsay denied the latter charge as "preposterous," dismissing allegations made by a government member of the House of Lords that he "had undertaken to be Gauleiter of Britain." Although he denied any knowledge of Wolkoff's communications with Joyce in Berlin, the evidence MI5 had obtained of her efforts to contact the Germans and the Right Club sponsorship of her poster campaign were considered sufficient legal justification for keeping him in prison without trial for four years.[26]

Ramsay's arrest was a warning to the other members of the Right Club that they faced the same threat. Since the Metropolitan Police files have yet to be released, it is not clear how many other members of the club were taken into custody. But there is now evidence that some members of the Right Club were highly placed government officials and influential Members of Parliament who were active in calling for a negotiated peace with Hitler.

On the morning the War Cabinet took the decision to amend the law to make it easier to detain German sympathizers, one of the more prominent members of the Right Club was with the delegation of M.P.s in the all-party "Peace Lobby" that went to see Lloyd George. Sir Ernest Bennett, a National Labour M.P., joined with the Labour peace activists Richard Stokes and Rhys J. Davies and the Tory C. T. Culverwell in an effort to persuade the former Prime Minister to renew his call for a negotiated settlement in the light of the Allied military reverse in France. Lloyd George, whom Churchill was entreating to join the War Cabinet precisely to prevent him becoming the focus of a peace plot, disappointed his callers. "The idea that we could sign a humiliating peace was ridiculous," Lloyd George said. He was in favour of giving back former German colonies, he told the delegation, but unless there was disarmament and world peace, "we should fight to the bitter end."[27]

A "hornet's nest" of rumours and speculation about a dangerous Fifth Column was part of a deliberate campaign whipped up by MI5 on the back of Kent's arrest. It brought General Kell to 10 Downing Street for a conference with Chamberlain on 24 May. The details of their discussion are still so sensitive that they are not a matter of public record. But the clues in the Confidential Annexe discussion of the Kent affair pointed to some alarming evidence uncovered by MI5 that Ramsay, and by implication, other members of the Right Club had been engaged in what Chamberlain darkly described as "treasonable practices." Just what these unspecified "treasonable practices" were remains unclear. Neither the report given by Knight to the American Embassy nor the admissions at Kent's and Wolkoff's trial explain what treachery Ramsay had committed. The Right Club founder was never charged with any crime during his four years' prison detention, and he successfully sued the *New York Times* for printing a story on 25 August 1940 claiming that he had "sent to the German legation in Dublin treasonable information given him by Tyler Kent." The judge was obliged to find in Ramsay's favour, awarding him derisory damages of a farthing.[28]

"I am convinced that Hitler would call Captain Ramsay a friend," Mr. Justice Atkinson declared. "He was disloyal in heart and soul to our King, our Government, and our people." Whether he was or not, disloyalty "in heart and soul" was not a criminal offence, even under Britain's draconian Defence of the Realm Regulations. No evidence was ever produced to support a charge of treason, let alone convict the Conservative M.P. His son, Colonel George Ramsay, said he could "remember him saying that Hitler was doing the right things in the wrong way . . . but he was a patriot. I remember that we were all told by him that we were to fight for our country."[29]

The failure to charge Ramsay, despite Chamberlain's allegations of "treasonable activity," is yet another indication that Kent's arrest and Ramsay's detention were part of a charade orchestrated by the security services. Those few records that have been declassified suggest that the whole affair was inflated out of all proportion at the behest of Churchill to panic the Cabinet into giving him the power to lock up Ramsay as an example to the other Members of Parliament in the Right Club who were sympathetic to striking a deal with Hitler. In this connection it is significant that the Home Secretary detailed among the "incriminating documents" discovered in Kent's possession "a sealed packet containing a book in which were recorded the names and addresses of the members of the Right Club." The list that Ramsay had padlocked

160

for secrecy in his red leather ledger holds the key to explaining why the Kent case was so important for Churchill.[30]

On his release from Brixton Prison on 26 September 1944, Ramsay claimed that the names in the so-called Red Book would have "shrieked aloud" if he had divulged them to the newspapers. But he stuck to his word as an officer and gentlemen until he died in 1955 to protect the membership list "from becoming known to the Jews." When interviewed in 1982, Kent, who claimed not to know more than a handful of the names, was convinced that if it ever came to light, the missing Red Book would show that the Right Club contained many influential members of the British establishment.[31]

The Red Book, which had vanished for fifty years, turned up during the clean-out of a safe at a firm of London solicitors. It was sent to Professor Richard Griffiths of King's College, London University, author of *Fellow Travellers of the Right*, an authoritative study of "British enthusiasts for Nazi Germany." The names it was found to contain reawakened the half-century-old controversy when Dr. Griffiths was filmed for *Divided We Stand*, an ITV documentary on the peace movements of 1940. The leather ledger was shown on television, its cover still bright red but its lock damaged exactly according to the description given in the U.S. Embassy report of how it was broken open before Ambassador Kennedy. Libel considerations restricted the camera to scanning only a few safely deceased names among the 200 members, 100 of them women, who are listed in Ramsay's slanting handwriting.[32]

For the first time it is possible to see why Ramsay guarded the names of the Right Club members with such tenacity. Many of the most prominent names were Old Etonian former Guards officers, and like himself members of prominent London establishment clubs, many from the Carlton, the senior Conservative club for government ministers. There were sixteen Members of Parliament, ten from the Commons and six from the House of Lords. (See Appendix 6.)

The historical importance of the Red Book is not so much whether Ramsay or any of the Right Club members actually engaged in "treasonable activities." It is significant that because MI5 had evidence of Wolkoff's communication with the Germans, *every member* in the ledger could be threatened with detention under the revised Regulation 18B. In the panicky climate of May 1940 it mattered not whether individual members really were anti-semitic, pro-Hitler or anti-Churchill – or even whether Ramsay may have padded the list. What counted was that Scotland Yard could portray the Right Club as a miniature "Who's Who" of the landed right-wing gentry that ranged from a member of the Royal Family, through Conservative Party chiefs, to prominent peers and junior members of the government. Only now that the list has finally become available is it possible to appreciate why the ledger that Kent had been given for safekeeping assumed such importance in the critical summer months of 1940. The Right Club's links to Kent and Wolkoff made it plausible "proof" of the sinister "enemy within" the upper reaches of the British establishment. The subsequent wave of detentions, particularly that of a right-wing Conservative M.P., enabled Churchill to send a very clear warning to any groups favouring a negotiated peace that they risked being locked up.

Churchill was confident that Progress had been made that Wednesday to deal with the "enemy within" as well as the "enemy without." At the beginning of the evening meeting of the War Cabinet he gave a very optimistic assessment of his trip to France. Reporting that he was "most favourably impressed" by General Weygand's "vigour and confidence," he read out the four-point summary of the counterattack plan that had been agreed that afternoon at Vincennes.[33]

It fell to General Ironside to puncture the Prime Minister's "almost buoyant spirits" by announcing that "so far as is known, no preparations had been made for these attacks at noon that day." As he saw it, the French plan was "still all *projects.*" In order to satisfy French wishful thinking, the British Expeditionary Force, which was running low on food and ammunition, was losing "a chance of extricating itself." Ironside was not without support in his delicate mission of trying to educate Churchill; Anthony Eden came to his aid by reporting a telephone conversation he had had at five that afternoon with a member of General Gort's headquarters staff who had driven to the Belgian coast to make the call on an unscrambled open public telephone line, because all direct lines of communication had been cut.[34]

"The situation was very grave," Eden reported. There were serious shortages of food and ammunition. Liaison with the main French force had broken down because their "coordinator has had an accident and coordinated no longer." Although Gort had failed to meet Weygand yesterday, he had come away from the conference at Ypres with the impression that there was "very little doing." King Leopold had agreed to a partial retreat to shorten the British line by thirteen miles, but described his conference with Weygand as "four hours of confused talking." Eden was told that a minister should be sent out to see for himself that conditions really were "very grave." Gort was relying on the French to clear his lines of communication. "As yet, however, they were not prepared to fight" was the B.E.F. commander's urgent message, "nor did they show any sign of doing so."[35]

"I hope the French will act," Chamberlain observed, "all reports show that they will not." His vexed diary entry that night reflected the pall that had fallen over the War Cabinet. Their mood of gloom was not relieved by Churchill's insistence that it was "good common sense" to press the Norway commanders for some "small success" that could provide an "en-heartening contribution" to the troops in France. Another indication of Britain's parlous military predicament was that the need for additional fighters was so desperate that the Cabinet were prepared to consider appealing to the Russians. The outcome of the Battle of Britain might have been very different if the R.A.F. had been obliged to rely on untried Soviet Migs and Yakolevs to defend British skies against the Luftwaffe. The very idea of going cap-in-hand to Moscow sent a collective shiver through the War Cabinet. Nonetheless they agreed to make it part of Sir Stafford Cripps's mission to float the idea to Stalin that the Soviet fighters would be purchased by the Chinese, who would then allow them to be resold to the British government.[36]

Britain's plea for Soviet fighters was to fall on deaf ears in Moscow, and General Ismay gloomily predicted that no amount of additional fighters could redress the balance in France. He said he was "really worried" about whether the French Army would fight. "He was afraid the Germans would offer the French generous terms," Colville wrote. Ismay's "dismal and depressing" mood did not brighten the next day when he awoke to find the situation in France "still blacker."[37]

DAY 4
"Falling Between Two Stools"
23 May

Early on Thursday morning German infantry units finally arrived at Amiens, hard on the tracks of the armour that had captured the town two days before. At nightfall the previous day the leading tanks of the 2nd Panzer Division reached the outskirts of Boulogne, while the vanguard of the 10th Panzer Division arrived at dawn in the suburbs of Calais. Boulogne was garrisoned by just two battalions: one from the Irish Guards and another from the Welsh Guards. Fighting street by street through the port, they put up a stout defence that prevented the Germans from completing their occupation of the port for the next two days. At Calais, a tank regiment and three rifle battalions commanded by Brigadier Claude Nicholson were to tie down an entire division of German tanks for four days. This proved a decisive factor in forcing General Guderian to commit his only reserve force, the 10th Panzer

Division, which he ordered into the battle for Calais, switching the 1st Panzer Division northward to Dunkirk. This was the last Channel port in France that remained open to supply the British Expeditionary Force – and it was just a twenty-five-mile drive up the coast road from Boulogne. But after advancing fifteen miles, the German tanks ran into heavy opposition from a unit of French troops dug in along the Aa Canal, which cut inland midway between the two ports. Had Guderian's two other Panzer divisions not been tied down at Boulogne and Calais, the British Army's Dunkirk escape route could have been cut off.

Cross-channel communication difficulties plagued Churchill and his chiefs of staff throughout that Thursday as crisis piled on crisis. The Upper War Room of the Admiralty was a scene of continual drama as the Prime Minister struggled to keep abreast of what had become a race by the Germans to encircle and trap the Allied armies in northern France.

"The signs are not good," General Ironside reported to the Prime Minister that morning. "Boulogne was isolated by German tanks this morning at 8 a.m." Sixty miles to the east, two divisions of B.E.F. infantry which had been battling south of Arras for two days were ordered back from the unequal struggle, which risked the encirclement of the "Frankforce" by Rommel's armoured division. Churchill later admitted that he never had "any knowledge of progress of this forlorn attempt at Arras to break the encircling line." But what did become clear to him early that morning was that the German advance on Boulogne was a "peril" that threatened to cut off the British Expeditionary Force. He minuted Ironside that the coast "must be cleared up if the major operation of withdrawal is to have a chance." This is the first indication that Churchill considered the safety of the British Army in France a greater priority than its participation in the Weygand plan.

"Communications of the Northern Armies have been cut by strong enemy armoured forces," Churchill then cabled to Reynaud. "Salvation of these armies can only be obtained by immediate execution of Weygand's plan. I demand the issue to French commanders in north and south and Belgian G.H.Q. of the most stringent orders to carry this out and turn defeat into victory. Time vital as supplies are short."[38]

The situation that had developed around the Channel ports was "so critical," the Prime Minister announced to the 11.30 War Cabinet, that he had instructed General Ironside to remain at the War Office to "supervise the conduct of these operations." The British Ambassador in Paris had confirmed that Weygand believed the conditions for going ahead with his plan "were more favourable than on the previous day," but expressed his concern that the French "showed no signs of taking the offensive." Churchill warned the Cabinet that if the plan failed "it would be necessary to make a fresh plan with the object of saving and bringing back to this country as many of our best troops and weapons with as little loss as possible."[39]

At the Chiefs of Staff conference that afternoon, the Secretary of State for War read the latest message from Boulogne, now under heavy shellfire from surrounding German tanks. The Germans had called upon the encircled British garrison to surrender. "The answer is no," Brigadier Nicholson had replied, "as it is the British Army's duty to fight as well as it is the German's." Eden said that Calais was also under attack, and the prospects of withstanding the siege were grim. The city was full of French troops and refugees, "all of whom seemed completely demoralized." In the north the B.E.F. forces in Belgium had been "heavily hammered" at Courtrai. The situation was not much better at the southern end of the British front. "The main difficulty had been to induce the French First Army to attack," according to Eden. "It had advanced on a two division front against Cambrai, but Lord Gort had little confidence that it would remain there." The B.E.F.'s supply situation was "very anxious," and the 2nd Armoured Division that was being landed at Cherbourg was too far removed to be brought into the battle.[40]

Clement Attlee, who had fought at Gallipoli and in the trenches at Lille, sensed the dangerous confusion that was overtaking Britain's military policy. He pointed out the "danger of falling between two stools" if the Weygand plan was not followed through or if concentrated attention was not turned to holding the Channel ports. General Dill believed that the best hope lay in carrying out the plan agreed with Weygand. "If Weygand can stage a good counterattack on the flank in the next 24 hrs, we may avert complete disaster," Cadogan noted. "But that is all the time he has got." His assessment summed up the "wait-and-see" position to which the War Cabinet had been reduced by the pace of events across the Channel. When the Minister of Information asked what he was to tell the press, the Prime Minister told him he would give the guidelines in his afternoon statement to the House of Commons.[41]

The gravity of the military situation was already producing a worried reaction from the Dominion prime ministers. The Australian Premier wanted a collective appeal to be made to the United States to release "every available aircraft." Churchill was not persuaded that they had "yet reached a situation in which a public appeal would be justified," but he cabled to the Dominion leaders that he would "welcome private appeals to the President from the Dominion Prime Ministers."[42]

With the evacuation of the B.E.F. hanging on the French, the War Cabinet, as Cadogan recorded, "decided in principle to get out of Norway." Because of the disastrous effect this decision would

165

have if news of it leaked out, it was agreed that the "utmost secrecy should be observed in regard to any suggestion that we might withdraw from Norway." This final dénouement of the disastrous Scandinavian adventure had been forced on the War Cabinet by an appreciation drawn up by the Chiefs of Staff, who proposed that all the forces in the fjord be concentrated on taking the port before withdrawing. This would at least bring the "political advantages of being able to say that we had captured Narvik." Churchill thought that the "advantages had been considerably minimized by the situation on the Western Front." He "deprecated asking troops to incur heavy losses in assaulting a town which it was planned to evacuate immediately afterwards."[43]

The Foreign Secretary, however, saw "considerable political advantages in capturing Narvik, if this could be done without heavy losses." It was a pointer to the way Lord Halifax was approaching the military disaster overtaking the Allies in France that he argued that Narvik would be a "valuable lever in connection with the Dahlerus plan for the withdrawal of both Allied and enemy forces from Northern Norway." Contending that it would be a "valueless lever if it was known that we intended to withdraw," the Foreign Secretary wanted "authority to pursue enquiries with both the Swedes and Norwegians as to the practicability of the Dahlerus plan." Chamberlain pointed out that the situation on the Western Front was "so bad that Hitler would not for a moment consider the Dahlerus proposals." Significantly, Churchill made no comment for the record. But the Foreign Secretary was told he "should not take further soundings in regard to the Dahlerus plan for the neutralization of Northern Norway." Halifax's willingness to relaunch an appeasement strategy as the Allies approached the brink of military defeat was underscored in his diary.[44]

"Winston's courage is very good," Halifax reflected, "but there is no minimizing the gravity of the situation." He communicated his pessimism to the American Ambassador at their meeting that afternoon. The Foreign Secretary's gloom was eagerly seized upon by Kennedy to fire off another defeatist telegram to Washington, warning Hull that the "situation *according to the people who know* is very very grim." In Kennedy's view, the "mass of the people just never seem to realize that England can be beaten or that the worst can happen to them." He did not "underestimate the courage or the guts" of the British, but "it is going to take more than guts to hold off the systematic air attacks of the Germans coupled with their terrific air superiority."[45]

Kennedy's forecasts that Britain would quickly succumb to the Luftwaffe were now being taken seriously by some members of the State Department. Germany's "dominance in the air" persuaded former Moscow ambassador Joseph E. Davies to send the President that Thursday his devastating conclusion that "short of a miracle both France and England will be occupied or destroyed this summer." He suggested that "prior to the initiation of any peace negotiations" Roosevelt should make provisions for the British and French "to sell or assign" their fleets and possessions "which are vital to our defense in consideration of the relinquishment of their obligations to us."[46]

However, the vaunted Luftwaffe which had caused other State Department officials beside Davies to write off Britain was already showing signs that it was overextending its resources. The previous day, when French light tanks made a thrust into Cambrai, they were driven back with the assistance of Henschel 123 biplanes. Heavy Stuka losses had obliged the Luftwaffe to send in these obsolescent dive-bombers to help the German infantry division to hold on to the town. The attack had been mounted as a belated effort by the First Army to support the faltering British push towards the Somme.[47]

At B.E.F. headquarters on 23 May General Gort was unaware that the French had made any effort at all to support his attack on Arras. What worried him was the lack of any sign of the promised French counterattack north across the Somme. The five divisions of the French Seventh Army commanded by General Aubert Frère advanced towards the south bank of the river that Thursday morning and Senegalese troops reached Amiens, where the Germans had established a bridgehead across the Somme. But Gort concluded that the French forces ranged south of the river had "no intention of attacking but were trying to prevent the Germans from advancing on Paris."[48]

The reason for the delay, although it was not communicated to Gort's headquarters, was that Weygand's plan was taking longer to put into operation than he had at first predicted. This was still unknown even to the French Cabinet, which that morning had reviewed plans for a mass exodus from the Paris region not just of ministries but of ammunitions factories. Reynaud, who still had every confidence in Weygand, had stalled a decision. He sent Baudouin to Vincennes for an urgent conference with the commander-in-chief, who explained that the "larger part of the German armoured divisions" were concentrated in the coastal sector around Abbeville and Boulogne. He said "the moment had come to try and cut them off from the bulk of the German army." He was confident that "if the English make a determined attack towards the south-east and if the Belgians hold their ground against pressure from the east, we shall be able to cut the German armour off from its base." With so much German armour already at the coast, Weygand admitted that the risks were very great, but he saw "no other way out of the present situation." He needed Reynaud's authority to go ahead with his strategical plan "whatever the cost."[49]

167

Baudouin returned to Paris to brief Reynaud. The Prime Minister approved Weygand's request "without demur" and he was given the go-ahead before four o'clock that afternoon. That Weygand waited almost half a day before getting authority for a plan that would take at least another day to get launched was astonishing, since he was aware that his communications with the encircled Allied armies were breaking down by the hour.

Weygand received authority to execute his plan that afternoon while Churchill was assuring the House of Commons that the Allied Commander-in-Chief "is conducting the operation involving all the Allied armies, with a view to restoring and reconstituting their combined front." When he returned shortly after four to the Upper War Room of the Admiralty, the Prime Minister was told that the Germans had captured the fort at the north of Boulogne harbour, effectively closing the port. He was even more dismayed to learn that there was still no news of the French attack. He telephoned Reynaud at 4.50 p.m. to know what had happened, and told him that Gort had "received no information from Blanchard." Since German tanks were in Boulogne and Calais, he asked "if it would not be better if the British Army fought in retreat towards the coast."[50]

"Weygand is satisfied. We ought not to change anything," Reynaud told Churchill repeatedly. "We must follow the path we have traced out. We *must* go on."

"The British Premier has got the impression of irresolution," Reynaud told Baudouin after putting down the phone on London. Failing to grasp the extent of the breakdown in inter-Allied communications, he told Baudouin that he had personally assured Churchill "that at the end of the morning General Weygand had said that the armies of Blanchard and Lord Gort were working hand-in-hand." To reinforce his point, Reynaud fired off a cable to London insisting it was "absolutely necessary to adhere to the plan adopted the previous day." Baudouin then telephoned Weygand to "warn him of Mr. Churchill's anxiety." If he received a direct call from London, Reynaud wanted him to "make an extremely firm stand" to the British Prime Minister. As Reynaud foresaw, Churchill did put a call through to Vincennes at six o'clock. Weygand, following his instructions to the letter, stretched the facts to try to convince him that all was going well with his planned operation. He claimed that the northward movement was already under way and "the French had recaptured" the Somme bridgeheads of Amiens and Peronne.[51]

"If true the news is stupendous," Colville noted sceptically that evening in his diary. General Ironside also doubted whether the French were moving. But after telephoning Weygand, he reported to the Thursday evening meeting of the War Cabinet that the French had "taken Amiens, Albert and Peronne and the manoeuvre was continuing under good conditions." Weygand, he noted, seemed unimpressed by the weight of German armoured forces moving up the coast towards Dunkirk, believing they were "reduced by casualties." He had also insisted that Blanchard's army could be supported from the sea, brushing aside Ironside's warning that there was "little chance of doing much." Weygand remained "confident," and "demanded" that the agreed plan be continued. "The rest," he said, "was disaster."[52]

The War Cabinet were now faced with having to make an impossible decision on conflicting information. The Chiefs of Staff recommended that the operation should continue as Weygand had requested. If the British Expeditionary Force had to retire to the Channel ports "it was unlikely that more than a small part of the force could be got away."

Just how bad the military situation was getting across the Channel became clear from the Prime Minister's report on the "catastrophic situation at Boulogne." At Calais there had been no up-to-date report of the fighting other than that a quarter of a million army ration packs had been landed, along with a tank regiment. But it had proved impossible to get the food supplies through to the B.E.F. because of heavy German armour ranged up three miles outside the town.

Churchill conceded that "even regarding the latest news in its most favourable light, there was little ground for confidence." However, he felt they had "no choice" but to go along with the French at this stage. "Any other course," he said, "would wreck the chance of General Weygand's plan succeeding." Unwilling to risk the consequences of reneging on the French, and misled by Weygand, Churchill and the War Cabinet took a decision that Thursday evening that could have cost Britain the loss of most of her Army. But that decision, fortunately for Britain and the fate of the West, had already been taken out of their hands by their commander in the field.

John Standish Surtees Prendergast Vereker, 6th Viscount Gort, may not have been the cleverest general in the British Army; but he was one of the more fiercely independent and courageous. In the Grenadier Guards during the First World War he had been wounded four times, mentioned in dispatches nine times and decorated with the Military Cross, two Bars of the Distinguished Service Order and the Victoria Cross. Until he was put in charge of the British Expeditionary Force in 1939, at the age of fifty-three, he had never commanded any force larger than a brigade. Jovial and charming, he was known affectionately as "Fat Boy" in the Guards mess. His more cerebral subordinate General Sir Alan Brooke (who was later to become Chief of the Imperial General Staff) admired him for his "great powers of leadership," although at times he seemed "incapable of seeing the wood for the trees."[53]

Fortunately, that Thursday and during the next ten days this archetypical bulldog of a British general not only saw the layout of the military wood very clearly but had also determined to steer his army to safety through the trees of conflicting orders and inter-Allied confusion. Harbouring a native, rather than a malicious, distrust of his French ally, Gort had on 20 May already begun reinforcing his secondary defence line. This was the Aa Canal, which skirted the left flank of the sector held by the British Expeditionary Force, running approximately north-south from the ancient port of Gravelines on the coast through St. Omer to Aire, where it joined the river system swinging westwards to La Bassée and the sector held by Blanchard's First Army.

The French, especially Weygand, would detect in Gort's every action evidence of British perfidy and determination to retreat rather than stand and fight according to the agreed plan. But the commander of the British Expeditionary Force was no less sceptical of French ability and willingness to mount and sustain a coordinated counterattack on the scale demanded by Weygand and Churchill. Gort was not a "political general." He simply saw it as his duty to do whatever was necessary to keep open a secure line of retreat. With his artillery down to less than four hundred rounds per gun, he responded to options dictated by military arithmetic, not international politics.

"We are tactically in an impossible position" was how Gort's chief of staff, Lieutenant General Sir Henry Pownall, summed up the predicament of the British Expeditionary Force that Thursday evening. He had ordered the troops on to half-rations that morning when headquarters received an "extraordinary telegram" from the Prime Minister sending his "best wishes" for the success of the Weygand plan. "The man is mad," Pownall responded angrily. "How does he think we are going to collect eight divisions and attack as he suggests? Have we no front to hold which if cracked would let in the flood?"[54]

Gort and his staff soon realized that Churchill could have no conception of the situation of their headquarters. So he decided there and then to make himself responsible for the destiny of his men. His gut instinct as a front-line soldier convinced him that London and Paris were so out of touch that it was his prerogative as the commander in the field to stick his neck out and say so. He therefore sent a telegram directly to the Secretary of State for War expressing his concern and insisting that "co-ordination" was essential if the armies of three nations were going to execute this complex manoeuvre, calling for General Dill to be flown over to see the problems for himself and report them to the Cabinet.

"My view is that any advance by us will be in the nature of a sortie," Gort bluntly warned Eden, "and relief must come from the south as we have not, repeat have not, ammunition for serious attack." This cable jolted the Secretary of State for War into a stark realization of the military facts facing the British Army in Flanders. Eden's concern was heightened by the lack of any definite French move that had prompted Churchill's telephone calls to Reynaud and Weygand. Although the French said they were moving according to plan, Eden was not so sure. That evening he sent Gort a cable that was to have far-reaching implications.[55]

After reporting what Weygand had told Churchill at six, Eden instructed the B.E.F. commander that the agreed plan was still in place. At the same time he provided Gort with an escape route. The crucial decision of whether and when to order a withdrawal in the event of the French plan collapsing was to be left to him. Eden took care to put these instructions on the record during that evening's War Cabinet; no disagreement was registered. Thus Gort was given the option that "if he found it impossible to continue operations in accord with General Weygand's plan, he should inform the British government so that the French could be informed, and all possible naval and air steps taken to cover the move to the coast."[56]

General Ironside's diary entry notes that this telegram effectively gave Gort "complete discretion to move his Army as he likes to try to save it." Convinced that Gort was "very nearly surrounded" but that "there is just a possibility that he may be able to withdraw through Ypres to Dunkirk," the Chief of the Imperial General Staff had already ordered more emergency rations to be sent to Dunkirk. But, as he recorded in his diary, "I cannot see that we have much hope of getting the B.E.F. out."[57]

Gort had too much bulldog tenacity to accept such a pessimistic assessment. That night he took the first step towards reorganizing his dispositions to prepare for an orderly withdrawal. Acting on the authority he had been given by the Secretary of State for War that evening, he ordered the abandonment of Arras and a fifteen-mile withdrawal of British forces to consolidate his rearmost flank along the Haute Deule Canal. It was a move that he knew would infuriate the French. Even Gort's able corps commander believed it was too late to make an orderly withdrawal. "Nothing but a miracle can save the B.E.F. now," General Alan Brooke reflected in his diary; "the end cannot be very far off."[58]

In London that evening the King, who had been kept posted with the dispatches coming into the War Office, found the news "so worrying" that he summoned Churchill to Buckingham Palace. The Prime Minister arrived at 10.30 p.m. and conceded that if the Weygand plan "did not come off, he would have to order the B.E.F. back to England." But he warned the King that this would result in

171

the loss of "all guns, tanks, ammunition, and store in France and that all depended on being able to hold onto the port facilities at Calais and Dunkirk."

"The very thought of having to order this movement is appalling," George VI wrote in his diary, gravely noting in his looping handwriting "the loss of life will be immense."[59]

After returning from Buckingham Palace, Churchill fired off another and sterner telegram to the French Prime Minister. Pointing out that there was a lack of communication between the British, French and Belgian armies, he demanded to know how this could be reconciled with the assurance he had been given earlier by Reynaud that "Blanchard and Gort are *main de la main?*" Although he had given Gort instructions to "persevere carrying out your plan," he reminded Reynaud that Gort had been told that any advance by the British Expeditionary Force "must be in the nature of a sortie and that relief must come from the south, as he has not (repeat not) ammunition for serious attack." The British chiefs of staff had yet to be given details of the Weygand plan, he complained. "We have not here even seen your own directive," Churchill concluded, "and have no knowledge of the details of your northern operation."[60]

The next day it was not the French who provided the "relief" that saved the British Army from encirclement. It was the decision by Adolf Hitler abruptly ordering a delay in the German advance that gave General Gort the opportunity to act unilaterally and save nearly a third of a million Allied soldiers.

Chapter 8

"A Wall of Sand"

DAY 5
24 May 1940

Early on Friday morning a bleak military report from France was given to Churchill by Colville, who encountered the Prime Minister in his dressing-gown and puffing a cigar on his way back to his bedroom after a pre-breakfast briefing in the Upper War Room at the Admiralty. The report contained some crumbs of comfort. A thousand troops had been evacuated from Boulogne during the night by Royal Navy destroyers under heavy fire, and at Dunkirk food and supplies had been landed and another ammunition ship was due to arrive that morning.[1]

No word had yet been received of the expected French counter-offensive. With reports of "tanks galloping all over N.E. France," Cadogan found the War Cabinet "pretty gloomy." Communications with Boulogne had been severed, and it was reported either to have surrendered or to be about to fall. In deference to French requests, no public announcement was to be made. An R.A.F. reconnaissance flight had reported a "definite halt" in the advance of the German armoured divisions towards Dunkirk. Whether this was due to "lack of petrol or the need for repairs," as the Prime Minister suggested, was unclear, but there were no Allied forces capable of stopping a full Panzer division of some 250 tanks pushing northward into Belgium across the rear of the British Expeditionary Force.[2]

The War Cabinet's main concern was the failure of the French to make their promised counter-offensive. In response to an urgent request from Sir Roger Keyes, the British government's special representative at the Belgian High Command, it was agreed that General Dill should immediately fly over to see General Gort to try and restore inter-Allied communication. The Belgian Ambassador in London had asked for contingency plans to be prepared for the evacuation of King Leopold and his ministers to England in the event of a military collapse.[3]

"The situation is very serious, for the English are falling back on the ports instead of attacking to the south," General Weygand whispered to Baudouin as they arrived for the Friday War Council meeting in Paris. The conference in the Prime Minister's office dragged on for over two hours as Weygand limned a sinister scenario of supposed treachery and deceit by General Gort. He said he had just learned from the French liaison officer with the Belgian Army that Arras had been abandoned by the British troops "without being compelled by the Germans to do so." The British Army appeared to be already retreating to the Channel ports, although no permission for these moves had been asked for by Gort when they spoke by telephone the previous evening. He declared of his British subordinate that he "would willingly have boxed his ears." Weygand could not believe that Gort would have acted in defiance of his orders without authority and so he laid the blame on the British chiefs of staff in London.[4]

"All this is most regrettable," Weygand complained, telling the War Council that the planned counterattack on the Panzer Corridor would have to be modified "in consequence of the retreat of the British army." The original junction point would have to be moved from Arras much farther down the Somme. The situation was one of "extreme gravity" because there would now be a further delay of several days while new orders were prepared and issued. As a result he foresaw that "it would be very difficult to avoid the capitulation of the Allied armies in the north for they were already suffering from a shortage of munitions and even victuals."[5]

Reynaud demanded that Weygand should tell him frankly what the military outlook for France would be if the Allied armies in Flanders were encircled and forced to surrender. The General said he was pessimistic. If the Germans broke across the Somme, then Paris must surely fall. As the meeting began to review alternative towns to which the government could be safely evacuated, the Prime Minister announced that it was his "fixed intention to fight on to the end, for the honour of the French army must be saved."[6]

Stung by this dire pronouncement that France was now facing defeat in the light of the alleged British retreat, Reynaud drafted a sharp and critical telegram to Churchill expressing Weygand's "surprise" that "contrary to this plan, Arras was evacuated yesterday by British troops" and reminding him of Weygand's order for Gort to make "a desperate effort to advance and effect a junction with the French forces which are marching south to north." In these "tragic hours," Reynaud insisted, that order must be obeyed.[7]

The accusatory tone of Reynaud's midday telegram caught the British Prime Minister off-guard. Still in the dark about the movements of Gort's forces, he immediately cabled Reynaud back to assure him that he had "told you all we knew over here." The War Office had only just confirmed the withdrawal from Arras, and he said Dill had been dispatched to see Gort to reaffirm that the B.E.F. had "no choice but to continue the southward move" according to the Weygand plan. Churchill's response reveals just how out of touch London was with the military events overtaking their army commander in Flanders. General Gort was no less ignorant that he was the focus of a row erupting between Paris and London.[8]

"The 'lice' are crawling and trying to get inside the fortress," General Pownall observed despondently of the advancing German tanks that Friday morning. At Gort's headquarters the situation looked black to his chief of staff. The coast between Dunkirk and Ostend was guarded only by scattered French forces. A single British battalion defended the twenty-mile stretch of the Aa Canal between St. Omer and the sea. The lower forty-mile stretch of the Canal d'Aire to Béthune, where it swung east to link up with the Deule Canal, was even more thinly covered and the many road bridges had not yet been dynamited. Tanks of the 10th Panzer Division had already seized four of the bridgeheads before the demolition parties reached them. There was nothing Gort could have done that Friday to stop the Panzers cutting across his rear to Ostend and cutting off his army's supply line and retreat to the sea – if the German tanks had pressed on to Dunkirk. But they did not.[9]

Just before midday, as the leading German tanks were approaching the town of Bergues, from where they could actually see the spires of the church at Dunkirk six miles away to the north, they halted in their tracks. B.E.F. headquarters was soon aware of this, because at 11.32 a.m. an intercepted enemy radio order had been picked up. Its urgency and origin were unmistakable. It had been transmitted *en clair* and not coded as such operational orders usually were. Within minutes of its transmission, Gort was passed the English translation: BY THE ORDER OF THE FÜHRER ... ATTACK NORTHWEST OF ARRAS IS TO BE LIMITED TO THE GENERAL LINE LENS-BÉTHUNE-AIRE-ST. OMER-GRAVELINES THE CANAL LINE WILL NOT BE CROSSED.[10]

"Can this be the turn of the tide?" Pownall wondered as he read the message. "It seems almost too much to hope for." The first assumption made by Gort's Chief of Staff was that the French attack had "tilted them off balance," panicking Hitler himself into intervening to halt the German advance. At B.E.F. headquarters they did not stop too long to ponder the reason, but seized on the German halt to redeploy their forces so as to reinforce the threatened sectors of the defensive line along the Aa.[11]

Hitler's order seemed so absurd that General von Kleist, overall commander of five of the Panzer divisions attached to Army Group A, at first made no effort to recall those of his forces who had pushed ahead. So German armoured cars succeeded in reaching the outskirts of Hazebrouck, where General Gort was heading that afternoon. The tank commanders who were already across the canal and within sight of their Dunkirk objective were all for pressing on. Then came a "curt telegram" to Guderian telling him that his "armoured divisions are to remain at medium artillery range from Dunkirk." Bewildered and angry, he ordered his advance forces to pull back from the northern side of the canal line, where they were to halt except for "reconnaissance and protective movement." His superior, von Kleist, was also given no choice, receiving "a more emphatic order that I was to withdraw behind the canal." The General would recall with contempt: "My tanks were kept halted there for three days."[12]

"This Political Move"

"We were utterly speechless" was how Guderian described his reaction to the order that stopped the 10th Panzer Division just short of its Dunkirk objective. There seemed no military justification for the "Führer Order." For almost three days the Panzer divisions remained impotently watching from the south bank of the canal line as the British demolished the remaining bridges and brought up artillery and troops on the far side to ensure that the next German crossing attempt would be fiercely resisted.[13]

What led up to the so-called Haltbefehl given by the Führer on 24 May 1940 became a matter of intense postwar debate. While the German generals and military historians agreed that it was Hitler's intervention that had robbed them of a quick victory, the reason for his seemingly irrational decision, which gave the all-but-encircled Allied forces almost three days to regroup their forces for a fighting retreat to the beaches of Dunkirk, is still disputed. For the British the "Miracle of Dunkirk" was a critical factor in enabling them to continue the fight against Hitler, who with his "Halt Order" had himself opened the way for one of the most remarkable evacuations in the annals of warfare. The simplistic explanation of this most puzzling enigma of modern military history is that the Führer simply got cold feet during the final stages of the Panzer dash for the Channel coast.

"Frightened by his own success" was how General Halder explained Hitler's intervention to rein in the Panzers after he had visited Army Group A headquarters at Bastogne on 17 May. The decision to call a temporary halt came the day after the Meuse defences had crumbled with unexpected rapidity. It cost Guderian a twenty-four-hour delay in starting his dash for the Channel ports to execute the planned Sichelheist by moving the armoured forces north along the coast to scythe off the British Expeditionary Force. The Führer's jumpiness during the actual French campaign was in stark contrast to his aggressive stance during its planning, when his bold demands had alarmed his generals. General Walter Warlimont, the Deputy Chief of Staff of O.K.W., attributed the Führer's first pause to his obsession with having what he termed a "pearl necklace" of infantry to protect the flanks of the advancing armoured division. Warlimont's superior, General Alfred Jodl, the O.K.W. chief of operations, noted that Hitler four days later again became "somewhat uneasy because the infantry divisions were not pushing forward fast enough." This was when the British had unexpectedly counterattacked from Arras on 21 May.[14]

General Halder's diary entry for 23 May confirms "Kleist's anxieties" about the "crisis at Arras which remains unresolved." It was reported as costing tank losses "as high as 50 per cent," depriving him of the reserves he would need if the French attacked the Panzer Corridor north across the Somme. Halder quickly moved to reassure Kleist that there was "no danger on the Somme" and that the "crisis will be over within 48 hours." Colonel (later General) Günther Blumentritt, operations chief of staff for Army Group A, concurred with O.K.H.'s confidence that their tank reserve strength was more than adequate to cope. Blumentritt's task was to supply "accurate figures" to Hitler each night of the French campaign, and he attested after the war that although losses "were often considerable," it should be emphasized that "the majority of these losses were of a transitory nature, i.e. technical, often repaired in the workshops within 24–48 hours."[15]

Hitler was understandably nervous that his armoured divisions could exhaust themselves in the north of France and would therefore lack strength for the advance on Paris. Attrition caused by the tremendous pace of the Panzer divisions' advance, resulting in worn-down tracks and mechanical breakdown, had actually outstripped battle casualties. But according to the testimony of the German generals, steps had already been taken to rectify that problem by 24 May. General Blumentritt categorically stated that "before Dunkirk the number of our tanks was growing again."[16]

Hitler had also expressed his apprehension about the risk to his precious Panzer divisions if they had to operate in the low-lying coastal terrain, where the reclaimed land was crisscrossed by dikes

177

and drainage canals. But this objection had been anticipated by Army Commander-in-Chief von Brauchitsch. On 23 May he revised the original O.K.H. plan by assigning to Army Group B a larger share in the final phase of the Sichelheist encirclement operation. The original O.K.H. plan had called for Field Marshal Feodor von Bock's twenty-one, mainly infantry, divisions to push westwards through Belgium to act as the anvil against which the entrapped Allied armies would be subjected to the hammer blows of the Panzer divisions, most of which had by now been concentrated under the command of Army Group A. The disproportionate increase of von Rundstedt's command to over seventy divisions created communications problems. These, von Brauchitsch feared, would become acute during the Kesselschlacht, or final "cauldron" phase, the battle when the two army groups moved into the mêlée to crush the broken remnants of the Allied armies. The Army Chief of Staff accordingly decided to reassign General Kluge's Fourth Army, with its two Panzer divisions (including Rommel's 7th and 5th), to von Bock.[17]

"At last the responsibility for fighting this battle to the end is placed in one hand," wrote von Bock. "It's a pity it wasn't done earlier. It would have saved a great deal of time." But the decision to reverse the original plan, giving von Bock the Panzer hammer and making von Rundstedt's army the anvil, did not please the commander of Army Group A. His sour comment was that he did not believe the revised order was "a particularly fortunate one at that given moment." Turning the original plan on its head made no sense, especially as the Allied line facing Army Group A was only thinly defended. Halder therefore argued for intervention to "restore harmony between the two forces advancing on the cauldron from different sides." He believed his chief was "too anxious to shift responsibility" and was also "surrendering the honour of success." When von Brauchitsch overruled him, the order went out from O.K.H. at midnight on 23 May effecting the change in plan without Halder's customary endorsement.[18]

Hitler was not consulted in advance about this last-minute change in plan. But since its result would spare the Panzer divisions during the Kesselschlacht, it cannot have played a major part in his decision to halt their advance next day. Nor can it be argued that the Führer blundered because he did not know the battle plan his generals were following. He had an amateur's fixation for military detail, and his concern to avoid any last-minute foul-up of the approaching victory kept him poring over the headquarters maps with a magnifying lens into the small hours of the morning. He must therefore surely have seen that the weakly defended twenty-five-mile stretch of coast between Dunkirk and Ostend was the back-door for the British Expeditionary Force. When the German tanks came within seven miles of Dunkirk that Friday morning Guderian was only a matter of hours from turning the back-door into a trap to seal forty-five Allied divisions in a thirty-mile-deep pocket, ready for hammering by the two German armies. So while Hitler may not have anticipated that the enemy could escape by sea, his decision to intervene personally to delay the closing of the trap represents an uncharacteristic rejection of a golden opportunity for a quick victory.[19]

The military situation gave no justification for his intervention. "Entirely satisfactory" was how Halder summed up the advance on the morning of 24 May, observing that "the enemy's fighting power probably does not count for much." Nor did O.K.H. see any need for the temporary close-up order issued by von Rundstedt the previous day, although the Army Group A war diary entry for 23 May cites concern that the continuing intrusion towards Arras was a prelude to a major French flanking attack developing across the Somme. Before the British withdrawal had become apparent, von Rundstedt had issued an order at 6 p.m. the previous evening that *"in the main* Hoth Group will halt tomorrow; Kleist Group will also halt, thereby *clarifying the situation and closing up."* The actual wording of this signal shows that the purpose of the order was for a temporary pause on the canal line to allow the right wing and centre of the Fourth Army to close up to consolidate von Rundstedt's forces. It was not interpreted by the Panzer Corps commanders as a full-blown halt order, because on Friday morning the leading units of tanks that had already established four bridgeheads across the Aa continued pressing their pursuit of the enemy for eight to ten miles on the far side of the canal line.[20]

Everything changed when the Führer arrived shortly after eleven that morning at von Rundstedt's headquarters at Charleville near Sedan. He was furious when he discovered that without informing him O.K.H. had decided to transfer the entire Fourth Army from the middle of von Rundstedt's line to Army Group B. This he considered a "mistake, not only militarily but psychologically." He told von Rundstedt that he would personally have the O.K.H. order countermanded before it went into effect at eight that evening. Although Hitler still expressed concern about the need to conserve the armoured divisions from the cauldron, he was, according to Jodl, "very happy about the measures of the Army Group which accord entirely with his ideas." The Headquarters war diary confirms that the Führer "agreed with" the need for a pause to allow the mobile forces to close up, but that he wanted to go further. It was Hitler himself who had seized on von Rundstedt's temporary "catch-up" instruction and transformed it into an all-embracing "Halt Order," which he justified "by insisting that it was in any case necessary to conserve the armoured forces for future operations."[21]

One factor that may have influenced Hitler's decision was a wilful need to intervene personally to demonstrate his supreme command authority, causing him to seize the opportunity to make Marshal von Rundstedt's temporary "catch-up" order of 23 May an excuse rather than the justification for the "Halt Order." The official British historian of the military campaign in France makes von Rundstedt the scapegoat for the decision, asserting that Hitler merely "confirmed" his order. When this verdict was published in 1953, it reflected the then conviction of many Allied historians that the German generals were conspiring to salvage their reputations by putting the blame on Hitler. Any suggestion that Hitler might have contributed knowingly to letting the British Army escape in 1940 was rejected out of hand. The "miracle of Dunkirk" had been transformed by wartime propaganda into a shining feat of arms for the British, despite their catastrophic loss of the battle and all their military equipment. Churchill, in his recently published memoirs of the war, had paved the way for the "official" explanation of Hitler's Haltbefehl by also ascribing all the blame to von Rundstedt. His views, not surprisingly, were therefore echoed in the official history, which implies that any other explanation would detract from "the fighting qualities of the Allied armies and the skill of British leadership," which were deemed to have been the decisive factors at Dunkirk.[22]

Such a variety of excuses has been offered for the "Halt Order" that it has diluted the credibility of any one of them as the decisive factor. To Warlimont, Hitler said it was the Flanders mud, to von Brauchitsch it was his reluctance to have the decisive battle on Belgian soil, to others it was the Luftwaffe; it has even been alleged that Hitler wanted to wait for the elite S.S. Leibstandarte brigade to arrive to share in the glory of the victory. It is curious that Hitler himself never blamed any of his generals for what turned out to be one of the biggest military blunders of the Second World War. This was regarded as most significant by Colonel Basil Liddell Hart, the pre-eminent military thinker, historian and strategist who interviewed many of the German generals after the war. (See Appendix 7.)

"Hitler's character was of such complexity that no simple explanation is likely to be true," Liddell Hart concluded. His exhaustive interviews and correspondence with generals and staff officers convinced him that there were a number of threads behind Hitler's Haltbefehl decision. "Three are visible – his desire to conserve tank strength for the next stroke; his long-standing fear of marshy Flanders; and Göring's claims for the Luftwaffe," wrote Liddell Hart, who believed that there was also an even more important and invisible "political" thread which must have played a critical part in the decision of 24 May. In 1948, when he first suggested, in his landmark study *The German Generals Talk*, that Hitler might have had a political motive in halting the advance on Dunkirk to set the stage for peace negotiations with Britain, it brought a storm of controversy.[23]

"If the British army had been captured at Dunkirk, the British people might have felt that their honour had suffered a stain which they must wipe out," Liddell Hart wrote. "By letting it escape, Hitler hoped to conciliate them." Liddell Hart's evidence for this startling conclusion was based on what the German generals told him of the extraordinary statements that Hitler had made during his visits on 17 and 24 May to Army Group A headquarters. On both occasions in his conversations with von Rundstedt the Führer departed from purely military matters to discuss his political goals in relation to England. Since his remarks in the hour-long conversation with von Rundstedt that Friday would have reflected what was on his mind when he issued the "Halt Order," Liddell Hart deduced that they might well have had a direct bearing on his decision.

"Hitler was in a very good humour," Blumentritt, who was present, told Liddell Hart. "He admitted that the course of the campaign had been a 'decided miracle,' and gave us the opinion that the war would be finished in six weeks." The Führer had looked forward to a "reasonable peace with France, and then the way would be free for an agreement with Britain." He then "astonished" Blumentritt by "speaking with admiration of the British Empire, of the necessity for its existence, and of the civilization that Britain had brought to the world." While conceding that the Empire might have been achieved by harsh means, the Führer had said with a shrug of his shoulders: "Where there is planing, there are shavings flying." He went on to compare the British Empire to the Catholic Church, saying he believed both were "essential elements of stability in the world."[24]

This was not the first time that Hitler had talked with von Rundstedt of his determination to come to terms with Britain. A week earlier, when he had also called a temporary halt to the German advance, General Georg Sodenstern, von Rundstedt's Chief of Staff, said that Hitler had "elaborated his views on England at some length." He intended there should be a "smooth and victorious run-off" of the French campaign. "England, after being decisively beaten in Northern France," Hitler declared, "would be ready for a settlement on the basis that 'England is the Seapower, Germany the policeman who will keep order on the continent.'"[25]

"The British can at any time have a separate peace," Jodl recorded the Führer as declaring three days later when news came that Guderian had taken Abbeville. Hitler was "beside himself with joy" and began busying himself with plans to have the French sign an armistice at Compiègne, on the very spot where the Germans were humiliated in 1918. On 24 May, when the Führer raised the subject for the second time with von Rundstedt, Blumentritt told Liddell Hart, he spoke in specific terms of the deal he believed he would strike with the British. His priority was for them to "acknowledge Germany's position on the Continent," but the return of Germany's lost colonies he considered "desirable but not essential," because they could not be held in war and "few Germans would settle in the tropics." Hitler even declared his readiness to dispatch German troops to support Britain if she got into difficulties with her Empire, restating that his "aim was to make peace with Britain on a basis that was compatible with her honour to accept."[26]

It was not illogical that Hitler should have felt the need to confide in von Rundstedt his plans to make peace with Britain in order to justify his "Halt Order." It was Army Group A which was directly affected, and von Rundstedt, as an officer in the Prussian tradition, would understand the importance of affording a respected enemy an honourable settlement now that the French were effectively beaten. After Hitler had left his headquarters that morning, von Rundstedt seemed to recognize as much by expressing his "relief and satisfaction" to his two staff officers.

"Well, if he wants nothing else," von Rundstedt declared to Sodenstern, "then we shall have peace." Blumentritt also told Liddell Hart that the more he thought back to what the Führer had said that Friday morning at Charleville, the greater his conviction became that the Haltbefehl had been called "for more than military reasons and that it was part of a political scheme to make peace easier to reach." Major Leyhle, an O.K.W. staff officer who was on particularly good terms with the Führer, assured Blumentritt that during May and June 1940 Hitler had "often talked to him about the idea of coming to an agreement with England."[27]

Historians and other writers have long been critical of this "political" theory, pointing out that Guderian flattered Liddell Hart on the contribution he had made to German tank tactics, although Blumentritt had no such claim. Liddell Hart's fellow countrymen were the most dismissive, perhaps because they recalled how, after the Fall of France, his reputation and patriotism became suspect. This was not just because of the irrational assertion that his theories of mechanized warfare were responsible for the German Blitzkrieg, but also because he was advising Lloyd George on the military and strategic odds against Britain ever being able to defeat Germany. Others have wrongly credited Guderian with the responsibility for having "elaborated a theory that Hitler let the British army escape from Dunkirk." Few have been willing to credit Liddell Hart's contention that Hitler's decision of 24 May was "mainly shaped" by his desire to let the B.E.F. escape from Dunkirk in the belief that this would facilitate a compromise peace agreement. One eminent German historian even declared that Liddell Hart's theory "should be banished to the realm of post-war fantasy."[28]

The fundamental inconsistencies in Hitler's decision argue that there could well have been a strong political thread to his "Halt Order." After all, Halder recorded at the time his belief that the order was a "political move," and Hitler himself alluded to such a motive in his so-called political testament of 26 February 1945, which expressed his deep regret that Churchill had been "quite unable to appreciate the sporting spirit" with which he had hesitated to destroy the British Army five years earlier. The "sporting spirit," it will be noted, made no reference to letting the British escape. This corroborates documentary evidence that modifies Liddell Hart's theory to suggest that while the Führer did not foresee the evacuation, he certainly intended to hold the British Army hostage to a diplomatic peace initiative.[29]

Fifty years after the event, the British still resent any suggestion that Hitler may have deliberately engineered the "miracle" enshrined by wartime propaganda as a national triumph which saved more than a quarter-million men from the jaws of defeat. But it is surely no insult to the heroism of the British forces to contend that but for Hitler they would not have had the chance to fight their way off the Dunkirk beaches to rally a nation at its darkest hour. To understand the significance of Hitler's probable political motive does, however, require a readjustment of the British propaganda image of him as the raving dictator hell-bent on the destruction of Britain and her Empire.[30]

"Reasonable Terms"

Now that it is possible to track the extent of the Anglo–German peace sounding that had been going on throughout the Phoney War, it is not "postwar fantasy" to argue that in May 1940 Hitler believed there was a good chance of striking a deal with Britain. We now know that the responses Berlin had received from the British Foreign Secretary to the succession of "peace envoys" such as Dahlerus and Mooney were not the unequivocal rejections they were later made out to be to protect postwar British political reputations. Berlin was also kept informed by Rome of the repeated efforts to buy off Mussolini and the signals of a willingness to talk in the right terms with Hitler that had been given repeatedly by R.A. Butler since October 1939.

As the prospect of military annihilation loomed in France, bankers, reeling from the ruinous cost of the war effort, were especially susceptible to the advantages of a negotiated peace. It had been City financiers such as Ernest Tennant who had provided the initiative and funding for the Anglo–German Fellowship which had given the Nazi propagandists a beachhead in pre-war English society. This was well known to the Reich's bankers, such as Puhl and Wolthart, who had played a key role as intermediaries with the peace efforts of Ambassador Kennedy and James D. Mooney's initiative to get negotiations under way with the British. Through Kennedy, via Mooney and Wolthart, the Germans would have known of the American Ambassador's close association with Montague Norman, the Governor of the Bank of England. Norman may have regarded Kennedy's Irish Catholicism and his "man-on-the-make" mannerisms with distaste, but they were in agreement that a protracted war might ruin capitalism and bankrupt Britain. While none of the British bankers would have opened themselves to accusations of treason by openly addressing the issue, their fears and their preference for a negotiated settlement circulated through the international banking community which continued to have dealings with Germany.

A cohesive "peace party" as such did not exist in Britain, but the undertow pulling in that direction grew more powerful as the prospect of defeat in France drew closer. It was given its most public expression in Parliament, where there had been repeated calls for a negotiated settlement during the Phoney War from M.P.s across the political spectrum. From Liberals such as the former Prime Minister Lloyd George to Labour members like Richard Stokes and right-wing Tories like Captain Ramsay, this lobby was becoming more active. That week an all-party group had again approached Lloyd George to take the initiative on the floor of the House. While the "peace lobby" was amorphous, it was not as insignificant either in terms of numbers or influence as Churchill later tried to make out.

Hitler, who had little grasp of the subtlety of British domestic democracy, would easily have misinterpreted these disparate but repeated stirrings as evidence of a sizeable parliamentary peace party. His willingness to believe in a powerful anti-Churchill opposition would have been reinforced by the calls for peace negotiations that had come so regularly from members of the House of Lords, including Lord Brocket, the Marquess of Tavistock and the Duke of Buccleuch, a Scottish banker whom Churchill had dismissed as High Steward of the Royal Household. The seemingly disproportionate number of peers who since the war began had been publicly and privately calling on the government to embark on serious peace negotiations would have appeared to Hitler to be the authentic voice of Britain's ruling class. This would have been an encouragement in May 1940 when Berlin, after the failure of so many attempts to lure the compliant Chamberlain into negotiations, had to face the intransigent Churchill as Prime Minister. The Wehrmacht's military breakthrough in France provided the opportunity for stepping up diplomatic as well as military pressure on Britain to negotiate. With France's army in retreat and Italy threatening to enter the war, Hitler calculated that the French government, if not their ally too, would be receptive to the offer of terms that permitted an honourable escape from total defeat.[31]

The first indication that France might be willing to negotiate brought a renewed German peace initiative on the back of a Swedish diplomatic initiative to neutralize Norway for which the British Foreign Secretary had failed to win Cabinet support. Hitler, it turned out, was not so interested in the neutralization of Norway, but had other objectives in sight. This was made clear to Dahlerus when he met Göring at Karinhall on 6 May. Göring said Germany now wanted Stockholm to permit the sending of supplies and ammunition by Swedish railway to German forces fighting to hold northern Norway against the Allied landing at Narvik. Five days later, the day after the attack on France began, Dahlerus was back in Berlin with a Swedish delegation that officially refused the German transit demands. This rejection fatally compromised Sweden's hopes for brokering a Norwegian neutralization.[32]

While the Swedish delegation were in Berlin on 11 May, Göring insisted on seeing Dahlerus alone and proceeded to lay before him the possibility of a new peace mission with far-reaching consequences. Göring said that all peace discussions were "impossible" just at that moment, but once the German Army had reached "the Belgian coast and Calais," the Führer intended to make a peace proposal to France. His terms would be very reasonable and would require the German annexation of Eupen and Malmédy in Belgium, the cession by France of Briey in the north-east corner of Lorraine and the return of the former German African colonies. "For the rest," Göring told Dahlerus, the Führer was "content on the whole to maintain the prewar status quo." But, he warned, if France rebuffed the peace proposal the war would engulf the civilian population and the French people "would learn what it cost to be so badly led." The intermediary who was chosen to carry Göring's proposals to the French was not Dahlerus but Raoul Nordling, the Swedish Consul General in Paris. He had been a member of the abortive "neutralization" mission and was in Berlin en route to France on 15 May when he received a summons to go to Luftwaffe headquarters. There he saw Göring, who promised to arrange transport for his immediate return to Paris if he would act as his personal emissary to the French Prime Minister.[33]

"Our armoured divisions broke through the French front on the

185

Meuse yesterday," Göring announced. "By the end of the month we will have taken Calais and Dunkirk. After that" – according to Nordling's account, Göring made a crushing gesture with his fist – "if M. Reynaud proposed an armistice at once," he said, Germany would grant France "reasonable terms." But the offer he was "authorized to make today" had to be taken up immediately. This was the only way for France to avoid occupation and total humiliation. If there was no response within two weeks, then, Göring said ominously, "conditions would be severe."[34]

The Swedish Consul General arrived back in Paris on 17 May. He immediately contacted the Prime Minister's office with the news that he had a "personal communication of the utmost importance." But such were the pressures on Reynaud that Nordling was not received until 20 May. His own report of the meeting recorded that the French Prime Minister rose up from his desk and paced his office in a state of "great agitation."

"The predicament of our armies is not nearly so black as they believe in Berlin," Reynaud said, raising his voice in anger, "and if you were not who you are, I would have you arrested on the spot for your defeatist proposal." Before dismissing Nordling he extracted a pledge that he would "speak to no one about the message he carried from Göring." The rejection persuaded the Swedish Consul General to regard his mission as completed. But the "très secret" report on "Possible German Peace Offers" uncovered among Reynaud's papers indicates that the German offer had "assumed a special importance in the light of events" that had occurred in the five days since the meeting with Göring. "In particular it raises the question," the note states, "whether the Duce may not be waiting for the moment when M. Hitler, considering himself the victor, puts forward his peace terms, to enter on to the scene himself."[35]

Göring's "invitation" to the French to ask for an armistice assumes an added significance in the light of the report of 18 May from the British Ambassador in Rome. Sir Percy Loraine had been informed by the Vatican Secretary of State that "if Hitler has some further success such as the capture of Paris" he would probably make some public offer of conditions for ending the war. Cardinal Maglione expressed the hope that "the offer would not be rejected out of hand." The same rumours of peace feelers being put out by the German diplomatic network were picked up and reported by the British Ambassador in Japan.[36]

While Berlin was busy laying the groundwork for a new peace offensive by leaking hints in the Axis capitals, the Foreign Office was predicting that Hitler's terms "will not be such as we can accept, short of capitulation." Hardliner Frank Roberts minuted his doubt that even if Hitler reached Paris he would "abandon his real objective, which is this country." He saw the rumours as part

186

of a subtle plan to "weaken allied resolution." But as he put it, in a perceptive turn of phrase, "the fox is the one person who is not able to call off the hunt – and we are now in the position of the fox."[37]

Hitler, with all the assurance of a huntsman on a clear scenting day, may have been happy to have the French fox run down on the battlefield, but he was less sanguine about letting his hounds maul their British ally. In his blueprint for Germany's future, Britain had been assigned a role as an unconquered and independent nation who would become Germany's maritime ally. She would act as buffer against the United States while the Führer completed his takeover of the entire continental landmass of Europe. Contemporary academic scholarship has demonstrated that, far from being driven by irrational Anglophobia, Hitler's foreign policy objectives were remarkably consistent – if megalomanic – throughout his career. The achievement of his ultimate goal of German world dictatorship depended on reaching an accommodation and forging an alliance with Britain. Hitler had set down the framework of his foreign policy eight years before the Nazis came to power, and he adhered to his goals with remarkable consistency. (See Appendix 9.)

"The goal is to bring England to its knees; to destroy France," Hitler had declared when he gave his generals their marching orders for the Blitzkrieg on the West. Once Germany was master of the Continent, he believed that Britain would see that she was her logical partner in a global alliance. The only alternative was for Britain to ally herself as the junior partner of the United States. Hitler believed that given the choice, her European heritage and Anglo-Saxon racial pride would inevitably drive England's leaders into his arms. Had the American "half-breed" Churchill not come to power, Hitler might well have seen his wish fulfilled. His conviction was based at least in part on his personal contacts with leading British statesmen. In 1936 he had charmed Lloyd George at the Berghof. The following year Britain had himself been impressed by the haughty aristocratic arrogance of Lord Halifax, with whom he had no trouble agreeing on the need for a common front against Bolshevism. Hitler had also received assurances from Halifax that Britain had no objections to German claims in Central and Eastern Europe provided they were realized peaceably.[38]

During the Phoney War the equivocal responses received in Berlin from the Foreign Secretary reassured Hitler that as long as Lord Halifax was a member of the British government German peace overtures were not falling on deaf ears. A report drawn up in November 1939 by Secretary von Weiszäcker and based on Foreign Ministry assessments reassured the Führer that leading members of the British Cabinet and a large number of

M.P.s wanted to make concessions to achieve a negotiated peace.[39]

Six months later, with the French Army crumbling, Hitler was on the brink of achieving his European goal. He had justification for believing that Britain would strike a deal this time. So confident was he that the British would come to terms that on 21 May, when Admiral Erich Räder sounded him out on the need to begin planning for an invasion of England, he was given no response. Hitler evidently believed that once the right-minded British were given the option, they would jump at the chance to save their country's independence, honour and Empire by displacing their warmongering Prime Minister. Just as Chamberlain had refused to deal with him, he would turn the tables by refusing to negotiate with Churchill. Hitler's preference was for someone like Halifax, whose experience as Viceroy would have educated him to the importance of Britain's imperial destiny.

"Seeking to Arrive at an Understanding with Britain"

It appears to be more than coincidence that in the days leading up to Hitler's discussion with von Rundstedt of his desire for peace with the British the German Foreign Ministry began sending signals of impending peace moves down the diplomatic sounding board at the same time as Göring dispatched his Swedish emissary to Paris. Hitler's peace-offer timetable appears linked to the arrival of the Panzers at the coast. So it is significant that Göring broached the subject of the French peace feeler just as the Germans broke out from the Meuse bridgehead. This allowed time for the diplomatic softening up to work. Sixty-mile-a-day advances by the German tanks, which would bring them to the coast in a matter of days rather than weeks, had not it seems, been foreseen by either Göring or the Führer. This suggests that one of the factors contributing to Hitler's well-documented anxiety in the week leading up to the "Halt Order" could have been the unexpectedly rapid collapse of the Allied armies that threatened to upset the timing of the peace diplomacy.

It is significant that Göring told Dahlerus the Führer's peace offer would be conditional on "seizing the Belgian coast and Calais," *not* on the surrender of the Allied forces. This implies that Hitler originally envisaged dictating his peace terms as soon as the Panzer advance to the Channel had boxed in the Allied forces between the hammerheads of the two German armies. Holding more than a third of a million Allied soldiers hostage to armistice negotiations would be a powerful inducement to the governments of France and Britain to accept the peace he intended to dictate. But the breathless pace set by the Panzer commanders put the military schedule way ahead of his political gambit.

Hitler's hopes for pulling off a diplomatic coup also depended on the Allied armies not being annihilated too soon. He would then also achieve his goal on the back of a military success for which he, and not the Army, could claim the lion's share of the credit. Reynaud's abrupt rejection of Göring's authorized "invitation" to France seems to have caught Hitler with his diplomatic hand short of the next card to play. It appears to be no coincidence that he made his first intervention to slow the German advance on 17 May – the same day as the Swedish Consul General put Göring's proposal to the French Prime Minister. On 24 May, when Hitler intervened again to delay the encirclement of the British Expeditionary Force, it appears to have been another effort to buy time for the diplomatic moves necessary for his peace offer to be reconsidered.

Further clues in the documentary paper trail that illuminate Hitler's "political" agenda suggest that he intended Italy to play a key role as the military events in northern France approached their dénouement. At the beginning of the attack on France, Mussolini had been supplied with very full details of the progress of Germany's military operations. Initially Hitler had meant this information to encourage the Duce to choose the moment to make good his promise to join in the war. But all this changed after the faster-than-anticipated breakthrough on the Meuse. The ease with which the Wehrmacht's armoured lance drove through the sandhill of French defences appears to have persuaded Hitler that he did not need his reluctant ally's assistance to win his military victory in the West. This change in strategy emerges in his letter of 18 May to the Duce in which he reported German military progress but, in contrast to his first communication of 9 May, omitted any appeal to Mussolini to "assume his responsibility" under the Axis pact and join the war.

The Führer was even "too busy" to receive Dino Alfieri, the newly appointed Italian Ambassador to Berlin. After his interview with Ribbentrop on 18 May Alfieri reported that, for the first time since the war began, the Reich's Foreign Minister had shown no desire to know when Mussolini would declare war; he merely advised that the Führer was "very satisfied with Italy's attitude." This the Ambassador took to mean that Hitler "at least for now" was not interested in any bellicose action by Italy. Mussolini, afraid of being left out, reassured the Führer next day that "the period of non-belligerency cannot last much longer." He promised "important news on the subject in a few days."[40]

This cannot have pleased Hitler. His abrupt change of policy towards Italy's entry into the war had already been communicated

189

on 21 May to the Army High Command by their Foreign Ministry liaison officer, Hasso von Etzdorf. He reported that Mussolini had been told he could expect no military aid from Germany if he went to war with Yugoslavia and "no Italian soldier would be needed in [the] German theatre." Furthermore, O.K.H. staff were told by Etzdorf that "some minor differences *begin to stand out* between ourselves and Italy." The probable cause, although not spelled out, is indicated by Halder's observation: "Italy's chief enemy is now Britain, whereas enemy Number 1 for us is France. *We are seeking to arrive at an understanding with Britain* on the basis of a division of the world."[41]

Just how the Foreign Ministry was "seeking to arrive at an understanding with Britain" is not detailed in Halder's journal, but it is further confirmation that peace feelers were being put out. Italy had also become a key factor in these behind-the-scenes efforts by Berlin to invite peace overtures from both France and Britain. Hitler's reason for backpedalling on his previous efforts to get Mussolini into the war may not have been just that he did not want to dilute Germany's military triumph. Italy's threat to declare war was now a more useful diplomatic lever on Britain and France than Mussolini's actually joining the fight, as Hitler sought to turn to his own advantage the Duce's hesitation to join in until he was certain of the Wehrmacht's victory. At the same time he realized that if Mussolini smelled the blood of an impending Allied capitulation his "jackal instinct" would bring him immediately into the war to claim his share of the kill. This would rupture the diplomatic channel through which Hitler had the best chance of pulling off simultaneously the surrender of France and his longed-for accommodation with Britain.

The groundwork had first to be laid by encouraging Mussolini to step up his blackmail of the Allies to see just how steep a price they were willing to pay to keep Italy out of the fight. Negotiations with London and Paris would show the Duce how tempting a prize he could win without firing a shot. The logical next step would be for Mussolini to secure the prize by proposing a general European peace settlement that would open the door to negotiations with Germany. The success of the strategy depended on two factors: keeping Mussolini out of the war, and the willingness of the British to make concessions to the French by trading off Mediterranean real-estate. The most critical element in the diplomatic equation was the time factor. Impatient by nature, Hitler had learned from past experience that he could achieve his goals by remorselessly stacking the deck with threats and then allowing the wheels of diplomacy to grind to his advantage.

"In six weeks," the Führer had forecast to von Rundstedt on 24 May, "there would be peace and he would make a gentlemen's agreement with England." When he made this confident prediction, just before issuing the "Halt Order" on that fateful Friday, the Führer was definitely not intending that German troops would stand guard over the encircled Allied armies in the Dunkirk area until mid-July. This is just as absurd as to suggest that he gave the Haltbefehl in order to let the British Army escape. Hitler no more believed that a large-scale evacuation was possible from the open beaches of Dunkirk than did the British. Even Churchill's most optimistic estimate at the start of rescue operations was that only 50,000 men could be saved. This interpretation makes sense of both the military and the diplomatic record and gives credence to Liddell Hart's theory of a powerful "political" factor in the Führer's decision. It can therefore be argued that Hitler did not intend to let the Allied armies escape, but rather to delay their annihilation so as to provide a breathing space for his peace diplomacy to produce results.[42]

The two-day delay ordered by Hitler before Dunkirk also coincided with a flurry of diplomatic efforts in London and Paris to start negotiations with Italy. The French records show that this move had been taking shape for more than a week, and it may therefore be very significant that Lord Halifax chose that Friday to begin his efforts to get War Cabinet support for a French initiative aimed at appeasing Mussolini. Whether the Foreign Secretary was responding to some secret signal or not, it is surely too remarkable a coincidence that he chose that morning to propose that the time had now come for Britain to offer an inducement to Italy to stay out of the war.

The deal had evolved after a week of manoeuvring by the appeasers on both sides of the Channel. With Halifax's approval, Butler had made a conciliatory gesture to the Italian Ambassador on 15 May by promising that the British government would "eliminate all inconveniences" Italy was subjected to by the Royal Navy's contraband control searches. Count Bastianini welcomed the move while at the same time smugly assuring the Under Secretary of State that his government was "not a pack of jackals waiting to join the hunt when their possible prey was suffering a reverse."[43]

Yet this was precisely what Mussolini's tactic amounted to. Immediately after the German offensive began, he had raised Italy's price for continued non-belligerence. The French Ambassador in Rome had warned Reynaud that for "any hope of success" the Allies would now have to include "the status of Gibraltar, Malta and Suez as regards Britain and Djibouti and Tunisia as regards France." After the receipt of André François-Poncet's report, members of the French government, including the Minister of Finance, discreetly let it be known that France was willing to pay the rising price of Mussolini's blackmail. This was reported to Rome on 17 May by the Italian Ambassador in Paris, as an earnest that the French would work on the British to agree to discuss the status of Gibraltar, Malta and Suez.[44]

So desperate was Reynaud to keep the Italian threat from breaking the resolve of France's shaky military leadership that the next morning he transmitted, via Baudouin, clear signals of his willingness to talk to the Italian Ambassador. Alfieri then telephoned Rome with the news that not only were the French now willing to open discussions, but assurances had come from the British that they were also agreeable to settling Italy's complaints about the "situation in the Mediterranean." Lord Halifax, the Ambassador stated, had agreed in principle that if Italy remained a non-belligerent she could have a place at the Peace Conference, where her claims would be considered.[45]

This concession by London prompted Daladier, the French Foreign Minister, to push for the immediate opening of direct "political" negotiations with Italy. Reynaud, on the other hand, wanted to move more cautiously by asking the United States to find out how close Mussolini was to declaring war or whether he would entertain formal representations that would get him most of what he wanted without fighting for it. This suggestion was put to Ambassador Bullitt, who was asked by Reynaud to sound out Roosevelt's willingness to act as a mediator and guarantor if serious peace talks with Italy got under way. Three days later Daladier formally approached the British Ambassador in Paris to ask Lord Halifax to obtain his government's approval.[46]

"Their idea is to get President Roosevelt to ask Signor Mussolini what his reasons are for being on the brink of entering the war against our Allies," the Foreign Secretary explained to the War Cabinet on Friday morning. "If Signor Mussolini recited his grievances, the United States Ambassador in Rome would then say that the President would be prepared to communicate the Italian claims to the Allied Governments or some other words which would at least have a delaying action." It is obvious that the lessons of appeasement had been forgotten, because the Foreign Secretary "did not think that much would come of it," but the soundings themselves "would be useful" if the President was also asked to convey to Mussolini the proposal that Churchill had hesitated to relay to Rome. This was the offer to consider "reasonable Italian claims" that would be settled at a peace conference where Italy would be welcomed on "equal terms with the belligerents" if she did not enter the war.[47]

In simple terms Halifax was proposing to bribe Hitler's ally with a rain-check to a jackal's feast if only he would stay out of the war. Only Churchill did not believe that Mussolini would take the offer seriously. He averred that the risk outweighed the possible benefits and warned that the approach would send a dangerous signal to Berlin about Allied weakness if the cable ended up in German hands. The War Cabinet nonetheless gave reluctant approval to the Foreign Secretary's initiative. Churchill's strong personal disinclination to let Halifax resurrect appeasement that Friday morning appears to have been tempered by his determination to do everything he could to help Reynaud during France's hour of crisis.[48]

Britain's Foreign Secretary was soon to play a far more direct hand in the negotiations with Italy. Within hours of the Cabinet decision to give tentative support to the French move, the Foreign Office that afternoon received an approach suggesting private conversations would be helpful. The "invitation" came, not from the Ambassador, but from the Press Attaché at the Italian Embassy.

"Van[sittart] approached by Paresci with the suggestion we should offer to discuss Mediterranean with Italy," Cadogan records; "I'm all for it – if it will stave off war with Italy for a few days." Paresci, who claimed to be speaking "without instructions," told Vansittart "there were still a great many influential people in Italy who desired to see a peaceful solution of the Mediterranean problem." He suggested that if the Foreign Secretary approached the Italian government with a view to exploring the possibilities of a friendly settlement, he would not be rebuffed. Vansittart duly reported this to Halifax, who then obtained the Prime Minister's permission for a second meeting. There had, however, been some hesitation before Vansittart received word from Paresci that they should meet for the second time. The Foreign Office theorized that the delay was because of the need to consult Rome, a strong indication that Paresci's efforts were officially sanctioned.[49]

Why Gabriele Paresci was chosen rather than a more senior Italian diplomat is not clear; nor is the postwar decision to excise all mention of the Italian Press Attaché's name from the published version of Cadogan's diary. There is also only an oblique reference to Paresci in the British official history, which mentions a "hint from a member of the Italian Embassy that some private discussion of this kind might be of use."[50]

Paresci's "backdoor invitation" to France and his unofficial meetings with Vansittart led to a formal meeting between the Foreign Secretary and the Italian Ambassador. In their talk, the records show, Halifax was to exceed the limited brief he had been given by the War Cabinet by raising the possibility of Italy acting as broker for a general European peace settlement with Hitler. The clear effort to camouflage that meeting underlines the sensitivity of the British to their involvement in peace overtures with Italy on the same day that Hitler halted the advance on Dunkirk.

That Friday the hints of peace were mingled with indications dropped by Daladier of an increasing willingness on the part of the French government to talk peace if advantageous terms were proposed by Hitler. Rumours that the French might be prepared to compromise with Hitler fluttered back and forth like doves of peace in the diplomatic cables. These had been encouraged two days earlier when a right-wing deputy and junior government minister had approached Spain's ambassador in Paris. Jean Ybarnégaray proposed to fly to Madrid for a meeting with Franco, whom he regarded as "the only proper channel" through which to establish contact between France and Italy. He claimed he had authority to propose the end of "the servitudes of Gibraltar and Suez" as the basis for restoring "lasting peace" in Europe.

The Spanish Foreign Minister at once informed the German Ambassador in Madrid of an inquiry that showed France's inclination to "conclude a separate peace." He reported that Franco was "well disposed toward the peace idea" but worried that a visit by a French Minister might compromise Spain's neutrality. A reply was sent to Paris designed to "leave all doors open" should Italy or Germany wish to do so. On 24 May the German Ambassador in Madrid reported that the Spanish Foreign Minister had let him know that the Italian government had received word of the French peace feeler. That Friday, too, the Italian Embassy in Paris reported that Pierre Laval had called for the French government to open urgent negotiations with Rome as "the only way to talk to Hitler." Then Berlin that same day learned via the German Ambassador in Spain that the Spanish Ambassador in Paris had also been approached by Pétain. The Marshal let it be known that the situation was "extremely grave" but doubted whether even if he were leader of France "the Führer would ever listen."[51]

Since the Foreign Ministry in Berlin knew of these French peace feelers, it must be presumed that Hitler did too. Nor were Pétain and Ybarnégaray the only members of France's government floating proposals for negotiation that Friday, as the corrosive odour of impending military defeat wafted its way through the French ministries. By early evening even Weygand had succumbed. At 6 p.m. he summoned Baudouin to Vincennes. "The situation is very bad," he told the War Council Secretary. To prove just how serious, Weygand produced a telegram he had received that afternoon stating that the British Army had "put into effect the strategy of a retreat of forty kilometres." This, he announced, had "compelled" him to abandon the counterattack plans set for 26 May.[52]

"General Weygand," Baudouin recorded, "seemed to me overcome by the defection of the English." The Commander-in-Chief wanted to make the Prime Minister aware of the enormity of the military disaster facing France. He explained that he could do nothing if the British retreat continued other than to order the

194

Allied armies to fall back on the Channel ports. This would result in the capitulation of the northern armies and leave France with only fifty divisions to defend a 540-kilometre front. He regretted not being able to see any hope of saving Paris or even conducting an orderly retreat if the Somme and Aisne broke. Weygand said it would be "a wall of sand" against 150 German infantry divisions supported by their ten armoured divisions. It was "criminal" to him that France had declared war without the necessary reserves of guns, tanks and planes to see it through. Weygand therefore considered it his duty to fight as long as the government ordered it, but with the military situation so bleak, he suggested, there might be little point. He therefore asked Baudouin to convey the true picture to the Prime Minister at once.[53]

"I wondered if the morale of the Army and of the country was good enough to withstand a surrender on the part of the forces in the north," Baudouin reflected, "above all if at the same moment Italy were to declare war and Germany were to launch a peace offensive." With tears in his eyes the General agreed on the need to "save the national honour." At the same time he feared that the Army and the civilian population lacked the morale to fight to the end as Reynaud intended. The unspoken alternative that was implicit in Weygand's dismal words was the possibility of an armistice with Germany. When he was examined by the French Committee of Inquiry in 1946, Baudouin admitted that though the word had not been used on 24 May he and Weygand were already reconciled to an armistice, because they agreed that the "struggle was lost."[54]

"M. Paul Reynaud himself on 24 May was certain we had lost the fight," Baudouin conceded. "He kept talking about fighting on to the end, of fighting to save our honour, but the battle for France was lost." The French Prime Minister, on the other hand, remained doggedly determined that France would fight on after receiving Weygand's grim assessment from Baudouin that evening. His first action was to fire off an accusatory cable to Churchill protesting that the British Army in France had made a "retreat of forty kilometres towards the ports at a time when our troops moving up from the south are gaining ground." It charged that Gort's withdrawal was "in direct opposition" to Weygand's orders and as a result he was "compelled to give up the idea of closing the gap" in order to restore a united Allied line. "I need not lay any stress upon the gravity of the possible consequences," Reynaud concluded, demanding again that "General Weygand's orders should be obeyed."[55]

"Gort is still persevering in southward move," Churchill cabled back that night to the French Prime Minister. Rejecting the inference of double-dealing in Reynaud's message, he declared firmly that there had been no movement of the B.E.F. "of which we are aware [that] can be any excuse for the abandonment of the strong pressure of your northward move across the Somme." He said General Dill that morning had been "wholly convinced that the sole hope of any effective extrication of our Army lies in the southward move." He gave Reynaud his word that "should I become aware that the extreme pressure of events has compelled any departure from the plan agreed I shall immediately inform you." To prevent further misunderstandings Churchill promised that he would send a personal emissary to Paris the next morning. He selected for this difficult mission Major-General Sir Edward Spears, a Francophile M.P. who in 1918 had been liaison officer between the British and French High Commands.[56]

General Ironside had issued a warning at the Friday evening meeting of the Defence Committee that "much of the British Expeditionary Force might be lost" if an evacuation had to be attempted from northern France. So when Churchill cabled the French Prime Minister he still believed that Gort's best chance of saving the army was to fight his way south. That he was so far behind the true situation facing Gort's headquarters shows how rapidly the military situation in France was deteriorating. Churchill's assurances to the French Prime Minister were therefore given in ignorance and good faith. Reynaud, however, had no excuse for his deliberately misleading claim that the French forces were actually advancing across the Somme that Friday; it was such a wild distortion that it can only have reflected his mood of anger and frustration.

Reynaud that evening confided to Baudouin a deep concern that had been gnawing at him. "In the event of a peace offer by Germany on moderate terms," he wondered whether French public opinion would permit him to reject it. The Secretary of the War Council must have added his own strong doubts to those of the Commander-in-Chief because Baudouin records the Prime Minister's prophetic declaration: "I would resign, for I have always advocated war to the end."[57]

"Thus I knew on the 24th," Reynaud would later write, "that Weygand, and with him Pétain, were to form a coalition in order to demand an armistice if, as unfortunately there was some reason to believe, the battle which was to be waged on the Somme was lost." This "cruel betrayal," as he termed it, was approaching faster than he anticipated, as peace moves began in earnest that weekend. This is yet another reason for believing that there was a strong "political" factor motivating Hitler's decision to leash the tanks back from falling on their prey in Flanders.[58]

Chapter 9

"Looking the Ugliest Facts in the Eye"

Day 6
"A Timely Miracle Would Be Helpful"
25 May 1940

"It's all a first-class mess up and events go slowly from bad to worse" was how that fateful Saturday began for General Pownall at B.E.F. headquarters. The immediate danger confronting them was the concerted assault by von Bock's infantry at the junction between the Belgian and French armies along the River Lys. At 7 a.m., in the midst of this crisis, General Dill arrived on his fact-finding mission for the War Cabinet. With Reynaud's petulant telegram in hand, he wanted to know the reason for the pullback from Arras and why Gort had not yet begun the agreed counterattack. Preparations to conduct the moves demanded by General Weygand must go ahead, Dill insisted. Later that morning General Blanchard – who had finally been confirmed as Commander-in-Chief of the Allied forces in northern France – assured him that he would make three French divisions available for the counterattack.[1]

"There is NO blinking the seriousness of situation in northern area," Dill cabled to Churchill. He then set off for Ypres for a meeting with the King of Belgium and his military advisers. What he did not know was that the French plans were already unravelling. That morning, Gort's liaison officer with the French discovered that Blanchard's promised two divisions were a mirage. All the French First Army had available for the impending counterattack was one understrength division. Pownall saw this report as another act in "a Greek tragedy in which the end seems inevitably to come closer and closer with each succeeding day."[2]

"I must know at earliest why Gort gave up Arras and what actually he is doing with the rest of his army," Churchill wrote to General Ironside first thing that morning. "Is he still persevering in Weygand's plan, or has he become largely stationary?" But no one in London that weekend could have accurately kept up with the rapidly deteriorating military situation in Flanders. Churchill himself admitted as much to the War Cabinet that morning when he reported that he was in the dark but believed that "Lord Gort was persevering in the southward move." Ironside confirmed that except for Dunkirk, all lines of communication to the B.E.F. headquarters had been severed. Boulogne had been given up (although it did not finally fall to the Germans until that afternoon), and only three tanks survived in Calais.[3]

Churchill dispatched a "heartening message" to the Calais garrison and its commander, assuring them that their gallant stand was "of the highest importance to our country and Army" because it was tying down an entire German armoured division. "The eyes of the Empire are upon the defence of Calais," his telegram to Brigadier Nicolson declared. "His Majesty's Government are confident you and your gallant Regiment will perform an exploit worthy of the British name."[4]

There was never any doubt about the outcome of the fierce struggle being waged at Calais that day. The War Cabinet debated how best to inform the public about a possible invasion, and whether to evacuate the south and east coasts of Britain. Calling on British soldiers to fight to the death and at the same time making overtures to the Italians seemed inappropriate to Churchill, but the Foreign Secretary announced that he had opened up a diplomatic line to Rome to assist the French in keeping Mussolini out of the war.

"Very likely nothing will come of all this," Halifax said, carefully cloaking his efforts to effect a démarche with Mussolini by implying that he was going through diplomatic motions to "gain time" and placate the French. Suspicious of any talk of appeasement, Churchill said that while he could not object to a guarded approach, he was very worried that "it would amount to a confession of weakness." The Prime Minister did not trust the Italians. His concern was that "at any moment Signor Mussolini might put very strong pressure on the French," who, he reminded the Foreign Secretary, were "in a very weak position."[5]

Churchill saw that if Britain allowed herself to be sucked into direct discussions with Italy it would be used by the wobbling members of the French government to force Reynaud to negotiate with Mussolini as Hitler's proxy. Daladier, now the French Foreign Minister, had been pressing for direct negotiations with Italy, and the day before had been headed off only by Reynaud's insistence on getting the British to support an indirect approach to Mussolini by Roosevelt. The British Ambassador in Madrid had reported that "it was the German plan that Italy should immediately offer a separate peace to France."[6]

Just how shaky Reynaud's fragile coalition had become was observed at first hand that morning by Churchill's personal emissary when he attended the midday meeting of the French War Council. General Spears did his best to reassure Reynaud that Churchill had not issued any orders to Gort that countermanded the agreed Allied plan. Sitting next to Marshal Pétain around the large Louis XV table of the French War Ministry, the British M.P. had been shaken to hear Weygand's bleak review of the military situation. It was interrupted when General Blanchard's liaison officer arrived – "the very embodiment of a catastrophe," according to Spears's account – and concluded his depressing report by bluntly telling his Commander-in-Chief: "I believe in an early capitulation."[7]

Weygand reacted, "in a voice like a saw on steel," with a tirade blaming the French government for being totally unprepared for war with Germany. He declared he would fight on, but was of the opinion that "a capitulation must soon take place" for Blanchard's armies. His own "quite inadequate reserves" would then make it "extremely difficult for the French armies to hold a front extending from the mouth of the Somme to Switzerland." Accepting that his planned counterattack was now doomed, Weygand asked permission to countermand his orders and to call for the northern armies to retreat on the Channel ports. It was only when Spears argued that this would bring terrible confusion to the Allied commands that Weygand was persuaded he should leave a withdrawal to the discretion of the Commander-in-Chief on the spot.[8]

"Blanchard's troops, if doomed, must go down with honour," Weygand said with regret and resignation. The best they could now hope for in the face of impending defeat was that the First Army would not bring disgrace on itself by having to "surrender in an open field." Before leaving the meeting, Spears insisted that Weygand and Reynaud should jointly dictate a seven-point summary of the War Council's decisions for transmission to Churchill. As he made his exit from the ornate council chamber, Spears noticed that Marshal Pétain was still sitting silent as carved stone, "his chin sunk forward, looking straight at the carpet in front of him."[9]

Weygand took the British representative's departure as the cue to launch into an even more pessimistic appreciation of the choices confronting France. He told Reynaud that when the Germans broke through the Somme defence line "it was impossible to imagine the Army retreating in good order and defending successive positions." The Prime Minister decided to postpone any further discussions on the military situation until the emergency Council meeting that evening. But he had won the support of the bluff

Interior Minister, Georges Mandel, for his plan that the government must prepare to evacuate to Bordeaux.[10]

If confusion and alarm were the order of the day for the Allies, that Saturday also brought confusion and recrimination to the German High Command. That morning von Rundstedt telephoned the Panzer commanders to remind them of the Führer's "Halt Order" of the previous day. Significantly, Hitler chose to mislead Mussolini by giving him the impression that the German attack on the Allied lines was still being pressed with the utmost vigour.[11]

"It is not possible to say how long Allied resistance will last in the encircled zone," Hitler wrote to the Duce in a letter which made no mention of the fact that he had called a halt to the Panzer attack. The British troops, he reported, were "miserably led" and, though proving "very brave and dogged in defence," they would "probably collapse in a few days under the weight of the attacks now beginning." Hitler clearly wanted to give Mussolini the impression that military events were moving to a swift conclusion that did not require Italian intervention. Throughout the day the Luftwaffe concentrated every available aircraft on attacking the Channel ports. A great deal of damage was done to the harbour installations at Dunkirk, but there was little activity inland to disrupt the frantic effort being made by the B.E.F. to turn the canal embankments into fortified positions.[12]

Observing this reinforcement from the other bank of the Aa, resentment welled up all along the chain of German military command. Throughout that Saturday efforts were made to persuade the Führer to reverse his "Halt Order" and get the attack moving forward again. The Commander-in-Chief of the Army went to Führer Headquarters personally to plead with Hitler to let Army Group B resume its advance. But von Brauchitsch was stonewalled by Hitler, who claimed that he had left it to von Rundstedt to decide when to move his Panzers forward again. The enormous respect in which the General was held would have been sufficient to silence the criticism of subordinates, yet General Warlimont found it odd that Jodl "made not a single reference" to von Rundstedt's being in agreement with the Führer's orders.[13]

Halder recorded how that day brought "painful wrangles between ObdH [von Brauchitsch] and the Führer on the next moves in the encircling battle." Hitler not only refused to lift the "Haltbefehl," but also rejected the revised O.K.H. plan for Army Group A to make "heavy frontal attacks, merely to hold the enemy, who is already making a planned withdrawal, while Army Group B, dealing with an enemy already whipped, cuts into his rear and delivers the decisive blow." Hitler's decision to put "political" requirements above the dictates of military strategy caused Halder to complain that their "tug-of-war" with the Führer was taking a higher toll of

200

nerves than the battle. "This is a complete reversal of the elements of the plan," he fumed, predicting that Army Group B would now find itself facing a "consolidated front" which would slow progress and bring "high casualties." Halder remained confident that "the battle will be won," but he was so exasperated that he shut himself into his office and for the whole morning was "not in for anyone." When he went to Führer Headquarters that afternoon, he was received "in a cool, almost hostile manner." Hitler, he noted, was "agitated" as he reviewed plans for the next phase of the French campaign and launched into a "long-winded recapitulation of all the dangers presented by a city like Paris."[14]

"Speed is of the essence," Halder stressed, but the Führer did not take the hint as far as the Dunkirk pocket was concerned. Göring was also deaf to the appeal made to him by General Wolfram von Richthofen, the commander of the Luftwaffe's VII Air Corps Stukas, who was prevailed on to intervene by General Kleist. His telephone call to Göring's chief of staff Jeschonnek only brought the response: "The Führer wants to spare the British a humiliating defeat."[15]

Hitler did not seem to be concerned that the British Expeditionary Force was using the let-up in the attack to reinforce its weak left flank. Had the Germans kept up the pressure on both flanks, General Gort would have had no reserves to stave off the puncture that threatened the right flank that afternoon when the Belgian line began to cave in. A wallet recovered from the body of a German staff officer was found to contain von Brauchitsch's orders for an all-out attack the following day on the weak point at the hinge of the Belgian and British lines in the Ypres-Menin-Courtrai sector. General Alan Brooke, Gort's II Corps commander in the threatened sector, personally took this alarming intelligence to B.E.F. headquarters. "I found the atmosphere entirely changed and was at once presented with the 5th Division for the defence of the Ypres-Comines Canal," Brooke's diary records. The decision to assign him one of the two divisions earmarked for the counterattack left Gort with a dilemma: he could not now comply with the orders he had received from the French and British governments.[16]

That afternoon Gort struggled to make a decision on which he knew the fate of his army – and probably his country – turned. In the villa that served as his headquarters at Premesques he sat at his table studying the maps, "bewildered and bitter" because, as one of his staff recorded, he resented not taking "an active physical part in the battle." The choice was simple: to continue to support the Weygand offensive plan, or to abandon it completely and concentrate his strength on shoring up the weak points in the Allied line. It was a decision that Gort faced squarely with the no-nonsense courage of a front-line soldier. There was no time to consult with Blanchard and face the inevitable political delays and wrangles that would result if his Allied superior referred the matter to the French High Command. To avert the impending disaster he exercised the authority he had been given by the War Office to put the safety of the British Expeditionary Force above the orders he received from General Weygand.[17]

At 6.30 p.m. that Saturday evening Gort decided to exercise his right to save his army. He ordered both the 50th and 5th divisions up to reinforce the Ypres front and sent word to Blanchard's headquarters that he was calling off British participation in the next day's offensive in order to hold the threatened Allied perimeter and secure the option of an orderly Allied retreat to Dunkirk.

Gort could not have appreciated at the time the pivotal influence the decision he took at B.E.F. headquarters that afternoon would have on the course of history. We can now see that it opened the way to saving the bulk of the British Army, and that the return of these trained soldiers was to be a crucial factor in Churchill's ability to rally the nation in the expectation that the United States would eventually join the war. But in Washington that Saturday no one in the White House or the State Department would have risked good money on the lengthening odds against Britain's survival.

President Roosevelt was tracking the situation in Europe very closely. In addition to the normal State Department reports, he was in direct personal communication by phone and cable with his ambassador in Paris, and he received daily military situation reports from the War Office in London, courtesy of the British Embassy in Washington. The increasing anxiety of the appeals for American help relayed by Bullitt and the litany of military disaster in the British reports gave Washington an alarming impression of impending Allied collapse.

"Churchill talking about moving the Empire to Canada; Reynaud going completely off the line; and Bullitt shrieking over the telephone every half hour," Berle wrote from the State Department. The Assistant Secretary believed the administration and the country were "just waking up to the fact that an Allied defeat threatened us, and now that seemed possible they are beginning to get frightened." The nightmare haunting Roosevelt was that the military defeat of France would drag Britain into an armistice with Germany, making Hitler not only master of Europe but admiral of the Atlantic, commanding a menacing Germany navy reinforced by the British and French fleets. Constrained by domestic politics from being able to send the fighters and destroyers for which Churchill had appealed, the President searched for a way to sustain Britain if France fell – and keep the British fleet out of Nazi control. Unwilling to bargain directly with Churchill, he decided to invoke the assistance of the Canadian Prime Minister.

He knew, from talks held secretly under the camouflage of an April "holiday" visit to the U.S. by the Canadian Prime Minister, that William Lyon Mackenzie King shared many of his fears.[18]

On Friday afternoon Secretary of State Hull had put in a call to Ottawa which interrupted a meeting of the Canadian Cabinet. Hull asked Mackenzie King if he would send to Washington right away someone in whom he had "the fullest confidence and could trust in every way" for a "talk with him and someone higher up." The Canadian Prime Minister had just received Churchill's cable addressed to all the Dominion Prime Ministers announcing that he expected "an early attack on these islands" and that "everyone here was resolved to fight it out." It added that "every form of intimate personal appeal and most cogent arguments" had already been made to the American President. "Roosevelt was doing his best" to carry Congress and public opinion but was "still much diverted by impending Presidential election." The Empire's premiers should, therefore, "follow up our appeal by a personal appeal from yourselves."[19]

After such a request, Mackenzie King had no difficulty persuading his ministers to agree to sending a special envoy to take up Hull's invitation. As the Canadian Ambassador in Washington was on sick leave, the Prime Minister selected Hugh Keenleyside of the Department of External Affairs. An experienced diplomat, he happened to have just returned from discussions with the President about Americans enlisting in Canada's armed forces. Keenleyside left by the overnight train for Washington on Friday afternoon. On Saturday he was met at Union Station by a White House aide and, to prevent his arrival being noted by the press, was smuggled into the ante-room of the President's Office. There he was greeted by Secretary Hull, who delivered his "sulphurous views about Europeans in general and the French in particular." The President, by contrast, was so affable it seemed, Keenleyside noted, "as though he had been sitting at his desk just waiting for me to return after my brief absence." Roosevelt may have put on a cheerful face, but what he told the Canadian envoy was full of doom.[20]

"There seems to be little doubt that within a week annihilation or surrender will be the only military alternatives," Roosevelt announced solemnly, predicting that the Germans would easily over-run the rest of France and would probably offer favourable terms to the French provided they disarmed and handed over their fleet. Britain would then come under all-out attack. Facing what Roosevelt said was the Germans' five-to-one air superiority, the British would, he thought, be unlikely to "withstand the assault for many weeks." They would then be forced to sue for peace. The President said that "based upon reports received from Berlin" the Germans would make two alternative offers. One would be a "comparatively reasonable one, conditional on the surrender of the Empire – and the handing over of the British Fleet"; the other would be of "the most Carthaginian nature," involving German occupation.[21]

Roosevelt was "afraid that the temptation to buy a reasonably 'soft' peace will prove irresistible." Such a decision, he said, "would mean not only the temporary extinction of civilization in western Europe, but its permanent destruction throughout the world." What the President and the Secretary of State desired to convey to Churchill was the necessity for the fleet to be kept in action during the aerial bombardment of the British Isles until the "last hope of successful resistance is gone." Then it should be sent overseas. They envisaged that in the worst-case scenario the British government would evacuate to Ottawa. In deference to historic American political sensibilities, Roosevelt thought it better that the King should take refuge not on the mainland of North America, but on the island of Bermuda. The British fleet, on the other hand, would find a welcome refuge and repair facilities in United States Atlantic ports, while the U.S. Navy would defend the Pacific during the "two or three years" that it would take to blockade Germany into submission.[22]

"It will be a period of horrible suffering," Roosevelt warned, "but it does offer hope." If the Nazis got control of the British and French fleets, that would mean the end of hope. The United States would have to arm and organize "on a colossal scale" to deal with the two-ocean threat posed by Germany, Italy and Japan. The Army at present had only 3,000 planes and none could be sent to help the Allies because of the need to maintain adequate national defence. American public opinion, the President told Keenleyside, "will not permit immediate intervention to save France and the United Kingdom." Opinion was shifting, "but not with sufficient rapidity to make effective aid possible – unless the United Kingdom can hold out for months alone." As Roosevelt put it, "the ultimate freedom of the British Isles will be dependent upon the United States and the Dominions getting control of the British, and if possible the French, fleet." Roosevelt said the Canadian Prime Minister would therefore appreciate why it was impossible for him to put this request directly to the British Prime Minister, but he was sure that Mackenzie King would be able to make the case with the aid of the other Dominion leaders.[23]

After the hour-long session, Keenleyside surreptitiously left the White House by a staff entrance. He was an experienced enough diplomat to suspect that he had been subjected to a certain amount of diplomatic window-dressing, but the message he was asked to relay to the Canadian Prime Minister underlined the gravity of the choices facing Britain. It was clear to him that the President and Secretary of State discerned little hope of Britain's survival after a military collapse of France, and that Churchill could expect no immediate American military support, or any destroyers or fighters.

That afternoon, as Keenleyside began the weary overnight train journey back to Ottawa, the American Ambassador in Paris gave his blessing to the draft cable appealing for Roosevelt's intervention with Mussolini. Instructions were simultaneously telegraphed to the French and British envoys in Washington that evening by both governments. They were told to see the President "at once" to propose that he should inform Mussolini that "he had reason to believe" that the Allied governments were prepared to address Italian grievances in the Mediterranean. Mussolini would be offered equal status at a peace conference at the end of the war which would consider "reasonable Italian claims." Roosevelt was to offer to sponsor and guarantee the fulfilment of the Allied promise as part of the general postwar settlement, "provided that in the meantime Italy had not joined in the war against the Allies."[24]

The indirect approach via the American President was also followed up that afternoon by Lord Halifax. The War Cabinet had approved only one informal meeting between Vansittart and the Italian Press Attaché, but the Foreign Secretary decided to intervene personally and "asked the Italian Ambassador to call."[25]

When Signor Bastianini arrived at the Foreign Office at five that afternoon, he found the Foreign Secretary very anxious to clear up what he claimed was "a misunderstanding." Despite the discouraging message received from Mussolini, the Ambassador was assured that His Majesty's government wanted to make plain "our desire that Italy should naturally take her proper place at a peace conference by the side of the belligerents." Halifax hoped that the measure of success achieved over contraband control issues "might serve to open the way to the treatment of other questions," because he wanted to ensure that "nothing had been left undone that could help to avoid any misunderstandings, or something worse."[26]

Despite the oblique language, the Italian Ambassador grasped the drift of Halifax's overture by saying that it was the Duce's view that "the settlement of problems between Italy and any other country should be part of a general European settlement." Was he now to inform his government that it was "opportune" for the British government to agree to this? To this direct question whether Britain was ready to agree to Mussolini mediating peace negotiations with Germany, the Foreign Secretary's response was elliptical, but not negative. Whether "such matters" could be discussed while the war was in progress, Halifax said, "would no doubt depend upon the nature of the issues raised and upon the course which any discussions might take." Picking up on this cue, Bastianini asked whether this discussion involved "not only Great Britain and Italy *but other countries.*" Halifax again tried to sidestep by saying that "it was difficult to visualize such wide discussions while the war was still proceeding." He left it to the Ambassador to draw the inference – and Bastianini did so by declaring that "once such a discussion were begun, war would be pointless."

Lest the Foreign Secretary be under any misapprehension over the proposal that was being made to him, Bastianini cited Poland as an example of Mussolini's concern. He told Halifax that any discussions would lead to a European settlement that "would not merely be an armistice, but would protect European peace for a century." That Halifax gave the clearest hint that he was looking for a negotiated end to the war emerges even from his own carefully worded version of the conversation. Reporting that he spoke for the French government as well as the British, he told Bastianini that "they would *never be unwilling* to consider any proposal made with authority that gave promise of the establishment of a secure and peaceful Europe," and "when we came to such discussions, Signor Mussolini would have an *absolutely vital part to play.*" The Foreign Secretary then gave another nudge to Bastianini by saying he "could certainly" tell his government that Britain "did not exclude the possibility of some discussion of the wider problems of Europe."[26]

Even the lapidary phrases of Halifax's official report show the degree to which he had exceeded the very limited brief he had been given by Churchill and the War Cabinet. His exchanges with Bastianini were not restricted to offering to settle differences with Italy, but had signalled the British government's willingness to agree to Mussolini taking the lead in a general European peace initiative. Lord Halifax was too well versed in the practice of diplomatic subtlety to have given such encouragement inadvertently. That he believed he had succeeded is evident in his report to Cadogan after the meeting that he believed his interview with Bastianini "wasn't unsatisfactory."[27]

This was not, however, the impression that Cadogan's private secretary was given by the Italian Press Attaché shortly after the meeting. From what Gladwyn Jebb relayed to him, Cadogan concluded that "H[alifax]'s conversation had *raté* [misfired] completely." The reason given by Paresci, who was clearly acting as a go-between in these delicate peace soundings, was that the Foreign Secretary had not yet offered the concrete proposals relating to Gibraltar, Malta and Suez that the Ambassador had been led to expect. Paresci also stressed that for progress to be made Mussolini had to be offered immediate satisfaction of his demand that the

British give up control of the Mediterranean. This, Jebb told the Press Attaché, Britain would certainly not do short of "total defeat in war."[28]

The impression given by the Foreign Office record of the exchanges with the Italians that Friday and Saturday is that Ambassador Bastianini and Paresci were acting in concert. Were they obeying instructions received from Rome, or was the Italian Ambassador independently angling for a diplomatic coup which he could present to Mussolini? Bastianini had promised Halifax he would "immediately pass on" the British government's willingness for Italy to participate in a "general European settlement." Yet the published Italian diplomatic exchanges omit this report, raising the possibility that the Ambassador was delinquent or else that in the postwar climate the Italian government considered Bastianini's report too sensitive to release when the selected diplomatic record was published in 1952. The suspicion that the latter explanation is correct is supported by French accounts that the British Ambassador had already confirmed that the Italian Ambassador's report, with very clear expressions of Halifax's willingness to negotiate, was received in Rome.[29]

The only clue that Halifax gives that he might have been more preoccupied with the consequences of the diplomatic initiative he had set in motion that afternoon than he officially admitted was that he "sat under a tree in Buckingham Palace Gardens for a quarter-of-an-hour" on the way back to the Dorchester Hotel that evening. "If only one could get rid of this feeling in the pit of one's stomach," he reflected, "the summer would be lovely."[30]

Lord Halifax also repeatedly sought to justify his diplomatic initiative with the Italian Ambassador with the excuse that he "did not want to give the French an excuse for complaining." He was to protest this too often for it to be a convincing justification of his real motives. His diary reveals how deeply he was affected by the collapse of the French Army – "the one firm rock on which everybody had been willing to build." He was shaken that the "Germans walked through it like they did through the Poles." Halifax's very logical train of thought appears to have left him without an answer to the question of how Britain was going to survive to carry on the war if she also lost the best part of her army and France was forced to sue for peace. A rationalist like Halifax, who prided himself on putting logic before emotion, could not avoid the spectre of defeat. This probably accounted for the nasty sensation in the pit of the Foreign Secretary's stomach as he sat in the royal arbour weighing a diplomatic alternative to a humiliating military surrender.[31]

While the Foreign Secretary may have mulled over such defeatist thoughts that Saturday, they were becoming a fearful reality in Paris for the French ministers who gathered in the President's council chamber at the Elysée Palace that evening. The emergency meeting of the War Committee began at 7 p.m. with a distressing review of the military situation by the Commander-in-Chief.

"It is my duty to prepare for the worst," Weygand announced, "that is to say for the eventuality that we may no longer have at our disposal the troops which comprise the northern group of armies." He gave what Reynaud described as "the most gloomy picture of the situation." France would be called to fight at odds of "three to one," he declared, predicting that the Army would be little better than "breakwaters" against the onrushing tide of the German armour. If Paris was abandoned, "each section of the Army must fight to save the honour of the country." France had "made the great mistake of going to war when she had neither the necessary material nor the necessary strategic plan." Now ministers ought to think "only of the resurrection of the country, and the courage with which it was defended would be the decisive factor in its revival." In what Reynaud took to be an expression of his preference for an early armistice, General Weygand declared that he was not in favour of the government evacuating Paris if the Germans broke through the Somme-Aisne defence line.[32]

"There can be no question of allowing the government to fall into Hitler's hands," Reynaud interjected. Cutting short further discussion, he called for the government to be evacuated to Bordeaux. The honour of the French Army, he believed, could be saved in such circumstances only by "a fight to the death." At this point the President, Albert Lebrun, interrupted the Prime Minister to ask what freedom the government would have to conclude a separate peace if it was offered. He said that "if Germany makes any relatively advantageous offer we ought nevertheless to examine it closely and objectively." But Reynaud reminded the War Council that France was "tied by a definite engagement" not to make a separate peace and would therefore be obliged to discuss any peace offer with the British. Marshal Pétain did not believe there was any need for reciprocity because England had fielded only ten divisions to the eighty of France, and the British had not fulfilled their promises.[33]

"One may be unfortunate, but one must not be disloyal," declared César Campincini, the Minister of Marine, announcing that he for one was against France unilaterally abandoning its treaty obligations if a peace offer were forthcoming from the Germans. Weygand suggested that Britain's ability to fight on would also be "seriously threatened by the loss of the whole of her present army which was to have been the nucleus of her future army." Reynaud said Churchill had told him he was "in favour of desperate resistance until the United States took the field." Ambassador Bullitt had been asked by the Prime Minister to ascertain whether Roosevelt would intervene if France was in danger. The answer was still awaited. The Prime Minister therefore felt that it was essential to have "an exchange of views" with the British government as to whether they were "ready to agree to important sacrifices to prevent the entry of Italy into the war."[34]

Reynaud agreed to fly to London next day and promised his increasingly jittery colleagues that he would "explain clearly" that despite the inequality of the three-to-one struggle, even if Paris fell, France would "carry on the fight, even if that were nothing more than one for honour." Weygand told him it was "essential" for him to stress to the British that "if the French Army was to fight to the end to save its honour this would inevitably mean the total destruction of all the French armed forces." When Reynaud walked out into the Elysée courtyard just after nine on that balmy May evening, he recorded, he was struck by the tragic realization that Pétain and Weygand were "in favour of asking for an armistice on the day that the battle for France was lost and of allowing the Government to be captured in Paris." With such ominous cracks opening up in his administration, Reynaud decided to use "Pétain's state of mind as an argument with Churchill" to press for "certain concessions in order to prevent Italy falling on us."[35]

The evening meeting of the Defence Committee in London began as the French War Committee was ending. For Britain the consequences of the disaster hanging over the Allied forces in Flanders may not have been so immediately ominous as those faced by the French. But Churchill and his advisers knew that the loss of the B.E.F. would cost the Army the bulk of its trained divisions and virtually all its tanks and artillery. The Channel was a broader bulwark than the River Somme, but in an age of air warfare England's ancient "moat defensive" was now less of a barrier than it had been to the invasion bids of the Spanish Armada and Napoleon.

The first-hand reports of General Dill, back from Belgium, and General Spears, whose dispatch had been flown in from Paris, confirmed that there was "no chance of General Weygand striking north in sufficient strength to disengage the Blanchard group in the north." Spears's memorandum predicted that such a strike would provide little more than a "breathing space before falling back to a line covering the harbours." Dill added the warning that the deterioration of the Belgian sector had left Gort with no option but to divert his forces to the northern flank. The failure of any southward thrust deprived Gort of the strength he needed to "cut his way north to the coast."[36]

The decision was now as clear to Churchill as it had been four hours earlier to the B.E.F. commander. On balance he came down heavily "in favour of an advance north to the ports and the beaches," saying that there was no other choice, given the "practical certainty that no effective French offensive is likely to be launched from south of the Somme for some considerable time." Gort was therefore to be alerted to be ready the following night to begin his march "north to the coast in battle order, under strong rearguards, striking at all forces between himself and the sea." The Royal Navy was meanwhile to be charged with preparing "all possible means for re-embarkation, not only at the ports but on the beaches," and the R.A.F. was to be ordered to "dominate the air" above the Dunkirk beaches.

At the time the decision was taken, even Churchill thought they would be lucky to get more than a fifth of the army back to England. Since the generals put an even heavier discount on the number of soldiers that could be evacuated, the Defence Committee decided that the six divisions of troops still in Britain were immediately to be armed with all available equipment and brought up to full strength. The Committee also began weighing the possibility of bringing home soldiers from overseas garrisons. After Spears had reported from Paris, Churchill said he would not be "at all surprised" if the Germans chose the moment of Italy's anticipated attack to offer France peace terms. If they did, he declared his intention of ensuring that the French government made it a condition of any armistice that "our Army was allowed to leave France intact, and to take away its munitions, and that the soil of France was not used for an attack on England."

What concerned the Prime Minister most was whether the French government would ever be in a position to impose those terms. If they were, and the Germans permitted France to retain her fleet and allowed the British Expeditionary Force to return to England, he said he "would accept it" since they "could hold out in this country once we had got our Army back from France." From his point of view that would be the only circumstance that would justify the Italian negotiations going any further than the guarded appeal already made to Roosevelt to intervene with Mussolini.[37]

The Anglo-French appeal to the President reached the State Department that afternoon. A messenger took it directly to Cordell Hull's Woodley Park residence, where he found the Secretary of State on the croquet green overlooking Connecticut Avenue. Hull, in his panama and whites, was defending his prowess as one of Washington's deadlier hands with a mallet in the annual tournament with his staff. The interruption to the game was greeted by one of the Secretary's earthy Tennessee profanities. He stopped play just long enough to announce that the Allied governments now wanted the President to make an offer on their behalf to the Italians. Taking up his mallet again, he told his staff they would discuss the proposal the next morning.

No details had been given by the British and French ambassadors of precisely what concessions they might be prepared to offer Mussolini. But Assistant Secretary Berle interpreted the proposal as "a veiled offer from the Allied governments that they would hand over to Mussolini – or at least discuss – Tunis, Suez, Djibouti, Malta, perhaps even Corsica and Gibraltar."[38]

While the State Department officials, on whose advice the ultimate fate of Britain would become ever more dependent, continued their croquet match on the wooded heights overlooking Washington, in London that night Churchill took action to counter the defeatism that he felt was invading the upper reaches of the British military. Earlier that evening he had agreed with his military chiefs that Britain's ability to fight on without France depended on rescuing as many as possible of the battle hardened troops of the B.E.F. No one, least of all the Chief of the Imperial General Staff, was willing to make an optimistic prediction.

"We shall have lost practically all our trained soldiers by the next few days – unless a miracle appears to help us" was the unvarnished opinion Ironside committed to his diary. But his trenchant pessimism had been grating on Churchill ever since their clash in April over the Norwegian operation. After the Defence Committee broke up that evening the Prime Minister moved swiftly to effect the removal of the Chief of the Imperial General Staff. At a late-night cabal in the Admiralty, Ironside supposedly "volunteered" to resign. Churchill later justified the decision to replace him with his deputy, General Dill, because of "a very strong feeling in the Cabinet and high military circles." What that strong feeling was he did not elaborate. But the gloomy predictions of disaster with which Ironside filled the pages of his diary that week suggest that his increasing pessimism was the real reason for his resignation.[39]

"No one could doubt that his professional standing was in many ways superior to that of Ironside," Churchill wrote. "As the adverse battle drew to its climax I and my colleagues greatly desired that Sir John Dill should become C.I.G.S." There is more than a hint here that he did not want to find himself saddled like Reynaud with a commander-in-chief who would insist on the hard military realities when the ride got really rough. The more compliant and politically attuned Dill was therefore promoted in place of the hard-nosed Ironside. Churchill had no need to read the General's defeatist private diaries to realize Britain's military commander-in-chief since the beginning of the war had an ill-concealed contempt for politicians who meddled in military decision-making. Ironside's offer to take on the thankless task of organizing Britain's home defences against the invasion threat was gratefully accepted by the Prime Minister, who rewarded him with a Field Marshal's baton.[40]

"Fortunately Ironside is gone, and Dill, who inspires great confidence, has taken his place" was Colville's reaction, reflecting the relief in Downing Street. But he did not envy Dill's responsibility for "salving the wreckage of the B.E.F." He felt that "a timely miracle would be helpful." Churchill's private secretary may have been anticipating the next day, Sunday, which was to be a day of National Prayer.[41]

"Ready to Consider Any Proposal"
26 May

"The English are loath to expose their feelings," Churchill wrote, but at Westminster Abbey next day for a service attended by the King and Queen he "could feel the pent-up, passionate emotion, and also the fear of the congregation, not of death or material loss, but of defeat and the final ruin of Britain."[42]

That Sunday, for the first time since war began, the British nation became collectively aware of the national peril that they were all facing. Yet only the Prime Minister and a handful of his senior ministers and military advisers had a true forewarning of how great the threat of ruin really was. Its harbinger had come that morning in a cable received from Paris announcing that the French Premier was arriving in London at lunchtime for urgent private talks with the Prime Minister. The reports he had received the previous day on the growing defeatism of the French government left Churchill in no doubt that Reynaud would raise the possibility of an appeal to Italy. Anticipating the consequences that might flow if the French stampeded the British into premature negotiations, Churchill immediately summoned an emergency Cabinet, which had met before ministers went to Westminster Abbey.

Churchill opened the meeting by announcing that the Chiefs of Staff had decided to order Gort to march his army to the sea. A telegram had just arrived from Admiral Keyes in Belgium warning that King Leopold had declined to leave for England because this might hasten the capitulation of the Belgian Army. The latter event would threaten disaster for the British Expeditionary Force, whose evacuation was now the Prime Minister's major concern.

Churchill declared to the meeting that "it seemed from all the evidence available that we might have to face a situation in which the French were going to collapse . . . We must do our best to extricate the British Expeditionary Force from Northern France." While Churchill could not foresee the outcome of the

212

battle in Flanders, he concealed his own pessimistic forecast and assured the War Cabinet that "there was a good chance of getting off a considerable proportion of the British Expeditionary Force." Nevertheless, he said they had to be prepared in case Reynaud was coming to tell them that "the French could not carry on the fight." He wanted the War Cabinet to be ready to reconvene that afternoon to meet Reynaud if necessary.[43]

Churchill anticipated that the French Prime Minister might be inspired by the Cabinet's united resolve to fight on whatever their ally decided. To allay any doubts amongst his ministers that this was a practical option, he announced that he had already asked the Chiefs of Staff to report on the worst-case scenario of Britain having to continue the war alone against Germany and probably Italy. Forecasting that Hitler would soon tempt France with generous terms to make peace, he cautioned that the terms he would offer Britain "would place her entirely at the mercy of Germany through disarmament, cession of naval bases in the Orkneys etc." Such an offer would be totally unacceptable. What Churchill wanted to know from the Chiefs of Staff was whether they could "hold out *reasonable hopes* of preventing serious invasion."

Alluding to what he called the "dark picture" of military disaster across the Channel, the Foreign Secretary put a very different construction on the choices facing Britain. The War Cabinet must "face the fact that it was not so much a question of imposing a complete defeat upon Germany but of safeguarding the independence of our own Empire and if possible that of France." It was possible, said Lord Halifax, that this objective might be best attained through a peace conference sponsored by Mussolini. This possibility had been hinted at by the Italian Ambassador the previous evening; Halifax had accordingly advised Bastianini that "we should naturally be prepared to consider any proposals which might lead to this, provided our liberty and independence were assured." Halifax added that he had already reported this discussion to the French Ambassador, and he requested approval for another meeting with the Italian Ambassador, who had asked for further talks, where he hinted he "might have fresh proposals to put forward."

Churchill, increasingly disturbed by Halifax's manoeuvring, announced that he was emphatically against any peace that might be achieved under a German domination of Europe. "That we could never accept," he declared. "We must ensure our complete liberty and independence." He was "opposed to any negotiations which might lead to a derogation of our rights and power." Chamberlain appeared to agree with Churchill's position, saying that he expected Italy to try to blackmail the French into negotiations with an ultimatum and that they would "have to watch them very carefully."[44]

Attlee too sought to cut off the Foreign Secretary's effort to seek approval for continuing talks with the Italian Ambassador by urging that they should wait to see what Reynaud and the Chiefs of Staff had to say about the "prospects of holding out if the French collapsed." Lord Halifax brushed the objection aside, contending that the French could play a strong card once Hitler was told that they were bound by treaty not to make a separate peace. "They might use this as a powerful lever to obtain favourable terms which might be of great value to us," he argued. Chamberlain shared Churchill's concerns but maintained a more cautious position, saying he believed that it was essential first to discover if the French were prepared to buy off Italy in order to keep the war going.

Halifax then attempted a second end-run by referring to the *aide-mémoire* circulated by the Chiefs of Staff in anticipation of the meeting with Reynaud. It was obvious to him that their ability to carry on the war single-handed against the Germans depended on maintaining air superiority in British skies. But he found that the *aide-mémoire* omitted to take account of the fact that once France was defeated the Germans would "switch the bulk of their effort to air production." Implicit in his criticism was his belief that the R.A.F. might soon be faced with insuperable odds and that Britain would be unable to carry on the war. The Foreign Secretary's defeatist line of argument caused the Chief of the Air Staff to remind the War Cabinet that the document circulated that morning "did not purport to cover those points." It had simply been drawn up "for the purpose of providing arguments to deter the French from capitulating and to strengthen their will to fight."

Attlee, who found the argument now being pursued by Halifax full of dangerous implications, tried to focus the discussion back on the point at issue. The strongest argument in the *aide-mémoire* to put to Reynaud was that "French capitulation would ultimately mean their destruction." Halifax was temporarily diverted by having to explain that as a "last resort" France should be asked to "put its factories out of gear." Chamberlain then pointed out that any such guarantees would be worthless, since the terms imposed by the Germans would inevitably prevent their fulfilment. The Prime Minister agreed. He was certain the Germans would make an attractive peace offer to the French, to "lay emphasis on the fact that their quarrel was not with France but with England."[45]

The pressure that the War Cabinet was now coming under from the Dominion leaders was evident in a cable received from the Prime Minister of Australia requesting a detailed report on the military prospects of the western front. In the present crisis it was agreed to delay giving Robert Menzies any detailed answer, and ministers adjourned after less than an hour to make the short walk to Westminster Abbey. Chamberlain, for whom that Sunday was "the blackest day of all," found he "could hardly attend to the service with the load on his mind."[46]

After the Abbey the Foreign Secretary "grappled" with the Belgian Ambassador, who wanted another cable sent to King Leopold to persuade him to leave Belgium before it was too late. Halifax and Cadogan then went into a midday meeting with the Italian Ambassador. Precisely what the Foreign Secretary expected to get from Bastianini is unclear, because the minutes of the meeting are still not declassified. What is evident, however, is that the Foreign Secretary was pursuing the Italians as a peace channel with a dedication and intensity that belied his protestations that he was simply window-dressing for the benefit of the French. Halifax hoped the meeting would produce the "fresh proposals" he had hinted at that morning, but he was evidently disappointed. "Nothing to be got out of him" was Cadogan's verdict. "He's an ass – a timid one at that."[47]

If Hitler was waiting on the British and French to give some clear signal that they were ready to parley with him via Mussolini, there was as yet no such sign. For two days the diplomatic wires had been alive with rumours of peace initiatives, but the German Foreign Ministry had still not detected a positive response. Sparing the British a humiliating defeat may well have been Hitler's intention, but he was not intending to let their army escape. There were ominous reports at Führer Headquarters that Sunday morning from his increasingly impatient commanders that the enemy was starting to slip out of their claws, the unclosed armoured pincers.

Army Group B was having a tough job breaking the Allied hinge on the Belgian front. That morning von Bock called up O.K.H. and urged von Brauchitsch to make his task easier by keeping up the pressure with an attack on the left flank of the Allied perimeter. "Unfortunately the armoured forces have been held back for two days," von Bock noted. "To this I say I regard the seizure of Dunkirk as absolutely necessary, otherwise the English might transport out of Dunkirk what they please, right under our nose." General von Brauchitsch agreed, saying he too wanted to push the attack on Dunkirk. That Sunday morning he and his deputy Halder brooded on another day of wasted opportunity, with the German armoured forces "stopped as if paralysed." Halder now worried that "cleaning out the pocket may take weeks, very much to the detriment of our prestige and our future plans." He sympathized with von Brauchitsch, who was "very nervous" that the orders he was receiving from the top made no sense. "In one area they call for a head-on attack against a front retiring in orderly fashion and still possessing its striking power," he wrote, "and elsewhere they freeze the troops to

215

the spot when the enemy rear could be cut any time you wanted to attack." Even von Rundstedt "could not stand it any longer" and had gone up to the front to discuss the next moves with his field commanders.[48]

It was noon, however, before the Führer finally reacted to the rising chorus of concern from his generals that the British were still landing supplies at Dunkirk in spite of the Luftwaffe attacks. He gave notice of his intention to rescind the "Halt Order" with a telephone order from O.K.W. to be relayed to von Rundstedt, authorizing him to resume a limited advance on the port. At 1.30 p.m. Hitler summoned von Brauchitsch to Felsennest. He found the Führer still cautious, but willing to approve an advance by the Panzers to artillery range to bombard roads and railway junctions leading to the harbour facilities. An hour later the Army Chief returned "beaming" to the O.K.H. command bunker and announced to Halder: "At last the Führer has given permission to move on Dunkirk in order to prevent evacuations."[49]

Hitler's order to resume Panzer operation on the left flank to seal off Dunkirk is yet another sign that even if he meant to spare the British a humiliating defeat he was certainly not intending to let their army escape. When he took the brake off the tanks that Sunday afternoon he knew that it would take more than half a day before the attack could be fully resumed. Most armoured units were resting; others were engaged in maintenance work with the tracks off their tanks. So it was to take many more hours before the German armoured pincer began to roll forward again.

Time was Hitler's ally when it came to the pressure that the French were now putting on their British partners to send a negotiating overture to Italy. Their sense of urgency made itself felt as Churchill lunched with the French Prime Minister in his private rooms at the Admiralty. Reynaud briefed his host on Weygand's bleak assessment of the military predicament and his agreement to fight on only "if ordered to do so" even if Paris fell. He warned Churchill that France's military command "did not think France's resistance was likely to last very long against a determined German onslaught." His own belief was that the "war could not be won on land."[50]

"Where then could France turn for salvation?" Reynaud asked rhetorically. He suggested that the time had now come to make an approach to Italy. If Mussolini agreed not to "stab France in the back," he said, ten army divisions could be released from the southern frontier to fight the Germans. Italy might agree to a non-aggression pact but only in return for the "neutralization of Gibraltar and the Suez Canal, the demilitarization of Malta and the limitation of Naval forces in the Mediterranean." This was a price Reynaud thought the British would have to pay. The French would also have to make concessions in their protectorate of Tunis and press Greece to do the same in the Dodecanese islands.

Precisely what was being proposed, Churchill wanted to know. Reynaud made it plain that he had been reliably informed that these concessions were the price the Allies would have to pay to keep Italy out of the war and France in the fight. The Germans might not abide by the Italian terms, Reynaud conceded, but while he himself "would not sign peace terms," he said, he might be forced to resign to make way for a premier who would accept Hitler's terms.

"I would have difficulties with my government if the Battle for France was lost," Reynaud stated bluntly. It was his duty to inform the Prime Minister that "Pétain would speak in favour of an armistice." Reynaud went on to elaborate what he saw as the increased dangers to Britain if the Germans occupied the French coast from Brest to Dunkirk. Churchill responded forcefully that Germany would then start attacking Britain and give the French time to regroup to defend Paris. This Reynaud thought unlikely because "the dream of all Germans was to conquer Paris." Undeterred, Churchill repeated his assertion that Britain "would rather go down fighting than be enslaved to Germany." Provided Britain and France stuck together, he asserted, they could survive the onslaught for the three months until there was a real prospect of the United States becoming committed.

Churchill had pulled out all the stops. But when he saw that he was making little impact he stopped and put the question point-blank. Had the Germans offered the French peace terms? "No," said the French Prime Minister. But he "knew that they could get an offer if they wanted one."[51]

Churchill then asked Reynaud to remain at the Admiralty while he consulted the War Cabinet, who were awaiting him at Downing Street. With the French Prime Minister so obviously weighed down with defeatism and the talk of negotiations, he decided against inviting him into the discussions, in case Reynaud's despondency should prove infectious. Churchill reported to the meeting briefly on his lunchtime discussions with Reynaud, advising that he did not think that Reynaud would now have any objection to the British Expeditionary Force being ordered to march to the sea. He gave a brief résumé of his later discussion with Reynaud over the French plan for a direct appeal to Italy, and then proposed that the Foreign Secretary should go directly to Admiralty House to have a few minutes alone with Reynaud and should then bring Chamberlain and Attlee round for a final talk.

Halifax, however, wanted first to settle the question of the approach to Italy, which he now favoured not just on behalf of France but because Mussolini's reluctance to see a German-dominated Europe could be exploited to "persuade Herr Hitler to take a more reasonable attitude." Churchill intervened to quash any further discussion by expressing his doubt that anything would come of an approach to Italy. He wanted the War Cabinet to take the matter up another time; the immediate priority was to get Reynaud's approval for the formal orders to Gort to retreat to the coast, "to make sure that the French had no complaint." Churchill asked Halifax to have a draft telegram for Reynaud to sign drawn up and sent over to Admiralty House at 3.15 p.m.[52]

The Cabinet then broke up, leaving the Foreign Secretary without the authorization he needed to proceed with the Italian peace negotiations. At the same time he had been given no specific instruction not to discuss his peace initiative with the French Prime Minister, so during his private session he made it the main issue of their conversation. According to Churchill's memoirs the British "were not able to show any favour to these ideas." He wrote that Reynaud "found my colleagues very stiff and tough." The Cabinet records and the account left by the French Prime Minister show that this was far from the case.[53]

"Lord Halifax told me that he *had already initiated advances on the previous day* towards the Italian Ambassador in London," Reynaud wrote in his memoir. He specifically cited the Foreign Secretary as telling him that he had indicated to Bastianini "that the Allies *would be ready to consider any proposal* for negotiation both as regards Italian interests as well as the basis of a just and lasting peace." The French Prime Minister thought Lord Halifax "was impressed by my arguments." He did not, however, receive any encouragement from Churchill, who was "hostile to any concessions to Mussolini."[54]

"My own feeling was that at that pitch in which our affairs lay, we had nothing to offer which Mussolini could not take for himself or be given by Hitler" is the contrasting version of the same discussion that appears in Churchill's memoirs. The approach already made via Roosevelt was as far as Churchill said the British government was prepared to go. Bargains were not made "at last gasp" and he foresaw that "once we started negotiating for a friendly mediation of the Duce we should destroy our power of fighting on." Chamberlain and Attlee expressed similar concerns to Reynaud when they joined the session at the Admiralty. The French Premier nonetheless detected that Chamberlain's negative attitude to approaching Italy was tempered "with some reservations." Although Halifax expressed support for the French scheme to approach Mussolini directly, the only assurance that Reynaud got that afternoon was that the Cabinet "would discuss the matter" and that he would be kept informed. By refusing to be stampeded into an agreement to mollify the French Prime Minister, Churchill

218

won time to continue the battle against Halifax's strong arguments for resurrecting appeasement.[55]

The Prime Minister had nearly as much difficulty persuading Reynaud to send a telegram instructing General Weygand to authorize General Blanchard to "formally order a withdrawal towards the ports." The French Prime Minister at first tried to blame Gort's unauthorized withdrawal from Arras for the collapse of the Allied counter-offensive. Even after Reynaud had "been persuaded to accept the British point of view," it took three drafts before he agreed to sign the cable, which was telephoned over to French headquarters at 4.05 p.m. To ensure that there was no confusion, Churchill had Eden telegraph Gort shortly afterwards: "You are now authorized to operate towards the coast forthwith, in conjunction with the French and Belgian Armies."[56]

Reynaud then left to fly back to Paris. He was met at Le Bourget by Baudouin, who informed him of the mounting pressure in the War Council to negotiate. Weygand, worried about anarchy, wanted Reynaud to reverse the decision to evacuate the government if Paris fell, suggesting that they should follow the example of the Roman senators whom the invading barbarians found sitting in their curule chairs. To save France's honour Weygand did not believe it necessary to "fight to the last cartridge;" but it was right "to stop in time to prevent a useless massacre." Marshal Pétain, Baudouin reported, had come "with tears in his eyes" to say that "talk of fighting to the last man" was stupid; he just did not believe in it. The same view had been expressed by Camille Chautemps, the minister responsible for coping with the refugee problem, who told Baudouin that he supported Pétain because "no civilian will have the requisite authority to negotiate and we shall have to do that soon."[57]

Baudouin, who was now inclined to agree with the growing lobby for negotiating France out of the war, was disappointed to hear that Reynaud, despite his "very trying interview," had failed to get British agreement for a direct approach to Italy. "Churchill holding back. Only Halifax is understanding" is how Baudouin summarized it in his note of their conversation. Later that evening he expanded on the account he had given in his diary. "The only one who understands is Halifax, who is clearly worried about the future, and realizes that some European solution must be reached," Reynaud had reported. "Churchill is always hectoring, and Chamberlain is undecided." Halifax had proposed to "internationalize the Suez Canal, Gibraltar, and Malta in order to be able to negotiate with Italy at once." Churchill would not agree, and "had taken refuge behind the War Cabinet," who would give their answer the next day. The British Prime Minister's stonewalling irritated Baudouin. With the backing of Reynaud's manipulative mistress Hélène de Portes, the former Banque d'Indochine director was playing an increasing role as the crisis grew more intense. He openly criticized Reynaud when he learned that there had been no discussion of whether France could be released from her promise not to make a separate peace. The Prime Minister, he charged, had "not fulfilled the mission with which the War Council had entrusted him."[58]

That night the British Prime Minister dispatched a telegram informing Reynaud that it was "impossible" for him to send the text of any proposal to Italy before Monday. "Will do my best, but feel convinced only safety lies in ability to fight," Churchill cabled. "All here most grateful for your visit and admire your calm courage amid these storms." The message of support arrived after the French Prime Minister had weathered another stormy meeting with Foreign Minister Daladier and Charles Roux. Discussion was "confused and harrowing," but Reynaud exerted his authority by insisting that they should postpone any move towards Italy until the next day, when the approval of the British Cabinet was expected.[59]

The discussion that took place in the Admiralty after the French Prime Minister left that afternoon was no less harrowing for the British Prime Minister. He closeted himself with Chamberlain, Halifax, Attlee and Greenwood for what the official record describes as "an informal meeting of War Cabinet Ministers." It seems that Churchill wanted to keep the discussion off the record, for, whether by accident or design, the Cabinet Secretary was not present for the first fifteen minutes of a discussion that quickly became heated.[60]

What the Foreign Secretary now proposed was that Mussolini should be invited to sound out Hitler on what terms he was prepared to offer not only to France, but also to Britain. Halifax later complained about the "discursive meeting of what was supposed to be the Cabinet." According to his diary the Prime Minister was "very jumpy," and with secretaries coming and going "the general atmosphere was like Waterloo Station." The Foreign Secretary found it "very difficult to do business" – no doubt because Churchill repeatedly expressed strong opposition to the back-door peace negotiations that Halifax was trying to press through. The official minutes pick up with Churchill lecturing Halifax that Britain still had the power to resist and attack, whereas the French did not. They might be offered "decent terms by Germany" but not Britain. "If France could not defend itself," he said, "it was better she should get out of the war rather than that she should drag us into a settlement which involved intolerable terms." The French might "hang on" but they must "take care not to be forced into a weak position in which we went to Signor Mussolini and invited him to go to Herr Hitler and ask him to treat us nicely." Above all, they must not "get entangled" before there had been any serious fighting.[61]

220

Though prefacing his response by saying he "did not disagree with this view," Halifax quickly made it very plain that he did. He attached "rather more importance than the Prime Minister" to permitting the French to try the Italian initiative. With lawyerly precision he then set about cutting away the underlying tenets of Churchill's "diagnosis" that Hitler was bound to put forward "outrageous terms." Not only did Halifax argue that this was not in Hitler's interests, but he agreed that if the German terms threatened Britain's independence they "would not look at them for a moment." He was strongly of the opinion that Mussolini shared Britain's concerns about Germany dominating the balance of power and that therefore there was "no harm in trying this line of approach."

"The problem was a difficult one," Chamberlain conceded, "but it was right to talk it out from every point of view." He worried that Mussolini could act as an independent mediator only with Hitler's forbearance. The French desire to make concessions of "certain named places" to induce Mussolini not to enter the war would give away "something for nothing." Serious consideration should be given to the Prime Minister's opinion that "we might be better off without France," provided certain safeguards were obtained.[62]

In a bid to terminate what was becoming an increasingly heated discussion, Churchill proposed that it was "best to do nothing until we saw how much of the army we could re-embark from France." Even so, Halifax persisted. He wanted to get Britain's position clear because they would soon have to deal with Roosevelt's response to the joint appeal. He also detailed his discussions of the previous day with the Italian Ambassador – who he said was standing by for an answer – but did not mention his meeting that morning. After listening with rising impatience, the Prime Minister responded to Halifax with all barrels blazing. This much is evident from Chamberlain's diary, which records more graphically than the laboured official minutes how Churchill punctured the Foreign Secretary's carefully argued case.

"It was incredible," Churchill was reported as saying, "that Hitler would consent to any terms that we would accept – though if we could get out of this jam by giving up Malta, Gibraltar and some African colonies *he would jump at it.*" This he believed was most unlikely while Hitler "thought he had the whip-hand." Churchill argued that the "only thing to do was to show him that he could not conquer this country," since it would be better to do without the French if they "tied us up with a conference which we should enter with our case lost beforehand."[63]

The Foreign Secretary countered that there "could be no harm in trying Mussolini" because if his terms proved "impossible we could still reject them." On the other hand if it was "found that we could obtain terms which did not postulate the destruction of our independence, we should be foolish not to accept them." Chamberlain now announced that he "supported this view," according to his diary, which recorded that "Attlee said hardly anything." The official record, however, shows that Attlee intervened in favour of Churchill's position, which was strongly backed by Greenwood, who declared that there was little to be gained and that British prestige would be badly affected once Hitler learned of the proposed concessions.[64]

With ministers so evenly split, Churchill decided that it would be imprudent to press the issue further that day. So while he said that he "did not raise objection to some approach" to Mussolini, he proposed they needed to find a formula not only to placate the French, but one "that would give them time to think." It was therefore agreed that the French Prime Minister would be told that the War Cabinet had not yet agreed. With this, Churchill said irritably, Reynaud "would have to be content." It was very "plain from his attitude that he had given up all idea of serious fighting." The meeting ended after agreeing that the Foreign Secretary would circulate the draft of his proposed communication before there was any further approach to Italy. In a move that was intended to reinforce his side of the argument, Churchill obtained the War Cabinet's approval for Sinclair, who was the leader of the Liberal Party, to attend the meeting next day, when it was agreed that they would again take up the whole question of peace initiatives.[65]

"Settled nothing much," Cadogan recorded when the meeting broke up at six o'clock. The Prime Minister was criticized for being "too romantic and sentimental and temperamental." Chamberlain was "still the best of the lot." The four-hour-long wrangle might not have resolved the issue of whether they should send a peace feeler to Hitler via Mussolini, but it had underlined the importance of saving the British Expeditionary Force to strengthen Britain's ability to fight on even if France pulled out of the war.[66]

As the War Cabinet meeting adjourned, the signal was sent to Vice-Admiral Sir Bertram Ramsay at his Dover headquarters: OPERATION DYNAMO IS TO COMMENCE. This set in motion the massive evacuation plans already drawn up by the quietly-spoken Ramsay, under whose efficient direction an armada of small ships was already assembling in the estuaries, creeks and ports of south-east England. In the next ten days every fishing vessel and private pleasure craft capable of crossing the Channel was requisitioned to join with Navy destroyers, passenger ferries and tugs in the race against time to rescue the troops from Dunkirk.

The all-out effort to save the British Expeditionary Force of necessity required abandoning the gallant defenders of Calais to their fate. Resistance in Boulogne had ended the day before, but that night the destroyers and transport vessels standing by to take off the troops at Calais received orders redirecting them to Dunkirk. For all Churchill's brave talk earlier of fighting to the last, reality was brought home to him that night when he approved the final order informing Brigadier Nicolson that his garrison was to be sacrificed to save the British Expeditionary Force. "Evacuation will not (repeat not) take place and craft required for above purpose are to return to Dover," the signal read. It concluded: "Government has therefore decided you must continue to fight. Have greatest admiration for your splendid stand."[67]

That evening at dinner the Prime Minister's silence and uncharacteristic distaste for food and drink were noted by General Ismay, who took it to be an indication of how deeply he had been affected by the strain of the day's events. Churchill himself wrote that he felt "physically sick." Stricken by the necessity of ordering men to lay down their lives, the Prime Minister can hardly have avoided feeling sick that the French and now even members of his own Cabinet seemed willing to give up without a proper fight.

Churchill was not the only high official to feel the mounting pressure. "It is a strain – daily and hourly looking the ugliest facts in the eye," Cadogan wrote. "A non-stop nightmare. God grant that I can go on without losing faith or nerve. But where to?" The Permanent Secretary of the Foreign Office was aware of the recommendation that had been circulating that week for plans to be made for the evacuation of the Royal Family and government to Canada. Items of "cultural and historical interest" such as the Crown Jewels, the Coronation Chair, the Doomsday Book and Magna Carta, "whose presence here is no help to prosecuting the war," should be transported across the Atlantic immediately. This suggestion met with strong opposition from some officials, who felt that it was premature and would send out signals of panic and "would produce the worst possible impression" in Canada and the United States.[68]

The Foreign Office was as yet unaware that President Roosevelt was already thinking along much the same lines, though his preoccupation was with saving the British fleet rather than the Crown Jewels. The British Ambassador, Lord Lothian, was summoned to the White House that evening to be told that the American Ambassador in Italy had been instructed to approach Mussolini offering the President's "mediation" along the lines agreed in London and Paris. Saying that he was "merely thinking aloud," Roosevelt then proposed that "if things came to the worst," Britain's surviving planes, warships and merchant vessels "should be treated not as British but as Empire possessions and transferred before they could be captured or surrendered to Canada or Australia."

What prompted Roosevelt to follow up on the message he had conveyed to the Canadian Prime Minister's envoy the previous day was a telegram from Paris. In a communication "for your most private ear," Bullitt warned the President that the Allied armies "will be obliged to surrender within two or three days" and that Paris would fall "within five or six days."[69]

"I regret deeply to feel obliged to express such an opinion," the Ambassador wrote, "but I think you ought to know just how serious the situation is." So while Lothian did not know the precise reason for Roosevelt's fears that the "whole edifice was collapsing," he tried his best to counter them. Would the United States come into the war "if such a catastrophe impended," he asked; such an assurance would "exercise a profound influence on the British decision," he suggested. The decision, said the President, rested not with him, but Congress, so he could give "no definite answer." But he "thought it probable." Popular opinion was "rapidly changing," and Germany, he predicted, would be bound to challenge some "vital American interest in the near future."[70]

Roosevelt refused to be drawn beyond this vague and unsatisfactory statement. He also put it in the record later that he had asked the British Ambassador "not to report the conversation to London." Since he believed that there was "just a chance" that Lord Lothian would obey his injunction, he obviously framed his remarks knowing that they might reach Churchill. The British Ambassador, however, regarded it as his duty to report on the strong current of the President's pessimism. He also considered it important to alert London to Roosevelt's "curious observation" that should it become necessary to evacuate the King and the "Imperial government," then Bermuda would be a better capital for the government than Canada.

"Canada might feel a difficulty about the transfer of Downing Street to Toronto," the President suggested. "The American republics may be restless about a monarchy being based on the American continent."

It was not the prospect of playing host to the Royal Family and Britain's government that alarmed the Canadian Prime Minister that evening after Keenleyside arrived back in Ottawa; it was the pressure Roosevelt wanted him to put on Churchill that caused him to feel "instinctively revolted" at the thought of the British going down and the idea of turning their fleet over to the United States. To Mackenzie King it appeared that "the United States was seeking to save itself at the expense of Britain," and that the President's appeal was to "the selfishness of the Dominions at the expense of the British Isles." Worried about the political reaction from the patriots of the Canadian Tory opposition, he was disinclined to act as Roosevelt's bag-man, considering that it "should be done direct with Churchill and the President and not through others." Taking refuge in the vacillation for which he was notorious, the Canadian Prime Minister sent Keenleyside away to write up a full report while he decided to "sleep on it."[71]

Asking the Canadian Prime Minister to put pressure on the mother country at the very time when Churchill was appealing to the Dominions to reinforce his appeals for help to the United States was a terrible request. It was as if, with the house in flames and Mother trapped inside, the Fire Brigade was asking the eldest son of the family to tell her that there was no water to douse the flames, whilst demanding that she throw down her jewelry box as down-payment for future rebuilding of the home.[72]

Chapter 10

"Winston Talked the Most Frightful Rot"

"A Tight Corner"
27 May 1940

"I was distressed to find the situation much blacker than when I left on Friday," Churchill's private secretary observed of the Monday morning after his return from Oxford. Colville found Downing Street in a crisis and alive with rumours of the impending French collapse – and worse. "The Cabinet are feverishly considering our ability to carry on the war in such circumstances, and there are signs that Halifax is being defeatist. He says that our aim can no longer be to crush Germany but rather to preserve our own integrity."[1]

Colville's confirmation that the Foreign Secretary was regarded by Churchill's staff as "defeatist" is consistent with the Cabinet minutes – but not with his own diary. There we find Halifax once again stating that when the French Ambassador came to see him that morning about the approach to Italy, he told him he "did not believe in it much himself." But since M. Corbin was "insistent" on getting Reynaud the answer that he had been promised, Halifax promised to "put it to the Cabinet."[2]

Churchill put off discussion on the Italian peace approach until the War Cabinet's afternoon meeting. If, as he anticipated, Mussolini rejected President Roosevelt's appeal of the day before, this would kill Halifax's argument without more wrangling. Churchill himself regarded any approach to the Italian dictator as pointless and dangerous, but to his intense irritation, the peace issue intruded under a different head at that morning's War Cabinet discussion.

The news from the western front was bad, but no worse than on Sunday. The evacuation of 25,000 men from Dunkirk overnight

226

gave rise to some guarded optimism on the first day of Operation Dynamo. Perception was as important as reality, and hopes rose after Dill, the new and more pliant Chief of the Imperial General Staff, reported that Calais was still holding out somehow, and that General Gort's forces had managed to contain the renewed German attack on the left flank of the British Expeditionary Force. On the right flank, however, the situation was becoming desperate. The Belgian front line south-east of Ypres was reported to be "in grave danger of collapse." This was worrying because the first stage of Gort's planned three-day withdrawal to Dunkirk was due to begin that night. Only two roads were available in the twenty-mile-wide corridor in which the French and British armies were now packed. The retreat would be "extremely critical," Dill cautioned, but "the troops of the B.E.F. are in good heart because they felt themselves more than a match for the enemy."[3]

The peace issue broke through again when the War Cabinet had to consider how to respond to the Prime Ministers of Australia, Canada, New Zealand and South Africa, who were pressing for straight answers on the alarming press reports from France. Chamberlain, reporting on an interview with the Empire High Commissioners, said that Stanley Bruce of Australia had "taken a most gloomy view of our prospects if France went out of the war." The Australian High Commissioner had urged that they should "'mobilize' President Roosevelt and Signor Mussolini before the fall of Paris." Chamberlain was instructed to call another meeting with the High Commissioners to inform them that there was "no prospect" of giving in; Britain would "fight on," even if France went out of the war. Although this was the Prime Minister's opinion, Halifax intervened to get a significant qualification: Churchill's statement was to apply only to "the immediate situation arising out of the hypothetical collapse of France." On the Foreign Secretary's advice, the Dominion Prime Ministers were to be told that "It would not mean that if at any time terms were offered they would not be considered on their merits."[4]

Churchill, alarmed at all this talk of peace terms by the Foreign Secretary during the week which would see the climax of the military crisis at Dunkirk, intervened to counter the corrosive effect this rider might have on government morale. He produced the draft of what he called "a general injunction to Ministers to use confident language," declaring his conviction that "the bulk of the people of the country would refuse to accept the possibility of defeat." When the War Cabinet approved the text, the Prime Minister announced that it would be circulated to all senior officials – and he reminded the ministers that he depended on them to set an example of resolution.

Churchill recognized that the will to fight was as important to

Britain's survival in this hour of national peril as the means. His determination to have no truck with any hint of defeatism brought him into conflict that morning not only with his Foreign Secretary but with the Chiefs of Staff.

Their report, "British Strategy in the Near Future," was an assessment of the nation's ability to sustain the war in the event of a French capitulation. But Churchill was unhappy with the military arithmetic because it spelled out the fact that the odds were long, if not hopeless. He set about challenging the figures, item by item, wherever he thought the Chiefs of Staff had been too favourable to the Germans.

Rejecting the Air Staff's assumption that the Germans would necessarily get air and naval bases from France, he contended that the French might be allowed to remain neutral. It was typical of Churchill's determination to put the best possible construction on the situation, to accentuate the positive even at the expense of ignoring or eliminating the negative. This caused alarm to some of his military advisers, but his resolution was driving and infectious, and he soon had the Chiefs of Staff climbing down over their figures for the Luftwaffe. German air superiority over the R.A.F., he declared, was not nearly so bad as four-to-one. Stabbing the offending figures in the dossier with his thick finger, he protested that the report was "misleading."[5]

The U.S. military's estimate was five-to-one; but Churchill chiselled away at the figures and criticized the report line by line until at last Air Vice Marshal Peirse conceded that the figures on aircraft production, training and operational tables were too generous to the Luftwaffe and not generous enough to the R.A.F. Churchill got his way and the comparative tables were reinterpreted for the record to show that the odds were actually only 2½-to-one in the Germans' favour.[6]

"If our airmen were shooting down 3 to 1," the Prime Minister declared, "the balance was on our side." Splitting numbers may have been good for the Prime Minister's morale and for the Ministry of Information press releases; but it worried Lord Halifax. He suspected that the R.A.F. was inflating its daily score of enemy planes destroyed – as in fact it was – in order to humour the Prime Minister. Churchill's incorrigible optimism, however good for morale it might be, could not change the fundamental military calculations that tipped the balance heavily in Germany's favour in every military department except the Navy.

The Prime Minister's assumption that President Roosevelt would eventually bring America into the struggle was no more reassuring to a sceptic like the Foreign Secretary than the admission by the Chiefs of Staff that, if France fell, Britain could continue the war only with United States aid. As Chamberlain pointed out, the report "was based on the assumption that the United States of America would be willing to give us full economic and financial support." This, he agreed, was "not an unjustifiable assumption" but he cautioned that "we might not obtain this support in the immediate future." The second major concern of the Chiefs of Staff was that if France collapsed there would be insufficient armoured forces in the country to repel an invasion. They anticipated an invasion, but predicted that the Germans would attempt a landing only if they could achieve air superiority. This demanded immediate attention to stepping up fighter aircraft production and protecting the factories from bombing raids.[7]

At the outset of one of the most critical weeks in British history, the inescapable problem facing the War Cabinet was how to secure the support from the United States without which the nation's economic and military capacity to continue waging war would quickly be exhausted. Not even Halifax disagreed that the priority had to be to "induce the Government of the United States to release destroyers, motor torpedo boats and aircraft, particularly fighters, from stocks now held by the United States." The question was whether Washington would deliver not only war matériel but also "active financial and economic assistance." A Committee of Ministers under the Foreign Secretary was detailed to consider setting up a special mission to go to Washington to supplement the efforts already being made through diplomatic channels and by the Anglo-French Purchasing Mission.[6]

Churchill maintained his confidence that Roosevelt would eventually come to Britain's aid. This was whistling in the dark to Lord Halifax, whose American Department officials were expressing anxiety about putting too much reliance on the United States, whose global interests were not the same as Britain's. In the circumstances it seemed curious that the Prime Minister rejected out of hand Lord Lothian's cabled suggestion that American support would be forthcoming if Britain ceded Trinidad, Newfoundland and Bermuda to the United States to pay off outstanding World War I debts. The Prime Minister was strongly opposed to making any such offer unless it could be part of a two-way bargain that would help Britain to obtain the fighters and destroyers she needed to wage the current war.

"The United States has given us practically no help in the war," he told the War Cabinet. "Now that they saw how great was the danger, their attitude was that they wanted to keep everything which would help us for their own defence." He was unaware as yet that this was precisely the position taken by Roosevelt in his secret talks with the Canadians. The President's already pessimistic assessment of Britain's ability to survive had just received a further jolt from the American Ambassador in London. Britain's military prospects were now hopeless, Kennedy had cabled that Monday, telling the State Department that "only a miracle" could save the Allied armies from being wiped out.[7]

American defeatism also worried the Canadian Prime Minister in Ottawa that day. He read and re-read the reports of Roosevelt's comments to Keenleyside before deciding to telephone the Secretary of State in Washington. When Hull came on the line he asked whether it was their intention for him to "communicate direct with Mr. Churchill or to get the Dominions together to make the representation referred to." The Secretary of State told him that their intention was not to make an "immediate presentation to Churchill," but "when the time came" to have the Dominion "tell Britain to stand firm and not part with her fleet and make a soft peace." This appeared to conflict with what Keenleyside had reported of the need for immediate action, so Mackenzie King called in the External Affairs diplomat and asked him to return to Washington to ask Roosevelt to clarify his request. Mackenzie King took care to inform Keenleyside of his concern that "the United States might be using Canada to protect themselves in urging a course that would spare them immediate assistance to Britain."[8]

The Canadian Prime Minister did not of course know that Washington's attitude had been coloured by the Anglo-French request for the President to act as an intermediary with Mussolini. At 11.30 that morning the American Ambassador in Rome went to the Chigi Palace to see the Italian Foreign Minister. He told Ciano that he had a "message of the greatest importance from President Roosevelt to give verbally to the Duce." When it was apparent that he would not get an audience with Mussolini, Ambassador Phillips took it upon himself to make the representation to Ciano. The boyish-looking Foreign Minister took careful notes, but when Phillips inquired deferentially if he could be given "some general idea" of what Mussolini's likely reaction would be to the President's appeal, he was brushed off. "It would be a categorical refusal," Ciano predicted with undiplomatic bluntness. The Duce, he said, had decided irrevocably to "discharge the obligations which were imposed on him by his alliance with Germany." The Foreign Minister assured the American Ambassador that "Nothing could now change the course of events."[9]

At one o'clock that Monday afternoon Ciano telephoned the American Embassy to confirm that the Duce had indeed rejected Roosevelt's offer. In his diary Ciano noted that he had told Phillips that Mussolini wanted war and "even if he were to obtain by peaceful means double what he claims, he would refuse." What he did not reveal was that the Duce had talked of 10 June as the day when Italy would enter the war. Nor did the Foreign Minister drop a hint of this to the French Ambassador, who called that afternoon and received the same abrupt response as the American Ambassador. Ciano observed in his diary that it was a reflection of the psychological situation in France that François-Poncet "made some very precise overtures," including an offer to "make a deal about Tunisia and perhaps even Algeria." Ciano told him it was "too late" and terminated the interview.[10]

No news from Rome had been received in Paris that afternoon when General Spears and the British Ambassador conveyed to Reynaud the latest telegram from Churchill. It was full of encouragement – but it stalled on the question of an Anglo-French appeal to Mussolini. The French Prime Minister was pale and dejected. Spears noted how he nervously jerked his neck, as though trying to escape a too tight collar, as he launched into an explanation of why it was vital for the British government to agree to internationalize Gibraltar and Suez to avert the "mortal danger" France faced from Italy. Churchill and Attlee, he said, were against the French appeal, but he assured Spears that Halifax was not "unfavourable." The Foreign Secretary, he said, was prepared to propose this to Mussolini "were Italy willing to collaborate in establishing a peace preserving the independence of Great Britain and France."

"It was left that your War Cabinet were to discuss an offer to Mussolini after I had gone," Reynaud explained. It came as a "shock" to Spears and the Ambassador to learn that Halifax was apparently ready to buy off Mussolini with Gibraltar or Malta – let alone make Italy a partner in the Suez Canal. Spears told Reynaud that he did not see the "mortal danger" to France from Italy that would justify such a desperate deal. The French Prime Minister was despondent and evidently under pressure from Daladier and those ministers who were urging the appeal to Italy in the hope that it would lead France to a negotiated way out of the war. He therefore stressed how important it was for Spears to convince Churchill "how desperately serious the French Government and Weygand consider the position to be."[11]

Reynaud was reacting to the dismal report delivered by the French Commander-in-Chief at that morning's meeting of the War Council, in which Weygand had predicted that the bulk of the six divisions of France's First Army would be trapped at the end of the Allied pocket if Belgian lines gave way. "Not only do the English not attack, but they retreat and the Belgians are giving way," he complained. "How are we to avoid disaster?" He complained that he was powerless to do more than send out "rigorous telegrams" to his British and Belgian subordinate commanders.[12]

Weygand's telegram had not yet reached General Gort, who that morning had shifted his headquarters north to Houtkerque along roads made all but impassable by swarms of French refugees. As the German attack began on Cassell, the British and French commanders met in the town to agree the plan for an evacuation from Dunkirk. The assault from the enemy air and ground forces had been winding up steadily since the early hours of Monday when the armoured divisions began pounding away again. They were now attacking along the whole length of the Canal Line from Gravelines on the coast to Carvin forty miles inland near the end of the deep pocket which contained the Allied armies.

Just as the German generals had forecast three days before, their second attempt to drive bridgeheads across the Aa ran into heavy opposition. Encountering "stronger resistance than expected," General Kleist's armoured divisions reported to headquarters. The tank crews were now paying the penalty for Hitler's Haltbefehl. "By noon the attack has made very slow progress," Halder recorded in his log. The British were now dug in along the canal and obstinately fighting for every foot of ground to keep the escape route to Dunkirk open. On the right flank von Bock's infantry were slowly pushing into the hinge between the French and Belgian armies inwards towards Ypres.[13]

"The enemy is beginning to break, but it is a slow process," Halder noted. "We must bear in mind that a total of four enemy armies are packed into this pocket and that there is nothing left for them but to fight back as long as there is any ammunition; it must give in eventually." It was not until late that afternoon the first cracks began opening in the two opposite flanks of the Allied pocket. On the left, Rommel's 5th Panzer Division succeeded in pushing a bridgehead across the canal in the Béthune sector at the junction of the B.E.F. and the French First Army. Some twenty-five miles to the north on the right flank the Belgian army was stretched to breaking point south of Ypres. When the hinge finally gave way and German troops burst through the Belgian line at Thiel, King Leopold decided that the time had come to call an end to the fighting before his army disintegrated into a rout.[14]

News of the impending collapse of the Belgian front exploded at Weygand's headquarters with the impact of a heavy shell shortly after six. Weygand immediately left Vincennes and drove to the Prime Minister carrying the telegram from King Leopold's French liaison officer predicting the "total capitulation" of the Belgian Army. A shaken Reynaud summoned the Belgian Prime Minister and his Minister of National Defence, who happened to be in Paris. General Denis was close to tears when Premier Hubert Pierlot declared that he was "in disagreement with the King who had betrayed Belgium." Later that evening, when General Spears and the British Ambassador had a further meeting with the French Prime Minister, they found him still "white with rage," repeatedly muttering "There has never been such a betrayal in history."[15]

No news of either the impending Belgian capitulation or Musso-lini's rejection of Roosevelt's offer had reached London by 4.30 p.m. when the War Cabinet assembled again. "Suggested approach to Signor Mussolini" was the only item on the agenda. In contrast to the prosaic billing, even the stilted record of the Cabinet secretariat could not conceal the fierce row that erupted as Churchill and Halifax collided again and again over the fundamental policy issue of whether the British government should investigate the possibility of a compromise peace with Hitler.

Churchill opened the discussion by letting the War Cabinet know that he was now more strongly opposed to the idea of a direct approach to Mussolini than he had been the day before. He declared that Halifax's draft letter to the Italians, setting out the terms of the overture suggested by the French, was "not unlike the approach which we had asked the President to make." He also wanted the proposal rejected because there was a "good deal of difference between making the approach ourselves and allowing one to be made by President Roosevelt, ostensibly on his own initiative."[16]

Lord Halifax at first took refuge in the French position, relaying Reynaud's latest request for "geographical precision," which had been conveyed to him that morning by the French Ambassador. The French wanted him to spell out the concessions Britain was prepared to make regarding Gibraltar, Malta and Suez in order to give added inducements for Mussolini to cooperate. The Foreign Secretary said he had advised M. Corbin that this would be unacceptable to the War Cabinet. But he expressed his concern that the French were preparing to blame Britain if the approach was not made and Mussolini declared war. He acknowledged that Roosevelt's appeal was in the process of being put through diplo-matic channels, but said he had received a "cryptic message" from the British Ambassador in Rome that suggested "nothing we could do would be of any value to us at this stage, so far as Mussolini was concerned."[17]

Chamberlain added that the Ambassador had also reported that General von Epp had come to Rome to inform the Italian govern-ment that Hitler did not want them to come into the war after all. If this were true they would be offering Italy concessions for nothing which would be rejected anyway. Chamberlain said he was convinced that Mussolini would also rebuff Roosevelt's overture because he wanted to wait until the Germans captured Paris before joining the war to get a share of the spoils. Approaching Mussolini now, said Chamberlain, "would serve no useful pur-pose" except to prevent the French from blaming Britain if Italy attacked them.

Was it worth taking the risk to "settle relations with a faithful

233

ally"? That was the question posed by Churchill – who answered, rhetorically, "No." He was supported by the Secretary of State for Air, who had been invited to join the critical discussion as leader of the Liberal Party; Sinclair also argued the "futility" of appealing to Mussolini "from a tight corner." It would be interpreted as an admission of weakness by the Germans, would upset the Dominions and could well undermine morale in Britain and the Dominions. "If the French were so weak that they could not await the result of President Roosevelt's intervention," Sinclair asked, "was it wise to go further with them and weaken our own position?"[18]

The Foreign Secretary disagreed. He questioned whether there could be "very much force in the argument that we must do nothing which gave the appearance of weakness, since Signor Mussolini would know that President Roosevelt's approach had been prompted by us."

Attlee immediately challenged the position taken by Halifax. Speaking as the leader of the Labour Party he said that an appeal to Italy would be "of no practical effect and would be very damaging to us." The deputy Labour leader, Greenwood, concurred. His position, like the Prime Minister's, was unchanged since their previous discussion of the issue; if anything, it had hardened against appealing to Mussolini, and he suggested that it would be "heading for disaster" to go any further.[19]

Churchill, confident of the backing of these three ministers, now set strongly about denouncing the futility of approaching Mussolini, which he argued would be of less help to the French Prime Minister than if Britain made a firm stand. Appealing to the Italians would "ruin the integrity of our fighting position," since "everybody would know what we had in mind," even if no geographical names were mentioned. It looked suspiciously like a manoeuvre by defeatists in the French government to get a separate peace despite the joint agreement not to do so. "If the French were not prepared to go on with the struggle, let them give up," Churchill said, adding that he "very much doubted that they would do so."[20]

"If this country was beaten, France became a vassal state," the Prime Minister declared, "but if we won, we might save them." In two or three months, by "showing the world that Germany had not beaten us," Britain could regain her prestige. "Even if we were beaten, we should be no worse off than we should be now to abandon the struggle," Churchill insisted, reinforcing his oratorical appeal. "Let us therefore avoid being dragged down the slippery slope with France. The whole of this manoeuvre was intended to get us so deeply involved in negotiations that we should be unable to turn back." They had gone too far already.

"The approach was not only futile, but involved us in deadly danger."[21]

The Prime Minister's rhetoric was interrupted by Chamberlain, who said that while he still believed "it would not serve any useful purpose," they should not give "a complete refusal" to Reynaud. He was in favour of going "a little further with it, in order to keep the French in a good temper." Halifax sensed that he had now found a powerful ally, and launched his own counterblast against the Prime Minister's intransigence.[22]

"I thought Winston talked the most frightful rot, also Greenwood," was how Halifax recorded the clash in his diary. "And after bearing it for some time I said exactly what I thought of them, adding that if that was really their view, and if it came to the point, our ways would separate." This implicit threat of resignation evidently took Churchill by surprise, and according to Halifax he "mellowed."[23]

The bitterness of the clash between Churchill and Halifax has been carefully toned down in the Cabinet minutes. Yet even the formal official account suggests how far the two were at odds over the issue of negotiations. The Foreign Secretary issued his challenge by declaring that they had "certain profound differences of points of view" that he wanted resolved. He felt the Prime Minister was deliberately distorting his position with the imputation that "we were suing for terms and following a line that would lead to disaster." Had not Churchill said the day before that "he would be thankful to get out of our present difficulties" and would agree to "territorial concessions" if the terms offered by the Germans did not affect Britain's independence and vital strength? This was very different from the position now taken by the Prime Minister, "that under no conditions would we contemplate any course except fighting to a finish."[24]

"If, however, it was possible to obtain a settlement which did not impair those conditions," Halifax declared that "he for his part, would not be able to accept the view now put forward by the Prime Minister." Two or three months might show whether Britain could stand up against the air attack. He was prepared to take that risk on if the nation's independence was at stake; if not, he believed it "right to accept an offer which would save the country from avoidable disaster."[25]

The Foreign Secretary had made his position clear. If the right terms were offered, he would strike a deal with Hitler. He had now challenged Churchill to say whether he was prepared to accept the principle that a deal which did not threaten Britain's independence would be in the national interest. The Prime Minister was in a trap. If he agreed with Halifax's position, it would start the slide to negotiations; if he rejected it, the Foreign Secretary would resign and precipitate a crisis that could be fatal for both Churchill and the nation.

Halifax had deliberately set himself on a collision course to define the parameters for the negotiation he now seemed to regard as inevitable. Churchill extricated himself from the trap as gracefully as he could by oiling the waters. He suggested they should try to settle the issue at hand rather than get involved in hypothetical situations and issues that were unlikely to arise.

"If Herr Hitler was prepared to make peace on the terms of the restoration of German colonies and the overlordship of central Europe, that was one thing," Churchill declared. "But it was quite unlikely that he would make any such offer." Chamberlain also intervened to cool the row by agreeing that it would be better to wait for concrete proposals before deciding on essentials. But Halifax would not be deflected. He persisted in pressing for an answer to the hypothetical question. If Hitler offered peace terms and the French government insisted that he should deal jointly with the Allies, "would the Prime Minister be prepared to discuss them"?

"No," said Churchill firmly. He "would not join France in asking for terms; but if he were told what the terms offered were, we would be prepared to consider them." It would be a mistake he argued, to take Hitler's bait by accepting an open invitation to discuss terms. On this principle the War Cabinet could agree. At this point Greenwood brought the discussion back to immediate objectives, reminding them they had to give an answer to the French. The Foreign Secretary again dug his heels in and said he was not willing to send a "flat refusal." Chamberlain was also doubtful about rejecting the French proposal outright. Churchill still did not want to sanction any approach to Mussolini other than the one already made, he believed ill-advisedly, by Roosevelt. Attlee, Greenwood and Sinclair were with him, so technically could have carried the decision. But he recognized that this would risk Cabinet unity, and he therefore decided to postpone a final resolution of the issue until Mussolini's response was known. Reynaud was to be cabled that it was an inappropriate moment for an Anglo-French approach that "would only confuse the issue and might well be resented by President Roosevelt, and was likely to create an impression of weakness."

The Prime Minister was alert to the dangers of sending peace feelers – even via Washington. This was underlined at the conclusion of the meeting when the Foreign Secretary circulated the latest cable from the British Ambassador in Washington, which reported the President's defeatist attitude and his concern over the fate of Britain's fleet. The value of his "bargaining counter" was confirmed, and Churchill declared that if Roosevelt thought he was doing them a favour by picking up the bits of the Empire, "It was as well that he should realize that there was another aspect to this question."[26]

Making it clear that Britain would fight on regardless of what happened to France was the way Churchill intended to bring that point home to the White House, and this was another reason for rejecting the appeal to Mussolini. But by the end of the meeting, little had been resolved on the fundamental issue. Churchill and his supporters were opposed, Halifax was in favour and Chamberlain was wavering between the two sides. The French could be stalled with an excuse, but the Prime Minister and Foreign Secretary had yet to find a way of resolving their differences over an issue that might yet bring the government down if they did not find a way to compromise.

"I can't work with Winston any longer," Halifax told Cadogan as the meeting wrapped up. "Nonsense," his Permanent Secretary said consolingly. "His rodomontades probably bore you as much as they do me, but don't do anything silly under stress of that." Immediately afterwards Halifax asked the Prime Minister to come with him into the garden for a talk.[27]

The only version of their conversation is Halifax's own diary account, which relates how he "repeated the same thing" and that "Winston" was "full of apologies and affection." Yet he was still confronted by Churchill's refusal to budge over the issue of negotiations. His frustration with the Prime Minister surfaced in his diary, noting how "it does drive me to despair when he works himself up into a passion of emotion when he ought to make his brain think and reason." Over tea in the Foreign Secretary's office that afternoon Cadogan counselled Halifax that he "hoped he really wouldn't give way to an annoyance to which we were all subject." Halifax promised to consult Chamberlain "before he did anything." This was some reassurance to the Permanent Secretary because, as he reflected, Halifax "wasn't one to take hasty decisions."[28]

The "affection" with which Churchill soothed Halifax in the garden of Number 10 succeeded in averting a government crisis at a potentially fatal moment. While both men recognized the need to bury the animosity that had flared up over the Italian negotiations, the Cabinet was now divided over a fateful decision. This was now hostage to differences of policy and of philosophical approach that were summed up in Halifax's complaint about Churchill's failure to bow to reason. The Prime Minister's "rodomontades" notwithstanding, he had put forward powerful arguments against falling into a negotiating trap which would fatally damage the image of national resolution he was trying to generate.

At the same time Churchill recognized that the most powerful argument he could marshal against negotiation was to get the

British Army back from Dunkirk. That afternoon he sent a telegram of encouragement and good wishes to General Gort "at this solemn moment." Offering helpful advice about using cannon "to kill tanks," he even urged sending a column to help the gallant defenders of Calais, unaware that the port had fallen the previous day. He also told Gort that he was sending a rallying message to King Leopold, calling for Belgian cooperation with the evacuation plan and "asking them to sacrifice themselves for us."[29]

The Belgian Army, however, had done all it could to help the British Expeditionary Force and was collapsing from the effort. At five that afternoon King Leopold, who had refused a last-minute offer of sanctuary from King George VI, summoned Admiral Keyes and asked him to warn London and General Gort that the military situation on their front was desperate. He announced that he had decided to ask the Germans for a cease-fire at midnight.

When the news reached Churchill, he immediately fired off a telegram to Keyes informing him that the Belgian government had "reassembled on foreign soil" to dissociate itself from the King's action. "By present decision the King is dividing the nation and delivering it into Hitler's protection," Churchill concluded sternly. "Please convey these considerations to the King, and impress upon him the disastrous consequences to the Allies and to Belgium of his present choice." But King Leopold had already told Keyes that his duty was to stay with his army and his people.[30]

Churchill reported the King's decision at an emergency meeting of the War Cabinet called at ten that evening to consider how to respond to Belgium's capitulation. Leopold's action was "certainly not heroic," according to the Prime Minister, but he said it "might well be the best that he could do for his country." Now they must "face the fact that it has the most serious consequences for the British Expeditionary Force." General Dill agreed that the collapse of Belgium would put Gort's army "in the most serious peril," since he had no troops to close the gap.[31]

The news that Calais had fallen had belatedly come from R.A.F. reconnaissance flights, which had confirmed that all fighting had ceased. The B.B.C. had broadcast the news of the Belgian surrender that evening, so the Minister of Information suggested that the public be made aware of the loss of Calais and the serious situation facing the British Expeditionary Force. Duff Cooper was worried that because the French press communiqués "still had a cheerful tone" the public were "quite unprepared for the shock of realization of the true position." While Churchill agreed that the Belgian armistice would have prepared the public for bad news, he was against "any detailed statement or attempt to assess the result of the battle until the situation had been further cleared up." He proposed to tell Parliament that the dangers facing Britain "had not been greatly increased by what has happened," while the means of meeting them had increased. He wanted the country to "take heart from the superior quality and morale of our Air Force which had been so clearly demonstrated."

Lord Halifax remained ominously silent at the meeting and made no comment in his diary on this extraordinary piece of wishful thinking. Earlier that day he had written that Churchill had been talking "rot," but that evening he must have wondered whether emotions had run away with the Prime Minister's brain. With the greater part of the British Army stranded at the mercy of the Germans on the other side of the Channel, the Belgians suing for peace and the French likely to do so at any moment, Halifax must have been astonished at Churchill's claim that Britain's means of fighting the Germans had actually improved. To state that the dangers had not increased seemed to be standing the logic of Britain's military balance sheet on its head. The Prime Minister knew as well as his Foreign Secretary that the war could not be won with emotional nostrums and wishful thinking about the United States.

At the end of that harrowing day Churchill retired with a whisky and soda. What Halifax consumed as a nightcap is not recorded. But Churchill's refusal to accept the reality of the military predicament confronting Britain can have given the Foreign Secretary precious little inducement to a sound night's sleep.[32]

DAY 7
"We Shall Fight It Out"
28 May

On Tuesday at 4 a.m. all resistance to the Germans by the Belgian Army ceased. The terms of the armistice personally negotiated by King Leopold with General von Bock stipulated that "German troops be allowed to proceed to the coast" and permitted "free passage to the coast." This opened the way for the Wehrmacht's effort to snap its steel pincers on Dunkirk, which began in earnest that morning. Belgian soldiers carrying white flags stood sullenly aside as troops of Bock's Sixth Army marched through Ypres heading for the port of Ostend twenty miles away. German air and ground forces were now moving at full tilt to seal off the Channel ports and lock off the enveloped British and French armies from any escape to the sea.[33]

Churchill and the War Cabinet in London could do little more than act as score-keepers in the deadly race to snatch the British Expeditionary Force from the disaster overtaking it across the

Channel. The first day's results were encouraging. At their 11 a.m. meeting that morning the War Cabinet learned that 11,400 men had arrived overnight at Dover and 2,500 were en route across the Channel from Dunkirk. A further 9,000 troops were sheltering from the Stuka bombing raids in the sand dunes or waiting to be rescued from the exposed Dunkirk beaches.

A heavy pall of smoke from the incessant waves of bombing attacks hung over Dunkirk that morning as five destroyers went alongside the jetties to take on a thousand men each. Added to the menace of the Luftwaffe were the fast torpedo boats of the German Navy, which that night had sunk a troop transport. Of the thousand men who embarked on it at Ostend, only thirty-three survivors had been picked up.

One of those who had made a safe overnight crossing of the Channel by Navy motor torpedo boat was Roger Keyes, who gave the War Cabinet a first-hand account of the valiant battle of the Belgian Army. He reported that Gort was in "good heart," but Keyes did not think he "rated very high the chances of extricating the B.E.F. from their dangerous situation."[34]

"No doubt history would criticize the King for having involved us and the French in Belgium's ruin," the Prime Minister predicted, but "it was not for us to pass judgement on him." Churchill's magnanimity contrasted with the vitriolic public denouncements of the French Prime Minister. That morning Reynaud had broadcast to the French people branding the Belgian surrender "an event without precedent in history." King Leopold was made the scapegoat; a decree was drawn up to deprive him of his membership of the Légion d'Honneur. History, however, was to vindicate the King to some degree – as Lieutenant-Colonel George Davy intimated to the War Cabinet that morning. The former British military liaison officer at Leopold's headquarters called for credit to be given to the Belgian Army in any public announcements. "The King had done all he could," Davy reported, "ever since it had become apparent that the British Expeditionary Force might have to fall back on the ports, to support its withdrawal."[35]

Churchill was less concerned with recriminations against the Belgians than with ensuring that Britain's armed forces bent every sinew to hold Dunkirk as Operation Dynamo went into full gear. His order that continuous fighter patrols be maintained over Dunkirk and three miles east and west of the beaches was made in spite of protests from the chief of Fighter Command, Air Marshal Dowding, who was "deeply concerned at the effect of the order on the air defence of Great Britain." The Chief of the Air Staff had also overruled Dowding, rejecting his claim that "our fighter defences are at cracking point." The R.A.F. was now Churchill's main hope not only for helping to save the B.E.F., but for denying the Germans

240

the air superiority over Britain that they would have to win before mounting an invasion attempt. That day's warning from military intelligence of a possible German raid on Scotland from Norway underscored the fact that direct attacks by landing forces would probably be Hitler's next move. Reconnaissance flights revealed that the alert was a false alarm, but invasion jitters hung over the meeting that morning as ministers reviewed the steps taken to deal with the Fifth Column and set up the Home Defence Executive. The shortage of destroyers, which would be crucial in thwarting seaborne landings, was growing more acute as losses mounted from German bomber attacks on Channel operations. Without discussion the War Cabinet took note of the First Lord of the Admiralty's decision to suspend all construction of battleships and aircraft carriers and to concentrate on building destroyers and escort craft.[36]

In the midst of gearing Britain up to continue the struggle against Germany, there was a note of relief for the Prime Minister when the Foreign Secretary reported that word had been received from the British Ambassador in Washington of Mussolini's "entirely negative response" to the President's appeal. The French had been informed, Halifax said, and the War Cabinet must now give Reynaud an answer on the question of the direct approach to Italy. Churchill put off the third round of what had now become a three-day wrangle over peace negotiations until a special meeting to be called that afternoon.[37]

On the day when, Churchill said, the "escape of the British Army hung in the balance," it was significant that the morning meeting of the War Cabinet concluded with what amounted to a pre-emptive move against Halifax and others who were considering a negotiated peace. The "shot across the bows" was delivered in the form of a strongly worded personal letter from the Prime Minister to go to all ministers and senior government officials. This "Strictly confidential" injunction, endorsed by the War Cabinet, stressed the need for maintaining "a high morale" while "not minimizing the gravity of events." It required the recipients to display "confidence in our ability and inflexible resolve to continue the war" until the German will had been broken. "No tolerance should be given to the idea that France will make a separate peace," Churchill warned, and his letter concluded: "whatever may happen on the Continent, we cannot doubt our duty, and we shall certainly use all our power to defend the Island, the Empire and our Cause."[38]

The Prime Minister's injunction "not to talk or look defeatist" might have been aimed directly at the Foreign Secretary's willingness to support French calls for the appeasement of Mussolini as a way of starting negotiations with Hitler. Hugh Dalton, the Minister of Economic Warfare, was not alone in his alarm at the "streaks of defeatism" he found appearing in ministerial reports. His concern was shared by the Labour and Liberal members of the administration, who warmly endorsed the sentiments expressed so unequivocally in the Prime Minister's letter.[39]

Churchill's announcement that he intended to make a statement that afternoon in the House of Commons was another sign that he was moving to head off any parliamentary move to call for a negotiated peace in the wake of the anticipated debacle at Dunkirk. He directed that the Minister of Information should give a brief summary of the grave military situation in France on the B.B.C. one o'clock news, because he wanted the public to know that the British Expeditionary Force was "fighting its way back to the coast under the protection of the Royal Air Force," as the Navy was embarking the troops. "It would be idle to try and forecast the success of this operation at this stage," Churchill reminded his colleagues, stressing that he wanted no defeatist talk and that he himself intended to put as positive a construction on the news as was prudent in his Commons statement on the impending rescue of the British Expeditionary Force.[40]

The initial stage of the Dunkirk evacuation depended on executing one of the most difficult of all military manoeuvres – a fighting retreat. Like emptying the British and French armies out of a sack under heavy external pressure, the operation required keeping up just enough resistance to stop the sides being pushed in as the troops were steadily withdrawn through the mouth. The mouth of the bag was a twenty-by-four-mile perimeter around the port of Dunkirk which had to be defended and held as the thirty-mile-long sack was rolled up in a carefully controlled fighting retreat. At the bottom of the sack was the French First Army headquarters at Lille, which had the trickiest manoeuvre to execute.

Plans had already been worked out for rolling up the bottom half of the Dunkirk sack when General Blanchard arrived at Gort's headquarters on Tuesday morning. The French commander, who had heard nothing about the British evacuation plans from his own High Command, remained under the impression that the Allied armies under his command would withdraw to a fortress redoubt based on Dunkirk. When Blanchard learned that morning for the first time that the British Army was already being evacuated by sea, he was aghast and protested that "the bridgehead would be held with no thought of retreat." He was still reeling when he was told by Gort that the Belgian surrender had made it impossible to prevent the Germans from breaking through the right flank at Ypres and joining up with the Panzer division that was already pushing in the left flank around Béthune. If the French forces in the Lille sector could not make a fighting withdrawal of more than fifteen miles that night, the German pincer movement would break through and trap most of the First Army in the bottom half of the Allied sack.[41]

Blanchard at first demanded a twenty-four-hour postponement, claiming that General Prioux's First Army was too tired to make such a move. Gort contended that delay would be fatal. He told Blanchard bluntly that the British would go ahead with their plan whether the French joined them or not. Later that afternoon Prioux changed his mind and issued orders for the movement of the northerly portion of his army that night. By then half of the French First Army was in the Lille pocket. When Rommel's 7th armoured division broke through next day to join up with von Bock's forces north of Armentières, they were trapped.

"When one is let down by one's relatives, the usual thing is to address an appeal to one's friends," Baudouin advised the French Prime Minister that Tuesday morning. He suggested that France swallow her pride and use the Belgian capitulation as the pretext for asking Britain to join in an urgent appeal for the armed intervention of the United States to save France. Reynaud sent for the British Ambassador and General Spears to sound them out on the idea. Sir Ronald Campbell said he would have to consult with London; Spears said he was "entirely unfavourable." Only the U.S. Senate, he reminded Reynaud, not the President, could declare war. "To ask for the impossible knowing it was impossible," Spears cautioned, "would give the impression we had given up hope." Reynaud, who was under the dangerous misapprehension that the capitulation of Belgium would cause a wave of public indignation in the United States, was clutching at straws. It would have a "very bad effect on British morale," Spears told him, when America did not declare war.[42]

The increasing desperation of the French Premier was also apparent when he broached what he called the "more important question of Italy." He complained he had still not received an answer to the questions he had put to the British War Cabinet on Sunday. For Reynaud the matter of treating with Mussolini was now "very, very urgent." Hopeless though it might seem after the rejection of Roosevelt's appeal, he still believed the attempt should be made to keep Italy out of the war by proposing a Franco-Italian conference. What he needed to know immediately was whether the British would be prepared to make concessions concerning Gibraltar and Suez.

The British Ambassador advised that it would be a waste of time to make a direct approach to Mussolini – and there was a real danger that it would encourage Hitler to believe the Allies were ready to sue for peace. He cautioned that nothing should be done until an answer was received from London. But Reynaud had to deal with Daladier and senior Foreign Ministry officials, who had already tried to bypass him to make a direct approach to Italy. A copy of the French Foreign Minister's appeal had been telegraphed to the French Ambassador in London to give to the Foreign Secretary. After Corbin saw Lord Halifax that morning he reported back confirming that Britain's Foreign Secretary had on Saturday independently sounded out the possibility of a direct approach through Bastianini. Halifax had told him that morning that when he received no reply he had asked Sir Percy Loraine in Rome to follow the matter up with the Italian Foreign Minister. "Ciano had replied that he had indeed received a cable from Bastianini on this subject," Charles-Roux wrote in his memoir, "but that this was now under the general embargo which Mussolini had placed on all discussions with the Allies."[43]

This French confirmation that the British Foreign Secretary had indeed made what amounted to an independent approach via Bastianini during his meetings of 25 May indicates how far Lord Halifax had gone in acting independently of Churchill and the War Cabinet, who had been stalling the French. As it happens, Ciano had told the British Ambassador in Rome that "in the circumstances it seemed useless for him to reply to Lord Halifax's overtures, even out of politeness." This is corroborated by Ciano's diary, which records that on 28 May he received the British Ambassador, who "complained about the interruption of the negotiations." Loraine had visibly paled when Ciano caught him off balance by stating that "all this was useless because we are on the brink of war." Recovering his composure, the British Ambassador declared "We shall answer war with war."[44]

When the French Ambassador arrived shortly afterwards that Tuesday afternoon, he was "the picture of distress," according to Ciano, when he was told there was no offer from France that would be acceptable. That evening the Italian Foreign Minister gave the German Ambassador a blow-by-blow account of the rejection of the American and Allied peace feelers. Ciano emphasized that they "were particularly interesting from the psychological point of view." He boasted how the French Ambassador, who promised that "the Italians could have all they wanted," was rebuffed with the declaration that "even if he served him up Tunis, Algiers, Corsica and Nice on a platter, he [Ciano] could only say no, because there was only one thing for Italy now and that was war." The British Ambassador had been "high and mighty," attempting to argue that "surely it was not necessary" for Mussolini to go to war to settle his disputes with the British and French. Ciano claimed that he had "profoundly impressed" Sir Percy by telling him that "settlement by force of arms was unavoidable." His statements to the British and French Ambassadors were "tantamount to a declaration of war," Ciano assured the German Ambassador, and he said the Duce was preparing a letter for the Führer that would name the day when he would join the struggle.[45]

The Italian Foreign Minister may have been right about the psychological significance of the Allied overtures to Mussolini, but his arrogant snubbing of the British and French Ambassadors put an end to any hopes Hitler may have had for exploiting the entrapment of the Allied armies at Dunkirk as a bargaining counter. By rejecting the French bribes and refusing even to acknowledge Lord Halifax's clear and direct overture, Mussolini had unwittingly come to Churchill's aid and torpedoed the British Foreign Secretary's efforts to use Italy to manoeuvre Britain into indirect negotiations with Hitler.

Churchill's defiant speech in the House of Commons that Tuesday afternoon sent a second torpedo blasting into the Foreign Secretary. Since it was delivered only an hour before the scheduled War Cabinet showdown over the Italian initiative, Churchill's uncompromising choice of words sent a strong "no-surrender" message to Lord Halifax and the other would-be appeasers in Parliament.

After paying tribute to the Belgian Army, which had "fought very bravely," the Prime Minister did not flinch from acknowledging that the effect of the defeat of Belgium on the British Expeditionary Force "adds appreciably to their grievous peril." He was encouraged by the reports that the troops were fighting their way back to Dunkirk "with the utmost discipline and tenacity," but he did not minimize the dangers that lay ahead. "The House should prepare itself for hard and heavy tidings," he said, issuing a solemn assurance of his resolve not to give up the struggle whatever the outcome in France.[46]

"I have only to add that nothing which may happen in this battle can in any way relieve us of our duty to defend the world cause to which we have vowed ourselves," Churchill declared, "nor should it destroy our confidence in our power to make our way, as on former occasions in our history, through disaster and through grief to the ultimate defeat of our enemies." His statement of dignified defiance, in which he declared his resolve that Britain would fight on whatever the outcome in France, brought immediate speeches of support and praise. A Labour member claimed that they had "not yet touched the fringe of the resolution of this country." The Chief Liberal Whip declared that Churchill had given expression to "not only the feeling of the whole House but the feeling of the nation."[47]

Buttressed by this reception in the House of Commons, Churchill had reason to be confident that he had consolidated his position by the time the War Cabinet reconvened at 4 p.m. In renewing his call for a joint Anglo-French approach to Italy, the Foreign Secretary

245

now found he was batting on a much more slippery pitch than the previous day, because the Prime Minister's prediction that Mussolini would reject Roosevelt's offer of mediation had just been confirmed by the British Ambassador in Rome.

What the Foreign Secretary did not yet know, however, was that his own direct soundings through Bastianini had also been turned down. To support his contention that it was still not too late for direct negotiation, Halifax reported that Vansittart had met once more with the Italian Embassy official. The message had been relayed back that a further approach was not "hopeless" if the British offered concrete concessions to give a "clear indication that we should like to see mediation by Italy." Churchill, taking a firmer line than during the previous discussions, insisted that the French were trying to get Mussolini to act as an intermediary to negotiate with Hitler. He said he was "determined not to get into this position" because it would be the "the slippery slope" of negotiations leading to humiliation. The situation would be "entirely different when Germany had made an unsuccessful attempt to invade."[48]

Chamberlain at first swung back and forth between agreeing with the Foreign Secretary's wish to approach Italy so as to stave off defeat for the French and Churchill's fear that any negotiating move would weaken the national resolve to fight on if France fell. On the one hand, he said that concessions to Italy of Gibraltar and Malta would have no value if they left Britain still at war with Germany. On the other, the former appeaser argued that Mussolini's rebuff to Roosevelt did not necessarily mean he would reject a direct offer by the French if it was tempting enough. But he said he was inclined to agree with the Prime Minister that Reynaud's aim was to "try and turn those conversations into a peace Conference."

Seeing that the War Cabinet were moving decisively against an immediate appeal to Italy, the Foreign Secretary tried to get his colleagues to accept the principle that it might be necessary to negotiate with Hitler at some future date by addressing "the large issues involved." In a hypothetical situation – one which he was careful to characterize as unlikely – Halifax asked what their reaction should be if Mussolini set himself up as a "mediator" who was able to "produce terms which would not affect our independence." Surely, he argued, they would get better terms "before France went out of the war and our aircraft factories were bombed, than we might get in three months time." But the Foreign Secretary found no support among those who were opposed in principle for the hypothetical agreement he was searching for. Churchill reiterated his warning that simply getting into negotiations was a trap. Once they had been lured to the conference table they could not, as Halifax repeatedly asserted, walk away if the terms were not acceptable, because "all the forces of resolution which were now at our disposal would have vanished." This was an argument whose merits appeared to move Chamberlain decisively in support of the Prime Minister. It was so persuasive, he said, that it overcame his earlier inclination to do everything possible to accommodate the French.[49]

"Mediation in the presence of a great disaster," at a time when it appeared Britain had no resources left, Chamberlain said, "could only have the most unfortunate results." But he believed that if the British could hold out they would be able to get better terms. "The present was not the time," he finally declared, "at which advances should be made to Signor Mussolini." Chamberlain's view met with concurrence around the table; only the Foreign Secretary continued to have reservations.

Wrapping himself once more in the French cloak, Halifax then raised Reynaud's latest idea of appealing to Roosevelt to come into the war. Attlee said dismissively that the French Prime Minister was "too much inclined to hawk around appeals." He saw it as just "another attempt to run out." Churchill believed that Reynaud wanted to get out of the war, but did not want to break France's treaty obligation. If Mussolini came in as mediator he would not only "take his whack," but it was "impossible to imagine that Herr Hitler would be so foolish as to let us continue our re-armament." By continuing to resist, Britain could continue to inflict damage on Germany.

"A time might come when we felt that we had to put an end to the struggle," Churchill said, "but the terms would not be more mortal than those offered to us now." Halifax was still unconvinced by the argument. What was there in the French suggestion of "trying out the possibilities of mediation that the Prime Minister felt was so wrong"?

With the argument about to circle back on itself and become as rancorous as on the previous day, Chamberlain intervened with a compromise formula that would get the Foreign Secretary off the hook. In Chamberlain's view it was "clear to the world that we were in a tight corner," so they had nothing to lose by declaring openly that they "would fight to the end to preserve our independence but were ready to consider decent terms if such were offered to us." To general agreement, he argued that they should recognize that the alternative to fighting on "involved a considerable gamble."

"Those nations which went down fighting rose again, but those which surrendered tamely were finished," Churchill declared. Either option facing Britain was attended by great danger, said Attlee; continuing to resist was a gamble too, but "he did not feel that this was a time for ultimate capitulation." The Prime Minister added that he thought the chances of being offered decent terms were "a thousand to one." Halifax objected. He did not see how the course he proposed "could even be remotely described as ultimate capitulation." Attlee repeated that any hint of willingness to negotiate would critically harm civilian morale. "So far as the industrial centres of the country were concerned," Greenwood chipped in, "anything like weakening of the Government was a disaster."

It was at this point that Chamberlain put his weight decisively behind the majority. Their duty, he said, was "to look at the situation realistically." While he might agree in principle with Halifax that if they could get terms now that did not threaten British independence "we should be right to consider such terms," realistically they must conclude that "an approach to Italy was useless at the present time." Chamberlain's diary shows that he regarded Reynaud's proposed offer as "derisory" and "inopportune," but was unwilling to abandon Halifax completely in the War Cabinet. In a gesture intended to appease the Foreign Secretary, he suggested that it "might be that we should take a different view in a short time, possibly a week."

"We had a rather strong discussion, but finally agreed on a reply drafted by me," Chamberlain wrote, taking credit for the compromise solution to the impasse. Halifax found himself out-manoeuvred but not defeated yet on the principle that negotiations might still be necessary. So, after three days of bitter wrangling, the War Cabinet reached a consensus that Tuesday afternoon in which they agreed to inform the French that it was the wrong time to negotiate, "without rejecting their idea altogether."[50]

Once the dispute had been temporarily patched up, the Prime Minister had less difficulty in persuading his colleagues that it would be premature to make an appeal to Roosevelt until they knew the outcome of Operation Dynamo at Dunkirk. Churchill also rejected Halifax's suggestion that he should make a broadcast to the Empire that would be relayed to the United States. At 6.15 p.m., the Cabinet adjourned for three quarters of an hour to allow the Foreign Secretary to draft a reply for the French, and the Prime Minister moved to consolidate his position when the twenty-five ministers who were not members of the Cabinet packed themselves into his small office.

The tension in the Prime Minister's Room that Tuesday evening was highly charged. Through the mullions of the Gothic windows, the sight of anti-aircraft balloons wallowing like herds of silver elephants over the London skyline was a direct reminder that the capital was girding itself for the anticipated assault by the Luftwaffe. With a calm authority Churchill reported on the extreme urgency of Britain's military situation. He gave a full and frank account of the chapter of military setbacks that had brought the Allied forces to the disaster confronting the British Army at Dunkirk.

The French Army, the Prime Minister explained, had been "hypnotized by the Maginot Line" and stunned into paralysis and defeatism by the force of the German breakthrough at Sedan. He gave graphic accounts of his trips to Paris and his repeated effort to rally the French. Now there was a "grave danger" that the British Army would be surrounded before it could fight its way out to Dunkirk.[51]

"We should certainly be able to get 50,000 away," Churchill announced, but it was impossible to tell. "If we could get 100,000 away that would be a magnificent performance," he said, giving a vivid picture of the aerial battles going on over the Dunkirk beachhead. "It was clear that we had killed off most of the best Nazi pilots," he said, claiming the R.A.F. fighters were "clawing down" the Luftwaffe at rates of "3:1, to 4:1, and lately 5:1." There could be no disguising the fact that they might still meet with "the greatest British military defeat for many centuries," and the country had to be prepared for setbacks and "other events of great gravity in Europe." There was, he intimated, the probability of a French collapse. Disastrous though this might seem, Churchill suggested that it might be "easier to defend this island alone," and they could count on "an immense wave of feeling" which might even bring the United States into the war. All this was speculative, the Prime Minister declared. What they had to do was to prepare themselves against the reality of a German invasion. They could rely on their strong navy, mines, air defences and "good troops," reinforced by soldiers from the Dominions and British garrisons recalled from overseas. Stocks of food and oil were ample, and aircraft production was rising.

"It was idle to think that if we tried to make peace now we should get better terms from the Germans than if we fought it out," Churchill declared. Rehearsing many of the arguments he had used in the War Cabinet, he predicted that negotiating peace with Germany would lead to Hitler stripping Britain of her fleet to make her a "slave state" under a puppet like Mosley. The country deserved better; they had "immense reserves and advantages" and he believed they must continue the struggle.

"We shall go on and we shall fight it out, here or elsewhere, and if the long story is to end, it is better it should end, not through surrender, but only when we are rolling senseless on the ground," the Prime Minister concluded. His ringing peroration brought a loud chorus of approval from around the table.

"No one expressed the faintest flicker of dissent," according to Dalton. There was further approval when Churchill declared that

249

"mere bombing" would not cause the government to evacuate London. Noting that neither "Old Umbrella" nor any other members of the War Cabinet were present, the Minister of Economic Warfare assumed that Chamberlain had "wanted to run very early" and that was why the Prime Minister needed their support. As they rose to leave, Dalton patted the shorter Churchill on the shoulder, telling him he ought to get the Low cartoon that showed them all rolling up their sleeves. "Yes, that was a good one, wasn't it?" the Prime Minister said with a grin. "He is a darling," Dalton noted admiringly in his diary.[52]

"There is no doubt that had I at this juncture faltered at all in the leading of the nation, I should have been hurled out of office," Churchill was to write of the spontaneous response of the ministers to his exhortation. "I was sure that every Minister was ready to be killed quite soon, and have all his family and possessions destroyed, rather than give in." His appeal for Britain to fight on had received unanimous support, fortifying his belief that he would now be able to carry the Commons in any fight to oppose peace negotiations. But despite his assertion, made a decade later, about "a white glow, overpowering, sublime," he still had to stoke the dying embers of the Foreign Secretary's furnace.[53]

After the adjournment, Churchill glowed with renewed vigour when he assured the War Cabinet that the junior ministers had "not expressed alarm at the situation in France, but had expressed the greatest satisfaction when he told them that there was no chance of our giving up the struggle." He told his colleagues that he had never before heard such a gathering of politicians express themselves "so emphatically." To drive home the corrosive impact that defeatism was having on the French government, he read out General Spears's two alarming reports before the War Cabinet approved, without further discussion, the draft of the telegram he sent to Paris rejecting any further approach to Mussolini.

Churchill had not won an outright victory. Chamberlain's compromise only ruled out further peace feelers pending the outcome of the Dunkirk evacuation. The cable dispatched to Reynaud specifically stated that, "without excluding the possibility of an approach to Signor Mussolini at some time," the British War Cabinet did not believe that "this would be the right moment." The minutes also reveal that the Foreign Secretary persisted in trying to open the path for negotiations by backing the French appeal to President Roosevelt to intercede with Hitler. The Prime Minister rejected any such move.[54]

"If we made a bold stand against Germany, that would command admiration and respect," Churchill reminded Halifax. "But a grovelling appeal, if made now, would have the worst possible effect." A draft dispatch had been submitted by Halifax in anticipation that the "complete collapse" of France would prompt Hitler, "in conjunction with Mussolini," to offer peace terms to Britain as well. The Foreign Secretary therefore wanted the Prime Minister to suggest to Roosevelt that he might "feel able to play a decisive part" by informing Hitler "at the chosen moment" that "terms that were intended to destroy the independence of Great Britain or France would at once touch the vital interests of the United States."[55]

This draft telegram is further evidence that the Foreign Secretary was committed to "better terms, not . . . victory" in his assiduous efforts to lay the groundwork for the negotiated settlement he believed inevitable if France capitulated. It is not surprising to find that, ten months after drafting this cable, Halifax was anxiously trying to retrieve it from Washington, where he had been sent as ambassador in January 1941. His former private secretary was given the delicate task of retrieving the potentially embarrassing document. The Foreign Office copy had already been removed from the files so Nicholas Lawford had to ask the Prime Minister's office for his former master's grovelling appeal for "American action in the event of Hitler trying to impose peace terms on us after the Fall of France" by explaining that it had been drafted "at a bad time in June."[56]

Halifax's "grovelling" appeal is further evidence that defeatism motivated his backstairs manoeuvring with the Italian Ambassador and his vigorous three-day campaign to persuade the War Cabinet to agree that if Britain's independence was not threatened a negotiated settlement would be preferable to fighting on against Germany. Halifax had evidently sounded out the American Ambassador along these lines, because Kennedy in his 24 May report informed Washington that the Foreign Secretary was "definitely of the opinion that if anybody is able to save a debacle on the part of the Allies if it arrives at that point it is the President."[57]

Chamberlain too had come to the painful conclusion that if France fell, Britain would be "fighting only for better terms, not victory." Although he was more circumspect than the Foreign Secretary in Cabinet, his diary reveals that he had decided that "if the French collapsed our only chance for escaping destruction would be if Roosevelt appealed for an armistice." Since both Chamberlain and Halifax were anticipating the necessity of eventual negotiation with Hitler, this explains why Churchill had faced such an uphill fight in more than eight hours of back-and-forth argument in the War Cabinet. It was a reflection on the relative weakness of his authority as Prime Minister that although he commanded the majority of votes and the loyalty of the junior ministers, he dared not ride rough-shod over the two most powerful members of his government. It also underlines the significance of his summoning Lloyd George that Tuesday to suggest he take a position in the

War Cabinet "subject to the approval of Neville Chamberlain." He hoped to bolster his authority and at the same time remove the potential "prime-minister-in-waiting" from becoming the focus of the parliamentary group who wanted to strike a deal with Hitler. That the canny Lloyd George found an excuse to decline the offer was further indication that he was still anticipating that his turn would come when Churchill's coalition crumbled.[58]

While Churchill could have carried the majority of the government on his opposition to negotiations, forcing the issue to a vote might have precipitated Halifax's threatened resignation. The urge to appease died hard among those ministers who had made it their article of faith for so many years. History had shown that neither Hitler nor Mussolini could be trusted, but the record shows how Churchill had to battle through that long crisis-filled weekend to forestall Halifax's attempt to resurrect the discredited policies. At the same time he knew that if he went over the heads of the Foreign Secretary and Lord President, it might have triggered a rancorous parliamentary showdown. If this had erupted during the critical days of the Dunkirk evacuation, it must be doubted whether even Churchill's rhetoric or the support of the opposition parties could have sustained him if the Conservatives in Parliament had turned against his leadership. Among the leading Tories who regarded Churchill as a dangerous usurper was Halifax's deputy Butler. He was one of those suspected of encouraging anti-Churchill opposition with rumours of "a definite plot afoot to oust Halifax and all the gentlemen of England, from the government, and even from the House of Commons."[59]

If there had been a showdown with Halifax, Chamberlain, whose objections to negotiating a compromise settlement appear to have been more of timing than principle, might well have decided that his duty was to rally the Tory faithful behind Halifax in order to save the nation and the Empire. While Churchill and the Labour leaders would have argued that it was treachery even to consider peace feelers while Britain was still unconquered and her air force and navy still had the sinews and muscle to fight, Halifax and Butler had for months been sending and receiving peace feelers. Shaken by the French collapse, for the Foreign Secretary the overwhelming negatives of the military equation dictated negotiating with Hitler while Britain and her Empire were still intact. He wanted to find out what terms Hitler would offer, arguing that they would be less harsh than if they tried to hold out, only to have their towns and factories pounded into rubble by the Luftwaffe. Logic and prudence dictated that the Allies should at least inquire what terms Hitler would offer.

This appears to have accorded with Lord Halifax's eighteenth-century view of war when European states dispatched armies to do fight on the chessboard of conflicting national ambitions and interests. Once the great set-piece battle was over, the diplomats assembled for a peace congress in Vienna, Paris or Berlin, to parcel out territory and colonial possessions according to a rationally agreed formula.

Yet by 1940 it was no longer true to say, as Churchill had in World War I of Admiral Sir John Jellicoe's Grand Fleet, that a commander could "lose the war in an afternoon." The fate that had so swiftly overtaken the French Army because its battle-plan was pinned to the flawed Maginot Line strategy was without doubt a great military disaster. But it need not have been a fatal one for France. Had General Gamelin rallied his reserves and massed his tanks to counterattack in time, the German Panzer thrust could have been severed and the Allied armies in northern France saved from the catastrophe now facing them. Confronting a military catastrophe on such an epic scale, Lord Halifax and General Weygand, because they viewed the struggle in a Napoleonic context, were both arguing that the struggle against Hitler was all but lost and a gentlemanly deal could be struck with Hitler before their trapped armies were annihilated.

Churchill, however, was determined to capitalize on the disaster by harnessing national anger and collective resolve to continue the fight whatever the outcome in France. He did not believe that Britain – or France either, for that matter – should countenance capitulating after a single military defeat. As long as there was homeland territory to be defended, bombs to be dropped, shells to be lobbed and soldiers and civilians to fight, he was determined Britain would never surrender. Time and again in his rousing speeches Churchill would remind the nation that the Germans were suffering casualties too and would be made to pay a terrible price if they attempted to invade Britain's beaches, villages and hills.

Churchill was not a compromiser by experience or by inclination. When Halifax – and Weygand – argued the logical case that there was little point in continuing to sacrifice lives and treasure because the Allies, collectively and individually, lacked the arms and resources to defeat Nazi Germany, they were making a fundamental miscalculation about Hitler's war machine. By instinct rather than logic, Churchill refused to accept the assumption that Germany was now unbeatable. He was to be vindicated when "total war" proved that, as a strategic formula rather than tactical concept, Blitzkrieg warfare was a flawed weapon. It was a strategy that Hitler and his generals had devised for winning European victory on the cheap, with a series of lightning campaigns that did not require the full economic and military mobilization of the German economy for total war. What Churchill foresaw was that neither Hitler nor Germany would be able to sustain the easy victories once the struggle became a global slogging match.

It was this conviction that drove Churchill to fight on alone, however unequal the struggle, inspired by the belief that sooner or later the United States would be obliged to join the struggle against totalitarianism rather than see her own cherished democracy challenged. What Halifax had not grasped – but Churchill and Hitler had – was that the "total war" was governed by less than gentlemanly rules and fought by more abstract forces. Battles were no longer decided on some corner of a foreign field in an afternoon, but had become campaigns lasting for months and years, reaching across continents and oceans, in the skies and in the factories of the homeland where non-combatant citizens threatened by enemy bombers had to be enlisted like troops into the front lines of the production battle. In total war, mobilization and motivation of the civilian population were going to prove as decisive a factor as the brigades of tanks and squadrons of aircraft on the military balance sheet.

In berating Churchill's emotional approach to war, Halifax, who himself acknowledged his inability to tap the hidden national springs of determination, showed that he did not possess, or understand, the essential qualities of a twentieth-century warlord. In what was to become the supreme struggle for the minds as well as the lives and loyalties of whole nations, the charisma of a Churchill or a Hitler was as vital to deciding the outcome as the tactical ability of generals or the bravery of front-line troops.

Yet to sustain Britain's war on the battlefronts, Churchill knew he had first to win the fight against the defeatists in his own Cabinet and party. Although he emerged the winner of the first round, he had failed to score a knock-out victory. He knew that Chamberlain had sided with him over the futility of immediate negotiations, but had made it clear that he did not disagree with the Foreign Secretary's contention that it might soon be in the national interest to make peace with Hitler on terms that did not threaten Britain's independence. But for the time being Chamberlain had accepted Churchill's argument that Hitler was most unlikely to offer anything approaching acceptable terms on the eve of his military triumph in France. But his support might evaporate if the military situation worsened and Germany offered generous terms.

The record shows that Churchill was wrong. Hitler was even then already telling his conquering generals that he had no intention of imposing a Carthaginian peace on Britain. The evidence now suggests that Halifax was correct in his argument that Germany was prepared to offer terms that did not threaten British independence. From what is now known of Hitler's diplomatic initiatives in the week leading up to Dunkirk, it becomes chillingly apparent that during the three critical days that weekend, the British War Cabinet teetered on the brink of the slope that could have led to a deal being

254

struck with Germany. If Mussolini had not been so blind to the prize that the British and French were holding out to him, the diplomatic stage was set as Hitler appears to have intended when he issued the Halt Order that checked the Panzer divisions from crushing the surrounded Allied armies.

Lord Halifax was dangerously close to the truth when he argued that the Führer's diplomatic and military equation could be satisfied if Britain retained her independence and recognized his hegemony over the Continent. Making Germany a bulwark against the incursion of Communism into Europe even had a certain strategic appeal for Halifax, as it did for many Tories and City bankers. With the military disaster of Dunkirk hanging over them, and pressured to save the French from a knockout blow from Mussolini, Churchill saw only too clearly the dangers of the "slippery slope" of peace negotiations. Once embarked upon, the Allied peace feelers, however tentative, would reinforce the appeasing inclinations of the Foreign Secretary and sap the collective resolve of government, parliament and nation that Churchill had been striving for. The reports from Paris showed how quickly defeatism was draining France's collective will to sustain the fight.

Yet even if Churchill had not yet won the battle against the defeatists in his government, 28 May 1940 marked a critical victory in the political struggle for Britain's survival. Blocking the Anglo-French démarche with Italy checked the British government as the Foreign Secretary was trying to grease the slipway to the compromise peace which Hitler wanted – and which both Churchill and Roosevelt feared would be disastrous for the cause of democracy.

The French Premier, unlike the British Prime Minister, was unable to hold the brakes on the powerful members of his Cabinet who argued with the same logic as Lord Halifax for a compromise peace. It is now evident how the fate that overwhelmed the government in France in the next two weeks might well have overtaken the British. The records leave little doubt that, but for Churchill, World War II would have ended during the first half of June 1940, setting the whole course of global history on a different and more sinister course.

Chapter 11

"A Certain Eventuality"

"Companions in Misfortune"
29 May–2 June

"Our success must depend on our unity, then on our courage and endurance," Churchill urged the French Prime Minister. His telegram rejecting any Anglo-French appeal to Mussolini reached Paris in the early hours of 29 May. Reynaud was told that "neither we nor you would be prepared to give up our independence without fighting for it to the end." This "very fine message" from Churchill strengthened Reynaud's convictions, but not for long. The following evening Foreign Minister Daladier handed the Italian Ambassador a diplomatic note formally proposing that "negotiations should begin in the near future." Rome remained deliberately deaf to the approach as rumours of Mussolini's intention to attack multiplied, despite a second French appeal through the Vatican.[1]

Pressure mounted on the embattled Reynaud. That Wednesday morning General Weygand gave him a memorandum calling for the British government to send "two or three divisions." More tanks, anti-aircraft guns and fighter aircraft were needed to reinforce the French Army reserves that were massing along the Aisne and Somme to defend Paris. Churchill was to be warned that "a moment might come after which France would find herself, against her will, unable to put up a fight which would be of any military use in the protection of her soil." The memorandum, endorsed by Marshal Pétain, advised that in those circumstances an armistice would have to be solicited. Reluctant to risk "a rupture" with his military chief, Reynaud passed the demand for additional forces to the British Ambassador. At the same time he directed Weygand to consider plans for "a national redoubt" in the Breton peninsula.[2]

In London there was guarded optimism at the 29 May meeting of the War Cabinet. Churchill announced that Narvik had finally been occupied at 10 p.m. the previous evening. The British and French divisions in Norway could now be evacuated and transferred to France. During Wednesday the number of troops rescued from Dunkirk passed the 40,000 mark and the evacuation was progressing "at the rate of about 2,000 an hour." Churchill's confidence was rising that much of the army could be snatched from Dunkirk. It made him "theatrically bulldoggish," according to Cadogan, when it came to issuing orders to General Gort. In such a "desperate and distressing" predicament, he declared, the B.E.F. commander "should not be offered the difficult choice between resistance and capitulation" but should fight to the end to get every last man off the beaches. The Foreign Secretary countered that it "would not be dishonourable to relinquish the struggle in order to save a handful of men from massacres." The orders finally issued to Gort that evening made him "the sole judge of when it was impossible to inflict further damage upon the enemy."[3]

The Prime Minister told the War Cabinet that he had rejected Lord Lothian's suggestion for leasing rights to bases in Newfoundland and the British West Indies as a gesture to the United States. He wanted no empty concessions for American favours, dismissing as "fantastic" the French Ambassador's proposal that Roosevelt should be asked to send the U.S. Atlantic Fleet to the Mediterranean. Lothian was to be instructed that "a definite assurance of assistance should be a prerequisite of any concessions." Still smarting from Roosevelt's rejection of his plea for destroyers, the Prime Minister laid down that the subject "should not be broached to the President" at the present time.[4]

Churchill's belief that the British fleet was his strongest bargaining counter was made very clear to Hugh Keenleyside that morning during his ninety-minute meeting with Roosevelt. The purpose of this third visit by the Canadian envoy to the White House was to discover how far Roosevelt wanted his Prime Minister to go in "promising U.S. cooperation after Britain saves the fleet while sacrificing its own independence." The President, who was certain that France would have to capitulate within the week, was asked what steps he could take to save Britain. "Even limited aid now will have a very great value," Keenleyside told Roosevelt and Hull, reminding them that "one plane today would be worth ten planes in two months."[5]

American public opinion, the President declared, was "not yet ready" for the level of aid that Churchill and Mackenzie King were asking for. This he saw as another reason why he could not bring pressure to bear on Churchill to reject any consideration of a "soft peace" and send the fleet to sanctuary across the Atlantic. "If you don't help us at once we will let the Germans have the Fleet and you can go to Hell" was the reaction he would get from the British. While Roosevelt expressed sympathy with Churchill's position, he said it would not be "very helpful" because Britain's "bargaining proposals" could not be met. "To be effective this argument must come from Canada," the President told Keenleyside, emphasizing "as representative of Canadian opinion."[6]

"'Keep the Fleet from the Germans,' thus 'Save the Empire' and 'Win the War'" was the message the President wanted Mackenzie King to relay to the British Prime Minister "at once." He said that a similar appeal was being put to France. But if the Germans took "any unusual or particularly vicious action" against Britain after it had laid down its arms and sent the fleet to the United States, Roosevelt promised that "public opinion in America would demand immediate intervention" and participation in the blockade. This he believed would "bring ultimate victory to the Allies." It was "the only plan that can save democratic civilization – unless the Allies can hold the Germans on the western front throughout the present summer."

When Keenleyside communicated the President's grim injunction to Mackenzie King in Ottawa the next day the Canadian Prime Minister was worried about how to meet the President's wishes and at the same time "have the message appear to be from myself rather than from him." He failed to reconcile his dilemma, and two days later, on 31 May, he cabled to Churchill a summary of Roosevelt's position as it had been set out in Keenleyside's report.[7]

The President's pessimistic view of Britain's chances of surviving a French military collapse reflected the bleak assessment of the U.S military and the State Department. Confirmation of this came that day from the Chairman of the Anglo-French Purchasing Board in Washington. After a meeting with the Treasury Secretary, a staunch supporter of the Allies, Arthur Purvis cabled that Morgenthau had warned him that the President had decided he could not obtain Congressional approval for selling equipment from U.S. Navy and Army stocks. Furthermore it would be "useless and dangerous" for Churchill to "attempt the impossible" by pressing the issue with Roosevelt. The only crumb of comfort that Purvis was able to report was that General George Marshall, the U.S. Army Chief of Staff, was "sympathetic to the Allied cause," and was searching for a way to supply equipment to the Allies "within the existing law." Next day Purvis cabled that as far as munitions were concerned, Marshall was "prepared to stretch a point." By declaring them "surplus" to U.S. army requirements he would make immediately available for Allied purchase 100 million rounds of ammunition, 500,000 Lee-Enfield rifles, 10,000 Browning machine-guns and 500 field guns.[8]

This was very welcome news for the War Cabinet, faced as they were with rearming the troops being rescued from Dunkirk. Over a hundred thousand had arrived back in Britain by 30 May, but only two thirds of them brought back their weapons. Over a thousand field guns and all heavy guns and mechanical transport were abandoned on the beaches. That afternoon General Gort was instructed that once his forces were reduced to the equivalent of three divisions he was to transfer his authority to a corps commander and return to England, since "it would be a needless triumph to the enemy to capture you when only a small force remained under your orders."[9]

Chronically short of guns and heavy equipment though the British Army was, Churchill had cabled the French promising that Britain would "build up a new B.E.F." with equipment sufficient for five divisions, to include Australians and Canadians, "for reinforcement of our troops in France." Reynaud had appealed for three divisions immediately, so the telegram gave him "neither satisfaction nor solace," even though General Spears conveyed the Prime Minister's assurances of Britain's "inflexible resolve to continue" *whatever* the outcome for France.[10]

Demonstrative proof of the Prime Minister's resolution are the slashes of bright red ink across the Australian High Commissioner's report calling for the United States to back an international conference "to formulate a peace settlement." Churchill had struck out Stanley Bruce's offending paragraphs with a very large "No" and scrawled "Rot" against his conclusion that to save unnecessary "further shedding of blood and the continuance of hideous suffering," Roosevelt should call on the belligerents to "cease the struggle."[11]

Churchill had that day also received Lloyd George's formal rejection of the invitation to join his administration as Minister of Food. He said he could not serve in the same Cabinet as Chamberlain and Halifax, whom he regarded as the two "architects of this catastrophe." If Churchill had suspicions that the former prime minister was really holding himself aloof from the government in order to await the call to supreme leadership, he was careful to conceal them. He sent Lloyd George a friendly letter regretting his decision and promising "to keep in personal contact, so that I may acquaint you with the situation as it deepens."[12]

Just how deep the crisis might become the Prime Minister revealed to the meeting of the War Cabinet that evening when he instructed the Chiefs of Staff that they should "not hesitate to contaminate our beaches with gas if this was to our advantage" in repelling a German invasion. The Prime Minister's immediate concern was the French: their High Command had not yet given specific orders for the evacuation of their troops at Dunkirk, and Daladier was reported to be making an independent appeal to Italy. The British Ambassador in Paris acidly commented that Reynaud was "hardly up to the Herculean task of galvanizing his rather flabby team." Churchill decided that he must fly to Paris next day to do the galvanizing himself.[13]

Later that Thursday evening the Defence Committee received news that 860 vessels were now involved in the Dunkirk operation and that 4,000 men had been embarked the previous hour. Once more Churchill laid down the "urgent necessity of getting off more French troops," in order to avoid "irreparable harm to the relations between ourselves and the Allies." The German High Command had only just begun to appreciate the true scale of the British rescue operation. "Le Débâcle" was how the "disintegration of the bottled-up enemy forces" at Dunkirk was reported to General Halder at O.K.H. that evening. "Some of the British units in there are still fighting stubbornly and with determination, others are streaming back to the coast and try to get across the sea in anything that floats." It was von Brauchitsch who feared that Dunkirk was turning into a fiasco for the German army. He had angrily protested at his morning conference with the Führer that the British were escaping in large numbers because of the "blunders forced upon us by O.K.W." in holding back the tanks, which had cost two vital days in sealing off the pocket. "Worse," the Army Chief declared, "the bad weather has grounded our Air Force and now we must stand by and watch how countless thousands of the enemy are getting away to England right under our noses."[14]

Some 150,000 Allied troops had reached England by 12.30 p.m. on Friday, when Churchill's plane touched down at Villacoublay airport. The Flamingo carrying the Prime Minister, together with Attlee, Dill and Ismay, escorted by a posse of Hurricanes, had been forced to make a wide detour to the south of Paris to avoid German air patrols. When the Prime Minister stepped out of his plane "fresh as a daisy," Spears observed how danger and the evocation of battle "acted as a tonic and stimulant to Winston Churchill."[15]

After lunch with Ambassador Campbell at the British Embassy, the Prime Minister was driven to the Ministry of War, where Reynaud and Pétain were waiting with Weygand and Darlan to begin the Supreme War Council. After Churchill had given him the latest Dunkirk figures, Reynaud carped over the fact that only 15,000 French soldiers had been evacuated so far. This glaring disparity in numbers, he was afraid, "might entail grave consequences in the political field."[16]

"We are companions in misfortune," the British Prime Minister responded; "there is nothing to be gained from recriminations over our common miseries." The French commanders, he explained, had yet to give their troops evacuation orders, but he promised that during the remaining forty-eight hours of the operation the Allied forces would be taken off the beaches "on equal terms between the British and French – '*bras dessus bras dessous*'." Reynaud would later write that it was with "tears in his eyes" that Churchill declared that, despite their previously agreed plan for four French divisions to act as the Dunkirk rear guard, he "did not wish to see French troops bear new sacrifices." Orders would therefore be given that British troops "as far as was possible" would hold the rear of the beach perimeter.[17]

The Prime Minister confidently assured the Supreme War Council that the decision to begin the evacuation of Norway on 2 June, would release a further 16,000 troops to join the battle for France. Reynaud "begged" that the 200,000 British soldiers saved from Dunkirk should also be immediately sent back to France. He reiterated Weygand's demands for additional British tanks, guns and fighter aircraft.

Churchill responded to these impossible demands with encouraging general statements rather than specific promises. Immediate commitments, he said, "would of necessity be small." He explained that if Britain did not keep sufficient forces to resist a German invasion attempt "all would be lost." Two British divisions, one of them armoured, were already on the new Somme front line. Of the original nine divisions of the British Expeditionary Force, "there might perhaps be only 4 or 5 divisions left." Re-equipping them for battle in short order would be impossible, since twice the amount of artillery available in England was having to be abandoned on the beaches of Dunkirk. The Home Forces that would have to defend Britain in the event of an invasion consisted of only two fully equipped divisions, with fourteen still in training and equipped only with rifles. The R.A.F. would have no fighters to spare after the losses in the aerial battles over the Dunkirk beachhead. Of the ten R.A.F. squadrons sent to France, "little was left." Only twenty-nine of the thirty-nine squadrons originally considered the minimum for home defence were now available.[18]

Churchill argued that the Allies had only to hold the Germans at bay through the summer for the United States to come to their aid. The Americans were so "roused," he predicted, that even if Roosevelt could not declare war he "would soon be prepared to give us powerful aid." Even if Britain and France ran out of cash, the United States, he predicted, would "continue to deliver" if English towns were attacked, because the names they shared with many in the United States "would have a still profounder effect." He then launched into what Campbell described as a "most magnificent peroration on the implacable will of the British to fight on to the

261

bitter end." Britain and France "had only to carry on the fight to conquer;" neither side must abandon the struggle and be "reduced to the status of vassals and slaves for ever." If England was "laid waste" she would wage war from the New World. Better, Churchill declared, for European civilization to go down fighting to a "tragic but splendid end" than that "the two great Democracies should linger on, stripped of all that made life worth living."[19]

Spears recorded that even the interpreters fell silent, "deeply moved, carried away by the emotion that surges from Winston Churchill in great torrents." The passionate ferocity of the Prime Minister's exhortation made Attlee's endorsement and observation that the Germans "killed not only men but ideas" seem an anticlamax.[20]

"Never before had their two countries been so united and determined as in the present hour of danger," Reynaud was roused to declare enthusiastically. Echoing Churchill's emotion, but speaking, the British Ambassador thought, with "his head rather than his heart," he vowed not to abandon the struggle if one country went down; with British help the French would hold the Somme, provided the United States moved quickly "to make good the disparity in arms."[21]

Churchill continued to rally Reynaud's spirits over dinner. But Spears knew from the Prime Minister's tone as he bade him good night that "he realized in his heart that the French were beaten, that they knew it, and were resigned to defeat." If the Prime Minister had written off the French, however, he gave no hint that his confidence in Reynaud was shaken when he returned to London next morning and reported on the Supreme War Council to the 1 June meeting of the British War Cabinet.[22]

"Considering how critical the situation was the results were most satisfactory," Churchill concluded, outlining the agreements reached on Norway. "Since we had got off such a large proportion of the British Expeditionary Force we should send some additional troops to France," he urged, "complete with the necessary air component." The Chief of the Air Staff was reluctant and advised that the R.A.F should restrict any additional participation in the battle for France to long-range bombing attacks on German industry and raids on Italian industry when Mussolini launched his attack.[23]

General Gort, who had arrived from Dunkirk overnight after handing over his command as instructed, came to deliver his report in person. The whole Cabinet rose as a man to greet him, and Churchill paid generous tribute to the "skill and determination of his leadership." Gort predicted that the Germans could probably not be held off the beachhead for more than twenty-four hours. The embarkation "must be finished that night and . . . there was no hope for any French troops that were still outside the perimeter."

"We had achieved our purpose and saved our Army," the Prime Minister observed, drawing attention to the R.A.F's success over Dunkirk in its "first real trial of strength" with the Luftwaffe. "This represented a signal victory for the Royal Air Force that gave cause for high hopes for the future." The report from the Chief of the Naval Staff was less sanguine. The large numbers of craft wrecked or sunk by enemy air action included six destroyers, and nearly every warship engaged on the rescue operation had suffered bomb damage. This severe reduction of the Royal Navy's destroyer strength was very worrying because they depended on the remaining flotillas to deter a German invasion force crossing the narrow seas. Only the United States could supply replacement destroyers.

The Foreign Secretary said he had asked Ambassador Kennedy the previous day to inform the President "that the psychological moment had now arrived and that any material assistance which the United States could afford the Allies within the next week would be worth ten times as much as similar assistance in a month's time." Halifax had followed up with a letter suggesting that Kennedy might sound the President out to see whether he would consider "putting in hand the reconditioning of the older destroyers" to save time, "if, as I dare to hope, that decision is favourable." To this appeal Kennedy responded equivocally that "if and when Italy came in" the President might have a chance to do a good deal more "with the general assent of U.S. opinion."[24]

"Dunkirk was worth forty appeals to the Allies from the United States," Kennedy assured Halifax. Churchill decided to put this to the test by cabling Roosevelt that night to remind him of "our urgent needs." If America were to supply immediately 200 Curtis P.40 fighters, he said, they could account for "something like 800 German planes." While he appreciated Roosevelt's difficulties, "legal, political, financial, regarding destroyers," he said, "the need is extreme."[25]

This "Former naval person" telegram of 1 June is very significant, not just because it was the only one Churchill sent to Roosevelt during the three weeks between 20 May and 10 June, but because it was *not* relayed through Ambassador Kennedy and the U.S. Embassy. The reason for this may have been the warning of Assistant Secretary of State Sumner Welles, relayed via Lord Lothian a week earlier, that the U.S Embassy channel was not secure, for reasons "of which Scotland Yard are aware." The reference to the arrest of Tyler Kent prompted Churchill to dispatch his confidential and secret message to Washington via the secure Foreign Office cipher. Sending the cable at this juncture, according to Colville, was part of the Prime Minister's strategy "to bring the U.S. into the war by painting to the members of the Administration the most sombre portrait of what we expect from Germany and by harping on the possibility of France giving up the struggle."[26]

Confirmation had been received that day from the Canadian Prime Minister that the stratagem the Foreign Office regarded as "blackmail" was finally making the President sweat over the fate of the British fleet. According to Mackenzie King's cable reporting Keenleyside's White House discussions, Roosevelt felt "it would be disastrous to surrender the fleet on any terms" in the event of "France being overrun and Britain so situated that she would not be able to repel mass attack from the air." The Canadian Prime Minister warned that the President "cannot, it is considered, give immediate belligerent aid." Britain and France would have to "hold out for some months" before it would be politically possible for the United States to send over the degree of support they were appealing for. The cable from Ottawa was a reminder of the Foreign Office's warning to the Prime Minister that his blackmail strategy might backfire if the President "is or was under the illusion that Canada, South Africa, New Zealand etc could insist on the British Fleet being sent to Canada if Great Britain was overcome." Churchill simply marked "noted" on the minute from the American Department cautioning that an appeal "from weakness to the Americans will fail."[27]

The Prime Minister may have been keen for the White House to sweat over the prospect of what would happen to the British fleet if Britain went down to defeat, but he reacted vigorously to any such speculation by his own officials. That Saturday he rejected the secret Foreign Office proposal to draw up plans to evacuate the Royal Family and prepare for the "removal now from this country to another part of the Empire" of the Crown Jewels, bullion and securities. "I believe we shall make them rue the day they try to invade our island," Churchill penned in red on the minute, ordering, "No such discussion can be permitted." For the same reason he emphatically rejected the National Gallery's proposal to ship its most valuable paintings to Canada. "No, bury them in caves and cellars. None must go. We are going to beat them."[28]

"A Matter of Life and Death"
3–9 June

It was not only the destroyers but whether the United States could be persuaded to supply the weapons needed to rearm and re-equip the army rescued from Dunkirk that were the immediate concern for Britain's military chiefs. The total number of Allied troops snatched from the bomb-trap beachhead passed the quarter-million mark on 2 June. That Sunday evening the War Cabinet were told that the enemy bombing was now so intense that daylight operations at Dunkirk had been suspended. When the flotillas of small craft headed off for the beaches again at 9 p.m., it was hoped to pick up another 22,000 men under cover of darkness. The French request to keep the operation going through Monday so as to save as many of their 25,000 remaining troops as possible was strongly endorsed by Churchill. At the Chiefs of Staff Committee that had preceded the Cabinet he had discussed Reynaud's latest appeal for the immediate return to the Somme front of three divisions "of tested fighting value," and for R.A.F. fighters to operate from airfields in France. These "grasping" demands annoyed the Prime Minister, but he felt that some gesture to help the French was essential to sustain their morale.[29]

"Were we to decline to respond to M. Reynaud's appeal there was a considerable danger that a point might be reached at which French resistance might collapse," Churchill told the War Cabinet. "We might eventually be faced with a French government, not merely out of the war, but actually hostile to us." But he was becoming a little too "sentimental" about the French for some of his Cabinet colleagues. Attlee was prepared to offer "one or two divisions" as a "token of our sincerity," but declared it was impossible to meet Reynaud's demands without impairing the "essential fighter defences of this country." When Halifax and Chamberlain supported Attlee, Churchill agreed to defer an answer until they had seen the "considered view of the Chiefs of Staff."[30]

When the War Cabinet met at 11.30 next morning, the Prime Minister was able to announce what he had not even dared to hope a week earlier. The British Expeditionary Force "had now been withdrawn practically intact, except for their losses through casualties in action." The French, however, "had not made anything like full use of the facilities available for the evacuation of their troops the previous day and night," but he would urge Reynaud that Tuesday night's evacuation would be their last chance to get their soldiers out. The Prime Minister's continued willingness to defer to the French was evident in his refusal to accept the recommendation of the Chiefs of Staff that only two divisions could be sent to reinforce the Somme front. This was "not sufficient," he told them, demanding a third division. Eventually the War Cabinet agreed; but the Prime Minister could not budge his colleagues when it came to sending more fighters to France. Air Marshal Peirse held firm that the commitment must be limited to "six squadrons of Battles and three fighter squadrons," because of the heavy fighter losses in France and high casualty rates over Dunkirk.[31]

In support of the Chief of the Air Staff, Air Chief Marshal Dowding produced an alarming graph showing that 250 Hurricanes had been lost between 8 May and 18 May. This was more than six times the rate at which replacement fighters were being produced, to say nothing of the pilots killed. As of 1 June, the R.A.F. could muster 244 Hurricanes and 280 Spitfires to guard the whole of the British Isles. Fighter Command faced a "bottleneck" of trained pilots, and Dowding, its Commander-in-Chief, issued a dire warning: "If the enemy developed a heavy air attack on the country at this moment," he "could not guarantee air superiority for more than 48 hours."

Dowding's intervention struck a chill into the War Cabinet and proved decisive. His stand against sending any more fighter squadrons to France was endorsed by Lord Halifax, who warned of the dangers of "falling between two stools." Whatever help was given to the French, he said, would prove inadequate and it could only weaken, perhaps fatally, Britain's own defences. The Prime Minister bowed reluctantly to the majority view and undertook to tell Reynaud that the R.A.F's resources were sufficient only to bring up to strength the three fighter and six bomber squadrons already in France. But he expressed his concern that "we had some 500 fighters of incomparable quality which we would be withholding at a moment when they would be making the supreme effort on land." He therefore said he would tell the French that the matter would be reviewed "in ten days." That afternoon he cabled to Spears: "You should prepare them for favourable response Army but disappointment about Air."[32]

Halifax had sided so strongly with Dowding against him that Churchill gave him a written rap on the knuckles. Reminding the Foreign Secretary that it was his "responsibility as Minister of Defence for advising the Cabinet on the main grouping and development of our Forces," he wrote that it was now essential to build up the British Army in France. "I hope I may be given some help in this, and be allowed to view the War situation as a whole." When Cadogan learned of this, he feared that relations between the Prime Minister and the Foreign Secretary had "become rather strained." He commented that Churchill's "theatricality" was the principal fault. For Halifax it was the Prime Minister's "disorderly mind" that prompted him to carp in his diary: "I am coming to the conclusion that his process of thought is one that has to operate through speed . . . As this is the exact reverse of my own it is irritating." The Foreign Secretary's frustration was increased by Churchill's refusal to give up.[33]

"We could never keep all that we wanted for our own defence

while the French were fighting for their lives," the Prime Minister argued in the War Cabinet next day, opening up the issue all over again. This time Halifax kept a lower profile and left it to the Secretary of State for Air to argue for restricting the number of squadrons in France to the previously agreed three.[34]

Some consolation for Churchill came on 4 June in a cable from Arthur Purvis in Washington reporting that the first consignment of rifles, ammunition and machine-guns was being readied for shipment as soon as the legal obstacles could be cleared. The next day Purvis reported that on the subject of the destroyers Treasury Secretary Morgenthau had assured him that for "the first time" Roosevelt had hinted that he would "try to find a way to work out getting ten for you." The snag was that the U.S. Navy baulked at declaring even obsolete vessels as surplus to requirements, and the Attorney General could not sanction their sale to the Allies without prior advertisement as he had the arms shipment the day before. Next day the Senate Foreign Relations Committee moved to block the White House plan by rejecting the administration's proposal to sell ships and planes to Britain as well as rifles, guns and ammunition. Purvis passed on Roosevelt's "regret" that as far as destroyers were concerned the United States of America could not spare any.[35]

The trainload of weapons and ammunition rolling northwards to New Jersey and the Raritan wharfs that weekend was the first tangible proof that the President was at last moving to get aid to the Allies. This news from Purvis boosted the Prime Minister's confidence that Tuesday as he prepared for his critical statement that afternoon to the House of Commons. It can only have been because of Halifax's agitation for a compromise peace that Churchill invited both the Foreign Secretary and his deputy to join him in the garden of Number 10 as he rehearsed his "we shall never surrender" speech. "There we were, the lanky Edward, the stocky Winston and myself," Butler recalled in his memoirs, describing how Churchill, in the midst of his peroration about fighting the Germans on the beaches, had suddenly stopped and turned to address them.

"Would you fight in the streets and on the hills?" he asked. Butler said he and his master "warmly agreed." The Prime Minister resumed marching round the garden after they had obediently chorused: "Yes, certainly, Winston."[36]

The Prime Minister, unfortunately for history, left no record of his view of the apparent conversion of the two arch-appeasers in his government. But Halifax, in his diary that evening, did single out for criticism the end of Churchill's speech, "where he talked about the possibility of us fighting alone." He complained that the French Ambassador would be upset at this intimation that the British expected his country to be defeated. His worry that the

Germans would also exploit it suggests that the Foreign Secretary was not comfortable with the Prime Minister's rhetoric designed to fix his "no-surrender" doctrine as the immutable cornerstone of British policy.

Churchill's speech proved to be one of his greatest oratorical and political triumphs. What he had feared only a week earlier might have to be a report of "the greatest military disaster in our long history" became a celebration of the "miracle of deliverance" achieved by the valour and perseverance of British soldiers. He paid tribute to "the unconquerable fidelity" of Gort and the B.E.F., but reserved his highest praise for the R.A.F. fighter pilots who had emerged the victors in "a great trial of strength between the British and German Air Forces." Comparing them to the "Knights of the Round Table" he assured the nation that "the cause of civilization itself will be defended by the skill and devotion of a few thousand airmen."[37]

"Wars are not won by evacuations," Churchill cautioned, acknowledging the "colossal military disaster" that had exposed the heartland of France to the German assault and opened up the prospect of an imminent attack on Britain. A major part of the speech detailed the anti-invasion preparations, including Churchill's promise to use the powers Parliament had given "to put down Fifth Column activities with a strong hand . . . until we are satisfied, and more than satisfied, that this malignancy in our midst has been stamped out."

After sending this strong warning to those who would make peace with Hitler, Churchill drew his speech to a climax with a rousing peroration. He promised that "every man" in His Majesty's Government was resolved "to defend our island home, to ride out the storm of war, and outlive the menace of tyranny, if necessary for years, if necessary alone." Britain and the French Republic would "defend to the death their native soil, aiding each other like good comrades to the utmost of their strength." Tracts of Europe might fall "into the grip of the Gestapo and all the odious apparatus of Nazi rule," but as long as he was Prime Minister, Britain "shall not flag or fail."

"We shall fight on the beaches, we shall fight in the fields and in the streets, we shall fight in the hills, we shall never surrender," Churchill declared in a coda of eloquent resolution. "And even if, which I do not for one moment believe, this island or a large part of it were subjugated and starving, then our Empire beyond the seas, armed and guarded by the British Fleet, would carry on the struggle, until in God's good time, the new world, with all its power and might, steps forth to the rescue and the liberation of the old."

When the Prime Minister resumed his seat, a wave of enthusiasm swept across the Chamber and the packed Peers' Gallery.

The speech that one Labour member rated as "worth 1,000 guns" was an inspiration to everyone who heard the B.B.C. announcer repeating its rousing finale on the evening news broadcast. It was impossible not to be stirred by the almost physical impact of Churchill's "Elizabethan phrases," which Vita Sackville West, Harold Nicolson's wife, felt had "the whole backing of power and resolve behind them, like a great fortress."[38]

It was a roar of defiance that reverberated across the Atlantic. Halifax's reservations about the allusions to the United States as Britain's ultimate salvation proved groundless. The Prime Minister's speech had a powerful impact in the American press and the White House, reinforcing the belief that Britain's war leader would fight on. It also contained the message that Roosevelt wanted to hear: as Interior Secretary Ickes discerned, Churchill had "really served notice that the British fleet, whatever might happen, would not be surrendered to Hitler."[39]

Churchill followed up his speech by cabling Mackenzie King that they "must be careful not to let Americans view too complacently [the] prospects of a British collapse, out of which they would get the British Fleet and the guardianship of the British Empire, minus Britain." He wanted it relayed to Roosevelt that "if America continued to be neutral, and we were overpowered, I cannot tell what policy might be adopted by a pro-German administration such as would be undoubtedly set up." The President might be "our best friend," but, as Churchill pointed out, "no practical help has been forthcoming from the United States as yet." This was also the excuse he gave his ministers for blocking the request of his scientific adviser for the exchange of technological secrets with the United States. He minuted that he was "disinclined to this at the moment" because he was "waiting for further development of the American attitude."[40]

The Allies' urgent need for immediate American military aid was underlined by the German attack on the Somme defence line, which began next day. Reynaud responded to the 5 June offensive by issuing an urgent appeal for more British military assistance. He also reshuffled his Cabinet, finally sacking Daladier, along with others he regarded as defeatists, and bringing in Colonel de Gaulle as Under Secretary of War to stiffen the resolve of his ministers. Unable to rid himself of Pétain, who had become his albatross, he offered to make him Foreign Minister in a bid to retain his commitment to the war. When the shuffling war hero refused on the grounds that he was a soldier, not a politician, Reynaud realized that Pétain and Weygand were already preparing to call for an armistice and acting as an axis of defeatism in his own cabinet, which infected other ministers, who "would be ready, when the time came, to join forces with these two."[41]

"How can we help the French in the battle?" Churchill asked his military chiefs that Wednesday morning. He wanted to do something "without hurting ourselves mortally, and in a way that will encourage the French to feel that we are doing all in our power." A division of Highland troops was engaging the Germans on the French right flank from Abbeville to the Channel, but now Reynaud had asked for the immediate dispatch of more British soldiers and additional R.A.F. fighter squadrons. At Churchill's insistence it was agreed that he could cable the French Prime Minister that two fighter and four bomber squadrons were "at full strength ready to intervene from this country." Reynaud responded like a hungry fledgling rather than a fighting cock by demanding ten squadrons "immediately," to be followed "as soon as possible by ten further squadrons." This amounted to asking for half the total fighter strength of the R.A.F. and was "altogether unreasonable," Churchill told the War Cabinet that afternoon. He telegraphed Reynaud explaining that "British fighter aviation has been worn to a shred and frightfully mixed up by the needs of maintaining standing patrols over Dunkirk." No more planes were to be spared for France, but he could promise to send over an additional Highland division, which would begin embarking the following morning.[42]

After the formal meeting of the War Cabinet was over, Churchill kept his ministers back for a private exhortation. His particular concern was to appeal to Sinclair and Attlee for their help in putting an end to what he called a "heresy hunt," the campaign to oust the "Men of Munich" still in the government, which was still being conducted in the Labour *Daily Herald* and Liberal *News Chronicle*. Churchill's dressing down of the Labour and Liberal leadership was fulfilling an obligation to Chamberlain, who, for his part, had reluctantly agreed to drop his objection to Churchill's efforts to bring Lloyd George into the War Cabinet. Halifax must have regarded Lloyd George as a rival when it came to his potential for making a deal with Hitler, because he insisted that the former Prime Minister must agree "that any peace terms, now, or hereafter, offered, must not be destructive of our independence."[43]

Lloyd George had spent over an hour with the Prime Minister after his rousing House of Commons speech the previous day. He rejected Churchill's appeal to join his administration, citing his antipathy to Chamberlain and Halifax. He was aware that if he entered the government he would no longer be the prime minister of last resort for the thirty M.P.s and peers still secretly campaigning for negotiations with Hitler. As he had made clear to the parliamentary peace delegation, he expected a military stand-off and did not believe that Britain should seek a humiliating peace in the aftermath of the defeat of France, which he foresaw approaching rapidly.[44]

So did the Germans.

"The days to come will show if the enemy is accepting a battle of decision at the Somme and Aisne," General Halder noted with confidence during the opening hours of "Operation Red," the second phase of O.K.H's plan for the battle in France. Anticipating that the Panzer divisions would soon smash open the road to Paris, he predicted that the French "will be beaten on this line which will be breached probably east of Rheims and perhaps simultaneously also in the direction of the lower Seine." The French High Command also anticipated the German strategy; and it greatly unnerved them.[45]

"There should be no limit to human efforts when it is a matter of life and death, and that has been the position since the decisive battle began yesterday morning," the French Prime Minister told his War Council on 6 June. He turned to General Spears to ask "What can you give us?" Before Churchill's emissary could respond, Weygand declared that the "common cause of the Allies was in deadly peril." The British, he said, could not now hesitate to send over the air and ground reinforcements without which Paris would fall. What then?[46]

"England and the United States would send us arms," Reynaud insisted, "but we must hold out in some part of France." He called for preparations to be made for a fighting retreat to the Breton redoubt. Weygand described this as a "fantasy." Pétain intervened to opine that if the present battle was lost "there would be nothing to do but to treat with the enemy."

"No fighter aircraft and no fresh divisions" had arrived from Britain, Weygand told Reynaud that morning. But as the British War Cabinet concluded that afternoon, there was precious little they could send the French except promises and encouragement. Churchill telegraphed them that the 52nd Highland Division would be followed by Canadian troops the following week and that R.A.F. fighter and bomber squadrons would intervene in the battle from their bases in England. The response from Paris was yet another urgent appeal for more air support, which exasperated the British Chiefs of Staff.[47]

"We should be insane to send them all our fighters," General Ismay told Churchill that evening. "If they were lost the country would be beaten in two days, whereas even if France surrenders we should still win the war – provided our air defences are intact." The point was taken by the Prime Minister. At next morning's War Cabinet he confessed he was worried that the French "would try and put the blame on us if they lost this critical battle."

271

It was agreed that he could tell the French Prime Minister it might be possible to assign four additional fighter squadrons operating from Britain to refuel at French airfields south of the Somme.[48]

That Friday, 7 June, two German armoured divisions broke through to Forges and Les Eaus, opening up the road to Rouen and the lower Somme. "I am convinced that the battle is lost:" with these words Under Secretary Baudouin broke the news to his despondent Prime Minister. By Saturday, 8 June, a yawning gap had been torn in the line held by France's Tenth Army. Orders were issued for the retreat to the lower Somme. Cut off from the French, the British Highland division had to fall back on Le Havre. With the prospect of another Dunkirk-style rescue looming, Weygand moved his own headquarters a hundred kilometres south of Paris to Briare. Putting the bleakest construction on Friday's developments, he told Reynaud that the French Army were now "at the end of their reserves."[49]

"It is useless, and we ought to stop before the whole country is destroyed," Minister Camille Chautemps confided to Baudouin that evening. The despair of the commander-in-chief and the ministers was deepening by the hour, as they looked to France's military hero for a solution. Baudouin too was becoming infected by Chautemps's assurance that "Marshal Pétain saw the position the clearest."[50]

Ironically, that Saturday found the German High Command also in a state of indecision and tension. Seeing their forces on the brink of one of their "typical breakthrough situations which first look quite critical but after a while turn into a picture of complete success," Halder and von Brauchitsch went to see the Führer. They tried to convince him to use the Panzer divisions to spearhead an additional push to exploit the breakthrough on the lower Seine. A cautious Hitler insisted on sticking to the original plan; Paris would not be attacked until the German forces had broken through on the River Marne to the north of the city.

In London the Defence Committee that evening considered, but rejected, the increasingly desperate appeals from Paris for more military help. That Saturday was the final phase of the Norwegian operation. But embarking the last of the Allied forces at Narvik had cost the Royal Navy the aircraft-carrier *Glorious* and two destroyers sunk. In circumstances that were far from optimistic, the Prime Minister summed up the choice that had to be made. They "could regard the present battle as decisive for France and ourselves, and throw in the whole of our fighter resources in an attempt to save the situation." If they failed, Churchill warned, "we should then have to surrender." The alternative was to regard the land battle

272

as "of great importance" but "not decisive one way or the other" for Britain. "If it were lost, and France was forced to submit," he still saw "good hopes of ultimate victory, provided we ensured that our fighter defences in this country were not impaired."[51]

"If this country were defeated, the war would be lost for France no less than for ourselves," Churchill concluded, "whereas, provided we were strong ourselves, we could win the war, and in so doing, restore France to her position." He therefore had decided that it would be "fatal to yield to the French demands and jeopardize our own safety." As this was also the unanimous view of the Defence Committee, it fell to the Prime Minister to break the news of the British decision to the French.

"We are giving you all the support we can in this great battle," Churchill cabled Paris, "short of ruining the capacity of this country to continue the war." He said he could see "only one sure way through now, to wit that Hitler should attack this country, and in doing so break his air weapon." To Jan Smuts, the South African Prime Minister, who had been urging that air reinforcements be sent to France, Churchill replied that if the Luftwaffe was defeated, Hitler would be "left to face the winter with Europe writhing under his heel, and probably with the United States against him after the Presidential election is won." This was the rationale behind the British strategic decision which was cabled to South Africa on 9 June.[52]

"It is vital to our safety that the United States should be involved in the totalitarian war," the Prime Minister minuted to the Dominions Secretary, under whose name the cable to Smuts was dispatched. But, as Churchill knew full well, involving the United States depended as much on American public opinion as it did on Roosevelt, who had to keep his weather-eye on the electorate as well as Hitler. That Sunday evening Ambassador Bullitt telephoned the White House that the French government had begun leaving the capital, because "German forces are approximately 25 miles from Paris."[53]

The decision had been taken by the French War Council to begin the evacuation of Paris only after Marshal Pétain had tried to dissuade the government from abandoning the capital, arguing that an armistice was the more logical and honourable solution. Reynaud contended that "no honourable armistice could be expected from Hitler," because his plans "were to destroy France utterly." It would be "imprudent," he argued, to cut France off from her allies. The Marshal disagreed. "England has got us into this position," he declared. "It is our duty not to put up with it, but to get out."

It was at this point in the debate that General Weygand joined the meeting to report that the defence line was still holding on the Marne north of the city. If it was lost, he warned, France's armies "would inevitably be separated and condemned to rapid destruction." Reynaud again called for a retreat to the national redoubt in Brittany, where they could hold out while awaiting reinforcements from Britain and the United States. Weygand countered that if the present battle were lost, there would be no way of transporting the troops to garrison the Breton fortress. Baudouin's own faith in the Prime Minister was slipping away. He observed that to "secure the destruction of Hitler and Nazism," Reynaud "would bleed France white." He decided that he was "less fanatical."[54]

"C'est la Dislocation"
10–11 June

Monday, 10 June, began badly for the Allies, with reports that German tanks had crossed the Seine at two points, forcing the rapid retreat of the French armies north and south of Paris. General de Gaulle returned from London with more bad news. Churchill had "flatly refused to empty England of fighters, for the Battle of France was no longer of great importance in his eyes." With German air supremacy rapidly exhausting French troops, and news that the British Highland division was preparing to evacuate from Le Havre, despair gripped the French leaders. Weygand said that it was his duty to warn the Prime Minister that "the final rupture of our lines may take place at any moment" and that the crossing of the lower Seine could bring the Germans to the gates of Paris in twenty-four hours.[55]

Sunday's pitch-dark weather over England was as bleak as the news reaching London from Paris. Reviewing the reports for the afternoon War Cabinet, Churchill announced that he had considered flying to France but had decided not to do so because "the French would certainly press us to give them help with fighter squadrons beyond what we could agree to." Earlier he had been roused from his afternoon nap to be told that Mussolini was about to enter the war. The British and French ambassadors in Rome had been summoned by the Italian Foreign Minister and informed that Italy would commence hostilities against the Allies at midnight. Sir Percy Loraine had gallantly, if undiplomatically, retorted: "England is not in the habit of losing her wars."[56]

Churchill was no less scathing. "People who go to Italy to look at ruins won't have to go so far as Naples or Pompeii again," he growled when Colville brought him Loraine's cable. But the announcement from Rome raised the Prime Minister's concern that it would be the final straw for the French. As the midnight deadline approached, Churchill's temper improved when he listened to the American network broadcasting Roosevelt's strong denunciation of Italy. The President, his voice breaking through the waves of transatlantic static, declared that "the hand that held the dagger has struck it into the back of its neighbour." His firm tone beamed a message of hope to Britain and France from the steps of the University of Virginia, where he delivered the commencement address for the graduation class of his son Franklin Jr. Brushing aside the agonizing of the State Department, he seized the opportunity to make public the assurances he had so far only given privately. In calling for an acceleration of the rearmament of U.S. forces, he reminded Americans that it was in the interests of national defence to support the Allies in their struggle against the Axis.[57]

"We will extend to the opponents of force the material resources of this nation," the President announced. "We will not slow down or detour. Signs and signals call for speed: full speed ahead." Churchill found Roosevelt's speech "a strong encouragement in a dark but not unhopeful hour." He cabled immediately to tell Roosevelt how much he had been "fortified by the grand scope of your declaration." He now urged the President to do everything he could to keep France in the fight, warning that there would be pressure to parley with the Germans if Paris fell. He promised to have "a strong British army fighting in France for the campaign of 1941." For this, however, Britain would have to survive, and Churchill reminded the President of his recent appeal. The need for destroyers, he said, was "even more pressing" in order to deal with the new Italian submarine threat. "Not a day should be lost," Churchill concluded expectantly, sending his "heartfelt thanks" for what Roosevelt might already be doing to support "what we now indeed call the Common Cause."[58]

When this cable reached Washington the White House had already been forewarned by Ambassador Kennedy's telegram that Churchill "is still pleading for destroyers, and I judge from his conversation that he believes with the bombing of well known places in England that the United States will come into the war." He reported how the Prime Minister had told him that "as long as he lived the British Fleet would not be handed over to the Germans," but that he could not rule out that a Mosley government "might turn over anything that Hitler wanted in order to save England from destruction." Kennedy fretted that Churchill intended to make the Americans "patsies" – if Britain went down to defeat. "I can visualize their possible eventual acceptance of a German victory," he said, "but they will never forgive us for not having come to their aid."[59]

"ITALY AT WAR, READY TO ATTACK, STAB IN THE BACK SAYS ROOSEVELT, GOVT. HAS LEFT PARIS" was how the *New York Times* headlined the new crisis. Urgent pleas for help were flooding in to the White House. Ambassador Bullitt had relayed an "enemy almost at the gates" *cri de cœur* from the French Prime Minister. "We shall fight in front of Paris; we shall fight behind Paris," Reynaud wrote, imploring the President "to declare publicly that the United States will give the Allies aid and material support by all means 'short of an expeditionary force'." At a loss to know how to deal with such a wrenching appeal, the President turned it over to the State Department. While the officials debated for two days what response to make, the French government was rocking on the brink of collapse. Just how shaky Reynaud's authority was becoming was clear the following morning in London when a cable arrived requesting a Supreme War Council meeting that evening at General Weygand's Briare headquarters.[60]

"We shall have to concert with them on a grand strategic plan for the future conduct of the war," Churchill told the Tuesday War Cabinet. He promised to "give them every encouragement to continue the struggle and discourage any signs of movement towards making a separate peace."[61]

The British Prime Minister's party, which included Eden, Dill and Ismay, landed late that afternoon at a deserted airfield in the Loire valley south-west of Orleans. A French colonel greeted them like poor relations arriving at a funeral reception. Weygand's headquarters were in the Château du Muguet, where the Supreme War Council assembled at 7 p.m. The French were ranged around the table, looking, as Spears observed, like prisoners "hauled up from some deep dungeon to hear an inevitable verdict." The British gave a frosty reception to Reynaud's request that the R.A.F. should call off that night's planned bombing attack on northern Italy because the French feared a heavy retaliatory raid. Churchill tried his best to cobble together reasons to hope that the military front would soon be stabilized and the R.A.F. would break Germany's might in the air, allowing the British Army to return to France in force by 1941. All the French had to do was to hold the German advance.[62]

"It is a race between the exhaustion of the French and the shortness of breath of the enemy divisions," Weygand retorted, saying that there was nothing to stop the Germans reaching Paris – or continuing beyond into the heart of France. "We are fighting on our last line and it has been breached," he declared with resignation. "I am helpless. I cannot intervene, for I have no reserves. *C'est la dislocation*" – the break-up.[63]

Churchill was appalled by this Niagara of despondency from the Allied Commander-in-Chief, which he received with an expression that General Spears wrote "was not benevolent." The Prime Minister then looked to General Georges to shed some ray of hope into Weygand's dark landscape of France's military despair. But his old ally said it was his duty to dispel any remaining British illusions. Adding up the arithmetic of military defeat Georges declared that the Germans had a superiority of three to one in ground forces. The French Air Force was down to 180 fighters and its pilots were dead-beat.

"We must not be hypnotized by our defeats," Churchill countered, hoping to rally the French by paying tribute to their "heroic resistance" and regretting that the British had not yet been able to play a bigger part in the struggle. This would all change, he promised. "French and English phrases tumbling over each other like waves racing for the shore when driven by a storm," was how Spears described Churchill's bravura performance. He dredged the annals of military history from Sparta to the Great War and his own personal experience for examples to show how continued resistance in the face of an overwhelming enemy ultimately led to victory not defeat. The French must fight on, he argued, even if Paris fell. But the only French general present who responded favourably to his call for a "war of columns" and guerrilla actions to tie down the German Army was Charles de Gaulle.[64]

General Weygand made it plain that he had no taste for guerrilla warfare, and he remained unshaken in his belief that France was facing a "war of fronts" that had been all but lost. The only hope of turning the tide was with large-scale air attacks. Was Britain, he demanded, now prepared to send every plane she had to France for the decisive battle?

Churchill was unaware that Weygand had already effectively ordered that Paris was to be spared destruction by declaring it an open city. But Weygand's defeatism stung the Prime Minister into responding that it was not today's battle for France, but tomorrow's battle for Britain, that would decide the fate of the war. "If we won that battle," he declared, "all we had now lost would be retrieved." If France "in her agony" decided her Army should capitulate, "let there be no hesitation on our account." He announced with angry determination: "Whatever happens here, we are resolved to fight on for ever and ever." The French Prime Minister, who had already been assured by Admiral Darlan that if Britain fought on alone she would quickly have "her neck wrung like a chicken," intervened. "If we capitulate, all the might of Germany will be concentrated upon invading England," Reynaud said. "And then what will you do?" Churchill thrust his jaw forward and growled, "Drown as many as possible of them on the way over, and then . . . 'frapper sur la tête' anyone who managed to crawl ashore."[64]

This was one of the few moments of levity in the "miasma of despond" that, Spears recorded, had fallen on the conference "like

277

a fog." The mood lifted only slightly when the council adjourned for dinner at nine with little accomplished and nothing agreed. Before they retired for the night at the château, Reynaud confided to Churchill that Pétain was pressing for an armistice. The Marshal did not raise the subject during the short session of the Supreme War Council the next morning when Churchill made a final effort to rally the French with promises to send fresh divisions from England as soon as they could be re-equipped. The Marshal, like Weygand, remained impassive. France's only hope lay "in the industrial resources of the U.S.A.," Reynaud concluded after Churchill promised to send another message to Roosevelt. But first he insisted that the British must be consulted before the French took "decisions of great moment" – everyone present knew that Churchill was referring to an armistice, but the shameful word was not uttered. With Reynaud's solemn assurance that this would be done, the Supreme Allied War Council broke up. Only then did General Georges make the disquieting observation that he regarded "an armistice as inevitable." Churchill then sought and obtained a personal commitment from Admiral Darlan that any surrender of the French fleet "would be quite contrary to our naval tradition and honour."[65]

The question of an armistice was openly discussed at the six o'clock Council of Ministers that Wednesday evening. The evacuated French government had assembled at the Château de Cangey outside Tours, 120 miles south-west of Paris in the rolling vineyards of the lower Loire region. Weygand tabled his request that the Germans be asked for an armistice before the French Army completely disintegrated. Reynaud rejected the idea, comparing it to dealing with Genghis Khan. Not only could they not trust Hitler, but to seek peace at this stage would be dishonourable and futile. If Paris fell, the army would withdraw to Brittany or, if that proved impossible, to North Africa. He wanted France to continue the struggle indefinitely from Algeria.

Marshal Pétain then rose to call for an armistice "without delay in order to save what was left of France." Ministers were crushed and divided. Since Paris had not yet fallen, some felt, such capitulation would be precipitate. Reynaud won an agreement that they should not in any case make the momentous decision until they had fulfilled his promise to consult again with the British. "France must never be separated from England and the United States," he insisted. "The Anglo-Saxon world will save France, and it alone can restore her."[66]

"France was near the end of organized resistance," the Prime Minister reported to the War Cabinet after arriving safely back in London. Reynaud "seemed quite determined to fight on" but the only support he had received from the French military was from de Gaulle. Churchill predicted that de Gaulle would be put in command when the Somme front collapsed. He described Pétain as a "dangerous man" who "had always been a defeatist" and was now manoeuvring for an early armistice, to save France from systematic destruction.

"We must now concentrate everything on the defence of this island," Churchill told his colleagues, obtaining their agreement that "for a period we might still have to send a measure of support for France." In a last-ditch effort to strengthen Reynaud's hand and stay Pétain's bid for an armistice he obtained Cabinet approval to put the desperate situation squarely before Roosevelt. "A declaration that we were firmly resolved to continue the war in all circumstances," the "Former naval person" cabled to the President, "would prove the best invitation to the United States to lend their support."[67]

"If there is anything you can say publicly or privately to the French now is the time," Churchill pleaded in his cable to the President. He told Roosevelt that the French generals saw their situation "in the gravest terms." Weygand believed that France could no longer sustain a "coordinated war." The "aged Marshal Pétain" was ready to make peace with the Germans. Churchill told the President that now was "the moment for you to strengthen Reynaud the utmost and try to tip the balance in favour of the best and longest possible French resistance." Darlan, he reassured Roosevelt, "will send the French fleet to Canada" rather than see it fall "into bad hands." He himself had promised the French that "we shall continue whatever happened and that we thought Hitler could not win the war or the mastery of the world until he had disposed of us."[68]

The Prime Minister was hoping, according to Colville, that the Americans "will come in now – at any rate as a non-belligerent ally." This may have been over-optimistic, but Churchill had some cause for confidence. He had just been handed the report that the rifles, machine guns and ammunition whose release had been authorized by the President were already being loaded aboard British and French freighters docked at the New Jersey piers. But all the arms and munitions in those 600 railroad freight cars were no more than a drop in the Allies' ocean of need. Churchill would later pay tribute to Roosevelt, recalling that it was a "supreme act of faith and leadership for the United States to deprive themselves of this very considerable mass of arms for the sake of a country which many deemed already beaten."[69]

Ambassador Kennedy, through whom Churchill sent this telegram to the President, was busily working to foreclose the Prime Minister's appeal by cabling to the State Department that British "preparedness for carrying on a war is pitiful," and that Churchill "urged me strongly to present again his crying need for destroyers."

He added his opinion that, "short of a miracle," England was only holding on in the hope of the United States coming in. "Churchill said quite definitely to me he expects the United States will be right in after the election," Kennedy reported. "When the people of the United States see the towns and cities of England, after which so many American cities have been named, bombed and destroyed, they will line up and want war." British newspapers, he warned, were reporting that all it needed was an "incident" to bring America into the war. "If that were all that were needed," he hinted darkly, "desperate people will do desperate things."[70]

The scurrilous implication that Churchill might be preparing to arrange another *Lusitania* incident was discounted by the President, who had become inured to Kennedy's clumsy slurs. The sour tone of the Ambassador's telegram was the result of his becoming "very sore at not having been seen enough" by Churchill. That was the Foreign Secretary's explanation of why that afternoon the Ambassador "blew off with every expletive for about twenty minutes." After the back-street vocabulary had exhausted itself, the imperturbable Halifax, who realized that "argument would be of no immediate value," remarked coolly that Kennedy "must now feel much better." The American envoy "saw the humour of this and we got on well," Halifax recorded.[71]

But the last laugh appears to have been at the Ambassador's expense. The "Former naval person to President" message that he was given that evening to smooth his ruffled feathers was the first to be sent through the U.S. Embassy since the arrest of Tyler Kent. The records show that this 12 June cable was transmitted in "Grey Code," while Kennedy's own report to the State Department went by secure naval machine cipher. Churchill's message could therefore be easily read if it was intercepted by hostile eavesdroppers, but Kennedy's could not. The German codebreakers, we now know, did not need a spy like Kent in the U.S. Embassy Code Room to read the Grey Code. The next day the Prime Minister sent another brief message to the White House by the same route, although his files confirm that he was well aware that the U.S. Embassy channel was not a secure way of communicating "Personal and secret" information to the President.

Foreign Office records confirm that Churchill adopted Roosevelt's stratagem of using the insecure Grey Code to let Hitler "know and understand how close our liaison with the Americans is." The desire to get this message through to Berlin would explain the otherwise disconnected addition that the Prime Minister appended to his 13 June cable announcing that the "crisis has arrived" and that he was off to France again. Unless he wanted to warn Hitler off, what can explain his call for Roosevelt to send "an American squadron" to the port of Berehaven in Ireland? (See Appendix 9.)

"The Darkest Hour"
13–14 June

"Anything you can say or do to help [the French] now may make a difference," Churchill told the President in the telegram that reached the U.S. Embassy that Thursday afternoon while he flew on a long westward detour over the English Channel to avoid German fighters. Reynaud's summons to Tours had arrived late the previous evening after the devastating news that Britain's 51st (Highland) Division in France had surrendered to Rommel's Seventh Panzer Division. A thunderstorm broke with ominous portent as the two planes carrying the Prime Minister's party landed at the airfield outside Tours, still pock-marked with bombcraters from the previous night's raid. Churchill, Beaverbrook, Halifax, Cadogan and an interpreter were crushed into a small motor car for an uncomfortable journey to the Préfecture. On arrival they found that the French government members had not yet turned up.

"However difficult the decisions we have to take later there is one about which we have no doubt," the Prime Minister declared: "we want luncheon." The British party made its way through pouring rain and streets crowded with refugees to a nearby restaurant for cold chicken and bottles of the local Vouvray wine. Baudouin arrived at 2.30, ruining Churchill's lunch with his "outpouring of oily defeatism," according to General Spears, who turned up shortly afterwards with the British Ambassador, just before Reynaud and Mandel.[72]

It was 3.30 p.m. before the final meeting of the Supreme War Council began its sepulchral deliberations. That not a single French general was present that afternoon was taken as an ominous portent by the British delegation. Their fears were confirmed when Reynaud reported that General Weygand had requested an immediate armistice. "Our only chance of victory is the prompt entry of the United States into the war," he said. "President Roosevelt must realize this and accept the responsibility." Weygand asked Churchill to join in making a final appeal to the United States, although he feared it might already be too late to save France. Reynaud then asked whether Britain would release France from the promise he had made not to make a separate peace with the Germans.[73]

Sidestepping the capitulation issue, Churchill made another bid to rally the French until his stream of oratory was interrupted. "I did not ask what England is going to do or how she regarded the future," Reynaud impatiently interjected. "I ask your permission to withdraw from the struggle by a separate armistice, while maintaining the solidarity caused by agreement."

"France has been sacrificed in the struggle against the common

281

enemy," the British Prime Minister acknowledged. "Whatever may be her attitude after her defeat, Great Britain will in any event restore her to power and greatness." He assured the French that whatever the outcome "there shall be no recriminations," promising to add his own appeal to President Roosevelt. But he asked the French to postpone any armistice decision until they had Roosevelt's answer. Reynaud responded that he was grateful for the declaration, but feared the enmity that might arise between their two countries if America did not step in to save the situation. Churchill wanted to know how long Weygand would hold out before he asked the Germans for an armistice. "Was another week possible, or less?"[74]

When Reynaud did not give a precise answer, the Prime Minister launched into a recital of the dire consequences of France's military collapse. This still did not answer the French Prime Minister's demand to know whether the British would release him from the solemn obligation not to make a separate peace with Germany. Spears, concerned that if the French did not get a clear response they might join the common enemy, passed a note to Churchill suggesting they adjourn for a discussion. For twenty minutes the British delegation paced the wet garden arguing whether Reynaud's authority had already been too far undermined by the absent Weygand and Pétain. It was Beaverbrook's "voice of common sense" that put an end to the soul-searching. "Tell Reynaud that we have nothing to say or discuss until Roosevelt's answer is received," he advised. "Don't commit yourself to anything."[75]

When the Council reassembled, Reynaud's fortitude had been temporarily restored by the arrival of de Gaulle. The meeting concluded on a note of renewed, if shaky, optimism: that on the joint appeal to the American President would rest France's salvation. Churchill admitted that it was the "darkest hour for the Allied cause" but continued to declare that his confidence that "Hitlerism would be smashed and that Nazidom could not and would not over-rule Europe remained absolutely unshaken." This inspired Reynaud to announce, with noticeably less conviction, that his confidence was "equally firm."[76]

"*L'homme du destin,*" Churchill told de Gaulle under his breath as the British party were ushered through the noisy crowd of French government officials gathered in the Préfecture courtyard. It was then that Reynaud's mistress thrust herself at him, crying that "my country was bleeding to death." The Prime Minister made out that he had not heard the Comtesse de Portes as he climbed into the car beside Reynaud.

"Don't give in, don't go over to the enemy. Fight on," Churchill kept on repeating to the French Prime Minister during the drive to the Tours airfield. Of the Hélène de Portes episode, he later remarked, during the two-and-a-half-hour flight back to England, "She had comforts to give him that were not mine to give."[77]

There was no comfort for the French Prime Minister when he confronted the Council of Ministers at the Château de Cangey that evening. When they heard that the Supreme War Council had decided only to issue an appeal for American belligerency, Pétain and his supporters were furious. They denounced Reynaud for not yet gaining British approval for an armistice approach. News that German troops were about to enter Paris added to the confusion and fierce partisan debate. The outcome was the decision not to fight on in the Brittany redoubt but to retire the government immediately to Bordeaux. The Council nonetheless heeded the Prime Minister's arguments in favour of postponing a final decision on the armistice issue for twenty-four hours until Roosevelt's decision was known.

Waiting for Churchill when he arrived back in London shortly before nine that Friday evening was a telegram from the White House with the President's response to Reynaud's 10 June appeal. Roosevelt said he had been "deeply moved" by the French Prime Minister's message and that "this Government is doing everything in its power to make available to you and the Allied Governments the material they so urgently require." But the President's message, while long on expressions of admiration for the "magnificent resistance of the French and British armies," was short on the pledges of support needed to keep France in the fight. It also pointedly reminded the two prime ministers that "the French and British fleets continue the mastery of the Atlantic." Appended to Churchill's copy was a polite refusal to send a U.S. Navy squadron to Irish ports because the Pacific Fleet had to maintain its full strength against Japan.[78]

Churchill wanted to read more into this telegram than the President intended, as became apparent when, calling it a "remarkable message," he read it aloud to an emergency session of the War Cabinet that evening. He announced that it "came as near to declaration of war and was probably as much as the President could do without Congress."[79]

"The President could hardly urge the French to continue the struggle and to undergo torture," Churchill declared, "if he did not intend to support them." He professed his confidence that if Roosevelt "were not disavowed by his country then it was clear that he would bring them in on our side in the near future." Beaverbrook said he was in complete agreement with this wildly optimistic interpretation of the President's message. "It was now inevitable that the United States would declare war," he concluded, adding that Roosevelt's telegram provided "complete justification" for the position they had adopted with Reynaud a few hours earlier at Tours. Ministers who had not been at the Supreme War Council meeting were far more sceptical. They pointed out that Roosevelt "had not stated in [direct] terms that the United States would declare war." Their doubts were brushed aside by the Prime Minister, who contended that "no head of State could send such a message to France urging her to continue her agony unless he was certain that his country was coming to her aid."

What was clear to the "Anglo-Saxon mind," argued the sceptics in the Cabinet, might appear "in a rather different light to the French who would be looking for something more definite." Churchill's doubting colleagues nettled him. Mindful that there were still 150,000 British troops of the 52nd Division on the Somme, he was desperately clutching at straws to give the French a reason for continuing to fight. Reynaud was therefore cabled immediately that Roosevelt's message "fulfilled every hope and could only mean that the United States intended to enter the war on our side."

At this point the Prime Minister slipped out of the Cabinet Room to seek confirmation of his assertions from the American Ambassador, who had been summoned to Downing Street. Churchill told Kennedy that publication of the President's message would provide a dramatic counter to the German occupation of Paris and that he was going to bolster the French by announcing that "Britain and France are one." Kennedy, who had just spoken to the White House on the transatlantic telephone, said that the President was "agreeable" to publication, but that he had had to bow to the advice of the Secretary of State; and Cordell Hull had flatly refused to have the telegram made public.[79]

"If he will consent to have this published it pretty well commits America to war," the Foreign Secretary had assured the War Cabinet. But the Prime Minister returned to tell them there was a setback, which he hoped could be removed once Roosevelt knew "how critical the situation was." The American Ambassador, he explained, was returning to the Embassy to communicate this to the President with a full report of the Supreme War Council at Tours. Anticipating that this would bring a favourable response from Washington, the War Cabinet gave its approval to a series of crucial telegrams that Churchill and the Foreign Secretary worked on until 2 a.m.[80]

One went to Reynaud reassuring him that Roosevelt's cable really was the light shining at the end of the tunnel and the Cabinet was "united in considering this magnificent document as decisive in favour of continued resistance of France." A simultaneous dispatch told the British Ambassador in France that Roosevelt's message "seemed very near to the definite step of a declaration of war." Another cable, addressed "at this solemn hour" to the French government, declared an "indissoluble union of our two peoples and our two Empires."[81]

Churchill then made his personal appeal to Roosevelt, warning him that the French, who were "very nearly gone," were asking to be released from their "obligation about not making a separate peace." They could only continue the fight if "hope of ultimate victory" was "kindled by American intervention up to the extreme limit open to you." Churchill asked permission to use Roosevelt's "magnificent message" as the kindling by publishing it "tomorrow June 14," when it might "play the decisive part in turning the course of world history" by denying Hitler a "patched-up peace" with France.[82]

Churchill's appeal was cabled from the American Embassy in Grey Code during the early hours of 14 June. Since Churchill had specified its routing via Kennedy, it can be presumed that it was intended to be intercepted by the Germans. Its hyperbole suggests that it may well have been designed not just to persuade Roosevelt to change his mind but also to impress Hitler with how closely the President was privately allying himself to the Allied cause. The encrypted cable which revealed the true situation to the Secretary of State was sent by Kennedy in the secure Naval Attaché's cipher. It was much more negative in tone and content, reporting that Churchill was "terribly disappointed" at the refusal to publish the President's message to Reynaud, because "conveying such a message now to the French would merely dampen what fires remained."[83]

"The danger of publication of your note to Reynaud as I see it is that Churchill sees in your note an absolute commitment of the United States to the Allies that if France fights on the United States will be in the war to help them," Kennedy warned the President, adding "I see a great danger in the message as a commitment at a later date." His disclosure that the Prime Minister was now so desperate to keep the French in the fight that he was determined to portray the President's message as a commitment to United States belligerence greatly alarmed the Secretary of State. Hull had been growing increasingly uneasy about the political repercussions for the President after his commitment to send the Allies more war supplies in his "stab in the back" Charlottesville speech. Roosevelt, preoccupied with the possibility of the Germans capturing the French fleet, had pressed Hull to go to the limit in pledging the French more supplies. The President had an ally in Sumner Welles, who egged him on, behind the Secretary of State's back, much to Hull's annoyance.

"Welles and the President are emotionally much more engaged than the Secretary," noted Assistant Secretary Berle, who saw a "difference of principle" in their commitment to the Allies from his own. That principle was to be put to the acid test that Thursday evening in Washington when the French Prime Minister's emotional appeal reached the White House.[84]

"I must tell you," Reynaud telegraphed, "that if you cannot give France in the hours to come the certainty that the United States will come into the war within a very short time, the fate of the World will change. Then you will see France go under like a drowning man and disappear, after having cast a long look towards the land of liberty from which she awaited salvation." Despite the President's concern to do everything he could to save France, he knew he must stop short of making anything like a pledge that could be interpreted by the isolationists as a commitment to go to war. The warning that Kennedy had sent prompted the Secretary of State to intervene immediately to persuade Roosevelt to stand firm and discount Welles's arguments for Churchill's appeal.[85]

"My message to Reynaud not to be published in any circumstances," the President told Kennedy that evening in a triple priority cable. "It was in no sense intended to and does not commit this Government to the slightest military activities in support of the Allies." Only Congress had the constitutional authority "to make any commitment of this nature," and if there was "any possibility of misunderstanding" the Ambassador was to "insist that Churchill at once convey this statement to the appropriate French officials."[86]

When the American Ambassador arrived at Downing Street next morning at 9.20 a.m. he "made perfectly clear" to Churchill the President's attitude regarding publication of his message. He also told the Prime Minister that Roosevelt hoped he would "explain the position" to Reynaud. This Churchill refused to do. "If President Roosevelt now appeared to be holding back," Churchill said, "this would have a disastrous effect on French resistance." That was what he reported to the 14 June morning meeting of the War Cabinet, adding that in his view the British Ambassador in Paris should be told right away that Roosevelt's message of 13 June "gave M. Reynaud the assurance of further support which he considered essential." Campbell was also instructed to deny the "pernicious reports" circulating in French government circles that "if America should not declare war" Britain would release France from the commitment not to make a separate peace.[87]

What the Prime Minister now suggested to keep their waning ally fighting was a fresh promise to send more troops to join the 150,000 already battling with the Germans along the Somme. But even as the War Cabinet gave its blessing, the gesture became futile. Columns of field-grey German troops, led by a procession

286

of tanks, had reached the outskirts of Paris at nine that Friday morning.

General von Küchler's Eighteenth Army found no opposition in the open city. The German soldiers made a point of marching right through the middle of the Arc de Triomphe, trampling the sacred flame under their jackboots. As they debouched down the Champs Elysée there were no cheering crowds, only silent, funereal groups of elderly Parisians whose tear-filled eyes attested the humiliation of the sacred flame as the dark cloud of Nazi occupation settled over the "City of Lights." The second desecratory act of the occupation forces was to hoist a huge swastika flag from the top of the Eiffel Tower as a symbol of the Führer's military triumph. The Nazi banner replaced the *tricolore* over the fortress of Verdun next morning. During the next seven days the Nazi banner usurped the French flag in French towns from the Atlantic to the Swiss borders. As the German advance flooded down France, only the fortresses of the Maginot Line remained as unconquered islands breasting the four-hundred-mile-wide grey tide.

Ambassador Bullitt remained in Paris as the city's self-appointed provisional mayor when the diplomatic corps decamped with the fleeing government to Tours. With the second move of the government there was no meeting of the Council. The intriguing of the "softs" continued as Pétain enlisted Baudouin to his supporters, who already included Weygand, Chautemps, and Ybarnégaray, all now calling for an immediate armistice. Aided by the insidious lobbying of the Comtesse des Portes, their confidence grew. Next day they squared off for a showdown with Reynaud's "diehards," led by Ministers Mandel, Campicini, Marin and de Gaulle.

Reports came from British headquarters that Friday afternoon that the French Army was "disintegrating into disconnected groups." Churchill could now only hope that the news might persuade Roosevelt to reconsider and make some gesture of intervention. When none came by Friday evening, the Defence Committee decided that the time had come to risk French charges of desertion by ordering the 150,000 British troops still engaged in France to make a fighting withdrawal to the Atlantic ports for evacuation. The crumbling Allied military command left Churchill no choice but to cable Reynaud that he was stopping the disembarkation of any further British forces in France "till the situation is more clear."[88]

Amidst alarming rumours of an imminent collapse in France, the Foreign Secretary met the Dominion High Commissioners, who raised for the first time the possibility of Hitler making a peace offer that included Britain. According to his own account, Halifax discussed the various forms that this might take. While careful to say that it was "at present a totally unreal hypothesis," the Foreign

Secretary did nevertheless advise that there "would be a reasonable time to consider," a further indication that he was anticipating a "soft" rather than a "hard" German peace feeler.[89]

Lord Halifax had by now had ample opportunity to reflect, with the other members of the War Cabinet, on the sombre military and economic equations set out in "British Strategy in a Certain Eventuality." This "To Be Kept Under Lock and Key" *aide-mémoire*, prepared three weeks earlier, now assumed the magnitude of a self-fulfilling prophecy, because what had begun as assumptions were now a reality. The report addressed the grim question whether Britain "could continue to fight single-handed if French resistance were to collapse completely." In eighteen succinct and coldly unemotive pages, the Chiefs of Staff had set down the strategic balance-sheet on which the British government would have to determine whether it was practical to fight on against Germany. Their fundamental assumption, italicized for emphasis on the front page of the report, was that Britain could not continue the struggle unless "America is willing to give us full economic and financial support, without which we do not think we could continue the war with any chance of success."[90]

Even fifty years later, the assumptions about Britain's chances of survival made by the British military planners in May 1940 amount to little more than a depressing set of uncertainties. It is therefore possible to appreciate the stunning impact that "British Strategy in a Certain Eventuality" must have had on minds such as Lord Halifax's, whose decisions were based on logical certainties, rather than emotive instinct like Churchill's.

To survive, the Chiefs of Staff concluded, Britain would have to face the onslaught of overwhelming German military superiority in the air and on land. The prime condition set by the report was reliance on American support. Then the morale of the British people had to "withstand the strain of air bombardment." Imports of commodities "necessary to sustain life and keep our war industries in action" had to be maintained despite the U-boats, and Britain had to muster sufficient military forces to "resist invasion." When it came to the question of Britain's capacity not just to survive but to defeat Germany, the military prospects were even more unpredictable. The conjecture put forward by the Chiefs of Staff was that victory might just be possible, by "a combination of air attack on economic objectives in Germany and on German morale and the creation of widespread revolt in her conquered territories." The Chiefs of Staff once again emphasized "that these conclusions as to our ability to bring the war to a successful conclusion depend entirely upon full Pan-American economic and financial co-operation."

Lacking Churchill's uplifting rhetoric, the cold analysis of "British Strategy in a Certain Eventuality" cannot have seemed a reassuring prospectus on 14 June 1940, when the War Cabinet decided to risk sending a copy of it to Washington to spur on the British Ambassador's efforts to secure American support. It was never intended to be shown directly to Roosevelt, but was meant to remind Lord Lothian that American backing – sooner rather than later – was absolutely critical to Britain's survival.

Reacting to the new priorities imposed on him by the impending French capitulation, the Prime Minister spent part of the evening drafting his longest telegram yet to the President. Skilfully weaving his case with arguments that ranged from regret, appeals to American self-interest and flattery to unashamed solicitation, with more than a hint of blackmail, Churchill made a final eloquent effort to persuade the President to take a major step towards belligerency. Whether he believed he had any chance of success is less clear than that the tone and content of the message to Washington may have been intended to give Hitler pause. Like Churchill's two previous messages, this telegram was sent through the U.S. Embassy in the Grey Code accessible to the Germans.

"A declaration that the United States will, if necessary, enter the war might save France," Churchill advised the President. He reminded Roosevelt that Hitler might bargain an easy peace for the French fleet. When it came to the much more powerful British fleet, he reiterated his "nightmare" scenario of a defeated government, of which he was no longer head, striking a deal with the Germans. In those circumstances, Churchill warned, the "overwhelming sea power" of the Axis "would be decisive on the future of the United States." More than half this telegram was devoted to statistics, supplied by the Admiralty, backing up the argument that the obsolete U.S. Navy destroyers were now more essential than ever "to bridge the gap until our new constructions come in at the end of the year." If French resistance ceased, "this island will be the only hope of averting the collapse of civilization as we define it."

"We must ask therefore as a matter of life or death to be reinforced with these destroyers," Churchill pleaded. "We will carry out the struggle whatever the odds but it may well be beyond our resources unless we receive every reinforcement and particularly do we need this reinforcement on the sea."[91]

"The Hour Has Come"
15–16 June

This was the Prime Minister's strongest appeal yet for help from the United States. The following morning it was approved by the War

Cabinet after Churchill had read the President's overnight cable that he was doing his utmost "to furnish all the material and supplies that can possibly be released to the Allied governments." Roosevelt suggested that the French could keep their fleet out of German hands, arguing that "if a general seeks an armistice for his land forces, he does not control or include the disposition of his naval forces."[92]

"Nothing short of a declaration of war by the United States," Churchill now told the War Cabinet, "would be likely to sustain the French much longer." The President's latest response gave very little hope of this. As the Minister of Information reported, the Germans had now launched their own bid to rouse American public opinion against Roosevelt's alarmist predictions.

HITLER DISCLAIMS ANY DESIRE TO INVADE THIS HEMISPHERE; TERMS "FIFTH COLUMN" FEARS AS STUPID; DENIES AIM TO SMASH THE BRITISH EMPIRE were the banner headlines that had appeared on the front page of the Washington *Times Herald* the previous day. Hitler, in what purported to be an interview with an American journalist, denounced as British "lies" the idea that Germany was any threat to the United States. The Führer declared that he believed in a reciprocal application of the Monroe Doctrine, "The Americas to America. Europe to the Europeans." The interview had already been seized on by the isolationists to brand Roosevelt as an alarmist, and the Minister of Information advised the War Cabinet that Britain must now face more of these tactics as Germany resorted to propaganda offensives to make it more difficult for the President to send aid to the Allies.[93]

American public opinion was only one of the considerations that Churchill had now to take into account in preparing for the psychological reaction to the impending German victory in France. That day he dictated a pre-emptive message of encouragement to the Dominion Prime Ministers saying that, if France fell, Britain would not only be able to fight on alone but could eventually wear Germany down. "No one can predict or guarantee the course of a life-and-death struggle of this character," he declared, "but we shall certainly enter upon it in good heart." The message ended by expressing confidence that Britain and the Empire could continue the war and the blockade "in conjunction with the United States, until the Hitler régime breaks under the strain."[94]

That afternoon, at a meeting of the Council of Ministers in the Bordeaux Préfecture, the French government all but cracked apart, riven "from top to bottom" over the armistice issue. Reynaud could not forestall a discussion until after receiving the reply they had agreed to wait for from the President of the United States. The "diehards" supported Reynaud's claim that to appeal to Hitler for terms was to "invite a rebuff" and that "there was nothing for it but to fight to the end." Chautemps challenged him to prove this by asking the Germans for the conditions on which hostilities could be ended. The majority of ministers indicated that they favoured this course. Reynaud countered by declaring that he was ready to resign if the vote went against him because he could not break the Anglo-French agreement. The President of the Republic then stepped in to avert the breakdown of the government.[95]

"We must not divide the country by dividing ourselves," Lebrun declared, announcing that he would not accept the resignation of the Prime Minister. The President's intervention stayed the critical vote when the Council adjourned until eleven the next morning after agreeing to ask the British government to release them from the promise not to enter into separate negotiations. When the stormy session ended, Reynaud's administration was barely afloat. He relayed to London via the British Ambassador another warning that unless the United States came into the war "at a very early date" France would not be able to continue. Churchill received this ominous news as he was preparing to set off for a weekend rest at Chequers. He delayed his departure to draft a last appeal to the White House.[96]

"If your reply does not contain the assurance asked for," the Prime Minister cautioned, "the French will very quickly ask for an armistice, and I much doubt whether it will be possible in that event to keep the French Fleet out of German hands." What commitment he expected Churchill did not specify, but he assured Roosevelt that it did not have to be an "expeditionary force," which he knew "to be out of the question."[97]

Early the next morning a telegram from Bordeaux was delivered to Chequers by motorcycle dispatch rider from the Foreign Office. It was from Ambassador Campbell relaying a request from the French government that the United States should be asked to act as intermediaries to find out "what armistice conditions would be offered to France by the enemy." After reading this, Churchill abandoned his Sunday in the country and drove back to London, having first summoned ministers to consider what Halifax called "the French S.O.S. telegrams."[98]

"We are fighting for our lives and it is vital that we should allow no chink to appear in our armour," Churchill warned the first meeting of the War Cabinet on 16 June. That, he explained, was why he rejected the French request for the United States to act as intermediary; Roosevelt might be tempted to use the approach as a "trump card" to ensure that Germany did not seize the French fleet and to pressurize Britain into joining a European peace conference. The French were to be granted only a limited and conditional release; the telegram that was drawn up allowed Reynaud only to take soundings to discover Germany's peace terms, "provided, but only provided, that French fleet is sailed for British harbours pending negotiations." Churchill insisted there was to be "no kind of suggestion that the United Kingdom had any part or lot in the enquiries or negotiations." It must be made clear that these soundings were initiated by France "alone on her sole responsibility, His Majesty's Government being resolved to continue the war." France's honour was to be at stake in observing these conditions.[99]

In the Bordeaux Préfecture the French Council of Ministers was still debating the crucial armistice issue even as the British War Cabinet was deliberating in Downing Street on its consequences. Reynaud announced that the United States President had responded to his 14 June appeal with promises of material assistance, but no military help. "The reply is in the negative," he conceded. When pressed, he admitted "it is a reverse." The British, he reported, were now considering France's request to be relieved of the promise not to negotiate. He hoped that by the time he met Churchill that afternoon in Nantes he would have the answer from London. The "softs" on the Council denounced this delay as just another attempt by the Prime Minister to stall the inevitable. Baudouin suggested that the British were playing for time by retreating from their earlier agreement that an armistice decision should depend on Roosevelt's response. Pétain concurred, and tried to force the issue by standing up and reading his letter of resignation.[100]

"The hour has come," the Marshal declared, "for the Council to make up its mind." The majority of ministers indicated their agreement. Reynaud's side objected to taking a vote, knowing they would lose it. Eventually President Lebrun prevailed on Pétain to withdraw his resignation. The vote should await the formal British answer, which would be considered that afternoon when the Council met again at five to decide "whether final resistance was possible."

The Council adjourned at lunchtime in a mood of anger and frustration. In Bordeaux and in London, ministers believed that only a miracle – or an immediate declaration of war by the United States – could rescue Reynaud's administration and save France from having to appeal to Hitler for an armistice. In a final act of magnanimous resolution, Reynaud had dispatched General de Gaulle to London with the full authority to divert to Britain all the aircraft, armament and war supplies that France had ordered from the United States. It was over lunch with the Prime Minister and his entourage in the Carlton Club that de Gaulle suggested a dramatic gesture that could sustain Reynaud and avert an armistice: to transform into reality Churchill's earlier offer of an "indissoluble act of Union of the French and British peoples."

Churchill was at first sceptical. But Reynaud, when reached by

292

telephone, was by now straw-clutching with the desperation of a drowning man, and he enthusiastically endorsed de Gaulle's idea of making Britain and France one country. The Prime Minister was persuaded, and work began at breakneck pace to write a "Declaration of Anglo-French Unity" that would be the miraculous formula to keep France fighting from her overseas Empire. A special session of the War Cabinet was summoned and the British Ambassador was told to "suspend action" on the telegram giving the French the authority to sound out Germany for terms. In this race to beat time and the odds, Churchill did not disguise the mountainous constitutional and legal questions of citizenship, financial and legal systems and conflicting government mechanisms involved in the proposal.

"In this grave crisis," the War Cabinet were told, "we must not let ourselves be accused of a lack of imagination." A draft of the Proclamation of Franco-British Union was produced and approved by the War Cabinet at 4.30 that Sunday afternoon. Its text was telephoned over to Bordeaux in time to meet Reynaud's five o'clock deadline. If the Council of Ministers would accept it, this astonishing document would make Britain and France – on paper at least – one nation at the stroke of a pen.[101]

"At this most fateful moment in the history of the world," the Proclamation declared, Britain and France were to constitute themselves a single country to "concentrate its whole energy against the power of the enemy, no matter where the battle may be." Enthusiasm was running high in Downing Street late that afternoon as de Gaulle set off to fly back to Bordeaux with a copy of the Proclamation. The Prime Minister, accompanied by Attlee, Sinclair and by senior officials from the Foreign Office, headed for Waterloo Station. A special train stood ready to take them to Southampton, where one of the fastest cruisers in the Fleet had been laid on to ferry them across the Channel. Churchill's plan was to pick up the French Prime Minister at Nantes next morning for a historic on-board treaty signing ceremony at noon the next day.

"We might yet see the Fleur de Lys restored to the Royal Standard," Colville wrote expectantly in his diary. But it was not long before he was telephoning the station master at Waterloo to hold up the departure of the Prime Minister's train. Sir Ronald Campbell in Bordeaux had cabled that the meeting with Reynaud was now "impossible" because of a ministerial crisis. As the Prime Minister's party glumly made their way back to Downing Street Reynaud's government went through its death throes in Bordeaux.[102]

An hour before the scheduled Council of Ministers meeting Baudouin had learned from Reynaud that the British had withdrawn their earlier negotiating authorization. He had also found out that Reynaud was intending to put forward the declaration of an Anglo-French Union. The proposal was "so fraught with consequences" that Baudouin dismissed it as "not the problem of the moment," since the ministers were committed to asking Germany for armistice terms. When he warned Reynaud that a majority of the Council would go against him, the Prime Minister deflated like a punctured balloon, wearily acknowledging that if the vote went against him he would resign and make way for a Pétain government.

Reynaud was therefore uncharacteristically subdued as he read out Churchill's "generous offer" to his ministers an hour later. As if he was an actor with the wrong script, his speech in support of the Anglo-French Union was irrelevant to his fellow players. They already had their act together and were impatient to put an end to France's military agony, whereas the Prime Minister wanted to prolong it at the cost of thousands more French lives and treasure.

What Baudouin described as the "marriage of fire and water" under which the Council had been labouring for more than a week finally broke down in the impassioned accusations of cowardice and lack of patriotism that were hurled at each other by Mandel and Chautemps. With a weariness that was visible to everyone in the Bordeaux Préfecture, Reynaud suddenly gave up. He conceded that the majority favoured an armistice. Since he could not agree to this in breach of the solemn agreement he had signed with the British, he asked President Lebrun to nominate Marshal Pétain as his successor.[103]

When the Council of Ministers adjourned shortly after 7 p.m. that fateful Sunday evening, the French government had effectively resigned. Three hours later the President of the Republic finally accepted Reynaud's resignation, and invited Marshal Pétain to form a government.

"I have seen the list of future ministers," Reynaud announced to Baudouin on his way out of the meeting with Lebrun, "and it is a Laval administration." He congratulated his Under-Secretary on becoming the Minister of Foreign Affairs. After a ten-minute meeting with the pro-German Pierre Laval, the new Foreign Minister summoned the Spanish Ambassador to request that his government should make representations on behalf of France to the German government. Baudouin then held an icy meeting with the British Ambassador to promise that the French "would never hand over either all or part of the French fleet." He assured Sir Ronald Campbell that Admiral Darlan had already taken the necessary measure to ensure this. Then he told Ambassador Biddle (who was acting for the United States in Bordeaux while Bullitt remained in Paris) that he was also authorized to pass on to President Roosevelt "our promise not to hand the French fleet over to Germany."

The "Certain Eventuality" envisaged by the British Chiefs of Staff had come to pass. Britain was now facing Germany alone. The

Foreign Secretary was woken up in the early hours of Monday morning – "quite unnecessarily," he complained – to be told the names of the Cabinet members of Marshal Pétain's new French government.

"This," Lord Halifax noted, "raises all one's worst fears."[104]

Chapter 12

"Common Sense and Not Bravado"

Day 8
17 June

"The enemy is retreating along the entire front in a state of complete disorganization and under constant bombing by our air force," General Halder recorded at O.K.H. on Monday, 17 June. It was obvious to him that Allied resistance in France had crumbled. Guderian's Panzers had reached the Swiss frontier, and Kleist's forces had cut their way down France to the upper Loire. Almost a quarter of a million prisoners had been taken. A rout was inevitable, but how much longer the French government would hold out was not yet clear to Halder and his staff.[1]

The Spanish government's cable relaying the French armistice request had reached Berlin during the early hours, but it was not until just before noon that O.K.H. received the news in a telephone call from "Forest Meadow," Hitler's new advance headquarters in southern Belgium. In the woodland clearing ringed by anti-aircraft guns and barbed wire, the Führer and his "political command" were in a state of rare emotion. When the news of the armistice request was given to Hitler, to the astonishment of his aides he actually hopped with delight.

There was no jumping for joy in London that Monday morning. Yet the mood among the military leaders was more relief that they were free of a burdensome ally rather than gloom that the Battle of France had been lost. This was eloquently expressed by the Chief of Fighter Command in a letter to Churchill that began: "Well! now it is England against Germany, and I don't envy them their job." The mood was much the same in the Foreign Office, where Cadogan

296

recorded: "It will almost be a relief when we are left alone to fight the Devil and win or die."[2]

BRITAIN FIGHTS ON TO WIN, the *Daily Herald* proclaimed, echoing the optimism of many newspapers that France's exit from the war would help rather than hinder the national cause. The British population, for centuries conditioned to think of the French as the historic enemy, took heart that they were now free to concentrate on fending off a German invasion.

Regret, relief and resolution was the message the Prime Minister gave to the Monday War Cabinet, which decided to order the immediate evacuation of all British troops from France while Marshal Pétain's new government was negotiating over the armistice terms. Once more the flotillas of small craft set out across the Channel from the harbours and creeks of southern England to rescue British troops stranded in France. Many of their skippers were veterans of Dunkirk, but "Aerial," as the operation was codenamed, never attracted the publicity of "Dynamo," although on the longer crossings the danger from enemy air attacks was no less. That afternoon the bombing of the liner *Lancastria* cost the lives of most of the 5,000 evacuees boarded at St. Nazaire. For over a month the news was kept from the public by government censorship after the Prime Minister had personally intervened, minuting: "The newspapers have got quite enough disaster for today at least." There was no shortage of gloomy news for Churchill and his government that Monday. In the morning the German news service in Berlin had announced that Hitler and Mussolini were to meet next day, fuelling British concern that the two dictators would agree to carve up the French fleet between their navies. As the War Cabinet deliberated past midday on whether Britain could rely on Admiral Darlan's assurances that they had "nothing to fear" as long as he was Minister of Marine, Marshal Pétain was broadcasting to the French Army his call for a cease-fire.

"It is with a broken heart that I must tell you that fighting must cease," the Marshal had ordered in a reedy funereal voice all but cracking with emotion. A transcript of his broadcast was rushed into the War Cabinet meeting. It was agreed that the British Ambassador would redeliver the previous day's telegram making British agreement to armistice negotiations by the French conditional on their sending the fleet to British harbours.[3]

Churchill then addressed a personal appeal to "the illustrious Marshal Pétain and the famous General Weygand." These were the most polite words in a "snorter" of a cable, which the Foreign Office tried, but failed, to tone down. The cable ended by admonishing Pétain and Weygand that should they hand "their fine fleet" over to the enemy it "would scarify their names for a thousand years of history." In a speech that afternoon to the House of Commons, the Prime Minister took care to sympathize publicly with the plight of the French nation as a whole.[4]

"The news from France is very bad," Churchill admitted with heartfelt solemnity. "I grieve for the gallant French people who have fallen into this terrible misfortune." Nothing, he said, "would alter our feelings towards them or our faith" that "the genius of France will rise again." He told the House that what had happened in France "makes no difference to our actions and our purpose."[5]

"We have become the sole champion in arms to defend the world cause," Churchill announced. "We shall defend our Island home, and with it the British Empire shall fight on unconquerable until the curse of Hitler is lifted from the brow of mankind. We are sure that in the end all will come right." That evening he delivered his speech again in a B.B.C. world broadcast. His message that Britain would fight on was directed not just to the British nation but also to German and American ears. Before making the broadcast Churchill had assured Ambassador Kennedy of his intention personally to tell every American journalist in London that Britain was going to fight on until victory.[6]

"Why, if I don't say that, the people of England would tear me to pieces," Churchill said, half-joking. He made a point of asking Kennedy about destroyers when he suggested that the President would do well to send a warning to Pétain about the French fleet. The Ambassador's reluctance to let the British Prime Minister appeal directly to the American press was, as his report to the State Department that day reveals, a further indication that he did not believe that fighting on alone was the right course for Britain to take. He put this view strongly to the Foreign Secretary. Cadogan records in his diary that Lord Halifax afterwards went to see Churchill, but does not say what it was about. That the possibility of a peace initiative was discussed appears likely, not just from Kennedy's defeatist stance, but because this entry was censored from the published version of Cadogan's diary.[7]

What Halifax and Kennedy discussed that afternoon may be only hinted at in the carefully composed sentences that appear in the Foreign Secretary's private diary. It records that he found the Prime Minister "very robust and almost convincing himself that we shall do better without the French than with them." Halifax's own view was less rock-firm: "I *think* he is right in feeling that *if we can*, with our resources concentrated, hold the devils for two or three more months there is *quite a chance* that the situation *may turn* in our favour." That he hedged his own prognosis with so many conditionals suggests why he concluded: "Anyhow for the present, at least, there is no alternative." The evidence, as we shall see, shows that this may not have been the case, and that Halifax was already actively collaborating with his deputy Butler in putting out fresh peace feelers. Nor were the Foreign Secretary's doubts dispelled by Churchill's exhortatory speech the following day.[8]

The Prime Minister began by assuring the Members of Parliament that he had nothing to fear from the "dread balance sheet" now that the Battle for France was over and the Battle of Britain was about to begin. The rhetoric of his ringing call to arms conjured up reassuring visions of "immense, continuous and increasing" arms supplies flowing across the Atlantic, matched by the "individual superiority of our aircraft and pilots." He declared that even "contemplating our dangers with a disillusioned eye, I can see reason for great vigilance and exertion but none whatever for panic and despair." He portrayed the battle that had begun as a struggle not just for Britain and her Empire, but for the very survival of Christian civilization.

To strengthen the national resolve to withstand the "whole fury and might of the enemy," Churchill avowed that Hitler must break Britain or lose the war. Welding defiance, exhortation, hope and inspiration into rhetorical armourplate, he forged a magnificent speech that fired the British nation physically and spiritually for its lone fight with Hitler. "If we can stand up to him, all Europe may be free, and the life of the world may move forward into broad sunlit uplands," he prophesied; "but if we fail, the whole world, including the United States, and all that we have known and cared for, will sink into the abyss of a new dark age made more sinister, and perhaps more protracted, by the lights of a perverted science."[9]

"Let us therefore brace ourselves to our duties, and so bear ourselves that, if the British Empire and its Commonwealth last for a thousand years," Churchill concluded, "men will still say, 'This was their finest hour.'" Inspiring and courageous though his words were in June 1940, he himself later admitted that "rhetoric was no guarantee" that the nation would heed his call to arms. He even foresaw the possibility that his words would be interpreted abroad as "only a bold front, set up as a good prelude to peace negotiations."[10]

Ten years after the critical days following the Fall of France, Churchill was to acknowledge that his worst fear had been that Hitler "was in a position to offer the most tempting terms." He wrote that "it did not seem impossible that he would consent to leave Britain and her Empire and Fleet intact and make a peace which would have secured him that free hand in the East." This admission stands in striking contradiction to the arguments he employed at the time to swing the War Cabinet against Halifax's determined arguments in favour of seeking out Hitler's terms. It was the same challenge made to Reynaud the day before his government collapsed, and it was Churchill himself who conceded that he too might have been swept aside by the argument that "the war mongers have had their chance and failed." But in his memoirs he only raised the possibility in order to deny that the British government had *ever* found itself approaching that situation. Yet, as can now be seen, he was denying the historical record with his sweeping assurance that when it came to the question of peace negotiations "we never thought it worth a place upon the Cabinet agenda, or ever mentioned it in our most private conclaves."[11]

Churchill had good reason to bury not only the bitter three-day debate over whether to seek out Hitler's terms at the time of Dunkirk, but also an actual peace feeler that had been launched at Halifax's instigation on the day that France asked the Germans for armistice terms. The Foreign Secretary, it seems, had put a different cast on the "dread balance sheet" of British military arithmetic. Shortly after Churchill had announced that Britain's 'finest hour' was at hand, Lord Halifax was at Buckingham Palace sounding out the King, who shared his belief that Britain had "nearly touched bottom." According to the Foreign Secretary's private record, George VI "complained a good deal of the difficulty making contact with Winston!" Next day Halifax discovered "intrigues that are going on in the House of Commons" against Chamberlain – and, he assumed, himself. He was critical of Churchill's "discursiveness" and "extraordinary brain" which he found "a most curious mixture of a child's emotion and a man's reason."[12]

Such a litany of criticism at the hour of supreme crisis for Churchill and his government suggests that Lord Halifax's disillusionment had more to do with his own sympathy for the rational decision of the French to negotiate an armistice than with Churchill's emotional and childish refusal to face up to reality. In the two weeks since Halifax had argued for sending out non-committal peace feelers to ascertain Hitler's terms, Britain's Army had lost most of its weapons and Roosevelt had refused to become engaged. To Halifax it seemed more urgent now to try to discover if there was an acceptable alternative to Churchill's call for fighting on the poisoned beaches, the blasted hills and the bombed-out ruins of English towns and cities. While Britain and her Empire were still intact, reason rather than emotion argued for him to find an alternative before paying such a terrible price.

"Common sense and not bravado" was the actual phrase that the Foreign Secretary used for the alternative he envisaged, according to the report that Sweden's Minister in London cabled to his government on the evening of 17 June. Those English words and "diehards" leap out from the yellowing Swedish ticker-tape strips in the deciphered Foreign Ministry cable, which summarizes the "conversation" that Björn G. Prytz had with the Under Secretary of State at the Foreign Office that calamitous Monday afternoon.

The unenciphered original in the records of the Swedish Legation in London characterizes the talk as "highly confidential." This was clearly no routine meeting with the second most senior minister of the British Foreign Office. Prytz had developed specially close relations with Butler, socially and professionally. The Swedish Minister was an English-educated industrialist who dispensed with the formal stiffness of his professional diplomatist colleagues at the Court of St. James. A gregarious chain-smoker, he maintained a cottage in Surrey for his golfing weekends and, as a widely travelled and wealthy connoisseur, was a sought-after guest at dinner parties. His sporty two-seater Rolls Royce was a familiar sight outside the Mayfair homes of London society and Westminster politicians, including Butler's gracious Smith Square house, which was adorned with some of the fine Impressionist masterworks his wife Sidney had inherited from her father, the textile magnate Samuel Courtauld.

It did not therefore surprise Prytz that Monday when the Under Secretary of State dispensed with the diplomatic formalities and began to unburden himself on the consequences of the French capitulation. Butler complained that Britain's ally had capitulated "without any reservations concerning her fleet or colonies." He suggested that this would seriously affect the British government's ability to continue the war alone, dropping broad hints that peace negotiations were now being seriously considered. That is how Prytz interpreted his remarks both at the time and to the end of his life. He maintained that Butler gave him that afternoon a clear and deliberate diplomatic signal, couched in terms that led him to inform the Swedish government that a British peace move was in the offing.

"Britain's official attitude will for the present continue to be that the war must go on," Prytz reported in his telegram. The reality, as Butler "assured" him, was that "no opportunity of reaching a compromise peace would be neglected if the possibility were offered on reasonable conditions." The Under Secretary of State had reinforced the point by stating that no "diehards" would be "allowed to stand in the way in this connection," because "Britain had greater possibilities of negotiations [today] than she might have later on and . . . Russia would come to play a greater role than the U.S.A. if conversations began."[13]

The impression Prytz received of imminent British peace moves was reinforced when the Under Secretary was called out to see Lord Halifax. He returned with what he said was the message from the Foreign Secretary: "Common sense and not bravado would dictate the British Government's policy." Halifax, through his deputy, had sounded the cautionary note that while his message "would be welcomed" in Stockholm "it should not be interpreted as 'peace at any price'." The Swedish Minister also reported, from his conversations with unspecified Members of Parliament, that "there is an expectation that, if and when the prospect of negotiations arises, possibly after 28 June, Halifax may succeed Churchill."

The handwritten notation on Swedish Foreign Ministry telegram 723 shows that the cipher cable was received in Stockholm at 10.20 local time that Monday evening and decrypted by 1 a.m. on 18 June. When the report reached Christian Günther, Sweden's Foreign Minister, later that morning, it was immediately taken as an authoritative and direct signal from the mouth of the British Foreign Secretary of British intentions to make peace. On the face of it, this was the only conclusion that Günther, a career diplomat of considerable experience, could draw. As the annotation on the telegram confirms, its contents were at once communicated by diplomatic bag to the Swedish Ministers in Moscow and the Nordic capitals. Günther then showed the cable to the Parliamentary Foreign Affairs Committee and discussed its significance with Arvid Richert, the Swedish Minister in Berlin, who happened to be in Stockholm to convey the latest German demands for transiting their troops through neutral Sweden to Norway.

The significance of this particular telegram is the controversy it created after the war when the former Swedish ministers claimed it had influenced their decision to bow to pressure from Berlin on 18 June 1940 and give transit rights to German troops. As one high official in the London Foreign Office revealingly minuted, the Swedes had "unearthed an unfortunate skeleton." The British government repeatedly tried to persuade the Swedes to rebury it, because Britain's "stoutheartedness when we stood alone is such a tremendous asset to our prestige in the world." Whenever it rattled, this skeleton called into question not only the Churchillian myth of the "finest hour" but also threatened to wreck the reputations of Lord Halifax and of his deputy Butler, a postwar Foreign Secretary and, according to his supporters in the Conservative Party, "the best Prime Minister Britain never had." (See Appendix 10.)

"Defeatist Views"

The telegram containing the Halifax-Butler peace feeler of 17 June 1940 is preserved for posterity in the Riksarkivet, the start of a documentary paper trail that leads the historian from Stockholm to the palm-ringed campus of California's Stanford University, then back across the Atlantic to the Wren Library of Trinity College, Cambridge, and eventually to a sixteenth-century cottage in a sheep-filled Cotswold valley. That investigatory trail began behind the huge steel blast doors in the missile-silo-like galleries of the Swedish national archives, which were carved deep into the bedrock of picturesque granite bluffs overlooking the dark waters of Mälaren Lake. Secure from nuclear attack in the deepest of these tomb-like subterranean chambers, one of the world's most secure repositories, are housed the campaign reports of Gustavus II Adolphus, the military genius who made Sweden a great power in Europe at the start of the seventeenth century. In an adjacent row of electrically operated stacks, opposite the fat leather-bound annals recording Sweden's golden age, are the more prosaic cardboard boxes containing the files of the Utrikes Department – the Swedish Foreign Ministry. These World War II files chart a less glorious period of Swedish history, when a fragile coalition government, conscious of its military weakness, struggled to navigate a neutral course.[14]

At no time during the war did this diplomatic balancing act require more delicate diplomatic footwork than in June 1940, when Sweden's government – a patchwork of Social Democrats, Agrarians, Conservatives and Liberals – juggled the conflicting demands made by Germany, Britain, and the Soviet Union. The menace of Russian expansionism loomed large in June 1940, as Stalin sent the Red Army in to seize the Baltic republics of Estonia, Latvia and Lithuania, this new threat coming barely three months after Sweden had helped negotiate the armistice that ended Russia's "Winter War" with neighbouring Finland. The Allied evacuation of Narvik also brought renewed diplomatic demands from the Germans to allow transit for their troops, pressure that the British Ambassador in Stockholm, Sir Victor Mallet, worked vigorously to counteract.[15]

Per Albin Hansson, the cautious Social Democrat Prime Minister, found himself in a delicate political situation when Richert arrived in Stockholm on 17 June to deliver Ribbentrop's latest demand for the Wehrmacht to use Sweden's railway system. Two days earlier, the Swedish Minister in Berlin had been summoned to the Belgian castle of Acoz near the Führer's headquarters during the final stage of the Battle of France. There had been no mistaking the menace in Ribbentrop's tone when he informed Richert that Sweden's continued refusal to grant transit rights could be regarded as "an unfriendly act."[16]

The Swedish ministers assembled in some trepidation at 9 a.m. on 18 June to hear Richert's report on his meeting with Ribbentrop. Even the three Social Democrats in the Cabinet reluctantly agreed with the majority that concessions had to be made to the Germans rather than risk attack and occupation. Their decision was taken after Günther had insisted "rather dramatically" on reading out the Prytz telegram. One Social Democrat minister recorded how this had "tipped the scales" in favour of a limited agreement allowing strictly regulated transits through Sweden to German troops on leave. However, Swedish claims that their concessions to Germany in 1940 were based on a "broad hint from His Majesty's Government that Great Britain might come to terms with the Nazis" were later vigorously rejected by the British as "entirely misleading." In June 1940 the Foreign Office moved swiftly to get Butler to deny Prytz's report. They acted after Mallet cabled London on 19 June that the Swedish Foreign Minister had called him in for clarification of Halifax's reported remark that British policy would be dictated by "common sense and not bravado." To Günther's attempt to find out whether Butler's remarks "were intended as a hint," the astonished British Ambassador responded by referring him to Churchill's B.B.C. broadcast declaring that Britain would fight on regardless of the French defeat.[17]

"Certainly no hint was intended" was the Foreign Secretary's reply to Stockholm the next day, endorsing the denial already given by Mallet. Drafted by Butler, this cable tried to put a totally different construction on what had passed between him and Prytz. Blaming the "apparent anxiety of Swedish Minister lest war should be perpetuated and extended," the Under Secretary claimed only to have said that "force must be opposed to force." Prytz, he said, had "exaggerated the coincidence and importance of any polite message conveyed to him by way of explanation."[18]

Simultaneously the Swedish Foreign Minister had telegraphed Prytz on 19 June informing him that he had "told Mallet the contents of his cipher message and cautiously sought to clarify whether the intention was that the British attitude was intended to be communicated further [i.e. to the Germans]. We need to know if this was the intention." Next day Prytz cabled back that his conversation was "probably to be regarded as an expression of his and Halifax's private attitude and not intended to be conveyed further," because the British government was awaiting the outcome of the Franco-German armistice discussions, and its attitude "has not yet crystallized."[19]

An explanation for this curious backtracking by Butler is offered by Professor Wilhelm Carlgren, who interviewed Prytz extensively before writing his account for the official history of Swedish foreign policy in the war years. A veteran of Sweden's civil service and former head of the archives of the Foreign Ministry, Professor Carlgren suggests that the message Halifax relayed to Butler on 18 June to pass on to Prytz may *only* have been intended for Swedish ears. Essentially it was sent to warn Sweden not to be too stiff in opposing the German transit demands because the British government was considering whether it could get the right terms for negotiating a peace with Hitler. The Foreign Secretary might

304

well have been intending to make peace soundings with Berlin, not through Sweden but through another neutral country, possibly Switzerland or Spain. Butler failed, either deliberately or intentionally, to make this clear to Prytz. So the Swedish Foreign Minister, assuming that he was expected to act as intermediary, took immediate steps to see that the message would get to Berlin, only afterwards asking the British Ambassador for clarification. By doing so he inadvertently crossed wires. Mallet raised the alarm with the Foreign Office, forcing Butler to beat a hasty retreat, sheltering behind Halifax and claiming that his remarks had been misinterpreted.

Mallet, who appears to have been personally hostile to the idea of negotiating with Germany (in contrast to the British Ambassadors in Spain and Switzerland), became even more alarmed when he learned that a *News Chronicle* journalist had heard from two members of the Riksdag's Foreign Affairs Committee that Butler had said that "Britain would continue the war only if certain of ultimate victory." He reported to the Foreign Office that he had warned the British journalist that the Germans might intercept his cabled reports, and pointed out the dangers of "drawing false conclusions" from rumour picked up from the Swedish parliament.[20]

Alarmed and understandably anxious to contain the damage resulting from his remarks, Butler saw Prytz next day to get him to agree to modify his account of what had been said at their previous meeting. This much is obvious from the regret expressed in his telegram to Stockholm that Mallet had "obtained the impression that Sweden is anxious to play a mediating role." Prytz expressed concern that his friend Butler was now embarrassed because his "extremely confidential" message had leaked out. "Butler has experienced unpleasantness since suspicion of defeatism is a serious matter in these days," he said, denying that Halifax's deputy had made the specific remark attributed to him by the Swedish press. He did not, however, show to Butler, or give him authority to deny, the statements that formed the substantive element of his 17 June cable.[21]

Yet, in the cable Butler sent Mallet two days later informing him of his meeting with Prytz, he nonetheless by clever implication expanded this limited denial to discounting the whole of Prytz's original message. The Swedish Minister, he wrote, "*had derived an exaggerated impression*" and he was "very surprised that the matter should have been put to the Foreign Affairs Committee of the Riksdag, who incidentally were sworn to secrecy and should not speak to the Press." According to Butler, it was Prytz who had suggested that "certain interested parties in Sweden had mixed themselves up in the affair in an attempt to make mischief," and he urged Mallet "to prevent any further exaggeration."[22]

"Björn Prytz was absolutely certain that he had reported accurately," Carlgren confirmed after reviewing the records of his extensive interview with the former Swedish Minister in London. Not only did Prytz assure Carlgren repeatedly that he *had* accurately reported his meeting with Butler, but he told him that his other sources in the Conservative Party had also led him to believe that the Foreign Secretary was considering the possibility of forming a government that would negotiate with Germany if Churchill continued to refuse to do so.[23]

Since neither the Foreign Office nor the British Ambassador in Stockholm knew until after the war the full contents of Prytz's cable, Butler was able to cloud the issue by treating Prytz's denial of the garbled statement given to the Swedish press as a blanket denial of *all* his defeatist statements of 17 June. This was the line he took when the matter came to Churchill's attention after reading the Stockholm Embassy cables.

"It is quite clear to me from these telegrams *and others* that Butler held odd language to the Swedish Minister, and certainly the Swede derived a strong impression of defeatism," Churchill wrote testily to the Foreign Secretary on 26 June asking him to "find out from Butler what he did say." The letter expresses particular anger because the Prime Minister had just given the House of Commons assurances that "the present Government and all its members were resolved to fight to the death." Alluding to "a silly rumour" from the Balkans that British peace moves were under way, he warned Halifax that "any suspicion of lukewarmness in Butler will certainly subject us all to further annoyance."[24]

The Prime Minister's letter reached the Foreign Secretary that evening and he at once showed it to his Under Secretary. Whether Halifax found his deputy's language "odd" or "lukewarm" is not clear from the laboured handwritten explanation Butler delivered to Halifax. Exonerating himself by denying he had given Prytz "any 'impression of defeatism'," Butler drew attention to the denial sent on 23 June to Mallet. He mentioned the "great distress to the Swedish Minister and myself that this matter has assumed the wrong significance that it has." There is something suspiciously convenient about his explanation that he "did not keep a record" of the discussion because it was the result of a chance meeting in St. James's Park.[25]

"I do not recognize myself or my conversation in the impression given," Butler protested, implying that "since no one else was present," his master could decide whether he would have exhibited any lukewarmness. "You may enquire why any conversation with a Foreign Representative took this line at all," Butler wrote, "and why I was reported as saying that 'common sense and not bravado' would dictate our policy." Significantly, he begged the question by referring only to the denial he had sent to Mallet. Prytz, he added, had "since agreed with me that this account of our talk is correct." Yet he gave no details of his remarks in those "few minutes" other than claiming that he had reminded Prytz that "if we were to negotiate, we must do so from strength, and that force must be met with force." Whatever it was he had said on the subject of "an ultimate settlement," Butler wrote that it was "nothing definite or specific or that I would wish now to withdraw."

"I now place myself in your hands," Butler concluded, stressing the need for Halifax to have "absolute confidence" in him. Anticipating that Churchill might read the letter, he declared that he would already have resigned from the government "had I not been ready to subscribe to the Prime Minister's courageous lead in the House of Commons." He awaited "your and the Prime Minister's final opinion after you have read this letter and made any further enquiries."

The Foreign Secretary chose neither to make any further inquiries nor to show Butler's letter to the Prime Minister. Instead he got his Under Secretary off the hook by writing to Churchill next morning, maintaining (falsely, as the records show) that he had a "full note of what passed between him [Butler] and the Swedish Minister." There had been "no divergence of views," he assured the Prime Minister, drawing attention to the Stockholm cable of 23 June – written by Butler – accusing Prytz of fabricating "an exaggerated impression" of what he had actually said.

"I should be very sorry," the Foreign Secretary wrote, "if you felt any doubt either about Butler's discretion or his complete loyalty to Government policy, of both of which I am completely satisfied." That this complete exoneration of his Under Secretary was on its way to Downing Street on 27 June, only a matter of hours after the receipt of the Prime Minister's complaint, indicates that Halifax moved very hastily to shield Butler from the Prime Minister's displeasure. It is even more surprising to find that Churchill took the Foreign Secretary's superficial assurances at face value. He let the matter drop. But to have taken the matter further would have meant challenging Lord Halifax again over the thorny question of peace negotiations.[26]

Yet despite Butler's self-serving and carefully constructed denials, the evidence now available makes it impossible to believe that Butler was simply "speaking too much" or that he did not realize that Prytz would report such a portentous conversation to the Swedish government. Moreover, the records show that this was by no means the first peace feeler that the Under Secretary had given to neutral intermediaries, and both he and Halifax must have known that their "common sense and not bravado" message to Stockholm would reach Berlin. A more credible construction is that their intention was to elicit favourable peace proposals from Germany that would satisfy the formula the Foreign Secretary had already raised in the War Cabinet. After the protracted row three weeks earlier at the time of Dunkirk, Halifax appears this time to have wanted to establish that Hitler *would* offer reasonable terms before confronting Churchill.

Prytz, after being put under pressure by Butler to modify his story and report to the Swedish Foreign Minister that the message he was given was "probably" not intended to be "conveyed further," did not find out until the end of the war how he had been made a scapegoat. Then it became clear that Halifax and his deputy had denied they had made him the postman for an unofficial British peace feeler. Prytz first realized how he had been set up during a dinner conversation in the summer of 1946 with "a well-known British conservative publicist with good American contacts who used to be close to Butler." Prytz's informant, whom he did not name in the report he filed with the Swedish Foreign Ministry on 28 August, disclosed that Halifax and his deputy had also asked him "the day after France's capitulation" to sound out Ambassador Kennedy about a compromise peace with Germany.[27]

Prytz took to the grave the name of the mystery informant. But the identity of the "conservative publicist" he referred to emerged by serendipitous chance at Stanford University in the personal papers deposited for safe keeping at the Hoover Institution by Kenneth Hugh de Courcy.

Among the voluminous de Courcy papers is a handwritten memorandum detailing the three "historic missions" that the Conservative activist undertook at the request of senior members of the British government. The first was to Paris during the Munich Crisis, when de Courcy claims that his informants in the French military confirmed that France was not prepared to go to war over Czechoslovakia. In January 1940 he claims he again received approval from Downing Street to travel to Rome, Sofia and Paris again, where he was shown a secret French military report by General Charles Brécard that led him to conclude that France would be unable to resist a massive German attack. His third secret commission came on the eve of the French collapse, when he was summoned to the Foreign Office and was asked by Butler to act as go-between with the American Ambassador because "both he and Lord Halifax consider a negotiated peace to be desired."[28]

When accessioned to the Hoover archives in 1984, the "Special Notes" recounting the curious role de Courcy had played as peace intermediary in June 1940 were placed in a file marked "World War 1939–1945." That folder and another, which named Soviet sympathizers in the British establishment, have since disappeared from the Stanford Archives. Neither the local police nor the F.B.I., which was called in by the Hoover Institution to investigate the missing files, have been able to come up with any leads. The apparent theft of these particular files puzzles the Bureau as much as the Hoover staff. Not only is security tight at the Institution, but none of the valuable autograph letters from the Duke of Windsor to de Courcy is missing.

When interviewed in 1989, de Courcy was inclined to believe that his missing files may well have attracted the attention of the British secret service, since his account of what really happened behind the scenes on the day that France fell contradicts the official record. A ruddy-faced and philosophical octogenarian, de Courcy relishes his reputation in the Gloucestershire press as something of an eccentric for his efforts to exercise his ancient rights as Lord of the Manor of Stow-on-the-Wold and collect dues from the municipal car park. He now lives in the heart of the Cotswolds, surrounded by a pack of boisterous black cocker spaniels, in a honey-stone cottage crammed with the souvenirs of his long career as a political lobbyist. In 1940, as the Secretary of the Imperial Policy Group and editor of its widely read *Intelligence Digest*, he had become a gadfly to the hardliners in the Foreign Office for the allegedly *défaitiste* policy promoted by his publications. Another irritant was the confidence de Courcy enjoyed from the diplomatic community in London, including his friend Prytz, who regularly supplied him with Swedish intelligence on the war. Ever since he had returned from a fact finding trip to Paris approved by Halifax in April 1940, he had been warning ministers that France would collapse. (See Appendix 11.)

The Under Secretary of State, who "saw merits in the Group's work," had been de Courcy's principal ear and protector in the Foreign Office, and for two years they had been meeting on a regular basis. But after de Courcy's return from France Halifax's deputy had been avoiding him, because of Foreign Office concerns over the lobbyist's defeatist views. In his letters, however, de Courcy had urged the Under Secretary to intervene to set in train a diplomatic solution. His appeals grew more frequent and increasingly strident after the events leading to Dunkirk vindicated his predictions. On 15 May, after an hour-long meeting with Bastianini, he wrote to Butler that the Italian Ambassador was ready to intervene to effect a diplomatic solution. On 21 May he called for Butler to use the "counters" by bringing the "Italian and U.S.A. Ambassadors into immediate consultation." The Under Secretary, he said, was the only one "with a cool enough head and sufficient courage to take the only and right course." Butler responded that "the counters to which you refer, together with any others that it may be possible to play, are not being forgotten."[29]

309

On 31 May de Courcy passed on to Butler a letter from the French Senator Henry Lemery, a friend of Pétain, supporting a diplomatic resolution of the war. This followed up his previous day's communication expressing the hope that the "counters were not being lost sight of." The "very great gravity" of the military situation on 2 June prompted de Courcy to write again, predicting that Paris would fall within three weeks, and arguing that "astute diplomacy" with the Italians might still save the Allied cause from disaster. The time had come, he contended, for considering an appeal to Hitler for an armistice: "I beg you to use your influence to keep the wild men from dragging this Empire further towards disaster." The next day de Courcy forwarded to Butler a gloomy report on the situation in France expressing General Brécard's views but written by his wife. On 5 June, after meeting with M. Chastenet, de Courcy asked to see Butler to convey a message that Daladier's envoy found too sensitive to give directly to the British government.[30]

On the formal acknowledgement that de Courcy received from the Foreign Office on 6 June, Butler had added a handwritten invitation to meet him the next day, which set in motion the sequence of events described in the missing Hoover Institution file. When de Courcy telephoned as instructed, he found it odd that Butler did not want to meet in his office, or at his own house, but suggested 5 Belgrave Square, the home of his Parliamentary Private Secretary, Chips Channon.

"How dare you delay seeing me for six weeks when the life of England is at stake?" de Courcy challenged Butler next day in Channon's grand reception room. The response that he received from the Under Secretary was as cool as it was cryptic: "The life of England has been at stake for some time." Indignantly de Courcy reminded Butler of his letters repeatedly warning of France's inability to sustain a drawn-out battle with the Germans. When asked what he thought the British government should do now, de Courcy says that he urged striking a deal with Hitler as soon as possible to extricate Britain from the "military mess" she was in. He proposed enlisting the aid of the United States and presenting Hitler with a formula similar to the one that President Woodrow Wilson's advisers had urged in 1916. This would require a peace conference to be called, and the Germans would be told that if they did not attend it they would face the United States joining the war on the Allied side. American sanctions would also be implicit in enforcing a settlement that required Germany to withdraw from the occupied nations of Western Europe and restore some form of independence to Poland. In their discussions Butler insisted that Hitler would also have to be bought off by giving Germany control of the mouth of the Rhine – a concession that de Courcy says he flatly refused to countenance.[31]

The Under Secretary of State nevertheless agreed that de Courcy should try to sell the idea to the American Ambassador, and as soon as the meeting in Belgrave Square was over he telephoned and asked to see Kennedy on a matter of grave importance. To his great surprise, the Ambassador not only agreed to a meeting at once but endorsed the peace scheme when de Courcy arrived at the Embassy. "This is a most intelligent idea," Kennedy told him. "I will recommend it at once to the President."

Quite by chance de Courcy was lunching at the Carlton Club Annexe in Pall Mall a few days later. Butler was sitting on the other side of the dining room, and when he spotted de Courcy, came over to congratulate him. "The Ambassador asked for an interview with my master," Butler said, telling de Courcy "how enormously impressed he was with the proposal that you made. My master thinks it highly desirable if you saw Kennedy again as soon as possible."

In response to the Under Secretary's suggestion, de Courcy agreed to contact the American Ambassador and to meet Butler for breakfast the following morning at the latter's home in Smith Square. As he returned across St. James's Park to the Imperial Policy Group office in Old Queen Street, de Courcy was relishing the role he anticipated he would play in ending the war. But his hopes came crashing down shortly after four o'clock that afternoon when he received a phone call from Victor Raikes, a Conservative M.P. who was on the Executive Committee of the Imperial Policy Group.

"Your breakfast meeting will not take place," Raikes told de Courcy. "Instead what you will do is walk in St. James's Park tomorrow morning. When you cross the bridge you'll see somebody you know and you must express surprise."

The following morning de Courcy followed his instructions to the letter. When he encountered Chips Channon waiting on the ornate iron footbridge, he duly expressed surprise. After exchanging pleasantries they sat together on a park bench.

"I've a message from my master," Channon explained ominously. "You have to go back to Old Queen Street and burn your file, with everything that has ever been written between you and Butler." He seemed relieved to learn that de Courcy had not yet seen Kennedy. He instructed him to cancel his appointment and leave for Scotland immediately. "If you do not, you will be in very great danger," Channon said; "so will my master and so will Lord Halifax."

"Are you mad?" de Courcy demanded. Butler's Parliamentary Private Secretary explained: "Churchill has found out everything and is even threatening to lock up Halifax and my master under the 18B regulation." This startled de Courcy. His initial reaction was that the whole affair was being overblown. But he was aware of the government's powers under the wartime emergency laws. He agreed not to see Kennedy again or to tell anyone about the peace discussion. But he did not flee to Scotland or burn his files. He said that Butler carefully avoided any contact with him for some time afterwards, although he continued to write to the Under Secretary. The letter he wrote on 24 June on the French armistice received only a cursory acknowledgement from the desk officer. It was thirty-two years before de Courcy dared to raise the matter again, after finally writing his memorandum and sending it to Butler, who was then Master of Trinity College, Cambridge.[32]

"I must say that I do not think you have the Prytz interview quite right," replied Lord Butler in a letter from the Master's Lodge on 23 September 1973. He acknowledged receiving de Courcy's account "to put in my files," but he said that they were "long out of date," and that "the facts are mentioned in full" in his book. This was not true; nor was Butler's assertion that he "had practically no knowledge of, or contact with Kennedy." Surprisingly, all evidence of this exchange of letters has been expunged from Lord Butler's surviving papers, now in the Trinity College archive. This lends some credence to de Courcy's story. "The Prytz telegram terrified Butler," de Courcy noted on the reply. "He had a great deal more to do with Kennedy and so told me in 1940." According to the memorandum, now missing from the Hoover Institution, de Courcy was unaware before that meeting with Channon that the Prime Minister had not sanctioned the peace initiative in which he had been involved by Halifax and Butler. "The only clue I ever had," he wrote, "was from Prytz, who told me that Churchill did not approve because Butler had expressly told him to tell the Swedish government that Churchill's warlike views would not prevail."[33]

"I said and did all I could to sound what I believed to be the proper warnings and I have done so up to the last moment," de Courcy protested in a letter to the Dominions Secretary on 28 June 1940. Assuring Lord Caldecote, another of his regular correspondents in the government, that he knew what "some of the problems were and still are," he announced that he had "quite withdrawn all interest in positive foreign policy for the present." This came as a relief to Foreign Office officials like Roger Makins (later Lord Sherfield), who recalled how de Courcy "used to bombard us with memoranda and was regarded with the utmost caution." The Dominions Secretary, it turns out, had been forwarding de Courcy's letters to the Foreign Office, because, as he minuted, they represented "a point of view which is by no means to be neglected."[34]

Interception of de Courcy's letters to Senator Henry Lemery and Madame Brécard had persuaded the Foreign Office that he was "an out and out defeatist" and should be brought to the attention of MI5. But the security service said it had nothing on its files to indicate that he was "in any way disloyal." In June 1940 Makins even paid de Courcy the back-handed compliment that although he was a "defeatist," the Imperial Policy Group's memoranda did make "some good points." They were the source from which the Foreign Office admitted it had first learned of Pétain's close connection with Laval. "Mr. de Courcy is very often right," one official commented, "but he is a bad influence."[35]

Butler rather too eagerly concurred in a minute whose hypocrisy was not apparent at the time. In 1989, when Lord Sherfield was asked for his view of the accounts de Courcy and Prytz had given of the Halifax-Butler peace initiative, he claimed not to have known of the affair at the time; but he conceded that "a lot of us in the Foreign Office didn't really cotton on to what was really going on." He did know that "Prytz was very close to Rab," which led him to believe that Butler must have been "operating on his own" with de Courcy, because he was certain that Halifax did not know of their close relationship.[36]

"Rab was a very ambivalent character," Lord Sherfield said, stressing that Butler was so "very elusive" that officials in the Foreign Office would not have known if he had taken matters into his own hands in the way the Prytz and de Courcy accounts suggest. He was less certain, however, whether the Foreign Secretary would have initiated the Prytz peace feeler, believing it much more likely that Halifax was led into it by his Under Secretary. He agreed that Halifax would have regarded it as his duty to shelter Butler once the storm broke, because the Foreign Secretary considered "Churchill as wild and [needing] to be kept under control." Halifax must have been actively involved, unless Butler was deliberately lying to Prytz about the "common sense and not bravado" statement – or de Courcy was manufacturing the Foreign Secretary's congratulatory message relayed to him at the Carlton Club. There is also evidence substantiating de Courcy's account in a telegram Kennedy sent to Washington which appears to reflect the outcome of his first meeting with de Courcy.

"For the first time this morning many people here realize they are in for a terrible time," the Ambassador wrote on 17 June. "If the English people thought there was a chance of peace on any decent terms an upheaval against the Government might come." This cable was sent after Kennedy's afternoon meeting with the Foreign Secretary, which appears to have followed his enthusiastic endorsement of de Courcy. This was the day after Halifax had returned from meeting the French at Tours, only hours after the news reached London that the Germans had entered Paris. So it would have been an appropriate occasion for Halifax to suggest to Kennedy his intention to send discreet signals to Washington about "decent terms." It also appears no coincidence that such a hint might have been given by the Foreign Secretary immediately after his meeting with the

Dominions High Commissioners for a confidential discussion of how Britain might react to a German peace offer.[37]

That same evening the Halifaxes had dined with the Chamberlains. Next day the former Prime Minister wrote a confidential letter to his sister that suggests that the Foreign Secretary might have raised the possibility that Britain might have to seek terms from Germany. "I really don't like to put on paper even to you anything about the situation as it has been or as it is, for it seems too dangerous," Chamberlain wrote with uncharacteristic reticence, adding "it is extremely difficult to see any light at the end of the tunnel." He followed this cryptic reference by reporting the speculation that Lloyd George was "ready to form another govt & make the peace for the terms which he would be able to blame on the maladministration of his predecessors." If it really had appeared hopeless for Britain to fight on alone, Chamberlain would certainly have wanted to prevent the resurrection of his old political foe as peacemaker. Did he therefore tacitly give his blessing to Halifax over dinner that night for the scheme devised by Butler to find out whether the Germans would propose reasonable terms?[38]

The answer may never be known with absolute certainty. But the choice of Prytz to relay a sounding signal to Berlin is consistent with Halifax's concerns about the irrationality of fighting on alone and Butler's close association with the Swedish Minister. The artfully constructed statements contrasting the attitudes of the "diehards" with those in the government who were for "common sense" echoed the arguments that the Foreign Secretary had put to the War Cabinet three weeks earlier and the complaints about Churchill in his diary.

Butler also made it very plain to the Swedish Minister that while "no opportunity for reaching a compromise peace would be neglected," Halifax and he were not interested in "peace at any price." His assertion that "no 'diehards' would be allowed to stand in the way" was taken by Prytz as a thinly veiled reference to the removal of Churchill if he opposed a reasonable German peace offer that guaranteed Britain's continuing independence. It was probably for the benefit of Berlin that Butler added his suggestion that Germany's ally Russia "would come to play a greater role than the U.S.A. if conversations began."

The content and construction of Butler's remarks to Prytz are yet another reason for believing that this was not the off-the-record impromptu chat he tried to maintain later, but a feline bid to use the Swedish Minister in London to relay a high-level peace-feeler to Berlin. Since both Halifax and his deputy knew that the Germans were pressing for transit rights, they cannot have been unaware of the importance that would be attached in Stockholm to a signal that the Foreign Secretary wanted to strike

314

a deal with Hitler and that the "diehard" Churchill would not be permitted to stand in his way.[39]

That was certainly Richert's conclusion when he saw a copy of the Prytz telegram before setting off for Berlin that Tuesday with the Swedish government's approval for limited German troop transits. The Secretary General of the Foreign Ministry and the Swedish Foreign Minister would later deny that either had given their Minister in Berlin any *specific* instructions to transmit the contents of that cable to the Germans. But they did pass on the gist of Prytz's message to the Italian Ambassador in Stockholm, because Francesco Fransoni's 19 June cable, which survives in the Italian archives, reports that the "British government is inclined to enter into peace negotiations with Germany and Italy." Fransoni adds that the Swedish Foreign Minister had assured him that the information was "of an official character."[40]

"Richert was a cautious man and a professional diplomat who was a good friend of Günther," Professor Carlgren pointed out, confirming that a specific instruction would not have been necessary, since the Minister was well aware that Sweden's interest lay in furthering a speedy peace with the Allies to allow the Germans to give attention to the Soviet Union. But Richert's 19 June dispatch to Stockholm from Berlin *after* his meeting that Wednesday at the Reich Foreign Ministry suggests that he was following a written directive to raise the matter at his meeting with State Secretary Ernst von Weizsäcker.[41]

"Referring to *your letter of 18 June concerning the British inclination to peace*," Richert reported that he had asked Weizsäcker about the British reaction to the "new situation" arising with the armistice negotiations in France. Citing Churchill's speech promising to fight on, the State Secretary said that he had not seen "any signs of a willingness to negotiate on the British side." This he deplored, since he predicted it would lead to "an abominable destruction of Britain." Mentioning Prytz by name, the Swedish Minister in Berlin told Weizsäcker he had seen a report from London which suggested that "in leading circles a certain 'common sense' and *Verständigungswillen* [willingness to reach an agreement] now existed." Weizsäcker was interested but "sceptical," telling the Swedish Minister that he very much hoped for a negotiated settlement as the wisest solution but that as yet they had received no signs of a willingness to negotiate.[42]

Weizsäcker nonetheless responded immediately to this interview by sending Ribbentrop, who was in Belgium aboard his headquarters train, a teletype reporting that the Swedish Minister had informed him that over the peace issue there was now "a return to sound common sense in authoritative circles in London." Ribbentrop must also have given the State Secretary instructions to try to discover more, because on 22 June Weizsäcker summoned Richert to the Foreign Ministry again. After a brief discussion on transit rights, he raised the subject of the British peace feeler, producing a London press report that suggested that Lloyd George was about to enter the government and take over as Prime Minister to conclude a compromise peace. Was this, Weizsäcker asked, what Richert had been referring to the other day?[43]

The Swedish Minister, expressing some surprise, said that "this version was new to him and he did not believe it" because his information was that a "peace trend was beginning in the present government." This caused Weizsäcker to speculate which member of the British Cabinet "could be willing and capable of supporting a 'commonsensepolitik'." Richert reported that the State Secretary had then tried to deduce the minister's identity by a process of elimination, but according to the captured German Foreign Ministry records it was the Swedish Minister who went down the list of the more important members of the Cabinet, eliminating "Churchill, Eden, Duff Cooper, Chamberlain and Simon as unsuitable for this, *and hinted that Halifax represented the peace trend.*" When Weizsäcker said that Berlin "knew nothing of such peace moves in England," it was again Richert who replied "more emphatically than at his last visit that we would soon hear something more of this, but of course he could not say in what way."[44]

"One can only wish that Halifax and his men [will] soon take the rudder and not wait too long," Richert appended to his report of the conversation, suggesting how enthusiastically he may have promoted the peace feeler. His sentiments were obviously in tune with those of Sweden's Foreign Minister. But Günther found himself in something of a diplomatic quandary after receiving Prytz's telegram strongly denying that Butler's message was intended to be relayed to Berlin. His own impatience for a settlement would explain why Günther had not waited for Mallet's confirmation *before* showing the cable to Richert – or at the very least warned the Swedish Minister in Berlin not to mention the matter to the Germans until approval had been received from London.[45]

The haste with which the Swedes moved may have reflected their own interest in passing the British peace feeler to the Germans, but they now had a double dilemma in trying to find a way to get the positive German response back to London. Günther could not pass such a message through official channels without running the risk of admitting that a private conversation with the Swedish Minister in London had been relayed to Berlin. His other problem was that since the original Prytz message a new dispute had snarled up the Anglo-Swedish diplomatic relationship.

"We Are Going to Make Peace with Great Britain"

The German response to the Prytz message arrived in Stockholm in the midst of a blazing diplomatic row. It had erupted the previous day when Lord Halifax formally notified the Swedish Minister in London that the Royal Navy had seized six Swedish naval vessels when they put into the Faeroe Isles to refuel. The flotilla consisted of four destroyers that Sweden had purchased from Italy, whose crews were ordered at gunpoint to embark on their attendant oiler and depot ship. The justification Prytz was given by the Foreign Office was the international law of angary, which permits a belligerent to seize neutral war materials to prevent them falling into the hands of the enemy. It was a thin excuse, since the rusty and obsolescent warships, none of which could steam on more than one turbine, would not have been of value to Germany, and the Swedish Naval Attaché in London had taken care to notify the Admiralty and obtain official clearance for the passage of the flotilla.

Prytz and Mallet were kept busy for three days as Sweden fired off a barrage of "energetic" diplomatic protest to the British government and appealed to the Labour leaders to protest at this assault on her neutrality. Assurances were also obtained from Berlin that the German Navy, far from having any intention of seizing the destroyers, would escort them through the Skaggerak minefields. Lord Halifax was the minister who found himself in the middle of a shrill diplomatic rumpus and on Churchill's instructions had had to stall Stockholm with tit-for-tat accusations about Sweden's un-neutral decision to permit German troop transits. He then offered to arrange for the release of the destroyers if the Swedish government would release to Britain aircraft ordered from the United States. Such a brazen attempt at diplomatic blackmail was angrily rejected in Stockholm. Mallet and Prytz relayed the Swedish government's mounting fears that the acceptance of such a deal would result in an "ultimatum" from Berlin that they must accept German "protection" and surrender their navy. The Foreign Secretary's argument that a German démarche on Sweden might be imminent finally convinced Churchill and the War Cabinet to release the flotilla on 24 June.[46]

The seizure of the Swedish destroyers was ostensibly unconnected with the Butler–Halifax peace feeler. But its timing suggests otherwise. The issue of whether the Swedish flotilla should be seized appeared on the War Cabinet agenda the day after Butler's conversation with Prytz. Two days later, when the decision was taken to proceed with the seizure, the diplomatic crisis that erupted strained relations between Stockholm and London to breaking point at the very time the British government was denying the peace messages relayed by Prytz. The crisis was finally resolved on 24

317

June, the day before the Swedish Foreign Ministry finally found a way to get the German response to the British peace feeler to Ambassador Mallet in Stockholm.

The Swedish destroyer row was remarkably convenient for Churchill, tying up the Anglo-Swedish diplomatic wires which might otherwise have accelerated the peace initiative. It also served notice to Berlin as well as Stockholm that as long as Churchill was in charge the British government would employ its naval power decisively and ruthlessly. Sweden's Foreign Ministry had to resolve the destroyer crisis before proceeding with the peace feeler, and this contributed to the three-day delay before the German response reached London.

The intermediary who acted as a semi-official go-between with the British was Marcus Wallenberg, a businessman from a Swedish banking dynasty. He was also well known to and trusted by Halifax, since he had been involved in the long and difficult negotiations with Britain arranging for Swedish trade to continue through the blockade. Wallenberg did not meet Mallet until 25 June, the day after the British had agreed to release the Swedish destroyers. He reported that he explained to the British Ambassador that he was conveying a "private" message because the Swedish government "did not want to be misinterpreted." At the same time they wanted to make sure the message from Berlin reached the British.[47]

Wallenberg said that Mallet was "free to take it or leave it," and then passed on the news that the Swedish Minister in Berlin had reported that the "German side was exceedingly interested to know whether the British were inclined to negotiate." The British Ambassador "could not believe the British government were willing to negotiate;" he said this belied his instructions from London, since "on the contrary everything implied its firm will to continue the war." He agreed, however, to transmit the message to London, and that same day he cabled direct to Halifax that the Germans were "keen to negotiate." His report stated that "they could not negotiate with Mr. Churchill, Mr. Eden or Mr. Cooper but would be ready to negotiate with your Lordship."[48]

The Foreign Secretary and Butler now had the expression of German interest in negotiations they sought, but still lacked any indication whether it would be on reasonable terms. Halifax made no reply, and this telegram was not filed with the other exchanges about the Prytz cable but buried away with other Northern Department traffic. This was not surprising since it was on the following day that Churchill fired off his reprimand to Halifax complaining of Butler's "odd language." The message from Stockholm thus became an embarrassment that neither of its parents wanted to acknowledge.

Churchill's complaint about Butler was clearly triggered by

Mallet's cable, but why had he waited for nearly a week after first learning from Mallet's 19 June cable that something odd was afoot? Churchill's extreme touchiness over the peace negotiation issue means that he must have had a good reason for withholding action. It is also known that he relied very heavily on his MI5 and MI6 contacts and his intelligence adviser, Morton, to alert him to potential appeasers, so it is unlikely that the very fishy contents of the cables going back and forth to Stockholm following Prytz's report would not have been brought to his attention for a whole week. Within this time frame he could also have received the decrypt of Prytz's original cable from the codebreakers of Bletchley Park. Unless and until the British wartime intelligence archives are declassified like those in the United States, it will be impossible to establish just how much of the neutral cipher traffic was being read by the British in 1940. But Sweden's communications must have been a prime target, and the decrypts of Prytz's cable could explain Churchill's curious reference to "others" besides the telegrams of the British Ambassador in Sweden.

The Prime Minister did not, however, need to know the contents of the original Prytz telegram to deduce that Butler and Halifax were playing their appeasement game again. If de Courcy's account is correct, shortly after the Fall of France he had found out the full extent of their peace plot and was threatening Halifax with detention under 18B for subversive activities. This makes it even more surprising that he took no sterner action than the relatively mild letter about Butler's "odd language." There were no confrontations or resignations. The matter was simply allowed to lie after the Under Secretary's evasive and grovelling letter of apology permitted the Foreign Secretary to dash off a face-saving denial to Downing Street. Had there been an investigation, Butler would at the very least have been obliged to resign for his indiscretions.[49]

Why did Churchill let the matter drop after firing no more than a warning shot across the Foreign Secretary's diplomatic bows? The logical explanation is that Churchill left Halifax and Butler in office precisely so that the Germans *could* believe they were sending out peace feelers. If he had sacked the two most prominent appeasers in the War Cabinet, it would have signalled to Berlin that there was no hope of a negotiated peace with Britain. And this was a message that the Prime Minister could not yet afford to send to Hitler; as long as the Germans believed there was a chance of coming to terms, they would postpone their invasion of Britain. As long as Halifax remained in the War Cabinet, Hitler would not give up hope that, despite Churchill's emotional public declarations, "common sense and not bravado" would in time prevail.

Evidence that Churchill was indeed resorting to such Machiavellian stratagems to bluff Hitler has come to light in his selection of certain of his cables to be sent to Roosevelt in the insecure American Grey Code. These were the ones that would reveal to any eavesdroppers in Berlin his close links with the President, whose primary concern was to stop the British and French fleets from falling into German hands. Indications that Churchill's message got through to Berlin appear in the German record of the exchanges between the Führer and the Duce when they met in Munich on 18 June to agree the French armistice terms.

Two pointers that emerge from the conference record argue that the Germans had indeed been eavesdropping on Churchill's exchanges with the White House. The first was that neither dictator discussed dividing up the world's fourth largest fleet to bolster their own navies; their preoccupation was with finding a formula that would permit the French to neutralize their own warships. That appropriation by Germany or Italy of France's modern battleships was not even discussed as an option may well have been influenced by Hitler's knowledge that it would drive the United States closer to an all-out commitment to the British. Still more persuasive is Hitler's reference to the "refusal of the United States to sell destroyers to Britain." Until late August, Britain's appeal for destroyers was a closely held secret in both London and Washington. How could Hitler have acquired this vital information other than from intercepts of the Churchill–Roosevelt Grey Code cables?[50]

"If London wants war it will be a total war, complete, pitiless," Hitler had declared, while stating his "many reservations on the desirability of demolishing the British Empire, which he considers even today to be an important factor in world equilibrium." This was what Ribbentrop told the Italian Foreign Minister during the Munich meeting. To Ciano's question whether the Germans' preference was for the continuation of the war or a compromise peace, Ribbentrop unhesitatingly said "Peace," also indicating that contact was already being sought with London through Sweden.[51]

Since the "common sense and not bravado" message from Butler and Halifax had reached the Swedish Foreign Ministry only that morning, Ribbentrop had either received some advance notice of it or he was himself considering Sweden as a possible intermediary. Goebbels' diary also confirms that Hitler was hoping for a negotiated peace with Britain. When he raised the question with the Führer on 16 June he had been told that the French must "first go down on their knees." Then, said Hitler, they would see "what England intends to do" when Germany had effectively struck "the sword out of her hands." He had already discussed his plans in detail with his military Chief of Staff, General Jodl.[52]

"The Führer had anything but the intention of completely destroying the British Empire as England's downfall would be to the detriment of the white race," Jodl's assistant told a meeting

The Invited Envoy? The wreckage of the Messerschmitt Me110 (A) from which Rudolf Hess (B) parachuted to Scotland on 10 May 1941. Reports from KGB informants in the British Secret Service that the Deputy Führer's peace mission to the Duke of Hamilton (C) was the result of an MI6 plot are corroborated by RAF operational logs and newly discovered German records.

Appeasers and Warmongers. Hitler's assiduous prewar courting of British leaders included former Prime Minister David Lloyd George (A) and Lord Halifax (B *left,* with arch appeaser Sir Samuel Hoare). Chamberlain's disastrous policy resulted in his sell-out of Czechoslovakia at Munich (C) in 1938. When Winston Churchill became Prime Minister after the behind-the-scenes intervention of Chamberlain's confidant Kingsley Wood (D, in bowler, with Anthony Eden) Hoare was sacked from the government while Halifax remained Foreign Secretary and with 'Rab' Butler (E) continued to press for a compromise peace with Germany.

Fifth Column Conspiracies.
Tyler Kent (A), an American
Embassy code clerk who was
released from a British prison
in 1945 (B) after conviction
with Anna Wolkoff (C) of
Official Secrets Acts offences
in 1940. Their arrest resulted
from an elaborate MI5 'sting'
operation masterminded by
Captain Max Knight (D)
whose undercover agents
included Joan Miller (E) who
penetrated the Right Club run
by Conservative MP Captain
Archibald Maule Ramsay (F)
and his wife. MI5's
uncovering of this 'dangerous'
pro-German conspiracy was
used by Churchill to get
draconian new powers to
threaten peace plotters in
Parliament.

A

The Wall of Sand. As France's massive army crumbled before the German Blitzkrieg in the West, Premier Paul Reynaud (A *centre*) steadily lost the confidence of (*left-right*) Commander-in-Chief General Maxime Weygand, War Council Secretary Paul Baudouin and Marshal Pétain. Hitler, at his headquarters during the Battle of France (B), intervened to halt the Panzers before the Dunkirk beach-head (C) so as to encourage an Anglo-French peace offer.

The Jackal's Feast. Lord Halifax and the French Foreign Minister tried to get Italy to act as a peace mediator with Hitler after Mussolini entered the war and German troops occupied Paris (A). After France sued for an Armistice the Italian dictator met Hitler in Munich (B) to claim his share of the spoils.

We Shall Never Surrender. After gloating in Paris (A) the day after the French Armistice was signed Hitler confidently awaited Britain's surrender while Churchill (B) rallied his fellow countrymen to fight on even if Germany invaded.

A Chinaman's Chance. The defeatism of Joseph P. Kennedy (A) was encouraged by the warnings his sons Jack and Joe Jnr gave of *Luftwaffe* invincibility. The American Ambassador worked to prevent the release to Britain of mothballed World War I destroyers (B). Roosevelt (D) was determined that the British continue fighting and he and Secretary of State Cordell Hull (C *left*) enlisted Canadian Prime Minister Mackenzie King (C *right*) to urge Churchill not to come to terms with Hitler to 'save civilization'.

The Battles for Britain. The RAF, whose aircrews included Poles (A), defeated the *Luftwaffe* although their Hurricane and Spitfire fighters (B) were outnumbered by more than 2:1. Yet even after Britain's victory in the air, Lord Halifax (C, with Sir Alexander Cadogan) sanctioned peace feelers to Berlin's intermediaries. This encouraged Hess (D, with Soviet Foreign Minister Vyacheslav Molotov in November 1940) to prepare for a spectacular bid for a settlement with Britain before the attack on Russia. A September 1940 letter sent to the Duke of Hamilton at the request of the Deputy Führer was intercepted and appears to have instigated a plot, sanctioned by MI6 chief Sir Stuart Menzies (E), that lured Hess to Scotland nine months later.

A

B

Calling the Bluff. After Churchill had ordered the Royal Navy's ruthless attack on the French Naval Squadron at Oran (A & B) the smiles of Hitler and Göring at the Berlin victory parade (C) conceal their displeasure at Britain's refusal to make their triumph total. But German Foreign Minister Joachim von Ribbentrop (D, with Italian Foreign Minister Count Ciano) launched a plot to restore to the British throne the Duke and Duchess of Windsor (E, with U.S. Ambassador to France William C. Bullitt).

Breaking Britain's Secret. Churchill concealed the truth about the Hess peace proposal from Stalin (A, at Yalta in 1945) who KGB archives show had been kept informed of the inside story by Soviet spy Kim Philby (B, the Russian commemorative stamp). The full records of the British interrogation of Hitler's deputy were kept from the Nuremberg War Crimes Tribunal, where the insanity feigned by Hess fooled even Göring (C).

of Naval Staff on 17 June. The "possibility of making peace with Britain after France's defeat and at the latter's expense, on condition that our colonies are returned and Britain renounces her influence in Europe" was the reason the Führer gave for not wanting the High Command to "undertake studies and preparations for an invasion of England."[53]

During Ribbentrop's 1945 interrogation he confirmed that Hitler was ready and willing to respond to a British peace offer at the time of France's capitulation. He had received Weizsäcker's 18 June report that the Swedish Minister had hinted there was a peace movement in the British Cabinet. The timing fits exactly with Ribbentrop's discussions with Hitler about making peace with Britain, which he says took place *after* Dunkirk at the Führer's headquarters "before Compiègne, before the armistice."[54]

"Do you know what we are going to do now?" Ribbentrop said Hitler had asked him when they were alone that evening.

"Yes," Ribbentrop replied. "We are going to make peace with Great Britain."

"Yes."

"Shall I sit down and sketch out an offer for Britain?" Ribbentrop asked.

"No, don't do that. I shall do that myself – only three or four points, very short," Hitler said, and proceeded to dictate the guidelines on which Ribbentrop was to work out peace with the British:

"Point one: Nothing must be done to violate the prestige of Great Britain. Secondly, immediate peace, of course, with Great Britain. Thirdly, the only thing I do want is to have one or two of the old German colonies because we do need some colonial materials and so on; and fourthly: an alliance with Great Britain."

According to Ribbentrop, the Führer's confident expectation that Germany would soon be able to make peace with England was confirmed by the fact that he had even decided whom to appoint as the Reich's future Ambassador to London. His preference was the candidate Hess had put forward: his Bradford-born deputy, Ernest William Bohle, the energetic English-speaking head of the Nazi Party's *Auslands-Organisation*.

"What do you think of sending Bohle as Ambassador there?" Hitler asked. Ribbentrop said he had enthusiastically endorsed the choice. It is unlikely he would have raised any objection even had he objected to Bohle becoming Gauleiter of Great Britain. The former wine salesman owed his position as Reich Foreign Minister to his slavish toadying to Hitler. "Germany's No. 1 parrot," as Göring called Ribbentrop for his regurgitation of the Führer's opinions, was now given orders to do everything possible to bring about the peace his master so earnestly desired with Britain. The Reichsausminister turned for advice to the so-called England Committee. This was a group of former ambassadors and British specialists in the Foreign Ministry who met every Friday throughout 1940 "to prevent anything that would turn British public opinion against Germany." It had been established in November 1939, and, according to a former member, it was also instructed "to keep an eye on the possibility of concluding a peace with England." The England Committee had advised Ribbentrop that contrary to Hitler's belief he could not make acceptable peace offers to Britain "camouflaged as propaganda." Not only was this advice turned down, but Hitler also rejected the Committee's opinion that Britain would negotiate for peace *only* if Germany showed some willingness to evacuate the conquered nations and restore the independence of Czechoslovakia and Poland. After the Swedish peace feeler came to nothing, Ribbentrop, who had accepted his committee's opinion, concluded that he had to find some way of making a dramatic breakthrough. He decided to galvanize what the Committee believed to be an extensive and highly placed faction in the British government opposed to Churchill which might be persuaded to negotiate if the right channel of communication could be found.[55]

So when Ribbentrop was able to tell Hitler on 22 June that Lord Halifax was the Cabinet minister behind the Swedish peace feeler, his hopes of striking a deal with Britain must have leapt. Anticipation that events were falling out his way may have accounted for his "boisterously happy mood" when Goebbels arrived at the Führer's headquarters two days later. "Negotiations were already under way on these issues, via Sweden," Hitler assured his Minister of Propaganda, explaining that his terms were "England out of Europe, colonies and mandates returned," together with "reparations for what was stolen from us after World War I."[56]

Hitler warned Goebbels that it was not yet clear whether the negotiations would be successful. He would have been encouraged that the peace feeler through Sweden had come from the same British Foreign Secretary who had executed the policy of appeasing Germany and who now appeared to be willing to split with the warmonger Churchill. Even the most tentative of peace overtures from such a source as Britain's noble Foreign Secretary would have been taken very seriously. Halifax had the right credentials. As a high Tory aristocrat and a former Viceroy of India he could be expected to agree that Britain's destiny as an imperial and maritime power was complementary to and not in conflict with Germany's demand for authority over Europe.

The fact that Lord Halifax was the source of the Swedish peace feeler, combined with Ribbentrop's craving to please the Führer, would have spurred him to do everything possible to encourage the approach. The records show that hints of an imminent British peace move *were* leaked into the Berlin diplomatic rumour mill. Within days newspapers around the world were carrying the story that the hardline Churchill was facing a serious challenge from Chamberlain and Halifax over the peace issue. The rumours were not only timely but credible now that Britain's sole ally had gone down to defeat.

Yet in spite of all the efforts made by the German Foreign Ministry's so-called "peace campaign," they failed to produce the gesture that Churchill feared most. That was to respond to the Halifax-Butler peace feeler with specific assurances of Britain's independence. Only if the Foreign Secretary had received such a guarantee would he have been able to challenge Churchill by resurrecting the peace issue in the War Cabinet.

Chapter 13

"The Supreme Struggle"

"No One Is Downhearted Here"
21–30 June 1940

"Germany does not intend to give the armistice terms or negotiations the character of an abuse of such a gallant enemy," General Keitel declared at Compiègne on 21 June 1940 as he delivered the German armistice terms to the French delegation, led by General Charles Huntziger. The words were Hitler's; he had not only written the script for his chief of staff but had personally devised the ceremony to humiliate France.[1]

Sweeping up in a big open Mercedes through the avenues of trees lined with grey walls of Siegheiling troops, the Führer alighted and strutted with disdain across the sunlit clearing in the forest north-west of Paris, the exact spot where the German generals had surrendered to the Allies in 1918. Giant Nazi war banners shrouded the statue representing Alsace-Lorraine and provided the backdrop to the wooden World War I railway dining-car, which had been brought out of its museum to serve the same purpose twenty-two years later in this symbolic reversal of history. Seating himself in the wooden chair occupied by Marshal Foch in 1918, Hitler received the French delegation into the carriage. Their stony stares betrayed their shock at finding themselves in a picaresque charade. Satisfied with the spectacle he had orchestrated, the Führer departed after Keitel's speech, leaving his military staff to inform the French of the fate he had detailed for them.[2]

Paris was to be occupied, despite the pleas of Marshal Pétain. The French army would be demobilized, except for the bare military necessities for the protection of France's overseas empire. All tanks, guns, ammunition and military aircraft were to be surrendered to the Wehrmacht, whose forces were to remain in control of the greater part of metropolitan France. From Dunkirk to the Pyrenees the coast was to be under German military control; Pétain and Laval's government were granted authority over the portion of France south of the Loire to the Mediterranean. Under Article 8 of the Armistice the French fleet was to be sent to its home ports to be "demobilized and disarmed under German and Italian supervision." When Hitler had told Admiral Raeder the day before that the Kriegsmarine would not get a single French warship, he had sarcastically suggested that the best thing would be for it to be scuttled by its own crews. He rejected the French counterproposal that the fleet should be sent to North Africa.[3]

Next day, after Hitler had made his furtive dawn foray to gloat over Paris, the French delegation at Compiègne struggled valiantly through a day of frustrated attempts at negotiations. The Germans would brook no interference from the hostage government in Bordeaux. The *Diktat*, as Foreign Minister Baudouin described it, was finally initialled at 6.50 p.m., after Keitel had given the French a one-hour ultimatum. "Forced by the fate of arms to cease the struggle," General Huntziger announced, he was signing only under the direct orders of his government. "France," he protested, "sees imposed on her very hard conditions."[4]

"Diabolically clever" was Churchill's assessment of the German terms, which would come into effect two days later on the signing of France's separate armistice agreement with the Italians. It was Article 8 that caused him and the War Cabinet most concern at their 22 June meeting. Solemn assurances had been received from Admiral Darlan and Marshal Pétain that the fleet would never end up in the hands of Britain's enemies. The question was whether the French could now be trusted to keep their word. The fate of the warships was "vital to the safety of the whole British Empire," Churchill declared. He worried that the most powerful battleship afloat was lurking in the French West African port of Dakar; *Richelieu*, he told his ministers, "must not be allowed to get loose."[5]

With the unfinished battleship *Jean Bart* reportedly heading for Casablanca and the French Navy's heavy cruiser squadron at Oran, Churchill ordered the Admiralty to put in hand precautionary measures to ensure that these powerful battlewagons did not fall into German hands. He hoped that this outcome could be averted if the French Navy responded to the appeal of General de Gaulle, who on 18 June, in a B.B.C. broadcast beamed to France over the strong protests of the French Ambassador in London, had called on his fellow countrymen to join his Free French forces. If this appeal did not succeed, Churchill intended that a powerful Royal Navy task force would be ready to confront the French fleet.

"If Britain could get through the next three months," the Prime Minister had told the secret session of the House of Commons on 20 June, she could "get through the next three years." Maintaining control of the sea lanes and the airspace over Britain was the cornerstone of his military strategy. Emphasizing the importance of "transatlantic reinforcements," he predicted that as far as the Americans were concerned "nothing will stir them like fighting in England." Appealing for United States help when "down and out" would not work, but a "heroic struggle" was the best way of "bringing them in."[6]

That same day in Washington Roosevelt made an announcement that seemed likely to help Churchill to fulfil his promise. The vigorous seventy-three-year-old former Secretary of State Henry L. Stimson was made Secretary of War for the second time in his career, and the Chicago publisher Frank Knox, a former "Teddy" Roosevelt Rough Rider, became Secretary of the Navy. The appointments captured the political headlines on the eve of the Republican convention; Roosevelt had not yet declared whether he would seek the Democratic nomination, but bringing these two prominent Republicans into his administration was a clear pointer to his intention to run again. Knox and Stimson were both internationalists who would back the President's policy of stepping up aid to Britain.

The move also reflected the President's growing confidence that the British might after all fight through – a view he had committed to paper the previous week. The document provides an insight into the development of Roosevelt's strategic assessment, since it envisaged that the United States navy and air forces would be taking an active part in the war by the winter of 1940. Written four days before the French capitulation, it assumed France would fight on in Morocco with the British Isles "used as bases of supplies shipped from the Western hemisphere." In Roosevelt's scenario the U.S. would be "providing most of the forces for the Atlantic blockade." Four days after passing his memorandum to the sceptical scrutiny of the Army and Navy, the President made another significant gesture: through Lord Lothian he proposed sending a team of military analysts to Britain for secret Anglo-American staff talks.[7]

"The President said he thought this would be a good thing and it ought to take place at once," the British Ambassador cabled approvingly from Washington. But when Halifax raised Roosevelt's proposal with Churchill, he was apprehensive. "I think they would turn almost entirely on the American side upon the transfer of the British Fleet to transatlantic bases," he minuted on 24 June. "Any discussion of this is bound to weaken confidence here at the moment when all must brace themselves for the supreme struggle." Five days later Churchill was persuaded to change his mind by his military advisers and the Foreign Office, who warned that rejection might cool the President's new-found enthusiasm for Britain.[8]

Lothian was instructed to accept Roosevelt's offer, and the staff talks that began in late August would mark a significant milestone on the road to full Anglo-American military co-operation. By the end of June, after prodding by the Admiralty and Beaverbrook, Churchill also finally gave approval for Sir Henry Tizard's plan to share technological secrets with the Americans. He had kept the scheme on ice for more than a month and even now agreed grudgingly and on condition "that the specific secrets and items of exchange are reported [to me] beforehand." But when Lothian on 23 June resurrected his earlier suggestion that Britain could foster American goodwill by offering bases on her West Indian islands to the United States, he was slapped down again. The Prime Minister agreed with the Admiralty that such facilities were far too valuable to be given away, contending that they should be traded for destroyers or financial credits.[9]

Churchill appeared to prefer using the "blackmail" of the fleet rather than the offer of bases to bring home to the President the urgency of Britain's need for war material to fend off the anticipated German attack. Touring troops in Kent and Sussex on 23 June he found not a single anti-tank gun in the areas most threatened by a German invasion. The next day he cabled to ask the Canadian Prime Minister "to impress this danger upon the President, as I have done in my cables to him."[10]

"I shall obviously never enter into any peace negotiations with Hitler," Churchill told Mackenzie King, "but obviously I cannot bind a future Government, which, if we were deserted by the United States and beaten down here, might very easily be a kind of Quisling affair ready to accept German overlordship and protection." A similar message was sent four days later to Lord Lothian after he had warned that the White House was reacting to "a wave of pessimism passing over this country to the effect that Great Britain is inevitably defeated." The British Ambassador gave this as the reason why the President had bowed to political pressure in Congress to abandon the plan to send Britain twenty motor launches. To counter public pessimism, Lothian called for the Prime Minister to issue "a reasoned confidential statement showing not only our determination to fight to the finish but giving ground for hope and confidence."[11]

"Too much attention should not be paid to the eddies of United States opinion. Only force of events can govern them," Churchill cabled back. "Never cease to impress upon the President and others that if this country were successfully invaded and largely occupied after heavy fighting some Quisling government would be formed to make peace on the basis of our becoming a German protectorate."

The fleet, he said, might have to be used to buy lenient peace terms. He reminded Lothian that Britain had not "really had any help worth speaking of from the United States so far," although he conceded that the President was Britain's best friend. "What really matters is whether Hitler is master of Britain in three months or not. I think not," he added emphatically, advising Lothian to be "bland and phlegmatic."[12]

"No one is downhearted here," Churchill concluded his riposte, although he already knew that Halifax and Butler were less stout-hearted and that Berlin had responded to their peace feeler by leaking stories about an opposition group in the British government which wanted a peace deal. At the same time he cannot have been unaware that the rumours added an edge of credibility to the blackmail implicit in his message about the fleet. The State Department records confirm that U.S. ambassadors were reporting the same stories that caused anxiety in the Foreign Office in the two weeks immediately following the French armistice. The United Press Agency in New York carried a report on 27 June that Chamberlain was attempting to overthrow Churchill to form a cabinet that "would enter into negotiations with Germany." The story appeared next day in Tokyo newspapers, and from Lima in Peru came reports that the Anglo-German peace would be signed in ten days. The Foreign Office ordered British ambassadors across the globe to issue categorical denials, noting "this scare to have been pretty widely diffused."[13]

"Your Lordship and the Lord Chancellor are advising the King to make peace" was the tongue-in-cheek message the Foreign Secretary received from the British Ambassador to Yugoslavia. Considering how near the bone the rumours were, Lord Halifax must have been quite discomfited to receive similar reports from Sofia and Bucharest. Five days later from Athens came reports of a peace faction forming in the British Parliament, and the British Minister in Switzerland, who had already received one approach from the Papal Nuncio proposing that the Vatican should act as a peace intermediary, reported receiving a second visit on 22 June. Sir David Kelly trotted out the standard denial, but he found the Nuncio so insistent that he asked the Foreign Office if it might not be wise to follow up the Vatican proposal.[14]

"I see no reason for any such enquiry," Churchill wrote across the bottom of the telegram in his scarlet ink. "If Hitler has anything to talk to us about he can easily do so. It only betrays nervousness to ask." It was the Prime Minister's intention to make it very difficult for Hitler to get his insidious peace hints through to any British diplomat. Five days after this rebuff, the German Foreign Ministry tugged at its line to the Vatican once more: the Papal Nuncio contacted Ambassador Kelly again. This time he was more specific, asking if "His Majesty's government might be willing to find out privately through [a] third power without committing themselves what Herr Hitler really wanted."[15]

The Nuncio's approach was so persistent that Kelly decided to forward the offer to London on 26 June with his recommendation that the "Vatican's sympathies are worth cultivating." Implying that the Vatican's persistence indicated that a genuine peace offer might be obtained with little risk, he advised the Foreign Secretary that it might be "unwise to persist in discouragement now that the situation has been made so clear." Evidently Halifax agreed that the Pope's tentative lead was worth considering. "Silly old H. evidently hankering after them," Cadogan noted in his diary after the Pope's initiative. The Prime Minister was all for stamping on the suggestion. He wanted to avoid all contact with what might prove the sticky tentacles of Vatican peace feelers. He took strong exception to the presumption shown by the British Minister in Berne.[16]

"I hope it will be made clear to the Nuncio that we do not desire to make any inquiries as to terms of peace with Hitler," Churchill minuted to the Foreign Secretary; "all our agents are strictly forbidden to entertain any such suggestions." To leave Kelly no room for doubt how he should react, Churchill circulated his approved response to the War Cabinet: "His Majesty's Government has made it quite plain that there is no intention here of approaching Hitler to ascertain possible terms of peace."[17]

When the rebuff percolated back along the Vatican diplomatic channel to the Wilhelmstrasse, Reichsausminister Ribbentrop was furious. His irritation surfaced in the directive he dictated on 30 June for Weizsäcker to circulate to his staff: "Germany is not considering peace. She is concerned exclusively with preparation for the destruction of England." The same day the State Secretary assured General Halder that "Britain probably still needs one more demonstration of military might before she gives in and leaves us a free hand in the east."[18]

In the midst of the German peace manoeuvres it was the American Ambassador in London who appeared more certain than the Germans that Britain should take advantage of Berlin's invitation and throw in the towel. On 1 July he told Chamberlain that "everyone in the U.S.A. thinks we shall be beaten before the end of the month." Significantly, that week saw the first of many false alarms that a German invasion was imminent, throughout which Churchill maintained a nonchalant optimism that the attackers would be speedily hurled back into the waves. He devoted considerable time and energy to vigorous preparations to counter any military force that the Germans chose to direct at England from the sea or the sky. He toured southern England, rallying Britain's forces to resist and posing in bulldog stance clutching a tommy gun as an example of the reception awaiting any German who set foot on British soil.[19]

The reality was rather different. The Army was short of tanks and heavy artillery; there were fewer than forty tommy guns and not enough rifles in the country to equip even regular soldiers. Men over military call-up age who were being recruited into Local Defence Volunteer units were lucky if they even had shotguns. Drill had to be conducted with wooden rifles, and farmers on anti-parachutist night patrols had to rely on pitchforks and shotguns. By day the civilian recruits practised blocking streets with carts and blowing up improvised "tanks" made from perambulators, with "mortars" made of drainpipes and firing tin-cans of gunpowder.

Thousands of armbands had already been ordered for the War Office when Churchill decided that "L.D.V." was not an inspiring enough name for men who might soon have to defend their homes and streets from a well-armed invading army. "Don't hesitate," he minuted to the war minister Anthony Eden, "to change on account of already having made armlets etc. if it is thought the title 'Home Guard' would be more compulsive." The men of "Dad's Army," as it later came to be called, may not have been a match for the German invader, but they played a crucial role in galvanizing the nation's collective defiance and willingness to heed the Prime Minister's call to fight on the beaches, in the hills, towns and cities and never surrender.

Invasion preparations and the fate of the French fleet were the twin priorities for Churchill during the lull in the battle in the uncertain weeks after the Fall of France. Daily updates in the War Cabinet minutes on the disposition of their former ally's warships reveal how great a threat he and the Admiralty perceived the French fleet to be. Repeated assurances that it would not fall into Axis hands had been sought and received from President Lebrun and senior members of Pétain's government, including the Marshal himself: all had unhesitatingly pledged that the fleet would never be handed over to Germany or Italy but would be neutralized according to the terms still being hammered out by the Franco-German Armistice Commission, which was meeting at Wiesbaden.

Churchill had also received solemn personal promises from Admiral Darlan that the French warships would be scuttled by their crews before being permitted to come under German or Italian control. But private assurances were not guarantees, as the Prime Minister repeatedly reminded his ministers. His confidence that Pétain's regime would have the inclination, let alone the military strength, to stand by its promises had been shattered by the rejection of British demands to approve the armistice terms before they were agreed upon. The two former allies were now at loggerheads, with the British government backing General de

Gaulle's Free French forces. At Churchill's behest, plans were drawn up for landing 25,000 British troops in Morocco to establish an alternative French government on French territory. He saw this as the best way of rallying the loyalties of the officers and men of the French Navy, whose major warships were at overseas bases, out of reach of direct German control. But although the Prime Minister vigorously pressed the merits of "Operation Susan," as the North African plan was codenamed, the Chiefs of Staff killed it, declaring that such a commitment of the hard-pressed British forces "was not essential to the prosecution of the war."[20]

Yet for Churchill the fate of the powerful French fleet had now become as much a symbol as a strategic concern. If its officers and men could be persuaded to throw in their lot with the Royal Navy, it would send a powerful message to the world. But if the fleet ever fell into German hands, it would increase the military odds against Britain's chances of resisting an invasion. The Prime Minister could not know that Hitler had never had any intention of prejudicing the pacification of France or rousing the hostility of the United States by seizing the French fleet. Churchill was worried that a French government stripped of its military power might not be able to deny its warships to the Axis once they had returned to the ports of metropolitan France, as required by the armistice. The promises Pétain had made were no guarantee that the Germans or Italians would not seize the fleet on the excuse of some technical infringement of the French armistice terms. Such were the uncertainties preying on Churchill's mind when he told the War Cabinet that "in a matter so vital to the safety of the whole British Empire we could not afford to rely on the word of Admiral Darlan."[21]

The Prime Minister did not want a Britain under threat of invasion held hostage to such uncertainties. The only guarantee was to seize, or dispose of, the most powerful units in the French fleet. Not only did the Royal Navy command the forces necessary to achieve that end; seapower was the one area where Britain could demonstrate her military superiority. The temptation to make that demonstration, even at the risk of turning a former ally into an enemy, was to prove irresistible to Churchill. He also recognized the symbolic advantage to be gained, especially in the United States. Roosevelt had considered making an offer to buy the fleet outright, but Churchill determined that the French warships would be brought under British control or sunk. He was confident that when the French admirals were given the option of fighting alongside the Royal Navy or losing their ships, they and their crews would defy their commander-in-chief and their government's armistice pledges. It was a mistaken assumption that led to a tragedy whose scars persisted long after the war was over.

Day 9
"A Single Stroke of Violent Action"
3 July

At the Prime Minister's urging, the War Cabinet on 25 June authorized the Admiralty to take "the best measures" to capture the two
big French battleships. The following morning Admiral Sir Dudley
Pound, the First Sea Lord and Chief of Naval Staff, reported that by
3 July the Royal Navy would have assembled Force H, a battleship
and carrier force based on Gibraltar that would be "far stronger"
than the most powerful section of the French fleet then at the
naval base of Mers el-Kébir near Oran in Algeria. Planning began
at the Admiralty for "Operation Catapult" and the simultaneous
"Operation Grasp" to take over the French warships then still in
British home ports and in Alexandria harbour.[22]

"Catapult" was a bullying operation in which the powerful French
force at Oran was to be confronted by a superior British fleet and
given an ultimatum. The four choices offered would be: sailing out
to join the Royal Navy; proceeding to a British port and handing the
ships over; demilitarization under British supervision; or scuttling
the ships in the port. On 30 June the Chiefs of Staff reviewed the plan
and decided that "on balance the operations contemplated should
be carried out." They justified their recommendation on the grounds
that, French promises apart, there was no way of knowing that the
warships had really been rendered unserviceable if it was not done
under British supervision before they were sailed to ports in France.
At the Prime Minister's insistence, the War Cabinet agreed that
"Operation Catapult" should be executed "as soon as possible."[23]

Vice Admiral Sir James Somerville was dispatched by air the
same day to Gibraltar to take command of Force H. When he
arrived to explain the "Catapult" plan to Vice Admiral Sir Dudley
North, the Flag Officer North Atlantic, he was deeply disturbed,
and told Somerville that he was "absolutely opposed to the use of
Force." It was his belief that the French "would probably fight,"
because Admiral Marcel Gensoul, who was in command of the
cruiser squadron in Oran, had already declared that "he would
submit to no other power taking control of his ships." According
to North, at a conference that evening aboard H.M.S. Hood, "all
the Flag Officers and Captains present were opposed to the use of
Force." Their reaction was "so strong" that he considered sending a protest to the Admiralty next morning. He did not do so,
because he understood that Somerville was telegraphing his own
objections to the Sea Lords.[24]

Next day, when the final orders for Force H were received at
Gibraltar, North realized that it was too late to lodge his own protest.

The instructions given to Somerville showed that the government in London was "determined to use force and that this decision had been come to after the receipt and consideration of the Message from Vice-Admiral, Force H." The Commander-in-Chief Mediterranean, Vice Admiral Sir Andrew Cunningham, had also signalled to the Admiralty that he was "most strongly opposed to proposal for forcible seizure of ships in Alexandria." "Catapult" nonetheless went ahead over both admirals' clearly stated objections.[25]

On 2 July Somerville received his final orders to sail next day to confront the French fleet in its base at the Mers el-Kébir harbour. But there was one last-minute modification to the ultimatum he was to present: a fifth alternative, to be offered to Admiral Gensoul only if he refused all of the first four choices. This was intended to be a face-saving option, permitting Gensoul to agree to neutralize his warships at their North African base provided "the measures taken for demilitarization can be carried out under your supervision within six hours." If this option was also declined, Somerville's orders stated, "you are to endeavour to destroy ships in Mers el-Kébir but particularly *Dunkerque* and *Strasbourg*, using all means at your disposal."[26]

For Somerville, who had been in charge of the evacuation of French troops at Dunkirk, this was a heart-wrenching commission. As Force H steamed that afternoon past the lighthouse on the Gibraltar mole, he could only hope that the diplomatic language of the authorized approach would have a benign influence on the French. He was to put it to Gensoul that "the greatness of and territory of France" necessitated that the ships under his command should not fall into the hands of the common foe. "You are charged with one of the most disagreeable and difficult tasks that a British Admiral has ever faced," Admiral Pound signalled to Somerville, "but we have complete confidence in you and rely on you to carry it out relentlessly." Somerville was instructed to keep the Admiralty apprised of each stage of the operation, since the War Cabinet would be "impatiently awaiting news of 'Catapult'."[27]

In the early hours of 3 July, as the phosphorescent wake of Force H scored across Mediterranean waters dark and smooth as molten pitch, armed Royal Navy boarding parties overpowered the crews of the French warships in Portsmouth, Falmouth and Plymouth. There were only two casualties. There might have been more had the boarding parties not presented themselves as members of the Red Cross, a ruse which, while it saved lives, was bitterly resented by the French. There was great outrage at the piratical way they had been wrested from control of their vessels, which included the world's largest submarine, *Surcouf*. At Alexandria, where Vice Admiral René Godfroy commanded a squadron of France's Mediterranean fleet, a standoff occurred. As the French warships were moored in close proximity to the British there could be no shootout; nor could the French vessels steam away. Protracted and bitter negotiations with Admiral Cunningham resulted in Godfroy agreeing to an interim immobilization of his ships by discharging their oil.

At the western end of the Mediterranean that Friday morning the rising sun turned Force H into silhouettes, accentuating the graceful lines of the battlecruiser H.M.S. *Hood*. The long bow of the proudest ship in the Royal Navy carved ahead of two battleships, two cruisers, the aircraft carrier *Ark Royal* and two flotillas of destroyers. Captain C. S. Holland, who had been appointed negotiator, was detached aboard the destroyer *Foxhound* to make for Oran at full speed. He may not have been the happiest choice as emissary: the animosities he had generated as the last British naval attaché in Paris were to hinder rather than help his delicate mission.

Approaching the mole guarding the harbour entrance at Mers el-Kébir shortly after nine, *Foxhound* signalled to Admiral Gensoul the prepared message of salutation. It was sent by both Aldis lamp and radio because North and Somerville had agreed that the message was to be read and understood by all the French warships and their crews. The yeoman was slow and deliberate in clacking the shutters on the signal lamp to spell out in morse the French phrases requesting a meeting to discuss the possibility of Admiral Gensoul's bringing his squadron to join the British fleet off Oran, which he was assured was "waiting to welcome him."[28]

It was not the sort of welcome best calculated to please Admiral Gensoul, who was a stiff and loyal Frenchman and felt duty-bound to decline an invitation that would violate the terms of his country's armistice. He sent his Flag Lieutenant by motor launch to receive the British proposals and the six-hour deadline attaching to them. The choices as they appeared on the document that Gensoul read included the four options, but not the fifth, which Somerville had been instructed to hold in reserve. The document did set out the option that he could sail his ships to a port in the French Antilles such as Martinique, "where they can be demilitarized to our satisfaction, or perhaps entrusted to the United States." In this and the other cases the British offered to repatriate the crews. But Gensoul was so affronted at being given an ultimatum that he did not consider the so-called Antilles option or mention it when he signalled to the French Admiralty at 9.45 a.m. that there was a powerful British force off Oran. His message suggested that he had only been presented with the crude ultimatum "Proceed to sea with your vessels, six hours grace, or we shall be obliged to compel you to do so by force."[29]

"French vessels will reply with force to force" was the reply Gensoul dictated to his Flag Lieutenant. Shortly after 10 a.m. the

French Admiral's written answer was handed to Captain Holland. It confirmed the assurances already given that the French would not allow their ships to fall into enemy hands, and warned that the "first round fired would alienate the whole of the French Navy." After this failure of his first attempt to negotiate, Captain Holland returned to *Foxhound* to await further orders.[30]

Aboard H.M.S. *Hood*, steaming back and forth across Oran Bay at the head of Force H, just short of the firing range of the French guns, concern was mounting over Gensoul's intentions. Somerville had received from an *Ark Royal* reconnaissance flight a report of the furling of awnings and hoisting of boats on the French battleships, indicating that they were preparing to sail. The report, relayed to the Admiralty in London, greatly alarmed the War Cabinet, which was in continuous session, with Churchill anxiously monitoring developments.

"If you consider that the French Fleet are preparing to leave harbour, inform them that if they move you must open fire," Somerville was instructed. His immediate response was to order aircraft flown off *Ark Royal* to mine the entrance of Mers el-Kébir harbour. This action seemed a further affront to the already infuriated French Admiral.[31]

"Gensoul reply refuses our conditions and repeats assurance re sinking of ships," Somerville signalled just before noon. "States he will fight. I am prepared to open fire at 1.30 p.m."

A bloody outcome to the standoff at Oran now seemed inevitable. Apprehension increased when the War Cabinet learned that the Admiralty had intercepted a signal from Admiral Darlan to the Admiral commanding French forces at Dakar ordering him and his crews "to pay no attention to the British demands and to show themselves worthy of being Frenchmen." As Britain and France headed towards a clash of arms that might see the former allies at war, Churchill received a timely reassurance in a cable from Lord Lothian telling him that Roosevelt "would support the forcible seizure" of the French ships.

Off Oran, a peaceful outcome suddenly seemed possible on the flag-bridge of H.M.S. *Hood* after a midday report that the closing of the harbour boom indicated that the French ships were not going to try to put to sea after all. Somerville flashed another message to *Dunkerque*, Gensoul's flagship, reminding him that he now had until 3 p.m. to reply to the British proposals. Acceptance could be indicated by hoisting a large square flag to the masthead of the battleship. Twenty minutes before the deadline expired, no flag had been run up, but Gensoul signalled his readiness to receive a delegate for "honourable discussions."[31]

"I debated in my mind whether this was merely an excuse to gain time," Somerville wrote in his report, "but decided that it was quite possible Admiral Gensoul had only now realized it was my intention to use force." Captain Holland had to make a seven-mile detour by motor boat around the British minefield. As he passed the battleships in the harbour, tugs were standing by, suggesting that they were preparing for sea after all.

When Holland was piped aboard the French flagship it was past 4 p.m. and time was pressing. The Royal Navy Captain found Admiral Gensoul "extremely indignant" at being given an ultimatum and having his harbour mined. Discussions went nowhere with painful slowness, in large part because Gensoul insisted that he was bound by his orders and by France's obligation to observe the strict terms of the armistice. The French Admiral, who had not heard his government's response to his morning signals, believed he had no other choice than to abide by his orders. The only concession to the British terms he appeared ready to consider was the "Antilles Option," but only to the extent that his ships "would proceed to Martinique or the United States *if* threatened" with takeover by the Germans. A signal to this effect was being drafted when Captain Holland received instructions from Somerville that the deadline was approaching and he must return to *Foxhound* at once.[32]

Just before five, while Holland was still parleying in Gensoul's cabin, Somerville had received a warning from London: "Settle the matter quickly or you may have French reinforcements to deal with." The Admiralty had intercepted another signal sent to Gensoul from the Ministry of Marine alerting him that all French naval forces in the Mediterranean were on their way "in fighting order" to join him. "You are to answer force with force. Call in the submarines and air force if necessary."[33]

Admiral Gensoul had opened a glimmer of hope that the "Antilles Option" might offer a basis for negotiation, but since he had not forewarned his government of this choice, without higher authority his hands were tied. As the final minutes of the deadline ticked away, his truncated version of the British terms was being discussed by Pétain and his ministers, who had belatedly gathered for a conference half an hour before Somerville's ultimatum expired. Darlan reported that Gensoul had been given the stark choice "either to join the English Fleet or to scuttle his ships." He had approved Gensoul's defiant response that force would be met by force. Baudouin, who was present at the discussion, recorded how they were "completely overwhelmed" by the lack of time and communication facilities. The armistice terms forbade radio communications, and cable traffic would have proved too slow for any exchange. They could do nothing other than file a report to the Armistice Commission and assume as their meeting broke up that the destruction of Gensoul's squadron "was an accomplished fact."[34]

Events had rushed past the point of human intervention. When Gensoul's version of the "Antilles Option" reached Somerville, he decided that "it did not comply with any of the conditions laid down." The air strike waiting to be flown off *Ark Royal* was ordered up, and he signalled to Gensoul that if he did not accept the terms "fire would be opened at 17.30." The message reached the French admiral fifteen minutes before the ultimatum expired. Since Gensoul's reply, making a conditional offer to agree to the "Antilles Option," did not meet the strict terms of the ultimatum set down by the Admiralty, Somerville decided he had no choice but to order *Ark Royal* to fly off an attack. Klaxons blared as Force H went to action stations. *Hood*'s fifteen-inch turrets trained round to menace the Mers el-Kébir harbour, and the upperworks of the French battlecruisers, clearly visible over the top of the mole.

"I do not believe that he thought that fire would be opened," Captain Holland reported of Gensoul's cordial manner when he left the *Dunkerque* at 5.25 p.m. "Action Stations" were being sounded off as the *Foxhound*'s motor boat sped through the harbour towards the net defences. Captain Holland was barely one mile to seaward when the guns of Force H opened fire at 5.54 p.m.[35]

Salvoes of fifteen-inch projectiles hurtled over *Foxhound*'s launch with the roar of an express train. A minute later the French shore batteries opened up. Two minutes into the action a direct hit on the battleship *Bretagne* sent a hundred-foot column of smoke and flame skyward. It was followed by a huge second explosion as a destroyer blew up. Waterspouts then began erupting in the wake of Force H as the French guns closed range. Dense clouds of smoke mushroomed over the harbour, hampering the incoming waves of attacking aircraft. In the confusion a French battlecruiser and destroyer managed to escape through the minefield, unseen by Force H through the fog of battle. After thirty-six fifteen-inch salvoes had rained sixty-three tons of high explosive down on the captive French ships, firing ceased and Somerville called a halt to the ten-minute gunnery duel. *Ark Royal*'s Swordfish torpedo bombers then pressed home their attack when Somerville received a signal from the Admiralty: "French ships must comply with our terms or sink themselves or be sunk by you before dark."[36]

That afternoon's naval action at Oran put three of Gensoul's four capital ships out of action (the *Strasbourg* and her destroyer escaped to Toulon). British bombs and shells took the lives of more than twelve hundred French sailors. There were no victory cheers from those aboard the warships of Force H who had opened fire on men who had so lately been their comrades in arms. In London Churchill worried that Britain would find herself at war with France, as a message intercepted in the course of the action referred to the British force as "the enemy." By the same token, and no doubt from force of habit, the words "enemy fire" appear in Admiral Somerville's report. An "after-action" protest made to the Admiralty on 4 July by Admiral North, to "place on record the views which prevailed here," asserts that Admiral Somerville had shared North's deep apprehension before sailing from Gibraltar and that "the carrying out of this operation was utterly repugnant to him."[37]

Their Lordships resented the Admiral's criticism and formally admonished North for his deprecating comments "on a policy which has been decided on by the Admiralty in the light of factors which were either not known or unknown to the officers on the spot." They stated that the Admiralty were "never under the delusion that the French Fleet would not fight in the last instance," and they considered that North's letter showed "a most dangerous lack of appreciation of the manner in which it is intended to conduct the war." Churchill was even more scathing. "It is evident that Admiral Dudley North has not got the root of the matter in him," he minuted to the First Lord of the Admiralty. "I should be very glad to see you replace him by a more resolute and clear-sighted officer."[38]

North responded that his "dislike of the operation" arose not from "sentimental attachment to our late allies, but from strong doubts as to its effect on the course of the war." That he was not immediately relieved of his command indicates that his fellow admirals had strongly sympathized with his predicament. But two months later North was recalled, after the failure of the joint Free French-British operation against Dakar, which Churchill blamed on North for allegedly misinterpreting orders and letting a French cruiser squadron pass unmolested through the Straits of Gibraltar to reinforce the Vichy units in Dakar.[39]

North's doubts about the strategic value of "Catapult" were to be borne out when Hitler reacted to the Oran action by ordering the suspension of the fleet demilitarization clause in France's armistice agreement. The French regained operational control of their still substantial navy, which had lost little more than eight per cent of its total tonnage to the British actions of 3 July. The Führer was now confident that the French were so hostile to the British that he need no longer worry that they might turn over their ships to the Royal Navy.

German and French wartime propaganda portrayed the British action at Oran as a deliberate atrocity engineered by Churchill. Half a century on, the view is widely held in France that the action was an unforgivable and unforgettable outrage – unforgivable because the ultimatum was an insult to France's honour and the pledges given by her representatives, and unforgettable because of the way an ally suddenly became a foe by killing so many Frenchmen. The British naval action shocked Marshal Pétain and his ministers. When the news arrived, his government was still in the process of setting up its ministerial offices in the faded suites of the grand-luxe hotels of the spa town of Vichy.

Foreign Minister Baudouin reacted furiously to the "useless and culpable aggression." Had not he, the Marshal and Darlan given the British Ambassador their solemn word? "Why shed blood between the two countries and that under the amused eyes of the Germans?" The next morning, he found Pétain and Laval with Admiral Darlan, who was still trembling with emotion. "I have been deceived by my brothers in arms," Darlan complained. "They have betrayed the trust I reposed in them." A French cruiser squadron had been ordered to sea to join up with the *Strasbourg* to make a reprisal attack on British ships. "*Does* this mean war with England?" Baudouin asked Pétain. The Marshal looked at Laval, who said "We have made up our minds to reply to yesterday's attack on us with an attack of our own." The Foreign Minister was told to announce the rupture of diplomatic relations – a hollow gesture, since on the day before the armistice was signed Sir Ronald Campbell and his Embassy staff had left Bordeaux for England in protest at the failure of the French to consult over the German terms. The Vichy government did not declare war on Britain, but satisfied its honour by ordering a token bombing raid on Gibraltar.[40]

"All this is perfectly hateful," the Foreign Secretary noted regretfully in his diary, "but it seems quite clear that we could not run the risk of allowing the French Fleet to fall into German hands." For the Prime Minister, if not for his admirals, the action at Oran was a price he was prepared to pay to make Britain less vulnerable to a German invasion. An even more important consequence for Britain was that it demonstrated Churchill's resolve to let nothing stand in the way of his unwavering determination to confront a ruthless enemy.[41]

That message of resolution was also conveyed by the Prime Minister's admonition "to maintain a spirit of alert and confident energy," which he drew up that day to circulate to every Member of Parliament, every peer, all Lord Mayors and senior civil servants. They were told that the Prime Minister "expects all His Majesty's servants in high places to set an example of steadiness and resolution." The circular called for the reporting of "any persons, officers, or officials who are found to be consciously exercising a disturbing or depressing influence, and whose talk is calculated to spread alarm and despondency." Only if such defeatists were rooted out would the country be worthy of the men in the armed services, who, Churchill declared, "have already met the enemy without any sense of being out-matched in martial qualities."[42]

The Prime Minister's speech in Parliament next day was an object lesson in accommodating the stern and unforgiving dictates of war.

The House was silent as he pronounced his "sincere sorrow" over "the measures we have felt bound to take in order to prevent the French Fleet from falling into German hands." There followed a stark outline of the breaches of faith by the Bordeaux government which prompted the Cabinet's unanimous decision to proceed with the previous day's action. Although Churchill had hoped that the French would accept the British terms without bloodshed, he paid tribute to the way in which the French had fought their ships, "albeit in this unnatural cause." He was confident he could leave the judgement of Britain's action to Parliament.[43]

"I leave it also," Churchill declared, "to the nation, and I leave it to the United States. I leave it to the world and to history." This was not the time, he said, "for doubt and weakness" but the "supreme hour to which we have been called." The action Britain had taken would dispose of "all the lies and rumours which have been so industriously spread by German propaganda and Fifth Column activities that we have the slightest intention of entering into negotiation in any form and through any channel with the German and Italian governments."

"We shall, on the contrary," Churchill concluded, "prosecute the war with the utmost vigour by all the means that are open to us until the righteous purposes of which we entered upon have been fulfilled." The cheering and waving of order papers and handkerchiefs that erupted when the Prime Minister sat down was the most rousing reception he had yet received from the House. Overwhelmed, his eyes filled with tears that afternoon as the tumultuous reception marked his parliamentary coronation as the British people's undisputed war leader. With what he termed "a single stroke of violent action," Churchill had confirmed his claim to leadership and radically transformed the United Kingdom's image overseas. By striking with such ruthlessness at his former ally, he had demonstrated that Britain was not trembling helplessly on the verge of surrender to Hitler, but was defiant and dangerous now that her Navy was firmly in command of the sea.

"It should show the Dominions and the United States that, after all the defeatism of France and elsewhere, the British mean to win," Colonel Raymond E. Lee noted in his diary. The U.S. army attaché in London was a shrewd military observer with a keen sense of history. He saw that Oran was "the second milestone" for Churchill after Dunkirk, one that he predicted "may easily mark the turning point of Hitler's career." According to Roosevelt's aide Harry Hopkins, the news of the attack on the French fleet had the same impact on the President, who would later tell Colville it was the single event that persuaded him that Britain really meant to "stay in the fight, alone and if necessary for years."[44]

"Only a Matter of Time"
4–12 July

On the day of the Oran action Churchill received word that the *Britannic* had sailed from New York loaded with the first large shipment of American munitions, rifles and field guns. He now decided to exploit the new climate of national resolution by pressing the President again on the destroyers. Deciding that this was a good moment "in view of the American approval of treatment of the French," he drafted his first cable to Roosevelt in three weeks. "It has now become most urgent for you to give us the destroyers and motorboats," he opened stridently, warning that the Royal Navy was now pressed even harder by U-boats operating from the French ports and did not have the reserves to repel an invasion force.[45]

"The consequences to the United States of our being hemmed in or overwhelmed are so grievous," Churchill wrote, "it seems hard to me to understand why this modest aid is not given at this time when it could be perhaps decisively effective." The draft shows that he had crossed out the simultaneous transmission "through F.O. and American Ambassador," initialling that this cable was to be sent by the secure channel to the British Embassy in Washington. This is further confirmation of Churchill's awareness of the possibility of German eavesdropping on the American ciphers. He evidently did not want Berlin to know of his concern that the Irish government "are reconciling themselves with the Germans." He alerted the President that "it might be necessary for us to forestall German action by a descent on certain ports."

When Halifax showed the draft to Ambassador Kennedy, he was appalled. His Irish sentiments aflame, he insisted that the reference to Dublin's alleged treachery be struck out. The Foreign Secretary agreed, passing the amended cable back to Churchill with a letter explaining that it had been necessary to tone down its stridency with changes that "might perhaps avoid possible misconceptions." Churchill disagreed with Kennedy's comments.[46]

"I fancy it was because it was not sent through him that he crabbed it," the Prime Minister minuted to the Foreign Secretary. He was piqued because he did not understand the point of the Foreign Secretary's pencilled corrections. "As it now stands I do not see much use in sending any telegram." His second thoughts may also have been influenced by reading Lothian's cable from Washington on 6 July, which reported that the "very influential people" who wanted to step up assistance to Britain would not get the support of American public opinion without assurances that the British fleet "would cross the Atlantic if Great Britain were overrun."[47]

Churchill was not prepared to see his blackmail called without

American guarantees to send Britain the destroyers and massive amounts of military aid in return. He did not appreciate how risky a strategy he was pursuing. The President and the American public might have been impressed by the recent British naval action, but the U.S. Navy chief was not; Admiral Harold R. Stark had yet to be persuaded that Britain could survive.

The pessimism of the top naval brass in Washington was also mirrored in the brash optimism among Hitler's chiefs of staff. "The final German victory over England is now only a matter of time," General Jodl confidently predicted in his diary at the end of June. The Führer had been waiting at his headquarters in the Black Forest, hoping for word of Britain's willingness to negotiate before making his scheduled triumphant return to Berlin on 6 July. He could not understand why it was taking Britain so long to accept the military logic that was so clear to his chief of operations and respond to the peace feelers that had been put out by Ribbentrop. His annoyance that the failure of the German sounding via the Vatican was spoiling his aspiration to outdo Napoleon's triumphs became apparent on 1 July, when he told the Italian Ambassador that he "could not conceive of anyone in England seriously believing in victory." His patience was clearly wearing thin, because that day he permitted O.K.W. to issue preparatory orders for an invasion of Britain. But these were surprisingly indecisive, merely stating that "a landing in England is possible, providing that air superiority can be attained and certain other necessary conditions fulfilled."[48]

Hitler's conviction that Britain would soon ask for peace terms had cost the German military staff two weeks' planning time after France fell. On 1 July the army and navy staff met for preliminary discussions to decide the basis for an operation against England. Air superiority was deemed to be the essential prerequisite to invasion.

"The Führer has decided that a landing in England is possible provided that air superiority can be attained," Keitel recorded that day. "All preparations to begin immediately." Halder's reaction to the news of the Luftwaffe's mission was "Then perhaps we can dispense with land warfare." His sardonic "Plain sailing" comment reveals his own queasiness as a soldier at the thought of shipping six army divisions across the notoriously unpredictable Channel in a thousand small steamers before the October fogs. Nor was he any more confident next day when he noted sarcastically: "Similar to a large-scale river crossing." With the navy unable to guarantee protection for the troop transports against the overwhelming superiority of the British fleet, he was evidently having second thoughts about the feasibility of an invasion of Britain. He therefore instructed the O.K.H. operation staff to consider the "other primary problem," which Halder recorded as "military intervention which will compel Russia to recognize Germany's dominant position in Europe." The army staff were as eager as Hitler himself to find an excuse to shelve an amphibious operation that depended on the admirals in favour of a true generals' war against the Russians in the east.[49]

The victory parade in Berlin on 6 July was a spectacular display of military might and ecstatic crowds cheering under acres of fluttering swastika banners. Yet the failure to make peace with England irritated the Führer. His restlessness was evident when he postponed the scheduled Reichstag session and left Berlin to brood at his Bavarian mountain retreat in the Obersalzberg. The confidential reason given to Halder for the Führer's action was a "probable reshuffle of the British Cabinet," so Hitler may have believed that Churchill would soon be ousted. The Foreign Ministry officials were not so sanguine. "Discord between Churchill and Halifax. Churchill has prevailed," was the gist of the briefing Halder received on 8 July from the Foreign Ministry liaison officer, von Etzdorf, who was now predicting "War to the finish." He reported increasing concern in the Wilhelmstrasse over diplomatic moves which suggested Britain and Russia were seeking a rapprochement. The possibility of an understanding between "the bear and the whale" worried the Führer just as much as it did the army general staff. At the naval staff conference at the Berghof on 11 July, Hitler asked Admiral Raeder if he thought a speech appealing for peace "would be effective." The Admiral suggested that prefacing it with heavy bombing raids on the British would reinforce its impact on them. Raeder was "convinced" that Britain could be made to sue for peace "simply by cutting off her import trade by means of submarine warfare, air attacks on convoys, and heavy air attacks on her main centres."[50]

The ferocious air attacks on a British Channel convoy that commenced on 11 July marked the "official" start of the Battle of Britain. For the Germans it was just the opening round of their Kanalkampf, the struggle for air superiority that was to rage over the Channel and the skies of southern England for the next nine weeks. It pitted the 1,576 bombers and 1,089 fighters of Göring's three Luftflotten against 800 aircraft of the five R.A.F. Groups that comprised Fighter Command. It was a campaign whose outcome was to be decided largely on the performance of the British pilots and of the seven hundred British Hurricanes and Spitfires, which were faced with nearly twice that number of Messerschmitt Me 109s and Me 110s. To defeat the Luftwaffe's bid to control the air over Britain the R.A.F. had to knock their opponents out of the skies at more than twice the rate of their own losses. This was the kill ratio achieved on 10 July, when the first day's swirling dogfights, involving more than a hundred aircraft, resulted in the

343

R.A.F.'s losing six planes to the Germans' thirteen. This set the target for the bottom line that Churchill knew had to be maintained if a German seaborne invasion was to be thwarted.[51]

"The Führer is greatly puzzled by Britain's persisting unwillingness to make peace," Halder commented after the army chiefs had met Hitler on 13 June. "He sees the answer, as we do, in Britain's hope on Russia; and he therefore counts on having to compel her by main force to agree to peace." Halder observed that this was "much against his grain," because Hitler foresaw that "a military defeat of Britain will bring about the disintegration of the British Empire." He had reiterated his reluctance to shed blood to accomplish the destruction of an institution he admired, whose collapse "would benefit only Japan, [and] the United States."[52]

Hitler's reservations about the invasion surfaced again in Führer Directive 16, issued on 16 July, announcing his decision "to prepare for a landing operation against England, and if necessary to carry it out." By mid-August, preparations were to be ready for Operation Sea Lion to eliminate Britain as a base for "the carrying on of the war against Germany." The directive announced Hitler's intention of occupying England completely, but again he added the caveat: "if it should become necessary."[53]

"Peace Reconnaissance"
13–19 July

The Foreign Office records reveal one reason why Hitler was still hoping in mid-July that an invasion would be unnecessary was Berlin's renewed offensive of peace feelers. Brushing aside Ribbentrop's petulant 30 June directive that "Germany was not considering peace," the Foreign Ministry, presumably in response to the Führer's wishes, had launched the most serious effort yet to encourage Britain to open peace negotiations. The "peace offensive" began during the first week of July when Weizsäcker dispatched a plane to Switzerland to collect the Acting President of the International Red Cross, Dr. Carl Burckhardt.

Ostensibly Burckhardt's three days of talks in Berlin were to discuss relief for refugees in France. But the Foreign Office files reveal that one of the objects was to brief him as a high-level intermediary to see whether he could get talks going with the British. Weizsäcker arranged for Burckhardt to have "long individual conversations" with the Gauleiters Koch and Greiser, a senior general and the State Secretary himself. They all gave him the same story: "Hitler had returned to his old idea and hesitated before attacking England because he still clung to the hope of a working arrangement with the British Empire as hinted at in his recent interview in Belgium with Carl von Weigand." The contacts all emphasized that the American correspondent of the Hearst newspapers, whose "interview" with Hitler had created a sensation a month before, had accurately reflected his views.

Hitler wanted Britain's co-operation in setting up his "European Federation," they said, asserting that apart from some "local demands of Italy" that he would be obliged to support, the Führer wanted "a white peace like Sadowa" – a reference to the generous peace treaty Prussia granted to Austria in 1866. Burckhardt was asked if there was any chance of his having Red Cross business in England, "when he might see if there was any hope of a reasonable arrangement." Burckhardt promised Weizsäcker that he would "talk to an English friend in Switzerland."[54]

Foreign Office files confirm that this friend was Sir David Kelly, who reported his meeting in Berne with the head of the International Red Cross and M. Paravincini, the Swiss Minister in London, on 8 July in Berne. It was Dr. Burckhardt who asked the British Minister to treat the approach with "the utmost discretion," stressing that his Red Cross mission to Berlin was "not a cover" when relaying the German peace feeler. Kelly was assured that the German government "really were hesitating with the preparations for an attack on England and they were willing to call it off if they could do so without the loss of face." He explained in his report to London that he had told Burckhardt that he thought "our distrust of Hitler, apart from anything else, was a fatal obstacle." Burckhardt responded by stipulating absolute secrecy; any publicity, he told Kelly, "would be disastrous for him personally." But he indicated his willingness to serve as an intermediary for a peace move by telling Kelly that he was due to return to Berlin shortly.

A week after Burckhardt's visit, Kelly received another intermediary from Berlin, this time at the request of Spain's Minister in Berne. This was none other than Prince Max Hohenlohe who had held secret peace talks with Butler in Lausanne the previous year. He began by reading out to Kelly a reply Hitler had given to his own memorandum on peace. The Führer had stated that he was "prepared to accept *Einigkeit* [a concord]" with the British Empire, but that time was very short and England must choose "in the next few weeks." Hohenlohe warned that Hitler had been told that an invasion was "technically possible" and that "England would be crippled industrially."[55]

In his cable of 14 July to the Foreign Secretary, Kelly said the Prince was "very insistent I should report him." He was also careful to describe Hohenlohe as a "prewar acquaintance." In the game of peace feelers, it seems that not even British diplomats could be trusted to report accurately. The German Foreign Ministry archive that has come to light includes a letter of 20 June from Walter Hewel, one of Weizsäcker's most trusted officials, reporting to the State Secretary that Hohenlohe had told him that Sir David Kelly had been requested by Under Secretary of State Butler to make discreet contact with Berlin to establish what peace terms Germany would now offer England. Hohenlohe, who had become a national of Liechtenstein, was technically not an enemy subject and according to Hewel was acting as an intermediary of the British with the Germans. There is no indication in the files so far declassified that the Foreign Office had any idea of this instruction or of the diplomatic intrigues being played by their Minister in Berne on the initiative of Butler, presumably with his master Halifax's authority.[56]

"It looks as though Germany wishes to sound the ground for peace talks before she launches any offensive against us," the ever-watchful Frank Roberts minuted two days later on the Kelly report. "Any conversations with Germany on such a basis as peace terms at the expense of France and Belgium would enable Hitler at once to unite Europe, including France, against us and deprive us of growing American sympathy and support." To Roger Makins (later Lord Sherfield) the German approaches relayed by their Minister in Berne were a "peace reconnaissance." He described Prince Max as "completely exploded," although he conceded that Burckhardt was "in a different category." He recommended nonetheless that there was "nothing to show that these peace feelers have anything behind them or amount to more than they have in the past."[57]

The British Minister in Switzerland was therefore instructed that there would be "no response to these trustworthy intermediaries." An indication of the extent of this German "peace reconnaissance" through Ambassador Kelly was the efforts made in July 1940 to involve the United States as a mediator. At the beginning of the month the British Ambassador in Washington had received a signal from the Italian Ambassador, relayed by Assistant Secretary of State Berle, urging the "importance of coming to terms with Germany at once." He advised that while his approach was unofficial, it was made with the "full knowledge" of the German and Italian positions. The Ambassador, Berle told Lothian, had said in the strictest secrecy that the United States "ought to insist on acting as intermediary." The Assistant Secretary of State then disclosed that the United States had also had a "similar communication on the same line" from Don Alfonso, the ex-King of Spain.[58]

Lothian's telegrams, like Kelly's, were now being circulated on "Special Distribution" to the War Cabinet, along with all the other reports considered by the Foreign Office to be serious peace feelers. This was to ensure that standard policy, as laid down by Churchill, was followed, and that no encouragement was given to any German peace feeler. Silence, he considered, was the most effective way of signalling Britain's lack of interest in Hitler's overtures. An exception, however, was made in the case of the peace feeler received from the German Embassy in Washington by the British Ambassador on 19 July, the day Hitler was scheduled to make his peace speech to the Reichstag. That afternoon Lord Lothian telegraphed to London that he had been approached by an intermediary who had assured him "in good faith" that the German Chargé d'Affaires "if desired . . . could obtain from Berlin Germany's present peace terms."[59]

The intermediary was Malcolm Lovell, the Executive Secretary of the Quaker Service Council in New York, who claimed to be in close contact with the German Chargé d'Affaires, Thomsen. The message Lovell relayed was the familiar one of carrot and stick. Hitler was "reluctant to break up the British Empire," but "England would be devastated" and "time was getting short." When the British Ambassador referred to the "impossibility of trusting Hitler's word," Lovell suggested that the United States should be approached to guarantee any terms reached. What made the Quaker's proposal different from the other peace feelers was its invitation for the British Ambassador to open up direct communication with a German diplomat who would be able to specify officially on what conditions Hitler would make peace. It was reinforced three days later, when Lovell made a second approach to report Thomsen's actual offer to provide Germany's terms. The British Ambassador indicated his own inclination to follow it, underscoring his belief in its seriousness by making a personal telephone call to the Foreign Secretary at the Dorchester that evening.[60]

"We ought to find out what Hitler means before condemning the world to 1,000,000 casualties," Lothian urged Lord Halifax, although he immediately followed up with a cable in which his personal feelings in favour of pursuing the German peace feeler were less strongly stated. Such was his concern not to let the Lovell peace feeler grow cold that he "contemplated secret talk between the Chargé and myself." This, as he admitted in a subsequent cable, "would of course have amounted to opening negotiations."[61]

Lord Halifax also considered that the peace feeler was serious and worth following up. He circulated Lothian's request to the War Cabinet along with his own reply, which conformed with the Prime Minister's ban on any peace negotiations, telling the British Ambassador to "ignore Mr. Lovell's advance and return no answer to the German Chargé d'Affaires' message." But Churchill did not relent. Lothian was instructed to stick to this line even at the risk of the Germans' "trying to make mischief by putting it about that we had ignored a genuine peace offer." If approached again, the Ambassador was to say that he had "no instructions."

The War Cabinet's response to the Foreign Secretary showed that, without exception, its members backed Churchill's hard line. They wanted the door slammed shut and locked against any hint of peace negotiations. But Halifax wanted nonetheless to keep the door open, and therefore added the rider to Lothian that he "would be at liberty to listen and report to me."[62]

Two days later, this was countermanded, apparently at Churchill's insistence, when the Foreign Secretary sent a more emphatic instruction to the British Ambassador telling him "we are not prepared to ask for, or show interest in, Hitler's terms." However, U.S. Navy intelligence records show that Lord Lothian not only ignored his very clear instructions, but concealed the fact that he had actually sought out Lovell and encouraged the German peace feeler. His role was not exposed until 1944, when Lovell explained how he had been involved with peace efforts made by the Quaker headquarters in New York. He said he was contacted by the British Ambassador some time after Dunkirk and asked if he would see Chargé Thomsen "in connection with a possible peace negotiation or treaty between Britain and Germany." Lovell clearly inflated his role by claiming that for some time afterwards he had acted "as a messenger between Hitler and Churchill." Lord Lothian, he said, had told him that "all the school books of the future would record this matter since it was making history." But, he explained, the "negotiations failed because of Churchill."[63]

Corroboration for the essential correctness of Lovell's account if not for its hyperbole appears in the German records. Weizsäcker's memoirs reveal that he put a red flag on telegram No. 1488 from the German Chargé in Washington reporting on Lovell's peace moves. That cable does not survive, having presumably been destroyed by Ribbentrop – or possibly removed by the British. But a thorough search of the State Secretary's files in the German Foreign Ministry archives in Bonn did produce a 23 July minute by Weizsäcker: "Lord Lothian has offered his good offices. If he is a normal British Ambassador, he must have had a high approval. We may proceed on the assumption that the Quaker is authorized to bring us together."[64]

The German and American records therefore both indicate that Lord Lothian must have responded to the German peace feeler on his own initiative *before* receiving his two clear instructions not to do so from the Foreign Secretary. Even that, it seems, did not stop his efforts to seek a negotiated settlement. Documents and F.B.I. files show that soon afterwards, with the aid of Sir William Wiseman, who had been British Intelligence chief in New York during World War I, James D. Mooney was involved in one of the most bizarre peace plots of the entire war.

It also appears to have been no coincidence that on Friday, 19

July 1940, the day Lord Lothian had his meeting with Lovell, Adolf Hitler and Franklin D. Roosevelt both delivered speeches that were to have a decisive impact on the course of Britain's struggle for survival.

"In times like these – in times of great tension, of great crisis – the compass of the world narrows to a single fact," Roosevelt declared in a public address in which he reminded America that "The fact which dominates our world is the fact of armed aggression, the fact of successful armed aggression, aimed at the form of Government, the kind of society we in the United States have chosen and established for ourselves." The President was speaking in front of a battery of microphones in the Oval Room of the White House, but his words, measured and serious, were carried a thousand miles by radio relay to the giant loudspeakers ringing the Chicago Stadium. They echoed out over the arena, where the Democratic Party convention was about to declare its presidential nominee. For more than six months Roosevelt had been keeping even his closest White House aides guessing over whether he really would run again for the White House. As the Nazis overran Europe, the President's interventionist inclinations had been held in check by domestic political considerations. He knew that to make a successful run for an unprecedented third presidential term, his party must draft him as their unchallenged candidate, and so he had held himself aloof from the nominating process. The previous evening Roosevelt's draft-call had come, raucous and triumphant, as the convention members roared their acceptance to his nomination after a landslide victory on the first ballot of 874 delegate votes over his nearest rival, James A. Farley. That Friday evening, in what was billed as his acceptance speech, Roosevelt kept the convention on tenterhooks by talking of his planned January 1941 retirement and recalling the sleepless nights he had spent asking himself whether he had the right as Commander-in-Chief to call on men and women to serve if he himself was not ready to continue in office.[65]

"Today all private plans, all private lives have been in a sense repealed by an overriding danger," Roosevelt said, delaying the moment of his acceptance until the last. "Only the people themselves can draft a President. If such a draft should be made upon me, I say to you, in the utmost simplicity, I will, with God's help, continue to serve with the best of my ability and with the fulness of my strength . . ." The tidal roar that erupted in Chicago echoed across the United States on millions of radio sets.

That evening Roosevelt secured the support of his party. Now he had to win the backing of the whole country for his interventionist policies. Until the November election was won, he still had to move dextrously and cautiously in meeting Churchill's demands for the increased aid needed to keep Britain in the fight against Germany. The future of the British was also on the Führer's mind that same Friday evening as he stepped up to the flower-bedecked podium of the Kroll Opera House in Berlin to make his long-awaited *Friedensrede* – his so-called "speech of peace."

"I now hear only a single cry – not of the people but of the politicians – that the war must go!" Hitler declared, addressing his peace appeal to the British masses. Voicing his "deep disgust for the unscrupulous politician who wrecks whole nations," he denounced Churchill among those who would "carry on with the war" from Canada if Britain was invaded. "I can hardly believe that they mean by this that the people of Britain are to go to Canada."

"Mr. Churchill ought, perhaps, for once to believe me when I prophesy that a great Empire will be destroyed – an Empire which it was never my intention to destroy or even to harm," said the Führer, explaining that he was now appealing "*to reason and common sense* in Great Britain." As the victor "*speaking in the name of reason*" and not the vanquished begging for favours he said there was "no reason why this war must go on."[66]

If Hitler's speech had dealt with the specifics of the favourable peace terms that Britain could expect and had been lighter on sarcasm and historical distortion, he might have attracted more attention among those British politicians like Lord Halifax who were less determined than Churchill to carry on the war to the last bullet. Hitler's appeal for peace, cleverly constructed to give the impression of sincerity, was an impressive performance, all the more effective because for once he did not resort to his usual hysterical performance style. There is no doubt that the Führer genuinely wanted to reach a peaceful resolution of the conflict with Britain. Ten days before delivering this speech he had wondered aloud to Ciano whether "it would be possible by a skilful appeal to the English people to isolate the English government still further in England." But if Hitler had known anything about British politics he would have realized the futility of a foreign dictator appealing to the masses of ordinary folk, who actually detested the Nazis more than their rulers did. So his *Friedensrede* fell on deaf ears, although, as far as the Germans were concerned, he had cast himself as the reasonable party who could not be blamed if the British rejected his appeal.[67]

There was another, more sinister dimension to Hitler's speech. Chance alone cannot explain why he so deliberately chose to echo and stress the "common sense and not bravado" theme of the peace feeler received from Stockholm a month earlier. If it was a coincidence, it certainly did not strike Churchill that way. "I do not propose to say anything in reply to Herr Hitler's speech, not being on speaking terms with him," he had minuted to Vansittart.

He decided instead that Lord Halifax should have the privilege of answering Hitler's "gesture."[68]

The B.B.C. broadcast the Foreign Secretary's statement on 22 July. Its text had been polished by the Prime Minister, who, according to Halifax, had reservations about its excessive emphasis on the power of prayer. Apart from toning down the underlying note of religiosity, the "artist in language" – as Churchill was referred to by his Foreign Secretary – made several additions, including a slighting reference to Hitler as "that man," who was out to "sap the might of Britain." This was one of the strongest lines in Halifax's rejection of Hitler's "summons to capitulate to his will." The Foreign Secretary's attempt to contrast the Nazi vision of Europe in slavery with the freedom that Britain was fighting for was an awkward performance, made even less convincing by his uneasiness in front of the microphones and the cinema newsreel cameras. Such "appurtenances of democracy," he complained, "are very distasteful."[69]

That it was the Foreign Secretary who rejected his peace appeal added to Hitler's sense of injury after the immediate "NO" that the Prime Minister had directed the B.B.C. to broadcast within an hour of his Reichstag speech. It sent an unmistakable signal to Berlin that Churchill had prevailed and he could no longer count on a sympathetic ear for further peace feelers in the British War Cabinet. But by 22 July Ribbentrop had produced an alternative intermediary, one who appeared for a few crucial weeks to offer the Führer hope that there might still be a chance of winning his battle of peace with the British government before resorting to an all-out attack on England.

Chapter 14

"A Prince over the Water": The Windsor Connection

"A Man After My Own Heart"

"We must get hold of him, we must get Franco to detain him," Ribbentrop declared excitedly when he learned on 23 June that the Duke of Windsor was heading for Spain.[1] Erich Kordt, who was then *chef-de-cabinet* to the Nazi Foreign Minister, recalled how a "Strictly Confidential" cable "electrified" his baleful master on the evening of 23 June. Relayed to Ribbentrop's special train from Berlin, the telegram from the German Ambassador in Spain asked for instructions "with regard to the Duke and Duchess of Windsor who were to arrive in Madrid today, apparently in order to return to England by way of Lisbon." He said that the Spanish Foreign Minister reported that when General Franco's envoy, General Vignón, had met Hitler and Ribbentrop on 10 June "certain impressions" had been given "that we might perhaps be interested in detaining the Duke of Windsor here and possibly establishing contact with him."[2]

"Is it possible to detain the Duke and Duchess in Spain for a couple of weeks to begin with before they are granted an exit visa?" Ribbentrop immediately cabled to Ambassador Eberhard von Stohrer in Madrid, cautioning him "to ensure at all events that it did not in any way appear that the suggestion came from the German government." Out of this enigmatic exchange developed one of the most controversial episodes of World War II. For the next seven weeks the Duke of Windsor and his wife were pursued, courted and almost kidnapped by German intermediaries and secret agents, so desperate was Ribbentrop to make the ex-King the focus of a royal peace initiative.[3]

When the Duke and Duchess arrived in Madrid on Sunday, 23 June, after fleeing from the German advance in France, they were welcomed at the Ritz Hotel by the British Ambassador, Sir Samuel Hoare. It happened to be the Duke's forty-sixth birthday, but the cable handed to him from Churchill was not a greeting but a polite instruction asking him "to come home as soon as possible." His Royal Highness was less than enthused by this unceremonious response to the telegram he had dispatched two days earlier from Barcelona after crossing the French frontier: "Having received no instructions have arrived in Spain to avoid capture. Proceeding to Madrid."[4]

The British Ambassador shared the Prime Minister's concern that the Windsors' arrival in Madrid would arouse unwelcome German interest. He had already asked the Foreign Office for guidance after receiving the Duke's 20 June request for assistance in making his passage across the Spanish frontier. Hoare now wanted confirmation from London that he was proceeding correctly "in view of the press articles here saying it is intended to arrest him on arrival in England." Rumours were multiplying in the Spanish capital like summer flies that the Duke was seeking an exile, having aroused Churchill's animosity because he favoured an accommodation with Hitler.[5]

"Steps must be taken to ensure the safe return to this country of the Duke of Windsor," the 19 June War Cabinet had decided, well aware of the Duke's willingness to succumb to Nazi blandishments. In 1937, less than a year after he had given up the throne to marry Wallis Simpson, he had made, in defiance of government advice and the pleas of his brother, the King, a well-publicized tour of Germany. The couple had been royally received by Hitler and the Nazi leadership, who had danced attendance on the couple and treated the Duchess like a Queen, addressing her as Royal Highness, a title she had been denied by George VI. That decision had opened up a bitter family feud, and the Duke had reacted like a "middle-aged Romeo" to this slur on his wife, according to his former equerry, Sir Dudley Forwood. Forwood was also present throughout the hour-long private conversation with the Führer at Berchtesgaden, when the Duke repeatedly slipped into fluent German to emphasize his blood ties with and understanding of Germany. Forwood observed that his master "thought that his wise counsel might sway the Führer from confrontation with England."[6]

The *New York Times* put it more bluntly: the Duke had "demonstrated adequately that the Abdication did rob Germany of a firm friend, if not indeed a devoted admirer, on the British throne." On his tour he had been "very critical of English politics as he sees them and is reported as declaring British ministers of today and their possible successors are no match for German and Italian Dictators."[7]

An authoritarian at heart, Edward without doubt admired the leadership Hitler had given Germany and especially his success in eliminating the long lines of jobless workers that had moved him, when Prince of Wales, to make his celebrated protest: "Something must be done." While it would be overstating the Duke's pro-German leanings to say he was an overt Nazi sympathizer, he shared the belief of many of his aristocratic countrymen that Hitler had at the very least saved Germany from the Bolsheviks. Hatred of the Soviet regime was deeply ingrained in the young prince after his aunt and uncles, together with his Romanoff cousins, were murdered in the Russian Revolution. Many of his German cousins had become ardent Nazis in reaction to the spread of Communism in the 1920s. They included Karl Edward, the Duke of Saxe-Coburg-Gotha, and Prince Philip of Hesse, both of whom held senior rank in the Sturmabteilung, the brown-shirted Nazi militia. Prince Philip was rewarded by being made Gauleiter of Hesse and a confidant of Hitler; his marriage to the King of Italy's daughter had made him the Führer's obvious choice as go-between with Mussolini at the time of the Austrian Anschluss in March 1938.

Early in his nine-month reign, Edward VIII had received his cousin Karl Edward and afterwards the pro-Nazi German Duke enthusiastically reported to Berlin that his royal cousin had expressed a wish to have a meeting with Hitler, because of his "sincere resolve to bring England and Germany together." The same message was reaching Berlin from the German Ambassador in London, Leopold von Hoesch, who confirmed that the new King "feels a warm sympathy for Germany" and was in favour of a rapprochement. "We should at least be able to rely on a ruler who is not lacking in understanding for Germany." Such was the Ambassador's warm personal friendship with both the Prince of Wales and Mrs. Simpson that Prime Minister Stanley Baldwin was warned by M15 of the real danger that Hoesch might be getting direct access to state secrets. When Germany reoccupied the demilitarized Rhineland in defiance of the Versailles Treaty in March 1936, shortly after Edward VIII's accession, the new King made his sympathies very clear by urging Baldwin that Britain should not intervene militarily. The reports reaching Berlin from the German Embassy in London of the firm position adopted by the King during the crisis earned the admiration of Hitler. He believed the new British sovereign was "a man after my own heart . . . one who understood the *Führerprinzip*, and was ready to introduce it into his own country."[8]

Even the Duke's official biographer concedes that one of the reasons why Hitler sent Ribbentrop to London was his belief that the latter enjoyed a special relationship with the King. So when the new German ambassador arrived in Britain he had high hopes that with the King's sponsorship he could realize the Führer's goal of forging an Anglo-German alliance. Six weeks after Ribbentrop had been formally received at Buckingham Palace, his dream was shattered when the King abdicated and left the country to begin his life as a frustrated exile in France. Hitler had "personally instructed" his ambassador to do all he could to prevent the abdication. And in Ribbentrop's estimation it was not so much the romance with Mrs. Simpson but rather the King's efforts to bring about a rapprochement with Germany that led to his losing his throne, because of the machinations of "dark forces hostile to Anglo-German Understanding."[9]

Four years later, after receiving Hitler's orders on the eve of the Fall of France to work for an Anglo-German settlement, the Reichsausminister therefore reacted joyfully to the news that the Duke of Windsor was heading for Madrid. The Duke's affections for the Nazi cause may have been only skin-deep, but the records show they were taken very seriously in Germany. Ribbentrop also knew that the former King believed Britain had already lost the war. With a little encouragement, Ribbentrop thought, he could be persuaded to take the diplomatic stage and effect a dramatic transformation scene. Ribbentrop had good reason to believe that the Windsors would fall in with Hitler's peace plan; some months earlier, dispatches from the German Embassy in The Hague had rekindled Hitler's belief that the Duke of Windsor might be a willing participant in his scheme to end the war.

The captured Foreign Ministry files uncovered a cable of 27 January from Julius Count von Zech-Burchesroda, the German Ambassador to the Netherlands, reporting that "through personal relationships I might have the opportunity to establish certain lines leading to the Duke of Windsor." He explained that the Duke was dissatisfied with his posting (as a Major General on the Staff of the British Military Mission at French Headquarters) and had recently been to London to seek a more active role. "There is something like the beginning of a Fronde forming around W," Zech-Burchesroda reported, "which for the moment of course still has nothing to say, but which at some time under favourable circumstances might acquire a certain significance." The report detailed that when the Duke of Windsor was in London he "had explained to him through an intermediary why it is completely utopian for England to attempt to effect a change of regime in Germany, and the statements of my intermediary are believed to have made a certain impression on him."[10]

While Zech-Burchesroda's mysterious German intermediary in London has not yet been identified, he does not appear to have been the source through whom the Ambassador received top-secret Allied military intelligence obtained from the Duke of Windsor. This was relayed in a letter to Berlin on 19 February that reported that "the Allied War Council devoted an exhaustive discussion at its last meeting to the situation that would arise if Germany invaded Belgium." The decision was therefore taken to concentrate "the main resistance effort in the line behind the Belgian-French border." The source most likely to have relayed this information from the Duke was Charles Bedaux, the American "time-and-motion" millionaire, who had befriended the Windsors at the time of their wedding. He had been their host at his château Condé, and was a frequent dining companion of theirs. This was at a time when the Duke was serving at Allied Headquarters by day and gossiping with indiscretion at the dinner table by night. Bedaux was a friend of Göring and had extensive German business contracts. During the spring of 1940 he was making frequent trips between The Hague, where Count Zech-Burchesroda was posted, and Paris.[11]

The reports received from the German Minister in The Hague would have reinforced Hitler's conviction that the Duke could at a suitable juncture be made an ally if it were suggested to him that he might be restored to the throne if he helped to bring about peace between Britain and Germany. The fact that Franco's envoy General Vignón had learned from his 16 June conversation with Ribbentrop that the Windsors were intending to go to Spain is revealing, since the Duke and Duchess applied for Spanish visas two days later. So Vignón's report must raise the possibility that the Germans had prior knowledge of, or perhaps even had a hand in directing, the Windsors' destination before they fled on 19 June for La Croë. The pair had beaten a retreat to their rented villa on Cap d'Antibes from Biarritz after the Duke abandoned his "futile role" at the British Military Mission two weeks earlier.[12]

"An Impossible Game"

The Duke's choice of Spain as a temporary refuge could not have better suited Ribbentrop's plans to lure the Windsors into Hitler's peace offensive. The Reichsausminister's England Committee would have pointed out, if it had escaped Ribbentrop's attention, that the British Ambassador to Spain had been one of the most outspoken appeasers in the Chamberlain government and happened to be well-known to the Duke. Nor would it have been overlooked that when Hoare had been unceremoniously dropped from the Cabinet by Churchill, it was to Lord Halifax, his old friend and fellow appeaser, that he reported from Madrid.

"Slippery Sam," as Hoare was known by his enemies in the Conservative Party, attracted condemnation as a "rat" and potential "Quisling" from Cadogan, who predicted that as there were so many Germans and Italians in the Spanish capital there was "a good chance of S.H. being murdered." Madrid was indeed a city seething with treachery and intrigue in the summer of 1940. The wounds of Spain's bloody civil war, which had ended fifteen months earlier, had no time to heal before the European war broke out. Fired by German propaganda and undercover agents, the Spanish fascists in the Falange Party were agitating to join Hitler by declaring war on Britain. Hoare and his formidable wife, Lady Maud, had arrived on 1 June to find their embassy besieged by anti-British demonstrators calling for the return of Gibraltar. The nervous volatility of the country was evident on the streets of the capital, which were alive with demonstrators and armed militia. Most of the Spanish press was slavish in its praise for Hitler, as General Franco steered an uncertain course against the diplomatic gale from Berlin and Rome trying to blow Spain towards war. The winds of peaceful neutrality were being fanned with equal vigour by the British and American ambassadors.[13]

Hoare's "Special Mission," as defined by the War Cabinet, was to do everything possible to keep Spain neutral, a task that at times seemed increasingly futile. At his first meeting with Colonel Juan Beigbeder y Atienza, the Spanish Foreign Minister, the British Ambassador had spoken "quite openly about the possibility of the English government moving to Canada" if Britain was invaded. The pro-German Beigbeder reported every word of their talk to the German Minister. Von Stohrer passed it on to Berlin with the comment that Hoare was suffering from "political depression." The new British Ambassador could certainly not be accused of Churchillian resolution. In his view, the "parting of the ways" of Anglo-Spanish relations, as he put it in a cable to the Foreign Office, was so close that he kept the plane that had brought him to Madrid standing by to fly him out. The pilot and crew were still on call at the airport a week later. It was typical of Hoare's evasiveness that when the Spanish Foreign Minister offered, a month later, to act as a peace intermediary, his rejection was less than unequivocal.[14]

"It is possible it may one day come to that," Hoare conceded to Beigbeder, who immediately reported the British Ambassador's defeatist attitude to von Stohrer. The Foreign Minister's habit of passing on confidential diplomatic discussions to the Germans encouraged Berlin to think that it would be a simple matter to get Spain to declare war on the Allies. Hitler, who had supplied military aid to the Nationalist army that had crushed the Republican forces in the bloody civil war, considered General Franco more an undeclared ally rather than a neutral. But domestic concern for

Spain's impoverished and war-ravaged economy made the Caudillo wary of declaring himself a full partner of the Axis when the British were prepared to pay Spain to remain neutral – a price that, Hoare hinted, the British government might pay not just in economic aid and food supplies but also with territory.[15]

What Franco coveted more than the chance to grab a piece of French Morocco was the return of Gibraltar. The two-and-a-half-square-mile promontory jutting into the Mediterranean had been a thorn in the side of Anglo-Spanish relations ever since Britain captured the Rock in 1704. The strategic importance of Gibraltar, so vital in the days of sailing vessels and coal-fired warships, had declined with the advent of oil-burning ships and airpower, but Britain has always refused to countenance Spanish claims to one of the most emotive symbols of her maritime empire. Hitler and Mussolini were both offering to help Franco to seize Gibraltar if he would agree to join them against Britain, and so the Rock became an ace in Hoare's hand as he prepared to play a desperate game to keep Spain neutral.

"We may have to play high cards and even they may not take the trick, but our only chance is to play them," Hoare cabled to Lord Halifax on 11 June. His request to play the Gibraltar card came only a day after the German Ambassador had reported to Berlin denying the rumours that the British had already agreed to cede Gibraltar to Spain. A week later "Slippery Sam" was asking for guidance on the issue. "I feel bound to sound a warning that this attitude may well prove decisive in certain circumstances as to further relations with Spain," he cabled the Foreign Secretary. "I fully realize the grave questions of prestige involved even in admission that we would discuss the problem of Gibraltar," he added in a telegram that suggested he was about to play the ace. He did not believe that the Spanish government would expect a resolution of its territorial claim "other than as part of a general peace settlement." The War Cabinet on 18 June were alerted by Hoare to the possible necessity of making the Rock serve as a gigantic carrot to dangle in front of Franco. He suggested that its return to Spain might be discussed as part of a postwar settlement in return for Spain's wartime neutrality.[16]

Since Gibraltar is still a thorny issue between Britain and Spain, it is not surprising to find that the discussions in the critical weeks of June 1940 have been expunged from War Cabinet Minutes. Even the index entry to the fifth item on the 18 June agenda has been removed from the version available to researchers at the Public Records Office. This has led some British writers to assume that, because the censored item follows discussions on the seizure of the Swedish destroyers, it deals with a German peace offer received in response to the Prytz sounding. That this is not the case became clear from the full version, which was inadvertently copied for the author from the *uncensored* microfilm.[17]

The "missing" and still officially secret minutes of 18 and 19 June summarize the discussion on the "Question of Gibraltar" in response to Hoare's request for "guidance." It shows that Hoare was instructed that he could tell the Spanish government that "we should be ready to discuss after the war any matter of common interest to Spain and ourselves (without, however, referring specifically to Gibraltar)." The implication is that the War Cabinet were willing to discuss the Gibraltar issue by inference as a last resort. The following day's entry, also excised from the released Cabinet minutes, records that Hoare reported that Franco was "determined to keep out of the war and had made no demand as to Gibraltar."[18]

Whatever else "Slippery Sam's" political legacy, we can now see it was thanks to his adroitness in playing his hand while keeping the Gibraltar ace face down on the bargaining table with Franco, that the Union Jack still flies over the Rock. His success was to cause much periodic annoyance to postwar Spanish governments, who may have suspected but never knew for sure just how close the Caudillo had come to securing Gibraltar's return. It is evident from Hoare's veiled references in a letter to the Foreign Secretary on 26 June that he thought he might yet have to turn his ace up. The arrival of German troops at the Pyrenees frontier that morning raised the possibility that Hitler might move to occupy strategic points, including Gibraltar, after setting up a Nazi puppet government in Spain. Hoare reported that the consensus in Madrid was that the Germans "will not attempt direct action in Spain until they have made their attack upon Great Britain." He warned that in the "present precarious position of non-belligerency with constant German pressure," he might yet be forced to declare his final ace. "If I am to play a hand with nothing higher in it than a five of clubs," he cryptically warned Halifax, "I must have a partner who will try to pull me out of an impossible game."[19]

"Slightly Unhinged"—Spain
22 June–1 July

The "game" Hoare was playing became still more impossible during the Windsors' nine-day sojourn in Madrid. The Ambassador had originally been directed to speed the royal couple on to neutral Portugal, where a flying boat would be standing by at Lisbon to fly them to England on 24 June. This plan was dropped after objections by the Portuguese dictator to the Duke of Windsor's presence in Lisbon, which would overshadow the visit of his younger brother, the Duke of Kent, on the occasion of the eight-hundredth anniversary of Portugal's independence. This was the official explanation given by the Foreign Office when they instructed Hoare to keep the Duke of Windsor in Madrid until his brother's departure. But deference to Dr. António Salazar's pro-British sympathies may have been only one part of the reason for preventing the meeting in Lisbon of the two royal princes during a time of great crisis for Churchill when, as we now know, the Foreign Secretary was sending out peace feelers to Berlin.[20]

The Duke of Kent was the black sheep of the royal family until his death on 25 August 1942, when his R.A.F. Sunderland flying-boat bomber crashed into a mist-covered Scottish mountainside. Prince George's addiction to morphine, cocaine and passionate affairs with both sexes – one of his devoted lovers was the playwright Noël Coward – had titillated British society until his "safe" marriage in 1934 to Princess Marina of Greece. The Duke of Kent adored his elder brother and aped his enthusiasm for Germany, which was encouraged by their Hesse cousins. Prince Wolfgang, Philip of Hesse's younger twin, admitted in 1979 that his brother had acted as an intermediary between the Duke of Windsor and Hitler, though it was "not mediation in the true sense of the word," Prince Wolfgang said, describing conversations that had taken place between his brother and the Duke of Kent.[21]

This connection may have been known to, or suspected by, the German Ambassador to Spain when he cabled the news to Berlin on 2 July of the Windsors' imminent departure for Lisbon, reporting that it was "to confer with the Duke of Kent." In fact Prince George had already left Lisbon, but the Duke of Windsor would no doubt have welcomed the opportunity to unburden himself about the great crisis in his life and that of the country he had once ruled. What confidences might have been shared if the meeting of the royal brothers had taken place can only be a matter for speculation. It is a matter of historical record that the ex-King maintained he still had a special regard for Britain's destiny – and he had made it no secret that his view was very different to the course being steered by the Prime Minister. The Duke was freely holding forth on his belief that the correct course for the British government was to seek a compromise peace with Germany. He made a point of delivering his defeatist views to anyone who would listen, including the representatives of foreign governments.[22]

"In the past ten years Germany had totally reorganized the order of its society in preparations for this war," he told a staffer from the American Embassy. "Countries that were unwilling to accept such a reorganization of society and concomitant sacrifices should

360

direct their policies accordingly and thereby avoid dangerous adventures." As relayed by the American Ambassador to the State Department, the Duke had also made it plain that this view – which could be described as sympathetic to the Nazis – "applied not only to Europe but to the United States also." The Duchess had chipped in that "France had lost because it was internally diseased and that a country which was not in a condition to fight a war should not have declared war." Such subversive statements would have been unforgivable for any British citizen. When they were promulgated from the lips of a former King who made no secret of his pro-German sympathies, it was tantamount to treason.[23]

That was the inference of the report sent to Washington by the American Ambassador. Alexander Weddell, a stolid career diplomat, expressed concern that the Germans "would make trouble" out of such statements. He even wondered whether such views might not be representative of "an element in England, possibly a growing one, who would find in Windsor and his circle a group who are realists in world politics and who hope to come into their own in the event of peace."

Given that the Dukes of Kent and Windsor shared a deep affinity for Germany and a mutual loathing for the stiff moral hypocrisy of the British ruling class, it is clear why Churchill moved to block a royal summit in Lisbon. The royal brothers' inclination to see the Nazis in a sympathetic light because they had saved Europe from a second Bolshevik revolution could have provided the critical mass for a royal peace conspiracy which would have delighted Ribbentrop and been exploited by Hitler. If only to deny another opportunity for German propaganda, Salazar's objection – whether prompted or not – provided a convenient excuse for keeping the two most Germanophile members of the House of Windsor safely apart. But delaying the Windsors in Madrid encouraged rumours that the former appeaser Hoare was conspiring with his old friend the Duke to open peace negotiations behind the back of the government in London.

"Spanish press is circulating German propaganda of peace negotiations being carried on by the Duke of Windsor and myself," Hoare reported to Halifax on 30 June. Three days earlier he had sent a confidential cable urging Churchill to get the Duke back to England without delay or "there will be a prince over the water who will be a nuisance and possibly an embarrassment." Far from becoming a conspirator, the Ambassador had found himself playing the role of intermediary in a bitter dispute that had broken out between the Duke and the Prime Minister on 24 June. While the text of these telegrams remains officially closed until 2016, the index to the empty Foreign Office file that contained them outlines the progress of the row.[24]

"The Duke insists there is no need to hasten his return to the UK" was followed on 26 June by his ultimatum that "he cannot return till the status of the Duchess has been regulated." Churchill responded: "It will be better for Your Royal Highness to come to England as arranged, when everything can be considered." Hoare then tried to reason with the Duke but failed, reporting on 28 June an "unsuccessful argument" with him. A partial revelation by Churchill's biographer of the contents of the still classified exchange indicates that Hoare had managed to persuade the Duke to drop his demand for an official post; his principal demand now was for royal recognition of the Duchess. As Hoare explained, "it boiled down to both of them being received only once for quite a short meeting by the King and Queen, and notice of the fact appearing in the Court Circular."[25]

Feuding with the royal family over the status of the Duchess took priority for the Duke over his country's life-and-death struggle against Hitler. This came as no surprise to Sir Dudley Forwood, who recalled the tearful scene at the time of the Duke's marriage three years before when he had conveyed the message from the Palace that there would be no H.R.H. title for the Duke's wife: "I am afraid my master was slightly unhinged," said his former adjutant, who sincerely believed that Britain was in debt to Mrs. Simpson "for taking from the throne a man who might have been an unstable king."[26]

Whether this instability could have prompted the Duke to cast his lot with Hitler may never be known for sure, but his stubborn determination not to return to England unless his wife was accorded royal status gave Ribbentrop the opportunity he was looking for. Prompted by Berlin, the Spanish Foreign Minister offered the Windsors the opportunity to remain and put the Palace of the Caliph at Ronda at their disposal "for an indefinite period." The Duke now had the prospect of living in the heart of Andalucia in a manner befitting a prince instead of having his wife ostracized by his family and being banished to another "futile" official posting. Beigbeder reported to the German Ambassador that the idea had a definite appeal for the Duke, who told him "that he would return to England only if his wife were recognized as a member of the royal family and he were appointed to a military or civilian position of influence." But, tempting though the offer of the palace was, the Duke said he had nonetheless decided to go to Lisbon first, as the British government ordered. According to the German Ambassador's 2 July report, he said he "intended to return." To take the edge off Ribbentrop's displeasure that the Duke had been allowed to leave Spain, von Stohrer was careful to add that "Windsor has expressed himself in strong terms against Churchill and against this war."[27]

"Windsors leave for Lisbon tomorrow," Hoare cabled to London on 1 July with evident relief because, as he reported, their visit "has stimulated German propaganda." He followed it up with a private warning to the Prime Minister. "I do not believe they will return to England without further assurances," he forecast, explaining how the Duke had told him that he was only going to Portugal "to await the reply in Lisbon to the questions about his future." Churchill responded by sending a curt telegram to await the Windsors' arrival in Portugal.[28]

"Your Royal Highness has taken active military rank and refusal to obey direct orders of competent military authority would create a serious situation," he reminded the Duke, making it plain that action would be taken if His Royal Highness refused to obey his government's instruction. "I hope it will not be necessary for such orders to be sent. I must strongly urge immediate compliance with wishes of the government." The threat of a court martial unless he returned to England stung the Duke. He later complained to Churchill that the threat had "amounted to arrest" and that he had stooped "to dictator methods in your treatment of your old friend and former King . . ."[29]

"A Centre of Intrigue"—Portugal
2 July–1 August

The Duke finally gave in. He agreed to return home without any preconditions about his wife's royal status. On 4 July the Windsors were packed and ready to leave Lisbon by R.A.F. flying boat when their plans were changed once more. When the Duke arrived at the British Embassy that morning he was given a telegram from Churchill offering him the appointment of "Governor and Commander-in-Chief of the Bahamas." For a royal prince who had once ruled over an empire it was an insult to learn that he was expected to take charge of one of the more insignificant of Britain's thirty-five colonial territories. But the Prime Minister's telegram gave him no option.

"Personally I feel sure it is the best [offer] open in the grievous situation in which we all stand," Churchill apologized rather curtly. "At any rate I have done my best." The former King, who was expecting at least to be Governor General of Canada or one of the other dominions, took more than half an hour to be persuaded to accept what he saw as a St. Helena-like exile.[30]

The chain of sandy islands off the Florida coast had far more amenities than the rocky outcrop in the South Atlantic to which Napoleon had been banished. The only physical hardship to be endured at Government House overlooking the sweeping silver strand of Nassau Bay was the mosquito-ridden summer heat, and the Bahamas boasted social diversions as the winter playground of American millionaires. But it was an exile nonetheless, and the Duke took it as another slight from the British government. In fact it was his younger brother who had instigated the idea. The appointment had been decided on at a meeting three days earlier at Buckingham Palace after the King had told Churchill that they must "keep him at all costs out of England." The draft of the telegram prepared for Churchill by the Colonial Secretary, Lord Lloyd, announcing the appointment to the Dominion Prime Ministers explained in unflattering language why the official decision was made to exile the Duke for the duration to his "St. Helena." The Governorship of the Bahamas was portrayed by the Colonial Secretary as the solution with "the least of possible evils."[31]

"The activities of the Duke of Windsor on the Continent in recent months have been causing H.M. and myself increasing uneasiness as his inclinations are *well known to be pro-Nazi and he may become a centre of intrigue*," stated the draft telegram. "We regard it as a real danger that he should move freely on the Continent. Even if he were willing to return to this country his presence here would be most embarrassing to H.M. and the government." After the Duke's acceptance had been received, Churchill struck out the two unflattering sentences. Instead of receiving a startling official admission of the Windsors' flirtations with the Germans, the Dominion Prime Ministers learned that "though his loyalties are unimpeachable, there is always a backwash of Nazi intrigue which seeks to make trouble about him." This was also the phrase that Churchill used in the courtesy message he dispatched to President Roosevelt notifying him of the Duke of Windsor's appointment to the Bahamas. The 9 July telegram was sent via the American Embassy just one day before his former subjects learned that their ex-King would be on war duty beneath the waving palm fronds of a sub-tropical paradise island.[32]

If the Germans did not intercept this cable, Ribbentrop was quickly alerted that the Duke was having second thoughts about his Bahamas appointment. On 9 July von Stohrer reported from Madrid that the Duke had contacted the Spanish Foreign Minister asking him to "send a confidential agent to Lisbon" and had "reiterated his intention to return to Spain."[33]

The Windsors had been accommodated in a stylish seaside villa at Cascais, up the coast road north of Lisbon, adjacent to the rock formation that was symbolic of their predicament, since it was known to local fishermen as Boca do Inferno (Jaws of Hell). The British Embassy was dismayed that they were guests of Ricardo Espirito Santo Silva, an ambitious banker who was close to the German Ambassador in Lisbon, Baron Hoyningen-Huene. The pink-stucco villa became the object of intensive surveillance by British intelligence agents. But the Germans had no difficulty obtaining information about the Windsors through Santo Silva's friendship with the Baron.

On 10 July the Ambassador reported to Berlin that he had learned from members of their entourage that the Duke believed that "his appointment to the Bahamas is for the purpose of keeping him away from England since his return would greatly strengthen the friends of peace." He had therefore declared his intention "to postpone his journey to the Bahamas for as long as possible" in anticipation of "an early change in his favour." The Duke was portrayed by the Baron, on the reliable authority of Santo Silva, "as a firm supporter of a peaceful compromise with Germany" who believed "with certainty that continued heavy bombing will make England ready for peace."[34]

The Duke himself wrote a firm "No" against this assertion when he saw the cable for the first time in 1953. But many of those who were with him attest to his defeatist and pro-German – if not pro-Nazi – sentiments. Viscount Eccles was the Economic Councillor at the British Embassy in Madrid charged with liaising with the Windsors during their stay at Boca do Inferno. He recalled the Duke explaining to him that it was hopeless for Britain to carry on the struggle against Hitler, and peace must be negotiated. He foresaw only endless defeat, suffering and eventual occupation if the British tried to continue the war against Germany. What was the purpose in continuing the fight, he had asked Eccles, since it was too late to save Poland? The Duke's words filled the diplomat with apprehension and foreboding because they echoed precisely the arguments Marshal Pétain had used six months earlier when he was France's Ambassador to Spain. Eccles did not question the Duke's patriotism but had tried "strenuously" to convince him that if Britain surrendered she would become another vassal state.[35]

"No one can understand the Duke's attitude at the time unless they realize that he honestly believed the war was lost," Eccles explained. "He did not want the Germans to win, but he thought that if they carried on the war they would." After attending one of the Windsors' dinner parties during their stay in Lisbon, the American Ambassador, Herbert Claiborne Pell, was so disturbed by the Duke's defeatist talk that he filed an immediate report to Washington. "Duke and Duchess are indiscreet and outspoken against the British government," he warned the Secretary of State. Their intention to visit America en route to the Bahamas he felt "might be disturbing and confusing." Pell urged that the Windsors' American visas should be cancelled because they had declared they would "remain in the United States whether Churchill likes it or not" to make peace propaganda.[36]

Ambassador Pell's warning was brought to the confidential attention of the British Ambassador in Washington. Lothian alerted the Foreign Office to the "icy character" of the reception that the couple would get in New York, and Churchill deferred to his advice. Without offering any explanation, he wired the Duke on 19 July with his travel arrangements. The American Export Line steamer *Excalibur*, sailing from Lisbon on 1 August, was to be diverted to Bermuda to connect with a Canadian vessel heading for the Bahamas. Next day the Duke objected forcefully. He pleaded with the Prime Minister to be allowed "to go to New York as I had originally arranged." The King urged the Colonial Secretary: "tell him to do as he is told."[37]

To humour His Royal Highness, Churchill conceded the Duke's demand that his two army batmen should be released from military service to accompany him to Nassau. But he would not be moved to agree to the Windsors' "landing in the United States at this juncture." The decision, the Duke was told, "must be accepted." The Duchess, however, could independently go for dental treatment to New York "if necessary." The Duke first accepted the arrangement, then tried to delay his departure from Lisbon for a week. He was politely but firmly advised that the sailing arrangements would not be changed.[38]

"I very much hope that you will be able to fall in with this proposal," Churchill cabled on 27 July. To ensure that the Duke followed his instruction, the Prime Minister sent him a personal letter carried by his legal adviser Walter Monckton, who had been pressed to fly out to Lisbon at Churchill's request. In the deferential opening paragraph, he promised to "do all within my power to serve your Royal Highness' true interests," assuring him that the Bahamas had "one of the most agreeable climates" and a "ceaseless flow of interesting people." The bitter pill was a stern injunction: the Duke could not visit the United States, because "the Presidential Election and the critical character of the war here have created abnormal conditions." Churchill also warned his old friend to take care to "express views about the war and general situation which are not out of harmony with those of His Majesty's Government." He said that "many sharp unfriendly ears will be pricked up to catch any suggestion that your Royal Highness takes a view about the war, or about the Germans, or about Hitlerism, which is different from that adopted by the British nation and Parliament."[39]

This letter and the other revealing exchanges with the Duke of Windsor from the still closed Churchill Archive were made public by Martin Gilbert, Churchill's official biographer. Its reference to conversations "reported by telegraph through various channels which might have been used to Your Highness' disadvantage" suggests that the Prime Minister was hoping to frighten the Duke into being more cautious in his defeatist statements. Churchill's "words of caution" were a thinly disguised reprimand to the Duke, who appeared to need reminding that his country was "passing through times of immense stress and dire peril when every step has to be watched with care."

The Prime Minister must have learned of the Duke's latest indiscretions, which allegedly predicted the fall of the Churchill government, which would bring Labour to power to negotiate peace, the abdication of his brother, and his own recall to the throne to lead a coalition of France, Spain and Portugal which would leave Hitler free to smash Bolshevik Russia. The report filed by members of the legation staff had it that the ideas were "put into the head of H.R.H. by Frenchmen and Spaniards who were playing Germany's game."[40]

Such alarming reports, exaggerated though they may have been by hearsay, were being passed on by British officials. This indicates that the Duke's defeatist views must have caused concern in London. Bitter at the humiliation of the woman for whom he had given up the throne, and frustrated that the British government was not prepared to take seriously his advice to end the war or to offer him a role in the war effort, the Duke of Windsor had become a dangerous liability as long as he remained in Europe.[41]

Whether the Duke is seen as a dupe, a foolish conspirator, or a treacherous one in the bizarre German plot that coalesced around the Boca do Inferno depends on the credence given to the statements he purportedly made which appear in the captured German Foreign Office records. When the so-called Windsor file was discovered in 1945, Churchill found it so distressing that, out of sentimental regard for the Duke of Windsor, he called for it to be expunged from the historical record.[42]

"I earnestly trust it may be possible to destroy all traces of these German intrigues," Churchill urged the then Prime Minister Attlee on 26 August 1945. This letter was written after he had read the file of original telegrams extracted from the German Foreign Ministry records on the instructions of General Dwight D. Eisenhower and passed to the Foreign Office by the American Ambassador in London. The originals were "placed in the Foreign Office," where they could be kept locked away with other captured German documents and files that the British government decided would be too sensitive ever to be released.[43]

The "Windsor File" escaped the British Foreign Office weeders because the existence of the telegrams was not known until they were discovered by the U.S. Army, which had custody of the captured records. The German diplomatic ciphers had defied the British codebreakers at Bletchley throughout the war, although the

Germans were breaking the Foreign Office cipher telegrams sent at the time to the Ambassadors on the Iberian Peninsula. The result was that the offending German telegrams were microfilmed by the U.S. Army *before* the originals were pulled from the collection on Eisenhower's instructions. It was in this form that they were discovered again by the team of Allied historians responsible for selecting and publishing the more important documents.[44]

In 1953, when Churchill was Prime Minister once again, he was infuriated to learn, just after the coronation of Queen Elizabeth II, that the cables detailing Ribbentrop's plot to snare the Duke of Windsor had not only survived but would appear in the official publication of selections of the German Foreign Ministry documents. President Eisenhower was "completely astonished to learn that a microfilm record was made of the documents." But he felt unable to grant Churchill's appeal, addressed to his "sense of justice and chivalry," to refuse "to allow the official publication of the telegrams or their revelation to anybody outside secret circles." The British editor in chief threatened to resign if the government interfered with historians' freedom to publish "on the basis of the highest scholarly objectivity." Churchill then tried to get publication delayed "for at least ten or twenty years." It was in fact only four years before, with one exception, all twenty-one cables were duly published by the British, the Americans and the French in 1957.[45]

The account given in the German records reveals that Ribbentrop, after receiving the 11 July report on the Duke from his Ambassador in Lisbon, unveiled his secret plan to the German Ambassador in Spain. Its ultimate aim was ill-defined, but its immediate objective was to entice the Windsors to return to Spain and to keep them there in territory where they were subject to direct German control. Ribbentrop ordered von Stohrer to arrange for this plan to be executed "as soon as possible, if necessary by force." Stealth was essential to avoid alerting the British secret service in Lisbon, who "then would prevent it at all costs." Once back in Spain, Ribbentrop said, the Duke and his wife "must be persuaded or compelled to remain on Spanish territory." The Duke was then to be told that "Germany wants peace," "the Churchill clique stands in the way," and the Führer was "determined to force England to peace by every means of power." When this goal had been achieved – presumably with the participation of the Duke – Germany "would be prepared to accommodate any desire expressed by the Duke, especially with a view to the assumption of the English throne by the Duke and Duchess."[46]

Abiding by Ribbentrop's instructions to deal with the matter "personally and confidentially," von Stohrer enlisted the aid not of the Spanish Foreign Minister, whom he considered too indiscreet, but of the Interior Minister, Serrano Suñer, Franco's brother-in-law. The Madrid district Falange leader, Miguel Primo de Rivera, Marqués de Estella – "a friend of the Duke for a long time" – was briefed to act as an intermediary. He set off for Lisbon on 14 July to invite the Windsors to return to Spain for a hunting expedition. Once in Spain they were to be confronted by Suñer for a discussion of the Gibraltar issue, during the course of which he would reveal a supposed British secret service plot to take the Duke's life. He would persuade the couple to remain in Spain for their own safety.[47]

Two days later Rivera reported that the Duke was coolly hostile to Churchill and favourably disposed to consider returning to Spain. On 23 July Rivera returned after a second visit to the Windsors to report that "the Duke has moved further and further away from the King and from the present English government." The Duke had referred to his brother the King as "utterly stupid" and was now "toying with the idea of dissociating himself from the present tendency of British policy by a public declaration and breaking with his brother." The Windsors "very much desired to return to Spain and expressed thanks for the offer of hospitality." Two days later Rivera reported that the couple were "astonished" when he advised the Duke to return to Spain, because he "might yet be destined to play a large part in English politics and even to ascend the English throne."[48]

Ribbentrop, who took the reports at face value, concluded that with the Duke nibbling on the bait the time had come to bring in professional assistance in the form of Walter Schellenberg, the young S.S. General whom Heydrich had made head of the foreign counter-espionage section of the R.H.S.A. After a briefing by Ribbentrop on 24 July, Schellenberg and two S.S. agents set off next day by air for Madrid. The final touches were put to the plot on 26 July, when it was agreed that the Windsors would be "invited" to set out for a "summer vacation" near the Spanish frontier. Then in the course of a hunting expedition they would cross the border with the aid of Portuguese frontier officials controlled by the Spanish secret service. Schellenberg left to coordinate operations in Lisbon, with the cooperation of the Portuguese police chief, whose connivance was arranged by Paul Winzer, the senior Gestapo officer in Madrid. A plane was laid on at Lisbon, ready to fly the Windsors to Spain in the event of interference by the British secret service.

The whole operation hinged on the Duke's reaction to a letter, intended to be "very skilfully composed psychologically," which would be handed over at an appropriate juncture by a second intermediary. Composed by de Rivera, it warned of a menacing but unspecified threat to the Windsors, who were offered the chance to escape to Spain by driving to a rendezvous with Rivera in the mountain border village of Guarda. In accordance with Ribbentrop's orders this letter not only contained no indication of any German involvement but specifically reassured the Duke that if Spain entered the war he would have the right to leave the country.[49]

The Duke received de Rivera's letter on Sunday, 28 July, from a Spanish Abwehr agent named Angel Alcázar de Velasco. He reported that the Duke read the letter three times, but it did not produce the psychological reaction intended. His Royal Highness, perhaps realizing for the first time the dimension of the intrigue he was being invited to step into, became indecisive and confused about what he should do. Without giving any indication that he would take up the offer of a Spanish refuge he told Velasco to come back in two days for his answer.[50]

At this climactic point in the pantomime, the Duke's trusted friend Walter Monckton arrived in Lisbon by air that evening with the exquisite timing of a fairy godmother flying in to rescue the prince from the evil magician. Whatever thoughts the Duke may have entertained of accepting the invitation to a hunting trip in Spain evaporated after his talk with his legal adviser. Monckton added his own cautions to the sternly worded counsel in Churchill's letter, warning the Duke that "there was a plot afoot against his security and that British influence, including possibly even some members of the Government, were implicated." Monckton did not offer any explanation as to who these members might be. After the war he significantly modified his story, saying that he told the Duke only "that the Germans might be plotting to keep him in Europe and possibly get hold of him."[51]

"'Willi' will nicht" is the 29 July entry in Schellenberg's surviving operational log. Information obtained from one of the agents planted among the domestic staff in Boca do Inferno alerted him that Monckton's arrival had thrown a monkey-wrench into his carefully laid plans. Next day the Duke told the intermediary Velasco that he would after all leave for the Bahamas, because "no prospect of peace existed at the moment." He excused himself from his starring role by saying that the "situation in England was still by no means hopeless"; therefore he could "not now, by negotiations carried on contrary to the orders of his Government, risk unleashing on himself the propaganda of his English opponents, which might deprive him of all prestige at the period when he might possibly take action." With time and the principal actor in his pantomime plot about to run out on him, Schellenberg resorted to ever more desperate stratagems to try to dissuade the Duke and Duchess from sailing from Europe in three days' time.[52]

"All things considered the simplest course will be to get a message to Willi to the effect that Germany is interested in making contact with him," he cabled Ribbentrop on 30 July. At his 1945 interrogation Schellenberg said that in his desperation to make contact with the Duke he "actually posted himself in the neighbourhood of his residence, but without success." Simultaneously he had set in motion a series of scare-tactics to frighten the Windsors into believing they were the target of a sinister assassination plot. Shots were fired at the windows of their villa. The Duke's fear of the 'Jewish Peril' was played on by sending him a list of the Jews who would be sailing with him. Flowers were sent to the Duchess with an anonymous note warning her not to sail; and one of the Duke's drivers was bribed to refuse to sail at the last moment after one of the Windsors' cars was sabotaged by Schellenberg's agents.[53]

Schellenberg even made plans for a bomb to be discovered aboard the liner as a prelude to a kidnap operation if the Windsors still refused to flee to Spain. Both plans proved impractical. In a final bid to keep the Duke in play, Ribbentrop finally authorized telling him that he was the recipient of a peace overture from an "authoritative German source." Ribbentrop's 'Most urgent top secret' cable arrived at the German Embassy in Lisbon on the evening of 31 July, while the Windsors were being feted at a farewell reception at the Hotel Aviz. It instructed the Ambassador to arrange for the Duke's host, Santo Silva, to "make the most earnest effort to prevent his departure tomorrow." He was to warn the Windsors that "reliable reports are in our possession to the effect that Churchill intends to get the Duke into his power in the Bahamas." He was then to explain that "Germany wants peace" and would "clear the way for any desire expressed by the Duke and Duchess." The Duke and Duchess were to be left in no doubt that this was a genuine appeal, made on the Führer's authority, to stay in Europe to "be prepared for further developments."[54]

At midnight the Windsors' party was still in full swing when Santo Silva received a summons from the German Ambassador. In the small hours of Thursday morning he saw Baron Hoyningen-Huene. After a thorough review of all possible courses of action they agreed on a final strategy that included asking Salazar to intervene with his own plea for the Duke to remain in Portugal.

Thursday was a day of frantic meetings after a flood of mysterious warnings designed to intimidate the Windsors into thinking again about sailing. Primo de Rivera flew in from Madrid to tell the Duke his life would be in danger in the Bahamas. He could not disclose his sources, but he urged His Royal Highness to delay his departure for "two or three weeks." Thoroughly alarmed, the Duke wanted to cable Churchill that he was not going to sail. Monckton, who had already arranged for a Scotland Yard detective to stand guard over the Windsors, managed to calm the badly rattled Duke into accepting that there was "no concrete evidence" that he or his wife were in any physical danger.[55]

The Duke's reaction to the appeal by Santo Silva not to leave for the sake of Europe was very revealing. On being told *for the first time* that he was the recipient of an authoritative German peace overture the Duke – according to the German accounts – was both flattered and impressed. "The Duke paid tribute to the Führer's desire for peace," admitting that it "was in complete agreement with his own," because he "was firmly convinced that if he had been king it would never have come to war." He "gladly consented" to the appeal to cooperate, but to disobey his orders "would disclose his intentions prematurely." The Duke had, however, regretfully come to the conclusion that it was too early yet for peace negotiations, because "there was no inclination in England for an approach to Germany." Nonetheless he was ready and willing to respond in future as an intermediary to an approach from either Germany or England, "which he thought to be entirely possible." He promised to remain in contact with Santo Silva and "agreed with him upon a code word upon receiving which he would immediately come back over." The Duke also relayed via his Portuguese host "an expression of admiration and sympathy for the Führer."[56]

This report was the most notorious of the cables. It is significant that Churchill dismissed as "tendentious and unreliable" the only telegram that purports to convey the Duke's reaction to a peace overture *after* the intermediary had revealed that it came from an "authoritative German source." It has been argued that this report is unreliable because the Duke's statements are being reported third-hand and that both the intermediary Santo Silva and Ambassador Hoyningen-Huene were *agents provocateurs* trying to put the best construction possible on their failure to keep the Windsors from sailing. But the defeatist statements attributed to the Duke had all been made before. His belief that if he had been king he could have prevented war with Hitler, his desire for a negotiated peace and his willingness to serve as an intermediary had all appeared in one form or another in the reports of the American ambassadors in Spain and Portugal. Only the effusive salutations to the Führer may be argued to be window-dressing.

What is relevant is that the Duke had this time reiterated his defeatist views *knowingly* to a self-declared intermediary of the Germans. That he had no hesitation in sending such a defeatist message to Berlin even *after* receiving Churchill's written warning about "sharp and unfriendly ears" may indicate whether he was a gullible fool or a calculating intriguer. Nor were his defeatist statements any more extreme than those attributed to him by non-German sources in Lisbon and Madrid. His argument in favour of a compromise peace accords precisely with the arguments used by Lord Halifax and R. A. Butler. In essence it was the "common-sense" rationale that since Britain could not win the war now, a negotiated peace was necessary to save the country from terror bombing and preserve the Empire. The Duke was saying no more than had already been said in the War Cabinet, in the corridors of Westminster and in City of London banks and boardrooms. The distinction is that the words were spoken by the Duke of Windsor to an emissary of the German Foreign Minister in circumstances that were close to treason if not actually so.

In the light of the statements made to Santo Silva on 1 August it cannot be credibly argued that the Duke of Windsor was an innocent dupe. Not even the most blindly devoted champions of the Windsors can deny that the Duke *did not* "just say no" to the German approach. If the tenor of his statements had been resolution and not defeatism, Schellenberg's Operation Willi could never have got off the ground. That it became a pantomime with too many conspirators is undeniable. But the record as it now stands, despite the Duke's denials in 1953, shows that at the very least he flirted with German conspirators. Whether he went further than flirtation is a matter of interpretation. But it is impossible to dismiss the suspicion that if at the beginning of Operation Willi the Duke had been made aware that he was being appealed to by the Führer, *it might have succeeded*; he might have been vain enough to accept the role of Hitler's royal dove of peace.

Schellenberg appears to have come to the same conclusion. That is why he staked out the Windsors' villa to try and engineer a face-to-face encounter with the Duke. But it was by then too late; Prince Charming had fallen under the protective spell of Monckton, who remained glued to his side until the royal party sailed. This Schellenberg noted, through powerful field-glasses trained from the tower room of the German Embassy, as he watched the Windsors boarding their steamer.

At 6.40 p.m. that bright Sunday evening, as *Excalibur* pulled out into the Tagus and a crowd of several hundred waved from the pier, two blasts on the steamer's siren should have brought down the curtain on Operation Willi. Or did it? Another cable discovered in the captured Foreign Ministry archives suggests that this was not quite the final act of the drama. On 15 August, the day the Windsors reached Bermuda, the German Ambassador in Lisbon received notice that "Willi" might yet be willing to play a part in Hitler's peace offensive. This is clear from Hoyningen-Huene's report that Santo Silva had just received a telegram from the Duke in Bermuda, "asking him to report as soon as it may become necessary for him to act." "Should anything be sent in reply?" the Ambassador asked Berlin.[57]

If Ribbentrop sent any reply to Lisbon for the Portuguese banker to relay to the Duke of Windsor, no trace of it now exists in the captured German archives. It is also puzzling that the Duke should have run the risk of sending such an incriminating cable through the vigilant British censors in Bermuda, the more so because this message simply repeated his confidential assurance to Santo Silva that he would remain in contact. The Duke's defenders contend that the lack of logic in this last cable proves that it was concocted and that this must surely undermine the credibility of all the others. But if the telegram was not sent by a disgruntled Duke, who was intent on thumbing his nose at British authority, could it have been sent *in his name* by British intelligence?

The Duke had been under close MI6 surveillance in Lisbon because of fears that he was "pro-Nazi and he may become the centre of intrigue." But once the Windsors were safely out of Europe and back under British control, a deliberately engineered provocation cabled in the Duke's name to his host Santo Silva would have furthered Britain's interests. The object of such a deception could have been the same as Churchill's decision to permit Halifax and Butler to remain at the Foreign Office.[58]

It would have encouraged Ribbentrop and Hitler to believe that all hopes of a negotiated peace with England were not yet dead. Until the Führer was certain there was no chance of a settlement he was holding back from launching the assault on Britain. Each day that Hitler delayed in calling for an all-out attack, Britain was making herself better able to resist, with munitions factories working round the clock to turn out the guns, tanks and aircraft necessary to repel the German invader. Hurricanes and Spitfires were being produced at the rate of a dozen a day; pilots were being trained at breakneck pace. Most important of all were the vessels steaming across the Atlantic deeply laden with the first instalment of American war supplies to arm the troops defending the British Isles against invasion.

Chapter 15

"Turning the Tide of War"
August–September 1940

"A Last Appeal to Reason"

The climax of the Windsor plot coincided with the two weeks that Hitler waited for a response after launching his "peace offensive" in the Reichstag. During this period the R.A.F. received over 150 new fighters, bringing an overall increase in front-line fighter reserves. Sixty-nine aircraft had been lost for 164 German planes downed in the air battles over the Channel convoys, a kill ratio of almost 2.4:1 in the R.A.F.'s favour during the opening round of the Battle of Britain. With the difference between victory and defeat hanging on so slender a margin, this early success played a vital part in the decisive second phase of the struggle, as the Luftwaffe launched an all-out attack on Fighter Command and its airfields.

Was it just coincidence that led Hitler to issue the orders for the all-out air offensive against England on the very day of the Windsors' departure from Europe? Or was there a connection with the failure of Ribbentrop's plot to use the Duke in a final bid for peace? The issuing of Directive 17 for the Luftwaffe campaign preparatory to the "Operation Sea Lion" invasion plans that were also promulgated from Führer Headquarters on 1 August suggests that the collapse of "Operation Willi" played its part in finally snapping Hitler's patience. To infer therefore that the Duke's flirtation with the Nazis actually saved Britain from being invaded because of Hitler's fatal delay would be to give too much weight to what appears to have been only one factor in the Führer's month-long procrastination, during which Britain's ability to resist grew day by day. But Operation Willi was arguably one of the elements that caused him to postpone a decision on the British attack until the peace feelers had been rejected.[1]

This is clear from Hitler's 21 July conference with the newly promoted Field Marshal von Brauchitsch in Berlin, when he specifically identified the "Duke of Windsor: Letter to King" as one of the factors in his peace calculations. The O.K.H. chief reported to his deputy, Halder, that the Führer seemed not unhopeful of the chances of peace because of the British press reaction to his speech, which, while "initially violent in its rejection, later turned on a softer tone." He said that Hitler had also cited Lloyd George and had revealed that the German Chargé d'Affaires in Washington had just reported that the British situation was "considered hopeless." This information from Washington must have come from the Quaker Lovell's discussions with Lord Lothian, because Thomsen quoted the British Ambassador as saying "Britain has lost the war." Hitler declared to his military leaders that Britain should "pay" but he wanted to do nothing "derogatory to her honour", since Thomsen had reported the possibility of a new British Cabinet being formed consisting of "Lloyd George, Chamberlain, Halifax."[2]

Hitler admitted that he had "no clear picture on what is happening in Britain"; that was why he now wanted preparations to be made "as quickly as possible" for a decision by armed force. But at the same time he had yet to make up his mind to proceed with the invasion; he told von Brauchitsch that it was "very hazardous" and would be undertaken "only if no other means are left to come to terms with Britain." He had also concluded that if Britain did not respond to his peace offer it would be because she was putting her hope in America and Russia.

"Stalin is flirting with Britain to keep her in the war and tie us down," Hitler explained. "Our attention must be turned to tackling the Russian problem and prepare planning." The Führer's ambivalence over the feasibility of the invasion and his growing belief that eliminating Russia was an alternative way of forcing Britain to come to terms were evident on 31 July when the army and navy staff assembled at the Berghof. Admiral Raeder reported that operational preparations for the invasion could be completed by 13 September, but he had strong reservations. The weather, and problems in finding enough barges and tugs were only two of the difficulties that were being encountered. There were differences with the army over where and at what time of day to make landings. His worst fear was that with only four destroyers currently available as escorts, the thirteen British battleships would swiftly make mincemeat of the vulnerable invasion force. The prospect unsettled the Führer. "Preparations were to proceed," he nonetheless decided, while the results of the air war would determine whether or not to go ahead. If the results were unsatisfactory, the invasion would be stopped; if the British started crumbling under the Luftwaffe assault, Hitler said, "we shall proceed with the attack."[3]

"To all intents and purposes," the Führer declared, "the war is won." Britain, he had now concluded, was only holding on because of Russia and the United States. "If Russia drops out of the picture America, too, is lost for Britain. With Russia smashed, Britain's last hope would be shattered. Germany would then be master of Europe and the Balkans." Accordingly "Russia's destruction must therefore be made part of this struggle." The Führer announced that "The sooner Russia is crushed the better." He therefore set a spring 1941 deadline for the military preparations for the great eastward campaign to be ready.[4]

Now that Hitler had settled on an alternative strategy for dealing with Britain, he issued Directive 17 setting the conditions "necessary for the final conquest of England." This called on the Luftwaffe "to overcome the British Air Force with all means at its disposal and as soon as possible." After winning air superiority it was to switch its attack to British harbours and "stand by in force for Operation Sea Lion." Simultaneously O.K.W. chief Keitel issued the directive calling for invasion preparations to be completed by 15 September. Two weeks after the launching of the air offensive against Britain, the Directive announced, "on or about 15 August the Führer will decide whether the invasion will take place this year or not; his decision will largely depend on the outcome of the air offensive."[5]

"The proposed invasion of England was nonsense because adequate ships were not available," Field Marshal von Rundstedt told Allied interrogators in 1945. "We looked upon the whole thing as a sort of game because it was obvious that no invasion was possible when our navy was not in a position to cover a crossing of the Channel or carry reinforcements." But if the invasion preparations ordered on 1 August were part of a gigantic bluff to frighten Britain into surrendering, Göring's Adlerangriff (Eagle Attack) plan had a more serious objective. This plan, a response to the Führer Directive calling for the concentration of the Luftwaffe "against [R.A.F.] flying units, their ground installations and their supply organizations and the aircraft industry", was based on Göring's conviction that his bombers and fighters would need only two weeks of concerted attacks to wipe out R.A.F. Fighter Command. The Adlerangriff directive issued on 2 August ordered the aerial assault to begin with a massive three-pronged strike against airfields, radar installations and aircraft factories as soon as a suitable spell of fine weather was forecast.[6]

On 2 August German bombers droned over England dropping

not bombs but newspaper-size propaganda leaflets headlined "A Last Appeal to Reason by Adolf Hitler" and detailing his final peace offer. For the next week, as the Luftwaffe waited on the weather to launch its all-out assault on the R.A.F., the pace of the air war over the Channel increased and the British government grew more anxious to know, not if, but when and where the Germans would make their invasion attempt. The Admiralty had supplied a list of dates and possible locations but even ULTRA provided few clues until 29 July. That day the intercept of a German Air Force *Enigma* cipher ordering bombers to avoid attacking the piers in the English south-coast harbours was interpreted by Military Intelligence as evidence that the enemy wanted them left intact for use during the intended invasion. This intelligence sharpened Churchill's conviction that, as Lothian had cabled from Washington, the time was ripe to press Roosevelt on the destroyer issue again. "I am sure that this is the moment to plug it in," Churchill minuted to the Foreign Secretary enclosing his first telegram to Roosevelt in over a month and a half.[7]

"The Common Cause"
29 July–10 August

"It has now become most urgent for you to let us have the destroyers, motor boats and flying boats for which we have asked," the President was told by the Prime Minister. He gave the Royal Navy's latest casualty list of eleven destroyers sunk or badly damaged in Channel air attacks, and asked Roosevelt for "50 or 60 of your oldest destroyers which could be used for escort duties releasing the Navy's modern ones to help thwart the invasion."

"Mr. President, with great respect, I must tell you that in the long history of the world, this is a thing to do now," Churchill appealed, saying that he was "beginning to feel very hopeful about this war if we can get through the next six months." The American rifles on the way across the Atlantic were to be used to arm the Home Guard, "who will take a lot of killing before they give up." He was certain the President would not "let the crux of the battle go wrong for the want of these destroyers."[8]

This cable, which significantly contained nothing that the Germans did not already know, was sent via the American Embassy. Perhaps to confuse Berlin's eavesdropping and to curry the Ambassador's favour, Churchill added that he was sending his message through Kennedy, "who is a grand help to us and the common cause." The Ambassador had been told three days earlier by Lord Beaverbrook that the Prime Minister, on his advice, was reversing

378

his tactics of making things look "as black as possible" for the Americans and instead putting the best construction on them. "Don't let anybody make any mistakes," Kennedy warned the State Department on 31 July. "This war, from Great Britain's point of view, is being conducted with their eyes only one place and that is the United States." This "grand help" was followed up by a further pessimistic message that preceded Churchill's cable, advising the Secretary of State that the Germans had the air power necessary to put the R.A.F. "out of commission." After this Britain's surrender "would be inevitable," because as the Ambassador graphically put it, without American support "they have not got a Chinaman's chance."[9]

This was not the view taken by William J. Donovan, a prominent Republican whose valour in World War I had earned him a Congressional Medal of Honour and the sobriquet "Wild Bill." Colonel Donovan, who had studied at Columbia Law School with Roosevelt, had declined the President's offer of the post of Secretary of War in June. That this dynamic and enthusiastic New York lawyer should make a fact-finding mission to England to dispel the gloomy defeatism of Ambassador Kennedy was the idea of William ('Intrepid') Stephenson, the MI6 representative in New York, who had sought him out. Donovan in turn enlisted the aid of his old friend Frank Knox, the Secretary of the Navy, who hawkishly believed that "the sooner we get into the war the sooner we shall get ready." He fixed a meeting at the White House with Donovan and Stephenson. The President enthusiastically agreed that Donovan would be his "unofficial representative." With a $10,000 letter of credit from the U.S. Treasury to cover his expenses, the Colonel left New York for Lisbon by Pan Am Clipper on 14 July, checking into Claridge's Hotel in London five days later.[10]

When Kennedy learned on 11 July from Secretary Knox that Donovan was coming over to "report on certain aspects of the British defense situation" he immediately saw it as criticism of his judgement and that of his military and naval attachés. The Ambassador cabled the State Department that Donovan's mission could only "result in creating confusion and misunderstanding on the part of the British." Kennedy would have protested even more strongly had he realized that Donovan's "fact-finding" mission had been instigated by the British Secret Service, and that it was the MI6 chief Sir Robert Menzies who had arranged a "red-carpet" treatment for Donovan and for Edgar Ansel Mower, the London correspondent of Knox's old paper the *Chicago Daily News*, who assisted the Colonel on his two-week fact-finding tour. As well as a meeting with the King and two long sessions with Churchill, the trip included visits to R.A.F. and naval bases and discussions with ministers and service chiefs. Donovan and Mower's conclusion was that although Britain's military situation was still shaky,

Churchill had inspired the nation with the will to resist. Donovan told the U.S. military attaché General Lee that he would go as far as saying that the odds were "2 to 1" that the British would beat off a German attack. This he also said to Rear Admiral John Godfroy, the Director of Naval Intelligence, who reported gleefully that Donovan was returning to Washington impressed by the "spiritual qualities of the British Race – those imponderables that make for victory which have evaded Joe Kennedy."[11]

When Donovan arrived back in Washington on 5 August to deliver his upbeat report to Roosevelt, he also passed on the Royal Navy's urgent need of old "four-pipe" destroyers. The basis on which the transfer might be arranged had been put forward by the Navy Secretary in an answer to the "almost tearful" pleas of the British Ambassador five days earlier. If Britain were to consider transferring her island bases in the Western Hemisphere in return for the fifty destroyers, Knox said a deal might be struck, because, he believed, Congressional approval would be forthcoming if it appeared that the United States would be getting the best of the deal.

Knox proposed the destroyers-for-bases deal at the 2 August meeting of Roosevelt's cabinet, and the President agreed. But as a further sop to congressional and public opinion he required that the British should make a public commitment that, if they were forced to surrender, the fleet would be sent to American or Empire ports. He also wanted to prevent the destroyers' becoming an election issue by arranging for advance agreement from the Republican presidential candidate, Wendell Wilkie. At his meeting with Donovan the President also admitted his concern that there would be a raucous partisan debate in Congress over the bill to transfer the destroyers, so Donovan had set a team of lawyers to work to find a legal alternative. Thumbing through the statutes, they discovered unrepealed emergency powers granted by Congress to President Andrew Jackson during the U.S. Navy's wars against the pirates of the Barbary coast of North Africa in the first decade of the nineteenth century. The Attorney General confirmed that this law would permit the President to transfer the destroyers by executive order, as the deal would enhance American security. But first the British had to agree to his terms.[12]

On 4 August the Foreign Office heard from Lord Lothian that the President had now asked for two British concessions that he characterized as "molasses", necessary to sweeten Congress into approval for a destroyer deal. The first required a "public assurance" that if things went badly the British fleet would not be handed over but would "continue to fight for the British Empire overseas." The second was that the British government would give air and naval facilities to the United States for "hemispheric defence" and that the "naval and air facilities in question would be made available to the United States as soon as we had obtained destroyers."[13]

When Churchill was told of the terms, he objected strongly. "Only a war alliance," he told the Foreign Secretary, "could justify any stipulations about the disposition of the fleet." He made it clear that he thought that Britain was getting the raw end of the deal by trading bases for "old destroyers." He did not want to give any guarantees about the fleet that would cause the United States to "relax in its efforts to help us." Lothian had meanwhile dispatched another request for a guarantee, only to be informed by the Foreign Secretary that the Prime Minister wanted the deal confined simply to the bases and would not go beyond his 4 June statement about the New World being "armed and guarded by the British Fleet." The Ambassador tried to put the best face on the embarrassing impasse by referring the President to Churchill's 4 June statement and by arguing that a public declaration about the fleet now would damage British morale.[14]

As the destroyer deal stalled, Churchill, in a tit-for-tat gesture, delayed the departure of Sir Henry Tizard's scientific mission "in view of the holding back of the American side." This attracted criticism from ministers, who pointed out the dangers of such brinkmanship when the American services delegation was about to arrive in London for the secret staff talks. It was only after Stephenson had reported on 8 August from New York that "Donovan believes you will have in a few days very favourable news" that the Prime Minister relented. "I am anxious they should start this mission as soon as possible and under the most favourable auspices," he minuted the same day, adding mischievously "The check of August 1 was only temporary."[15]

When the Prime Minister pulled out all the stops to put pressure on the President at this critical juncture, he played the political pawn that could threaten Roosevelt's re-election. It seems no coincidence that on 31 July, after more than two months' delay, the British finally informed the American Ambassador of their decision to prosecute Tyler Kent. When told of the decision at Brixton Prison by an official of the American Embassy, the former code clerk was "cold, self-possessed and completely non-committal." He was equally impassive when formally charged at Bow Street Police Station on 1 August on three counts under the Official Secrets Act. Kennedy's cabled report to Washington on the impending prosecution was a timely reminder to Roosevelt that the hostage to his political fortunes Churchill held would now be imprisoned rather than deported, which was a clear signal to Roosevelt at a critical moment in the bargaining over the destroyers that one political favour deserved another.[16]

At the same time Churchill knew he could not risk damaging the growing American confidence in his ability to lead Britain to survival. It was this concern that prompted him to react swiftly on 2 August when King Gustav of Sweden offered his services as a mediator. A simultaneous offer had been sent to Hitler, and the approach was to remain secret unless both parties accepted. Churchill minuted his resentment at the "intrusion of the ignominious King of Sweden as a peace-maker, after his desertion of Finland and Norway, and while he is absolutely in the German grip", injecting his own red-blooded lines into the anaemic diplomatic language of the rejection that the Foreign Office had drafted for King George to sign. "These horrible events have darkened the pages of European history with an indelible stain," he wrote. Accusing Hitler of "hideous crimes," he declared the British government's intention to "prosecute the war against Germany by every means until Hitlerism is finally broken." He added for good measure that "They would rather all perish in the common ruin than fail or falter in their duty." He reminded Halifax in his covering note that this was not the time "to enter into refinements of policy unsuited to the tragic simplicity and grandeur of the times and the issues at stake."[17]

"The Authentic Big Push"
11–27 August

The issues at stake were being decided, even as the Prime Minister wrote, by the R.A.F. pilots, who on 11 August brought down a record thirty-eight German planes over the Channel. But the R.A.F. lost thirty-one. On 12 August, in the planned precursor to next day's "Adlertag", the Luftwaffe turned its attention to trying to knock out the radar masts and stations which were giving the British early warning of incoming attacks. The British lost twenty-two planes for thirty-one German kills. By a superhuman effort the reserve radar stations were brought on line and the network was functioning in time to meet the new threat posed by the second round of the battle in the summer skies.

"Operation Eagle," Göring signalled to his air fleets on 13 August: "within a short period you will wipe the British Air Force from the sky." The weather refused to cooperate as the Luftwaffe meteorologists had predicted. Despite the confusion caused by heavy morning cloud, some fifteen hundred sorties to bomb the airfields of southern England were made that day. The R.A.F. downed forty-five enemy planes for a loss of thirteen, giving them the opening round. There was a relative lull the next day, when the Germans lost nineteen planes to the British eight. But 15 August saw one of the fiercest aerial battles of the war as Luftflotte 5 sent its planes from Norway to attack the north of England, while Göring's over-confident pilots hammered away from their bases in France, with their most powerful assault on the southern airfields. The R.A.F. shot down seventy-five enemy fighters and bombers for a loss of thirty-four. Churchill, who drove to Fighter Command Headquarters at Bentley Priory that afternoon to watch the underground operations room in action during the final stages of the day's operations, was assured by Air Marshal Dowding that the Germans had lost over a hundred planes; the press were given the figure of 144, against losses of twenty-seven for the R.A.F. Churchill would later pay tribute to Dowding for his prudence in keeping in reserve a fighter force in the north through all the weeks of action over the Channel.

"We must regard the generalship here shown as an example of genius in the art of war," he wrote. An article in that Thursday's *New York Times* – unfettered by British war censorship – dismissed the widely held belief that the aerial battles in the skies over England were the "prelude" to the invasion. "What we are now watching is the authentic big push," Major Alexander Seversky declared. "If Great Britain loses the present battle, she will in effect have lost the war, at least as far as the mother country is concerned."[18]

At the height of the Battle of Britain, on Adlertag itself, Roosevelt finally sent the word that Churchill had been waiting almost three months to receive. Two days earlier the behind-the-scenes legal parleying in the White House had resulted in a letter to the *New York Times* from Dean Acheson and three prominent lawyers. To forestall Congressional delays, it argued that the President had legal authority to transfer the destroyers to Britain. This prompted Roosevelt's 13 August cable, which announced: "it may be possible to furnish the British Government as immediate assistance at least 50 destroyers, the motor boats heretofore referred to, and insofar as airplanes are concerned, five planes of each of the categories mentioned, the latter to be furnished for war testing purposes." This assistance would be given "in return for the national defense and security of the United States" and on two conditions. Roosevelt wanted Churchill's private assurance that British warships would not be handed over to the Germans if the situation became untenable, in addition to ninety-nine-year leases on bases in Newfoundland, Bermuda, the Bahamas, Jamaica, St Lucia, Trinidad and British Guiana.[19]

Roosevelt proposed that the details about the bases should be settled by "friendly negotiation," and next day the Prime Minister urged the War Cabinet to put aside its doubts that the President was driving too hard a bargain. The terms were acceptable to him, he said, and he contended that the sale of the destroyers would be a decidedly un-neutral act which would have an "immense" impact on Germany. The United States would have made "a long step towards coming into the war on our side."[20]

"The worth of every destroyer is measured in rubies," the Prime Minister assured his dubious private secretary. It was a phrase he used again in his cable next day telling Roosevelt how "cheered" he was and grateful for "your untiring efforts to give us all possible help." The "moral value of this fresh aid" coming at this "critical time will be very great and widely felt." But Churchill made it clear that he was not easing up on his demands for "as many flying boats and rifles as you can let us have."[21]

"The spirit of our people is splendid. Never have they been so determined," Churchill assured the President. "Their confidence in the issue has been enormously and legitimately strengthened by the severe air fighting of the past week." The R.A.F. were keeping above the two-to-one kill rates with a 45:21 score on 16 August. The next day there was an unexplained lull in the battle, with only three Germans shot down and no British losses. The respite enabled pilots to get some rest while maintenance crews laboured to keep their Hurricanes and Spitfires airworthy and ground staff filled craters on runways and defused unexploded bombs. Next day seventy-one Germans were downed for twenty-seven losses before bad weather over England forced another temporary lull. During the next six days, the total score was thirty-two to eleven in the R.A.F.'s favour.

"Entirely satisfactory", was Roosevelt's response on 16 August to Churchill's cable. Even Morgenthau found the President "much more decisive" and resolved that he would announce the bases deal with the British at his press conference that very afternoon. Next day the public opinion polls revealed that he had the backing of 62 per cent of Americans for the sale of the destroyers to Britain, and his presidential rival Wilkie came out in favour, although not as unreservedly as the President had hoped. Roosevelt was full of optimism that morning as he and the Secretary of War set off by train for Ogdensburg on the banks of the St. Lawrence River. Officially they were going to upstate New York to observe large-scale army manoeuvres; unofficially the purpose of the trip was a secret meeting with the Canadian Prime Minister to agree on the terms of a mutual defence pact. Roosevelt told Mackenzie King that he had decided to sell the fifty destroyers to the British because the "public will accept it, given the fact that the United States is getting the naval bases it desires," and because Churchill "had at last given a sufficient pledge that he would under no circumstances surrender the British Fleet to the Germans."[22]

Yet even as Roosevelt was assuring the Canadian Prime Minister that his lawyers were working on ways to consummate the deal without the necessity of going through Congress, the Chief of the U.S. Navy was raising bureaucratic objections back in Washington. Admiral Stark, who was still doubtful that Britain could make it, with or without the destroyers, had baulked when he had been asked to prepare for the transfer of the destroyers by declaring them, as required by law, "obsolete and useless." He believed it would be unethical for him to declare the destroyers as surplus to requirements when he was asking Congress for a huge increase in emergency funds for naval construction. Stark's 17 August memorandum to the Secretary of the Navy announced that he could favour only a "clear-cut trade" for the "transfer of sovereignty" of the British bases, not ninety-nine-year leases on them. Stark also thought it politically expedient for the administration to obtain Congressional approval for the deal. As the Navy Department and the White House laboured over these bureaucratic hitches, Britain's immediate survival turned not on the old American destroyers but on the dwindling number of young fighter pilots and their Hurricanes and Spitfires.[23]

"Never in the field of human conflict was so much owed by so many to so few" was the indelible tribute Churchill paid to the courage of the R.A.F. pilots in the House of Commons on 20 August. Nearly six hundred had died since July, and the Prime Minister expressed the nation's gratitude "to the British airmen who, undaunted by odds, unwearied in their constant challenge and mortal danger, are turning the tide of war by their constant prowess and by their devotion." Britain, he declared, now "bristles against invaders, from the sea or from the air." Towards the end of a speech that had been unusual for its lack of oratory, Churchill alluded to the destroyer deal by expressing the hope that "our friends across the ocean will send us timely reinforcement to bridge the gap between the peace flotillas of 1939 and the war flotillas of 1941." He was careful to separate them from the decision which, he said, had been taken "some time ago . . . spontaneously and without being asked or offered any inducement", to lease naval and air bases in the West Indies to the United States.[24]

"This process means," Churchill prophesied, "that the two great organizations of the English-speaking democracies, the British Empire and the United States, will have to be somewhat mixed up together in some of their affairs for mutual and general advantage." He declared that he had no misgivings on this. "I could not stop it if I wished; no one can stop it." Churchill concluded, saluting the American aid which "Like the Mississippi . . . just keeps rolling along. Let it roll. Let it roll on full flood, inexorable, irresistible, benignant, to broader lands and better days."

Skating over the technicalities with rhetoric, the Prime Minister's speech only confused the delicate negotiations in Washington, where the legality of the transaction would unravel if Churchill insisted on decoupling the offer of bases and opening the way for awkward questions in Congress as to why the destroyers were being handed over.[25]

The President reacted by writing a personal letter to the Chairman of the Senate Naval Affairs Committee on 22 August comparing the destroyers-for-bases deal to the Louisiana Purchase. He painted the deal as a great bargain for the United States, which would acquire rights to bases whose value was far in excess of the quarter-of-a-million-dollar scrap value of fifty destroyers "which were on their last legs." The same day Roosevelt received Churchill's cable denying that he had "contemplated anything in the nature of a contract, bargain or sale between us." He foresaw "difficulties and even risks in the exchange of letters now suggested or in admitting in any way that the munitions which you send us are a payment for the facilities." This would set a precedent for computing the "money value of the armaments" given and received, and Churchill wanted to "trust entirely in your judgements and sentiments of the people of the United States about aid in munitions etc. you feel able to send us."[26]

What Churchill was determined to avoid was a specific *quid pro quo* arrangement, not just to avoid British criticism that he was selling the real-estate of the British Empire short, but because he hoped to use the destroyers to establish a precedent for the United States supplying war material to Britain without specific accounting of the cost. His insistence reflected the discussions of the War Cabinet on 22 August, when the Chancellor, Sir Kingsley Wood, had presented his report "Gold and Exchange Resources." This sober document made it plain that the reserves were running out faster than expected. The time was coming when Britain would be unable to pay for all the material and supplies being ordered in the United States.

The United States Treasury had been unrelenting in its insistence that the British orders were paid for, on the nail, in dollars, on a strict cash-and-carry basis. The bottom line, according to the Treasury calculations, was that even if the British liquidated *all* their gold and dollar assets – which they reckoned at $2,252 million (£563 million) in July 1940 – they had financial reserves for sustaining the war against Germany for little more than twelve months. In fact, as the War Cabinet learned on 22 August, the financial position was bleaker than the U.S. treasury estimates. Total gold and dollar reserves (including U.S. securities) had fallen from a total of £775 million ($3,100 million) at the beginning of 1940 to £156 million ($624 million) six months later. With the additional war supplies taken over from the French eating up the reserves at the rate of £80 million ($320 million) a month (four times the rate estimated by the U.S. Treasury) the Chancellor warned that Britain would run out of the money necessary to carry on the war by the end of the year.[27]

Chamberlain, who was convalescing from an unsuccessful cancer operation, provided the written advice that "It would be necessary for us to gamble to some extent on the willingness of the United States to give us financial help on an extended scale." The Chancellor then suggested that the government should requisition all gold wedding rings, coins and ornaments. But this measure would be only a drop in the bucket, and Churchill wanted it held over for use only "if we wished to make some striking gesture for the purpose of shaming the Americans." Lord Beaverbrook, the Minister for Aircraft Production, now elevated to the War Cabinet, proposed that the solution was to accelerate orders in the United States and thus make American industry so dependent that the U.S. government would have to step in to save Britain both militarily and financially. This was the policy the British government adopted in effect by ordering a thousand of the latest M3 "General Stuart" light tanks. The question of how Britain was going to meet the skyrocketing dollar bill for her war supplies was postponed. A solution was not forthcoming until Roosevelt came up with his ingenious scheme to "eliminate the dollar." This was to be enshrined in the Lend-Lease Bill passed by Congress on 11 March 1941, giving the President authority to "sell, transfer title to, exchange, lease or otherwise dispose of" defence articles to the government of any country. The consideration would be "payment or repayment in kind or property, or any other direct or indirect benefit" which the President deemed satisfactory. Churchill would hail the Lend-Lease Bill in Parliament as "the most unsordid act in the history of any nation."[28]

In the final week of August 1940, the Prime Minister's feelings about the United States were far less generous as the wrangle over the precise terms of the destroyer deal dragged on. "About five telegrams from Lothian to say Americans don't like P.M.'s procedure and must stick to the exchange of letters idea," Cadogan noted on 25 August, adding that Churchill "won't have an exchange of letters" and "doesn't mind if we don't get destroyers." The Prime Minister still objected to a formal exchange because it would give the Americans "a blank cheque on the whole of our trans-Atlantic possessions."[29]

"Could you not say that you did not feel able to accept this fine offer which we make unless the United States matched it in some way?" Churchill asked the President on 25 August. He evidently did not want to risk letting the Germans know that the destroyer deal was in danger of falling apart, because this cable was sent not via the U.S. Embassy but by the secure Foreign Office cipher to Washington.[30]

Churchill did not want to give any comfort to Berlin as the Battle of Britain moved into its most critical phase. The spell of cloudy weather that had curtailed air operations for two days lifted on 24 August, allowing the Luftwaffe to resume full-strength operations against R.A.F. airfields and send its bomber fleets by night to raid Birmingham's aircraft factories. The R.A.F. that day lost twenty-two planes for a score of thirty-eight, but more than half the German planes were bombers. When the German air assault resumed in all its ferocity during two days of clear skies, the R.A.F. kill rate of 61:49 fell below the critical two-to-one ratio for the first time. Fighter Command was under increasing strain as it faced up to the most critical days of the battle. Air intelligence had correctly predicted that the German decision to invade depended on the R.A.F.'s ability to defend the airfields and aircraft factories. On Hitler's express orders, London had so far been spared the raids inflicted on other British cities, but after a navigational error on 24 August the first German bombs had fallen on central London since the Zeppelin raids of 1918. "The War Cabinet," Churchill wrote, "were much in the mood to hit back, to raise the stakes, and to defy the enemy." Accordingly, the following night eighty R.A.F. bombers were sent to raid military targets on the outskirts of Berlin. On 27 August the Luftwaffe made a retaliatory night-time strike on London.[31]

The accelerating pace of the German air attack added to the fractious discussions in the War Cabinet over the terms of the destroyers-for-bases deal.

"I suppose we shall end up by getting the arrangements through, but it takes a long time," Lord Halifax complained after more fruitless exchanges with Washington on 26 August. "The American attitude simply infuriates me," Chamberlain wrote to Churchill, "but we can't win as we would wish without their help and I think your handling is admirable." The solution to the impasse was offered by Lord Lothian, who on 27 August relayed a State Department formula designed to satisfy Churchill's insistence on the gift and Roosevelt's need to have a specific trade in order to sign off legally on the destroyers. The British offer of bases: the leases for Newfoundland and Bermuda were to be considered a "gift," while those for the six West Indian bases would be a trade-off for the destroyers, motor boats and aircraft.[32]

Churchill cabled his acceptance in principle of the State Department formula the same day. "Even the next forty-eight hours are important," he told the President, but it was four days before the Prime Minister was persuaded to give Roosevelt the cabled guarantee that his 4 June statement on the fate of Britain's fleet "represents the settled policy of the British Government."[33]

DAY 10
"Memorable Transactions"
4 September

The deal was all but clinched on 31 August. That Saturday saw the heaviest fighting – and the worst single day's British losses – in the air war. Thirty-nine R.A.F. fighters were shot down in battles that cost the Luftwaffe thirty-one planes. The scales had tipped in the Germans' favour for the first time. During the remaining five days of bureaucratic haggling over the fine print of the destroyer deal, the Germans redoubled their daytime assaults against the airfields and their night-time raids against the aircraft factories of Merseyside and the Midlands.

Extensive damage was inflicted on four of the R.A.F.'s vital forward stations in southern England and six of its seven sector stations. According to the official R.A.F. history, the week of 28 August to 5 September marked the most desperate days of the entire Battle of Britain. In the official record it is referred to as the "critical period when the damage to sector stations and our ground organization was having such a serious effect on the fighting efficiency of the squadrons, who could not be given the same good technical and administrative service as previously." During that week the R.A.F. lost 193 planes to Germany's 237. The reserves of Hurricanes and Spitfires enabled the front-line strength of Fighter Command to be maintained, but its fighting efficiency was falling as attrition took its toll of combat veterans; casualty rates soared over 200, a total that exceeded the monthly output of trained but battle-innocent fighter pilots.[34]

Göring and his commanders, who had underestimated British aircraft production, concluded by the beginning of September that R.A.F. Fighter Command was approaching its final gasp. Adlerangriff might not have achieved air superiority in the two weeks promised, but the belief that the Luftwaffe was on the brink of victory led Führer Headquarters on 3 September to postpone Operation Sea Lion by six days, from 15 to 21 September. It was Göring himself who now decided on a major change of strategy. He concluded that the quickest way to finish off the R.A.F. fighters was to switch the Luftflotten to making massive raids on London. He reasoned that by concentrating his bombers against the British capital he would force the R.A.F. to commit the final remnants of its fighter strength to defending the heart of the Empire.

The R.A.F. raids on Berlin the week before had also stunned the Germans and enraged Hitler. His patience with Britain had finally snapped. Now he was willing to go along with Göring's new strategy of shifting the air war from military targets to the civilian population. This switch saved the hard-pressed R.A.F. from the defeat that would certainly have been its fate if the Luftwaffe had pressed on with its campaign of attrition against the British airfields and fighter squadrons. Neither the Führer nor Göring appreciated just how close to victory they were when they agreed on the decision that would change the course of the war.

"The British will know that we are now giving our answer night after night. Since they attack our cities, we shall extirpate theirs," the Führer told a wildly cheering rally of nurses and volunteer "Winter Help" workers at the Berlin Sportspalast on 4 September. His speech signalled the turning-point in the Battle of Britain, and next day, 4 September 1940, a directive from Führer Headquarters ordered the Luftwaffe to begin "harassing attacks by day and night on the inhabitants and air defences of large British cities." On the same day the announcement in Washington of the Anglo-American destroyers-for-bases deal marked another shift in the tide of war, because it increased Britain's prospects of survival and set the foundation for the alliance that would bring about Hitler's defeat.

ROOSEVELT TRADES DESTROYERS FOR SEA BASES; TELLS CONGRESS HE ACTED ON HIS OWN AUTHORITY; BRITAIN PLEDGES NEVER TO YIELD OR SINK FLEET: the six-column headline in Wednesday's *New York Times* broke the news of the President's 4 September message to Congress. Roosevelt had portrayed the destroyer deal to the legislators as "the most important action in the reinforcement of our national defense that has been taken since the Louisiana Purchase." His political strategy was vindicated. There were no legalistic objections to his exercise of executive powers, and by keeping the issue away from Congress he avoided the row on Capitol Hill that he had feared might damage his re-election campaign. The reverse proved to be the case: the transaction was greeted with universal enthusiasm by Americans, who believed that their national defence had been strengthened.

When the House of Commons assembled during an air-raid alert on the afternoon of Thursday, 5 September, the Prime Minister, with deliberate understatement, announced the conclusion of "memorable transactions between Great Britain and the United States . . . Only very ignorant persons would suggest that the transfer of American destroyers to the British flag constitutes the slightest violation of international law," he said delphically, adding that he had no doubt that "Herr Hitler will not like this transference of destroyers."[35]

Within hours of the President's formal announcement, the first flotilla of destroyers were sailed to Halifax, Nova Scotia, where British crews were ready on 6 September to effect the transfer of command. World War I four-pipe flush-deckers that Churchill had described as "measured in rubies" turned out to be wallowing rust-buckets that required four months of refitting in British shipyards before they were accepted as fit for service by the Royal Navy. But they more than made up for the numerical losses suffered during Dunkirk and provided a badly needed augmentation of the Atlantic convoy escorts during the winter battles against the U-boats. Even more important than their material value was their symbolic worth; the fifty destroyers provided a powerful reinforcement for Britain at a critical psychological juncture of the war.

"It would be impossible to overstate the jubilation in official and unofficial circles caused today by Roosevelt's announcement that fifty United States destroyers were coming to Britain in her hour of peril," the London correspondent of the *New York Times* reported. "It is very interesting," observed Secretary of War Stimson, "to see how the tide of opinion has swung in favor of the eventual victory of Great Britain. The air of pessimism which prevailed two months ago has gone."[36]

The peril of invasion was still a very real threat to Britain. On 7 September the bomber fleets assembled in formation over the Channel watched by Göring picnicking with his staff on the cliff-edge above Cap Gris Nez. This was the first day of the Luftwaffe's all out air assault on London. That Saturday evening the General Headquarters of the Home Forces issued the code word "Cromwell" – the invasion alert. It was another false alarm, but there was nothing deceptive about the savagery of the day and night air bombardment. A thousand enemy aircraft swarmed over the capital, dropping over 300 tons of high explosive and 13,000 incendiaries. London's dockland was set ablaze and 1,500 civilians were left dead and injured in the rubble of demolished homes.

It was the first night of what the British phlegmatically came to call "the Blitz." For the next week swarms of German bombers droned over the Channel to attack the ports of Southampton, Portsmouth, Merseyside and to hit London again. The R.A.F. still kept coming up to intercept. The Luftwaffe aircrews knew that Göring's promise to wipe the R.A.F. from the sky was proving to be an empty boast.

"Enemy fighter forces have not yet been completely eliminated," the Führer had told his military chiefs on 14 September, when he postponed taking the invasion decision for three days. "The prerequisites to Operation Sea Lion have not yet been completely realized," he admitted, blaming the weather and unreliable estimates of R.A.F. strength. He was not yet ready to call off the invasion. He would only postpone the decision, setting the new provisional dates of 27 September or 8 October. The next day the R.A.F. rose phoenix-like to win an undisputed victory by breaking up the largest raid yet mounted over London. Sixty German planes were shot down for twenty-six British losses. This was the highest score of the two-month-long campaign and marked the victorious climax of the Battle of Britain.[37]

"We may await the decision of this long air battle with sober but increasing confidence," Churchill announced to the House of Commons on 17 September. He was already guardedly optimistic about the eventual outcome of "one of the most decisive battles of the world." On the same day Hitler, while not yet prepared to concede defeat, postponed the invasion indefinitely on the grounds that Göring had failed to deliver the "prerequisite" of air superiority. To save face he insisted that preparations were to continue, then the very next day he bowed to pressure from the naval staff to begin the process of dispersing the invasion barges in the Channel ports, where they had become prime targets for the R.A.F. raids.[38]

The final decision over Operation Sea Lion dragged out for three more weeks, making it "unbearable" for the military staff. Finally, on 12 October, the Führer admitted failure by issuing the directive calling off any invasion operation until the following spring. He insisted, however, that "preparations for 'Sea Lion' shall be continued solely for the purpose of maintaining political and military pressure on England."[39]

Political pressure of a very different sort was being contemplated by the American Ambassador in London that October as the U.S. presidential election went into top gear. If Kennedy had made good his intention to intervene to try to prevent Roosevelt's return to the White House, he might have succeeded where Hitler failed, by forcing the British government to sue for peace. If Churchill had been deprived of the increasing flow of United States military supplies and Lend-Lease aid engineered by Roosevelt, within six months Britain would have run out of resources to continue her lone struggle against Nazi Germany.

"A Defeatist and a Crook"

The American Ambassador in London had grown increasingly resentful of Roosevelt's continuing to back Britain in the belief that Germany could be defeated if America shipped across the Atlantic enough military supplies. To the exiled financier it appeared to be as poor an investment as stuffing greenbacks down a rat hole. Britain, as Kennedy had repeatedly warned Washington, did not have the gold reserves to pay for that help and the United States would be sucked into the war if Roosevelt continued to back her hopeless fight against Germany. Kennedy had been furious when his advice was ignored and Roosevelt announced he was trading British bases for the destroyers that Churchill had been pleading for since May. He fired off a bitter complaint that he had been made a "dummy" because he had been bypassed in the negotiations.

In a personal letter insisting "there was no thought of embarrassing you" Roosevelt tried to soothe Kennedy's ruffled feathers by assuring the Ambassador "you are not only not a dummy but are essential to all of us in both Government and the Nation." Kennedy remained unassuaged and convinced that by the destroyer deal Roosevelt was dragging the United States one step closer to a war he was determined his country would not enter. Six weeks later he had had enough, and resorted to what can only be construed as political blackmail to effect his return to the United States with the expectation that he could trump the President by going over to the Republicans in a last-ditch bid to prevent Roosevelt's re-election.[40]

Kennedy's ace card was the bundle of the President's cables copied by Kent, which gave credence to the claim that Roosevelt was a warmonger. This was behind the threat Kennedy made on 10 October 1940 after cabling the President to demand to be recalled. He tipped his hand in a telephone call to Sumner Welles to tell him "he had written a full account of the facts to Edward Moore, his secretary in New York, with instructions to release the story to the press if the Ambassador were not back in New York by a certain date." A few hours later Welles relayed the message from the White House that the President "desires you to return to Washington for consultation sometime during the week commencing October twenty-one." Kennedy had already taken care to inform Halifax that he was intending to leave by 1 November, in the final week of the presidential election.[41]

"When I asked him what would be the main burden of his song," Halifax reported to Lord Lothian on 10 October, "he gave me to understand that it would be an indictment of President Roosevelt's administration for having talked a lot and done very little." After winning his hardball game with the State Department the Ambassador cabled his grudging thanks to Welles, adding he was "pretty sick and sore at a lot of things" – so sore that Kennedy evidently intended to go much farther than just making public his criticism of Roosevelt. For weeks he had been letting every American journalist in London know that he was fed up with the Roosevelt administration, hinting that he was considering returning to throw his support to the Republican challenger Wendell Wilkie. At a secret meeting with Claire Luce in London, Kennedy had arranged to give an exclusive interview on his return to New York to her husband's *Time* magazine, which backed the Republicans.[42]

Speculation was spreading in the American press that Kennedy's declared intention of arriving five days before the presidential vote was calculated to give the maximum impact to his declaration for Wendell Wilkie. The rumours reaching Washington about Kennedy's intended bid to sabotage Roosevelt's election caused anxiety at the White House. The October opinion polls had confirmed that Wilkie's "warmonger" charges against the President were cutting down his comfortable lead. Alarmed Democratic Party managers had finally succeeded in persuading the incumbent to abandon his stay-at-his-desk strategy, take to the campaign trail and make stump speeches during the final weeks of the campaign.

Churchill shared the Foreign Office nervousness that a hostile speech by Kennedy might tip the campaign to the Republicans and cost Britain her new-found champion in the White House. So it appears no coincidence that the *in-camera* trial of Kent and Wolkoff began on 23 October, the day after Kennedy left England for Lisbon and the Pan Am Clipper to New York. The Ambassador was therefore not available when Kent, who was challenging the legality of his arrest on the grounds that his diplomatic immunity had been violated, tried to have him called as a witness. Instead the Embassy's Second Secretary Franklin Gowen testified that the Ambassador had indeed made his request for State Department authority to remove Kent's diplomatic privileges and dismiss him from the Foreign Service "*on 19 May.*" He then went on to assure the court that it was "on 20th May *in the morning*" that the Department's reply was received stripping the code clerk of his diplomatic immunity. This was tantamount to perjury, because the originals of the cables reveal that this convenient fiction advanced the removal of Kent's immunity by nearly twenty-four hours, enabling the British judge to dismiss Kent's claim that his arrest was illegal and to order his trial under the Official Secrets Act to proceed.[43]

On Sunday, 28 October, the day before the British jury found Kent guilty, Kennedy stepped off the Boeing flying boat on to the dock of the Pan Am Marine Terminal in New York. He was immediately given a handwritten invitation to the White House for dinner that evening. There was another message from Senator James F. Byrnes, a Roosevelt confidant, reiterating the urgent communication from the President that Kennedy had been given at Lisbon. This "Dear Joe" letter urged that "no matter how proper and appropriate your statements might be, every effort will be made to misinterpret and distort what you say." In brusquely polite language that had been drafted for Roosevelt by Welles, it instructed Kennedy "specifically not to make any statements to the press on your way over or when you arrive in New York until you and I have had a chance to agree upon what should be said." The Ambassador was asked to come "straight through to Washington on your arrival since I will want to talk with you as soon as you get here."[44]

The long transatlantic flight and an enforced weather stopover in Bermuda had left Kennedy drained. He looked drawn and tense as he walked up the gangplank clutching a British air-raid siren as a souvenir. The flash bulbs popped as he was greeted by his wife and family, but the barrage of clamouring reporters failed to get the statement they had been waiting for. Nor did *Time* get its sensational cover-story interview, because Kennedy could not get himself off the hook after a telephone call to the President. Roosevelt told him there was a plane standing by to take him and his wife down to the White House for a "family dinner." The young Texas congressman Lyndon B. Johnson happened to be lunching in the White House with the President and House Speaker Samuel Rayburn when the call from Kennedy came through. Years later, he liked to recall that Roosevelt gave a theatrical throat-cut gesture and a hard grin as he put the receiver down on Kennedy.[45]

Just how Roosevelt succeeded in cutting Kennedy off from throwing his support to Wilkie is still a matter of debate. The only witnesses to Roosevelt's masterful performance over dinner were Senator and Mrs Byrnes and Rose Kennedy. They all maintained a tight-lipped discretion at the time. From what can be pieced together from those parts of the story they confided to friends, Roosevelt played the role of conciliator and friend to the point of unctuousness. He listened sympathetically to Kennedy's complaints about being ignored in London, then blamed it on the State Department officials, who he promised solicitously would be dealt with in a "real housecleaning." Rose Kennedy repeatedly reminded her husband of the debt of loyalty he owed Roosevelt. "The President sent you, a Roman Catholic, as Ambassador to London," she told him, "which probably no other President would have done." Byrnes flattered Kennedy by saying how helpful it would be for the Democratic campaign if the Ambassador would make a speech on Roosevelt's behalf the following night, announcing that air time on the radio networks had already been booked. The outcome was Kennedy's weary agreement to broadcast in support of Roosevelt's re-election, on condition that "I will pay for it myself, show it to nobody in advance, and say what I wish."[46]

This is a rather unconvincing scenario in the circumstances. Given the blackmail threat which Kennedy had employed to effect his return, it cannot tell the whole story of how Roosevelt twisted the Ambassador's arm to keep him from reneging. From Kennedy's sullen agreement to toe the party line it may be inferred that stronger appeals than loyalty were required to reverse the declared intentions of a resentful and determined former ally to desert the Roosevelt camp. It would have been in keeping with Roosevelt's subtly devious character to resort to a range of ploys to nail down his reluctant supporter. One was likely to have been the dangling of the bait of the 1944 Democratic nomination before Kennedy, at the same time hinting that if he became a Judas and deserted his party, it would not only wreck his own political chances, but those of his sons as well. Randolph Churchill, who was in a position to know, said that his father arranged for a "sheaf of tapped conversations of Kennedy's in which he expressed critical opinions of Roosevelt" to be passed to the White House.[47]

Now that there is documented evidence implicating Ambassador Kennedy in the billion-dollar Nazi gold loan and the trail of suspicion leading to his office from the information in the "Doctor" file, besides the evidence he was illegally playing the markets, Randolph Churchill's claim assumes a new significance. If the British had indeed passed on incriminating information obtained by MI5 on Kennedy, Roosevelt would certainly have been canny enough not to use it as a bludgeon. The President was adept at political scalpel strokes and would have planted hints to let Kennedy know he "had the goods" to destroy him if he jumped ship. With his sharp nose for a conspiracy, Kennedy would not have needed too many hints to realize that Roosevelt had been fed some of the riper sections of MI5's "Kennedy, Joseph P." dossier. Evidence that such a file still exists, and that it was voluminous after more than a year of phone-tapping and surveillance, can be found in the thick "Kennediana" Foreign Office file. Even the declassified sections – some parts are still closed – contain copies of Kennedy's private telegrams that were intercepted by the censor and sent to the Foreign Office for comment.[48]

Kennedy was an agile opponent who knew how to fight with the gloves off. Roosevelt also knew that, with his election campaign at stake, he could not afford to pull any punches. Whether the specific threat that brought Kennedy into line was the result of his fear of being branded an ingrate, a Judas, or a crook has to remain a matter of conjecture. The British will not declassify their secret intelligence archive and the F.B.I. file on Joseph P. Kennedy is suspiciously squeaky-clean for someone who had long been suspected of dealing in illegal liquor franchises. What is now a matter of historical record are the MI5 reports on the Kent case and "the Doctor." Evidence in both these files indicates the resources that MI5 put into keeping watch on the U.S. Embassy and its defeatist Ambassador as he held unauthorized secret talks with the Nazis.[49]

The British, thanks to Kent, would have been able to read the U.S. Embassy's most secret cipher telegrams – if their codebreakers were not doing so already. They would therefore have known the extent to which the American Ambassador had assiduously tried to suborn the President into believing that Britain was heading for defeat and had to be encouraged to make peace with Germany. It is a measure of Kennedy's brazenness that he could have announced after his return to Washington: "This is nonsense. I never made anti-British statements or said – on or off the record – that I do not expect Britain to win the war."[50]

Prejudiced though members of Churchill's government may have been, they knew better and had good reason for relief when the American Ambassador departed. On the record that has now come to light, Hugh Dalton, the Minister of Economic Warfare, appears to have been closer to the truth about Kennedy when he wrote: "I always regarded him as a defeatist and a crook."[51]

"Defeatist and Treasonable"

The American Ambassador's was not the only diplomatic effort to try to drive Britain out of the war in the autumn of 1940. As part of the "political pressure" that Hitler promised to sustain after the Battle of Britain was lost, the Foreign Office files detail another campaign of peace feelers put out from Berlin. The first had broken surface in London on 20 August, when Albert Plesman, the Dutch founder and director of K.L.M. airlines, after a three-hour meeting with Göring, drew up a peace proposal calling for a simultaneous appeal by Britain and Germany to Roosevelt to act as a mediator. Plesman's memorandum reached London via the British Legation in Stockholm and the Netherlands Foreign Minister in London. At the same time the British Ambassador in Turkey received through the Netherlands Minister in Ankara a peace feeler from Franz von Papen, the German Ambassador in Turkey. Reportedly Hitler, in a recent conversation with von Papen, had indicated that he was now prepared to restore a demilitarized independence to Belgium, the Netherlands and Poland so as to bring peace by October.[52]

Since Churchill by now had established his authority over the War Cabinet, not even Lord Halifax could risk hinting that the Foreign Office should respond to these peace soundings. Outside the government, however, there were still those who would have welcomed the chance to open up a dialogue. On 28 August Lloyd George had summoned Liddell Hart to his house near Criccieth in Wales, and during the final weeks of the Battle of Britain they had together drafted a memorandum advocating that peace negotiations should be undertaken now that Britain had won a temporary reprieve in the air battle. In contrast to the time of Dunkirk, Lloyd George believed it was time to talk terms with Hitler because Britain risked the possibility of defeat by the U-boats if she continued with the war. Lloyd George sent the Liddell Hart memorandum to Beaverbrook, who was non-committal. On 26 November, Lloyd George asked Liddell Hart for another copy, which he wanted to send to Roosevelt via his former secretary, Lord Lothian, in Washington. Early in 1941 a copy of the memorandum found its way into the hands of A.V. Alexander, the First Lord of the Admiralty, who passed it to Churchill. The Prime Minister called it "defeatist and treasonable" but did not take any further action because he considered its arguments were out of date.[53]

Churchill and the War Cabinet were evidently unaware of the peace plot being hatched by Lloyd George when on 5 September the Foreign Office received the clearest signal yet of Hitler's willingness to negotiate. What distinguished this message was that it was relayed through the impeccable authority of the President of the Swedish High Court of Appeal, Dr. Eckberg, who had called on the British Ambassador to tell him that a Berlin lawyer named Dr. Weissauer was in Stockholm waiting to arrange a meeting to present a comprehensive peace proposal to Britain. As Mallet reported to London, Weissauer was "understood to be a direct emissary of Hitler," to whom he reported directly. When Mallet did as instructed and made it plain to Dr. Eckberg that no useful purpose could come from the meeting, the Swedish Court President begged him to see Hitler's emissary, returning with copious notes which were claimed to be the actual words of Hitler and Ribbentrop. According to Weissauer the Führer's peace terms would permit Britain to retain her Empire "with all its colonies and mandates" provided Germany's continental supremacy was acknowledged. Hitler would in return recognize a Polish state, but Czechoslovakia had to remain a part of the Reich. The Foreign Office was extremely sceptical towards what appears to have been the first direct and specific peace feeler received from Hitler.[54]

"It looks as though all these so-called 'independent' moves, including that of M. Plesman, have been coordinated in Berlin," Frank Roberts of the Foreign Office minuted, adding "I see no reason to depart from the uncompromising attitude laid down in our reply to King Gustav." After Mallet's letter was passed to the King and members of the War Cabinet, Roberts's view prevailed; Cadogan instructed that "Mallet must not see Dr. Weissauer."

Hitler's most direct attempt to offer the British terms was cut off. But he continued to believe that he could succeed if only he could get his message through to the right group of people, those who were influential enough to bypass or overthrow Churchill. As Hitler began to focus his strategy for attacking Russia, the desirability of peace with Britain was discussed with his deputy. Hess was no less convinced than the Führer of the necessity of first making peace with England and had begun in August to take soundings of his confidential advisers with British contacts on how best to reach influential British personages who were hostile to Churchill and sympathetic to peace. Although they did not know it at the time, the British Ambassador in Washington was already sponsoring a peace move that was one of the most bizarre of the war. The mastermind was his friend, the former Cambridge boxing blue Sir William Wiseman, an unsuccessful playwright who had headed British secret service operations in New York during World War I before launching himself as a successful Wall Street financier.[55]

"Dangerous and Untrustworthy"

In 1939 Wiseman, hoping to get his old intelligence post back, offered his services as a propagandist to the British government. Shortly after Churchill became Prime Minister in May 1940, Lord Lothian wrote asking him to see Wiseman, who was then in London. Rather surprisingly, considering he had once been posted to New York as MI6 station chief, the Foreign Office considered Sir William "rather dangerous and untrustworthy – the sort of person who always goes beyond his terms of reference." Whether he ever saw the Prime Minister is unclear, but on 6 June he had lunch with Lord Halifax to discuss his British publicity work for Lord Lothian. It is clear from James D. Mooney's records that Wiseman was being used by the British Ambassador in Washington in a rather different capacity. Over lunch in the private dining room of the Wall Street bank of Kuhn, Loeb early in September, Wiseman offered to help Mooney in "finding some method of starting a negotiated peace move that would be effective." He explained that since Germany was the "irresistible force" and England the "immovable body," the war "was a draw." Wiseman contended that "the first utterances of peace must come from the German side", and they decided to cooperate in launching a simultaneous initiative to Britain and Berlin with the aid of the Vatican.[56]

Mooney then arranged a lunch with Cardinal Spellman at the Archbishop of New York's residence on 5 September, when their peace plot began rolling. On 21 September they had another meeting, at which Wiseman proposed that Mooney should go and talk over the scheme with his "friends" in Britain who also desired peace. At a meeting with Alfred P. Sloan the following week, the Chairman of General Motors agreed to cooperate when Mooney set down a set of terms he thought the Germans would find acceptable because they were based on the proposal he had personally received from Hitler that spring. On 10 October Wiseman met Mooney to tell him that now was not a "propitious time for negotiations in London." Mooney's records show that he gained the impression from Wiseman that it was Lord Lothian who wanted the brakes put on their scheme – a suspicion that was reinforced when he found out that the British Ambassador had left unexpectedly for London six days later.[57]

What Wiseman did not tell Mooney was that he had embarked on a freelance undercover mission. This time it was at the behest of Sir William Stephenson, the millionaire Canadian businessman, whom Churchill had in May 1940 appointed as Passport Control Officer in New York, the cover for the MI6 post that Wiseman had held in World War I. Stephenson operated on a much grander scale; his career as wartime head of the "British Security Coordination" intelligence network led to his postwar fame as "A Man Called Intrepid." What is not clear from Wiseman's records is the purpose of the undercover mission on which he set off for the West Coast in October 1940. Its immediate object appears to have been to make contact with the German Consul General in San Francisco, Captain Fritz Wiedemann, who had been Hitler's former adjutant until they fell out in 1939, when he was posted to San Francisco. Wiedemann had sent word through an intermediary that he was willing to act as informant for the British Government.[58]

The intermediary was Princess Stephanie von Hohenlohe-Waldenburg, the ambitious daughter of a Viennese dentist whose title came from her first marriage to a distant Hungarian relation of Prince Max von Hohenlohe. The Princess was a clever adventuress who had been a member of the entourage around Hitler shortly after he came to power. The Führer had flirted with her and expressed his admiration by presenting her with the Salzburg castle of Leopoldskron, which the Nazis had confiscated from the Jewish theatre director Max Reinhardt. She had then been taken up by Lord Rothermere when the English newspaper magnate, an unashamed admirer of the Führer, had visited at the Berghof. Through Rothermere's circle of English aristocratic appeasers, the Princess in 1938 had assisted Captain Wiedemann on his mission to explain Hitler's claims to Czechoslovakia. After her falling out with Rothermere led to a scandalous lawsuit and accusations that she was Hitler's spy, Princess Stephanie left England for the United States in December 1939. Frequently seen in the company of her old friend, who was now the German Consul General in San Francisco, she figured in West Coast newspaper stories about the "Nazi Princess".

The notoriety of Princess "Steffi" did not deter Wiseman when he had his first meeting with Wiedemann in San Francisco on 1 October. The report he sent Stephenson in New York suggests he did not make much progress with the German Consul, who was elusive and unforthcoming of any information. He talked only generally about Hitler, who now regarded him as "defeatist," denying that he had ever wanted to give information to the British. The Princess went to work on him again at Wiseman's suggestion. After returning from the West Coast, Wiseman resumed his contact with Mooney at the Metropolitan Club on 15 November, when he announced that it was time to revive their peace efforts. This caused Mooney to believe that Sir William must have received the green light from Lord Lothian. There was talk of Mooney going to Europe after stopping off in London on a mission for General Motors that would in reality provide cover for peace soundings. These plans were still fluid when five days later Wiseman received a telephone summons from Princess Stephanie.[59]

Wiseman flew out to San Francisco again on 26 November, unaware that his contacts with Hohenlohe had brought him to the attention of the F.B.I., whose director had kept the Princess under close surveillance ever since she arrived in the United States. The President had received regular reports that she was "dangerous and clever" and "as an espionage agent is 'worse than ten thousand men.'" Hoover's men had reason to believe she was acting as Hitler's courier to German espionage agents in the United States and was working in "association with Wiedemann" to undermine American interests. The F.B.I. had also discovered that Wiseman had been assisting the Princess in trying to recover jewels she had left in England. When they learned through phone-taps on Hohenlohe's residence that she would be meeting Wiseman in his suite in the Mark Hopkins Hotel, arrangements were made to eavesdrop on their conversation through concealed microphones.[60]

The F.B.I. transcript of the conspiratorial discussions makes an interesting contrast with the bland version that Wiseman submitted to British intelligence on 30 November. His own 3½-page report for Stephenson explained how he had met Hohenlohe to arrange that they would dine with Wiedemann the following evening, when the Princess would attempt to "draw him out." Hohenlohe "tried quite cleverly but the experiment was a failure." The F.B.I. version of what was discussed led it to conclude that sinister conspiracy was taking shape.

"These conversations pertain to the formulation of possible peace negotiations between Germany and Great Britain," Hoover wrote in his covering letter enclosing seventeen closely typed pages based on information picked up by the F.B.I. agents listening in on the microphones hidden in Suite 1024. Wiseman, for reasons that must cast suspicion on his loyalty and motives, had omitted in his report to mention his two long discussions with the Princess on 26 November, the day before. These focused exclusively on how she would help Wiseman to get his peace discussions with Hitler under way. Wiseman said he was "representing a group of Englishmen who believe that a satisfactory peace arrangement can be brought about between England and Germany." He asked the Princess to help in sounding out Wiedemann on the terms of a peace proposal that she would then personally carry to Hitler. They considered Lord Halifax, Sir Samuel Hoare and even Churchill as a last resort as possible channels for getting their proposal considered in London. In order to prepare a list of terms that would be pre-approved by Hitler, the Princess volunteered to go to Washington to alert Ribbentrop through Chargé Thomsen at the German Embassy.[61]

The following evening, according to the F.B.I. version, Wiseman told the German Consul General that he had confided to Wiedemann that he was the spokesman for "a British political group headed by Lord Halifax which hopes to bring about a lasting peace between England and Germany." Therefore he would send a record of their talk to the Foreign Secretary, who not only was "sympathetic" to their cause but knew Wiedemann. Halifax, said Wiseman, represented "a certain political party in the House of Lords and House of Commons which is very strong." The problem was how to persuade the British government that Hitler really could be trusted. This led to an extended discussion of Wiedemann's proposals for restoring the German monarchy that formed the substance of Wiseman's own dismissive report to British Intelligence.

The two conflicting reports suggest it would be an understatement to say that Sir William had lived up to the Foreign Office belief that he "exceeded his brief." The F.B.I. records show that the former British Intelligence agent was playing a deep and double game with his former employers by running two simultaneous peace plots whose sponsor was Lord Lothian. When checks were made, the British authorities washed their hands of any responsibility for Wiseman; a U.S. Army Intelligence report to the Bureau stated that "it had been definitely established through reliable contacts that the British government has not availed itself of his offer of his services in any way."[62]

Whether Wiseman was an *agent provocateur* for MI6 or double-dealing the British, whatever hopes he had entertained that the Princess might be a channel for communicating directly with Hitler were to be dashed when the F.B.I. arranged for her to be deported. She indiscreetly sought Wiseman's help to fight the order in a series of panicky phone calls that were tapped by Hoover's agents. She was eventually arrested, released, then interned as a suspect alien when the United States entered the war the following year.

When the F.B.I. moved against the Princess, Wiseman decided to revive his alternative intermediary with Hitler. On 3 December, after seeing Lothian in Washington, he told Mooney that "England's interest at that moment lay in the direction of peace." The problem, as he saw it now, was to find a way to get the peace initiative moving "without letting the Germans know in advance that the British were willing to entertain peace proposals." Mooney volunteered that he could approach the Duke of Windsor, with whom he was due to play in a charity Christmas golf tournament. They finally agreed that Mooney would arrange that Roosevelt should first be asked to put pressure on the British to talk terms with Berlin, because Churchill would "make a vigorous protest against the idea of discussing peace." But according to Sir William the Prime Minister "would be secretly pleased that he was being compelled."[63]

The latest round in the plot had just started to unfold when Lord Lothian died on 12 December from a kidney infection. As a Christian Scientist convert he had tried to cure himself by prayers and died at his post. It was not until Mooney's meeting with Wiseman on 8 January that he fully appreciated that Lothian had been the key figure behind Wiseman's peace initiative. The British Ambassador's death had left Sir William "rather confused as to what to do." Since Roosevelt had proved hostile to any peace feeler, to Mooney's intense frustration, his third effort to bring about peace between Germany and Britain was doomed.

The Wiseman-Lothian peace initiative can now be seen as yet another factor encouraging the belief of Hitler and his deputy Hess that there were highly placed and influential British groups who continued to plot to achieve a negotiated peace. It was this conviction, we now know, that was the genesis of the mission that was to bring the Deputy Führer to Scotland nine months later. The number of serious peace feelers emanating from British officials in 1940 explains why the cover-up of the real story behind the Hess flight began as soon as its principal landed in Scotland.

Chapter 16

"I Have Come to Save Humanity"

"I had *no recollection* of ever seeing him before," the Duke of Hamilton wrote on 11 May 1941 after his first encounter with Rudolf Hess. The Duke and Flight Lieutenant Benson, his intelligence officer, had set off on the drive from Turnhouse early that Sunday morning, arriving at Maryhill Barracks on the outskirts of Glasgow shortly after 10 a.m. They did not go directly into the guarded room in the barracks hospital where the German who was still claiming to be Captain Alfred Horn of the Luftwaffe lay propped up on an army cot, nursing an injured ankle and complaining of stomach cramps.[1]

The noble Wing Commander, who the previous night had disregarded R.A.F. Standing Orders requiring immediate interrogation of captured enemy flyers, now behaved like a regular detective, asking to see the German's personal effects before confronting the prisoner. He saw the wristwatch, Leica camera, small change and a travelling pharmacopoeia of patent medicine bottles and examined the two visiting cards bearing the names of Dr. Albrecht and Dr. Karl Haushofer, the snapshots of the pilot and his small son. He was most intrigued by the map of his own Dungavel estate, with his family seat ringed in red – later to be returned to the Duke as a souvenir.

"I could *not recognize* him," the Duke insisted after studying the photographs. Nor, he claimed, was he enlightened when he confronted Hess in the flesh. "I do not *think* I had ever set eyes upon him before," Hamilton said of the German he saw lying under the army blanket. Hess, however, seems to have had no

404

problem recognizing him: that is clear from Hamilton's account, which states that the prisoner "at once requested that I should speak to him alone". Hamilton said he "asked the other officers to withdraw."[2]

"The German opened by saying that he had seen me in Berlin at the Olympic Games in 1936, and that I had lunched in his house," the Duke recorded. "He said, 'I do not know if you recognize me, but I am Rudolf Hess.' He announced that he was 'on a mission for Humanity.' He declared that the Führer 'did not want to defeat England and wished to stop fighting.'"[3]

Hess then told the Duke that nine months earlier he had arranged for a letter to be sent from Albrecht Haushofer to the Duke proposing a meeting in Portugal. Hamilton was careful to emphasize in his report that "until this interview I had not the slightest idea that the invitation in Haushofer's letter to meet him in Lisbon had any connection at all with Hess." Explaining that he had made three previous attempts to fly to Dungavel to "stop the slaughter," Hess asked the Duke "to get together the leading members of my party to talk over things with a view to making peace proposals." Hamilton says he assured the German that Churchill was Prime Minister and "there was now only one party in this country." Hess nonetheless proceeded to announce Hitler's "generous peace terms that required Britain giving Germany a free hand in Europe." He expected the Duke to arrange for the King to "give him a 'parole' as he had come unarmed and of his own free will." He also asked for his aunt in Zürich to be informed without delay of his safe arrival and insisted that "his identity not be disclosed to the press."[4]

Apart from Hess's anachronistic belief that the rules of medieval chivalry applied in an age of total war, he did not strike Hamilton as mentally unbalanced. The Duke said he had found that Hess, "far from being mad, was a man of self confidence who had numerous proposals to make which would have been highly favourable to the Nazi leadership, although certainly not to anyone else." Interestingly, he omitted this opinion from his official report, which also fails to mention that Hess condemned Churchill's folly in the "buying of fifty second-rate destroyers from the U.S.A.," because he "could say with complete certainty what Hitler's peace terms would be, and what conditions Hitler would be prepared to accept in order to finish the war."[5]

The fact that neither of these points, which appear in the version given by Hamilton to his son, which was published nearly thirty years later, is in his 1940 report raises questions about what else Hess might have said to the Duke in their unwitnessed first conversation. After an hour the Duke brought the interview to an end, promising to "return with an interpreter and have a further conversation." The only surviving version

405

of their talk is the two-page brief that Hamilton had typed up when he returned to R.A.F. Turnhouse. How far it can be relied on as a full and accurate record is an open question; it has to be considered against the reliability of the Duke's statements about Hess's arrival the previous evening, which can now be seen to be seriously at odds with the R.A.F. records. Then too there is the matter of his failure to interview the captured pilot the night before, which became the subject of an official army complaint. But most damaging to Hamilton's credibility is his denial of ever having seen, recognized or met Hess before that Sunday morning at Maryhill Barracks. It is significant too that every one of these denials, whether contemporary or made many years later, appears to have been carefully qualified.[6]

"I had *no recollection* of ever seeing him before," the Duke stated in his 1941 report; "I had never seen Rudolf Hess, *so far as I am aware*," he wrote in a 1945 memorandum to the Air Ministry. The same subtle equivocation appears in a statement he authorized for publication more than twenty-five years later: "*I do not think* I had ever set eyes on him before." It is curious that the Duke appears never to have been able to make categorical denials himself; he always left that to others to infer or state. "The Duke *did not* recognize the prisoner (Hess) and had never met the deputy Führer," the Secretary of State for Air told the House of Commons ten days after Hess had parachuted into Scotland. Two years later the issue of whether Hamilton was telling the truth was raised in the War Cabinet after conflicting "information about Hess which had not hitherto been disclosed" appeared in the British and American press on 29 August 1943. Surprisingly, the source was none other than Britain's Minister of Information, who stated during a New York press conference that "Hess once met the Duke of Hamilton." The minister was Brendan Bracken, who had been at Churchill's side as his most trusted aide the night Hess arrived, a fact which did not escape British journalists. They seized on Bracken's statement, and it prompted awkward questions from Members of Parliament about who was telling the truth, the minister or the Duke?[7]

"The question whether the Duke 'saw' Hess or whether he 'met' him is surely a very unimportant one" was the written answer given by the Secretary of State for Air in a reply which, in the Whitehall tradition, now appears economical with the truth. The reason why the government and the Duke were so coy about the issue was known to Chips Channon, who in 1941 was a parliamentary official in the Foreign Office. Five years earlier, as a fellow Conservative M.P., he had travelled with the Duke (then the Marquess of Clydesdale) to Berlin for the 1936 Olympic Games. "The world does not know that the Duke IS thus concerned in the story," Channon recorded in his diary three days after the Hess story broke, recalling the invitation they had both received to luncheon with the Deputy Führer. Channon noted that he had declined, "but *I remember that 'Duglo' Clydesdale, as he then was, did go.*"[8]

Channon's diary is supported by newspaper accounts of the time. Lord Clydesdale's name appears among the half-dozen British V.I.P.s who also attended the banquet at the Chancellery hosted by Adolf Hitler and the Nazi leadership on the evening of 12 August. "Opportunities for meeting them were provided by the banquets and receptions that have been given daily in connection with the Olympic Games," the London *Times* correspondent reported.[9]

Hamilton, as one of the prominent figures at dinners of the Anglo-German Fellowship, would have enjoyed an especially warm welcome in Berlin. Like many members of Britain's social and financial elite, Hamilton worked for a rapprochement between Britain and Germany – not so much out of admiration for the Nazis, but because of the widespread belief that Hitler would be a bulwark against the spread of Bolshevism. With the encouragement of the Nazi leaders, the Fellowship and its German sister organization had been formed a year before by well-heeled leading city bankers and prominent members of the London and Berlin social elite. "The Anglo-German Fellowship is a post-Nazi creation and more or less replaced the old Anglo-German Society," the London *Evening Standard* reported on 28 November 1935, singling out for special mention "the Marquess of Clydesdale and several city bankers including Mr Samuel Guinness." Shortly before the Olympics in July 1936, *The Times* had listed "The Marquess of Douglas and Clydesdale" and his two younger brothers among the Fellowship members who dined at the Swastika-bedecked tables of the Dorchester Hotel. Seated amongst them were Reichführerin Gertrud Scholtz-Klink, the Nazi Women's League leader, and Hitler's aristocratic German cheerleaders, the Duke of Brunswick and Prince Otto von Bismarck. In the following month Hamilton was in Berlin junketing with other Anglo-German Fellowship V.I.P.s at the Olympic Games in Berlin.[10]

"Hess may have seen Clydesdale across the room when Hitler gave a special dinner in honour of Sir Robert Vansittart" is all that Hamilton's son was prepared to concede. This assertion begs the questions raised by Channon's diary and the *Times* reports. But even if Hamilton had only seen Hess across a dinner table it would be astounding that he could have forgotten the tall figure whose glaring eyes and beetling brows made the Nazi Party chief such a prominent member of Hitler's entourage. Even photographs taken in his withered old age betray Hess's unmistakable features. Why

then did Hamilton go through such a pantomime of semantic perjury after 11 May 1941 to conceal that he had ever seen, recognized
or met Hitler's deputy?[11]

The answer may lie in the curious relationship the Marquess
of Clydesdale struck up with Albrecht Haushofer, whom he also
met in Berlin in 1936. His younger brother, Lord David Hamilton
(another attender of the Anglo-German Fellowship), introduced
them at an "official dinner reception." This was according to the
account written by Hamilton's son while the Duke was still alive.
James Douglas Hamilton characterizes the thirty-three-year-old
bachelor Albrecht Haushofer as having a "certain fascination"
that evidently appealed to his father, who was the same age, also
unmarried, and a handsome man. As Reader in Political Geography
at Berlin University, Haushofer was an anti-Nazi intellectual who
wrote classical tragedies in blank verse. As the son of General
Karl Haushofer, Professor of Geography at Munich University and
the mentor of Hess, who attended the University after serving
in the First World War, he was a friend of the Deputy Führer.
The older Haushofer had developed the theories of "Geopolitics"
which had influenced Hitler's thinking on the German doctrine
of *Lebensraum*. As Nazi party chief, Hess became the family's
protector, arranging for dispensation from the Nazi race-laws
for Karl Haushofer's half-Jewish wife. He had also intervened
to get Albrecht reinstated in his post in the Information Section of the Foreign Ministry, where he operated as something
of an *éminence grise*. Like many of the senior bureaucrats in the
grandiose Auswärtiges Amt building on the Wilhelmstrasse, he
regarded foreign service as one of the last redoubts against the
upstart Nazis.[12]

Hitler distrusted the Prussian conservatives who ran the Foreign
Ministry, such as State Secretary Weizsäcker, but approved their
efforts at repairing Anglo-German relations. This objective was
shared with the group of Conservative M.P.s and Anglo-German
Fellowship members who celebrated with the Nazis at the Berlin
Olympics. The Marquess of Clydesdale was evidently struck by
Albrecht Haushofer's flattering attention and his claim to have
the ear of the German Foreign Minister as well as personal contact
with Hess. The anti-Nazi academic arranged for the Scottish M.P.
to meet Hermann Göring, who enthusiastically agreed to arrange
a tour of Luftwaffe bases for the Auxiliary Air Force officer, who
had flown over Mount Everest and commanded 602 City of Glasgow
(Bomber) Squadron.

According to his son's account, Hamilton used the opportunity
to conduct freelance espionage, passing on intelligence about
German bases he visited to the R.A.F.'s air attaché in Berlin. If
Hamilton was recruited as a freelance agent for MI6, it was a

particularly fortuitous coup, because the relationship he struck up with Haushofer took the Marquess of Clydesdale back and forth to Germany many times before the war. Interestingly, it was Hamilton who cemented what became a close friendship by proposing a second meeting in Munich in January 1937 after his ski trip to Austria. Apart from a shared passion for the slopes, another factor has emerged which could explain the blossoming of their personal relationship that is evident in three years of frequent and familiar correspondence.

The remarkably affectionate tone of Haushofer's "My Dear Duglo" letters suggest that there was a homosexual element in their relationship. Haushofer's brother admitted that Albrecht, who never married, was the subject of a 1941 investigation by the Gestapo into his alleged homosexuality. After the war Lord Beaverbrook told a British journalist whom he encouraged to write about the Hess mission that he had it on reliable authority that Hamilton and Haushofer had been members of the same homosexual network patronized by select members of the British ruling class. While this does not constitute proof, it reinforces the suspicion that this could be the reason why Hamilton's end of the three-year correspondence has never been released by his family. Haushofer's letters to Hamilton do confirm that the two men achieved a very close rapport that could have been inspired as much by a mutual homo-eroticism as by the undisputed fact of their shared vision of European politics.[13]

When Haushofer arrived in London in March 1937 on a private mission for Ambassador Ribbentrop, the Marquess of Clydesdale introduced him to his influential friends in Parliament and the Anglo-German Fellowship. During their meeting and in their letters over the next two years they frequently discussed ways of averting the inevitable collision between the British Empire and Nazi Germany. From his sources inside the Foreign Ministry, Haushofer kept Hamilton *au courant* with the efforts being made by the professionals to smooth over Ribbentrop's diplomatic blunders. Hitler's new envoy had arrived in London just before the abdication of Edward VIII in 1936, anticipating from the reports reaching Berlin of the new monarch's pro-German sympathies that he could establish a rapport with the encouragement of the King's German cousins and fulfil Hitler's hope of an Anglo-German alliance against Bolshevik Russia. The former champagne salesman was a gauche ambassador who shocked the British public by giving the Nazi salute – at Hitler's express instruction, he claimed – at Buckingham Palace. Ribbentrop's diplomatic and social gaffes did not assist the cause of the Anglo-German Fellowship, but Hamilton and his friends did not give up trying. For this he was honoured by the Ambassador, who sent a handsome gift of "silver gilt porringers" when the Marquess of Clydesdale married the sister of the Duke of Northumberland in December 1937.[14]

The following year, as the Nazis stepped up their anti-Jewish repression, the Anglo-German Fellowship went into decline, and it was finally discredited when public support for "appeasement" evaporated after Hitler marched into Czechoslovakia in the spring of 1939 in blatant disregard of the agreements signed less than six months before in Munich. It was a lesson to Chamberlain and Halifax that buying off a dictator could not guarantee "peace in our time," and the rising protests from the Labour Party, the trades unions and the Tory faction led by Winston Churchill shamed the British government into abandoning appeasement and giving firm guarantees to Hitler's next victim – Poland – in the spring of 1939. This made a collision with Hitler inevitable as the British government rushed rearmament ahead at breakneck speed. Yet even as late as July 1939 Hamilton responded to Haushofer's secret plea for British flexibility over Poland. Alerted in a letter that war could erupt "on any date after the middle of August," Hamilton passed this warning on to the Prime Minister and the Foreign Secretary. This was on the advice of Churchill, to whom he had first shown the letter.

A month after war had erupted, Hamilton became one of the first parliamentarians to raise publicly the issue of a negotiated peace. In what he would later claim was an attempt to give succour to anti-Hitler Germans, including his friend, he "tried to suggest the essentials of a just peace" in a letter published by *The Times* on 6 October 1939. While condemning Hitler's aggression, Hamilton proposed recognition of Germany's need for *Lebensraum* and her claims for "colonial settlement" as an olive branch when "a healing peace is negotiated between honourable men." The Prime Minister had vetoed Hamilton's original intention to have his proposal signed by "every younger Member of the House of Commons who was then in the Services." While the letter did not condone Nazism, that a Tory M.P. and officer in the auxiliary air force should have made such a peace appeal is indicative of Hamilton's affection for Germany and Germans.[15]

Ironically, on the very day the Marquess of Clydesdale's letter created a minor sensation in London, Hitler launched his own "Peace Offensive" in Berlin. But official and unofficial efforts to bring about a negotiated peace foundered because the British government drew the line at negotiating with Hitler. But, as this account has documented from German and British records, time and again during the Phoney War and again in the first months of the Churchill administration, the willingness of Halifax and Butler to nibble at the German peace feelers had convinced senior Nazis that there were "weaker vessels" in the British Cabinet who were still prepared to negotiate. While Churchill held stoutly to his defiant promise that "we shall never surrender" as we have seen, the signal from Lord Halifax was that as long as he remained Foreign Secretary "common sense and not bravado" might prevail.

Even after Hitler's July and September peace offensives had been rebuffed by an increasingly dominant and politically secure Churchill, Berlin continued to receive enigmatic peace feelers from senior British figures including Butler and Ambassadors Kelly and Lord Lothian. These reinforced Hitler's belief that if the opposition to Churchill could be mobilized by some dramatic gesture to overthrow him, he could still come to terms with Britain. The Nazi leader who devoted most effort and thought to finding an effective way to hold out a tempting olive branch to the British was Rudolf Hess. War had brought an inevitable decline in the Party Chief's status in the Nazi hierarchy. Finding a way to get peace negotiations going would give him the chance to restore his slipping prestige and earn the Führer's eternal gratitude. He was deeply disturbed by the pact of convenience engineered with Stalin by Foreign Minister Ribbentrop, believing that Germany's destiny lay in persuading Britain to join Hitler's intended crusade against Bolshevism.

Secret discussions with Hess's "geopolitical" mentor Karl Haushofer convinced him that the best way to rally the presumed anti-Churchill factions in Britain was by enlisting the services of Albrecht Haushofer and his friend "Duglo." One factor that influenced his choice was that Hamilton had just become Duke on the death of his father. Like many Germans too cognizant of their own history, Hess and Haushofer laboured under a very continental misconception about the power of Britain's constitutional monarch. They believed that "Der Herzog," as Scotland's premier peer, recently elevated to be Lord High Steward, would be able to appeal over Churchill's head direct to the King. He was also thought to wield great influence in the House of Lords, whose members were known to be more sympathetic to peace overtures than the lower chamber, where Churchills' rhetoric held powerful sway.

On Hess's instructions, Haushofer addressed to the Duke at the House of Lords a letter enclosed in an envelope sent to "Mrs. V. Roberts, Lisbon, Caix Postal 506." Her instructions were to send it on via the British travel firm "Cook's Mail" to London, thereby avoiding a German postmark. This cryptically worded "My Dear Duglo" missive, dated "B[erlin]. 23 Sept.", asked Hamilton, in surprisingly unsubtle terms, "whether you could . . . have a talk with me somewhere on the outskirts of Europe, perhaps Portugal." It was signed "Yours ever, 'A'" with instructions that the reply be addressed to "DR. A.H." (Albrecht Haushofer) care of a Lisbon company address.[16]

A letter could hardly have been written in a manner more calculated to advertise itself to a censor's distrusting eye. On 2 November 1940, when it was opened by a British postal examiner – described as "just one of our ordinary staff" – he deduced correctly that the "B" stood for Berlin. On 6 November the original was sent to MI5 with a photostat to the Foreign Office. The interception of the Haushofer letter would enable Hamilton later to deny that he had ever "been in correspondence" with Hess, while admitting that "It is certainly true that one man whom I knew in Germany was well acquainted with him." While Hamilton was technically correct in insisting that he had "never received a letter from Hess," he cannot, after three years of intimate exchanges, have been unaware of Haushofer's connection to the Deputy Führer.[17]

It is unlikely therefore that the Duke was ignorant of the connection between Haushofer and Hess in "mid-March" 1941 when he was summoned to the Air Ministry and, he said, "surprised" with "a photostat" of Albrecht's 23 September letter. It referred to Haushofer's July 1939 letter and invited Hamilton's "friends in high places" to "find significance in the fact that I am able to ask whether you could find time to have a talk." This was an unmistakable peace feeler. The Duke was clearly uneasy to find that "the Intelligence authorities were of the opinion that Haushofer was a significant person who had close relations with the German Foreign Office" and that they had decided that it "might be of considerable value to make contact with him."[18]

A month went by, according to the Duke's version, before he was "ordered" to attend another meeting in the Air Ministry at the London School of Economics in Houghton Street on 25 April. He was confronted by Captain D.L. Blackford of Air Intelligence and Major T.A. Robertson of MI5, who proposed that Hamilton should cooperate in springing a trap which required that he should "*volunteer* to go to Portugal in order to acquire all information possible from Albrecht Haushofer." Robertson, known as "Tar" to his colleagues in the British secret service, was the mastermind behind the legendary "Double Cross" operation that "turned" German agents caught in Britain and used them to feed false information to Berlin. His access to the MI5 Registry files would have revealed Hamilton's links to the Anglo-German Fellowship.[19]

Even if the Duke had not admitted it, MI5 must have known of Haushofer's direct connection to Hess, and if there had been a homosexual element this would have added to Hamilton's reluctance to act as bait in a plot to snare the Deputy Führer of the Third Reich. The Duke told Robertson he would go to Lisbon only "if ordered." This caused some surprise to the MI5 officer, and Hamilton was told that "for this type of job people volunteered and were not ordered." The Duke asked for time to think the proposition

412

over, knowing that the British secret services had a penchant for disowning "chaps" if an operation misfired or went sour. It was only after consulting his influential brother-in-law, the Duke of Northumberland, who had connections in the Foreign Office, that Hamilton wrote a temporizing reply setting down conditions for his participation. He expressed concern about how to frame a convincing reply to Haushofer after such a long delay, and he insisted on the prior approval of the Foreign Office and the British Ambassador in Lisbon before he agreed to go to Portugal.[20]

On 3 May Blackford of Air Intelligence sent Hamilton a 'secret' response distancing the Air Ministry from the operation by saying that the Duke's requests had been "passed to the Department concerned." That this letter was copied to "Captain Robertson" confirms that MI5 was involved. Robertson himself admitted that during this period he frequently turned for advice in his "Double Cross" operations to "Archie" Boyle, the head of Air Intelligence. So the Air Ministry's admission that the Foreign Office would not be able to give its approval "without Cabinet authority" suggests that *neither Air Intelligence nor MI5 had yet obtained Churchill's authorization* for its operation. Nor it seems, were they willing to risk asking him for it, because of his strong opposition to sending any hint to Berlin that might be misread as showing that the British government was putting out peace feelers. That much is clear from the "don't-call-us-we'll-call-you" tone of Captain Blackford's letter, which advised the Duke that the "matter was in abeyance." Should it "come forward again," Hamilton was told, "he would be informed."[21]

Now it was Hamilton who changed his mind about participating, and by 10 May he had replied to the Air Ministry: "I am of the opinion that a good opportunity might have been missed owing to the delay." He now volunteered to write to Haushofer explaining that his R.A.F. command had prevented him from getting abroad, but that an opportunity now presented itself to come to Portugal in connection with his duties. "If the proposition materializes and I am asked to go," he told Blackford, he thought it important to "avoid the appearance of waiting on the doorstep."[22]

The ink on his signature was barely dry when Hess parachuted to earth after trying to land at the Duke's Scottish estate. If Hamilton knew – as the evidence from the Observer Corps reports suggests he must have – the identity of the German pilot asking to see him, he was in a dilemma. It would be reasonable, from his contacts with Robertson, to suspect that MI5 might have a hand in the business, possibly even setting their operation rolling despite his initial reluctance to participate. Hamilton's name could have been used to lure Haushofer into triggering Hess's flight into the trap baited for him by the British secret service. If the secret

413

service had indeed played the Haushofer card, then the Duke knew that by confronting Hess without official authority his predicament would be made more awkward because of his pre-war association with the discredited Anglo-German Fellowship.

Fear that a plot might have been hatched by the devious minds of the British secret services would explain why Hamilton behaved so strangely on the night of 10 May 1941, ignoring the Army's repeated requests to interrogate the captured German who was suspected to be Hess until he had consulted with his contact in Air Intelligence. We are told by his son that the Duke "returned to bed, somewhat puzzled" but "in readiness for what the next day might hold in store." This at least admits the possibility that before turning in that night he had been busy on the telephone at his quarters. If he was instructed to do so, Hamilton would have had little choice but to deny having seen or met or even recognizing Hess before he entered the Maryhill Barracks on Sunday, 11 May.[23]

Yet despite Hamilton's claim not to recognize the prisoner, his own account shows that Hess had no doubt about the identity of his visitor that morning. Is it likely that someone as suspicious and meticulous as Hess on his "mission to save humanity" would have revealed his plans unless he knew with absolute certainty that the man at his bedside really was the Duke of Hamilton and not an impostor? Hess's certainty that he was speaking to "Der Herzog" can only be explained if he knew and recognized him. It is also odd that the R.A.F. Wing Commander who had been so concerned about being implicated in MI5's plan to use him as a lure would have conducted a possibly compromising exchange without witnesses *unless* he had received authorization to do so.

Hamilton's action immediately following Hess's arrival is so far out of character as to suggest that he must have been following instructions. Only if he was obeying secret orders is it possible to explain the extraordinary six-hour delay that Sunday before, according to his account, he attempted to communicate the momentous news to higher authorities in London. Since he "believed that the prisoner was indeed Hess himself" at 10 a.m., what could have held him back from reporting this startling news to the Foreign Office until around five o'clock that evening?[24]

According to the Duke's own account, when he left Maryhill Barracks about midday, he was in no doubt that the prisoner he had interviewed was Hitler's deputy. He must have been acting under some constraint from higher authority not to have revealed Hess's identity to the garrison commander, who was told only that "the prisoner was an important person and should be removed out of danger of bombing and put under close guard." Whether the Duke took his intelligence officer into his confidence is not clear, but they then drove together to the crash site, where Flight

Lieutenant Benson "removed certain parts that he thought might be of use." What parts were taken from the wreck is not revealed. It is clear that the Duke knew *before* he saw Hess that a team of R.A.F. intelligence officers from Ayr had already examined the Me 110 wreck. So there must have been some good reason for him to make a seemingly unnecessary diversion that added another hour or more to his delay in letting the authorities know that the Deputy Führer of the Third Reich was in a British Army hospital. Did Hess tell him there was a detailed peace plan, some letter or compromising list of highly placed British sympathizers that he had secreted in the cockpit before taking off and then overlooked in his panicky bail-out?[25]

Such an inference seems to be corroborated by Hamilton, who said that on the way back to R.A.F. Turnhouse he stopped off at his own quarters and "collected the letter Albrecht Haushofer had written in July 1939." His account also has him telephoning Air Vice Marshal Andrews, his superior officer, to ask permission to fly to London to deal with an urgent matter that he "could not divulge over the telephone, but which *should be reported as soon as possible* to the Foreign Office." This belated acknowledgement of urgency makes it yet more astounding that the Duke frittered away the best part of the afternoon visiting the wreck, going to his headquarters and then arranging for a W.A.A.F. to type up his confidential and carefully worded two-page report. If the Duke's account is to be believed, all this was done *before* he finally telephoned the Foreign Office some time around five o'clock. Why did he not make that telephone call five hours earlier from the Maryhill Barracks?[26]

It is so extraordinary as to be incredible that an R.A.F. Wing Commander really would have wasted so much time before reporting the capture of Hitler's deputy to higher authorities. It makes the Army report censuring the Duke for his failure to interrogate Hess promptly look mild in comparison. Yet there is no hint that anyone except Scottish Army Command ever criticized the Duke for what appears to have been a truly astonishing dereliction of duty on 11 May. There appears to be only one convincing explanation: that higher authorities already knew, either from the Duke himself or from other channels, that Hess was in Britain. It is simply not credible that a commanding officer of a fighter sector with the political experience and contacts that Hamilton had would not have reported the affair to his superiors before he claims he did, late that Sunday afternoon.

The first "official" reference to Hamilton's making a report appears in the manuscript version of the private diary kept by Sir Alexander Cadogan, whose frequent references to secret service activities do not appear in the published version. The entry for 11 May records how the Permanent Under Secretary of the Foreign Office was at home that Sunday afternoon when he received a telephone call from his private secretary: "5.30 Addis rang me up with this story: a German pilot landed near Glasgow, asked for the Duke of Hamilton. Latter so impressed he is flying to London & wants to see me at No 10 tonight . . . Half an hour later heard P.M. was sending to meet His Grace at airfield and wd bring him to Chequers [sic]."[27]

Hamilton records that his telephone call was stonewalled by John Addis, the duty secretary, who told him there was no possibility of seeing Cadogan until the following morning. In the midst of what the Duke described as a "tremendous argument" with the secretary, who "regarded the entire proposition with the gravest dubiety," another voice came on the line. It announced: "This is the Prime Minister's secretary speaking. *The Prime Minister sent me over to the Foreign Office as he is informed that you have some interesting information.*"[28]

How could Churchill have known that the Duke had "interesting information," unless his private secretary, Colville, was anticipating his call because the Prime Minister *already knew* about Hess's arrival? Colville does not say in his private diary or any published account that he was in the Foreign Office *that afternoon* at Churchill's request. His very specific recollection is of fielding Hamilton's call on *Sunday morning*. In his account, based on his wartime diary, Colville described in rather too much detail to be convincing how a night of incessant bombing had prompted a "waking dream" which he says was inspired by a popular wartime novel in which Hitler made a forced landing in England. After attending morning service, Colville wrote, "about 11 o'clock I walked over to the Foreign Office," where he found "Nicholas Lawford" in the midst of a heated telephone call.[29]

"Hold on a minute. I think this is your man," Colville records Lawford saying. With his hands over the receiver he explained that it was the Duke of Hamilton, "who had got some fantastic story which he refused to reveal in detail, and that he wanted the Prime Minister's Secretary to meet him at Northolt aerodrome."[30]

"Suddenly, my waking day dream came back to me," Colville wrote. "'Has somebody arrived?' There was a long pause. 'Yes,' he said, 'please be at Northolt to meet me.' He rang off." A quarter of a century later, Sir John Colville recorded: "I make no pretence to be a psychic power." He was still apparently amazed at the extraordinary parallel between Hess's arrival and the novel. But either he was mistaken in recalling that he fielded Hamilton's telephone call at around eleven that Sunday *morning* or both Cadogan and the Duke were lying in their contemporary accounts, which put the time of the call at 5 p.m. *that afternoon.* Further doubt was cast on the reliability of Colville's recollection of the affair by Nicholas Lawford himself, who said he was not in the Foreign Office that day and so could never have spoken the words attributed to him by Colville.

Lawford's own unpublished private diary shows that he was not even in London that weekend, which he spent breaking in his half-Arab colt Alexis on his parents' Hertfordshire estate. Lawford confirms Cadogan's account that it was his colleague John Addis who was on duty. While casting doubt on Colville's reliability, Lawford's correction raises the suspicion that Churchill's private secretary may have a good reason for concocting his "waking dream" fantasy about the E. Phillips Oppenheim novel. It suggests that Churchill had indeed learned about Hess that Sunday morning and that Colville's presence at the Foreign Office in the afternoon was prearranged so as to give the Duke of Hamilton's "official" version credibility.[31]

Colville's actual diary entry does indeed show him speaking with Churchill that morning to report on the devastation caused by the previous night's London raid. So the Prime Minister could have alerted him to expect the afternoon call at a prearranged time from Hamilton. There is further evidence from an independent source to indicate that the Prime Minister knew of Hess's arrival, that Sunday morning, most likely after Hamilton's interview had confirmed Hess's identity to MI6. That source was the wife of his host for the weekend, Nancy, Lady Tree.

Cadogan was also mistaken in assuming that the Prime Minister was at Chequers, the official country retreat of British Prime Ministers. He was actually weekending at Ditchley Park, the Oxfordshire home of his wealthy parliamentary supporter Ronald Tree. The previous November, German bombs had fallen in Kent near Chequers, and ever since then, whenever "the moon was high," Churchill spent his weekends at Tree's secluded Georgian mansion north of Oxford. This particular weekend his host happened to be in the United States, but Lady Tree was there and recalled that she was puzzled by "the strange request by the Prime Minister *on Sunday morning* that the Duke of Hamilton spend Sunday night at Ditchley."[32]

"Truth is sometimes stranger than fiction," Nancy Tree remembered the Prime Minister telling her very enigmatically that Sunday. She was not informed "why this peer from remote Scotland was being so suddenly, and importantly injected into Mr Churchill's councils." Nor, until later, did it dawn on her why she was also told by Churchill not to breathe a word to the guests. They happened to include Brendan Bracken, Roosevelt's special envoy, Harry Hopkins, and the Secretary of State for Air, Sir Archibald Sinclair. This has to be a suspicious coincidence, given that Churchill knew on Sunday morning that the R.A.F. Wing Commander would be coming to join them for dinner. Lady Tree's account puts the Prime Minister's knowledge of Hess well in advance of the first notice he received according to the "official" version of the event given by Colville, the call he made to Ditchley around five.[33]

"Well, who has arrived?" the Prime Minister demanded cryptically, instructing Colville to arrange for the Duke to be "driven directly there" after establishing he was "not a lunatic." Another reason for believing that the Prime Minister and his private secretary conspired in a charade is that Churchill's own account conflicts with the other records on a number of critical points. He claims in his postwar memoir that the first word he had about Hamilton came late *in the evening, after dinner,* while he watched a Marx Brothers film, "glad of the diversion" after a day of rising casualty reports from a still smoking London. This is not supported either by Colville's account or by Cadogan, who recorded with precision in his contemporary diary that by six he "heard the P.M. was sending to meet his Grace at airfield."[34]

The Duke took "an hour and a half" to reach Northolt airfield that Sunday evening, flying his own Hurricane down from Turnhouse, where he had taken off around five after making his telephone call to the Foreign Office. When he landed at about 6.30 p.m. he was instructed to fly on to R.A.F. Kidlington in Oxfordshire. Mechanical problems with an overprimed engine forced him to abandon his Hurricane and transfer to a slow trainer aircraft, which "landed at Kidlington in the dark." So it must have been well after nine before the car sent to collect him rolled down the long gravel drive at Ditchley Park. After taking off his leather flying jacket, the Duke was shown into the dining room, where brandy and cigars were being passed as the Prime Minister, "in tremendous form," cracked jokes.[35]

"Now, come and tell us this funny story of yours," Churchill had joked with over-deliberate humour. Hamilton suggested to the Prime Minister that it was "better to give him the information in private." When the other guests withdrew, he found himself alone with Churchill and the Secretary of State for Air. He then told his story, noting that the Prime Minister was "taken aback." Eyeing him "sympathetically," as if he might be suffering from war strain, the Prime Minister asked: "Do you mean to tell me that the Deputy Führer of Germany is in our hands?" Hamilton produced the photograph that Hess had brought with him, and both Churchill and Sinclair agreed that it certainly looked like Hitler's deputy.[36]

"Well, Hess or no Hess, I'm going to see the Marx Brothers," Churchill announced. He invited the Duke to join his party in the room where a film projector had been set up. When the rib-rattling *The Marx Brothers Go West* ended, around midnight, the Prime Minister took Hamilton aside for a private discussion. For three hours, according to the Duke, Churchill "went through every

418

detail and asked every conceivable kind of question." Hamilton mentions discussing the "copy of the letter sent by Haushofer in September 1940." Their three-hour interrogation presumably ranged across everything from the Duke's association with the Anglo-German Fellowship to MI5's request that he participate in their plot. The Duke volunteered his opinion that Hess was "an energetic fanatic and a stupid man," but not mad, and told the Prime Minister that Hess had insisted that a precondition of Hitler's willingness to negotiate peace was the removal of Churchill as Prime Minister.[37]

"Mr Churchill would not be very sympathetic to his point of view," Hamilton said he had warned Hess that morning. "By God I would not!" the Prime Minister thundered. Still uncertain about how to handle the affair, Hamilton recalls that he was "sworn to secrecy" by the Prime Minister. This was a rather unnecessary step in the circumstances since he was not anxious to reveal an involvement that could be made to look very compromising, and subsequent events were to show that the Prime Minister gave his personal assurance that the Duke's good name would be protected.[38]

Whether Hess had arrived with Hitler's blessing or not, Churchill was confronted with the dilemma of how to deal with what would be publicly seen as a spectacular German peace initiative at a time when the British were suffering a military defeat and after his own leadership of the war had been challenged in Parliament. If he acknowledged that Hess really had come to negotiate he would have to confront the clamour of those who still wanted to make peace in a war that not even his military advisers believed Britain could win without the United States. If Hess really was Hitler's emissary and Churchill rejected what the Germans would portray as a generous peace offer, he would alienate public opinion in America, where polls were showing a steadily building popular support for Roosevelt's increasing the U.S. Navy's role in the war against the U-boats in the Atlantic. Whichever course he took, Churchill was trapped. He must have regretted that the fighters under the Duke's command had not done a better job and shot Hess down in flames.

The one course not open to the Prime Minister was simply to ignore Hess and his "mission to save humanity," because once the press got hold of the story it would make blazing headlines in every newspaper in the world. In this quandary so fraught with potential political disaster, it is not surprising that Churchill's first reaction was to doubt the authenticity of the man claiming to be Hess.

"I don't believe the story," Churchill declared at his Monday morning meeting with Anthony Eden, now Foreign Secretary. He may well have been playing his scepticism for dramatic effect, because Eden, who had met Hess in 1935, confirmed right away that the photograph brought from Scotland by the Duke showed Hitler's deputy. The Prime Minister had alerted the Foreign Secretary by telephone the previous evening, and drove back to London at high speed next morning, accompanied by the Duke of Hamilton. Monday, 12 May, was a day of crisis and endless conferences at Downing Street. The Duke, who was there at Churchill's insistence, recalled: "I was closeted in a room with the First Lord of the Admiralty, the Head of the War Office and the Chief of the Air Staff. We were shown in one by one as the Prime Minister wanted us." Then the Duke was sent across to the Foreign Office with Eden to see Cadogan and "C" – Brigadier Stewart Menzies, the head of MI6. They decided that Ivone Kirkpatrick, who knew Hess well from his time in Berlin as the First Secretary of the British Embassy, would fly up to Glasgow with the Duke as soon as possible to "vet" the prisoner and "establish the man's identity completely." Kirkpatrick, a visceral anti-Nazi, was at that time attached to the Political Warfare Executive, headquartered at Woburn Abbey. So it was 3.15 p.m. before he arrived from Bedfordshire for the briefing by Eden and Cadogan. Hamilton, who was brought into the conference at four o'clock, observed with some surprise that "Kirkpatrick accepted the news very much as a matter of course."[39]

At 5 p.m. the diplomat and the Wing Commander were driven to Hendon airfield, where a plane was waiting to fly them to Scotland. The 132 m.p.h. top speed of the De Havilland "Rapide" belied its name, and it proved inadequate against the buffeting of strong headwinds, which forced a refuelling stop, extending the flight to Scotland to over four hours. When they finally landed at Turnhouse at 9.40 p.m., they learned that rumours about the identity of Captain Horn were flying thick and fast after the German radio networks had flashed out an eight o'clock bulletin announcing the "disappearance" of "Party member Hess," who had left on Saturday "on a flight from which he had not yet returned." Berlin's explanation implied that Hess had suffered a brainstorm, because he had left a letter which "unfortunately showed traces of mental disturbance which justifies the fear that he was a victim of mental hallucinations." Allegedly the Deputy Führer had been "forbidden by the Führer to use an aeroplane because of a disease which has become worse for years." The broadcast also announced the arrest of Hess's adjutants, "who alone knew of his flight."[40]

What has been overlooked in the quest for the true explanation of Hess's flight is why the broadcast was made at all. This is surely as significant as the question why Hitler waited a full day and a half *after* learning of his deputy's flight to Britain *before* authorizing the broadcast disclaiming his peace mission as the act of a madman. The German records and diaries confirm that it was early on Sunday morning that the unfortunate Karlheinz Pintsch, Hess's valet, arrived at the Berghof after an overnight train journey from Munich. At the Führer's awesome Obersalzberg mountain retreat, no one addressed the urgency of his mission, which was to personally hand to Hitler the letter Hess had entrusted to him before he took off from Hunstetten airfield near Augsburg at six o'clock the previous evening. Not until after midday did Pintsch finally manage to get admitted to Hitler's study.

According to Pintsch's account, Hitler reacted with surprising calm when handed the letter, commenting only that it was an "extremely dangerous escapade." He then invited Pintsch to join him for lunch. Only later that afternoon did he order the valet's arrest. General Karl Bodenschatz, Göring's adjutant, who was present when Pintsch handed over the two-page letter, said the Führer appeared "shocked," but he concluded that his "shock and surprise on hearing of Hess's flight was an example of superb acting." If so, Ribbentrop certainly appears to have been taken in. "The Führer knew nothing, nothing whatsoever," the former Nazi Foreign Minister insisted under interrogation in 1945. "The Führer rang me up and said 'Something has happened. You must come at once.'" Ribbentrop was in conference with a French delegation from Vichy led by the French Admiral Jean Darlan. "Leave Darlan, it doesn't matter, and come at once," Hitler ordered. "Hess has written a letter to the Duke of Hamilton in Scotland, and a quite fantastic thing, an extraordinary letter."[41]

Regrettably for history, all copies of this "extraordinary" letter have vanished. So too has the longer fourteen-page version that General Halder, the O.K.H. Chief of Staff, recorded had arrived at the Berghof the previous evening. Hitler, assuming it was some party memorandum, had left unopened the long letter that set out the full details of the peace proposal Hess intended to put to the British. Hess's wife Ilse found a copy of her husband's letter, which was later destroyed when their Munich house was bombed. Its final sentence had etched itself into her memory, she claimed, recalling vividly her husband's assurance: "And if, my Führer, this project – which I admit has very little chance of success – ends in a failure, if fate decides against me, there will be no harmful consequences for you or Germany; you can always deny all responsibility – simply say that I am insane."[42]

Frau Hess steadfastly maintained that Hitler did not know precise details of her husband's flight in advance, yet she conceded that he might have "mentioned such a plan in conversation with Hitler." The eye-witness accounts left by Pintsch and Bodenschatz also suggest that the Führer knew far more. So did Ernest William Bohle, the English-educated head of the Nazi

Party Auslandsorganisation and ambassador designate to a post-peace Britain. He recalled that his boss had discussed with him his intention of making some dramatic bid for peace. "I was always of the opinion that Hitler knew and I still believe this but cannot prove it," Bohle insisted in his 1945 interrogation; "Hitler is dead, and knowing Hess, he will never say a word about it." He said he could "scarcely imagine that Hess, who was always overcautious and shrank from personally making big decisions, would attempt an operation of such magnitude without consulting Hitler, much less carry it out."[43]

Alfred Leitgen, Hess's long-time adjutant, another member of the Deputy's entourage, had first-hand evidence for his belief that the flight was made with Hitler's approval. Shortly before his death in 1988, Leitgen spoke of a conspiratorial discussion between Hitler and his deputy in the garden of the Berlin Chancellery just before the flight. Although they kept their voices lowered, Leitgen was able to eavesdrop fragments that included the names "Albrecht Haushofer" and "the Duke of Hamilton." At one point, Leitgen claimed, he heard Hess insist there were "no problems at all with the aeroplane," rejecting Hitler's concern about how "dangerous" the mission would be. Leitgen said he had caught a loud interjection by Hess that concluded ". . . simply declared insane."[44]

With the exception of Ribbentrop, who was a bitter rival of Hess, the surviving eye-witness accounts of the Führer's entourage are remarkably consistent in suggesting that Hitler knew far more about his deputy's mission than he would later admit. This would explain the thirty hours he allowed to elapse before authorizing the German announcement that Hess had disappeared. Only if Hitler both knew about and sanctioned the mission would he have delayed reacting publicly as long as possible, hoping for some positive reaction from the British before having to brand his deputy, according to their prearranged plan, a madman. If Hitler did not know and approve of the terms set out in the letter he read at midday on Sunday, why did he not denounce Hess right away?

The accounts left by Hitler's top military aides, including O.K.W. chief General Keitel and General Halder, refer to the feverish mood of the discussions that took place at the Berghof throughout the afternoon and well into the next day. Hitler seemed unusually diffident and indecisive. In the absence of any news, he became progressively more preoccupied with the question whether Hess could have succeeded in reaching Scotland. Luftwaffe General Ernst Udet assured the Führer that the prevailing winds would have driven his deputy out to sea and oblivion. But Hitler would not accept this. Citing Hess's remarkable dedication and his "technical and mathematical abilities," he tried to convince his entourage that Udet was wrong and Hess was in British hands. What he most wanted to know was how the British would react.[45]

"He has done a very foolish thing because they'll put him in prison at once," Ribbentrop said he told Hitler. "It is quite an idiotic idea to go to the Duke of Hamilton to make a conspiracy against Churchill." Ribbentrop assured the agitated Führer that in spite of their differences over the alliance with the Soviet Union, he believed Hess to be "a man of integrity." As a member of the "Cabinet Council for the Defence of the Reich," Hess knew that Hitler was preparing to launch the Wehrmacht on the invasion of Russia. The fiercely anti-Bolshevik deputy regarded Ribbentrop's German-Soviet pact as a betrayal of Nazi principles and saw "the Russian affair as madness." He had argued that the Führer would court military disaster by launching Operation Barbarossa before Germany had come to terms with England.[46]

What neither Hitler nor his advisers could decide was whether Hess had survived and if so, how much he might betray to the British of Germany's strategic plans to attack the Soviet Union. If the Deputy Führer had crashed into the sea, then their dilemma was resolved, and any public announcement would court a propaganda disaster. Considering that this was the paramount concern of his staff, it is surprising to find that Dr. Joseph Goebbels, Germany's Minister of Propaganda and Public Enlightenment, was not brought into the discussion until well into Monday – yet another indication that Hitler wanted to wait as long as possible for a favourable response.

"We must presume him dead," Goebbels wrote after receiving the telephone call late in the day from a "shattered" Führer at his lakeside mansion at Lanke, north of Berlin. "Dreadful and unthinkable" was his immediate reaction to the news of Hess's disappearance that had already been broadcast as he prepared to fly south to the Berghof to take charge of the "damage control" publicity. "Führer's statement gives delusions as the reason for his action, some madness to do with illusionary peace feelers," Goebbels observed, worried that Hitler's decision to brand his missing deputy "a mentally disturbed man" could only do irreparable damage to the image of the leaders of the Third Reich. Hitler had shot himself in the foot by authorizing that Monday evening broadcast before there had been any admission by the British that Hess was alive. It suggests that the Führer could only have been acting irrationally, or else he was following Hess's suggestion that he should be declared insane if his mission collapsed.[47]

It is also interesting to find that Albrecht Haushofer was brought to the Obersalzberg that Monday on Hitler's orders. He was put in a small room with armed guards posted at the door. Hitler refused to see him, but gave instructions that he was to write a full report on his own role in the affair. "English Connections and the Possibility for Utilizing Them" was the prosaic title for a report that Haushofer might have guessed could be used as his death warrant. In it he summarized his many English connections, attempting to make a cogent and convincing case that justified the mission Hess had undertaken. He listed the numerous British contacts whose help and sympathies Haushofer himself had sought at various times before the war "on behalf of German-English understanding." Among the younger Conservatives he named, a surprising number were Scotsmen or had Scottish Constituencies, including Chamberlain's former Parliamentary Private Secretary Lord Dunglass, the Under Secretaries of State in the Air Ministry and the Ministry of Education, and high diplomats in the Foreign Office. David Astor, of the newspaper-owning family, who had been Parliamentary Private Secretary to Sir Samuel Hoare, was named, and so was the former Foreign Secretary Lord Halifax, who had since been posted to Washington as Britain's Ambassador.[48]

In the light of what the records have revealed about Butler's sustained efforts to negotiate a compromise peace, it is not surprising to find that Halifax's Under Secretary was singled out for special mention. Haushofer pointed out to Hitler that Butler, "in spite of his many public utterances is not a follower of Churchill or Eden." Three weeks later, by another curious coincidence, Butler was told that he was going to move from the post he had held for three years at the Foreign Office to Education, where it seems Churchill had decided he would have less temptation to pursue his "unorthodox" relations with Nazi Germany.[49]

Haushofer's memorandum was described by the Duke of Hamilton's son as a "mixture of truth, half-truths and camouflage," by which Haushofer hoped to save his own skin and protect his friends in the anti-Nazi opposition. But this is surely too glib a judgement. Although Haushofer was arrested for interrogation by the Gestapo, he was released after only eight weeks, remaining free though under suspicion until he was rearrested three years later. While exercising his discretion over German names, Haushofer certainly did not need to disguise the identity of the British contacts, since Butler and Halifax, to whom he ascribed leading roles in the British peace initiatives, are well documented in the Foreign Ministry files and were also familiar to Hess.[50]

The memorandum would therefore have given Hitler encouragement that Hess might have a good chance of succeeding in his mission. But the sequence of events appears to show that Hitler was reacting to a prearranged deadline which gave Hess twenty-four hours' grace. Why else would Hitler have brought on himself a public-relations disaster by authorizing the broadcast that evening? Only his fear that Hess might leak the Soviet

424

invasion plan or be used for propaganda could have prompted Hitler to self-destruct the mission by branding him as mad after the expiry of a prearranged time-limit. The statement broadcast by German radio on Monday evening that would detonate sensational headlines around the world also put the British Prime Minister on the spot. How best to handle the exposure story was the question that confronted the war leaders in London.

"Winston rang up, immensely excited and wanted us to issue something at once," Anthony Eden noted in his diary: news of the German communiqué on Hess had interrupted the Foreign Secretary's dinner. Ivone Kirkpatrick and the Duke of Hamilton were also sitting down to eat in the officers' mess at R.A.F. Turnhouse when a telephone call from the Foreign Secretary ordered them to go to Glasgow at once; Kirkpatrick was to interview the prisoner and report back as soon as possible.[51]

Eden summoned Cadogan and they went together to the Prime Minister's residence. Churchill presented them with a twelve-line summary of the Duke of Hamilton's report, which, although it omitted any reference to the Duke, stated that Hess "had come to England in the name of humanity hoping that a peace might be made between Great Britain and Germany . . ." The assertion that "the German officer in question is undoubtedly Hess" jumped the gun on Kirkpatrick and shows that Churchill had never entertained any real doubt about his identity. The Prime Minister's draft announcement, with its promise that Hess's "statement will be carefully examined," gave the Foreign Secretary heartburn.[52]

"How much we should tell of Hess's confused obsessions posed quite a problem," Eden would write, setting the precedent for the arguments that would dog the British handling of the affair. Churchill had even wanted to announce that Hitler's deputy had come to England "in the name of humanity." Eden and Cadogan were dead-set against any mention of a peace mission. "This won't do," Cadogan objected, recording that it "looks like a peace offer, and we may want to run the line that he has quarrelled with Hitler." They prevailed on the Prime Minister to remove the offending sentences.[53]

Shortly after eleven o'clock a hush fell over the throng of excited journalists from British and American news organizations packed into the conference room of the Ministry of Information. The Prime Minister's statement was read out by Britain's Minister of Information, Duff Cooper. It made no mention of peace. Within "two seconds," according to the New York Times reporter, Cooper and his Director-General Walter Monckton found themselves in a deserted room "as everyone made a wild scramble for the telephones." At 11.20 p.m. the B.B.C. broadcast the government's brief statement,

425

which threw no light on why Hess had arrived so unexpectedly in Scotland.[54]

The man at the heart of the tornado of rumour and speculation had already been moved for security to Buchanan Castle, a military hospital twenty miles north-west of Glasgow at Drymen. When Kirkpatrick and Hamilton arrived shortly before midnight, "dinnerless and rather tired" after the drive through the blacked-out roads, they had to clamber up a long flight of winding stairs to what had formerly been a servant's bedroom in the turreted country mansion. The naked glare of the single light bulb, crudely shielded by a newspaper, fell dimly on the iron bedstead. An army issue khaki blanket covered the sleeping form of the Deputy Führer of the Third Reich. The scene was so incongruous for Kirkpatrick, who had last encountered Hess surrounded by the ostentatious pomp of the Nazi leaders, that he surveyed the transformation in amazed silence for a few minutes.[55]

When they roused Hess, he was at first so dazed and confused that he did not recognize his visitor. Kirkpatrick reminded him of the last occasion when they met in Berlin. Two wooden chairs were brought in, and the hospital commandant and guard were asked to leave. Kirkpatrick then sat "sphinx-like," according to Hamilton, at the bedside of Hitler's deputy, who produced a sheaf of handwritten notes from a brown envelope. Despite his army flannel pyjamas, Kirkpatrick observed, Hess "appeared to be in the best of health" and was certainly not mad, since he "was able almost at once to plunge into the reading of a huge statement which he had prepared." This turned out to be a highly slanted review of Anglo-German relations and rivalry since the beginning of the century. As Hess approached his climax, a highly coloured explanation of how Britain had forced a reluctant Hitler into war, Kirkpatrick had to break off to take a telephone call. He could only inform an impatient Foreign Secretary that he had not yet discovered what was the true purpose of Hess's mission.[56]

"On returning I found Hamilton comatose and Hess itching to get on with his speech," Kirkpatrick wrote in his memoir. Not until 3 a.m., when Hess approached the bottom of his bundle of notes, did Kirkpatrick's patience finally snap. Interrupting the meandering lecture, he asked Hess to "define the object of his visit." Hitler's deputy answered with the simple statement that he had come "to convince the British government of the inevitablity of a German victory and to bring about peace by negotiations."[57]

It was six o'clock the following morning when the dog-tired Hamilton and weary Kirkpatrick reached Turnhouse to snatch a few hours' sleep. At 10.30 a.m. on Tuesday Kirkpatrick telephoned a brief report on his night's conversation to Cadogan at the Foreign Office. He summarized Hess's harangue in three parts: "a long recapitulation of Anglo-German relations from the time of King Edward VII to the invasion of the low countries" in 1940; a "lengthy explanation of the certainty that Germany would win the war"; and finally "proposals for a settlement whereby Germany should have a free hand in Europe and the British Empire should be left intact save for the return of the former colonies." Hess had also made it clear that the condition for opening peace talks was that "Hitler would not negotiate with the present government in England."[58]

Not a hint that Hitler's deputy had come to talk peace appeared in the Tuesday morning newspapers, which blazed with headlines such as HITLER'S DEPUTY ESCAPES TO BRITAIN. Conforming as expected to the government-inspired line, The Times speculated that the Deputy Führer had sought refuge after a split in the Nazi leadership. It challenged the official German claim that Hess was insane by pointing out that if this were the case he could hardly have made the long flight to Britain. "I have nothing to add at present to the statement on the wireless," the Prime Minister announced, refusing to be drawn on Hess during Tuesday questions in the House of Commons. "I think this is one of those cases where the imagination is somewhat baffled by the facts as they present themselves."[59]

"Churchill has little to say about the real motives," Dr. Goebbels noted with relief, observing that the British Prime Minister "has little use for talk of peace." Appalled by the "confused, schoolboy amateurism" of the letters Hess left behind, which he found "littered with ill-digested occult theory," Goebbels branded his former colleague a "failed Messiah," inspired by the "evil geniuses" of Professor Haushofer, his wife, his adjutants and his doctors. Yet Goebbels was most puzzled that although Hitler "condemns Hess in the harshest terms" he still "grants him a degree of realism." His advice to the Führer was that they should "stand together and keep calm." Ribbentrop was therefore dispatched to Rome to reassure Mussolini. Goebbels then flew back to Berlin to take command of what he anticipated would be a fiercely fought propaganda battle.[60]

"If I was the English Propaganda Minister, I would know exactly what to do," Goebbels bragged, laying down his own strategy to "wait and see" what salvos the British fired before responding. "What Hess wanted to say he put down very precisely in his letters," Goebbels told his staff. "If anything else is now put into his mouth, beyond those intentions, then it must be fabrication." To his astonishment and relief, not only was there no fabrication, but the British government refused to explain why Hess had risked his life to fly all the way to Scotland.[61]

HESS, DESERTING HITLER, FLIES TO SCOTLAND; BERLIN REPORTED HIM MISSING, the New York Times blared across the eight front-page columns of its Tuesday edition. It quoted the British Ambassador as saying that Hess had fled "because he saw the writing on the wall." But the predicted split in the Nazi hierarchy was wishful thinking inspired by the British government. Americans, thanks to an uncensored U.P.I. wire report, also learned on the same day the story broke that Hess had landed near the Duke of Hamilton's estate claiming he had brought peace terms that could end the war.[62]

"Yes, the maggot seems to be in the apple," the Prime Minister was quoted in the *New York Times* as having said when he ordered that the Hess story was to be exploited to the maximum. Churchill's double-edged remark could more appropriately have been applied to the opportunity that was being lost to capitalize on the Hess affair because of continuing pressure from Foreign Office officials, who had prevailed on the Ministry of Information to issue a directive to the British media not to speculate that the Nazi-Soviet Pact had prompted Hess's flight, because this was "a dangerous line" which encouraged those "who might want to stop the war because of their fear of the spread of communism."[63]

"We are dealing with dumb amateurs," Goebbels crowed with delight. "What we would do if the positions were reversed!" His own strategy, to "put a bar on all news at home and have the real facts discussed abroad," was working well.[64]

"Whatever he is, Hess is good news for England," the *New York Times* had declared. Its Wednesday edition devoted over 150 column inches to the story, ranging from reports from Berlin predicting a purge of the Nazi Party to predictions from London that the Prime Minister himself was going to hear the "fantastic story" from Hess's own lips. It also reported the government-promoted story of an R.A.F. Spitfire "stitching the fabric of Rudolf Hess's Messerschmitt with bullet holes." The gun battle was said to have "nearly robbed Britain of the war's most sensational prisoner."[65]

Most significant was the fact that the *New York Times* was the first to reveal that Hitler's deputy had flown to Scotland to see the Duke of Hamilton, who was identified with "the now condemned Anglo-German Fellowship" and "acquainted with Hess." But the British government's reluctance to exploit what the *New York Times* had dubbed the "story without counterpart in history" had surrendered the initiative. Goebbels picked up the slack to begin "sowing dark hints and denials." That afternoon the Bremen radio station reported that Hess had made his flight "under the hallucination that by undertaking a personal step in connection with the Englishmen with whom he was formerly acquainted it might be possible to bring about an understanding between Germany and Britain." Without mentioning the Duke of Hamilton, the communiqué hinted that the Deputy Führer had been "deliberately lured into a trap." In what appears to have been a final bid to test the British attitude to a peace feeler, the radio station emphasized: "Hess was better acquainted than anyone else with the peace proposals which the Führer had made with such sincerity."[66]

The German confirmation of Hamilton's involvement exacerbated the three-way dispute between the Prime Minister, the Ministry of Information and the Foreign Office over how to respond. "Hess is the bane of my life and all my time is wasted," Cadogan noted. Egged on by the Minister of Information, Churchill had decided to "make a statement tomorrow about Hess" to end a suspiciously deafening official hush. "What he dictated was all wrong," Cadogan wrote. "Hitler would heave sighs of relief," he advised the Prime Minister, because the Germans would say: "Then it is true what our dear Führer has told us. Our beloved Rudolf has gone to make peace." They might think Hess "rather silly" but they "won't think him a traitor, which is what I *want* them to *fear*." But the Prime Minister "brushed him aside." Churchill was determined to have his own way, telling Duff Cooper to return to Downing Street at midnight to collect a statement.[67]

The Prime Minister changed his mind after dining with Lord Beaverbrook, who was dead-set against making any statement. The Minister of Information came back to Downing Street as instructed, only to find himself in the middle of a three-way row. At 1.30 a.m. the Prime Minister, in "a raging temper," telephoned Eden, who had already retired, to read over his proposed statement on Hess. The Foreign Secretary was also not in favour of saying anything, "urging that the Germans be kept in the dark." Churchill insisted on going ahead and told Eden to draft an alternative. He recalled how he "struggled out of bed and produced it and telephoned it." Although Beaverbrook approved it, it was too anodyne for the Prime Minister. "Which was it to be, his original statement or no statement?" Churchill demanded. "I replied 'no statement'," Eden wrote, recalling how the Prime Minister had barked down the line "All right, no statement" before crashing his receiver down.[68]

"Now this is bad, since the belief will get around that we are hiding something and we shall be blamed in the Ministry," lamented Duff Cooper's parliamentary secretary Harold Nicolson. As a journalist Nicolson was apprehensive at leaving the initiative to Dr. Goebbels. "The real fact is that we cannot get maximum propaganda value out of this incident both at home and abroad," he complained. "I feel a terrible lack of central authority in all this." His fears were justified by *The Times'* headline, HESS'S 'NORDIC MISSION,' next morning. From a report that echoed the German broadcast British readers learned for the first time that Hitler's errant deputy "thought that the Duke of Hamilton could lead a group against 'the Churchill gang of warmongers'."[69]

The remarkable irony of the Hess affair is that it was Goebbels who revealed the truth about the peace mission. This suited his purpose because it threatened to expose cracks in Churchill's claim to be leading a nation united behind him in a fight to the death with Hitler. The Prime Minister was not unmindful of the damage that such stories might do in the United States. The sensational news of the Hess "peace" flight had already prompted Senator Burton K. Wheeler, the Republican leader of the isolationists on Capitol Hill, to call on the President to "seize the opportunity to negotiate peace out of the European war." Now there were reports from Washington that "until the significance of the flight will have been fully appraised," Roosevelt had judged it politic to postpone a speech he had scheduled for that Thursday, in which it had been predicted he would announce that the U.S. Navy was about to extend its area of operations into the eastern Atlantic to give badly needed assistance to the British convoys' battle against the U-boats.[70]

Churchill wanted to give no excuse for resurrecting criticism or revealing that there might be a dormant "peace party" in Parliament so soon after the no-confidence motion in the House of Commons. Roosevelt himself must have had some doubts about what lay behind the fantastic headlines. "If Hess is talking it would be very valuable to public opinion over here if he can be persuaded to tell your people what Hitler has said about the United States," the President had cabled to the "Former naval person" the day before. He wanted to know anything that might have been said about Germany's plans for "commerce, infiltration, military domination, encirclement of the United States." The Hess flight "has captured the American imagination," he told Churchill, advising him that "the story should be kept alive for just as many days, or even weeks as possible."[71]

The Prime Minister responded by directing the Foreign Office to make a "fairly full digest of the conversational parts" of Kirkpatrick's interviews with Hess, "stressing particularly the points mentioned by me in the statement I prepared but did not deliver." Before the text was transmitted, Churchill added his comment that if Hess "expected to contact members of a 'peace movement' in England whom he would help oust the present government," then "this is an encouraging sign of [the] ineptitude of [the] German Intelligence Service." He agreed, however, with Roosevelt's suggestion and would "let the Press have a good run for a bit" to keep the Germans guessing.[72]

A surviving White House memorandum shows that the President had hoped the British would obtain from Hess some propaganda ammunition he could use to stir American public opinion against Germany. Its writer suggested that such information was best obtained by skirting the more fastidious State Department officials.

The memo proposed the matter should be raised in a "telephone job between the President and Churchill." Since these transatlantic conversations were not recorded, it remains a matter of speculation whether the tête-à-tête between the two leaders was the reason for the overnight shift in the Prime Minister's position on Hess.[73]

At Thursday's midday meeting of the War Cabinet the Prime Minister announced that he had thought better of making a statement in Parliament. "P.M. in very good form – has got over his tantrums and admits our views are correct," Cadogan noted with satisfaction. The Cabinet minutes show Churchill explaining that he had decided to "wait a little while." He had decided Hess was to be treated as a "prisoner of State," to be kept in isolation and allowed only visitors permitted by the Foreign Office. The Minister of Information was instructed to "give guidance to the Press to refrain from any sentimental references lauding Hess, and to include reminders of his bad record as one of the Nazi leaders." The Cabinet also agreed that the Secretary of State for Air would "see the Duke of Hamilton" to discuss how to explain away his "connection with the affair."[74]

Immediately after the War Cabinet broke up, Lord Beaverbrook hurried off to Claridge's Hotel to chair a hastily summoned luncheon of newspaper editors and lobby correspondents. To everyone's surprise he announced that the Prime Minister was not, after all, going to make the anticipated statement, and he appealed to the Fleet Street editors to help spread "as much speculation, rumour and discussion about Hess as possible." He urged them to emphasize that "Hess fled for his life owing to a serious split in the inmost circle of the Nazi party." Cecil King, editor of the trenchant left-wing *Daily Mirror*, objected. He said they were being "invited to flog the dead horse," pointing out that government sources had released a "good deal of stuff about the Duke of Hamilton and so made it clear that the German story of a one-man peace bid is substantially correct." He said he had been personally assured by the Minister of Information that "Hess wrote a letter to the Duke of Hamilton which reached this country last September."[75]

Declassified Ministry of Information files confirm the muddle and conflict over managing the Hess story. The Duke of Hamilton now found himself the centre of a storm of slanderous speculation. He flew back to London on Thursday afternoon to see Cadogan. "Wanted to see the King," the Permanent Secretary noted. "I advised him to see the P.M. first." Churchill was unavailable, but the next day Hamilton received a summons to lunch with the King at Windsor Castle. "George VI was very curious to know what had happened," according to Hamilton. Three days later the Duke went to the Foreign Office again, "looking more and more like a Golden Spaniel," Cadogan commented waspishly. Churchill appears to

431

have wanted to distance himself from the Duke – who described him in his memoir as an "old friend" – and granted him only a "ten-minute interview." This took place on 20 May, in Churchill's car as it sped the short distance between Downing Street and Buckingham Palace. "What do you tell your wife if a prostitute throws her arms around your neck?" the Duke asked the Prime Minister, complaining at his treatment in the press. According to Hamilton, Churchill roared with laughter and ordered that "the press were not to be told a word."[76]

"This matter has now become so entangled in a mesh of half-truths, that I suppose it is impossible to make a clear and true statement," minuted an exasperated official at the Ministry of Information. Some redress for Hamilton was arranged by the Air Minister, who told the House of Commons that the Duke had "never met" and "never been in correspondence" with Hess. The Ministry of Information ducked the issue of its previous official statement by referring to "true facts" given in the statement of Sir Archibald Sinclair.[77]

This ministerial sidestepping encouraged the Communist Party of Great Britain to attack the Duke in a pamphlet which cited his membership of the Anglo-German Fellowship, together with his association with the "industrialists, bankers and aristocrats who have helped build up Hitler," as proof of his "friendship" with Hess. Hamilton immediately sued for libel. Harry Pollitt, the Communist Party Chairman, gleefully picked up the gauntlet, announcing his intention of calling Hess as a witness for his defence. The prospect of the public cross-examination of Hitler's deputy caused apoplexy in the Foreign Office. Cadogan urged the Prime Minister to order Hamilton to drop his case, but Churchill expressed reluctance to deprive even a Duke of the right to clear his name. After months of protracted legal wrangling, it was the Communist Party that finally climbed down. In an out-of-court settlement, Pollitt offered an apology, withdrew the libel and paid substantial damages.[78]

At the end of the week the government's "mesh of half-truths" and lack of consistency had already damaged its efforts to exploit the Hess affair, even before the War Cabinet took the decision to move the prisoner south from Glasgow. The Prime Minister had approved the War Office plan to lodge him temporarily in the Tower of London "pending his place of confinement being prepared at Aldershot." His treatment "will become less indulgent," Churchill minuted, ordering that Hess was to be kept "in the strictest seclusion"; the Prime Minister had to be personally informed "before any visitors are allowed." "The public will not stand any pampering" of "this notorious war criminal," Churchill cautioned, underlining in his scarlet ink, *except for intelligence purposes.*"[79]

The decision to move Hess overnight by rail from Glasgow to the Tower was ostensibly ordered by the Prime Minister for symbolic reasons. It also offered other possibilities. Churchill even appears to have considered bringing Hess to Downing Street in the hope that this would encourage him to open up. This is clear from a memorandum prepared by his private secretary on 18 May which advised that B.B.C. engineers could use the microphone circuits already installed in the Cabinet Room at No. 10 and the Cabinet War Room to set up "concealed apparatus whereby an interview with Rudolph [sic] Hess could be listened to by people outside the room." Whether the Prime Minister or the Foreign Secretary intended to confront Hess is not clear, but Churchill certainly considered it, because he marked the memorandum: "Keep handy for tomorrow" – a reference to the Monday meeting of the War Cabinet.[80]

The behind-the-scenes rows between the Foreign Office and the Ministry of Information destroyed any chance of making propaganda capital out of the Hess affair. Even before the end of the week, disturbing reports were coming in from the military security censors that revealed a growing number of letters "full of distrust and suspicion." Some servicemen wrote home expressing their belief that there "may be a collusion between our 'big-wigs' and the German ones." "There is something fishy behind it," one Scottish soldier commented. "I think his arrival was not so unexpected as we are supposed to think," said another letter.[81]

"The Hess affair is now at an end," Dr. Goebbels had declared smugly at the end of the week. "This is how quickly things happen these days," he observed as he promised himself that he would "stir the bloodhounds of the international press into cry" and bury the Hess affair by giving the world's media something else to write about. His boast was not an empty one. By the end of the week Hess had been supplanted from the headlines by reminders of the looming disaster facing the British forces in the Middle East. The encircled garrison at Tobruk still clung stubbornly to the battered North African port, but across the narrow seas in Greece German troops were assembling for the airborne invasion of Crete.[82]

By 19 May the pressure of events in the Middle East relegated discussion of Hitler's deputy to the bottom of the Cabinet agenda. Cadogan recorded that Churchill was "still hankering after his stupid statement about Hess," which he "insisted on reading with great gusto." The War Cabinet was not amused. As Cadogan put it, they were "*unanimous* against it and I think he has dropped the idea." Churchill decided that "Hess had already received so much attention in the Press that public opinion would favour giving the topic a rest." But he said they should go on "maintaining the anxiety of the German leaders" by planting stories that Hess was "talking freely" and "spilling Hitler's military secrets," even though this was discounted by "official" German sources; Berlin had repeatedly insisted that as Nazi Party chief "Hess had no knowledge of the war plans of the military leaders."[83]

Any statement at this critical juncture by Churchill would have run the risk of raising a discussion of peace terms at the time when Britain was confronted by the greatest military crisis since Dunkirk. Just how serious this was becoming emerges in the telegram the Prime Minister sent Roosevelt two days later on 21 May.

"There is anxiety here," Churchill admitted. "We are at a climacteric of the war when enormous crystallizations are in suspense but imminent." Noting the battle raging for Crete and the launching of the British action in Syria, and the "heavy cost" of the Battle of the Atlantic, he appealed for more support from the Americans to save the millions of tons of U.S.-built war supplies being lost to the U-boats. Concluding his assessment of the severity of the crisis facing Britain ten days after Hess's arrival, he concluded stoutly: "Whatever happens you may be sure we shall fight on and I am sure we can at least save ourselves. But what is the good of that?"[84]

We now know that the imminent climacteric Churchill was alluding to was not crystallizing in Crete, Syria or on the Atlantic, but in Germany's imminent attack on Russia. Yet how could Churchill be certain that the dramatic turning-point in the war was now at hand, when he had only been able to hint at it in his House of Commons speech of 7 May?

The Hess mission, as has now become clear, was the factor that provided the Prime Minister with irrefutable proof that Hitler, like Napoleon before him, was about to save Britain by dashing his military might against the boundless Russian hinterland. While only fragmentary clues surface in the British Hess files so far declassified, significant missing pieces of the jigsaw have come to light in United States and Soviet archives. For long it has been a matter of speculation that some of the pieces of the puzzle were held by the Russians, because the Hess mission was of such vital importance to Stalin. The Soviet archives were long considered even more impenetrable than the files of MI5 and MI6, but one of the more extraordinary results of Mikhail Gorbachev's *Glasnost* policy resulted in the Soviet Union's decision to produce their Hess file, whose British counterpart is still locked away.

The three-inch-thick card bound file No. 20566, "Black Bertha," had lain gathering dust in the vaults of the K.G.B. until sections of the N.K.V.D.'s dossier on Hess were made available to the author. In an unprecedented move, the first archival documents the K.G.B. has ever made available to western historians were produced, and they reveal that Stalin's well-placed spies inside the Foreign Office were keeping the Kremlin fully apprised of the true significance of the mission of Hitler's deputy.

Chapter 17

Spravka—Top Secret

On 14 May 1941 the Russian cipher clerks at N.K.V.D. headquarters in Moscow's Dzherzhinski Square decoded cryptogram No. 376 received from the Soviet Embassy in London. The Top Secret telegram had been transmitted in the one-time cipher pad system used by the Soviet intelligence services, which had not yielded to the British codebreakers who had been trying for fourteen years to penetrate the traffic emanating from the Russian Embassy overlooking Kensington Gardens. Unlike the American ciphers, the Soviet system had defied the best efforts of Bletchley Park because each message was encrypted using a fresh code sheet.

The British had no more success with cryptogram No. 376 than with any of its thousands of predecessors. If they had broken into its meaningless jumble of letters and numbers they would have uncovered the ring of Soviet "moles" who had burrowed up from Cambridge University into the very heart of Whitehall and the secret services.

This *Spravka*, as paraphrases made for security of original cryptograms are called in Soviet intelligence terminology, originated from Anatole Gorski and was sent after a meeting with Kim Philby. Known by his code name of "Henry," Gorski was controller of the network of Cambridge-educated spies that included Guy Burgess, then at the B.B.C., Donald Maclean and John Cairncross at the Foreign Office, and Anthony Blunt, the future royal art curator, who was then in B Division of MI5 working alongside "Tar" Robertson. Philby was not in London at the time, but at a Special Operations

Executive (S.O.E.) training camp at Beaulieu instructing exiled Europeans in guerrilla warfare. The 14 May cryptogram, which begins "VADIM reported from London," not only discloses for the first time the cryptonym of Ivan Chichayev, the N.K.V.D. Resident in London, but also reveals that he relayed from Gorski information obtained on Hess from Philby and other Cambridge contacts in Whitehall.[1]

> "Information received from SONNCHEN is that HESS arrived in England declaring he intended first of all to appeal to HAMILTON who he had become friendly with in connection with their common interest in aviation competitions in 1934. HAMILTON is a member of the so called Cliveden set. HESS landed near the castle of HAMILTON. KIRKPATRICK, the first person of the SAKULOK to identify HESS who tells him he has brought peace offers. We do not yet know the details of these peace proposals (Kirkpatrick is the ex-counsellor of the British Embassy in Berlin)."

"SONNCHEN" – the German diminutive "Little Sun" – was Philby's cryptonym; "SAKULOK" (Russian for "backalley") was the N.K.V.D. cryptonym for the Foreign Office. This 14 May *Spravka* shows that Philby must have been very fast off the mark in tapping his Foreign Office informants on Hess. In order for his controller Gorski to have made his report to Moscow Centre, Philby must have been in touch with his contacts at least twenty-four hours earlier, or possibly even before the German announcement was broadcast. When the report reached Moscow, the N.K.V.D. – as this *Spravka* records – reacted by instructing a Mrs. Ribkyna to notify their Residents in Berlin, London, Stockholm, America and Rome: "Try to find out all details of the proposals."

What the Kremlin urgently needed to know was whether the Hess peace mission was genuine, whether it was made with Hitler's approval, and whether the British were likely to consider negotiating a peace.

During the next few days Soviet agents responded to the call. One in the United States codenamed "GIT" reported from Washington that "Hess came to Britain in full agreement with Hitler to start peace negotiations because it was impossible for Hitler to offer peace openly without damage to German morale, so he chose Hess as his secret emissary." More credence was obviously given to agent "JUN," who telegraphed via the N.K.V.D. Resident in Berlin: "Chief of the American Department of the Ministry of Foreign Propaganda Eizendorf said that Hess is in a perfect state of mind and flew out to Britain with a definite assignment and proposal from the German government." Another Berlin agent, "FRANKFURTER," reported via the same secret channel, citing a staff general of O.K.W. who

436

said that "Hess's action is not a flight, but an undertaking made with the knowledge of Hitler with the mission of proposing peace to Britain." This view was echoed by "EXTERN" – considered to be a specially reliable agent by the N.K.V.D. "Hess," he reported, "was sent by Hitler to conduct peace negotiations and in the event of Britain's agreement Germany will immediately fall on the U.S.S.R."[2]

The reports from their agents in Germany, members of the Soviet underground network known as the *Rote Kapelle* (Red Orchestra), led the N.K.V.D. intelligence analysts to some disturbing conclusions. The mosaic they pieced together at Moscow Centre produced, according to Oleg Tsarev, who has researched the relevant archive files, a scenario that worried Stalin. "The Hess flight was not the act of a madman, nor an attempt to save his life from an intrigue," Tsarev asserts, "but the realization of a secret conspiracy by the Nazi leadership to strike a peace with Britain before opening the war with the Soviet Union."[3]

This was the assessment in the digest prepared for Stalin by the N.K.V.D., who were endowed with a special authority because of the penetration achieved by their agents into the German and British governments. The Soviet dictator considered Philby particularly reliable. Hungry for stolen secrets, which he believed had a special credibility, Stalin liked to receive their reports first-hand, dismissing as "dangerous guesswork" the conjectures of his intelligence chiefs. "Don't tell me what you think," Stalin would interject. "Give me the facts and the source."[4]

Stalin, who credited the British leaders with being as cunning as himself, had always harboured a pathological suspicion that Britain and Germany might eventually join ranks to turn on Russia. This fear was rekindled by the timing of the Hess flight, which coincided with the strain being put on the Nazi-Soviet Pact by Hitler's demands for a larger share of Russia's food, oil and war materials to feed the increasing appetite of the German war machine. Since their frosty meeting in Berlin the previous November, Vyacheslav Molotov, the People's Commissar for Foreign Affairs, had been involved in a fruitless round of negotiations with Ribbentrop over the terms of their joint trade agreement. A month before Hitler, on 18 December 1940, gave the directive for Operation Barbarossa, the *Rote Kapelle* sent the first warning of German intentions to attack Russia. In March the Kremlin analysts had interpreted the accelerating build-up of German forces in Poland as yet another example of Hitler's bullying diplomatic tactics. Many western diplomats shared this view, including the Foreign Office analysts in London.

Churchill, however, thought otherwise. Intelligence rumours had been reaching London ever since the Fall of France a year earlier that pointed to an eventual German attack on Russia. Originally scheduled for mid-May 1941, Barbarossa was delayed by a full month when the Wehrmacht went to Italy's aid against the advancing British forces in Greece and North Africa. The southward movement of German forces into the Balkans had also served as useful camouflage. So did "training operations" announced that spring in Poland for troops supposedly soon to be redeployed in the West for the renewed attempt to invade England. Yet by March 1941 evidence of an accelerating German build-up along the border of the Soviet Union had come in from a wide range of sources. And the Prime Minister, who was no less avid a devotee of intelligence than Stalin, had devoured them all to come up with his own conclusions of what was going on in Poland.[5]

"Up until March 1, I was not convinced that Hitler was resolved on mortal war with Russia, nor how near it was," Churchill wrote, admitting that he shared the belief of British military intelligence that "Hitler and Stalin would bargain at our expense rather than war upon each other." By April, however, he had changed his mind, convinced by intelligence from the British codebreaking operation which – with help from French and Polish intelligence officers – had succeeded in breaking into the German cipher traffic encrypted by the *Enigma* machines. To safeguard the potential war-winning weapon, only limited circulation was given to the intelligence obtained from the *Enigma* decrypts, which were codenamed ULTRA.[6]

Access to the "geese that laid the golden eggs and never cackled," as Churchill fondly called ULTRA, was restricted to the Prime Minister and his top military advisers. ULTRA remained a classified secret until 1974, so when Churchill wrote his own account after the war he could not reveal that an *Enigma* decrypt of the last week in March 1941 ordering another Panzer Division to Poland had "illuminated the whole Eastern scene like a lightning flash." Three days after receiving this Bletchley report, he passed, without revealing its source, a "short and cryptic" warning that was to be personally relayed to Stalin by the British Ambassador in Moscow, Sir Stafford Cripps.[7]

Stalin discounted these "facts" as yet another British provocation, because he refused to believe that Hitler would turn on him and open up a two-front war while Britain remained undefeated. British military intelligence analysts, who had direct access to ULTRA, also took this view. Their 1 April report concluded that the eastward move of German tanks was simply to "exert military pressure on Russia" and "there is *as yet no reason* to believe the numerous reports that Germany intends to attack Russia in the near future."[8]

The Prime Minister disagreed. His instinctive forecast was sharpened by April *Enigma* decrypts which revealed a growing concentration of German ground and air units in eastern Poland. Even as late as 22 May the Chiefs of Staff were still advising the War Cabinet that although Moscow-Berlin relations were "tense," reports of a rapprochement indicated that "Hitler has not finally decided whether to obtain his wishes by persuasion or force of arms."[9]

So when Hess unwittingly parachuted himself into the middle of the British strategic debate, Churchill concluded that the interrogation of Hitler's deputy would resolve the question once and for all. Declassified British files show that the Prime Minister personally directed the effort to "suck Hess dry" for intelligence. "I cannot doubt that there will be deep misgivings in the German Armed Forces about what he may say," Churchill advised Roosevelt on 17 May. Pumping Hess about Hitler's intentions towards Russia was one of the primary tasks for Kirkpatrick, according to Robert Bruce Lockhart, head of the Foreign Office's Political Intelligence Department. But he recorded that the diplomat was not well suited for the mission, because he had "no knowledge or understanding of psychology."[10]

Kirkpatrick nonetheless set out to discover what Hess had to say about German intentions towards the Soviet Union and in the early hours of 13 May tried to "draw him on the subject of Hitler's attitude toward Russia." When Hess announced that one of his preconditions for peace was that Hitler insisted on being given a "free hand in Europe," Kirkpatrick asked whether the Soviet Union was included in Europe or Asia.[11]

"In Europe," Hess replied, unaware that he was being led into a trap. When Kirkpatrick reasoned that therefore Germany would not attack Russia, Hess let only the cat's tail out of the bag by his admission that "Germany has certain demands to make of Russia, which would have to be satisfied either by direct negotiation *or as a result of war*." This is all that appears in the only available account of Kirkpatrick's interrogation, the version prepared for the Nuremberg tribunal. Significantly it also has Hess insisting that "there was no foundation for the rumours now being spread that Hitler was contemplating an early attack on Russia."[12]

Hess's response is suspiciously anachronistic. How could he have been privy to the debate in British Intelligence about whether Germany was going to attack Russia? It seems to have been deliberately inserted in the 1945 Nuremberg version to allay Soviet suspicions that Hess did betray Barbarossa to the British. This could also explain why there are no contemporary versions of

Kirkpatrick's report in the Prime Minister's files. Yet he must have been supplied with them, since Bruce Lockhart recorded that Churchill, "who hopes (perhaps too wishfully) to obtain valuable military information out of Hess has taken complete control."[13]

Kirkpatrick's published memoir has a much more demonstrative denial, with Hess insisting it was "out of the question" for Hitler to attack Russia. "I asked him again and again," Kirkpatrick wrote, "but he assured me that Hitler was a man who stuck scrupulously to his engagements." His book details how on 14 May he started shortly after 8.30 a.m. and "spent the rest of the morning preparing an account of Hess's statement which I dictated to a charming and competent WAAF stenographer . . ." The report was flown to London that afternoon. The two-and-a-half-page "Certified Mimeo copy" released by the Foreign Office in 1945 seems hardly to justify a morning's work for a "competent" stenographer, suggesting that the full – and still secret – report contains many more pages. Kirkpatrick also recounts how the Foreign Secretary ordered him next day to cut short a visit with the Duke to the aircraft carrier H.M.S. *Victorious* because "it was imperative that we should pursue our conversations with Hess."[14]

Yet the Nuremberg version of Kirkpatrick's 14 May interrogation, which is barely a page and a half long, does not mention Russia at all, and deals mainly with Hess's prediction that Germany would win the U-boat war. The only record released of the final Kirkpatrick interview on 15 May is only a single page. In it Hess denies that Hitler had any hostile intentions towards Ireland and the United States and requests two named Germans from British internment camps as translators to help him in peace negotiations. Again there is no mention of the Soviet Union, although it was the issue on which Churchill was burning with impatience to learn just how much Hess knew about Hitler's attack plan. The Duke of Hamilton, in a memorandum he prepared in 1945 in anticipation of questioning by the press during a visit to the United States for the R.A.F., also insisted that Hess "*made no remark* at all on Russia." Only when pressed had Hess "declared that Germany had certain demands to make on Russia," which, according to the Duke's rather too dismissive statement, "were not urgent." It is therefore noteworthy that even this denial was marked for deletion by the Foreign Office, another indication that anything Hess had said on the subject was considered taboo.[15]

"You will see that very little of this document touches on Hess's purpose," the Foreign Office letter accompanying the Duke's report advised the Prime Minister cryptically. Churchill, nonetheless, did not approve – either of the censored statement or of Hamilton's trip to the United States. He insisted that the Duke "should not, repeat not, undertake this task," because he did not want the Hess affair "stirred up at the present moment." The reason he gave is especially revealing. "The Russians are very suspicious of the Hess episode," he wrote, citing his "lengthy argument with Marshal Stalin about it in Moscow," when Stalin "steadfastly maintained that *Hess had been invited over by our Secret Service.*"[16]

Why should Churchill have been so sensitive about what Hess said on Russia when his concern is not borne out by what appears in the Kirkpatrick interrogation records supplied in evidence at Nuremberg? Without exception they all emphasize *how little* Hess knew about Hitler's strategic aims, particularly regarding the attack on Russia. The Prime Minister's extreme sensitivity could only be justified if he believed it was necessary to conceal even in 1945 *how much* the British had found out from Hess about Hitler's intended invasion of the Soviet Union.

This information had not yet been obtained "up until the evening of 14 May," according to Philby's Foreign Office contacts. This was the first item mentioned in his second report on Hess in cryptogram No. 338 from London received in Moscow on 18 May 1941. A photocopy of the original *Spravka* in the K.G.B. archives, cites Vadim's source as "information received by SONNCHEN [Philby] during a personal conversation with his friend Tom Dupree (the deputy chief of the Press Department of the Foreign Office) and as yet unverified." Dupree, who was serving in Madrid in 1936 and could have met Philby there, was not given a cryptonym, an indication that the N.K.V.D. did not regard him as an asset under Soviet control. Nonetheless, the information he supplied gave Moscow Centre cause for concern.

"During his conversation with officers of British military intelligence Hess declared that he went to Britain to confirm a compromise peace which was to stop the deprivation of the two belligerents and preserve the British Empire as a stabilizing force," Dupree reported, also relaying that "Hess declared his continued loyalty to Hitler."

"Beaverbrook and Eden visited Hess although this is officially denied," stated Dupree – a fact which added special significance to his other piece of information. "In his conversation with Kirkpatrick HESS declared that the war between two Nordic nations was criminal and that he believed that there was a powerful anti-Churchill party in England which wanted peace and would receive a powerful stimulus in the struggle for peace with his arrival."[17]

Anticipating that this would be Stalin's principal worry, Philby had helpfully quizzed Dupree "whether a British-German Union against the U.S.S.R. was what Hess wanted." The answer, as it was relayed by VADIM, cannot have given much comfort to the Kremlin, because Philby had cryptically said: "that is exactly what he [Dupree and the Foreign Office] wanted to get from Hess." This report also revealed that Hess had written a letter to the Duke of Hamilton "before Hess's arrival" which was "surely intercepted by the British counter-intelligence service," who had evidently not sent it on to the addressee for "some six weeks" and that Hamilton "within three days of receiving it passed it on to the counter-intelligence service." Philby's second report also noted that Churchill had been asked in Parliament who was detaining Hess. The Prime Minister's announcement that "Hess was my prisoner" was interpreted as "forewarning the opposition [to him] against any intrigues with Hess." Philby, however, advised "that it was not an appropriate time for peace negotiations." But he hazarded the opinion "that as the course of the war developed Hess could become the centre of intrigues for a compromise peace and would therefore be useful for the peace party in England and for Hitler."[18]

This *Spravka* is annotated by hand that a copy was put in the SONNCHEN [Philby] file with another to "Black Bertha." This was the codename the N.K.V.D. had assigned in 1941 to file No. 205666. Page 14 of this dossier contains an intriguing report from a Soviet German source that "Hess's past is very scandalous. He was a member of a group of '*Schwüle*' [homosexuals] calling themselves 'HOT,' among whom he was known as 'Schwarze Berta' [Black Bertha]. This was his nickname in those circles not only in Munich but also in Berlin." Hess's marriage in 1927 to Ilse Pröl, his friend of six years' standing, apparently "did not help his reputation," since, according to the report, "malicious Berliners continued to refer to Hess as 'she' and his wife as 'he'."[19]

This reference to Hess's homosexual connections appears to relate to the early days, before the homosexual Ernst Röhm was butchered in 1934. It is also significant that it was the British Foreign Office official Dupree who was the source for Philby's assertion that both Beaverbrook and Eden had visited Hess during the week after his arrival. None of the papers so far declassified substantiates this report, nor do any documents discovered in either Beaverbrook's or Eden's private papers. Such an inference could, however, be drawn from the Foreign Secretary's 15 May note that he had been "forgiven" by Churchill for dissuading him "from giving an account to the House of what Hess said," and that Churchill had "admitted that Max & I had been right." Then there is the curious anomaly that Eden penned his notes about Hess's arrival in the February section of his diary, raising a suspicion that, unless the Foreign Secretary was incredibly disorganized, this was a contrived afterword rather than an accurate contemporary reference.[20]

What Philby's second message does confirm is that even the

British intelligence officers conducting their surreptitious interrogations of Hess had apparently yet to report that he had let the
whole cat out of the bag regarding Russia. Yet Churchill, even
if he had not yet persuaded his chiefs of staff that the German
attack was imminent, was determined that Hess should be made
to disgorge the information which could justify his passing a
positive warning to Stalin. "P.M. rang up to ask whether I had
report of I.K.'s talk with Hess today," Cadogan recorded on 15 May,
observing that Churchill was "furious" to learn that Kirkpatrick
had not yet reported. It was 5 p.m. before Cadogan telephoned
the Prime Minister and reported that Kirkpatrick had "nothing
fresh."[21]

Since ULTRA had already disclosed that the Germans were under
way by that week to send in paratroops against the British forces
holding Crete, the only other source for the vital strategic intelligence concerning Russia was Hess. This explains why Kirkpatrick,
in his telephoned report of 13 May, had warned Cadogan "that Hess
was not very well informed on [the] German strategical plans" and
"would not open up very far with anyone evidently speaking for
the government." He suggested that if Hess "could be put in touch
with perhaps a member of the Conservative party who would give
the impression that he was tempted by the idea of getting rid of
the present administration, it might be that he would open up more
freely."[22]

"P.M. agreed we ought to draw Hess by pretending to negotiate, and he came out with my idea of J. Simon for the part,"
Cadogan recorded in a self-congratulatory note. Lord Simon, who
had met Hitler in 1935 when he visited Berlin as Foreign Secretary,
might well be regarded by Hess as sympathetic, since he was
one of the appeasers. The idea of using the Lord Chancellor as
"pseudo-negotiator" appealed to the Prime Minister. He "roared
with laughter," declaring Simon to be "the very man." The Lord
Chancellor himself was less than amused on 27 May when Eden
put the idea up to him, suggesting that he should drop hints that
would suggest to Hess that Simon was at loggerheads with the
Prime Minister.[23]

"All this will be kept most secret," Eden minuted to Churchill,
"and only Cadogan and I in this Office are aware of the project."
Nonetheless it took Cadogan more than a week of diplomatic solicitation to persuade the reluctant peer to cooperate. "Lord Simon
has now finally agreed to take on the job," the Permanent Secretary
noted on 4 June 1941. "Good," the Prime Minister scrawled on the
handwritten note passed to him by the Foreign Secretary.[24]

The "prisoner of state" had by now been transferred to specially
prepared quarters in Mytchett Place, which had been codenamed
"Camp Z." The former officers' residence in the countryside near
Aldershot was sealed off from the nearby army bases by high fences

and barricades of sharp barbed wire. Hidden microphones had been installed to record every word Hess uttered, even in his sleep. Major Frank Foley and Lieutenant Thomas Kendrick, two of the leading German specialists in MI6, had been detailed to act as his guard/companions, with instructions to coax him into talking as much as possible.[25]

"We'll wait and see what 'C's' men report," Cadogan had suggested. The Prime Minister, chafing to know whether the MI6 officers had extracted from Hess the all-important strategic intelligence about Russia, called for a full report from the head of the secret service. This brought Cadogan's assurance on 6 June that "full records" were kept of all Hess's conversations with the MI6 officers but he had "stuck to the line which he took in the original interviews." Since the transcripts were in German, "presumably the Prime Minister would not wish to read them." Cadogan expressed his own doubts that Hess possessed "any detailed technical knowledge of military affairs." He hoped that the forthcoming visit by Lord Simon might persuade him to "confess that he is on a mission from Hitler – if indeed that is the case."[26]

Three days later, on 9 June, Simon and Kirkpatrick arrived at the closely guarded gates of Camp Z and presented passes that identified them as Dr. Guthrie and Dr. Mackenzie, two psychiatrists. Hess, who had been informed that Simon was coming, was eagerly awaiting the "high political personage" in his Luftwaffe uniform and jackboots. The verbatim account of Hess's idiosyncratic interpretation of Anglo-German relations portrayed Hitler as a fatherly figure who had been forced into war by Britain. Hess had waxed mawkish about how he shared the Führer's determination to stop the war and avert the terrible vision of an "endless row of children's coffins with mothers crying behind." At the same time he spared no threats that the Luftwaffe would rain doom and destruction on Britain from the skies if his peace embassy was rejected. The news that the pride of the German navy, the battleship *Bismarck*, had been cornered and sunk after an epic chase in the Atlantic had in no way shaken Hess's confidence in ultimate German victory. He repeatedly assured Simon that the U-boats and the Luftwaffe would eventually starve and batter Britain into a conquered wasteland.[27]

"This cudgel of an olive branch" was how the Lord Chancellor described the four-point peace offer that Hess had signed and handed over to him. Simon's declassified report appears to show that he had failed miserably to elicit any strategically useful intelligence.

"I absolutely agree with the conclusions he has reached," Major Desmond Morton wrote after reading Lord Simon's report. Churchill had brought in his intelligence aide, who served as liaison with both MI6 and the codebreakers at Bletchley Park, to give his opinion of the Hess affair. A shadowy figure in the inner circle of the Prime Minister's most trusted aides, Morton had been retained as special adviser because Churchill distrusted what he described as the "collective wisdom" of the service intelligence organizations. Morton was one of the trusted and privileged few who had access to ULTRA, with instructions to "make a daily selection of titbits." From the information supplied by Morton, the Prime Minister would then form his own intelligence conclusion, "sometimes at much earlier dates" than his military advisers. His proudest achievement was deciding that the Germans would invade Russia when the British chiefs of staff were divided and the Foreign Office was convinced that Hitler was not intending to attack.[28]

"I submit that the time has now come to cash in on this wind-fall," Morton minuted to Churchill in a "Most secret" memorandum, proposing that the "ignorance, stupidity, falsity and arrogance of the Nazi leaders" should be exposed by publishing verbatim extracts of Lord Simon's interview. "The longer we wait, the rottener the apple," Morton advised. But his proposal was stalled by Foreign Office resistance and Beaverbrook's promise to Eden a month earlier "to strangle the infant" if Churchill revived the idea of making a statement about Hess. It was Morton who had concluded that Hess was not mad, believing that he had arrived "without the prior knowledge of Hitler" after being "completely misled" about British morale.[29]

So even if Hess was "not in the inner councils of Hitler or his Generals on high strategy," Morton concluded, he might "unwittingly possess knowledge of which he himself is unaware." To get to the bottom of the matter Morton set out to find the answers to two leading questions: What was Hitler's deputy so afraid of "in regard to the international situation"? and "why does he so earnestly desire a patched up peace *now*?"[30]

The answer, as Churchill and Morton suspected, was that Hess, because of his membership of the Nazi War Council, must have known whether Hitler planned to attack Russia without first reaching a settlement with England. The *Enigma* decrypts, the rumours coming in from the diplomatic grapevine and the penetration of the top-secret cipher reports sent by Japan's Berlin embassy to Tokyo, all continued to point to the imminent German invasion of the Soviet Union during the first ten days of June 1941, as the pieces of the intelligence picture began falling into line with Churchill's predictions. The day after Lord Simon's interview with Hess, Churchill's memoirs record that the Joint Intelligence Committee had reported on the Russo-German trade negotiations that: "*The latter half of June will see either war or agreement.*" Although this

10 June report was still ambiguous, Churchill wrote, it gave him the justification for authorizing the Foreign Secretary to pass on to Stalin the German order of battle on the eastern front, while carefully disguising its source. Churchill records that he authorized his extraordinary warning to Moscow *two days before he received the actual confirmation* from J.I.C. on 12 June that "fresh evidence is now at hand that Hitler has made up his mind to have done with Soviet obstruction and intends to attack her. Hostilities therefore appear highly probable, though it is premature to fix a date for their outbreak."[31]

But the justification Churchill gave for issuing his unprecedented warning to Stalin could not have derived from the source he so specifically identifies. This is the conclusion reached in the official *History of British Intelligence in the Second World War*, which states that "no record of a J.I.C. appreciation" such as that the Prime Minister singled out as the conclusive proof that Hitler was about to attack Russia was found. Professor A.H. Hinsley and his team of collaborators had access to all the J.I.C. reports, intelligence files and *Enigma* decrypts that remain classified in the British government's secret archives. Not only were Hinsley and his team *not* able to find the historically important 10 June J.I.C. report; it is clear that even two days later the War Cabinet was still uncertain whether Hitler really would attack Russia.[32]

What source of intelligence other than Hess himself could have prompted the Prime Minister's celebrated warning? That Lord Simon's report does not record Hess as having let the cat out of the bag regarding Russia is not conclusive proof that he did not do so inadvertently; it could have been excised from the report. Then too there are the records of the MI6 officers attending Hess which have never been declassified; either they or perhaps the full version of the Kirkpatrick reports could have provided the answers that were given in 1941 to Morton's two questions in a way that the Prime Minister decided was conclusive.

Churchill himself seems to have unwittingly provided the clue that Hess was indeed the source by protesting too much that no information regarding the invasion of Russia was obtained from him. "Considering how close Hess was to Hitler," he wrote, "it is surprising that he did not know of, or that if he knew he did not disclose, the impending attack on Russia for which such vast preparations were being made."[33]

The Prime Minister's extreme touchiness on the subject, which is evident in the declassified records, makes his archly constructed denial doubly suspicious in the light of the simultaneous declassification by the Americans and Russians of intelligence reports which show that Hess did indeed give warning of Hitler's intention to attack the Soviet Union.

446

"The Correct Story"

The key to the conundrum that has long puzzled historians is to be found between the buff covers of a U.S. Army Intelligence folder which was finally declassified at the end of 1989. It contains the letter written on 5 November 1941 by Captain Raymond E. Lee to Brigadier General Sherman Miles, Assistant Chief of Staff G-2, then chief of U.S. Military Intelligence at the War Department. It follows up his secret cable sent the previous day and reports that Hess *"gave warning of Hitler's intentions to invade Russia."* It explains how he drew up the enclosed notes on 28 October after "a conversation with someone whose intimate acquaintance with the affair is unquestionable." Assuring Sherman Miles that he had "every reason to consider this is the correct story," he cautioned his chief: "Will you please not duplicate this memorandum and show it only to such individuals as are really entitled to read it, as it would be a pity if it were traced back to my informant."[34]

The informant's identity can be found in Lee's private diary, which records "the source from whom I got all the information about Hess" as none other than Major Desmond Morton. Lee attests to Morton's reliability as "one of the discreet and shadowy figures who surround the Prime Minister, and who has a good deal to do with the Allied representatives around here." Lee also notes that he was told by Ambassador John G. Winant that "There was only one thing I did not know before and that is that Hess came over here to tell the British that the Germans were about to attack the Russians." After reading the report, he says, the Ambassador commented: "I never knew where the British got that information, but this must be their principal source."[35]

The K.G.B. archives reveal that Morton's report reached Moscow *even before* Lee's package arrived by diplomatic bag in Washington. The London source who supplied the information of what Morton said during a "lunch on 26 October" is identified only as "agent source" on p. 211 of the "Black Bertha" file, but a likely candidate is Colonel Frantisek Moravec ("Moravetz" in N.K.V.D. records), chief of the Czech military mission in London. Although not a Communist sympathizer, he had formed a secret marriage of convenience with the Soviets. In return for Russian assistance with the Czech underground, Moravec (codenamed "Accountant" in his N.K.V.D. file, No. 25344) throughout the war passed information obtained from his MI6 and Abwehr sources to the Soviets.[36]

The wording of the Lee and Soviet source's versions of Morton's Hess briefing is so similar that they must either have been at the same luncheon on 26 October or have seen the same written

447

briefing. Lee's diary entry of 31 October records his meeting with the *Time* magazine reporter who had lunched with someone "intimately associated" with Churchill. This explains why the two versions are identical, except for two paragraphs the K.G.B. have not released "for operational reasons." Both, for example, include Morton's retelling of a wisecrack of a hospital doctor. "We have a man in here who thinks he's Solomon," he said when the German pilot declared "I am Rudolf Hess."[37]

The Soviet and American intelligence reports of the 26 October Morton briefing shed important new light on the affair. They also explain the British government's subsequent decision to entomb the whole affair in official secrecy because Hess did disclose that Hitler was going to attack Russia.

"Hess landed and was captured just as the papers described," Morton had stated, confirming that the Duke of Hamilton had admitted not only that he recognized Hess, but that he had "met him up on a platform during the Olympic Games and maybe shook his hand." Morton's account also provides clues to what the British censored from the censored Kirkpatrick reports.[38]

"Hess said that he flew to the Duke to tell him that Germany was about to fight Russia," Morton disclosed, revealing that Hess *had* told Kirkpatrick that he "knew the Duke would see immediately that this was absurd and awful for England to continue to fight Germany any longer. For, if England continued fighting from the west, we should have to destroy England after we destroyed Russia." He believed that the Duke "could have gone to the King and told him about our plans to fight the Bolsheviks, and the King could have made peace with us." Hitler's deputy was apparently so ignorant of the British constitution that he was convinced that Churchill would be overruled. He argued that a deal could be struck, since the government represented "nobody but those fools who want to destroy Germany and therefore drag down the whole civilized world before the Bolshevik menace."[39]

"We immediately told the Russians that Hitler was going to invade Russia, but they wouldn't believe it," Morton assured the U.S. Military Attaché during their conversation of 5 November. The Russians, Morton explained, "seemed to think that we were trying to mislead them." Stalin, however, had evidently taken some notice; "that was why they were having military manoeuvres around Kiev in the month before Germany attacked them." The warning passed by Churchill on 10 June therefore appeared to have prompted the Russians to draw back many of their own divisions from the frontier to prepare their defence in depth. "If they hadn't had this warning," Morton ventured, "Hitler might have shattered many of Russia's best divisions by his surprise attack."[40]

Morton also disclosed, contradicting the official version, that he had himself interviewed Hess. The American and Russian versions record him confirming that he had "called on Hess several times." He gave a verbatim report of the fierce argument that had broken out when Hess insisted that in the Battle of Britain the British had lost 2,000 planes and the Germans only 500. When Morton pointed out that Britain only had a thousand front-line fighters in 1940, Hess erupted with irrational anger. "You're trying to trap me! You're trying to trap me!" he shouted. "I won't have it, you understand!" Then he sprang up and paced the floor violently, bringing this interview to an abrupt end. Hess appeared to be totally obsessed with the menace of Bolshevism, according to Morton, who added that during an interview with a leading British psychiatrist he had given a maniacal demonstration of the threat posed by the Soviets by clutching at his throat.[41]

"My mind is just like the Führer's, we think the same way," Hess had insisted repeatedly. "We have the same feelings. The Führer himself has said so." If, as Morton said he believed, Hess's mind was much like the Führer's "then it may be an explanation of Hitler's desperate drive into Russia, especially his push to Moscow, when a much more vital military objective would have been through the Donetz basin and down into the Caucasus." Only by crushing Moscow, which Hess said he "always believed to be the centre of the Jewish Bolshevik intrigue against Germany," would Hitler eliminate the Bolshevik menace reaching towards his throat.[42]

A further insight that Morton provided into the Duke of Hamilton's role, which has been underlined for emphasis in the Soviet version, describes the Duke angrily denying that he ever "had any correspondence with Hess or any of his acquaintances." He became still more upset when told that he had, because the "censor intercepted the letter from Hess's friend in which he asked you to come to Lisbon to meet Hess." Hamilton "demanded a meeting with Churchill about this" and was told he "could meet Churchill next morning if he went with him to Parliament." Evidently this was the meeting that the Duke recalled as taking place on the way to Buckingham Palace, when he made his quip about the prostitute. In the car with Churchill, Morton said, "Hamilton insisted he had never known Hess and had never had any correspondence with Hess." Churchill was impressed and "ordered Morton to investigate the matter." Morton discovered the Foreign Office official to whom the Haushofer letter had been sent by the censor. He "timidly admitted that he had forgotten to send the letter to Hamilton after making a copy of it." This cleared the Duke, Morton stated.

In what appears to have been a deliberate attempt to mislead for security reasons, Morton described Hess at the time as "living in a big mansion near Glasgow reserved for German officers."

Churchill, he also disclosed, had jokingly suggested that after the war "we can send Hess back into Germany the way he arrived here, and let the German people receive him from the skies." Ironically, it is now clear that this was just what the British government could not have done, because it needed to keep intact the Churchillian myth of wartime national unity.[43]

The possibility that Churchill used his aide Morton to spread disinformation that it was Hess, not ULTRA, who warned of the attack on Russia does not seem credible. Colonel Moravec's Czech intelligence service, via their Abwehr source Thümmel, had given the first warning of the German army's eastward movement. Concealing ULTRA from the Americans would have made no sense, because they knew that the British were breaking top-level German *Enigma*. In April 1941 U.S. Navy intelligence officers had visited Bletchley Park to exchange an American-built analogue of the Japanese "Purple" cipher machine for the GC & CS know-how to decipher the Atlantic U-boat Naval *Enigma*. Nor does the six-month delay in informing the U.S. Military Attaché make any sense if the British wanted to lay a false trail to camouflage ULTRA. It is moreover inconceivable that Churchill would have risked misleading the United States at a time when Britain was desperately trying to get American guarantees of support if her Far East possessions were attacked by the Japanese. Codebreakers on both sides of the Atlantic knew from intercepted Tokyo signal traffic that Japan was only weeks away from launching an attack in the Far East.[44]

"I always assumed that it was known that Hess came to warn us about Hitler's attack on Russia," said Sir Frank Roberts. His matter-of-fact corroboration that the Barbarossa warning is missing from the declassified Hess files is pertinent because he was once responsible for their security in the Foreign Office. Further documented confirmation for the admission made by Roberts can be found in the records kept by Lord Beaverbrook and Averell Harriman.[45]

When Lord Beaverbrook arrived in Moscow on 29 November to hammer out Russia's pressing claim to a bigger share of American Lend-Lease supplies, he and Roosevelt's envoy Harriman had a series of meetings in the Kremlin with Stalin. Anticipating that the subject of Hess would come up, Beaverbrook interviewed him beforehand, posing as Dr. Livingstone, the name he was assigned on his security pass. As a precaution, he took to Moscow the verbatim transcript of their conversation. Although their talk had produced little intelligence that might be used as a sop to Stalin, Hess had given Beaverbrook a rambling memorandum, *Germany-England from the Viewpoint of War Against the Soviet Union*, which he had compiled after the 21 June attack on Russia. It put forward a disjointed geopolitical argument that it was now in Britain's interest to make peace with Germany and join Hitler in his crusade against Bolshevism. German determination to crush the Soviet Union had, Hess claimed, been immensely strengthened by the "horrible machinations of the Bolshevik horde" that had "uplifted the spirit of resistance to the highest plane."[46]

Beaverbrook was therefore ready when Stalin made an oblique reference to Hess in one of their conversations in the Kremlin. "Do you intend to make peace?" he asked. Beaverbrook enquired the reason for this question. Stalin replied that "he concluded we meant peace because we kept Hess in our hands instead of shooting him." It is now evident that the Soviet dictator was alluding to the Philby *Spravkas* that suggested that the British might still be keeping their options open over a negotiated peace because as long as Hess was alive, he "was in the line of communication" and a potential link for negotiations with Hitler. Beaverbrook had to explain that even Germans could not be shot without a trial in Britain. Stalin then pointedly asked why Hess had come to England. *"To persuade Britain to join Germany in making an attack on Russia,"* Beaverbrook declared, handing him the Hess transcript and memorandum. "Thereafter we got on well," he wrote.[47]

Harriman's contemporary record of the conversation is even more revealing. "Stalin indicated that he thought Hess had gone not at the request of Hitler, but with the knowledge of Hitler, to which Beaverbrook agreed," he wrote. "The net of Beaverbrook's statement was that Hess had come thinking that with a small group of British aristocrats a counter-Churchill government could be set up to make peace with Germany which would be welcomed by the majority of the British. *Germany with British aid would then attack Russia."* Harriman records how Stalin "relished the amusing and detailed comments by Beaverbrook."[48]

Why, if Hess had not mentioned the attack on the Soviet Union before 22 June, when Barbarossa began, would Beaverbrook have provoked the distrustful Soviet dictator? Stalin and Molotov afterwards took it as their cue to derive a cynical pleasure from riling British ministers over the Hess affair.

"Over and over again within the next few years I was cross-examined about it by Molotov," the Foreign Secretary wrote, explaining that he had "told them all the details," even offering to show them all the statements. "I doubt if they were ever really satisfied that the incident was as unexpected and inexplicable to us as to them," Eden reflected in his memoir. Churchill also noted how the Russians "wove many distorted theories around it," recalling how Stalin taxed him on the affair in 1944 when he visited Moscow. "He asked me at the dinner table what was the truth about the Hess mission. I had the feeling that he believed there had been some deep negotiation or plot for Germany and Britain to act together in the invasion of Russia." Through the interpreter Churchill told the Soviet leader that when he made a statement of fact "within his knowledge" he expected it to be accepted. "There are lots of things that happen even here in Russia which our Secret Service do not necessarily tell me about," Stalin retorted with a wry grin. The very directness of the response evidently hit Churchill below the belt, because he records that he "let it go at that." He was unwilling to be dragged any further into a discussion that he must have realized would raise too many other embarrassing questions.[49]

The Prime Minister was of course unaware that Stalin's guile concealed the fact that he *knew* the innermost secrets of the Hess affair from Soviet moles like Philby who had penetrated Britain's Foreign Office and secret services. The British public did not learn until 1979 that the art historian Blunt, abetted by a bevy of his Marxisant Cambridge friends, was by May 1941 a trusted assistant to the director of counter-intelligence in MI5. Not only did Blunt have access to the most secret ULTRA; so did other Cambridge Communists the Russians had recruited as subsidiary agents and encouraged to get positions in military intelligence. The "Black Bertha" files declassified by the K.G.B. confirm the astonishing degree to which "Stalin's Englishmen" had alerted the Kremlin to the true objective of the Hess mission. The contemporary N.K.V.D. records reveal that it was a Soviet agent in the 2nd Bureau of the Vichy General Staff (France's military secret intelligence service) who first passed word that it was the British secret service who had played a crucial role in luring Hess to Scotland.

A Hess-related file contains six pages, in French, that were obviously stolen by an N.K.V.D. agent – who is not named, for "operational reasons" – from the Vichy General Staff intelligence files. The most significant is the report No. 398/B, dated "Le 5 Septembre 1941" and headed "ANGLETERRE Affaire HESS." This reveals that the source of the French information was a "longstanding friend of the British Trade Minister who was in touch with the Duchess of Hamilton." The source had "learned from the United States from a member of their entourage that in the aftermath of the Hess affair, the Duke of Hamilton, a captain in the R.A.F., was slapped in the face in the course of a reception at the Berkeley Hotel in London." After "several scandalous incidents of the same kind" the British government decided it was obliged – presumably to protect the Duke's reputation – to leak to "certain circles the truth of the Hess affair." The informant was described by French military intelligence as "very well connected with the high-ranking members of the British Secret Service in New York." Claiming that "this person had told him in August that the Hess affair was none other than a tremendous success for his service," he had proceeded to reveal how the British secret service had pulled off its spectacular coup:

"They, wishing to make up for the Best and Stevens affair [the Venlo incident of November 1939, in which the Germans had lured and captured two MI6 officers], had succeeded through an exchange of correspondence between imaginary Scottish conspirators (directed in the name of Lord Hamilton) and German agents, in convincing the German intelligence service of a fictitious conspiracy. In the course of eighteen months, the exchanges assumed the form of a serious conspiracy whose participants asked for and arranged for the arrival [in Scotland] of an important German representative to galvanize the conspirators. It was a source of great amazement to all concerned that this person turned out to be Rudolf Hess who was found within a few miles of Lord Hamilton's castle."[50]

That the report emanated from an MI6 source appears to have aroused Soviet suspicions that the British intelligence service had been playing dangerous games with the Germans. Yet the K.G.B. archives suggest that it was not taken seriously until October of the following year, when Moscow received corroboration from Colonel Moravec, who claimed to have actually seen the MI6 file on the operation involving Haushofer and Hamilton. On 21 October 1942 the chief of the Czech Military Intelligence Service, "Moravetz," "informed the N.K.V.D. Resident in London," according to cryptogram No. 450, that:

"The disseminated story that HESS arrived in England unexpectedly is not correct. Long before his flight HESS had corresponded about his mission with the DUKE OF HAMILTON. In this correspondence was discussed, in detail, all the questions to do with the organization of his flight. But HAMILTON was not himself a participant personally. All HESS's letters to HAMILTON did not reach him but were intercepted by the intelligence services where the answers to HESS in the name of HAMILTON were manufactured. In this way the British had managed to trick HESS into coming to England.

"Colonel MORAVETZ declared that he personally saw this correspondence between HESS and HAMILTON. According to MOREVETZ's declaration the HESS letters clearly represented that the plans of the German government were linked with their plans of their attack on the Soviet Union. The same letters set out the necessity of stopping the war between Britain and Germany. In conclusion Colonel Moravetz said that the English therefore have written proof of Hess and the other Nazi leaders' culpability in their preparations for the attack on the Soviet Union."[51]

This report of an MI6 plot behind Hess's arrival was considered important enough by the N.K.V.D. analysts to be immediately made the subject of a "Top secret" briefing for Stalin and Molotov. The summary from the "State Defence Committee of the U.S.S.R." was signed by the notorious "People's Commissar of Internal Affairs," Lavrenti Beria. Soviet intelligence took "Accountant's" report as convincing evidence of a British plot, since it was sent to Stalin and alluded to it in his cryptic remarks that Churchill might not have known what his secret service was up to. It also reflected the Kremlin's nightmare that elements in the British establishment had not given up hope of making peace and joining Germany in the attack on Russia.

Stalin's suspicions were also fed, as the "Black Bertha" file corroborates, by the many Soviet agents in the German intelligence services. The K.G.B. archives suggest that it could have been the "leaks" from the British secret service agent in New York that "inspired" not only the Montreal *Gazette* piece but also the *American Mercury* article with its assertion of a British secret service conspiracy behind Hess's arrival.

What credence can be given to the information in the Soviet records? The original, bound Hess and Moravec files were produced for examination at K.G.B. headquarters, and only half-a-dozen paragraphs out of over 400 pages were, "for operational reasons," covered by paper slips. Moreover, the information about British collusion derived from MI6 sources in contact with French and Czech military intelligence, and it squares with evidence from R.A.F. records and eyewitnesses that "normal action" does not seem to have been taken on 10 May 1941 to intercept Hess's incoming Me 110.

To this must be added other pieces of evidence that have come to light to corroborate a British plot to lure Hess to Scotland. The first of these is Haushofer's 20 September letter to Hamilton, written at the behest of Hess, which according to the Soviet sources began the MI6 plot. Other evidence has been found in the private papers kept by members of the opposition to Hitler in the Mittwochsgesellschaft (Wednesday Group). The diaries of Haushofer and his associates lead to the conclusion that he must have received some clear signal from a British source two weeks before Hess took off for Scotland. Whether this was the climax of a correspondence that had been going on for eighteen months, as the French learned from their MI6 source, or whether it was part of the fake correspondence to Haushofer, as Moravec claims he saw in the MI6 records, it must certainly have been credible enough for Haushofer to leave suddenly for Switzerland on 26 April 1941.[52]

It must be emphasized that Haushofer obtained official approval for his journey. This would not have been given without some tangible evidence of an offer made by his British contacts. At the same time it is clear that he ran an enormous risk because he undertook the mission both for the Foreign Ministry and in his capacity as a spokesman for the German underground opposition, for which he received help from Ulrich von Hassel's wife Ilse.

During an earlier trip in 1941 to Zurich, Ilse von Hassel had contacted the Swiss head of the International Red Cross, Dr. Carl Jacob Burckhardt, who, it is now clear, had secret channels to the London Foreign Office. She told him that Haushofer would be coming to see him "ostensibly for Hess," but actually on behalf of the Mittwochsgesellschaft. Burckhardt had told her he had been approached by "an agent of Himmler's who had come to him to find out whether England would perhaps make peace with Himmler instead of Hitler." This confirms that the Nazi leadership in Berlin knew that Burckhardt maintained a channel to London through the British Minister in Berne, Sir David Kelly.[53]

Burckhardt, as the Foreign Office records show, had been involved as the semi-official intermediary in communications to Germany via Switzerland that had been begun by Butler with his secret meeting in Lausanne in October 1939 with Prince Max von Hohenlohe. It was Burckhardt too who had been asked by Berlin to act as intermediary with the British Minister in Berne. This is confirmed in the correspondence of Walther Hewel, a ranking official of the Reich Foreign Ministry, who records a number of attempts by Kelly, on instructions from Butler, to make contact with Berlin in June and July 1940.[54]

Hess's decision to embark on his peace mission can be traced directly back to these June 1940 peace manoeuvres orchestrated by Butler. Ribbentrop's 1945 interrogation corroborates the assertion of Felix Kersten, Himmler's masseur, whose diary records that by 24 June 1940 Hess was determined to make his mission to make peace with Britain. More reliable confirmation for the role played by Butler's semi-official peace feelers via his Swiss friend Burckhardt comes from the British records. Despite his strenuous postwar denials that he was the principal British surrogate in this renewed game of peace feelers, Burckhardt, as head of the International Red Cross, did act as the intermediary for a series of discussions that took place between Kelly and Prince Max von Hohenlohe in the autumn and winter of 1941.[55]

The Hohenlohe–Kelly soundings centred on Hitler's plan for reaching peace in a European federation in which Britain would participate. The talks eventually stalled because Churchill insisted on rejecting any olive branches proffered by Berlin. But Ambassador

Kelly had nonetheless performed his mission so well that in September 1940 he received a "rap on the knuckles" when he was instructed not to leave any doubts about the British determination to fight on until the war was won. This did not stop British diplomats fron discreetly continuing to receive German peace feelers. Kelly, according to German records, approached Burckhardt again in December 1940, asking him to raise with Hohenlohe what Hitler's terms might be for a settlement. Three months later, in March 1941, we find Prince Max travelling once more to Madrid to detail proposals for a future settlement with Sir Samuel Hoare, the British Ambassador.[56]

The German record makes it very plain that during the spring of 1941 Berlin had received not one but several intimations that a compromise peace with Britain might yet be worked out. That they originated from the British ambassadors in Switzerland and Spain added to their credibility and must have made them seem very convincing to Berlin. This was why whatever invitation was received by the Berlin Foreign Ministry during the third week of April was considered credible enough by Hess – and Hitler – to authorize Haushofer to travel to Geneva to follow it up.

Haushofer, it should also be noted, left Munich for Switzerland on 26 April *the day after* the Duke of Hamilton was told by "Tar" Robertson that MI5 wanted him to "volunteer" to go to meet Haushofer in Lisbon. This coincidence may be further evidence that the baiting of the hook was being orchestrated by agents of the British secret services. Nor is this the only clue that suggests that the scheme outlined to Hamilton the previous day had already been set in motion and that a suitable morsel of encouragement was sent in Hamilton's name to be relayed to Berlin via Dr. Burckhardt. For it is this which appears to have brought Haushofer hurrying to Switzerland. For good measure, additional ground bait in the form of fresh rumours about a Scottish peace party opposed to Churchill were circulating in the eddies of diplomatic intrigue swirling about wartime Madrid. Nor does it seem unconnected with the chain of events that three days earlier the rumours that Hess himself had flown to Madrid with a letter from Hitler for Franco were denied by the official German Deutschlandsender radio station: "Reports concerning a journey to Spain by Hess are denied by authoritative German sources."[57]

What is also certainly a matter of record is that Haushofer had a meeting with Dr. Burckhardt on 28 April 1941. He reported finding the Swiss diplomat terrified that his role as an intermediary would be publicly exposed. At the same time Burckhardt expressed his doubt that any British government would be prepared to "renounce a restoration of the western European system." He said he had it on reliable authority that the British were no longer concerned with the fate of eastern Europe and that a restoration of former German colonies "will not present any overwhelming difficulties." He confirmed that he had met "a few weeks ago" with a prominent Englishman who he said was "close to leading Conservative and city circles." Although he declined to name him to Haushofer, Burckhardt said that the emissary from London had "expressed the wish of important English circles for an examination of peace" and that he had mentioned Haushofer as a possible channel. Burckhardt also revealed that the previous year he had had long conversations with Halifax when he was in London and with Henry Livingston, the English Consul General in Geneva, who was another supporter of a negotiated peace.[58]

Haushofer guaranteed Burckhardt complete discretion if he would arrange a meeting with the unidentified Englishman from London. Whether he did so is not recorded, but there must have been some productive message that Haushofer received from the Swiss intermediary the following week. Haushofer's mother noted in her diary a week later "Phone-call from Albrecht on his way back from his diplomatic mission – *which hasn't been without success.*" After talking to her son on 5 May, the day he returned to Germany, Martha Haushofer recorded: "The conversations of Albrecht have been fruitful."[59]

Since Haushofer had tried since September to arrange a meeting with a British intermediary, his belief in a "fruitful" outcome of his trip points in the direction of his having made a successful contact. While it is possible that this was with Kelly, the diplomatic cables of the British Embassy give no hint of it. An article published in 1946 by Switzerland's left-wing periodical *Die Nation*, by Erika Mann, daughter of the exiled German novelist, asserts that Burckhardt's favourable news had been provided by a meeting with Sir Samuel Hoare. The vehemence with which the Swiss diplomat immediately denied this charge suggests that he connived with the British to cover the tracks that led to Spain. Yet when Albrecht Haushofer returned to Germany on 5 May he certainly *believed* his talks pointed to an important diplomatic breakthrough. On the way back through Germany he met Albrecht von Kessel, with whom he raised the prospects of peace negotiations with the British. Kessel later recalled how Haushofer was obviously "delighted" with his talks and was carrying a very important package (*Kuriergepäck*) with him. Haushofer also reported on the Burckhardt meeting to Ilse von Hassel in Arosa, where she was nursing her asthmatic son. Confirmation of Albrecht's belief that he had achieved some success comes from Hitler himself, who called for an immediate report as soon as Haushofer had returned to Munich.[60]

Would one meeting with Burckhardt have justified Haushofer's enthusiasm, or were other players brought into the game? That Hess took off on his flight a week later suggests that the hook must have been cunningly baited. Since Hamilton had hesitated to go to Lisbon, the British secret service would have found a credible alternative in Sir Samuel Hoare, with whom Haushofer had floated his peace plan the previous year. Never completely trusted by either London or Berlin, Hoare found himself boxed in and watched like a hawk by his fellow countrymen as well as by the Spanish and German secret services. His meetings with Prince von Hohenlohe in early 1941 must have reinforced the German Foreign Ministry's interest in him as a conduit for peace. So it would have required only a gentle nudge of encouragement via Burckhardt to send Haushofer to Spain to sound out Hoare again. He could have flown unnoticed from Geneva under an assumed name, arriving in Madrid in a matter of hours.

That Haushofer did actually make the journey to Spain for a clandestine meeting with the British Ambassador was the conclusion drawn by Walter Wehrenberg, one of Haushofer's pupils and an associate of the secret Mittwochsgesellschaft. In a meeting with Haushofer shortly before the latter's execution by the Gestapo in 1944, Wehrenberg asserts, he told him in confidence how he had flown to Spain, arriving in Madrid on 1 May. But according to Wehrenberg, Haushofer's hopes of a fruitful meeting with Ambassador Hoare proved empty and his discussions in Spain led nowhere. Further indication that Haushofer did fly to Madrid to make contact with some senior British representative appears in a 10 May cable from the German Embassy in Madrid. Sent by Haushofer's friend Secretary Stahmer to Walther Stubbe, another Foreign Ministry confidant, it contained an invitation for Haushofer to make an early trip to Madrid for the purposes of delivering a lecture. The timing of such an unusual invitation does not appear to have been a coincidence; it seems that Stahmer may have been sending a prearranged signal of encouragement received from the British intermediaries.

Was the "invitation" to Haushofer really a veiled confirmation of the invitation to Hess to meet the Scottish peace plotters, sent when the Deputy Führer was already on his way to Britain? If so, it appears to be the final element in a two-week-long concatenation of interconnecting events that began on 25 April when Hamilton was asked by MI5 to go to Lisbon to meet Haushofer and elucidate what peace terms were on offer. The odds that such a chain of seemingly interlocking events was a coincidence are long. While not conclusive, it amounts to a persuasive case for arguing that the Soviet reports are correct and the invisible hand of MI6 was orchestrating the moves. The Duke's refusal to cooperate in the plot until the day of Hess's arrival did not prevent the hook being baited, the line cast and the strike made in his name. These were precisely the skills that the British were already employing to brilliant success in their "Double Cross" operation against German agents.

The unprecedented release by the Soviets of the original N.K.V.D. files adds more weight to this rationale for Hess's arrival in Scotland. The evidence that their agents in the French and Czech military intelligence obtained direct from MI6 sources reinforces their credibility. While not final confirmation, the "Black Bertha" and "Accountant" files in conjunction with the German records reinforce the theory that Hess arrived as the result of an MI6 fishing expedition. The curious anomalies in the R.A.F. records can also be construed as evidence that whatever it was that hooked the German negotiator, the arrival of some important Nazi figure must have been anticipated and his flight really was let in "by the back door" as part of some prearranged plan.

Churchill's own reactions suggest that he too was unaware of the MI6 plot and left at just as much of a loss as to how to deal with the public ramifications. This would explain his bitter conflict with the Foreign Office, which was nominally in charge of MI6. It also goes a long way to explaining why the British government decided to erect such a high and impenetrable wall of secrecy around Hess which was all the more remarkable because it was not breached in any significant way for fifty years.

For Hess himself, his mission proved a flight into oblivion made possible by the official explanation that his flight was the result of a brainstorm. Significantly Lord Beaverbrook said it was he who suggested this solution to Churchill's problem as they walked through St. James Park. Beaverbrook remarked that "anyone who came under the care of a psychiatrist was immediately written off as mad." This provided the official excuse to discredit Hess during the war, when a succession of psychiatrists were brought in and pronounced the Deputy Führer unstable, neurotic, paranoid, hypochondriac and finally mad. The irony is that this was the role that Hess told Hitler and his wife he intended to cast himself in if his mission failed.[61]

Disowned by Germany and accused of insanity by Britain, Hess spent the war in solitary incarceration feigning bouts of insanity. It was also politically convenient at the Nuremberg tribunal after the Allied victory in 1945 for the British to maintain the public belief that Hess was deranged. In this they had the unwitting cooperation of the accused, who only just escaped the death penalty demanded by the Russians for his part in the Nazi war crimes. The former Nazi Party chief was then sentenced to spend the rest of his days in Berlin's gloomy Spandau Prison.

The enigma surrounding Hitler's former deputy and his mission grew with the years. Whether the lonely prisoner was really Hess or a double became an increasing fixation for many investigators

459

attempting to penetrate the veil of suspicious secrecy that was maintained throughout the Cold War. The mystery was no nearer resolution on 17 August 1987 when the lifeless body of the last surviving leader of the Third Reich was found by his British guards in a wooden shed in the Spandau prison garden. Around the neck of the corpse was a twisted electric cable. The official autopsy concluded that Hess had died by his own hand. But the bizarre circumstances of his death gave rise to suspicions that, as with the events of May 1941, steps had been taken to prevent the truth ever being told. Rudolf Hess, who had outlived his mentor Hitler and his nemesis Churchill, managed his departure from the stage of history in a manner calculated to rekindle the flames of controversy about the role he had really played in World War II.

What is now clear is that, whatever role the British secret service played, the Hess mission had its genesis in the peace moves made by members of Churchill's government in 1940. The Soviet documentation shows that the inside story of the Hess flight was known to the Kremlin all along, making it unnecessary now for the British government to continue taking extraordinary steps to keep the true story a secret. For Churchill, disclosing the real story behind the Hess mission would have shattered the myth he intended to bequeath to posterity: that the "shining and sublime" resolution of a united British government saved the nation and the world from going under to Nazi tyranny in the summer of 1940. As long as the Cold War lasted, successive postwar British governments understandably had no wish to exhume the Hess skeleton by releasing records which would show that Stalin had justification for his suspicions that Hess had been lured over as part of a bizarre "Double Cross" plot by the British secret services.

In the post-Cold War era, as Britain increasingly moves towards becoming an integral part of the European community of nations, is it not now time to lay the bones of the Hess myth to rest once and for all? Now that the Soviet Union and the United States have set a remarkable precedent by opening their historic intelligence files, surely the British government should reconsider its obligations to history.

The K.G.B. claims to be serving the interests of historical truth. Why cannot the first of a new generation of British prime ministers seize the opportunity of the fiftieth anniversary of the Hess flight to order the release of the Hess files still withheld from the public archives?

APPENDIX 1

Did Chamberlain Want Churchill to Succeed Him?

S upport for the conventional view that Churchill succeeded to the premiership only because Halifax declined to accept the post on Chamberlain's terms is found in John Colville's diary. While Colville noted that "Halifax had categorically refused to form a Government" the previous afternoon, his refusal was evidently *not* final. The Prime Minister's lieutenants in the leadership crisis, Lord Dunglass and David Margesson, had not yet given up trying to persuade the Foreign Secretary to change his mind even as late as the afternoon of 10 May. Colville records how "the whole gang of hangers on" sat discussing a resolution to the crisis. As they saw it, the only possibility was for the King, who "is understood not to wish to send for Winston," to "persuade Halifax to recant his determination not to be P.M." Their fear of the danger of "rash and spectacular exploits" if Churchill should succeed Chamberlain by default was, it seems, only exceeded by their concern that "if Winston thought the P.M. were trying to hold onto the reins of power he would create such serious mischief in the House of Commons that a really serious crisis would arise."[1]

After news came in that Labour had agreed to serve under a new Prime Minister, Colville concluded that nothing could stop Churchill, "because of his powers of blackmail – unless the King makes full use of his prerogative and sends for another man." Chamberlain's men were, however, determined to make a last-ditch attempt to persuade "the unpersuadable Halifax" to reconsider before the Prime Minister left for the Palace. Under Secretary R.A. Butler was once again deputed to go and plead with Halifax – but he arrived at the Foreign Secretary's office only to find that he had "gone off to the dentist." Although Halifax's diary details the stomach ache brought on by Chamberlain's offer of circumscribed power, there is no mention of the pain migrating to his teeth. Since it was now well past six, outside the usual surgery hours, Halifax's decision to go to the dentist at the precise moment when the government crisis reached its denouement is decidedly odd. It is so out of character as to suggest that the Foreign Secretary invented a "diplomatic excuse" to duck out of the fray and nurse his injured pride.

Halifax had good reason not to revive the painful succession issue again because he knew it had already been decided. Chamberlain had the day before abandoned the uncooperative Halifax and cut a deal with Churchill. Amery's diaries and Churchill's own account provide the evidence for arguing that it was at his morning discussion with Sir Kingsley Wood at the Admiralty that the succession issue was definitively settled. This was the meeting at which Churchill struck the deal that so dismayed Amery and the Tory rebels: in return for becoming Prime Minister, he not only guaranteed Chamberlain – and, it would later emerge, Simon, another leading apostle of appeasement – a place in the new government, but promised that Chamberlain could be Chancellor of the Exchequer and remain party leader. The deal's broker was Kingsley Wood. The owlish Lord Privy Seal, who had for so long been Chamberlain's trusted political ally and friend, was – according to Boothby – an "extremely barometrical politician," but it needed more than a good political nose to take the decisive role that we now know he played during the final twenty-four hours of the leadership crisis.

"Suddenly we found an ally in Sir Kingsley Wood," Boothby wrote in his memoir, crediting the Lord Privy Seal with the most important role in bringing Churchill to power. His sudden appearance at the conspiratorial lunch with Churchill and Eden on Thursday is significant. It occurred *after* Halifax had rejected Chamberlain's offer of a "twilight" premiership and *before* the Downing Street cabal on Thursday afternoon during which Halifax counted himself out of the succession. That Kingsley Wood also briefed Churchill on exactly how to handle himself at that crucial afternoon meeting suggests not only that he knew the script but that he was coaching the new heir apparent with the full authority of Chamberlain. It has always puzzled historians why the Prime Minister, if he really intended Halifax to succeed him, should have bothered to bring him face to face with the rival contender. Now that it is known that Wood briefed Churchill exactly how to respond, this meeting appears to have been a charade.[2]

Why then was it staged? Given that both the Prime Minister and

Churchill knew in advance what was going to happen, the only logical purpose for that afternoon's meeting was to let Halifax shoot himself in the foot in front of the Chief Whip. Chamberlain could not then be accused of knifing the Conservative Party's favoured candidate in the back. Further corroboration that this was the real scenario appears in the accounts Churchill himself gave "several times" in confidence to Colville after he became his wartime private secretary. This version adds an important highlight to Churchill's published account and the one given by Halifax: a direct question that the Prime Minister asked after telling them that he was considering resignation and one or other must succeed him.

"Can you see any reason, Winston, why in these days a Peer should not be Prime Minister?" Chamberlain demanded. Colville was later told by Churchill that the question was a trap. If he answered yes, he would expose his own ambition, and if he said no, it would clear the way for the Prime Minister to recommend Halifax to the King. So instead of responding Churchill very deliberately turned his back and gazed out of the Cabinet Room window on to Horseguards Parade, waiting for Halifax to speak. What Churchill never told Colville was that his performance had been scripted by Kingsley Wood. So if Chamberlain's leading question was a trap, it could not have been set for Churchill. And with Churchill's silence, arranged by Kingsley Wood, Halifax fell right into it.[3]

Politics makes for strange bedfellows and subtle subterfuges. Yet few plots in British political history can have been so artfully executed or carried such momentous consequences as the Machiavellian intrigue that enabled Churchill to beat the odds-on favourite Halifax to succeed Chamberlain as Prime Minister. The principal factor determining the outcome was Chamberlain's limpet-like determination to cling on to the rock of party political power and Halifax's lofty reluctance to be a figurehead Prime Minister. Evidence that Chamberlain nurtured hopes of returning to Downing Street appears in his diary entry for 9 September, written after emergency surgery had disclosed the inoperable cancer that would kill him two months later. "Any ideas which may have been in my mind about possibilities of further political activity and even a possibility of another Premiership after the war have gone." This suggests that he had calculated in May that his chances of a future comeback would be best served by striking a deal with Churchill.[4]

According to hints made by Kingsley Wood, Chamberlain had harboured doubts about Halifax's will to fight Hitler shortly after the war began. This is the inference that can now be made from the testimony given in confidence by Kingsley Wood to Lord Beaverbrook shortly before he died in 1943. He confirmed the role he had played as Chamberlain's intermediary in striking the deal that brought Churchill to power – and for which he was rewarded by being made Chancellor of the Exchequer. Kingsley Wood also revealed another startling fact. "Quite soon after the start of the war Chamberlain himself told me that he would have to give way to Churchill," he told Beaverbrook. "He never intended that Halifax should be Prime Minister, he always intended Churchill to be his successor," he continued, asserting that "by the end of the year it had become obvious that the change was not far off, and I started negotiations with Churchill which resulted in the change." [5]

If Kingsley Wood's assertions are correct, then his friend and confidant Chamberlain must have been making contingency plans to relinquish the premiership since the beginning of 1940. This is so uncharacteristic as to suggest that some strands in the deeply laid plot to which Kingsley Wood alludes are still hidden. That Chamberlain was so determined, so early, that Halifax should not succeed him, suggests that he considered him a serious threat to his own long-term political goal of an eventual return to power. It could also be that Chamberlain had detected a threat of a very different order. Documentation has now come to light that in January and February 1940 the Foreign Secretary exceeded his brief by not only keeping the door open to, but actually encouraging, German peace feelers. There is now considerable evidence that the Prime Minister had good reason for his suspicions that if Halifax became premier he would take the first opportunity to negotiate peace with Hitler. Chamberlain, a shrewd politician, appears to have known that if Britain was ever brought to the brink of military defeat, the passionless Tory grandee Halifax would have rationalized it to be his duty to the Empire to strike a deal with Hitler.

APPENDIX 2

Pius XII and the German Generals' Plot

Pius XII has come under criticism for being "pro-German" because he failed to speak out and use the Vatican's influence to save European Jewry from the Nazi holocaust. But the record shows that he took considerable risks in acting as an intermediary in the 1940 conspiracy against Hitler. As Papal Nuncio in Munich and later Berlin after World War I, Archbishop Eugenio Pacelli's reputation for diplomatic surefootedness led to his appointment in 1930 as Cardinal Secretary of State. This brought him into direct conflict with the Nazis' and his "tenacity and mental elasticity" earned him the confidence of many Germans who were secretly opposed to Hitler. Among Cardinal Pacelli's personal contacts during his time as Nuncio in Berlin had been Admiral Wilhelm Canaris, the Abwehr chief, and General Ludwig Beck, the Chief of the Army General Staff. It was Beck's forced resignation in 1938 that removed the principal army opponent to Hitler's plans for war. When he was elected Pope shortly before the outbreak of the war, Pius XII did not allow his aversion to Nazism to diminish his faith in the goodwill of the German people. He was therefore the obvious choice of intermediary for General Beck and the group who began plotting to overthrow Hitler.

The dilemma for Pius XII – and the British government – was that the opposition in Germany had been forced underground by the Nazi police state, and was not a cohesive group with identifiable leaders. Many of its leading members in the Army and bureaucracy were right-wing Prussians. Their commitment to a restoration of the monarchy resurrected for the Allied governments the spectre of a Reich resurgent under a new Kaiser. The outbreak of war had brought a certain cohesion to the German opposition, but it was not until the victory in Poland that the various underground groups recognized that Hitler could be removed only by a coup organized by the discontented Army leaders who were becoming alarmed by the military plans of the jumped-up former corporal.

General Beck, the ousted Chief of the Army Staff, had remained the centre of disaffection in the Army. His principal contact in the High Command was General Franz Halder; other ranking Army sympathizers were Generals von Hammerstein, von Witzleben and von Falkenhausen, who commanded forces on the Western Front. The Abwehr was the principal hothouse of intrigue against Hitler, countenanced, if not encouraged, by its enigmatic chief, Admiral Canaris. The principal plotter was his Chief of Staff, Hans Oster, who exploited the protection afforded by the military intelligence organization to bring in accomplices such as Hans von Dohnanyi. An "aryanized" half-Jew, Dohnanyi was a former Supreme Court judge and the brother-in-law of Pastor Dietrich Bonhoeffer, the Nazis' most outspoken church opponent. Hans Bernd Gisevius, the German Vice Consul in Zürich, was another Abwehr officer who provided a contact point between the underground opposition and the Allies for the duration of the war.[1]

The civilian opposition was led by Ulrich von Hassel, the former German Ambassador to Rome, and Carl Goerdeler, an ex-Lord Mayor of Leipzig. Among the senior career bureaucrats who opposed the Nazis was Johannes Popitz, the Minister of Finance in the Prussian state. He and many other silent opponents of Hitler were members of the Mittwochsgesellschaft, the semi-secret Wednesday Group of bureaucrats, academics and industrialists. Representation was particularly strong from the Foreign Ministry, including Albrecht Haushofer.

Theodor Kordt, then Chargé d'Affaires at the German Embassy in London, had tried to open up a direct line from the opposition to the British government during the final months of peace. Vansittart had attended a series of clandestine meetings at the home of Dr. Philip Conwell-Evans, a leading member of the Anglo-German Fellowship Society. A former lecturer at Königsberg University, Conwell-Evans had been fired by enthusiasm for Germany and had tried with Kordt to avert war. After Kordt was posted to the German legation in Berne, Conwell-Evans maintained contact with him using a simple code. But Conwell-Evans's membership of the pro-Nazi Anglo-German Fellowship made the Foreign Office suspicious, and this suspicion dogged all his efforts to act as an intermediary for the German opposition. There is no evidence that he had received any encouragement from the Foreign Secretary when he travelled to Berne for a meeting with Kordt in January 1940. He had been reduced to sending messages to Kordt which, he claimed, Vansittart had supplied "on behalf of Prime Minister Chamberlain and Lord Halifax." They were forwarded to Oster and Beck, who took them as encouraging signals. But they turned out to be nothing more than rehashed extracts from Chamberlain's 12 October House of Commons speech.[2]

Another early effort to open contact with the British government was made by Adam von Trott zu Solz. This former Oxford Rhodes scholar and passionate anti-Nazi was a dedicated socialist and German nationalist, which set him apart from the conservatives and monarchists in the German Foreign Ministry, where he had become a protégé of the principal bureaucrat, State Secretary Ernst Freiherr von Weizsäcker. Von Weizsäcker was never a conspirator himself, but he was sympathetic to the opposition, and arranged for members of it to be posted to German embassies in neutral countries so that they could maintain contact with the Allies. It was Weizsäcker who sponsored von Trott, as a fresh recruit in the Abwehr, to make three "fact-finding missions" to England and the United States in 1939. Extensive contacts with British political leaders, including Chamberlain and Halifax, failed to convince the Foreign Office that von Trott was a representative of the opposition to Hitler. Nor did he have any more success in the United States after war broke out. Although he warned the State Department that there was "a very powerful group" in Britain that he feared might make a premature peace with the Nazis, he was regarded as an *agent provocateur* by the F.B.I., who, like the British secret service, suspected his credentials.[3]

"We were always very dubious about von Trott because he seemed to be travelling so much and so easily," explained Sir Frank Roberts. He was one of those in the Foreign Office who knew about the German opposition and its contact with General Beck. He did not share the view prevailing among many of his colleagues that all Germans were a "bloody lot of militarists." But when the Vatican line to the opposition opened up, he admits, he could never reach a satisfactory answer to the question: "What could they deliver?"[4]

The Pope's intervention highlighted the dilemma that trapped the German opposition and the Foreign Office in a classic "hen-and-egg" dilemma. The British were reluctant to provide any negotiating assurances without proof that the military conspirators could topple Hitler, and General Beck refused to move without such guarantees. "These generals," Von Hassel complained in exasperation, "would have the same government they wish to overthrow give them orders to do so." It was in an effort to break out of this paralysing circle of mutual distrust that the Pope's intercession with the British government was arranged. It had taken until December 1939 to establish the chain of contacts and cut-outs between the Pontiff and the German opposition leaders. The secret channel to the Vatican led through Dr. Josef Müller, a sympathetic Bavarian lawyer whose induction into the Abwehr was arranged to facilitate his travelling back and forth to Rome. His contact in the Vatican was Monsignor Ludwig Kaas, who communicated through Father Leiber, a German Jesuit in the Curia, as the direct link to Pius XII.[5]

This extraordinary "cloak-and-dagger" operation had been insisted on by the Pope himself to bypass the Cardinal Secretary of State, Maglione. He regarded it as essential to prevent the Gestapo, who were already very suspicious of the Vatican, from getting wind of his involvement. If the network had been discovered it would not only have compromised the papacy but would have proved fatal to the members of the German opposition. The obsessive secrecy insisted on by Pius XII did not make it any easier to convince the sceptics at the Foreign Office. After opening up the secret channel to London in January 1940, the Pope did his best to provide both sides with the assurances they demanded.[6]

"The results of the mediation are regarded as most favourable in Germany. The *coup d'etat* should come in mid-February," Father Leiber was informed by Müller in January. This proved a wild prediction, as Osborne found out when he received a summons to an interview with the Pontiff on 7 February 1940. In the papal study he learned from Pius XII that his contact with "German military circles" had reported that Hitler had now postponed his offensive on Belgium because a German officer who had made a forced landing had been carrying the plans, which "were genuine and the attack had been imminent." He still declined to name the source – it was probably Beck – nor would he show the "four-page typescript notes in German" which he read out to Osborne. According to his information, Hitler had boasted that he would be in Paris by summer, when he would go to the Louvre "to find a more worthy site to set up the Venus de Milo."[7]

The Pontiff provided sketchy details of the plot to "get rid of Hitler" in a coup that would be precipitated outside Berlin. It would establish a temporary "military dictatorship" until the danger of any civil uprising had passed. Then the generals would hand over to a "democratic, conservative and moderate" government of a "decentralized" and federal nature. It would agree to an independent Poland and non-German Czechoslovakia, but the military conspirators needed guarantees that the German state with which peace was to be negotiated would include Austria. "The Pope made no attempt to defend it or even recommend serious consideration," Osborne reported. "He said he intensely disliked even having to pass it on and he would no more expect an answer than on the previous occasion; but his conscience would not allow him to ignore it altogether lest there might be conceivably one chance in a million of it serving the purpose of sparing lives."

The British Minister to the Holy See forwarded to London the details of the offer relayed via the Pope. His advice was that this peace approach was serious. This was also confirmed by the King when he received a copy of Osborne's letter on 18 February. He wrote to Halifax that he was "very interested" in the generals' plot which he had already heard of from his cousin Queen Marie of Yugoslavia. Her source was the Yugoslav Counsel in Düsseldorf who had been told by a German General Staff officer that "the army were to take over from Hitler" and the Nazi leaders "would be done away with."[8]

But the diary kept by Ulrich von Hassel reveals that Halifax's favourable response *did* reach the conspirators. The entry for 16 March mentions von Hassel's discussions with Colonel Oster and Hans von Dohnanyi and "some extraordinarily interesting documents covering the conversations of a Catholic intermediary with the Pope." While von Hassel was impressed by the "surprising lengths" gone to by the Pontiff, he described Halifax's reply as "much more cagey." Nonetheless Goerdeler agreed to arrange for von Hassel to discuss the British response with General Halder. Then, at the last minute, the one member of the General Staff whose cooperation was essential to launching a military coup against Hitler unexpectedly cancelled the meeting.[9]

It is not clear from the surviving record whether General Halder feared that the S.S. or Gestapo had uncovered the plot, or whether his fellow generals had simply got cold feet.

APPENDIX 3

The Lonsdale Bryans Peace Mission

James Lonsdale Bryans was a globe-trotting dilettante with more polish than means, the kind of character who could have stepped straight off the pages of a Somerset Maugham short story. A self-proclaimed student of astrology and "sociological anthropology," he had arrived back from Sarawak in August 1939. Low on funds but not on initiative, he was looking up schoolfriends in the Foreign Office when he bumped into Lord Halifax. As one Old Etonian to another they chatted for a few minutes on the staircase about the worsening Polish crisis. After war broke out, Lonsdale Bryans tried to cash in on this conversation by offering his services as a peace intermediary. When he was rebuffed by the Foreign Office, he headed for Rome. After six weeks of social ferreting through the diplomatic community there, he found a junior Italian official who claimed to be in direct contact with the German opposition. This was Detalmo Pirzio-Biroli, who was engaged to the daughter of Ulrich von Hassel. With scant regard for security the Italian told the Britisher all about the planned *coup d'état* involving his future father-in-law, whom he identified only as "Charles."[1]

Armed with Pirzio-Biroli's typed memorandum setting out the peace terms and guarantees the plotters wanted from the British government, Lonsdale Bryans arrived back in London at the beginning of 1940. After plying his Foreign Office friends with the amazing details of the German generals' plot, he was informed that the Foreign Secretary was too busy to see him. He then enlisted the support of Lord Brocket, who was one of the most vociferous campaigners in the House of Lords for a negotiated peace. Brocket's 4 January letter of introduction, which succeeded in getting his young friend in to meet Halifax, remains, surprisingly, closed until 2016. So it is still impossible to know for sure what changed the Foreign Secretary's mind about giving his personal blessing to this amateur peace mission. Lonsdale Bryans's own account provides clues which suggest that Halifax wanted to open up an avenue for negotiations that would be free of the interference of his hardline officials.[2]

"No one wants peace more than I do, but it must not be a patched-up peace," Lord Halifax told Bryans at their meeting on 8 January, adding cryptically: "I know there are people who think this war need never have been declared." He conceded that it was "a tricky business," but he was sufficiently impressed by Pirzio-Biroli's memorandum to agree to give his personal support for Lonsdale Bryans to meet "Charles" as a semi-official intermediary. He also promised government approval of his travel visas and currency documents.

"It can do no harm, and it may do a lot of good," the Foreign Secretary said, according to Bryans. He was, however, later told by the Foreign Office that it was "not the policy of His Majesty's Government to approve contacts with German nationals." As Bryans had arrived in London before the Pope's offer to act as an intermediary, it seems that Halifax seized the opportunity to communicate with the German opposition. This would have been in keeping with what Sir Frank Roberts recalled of Halifax's standard reaction to German peace feelers: "Let's keep the door open, we have nothing to lose by it."[3]

In the case of Bryans, the Foreign Secretary's endorsement on his travel passes enabled the tyro-diplomat to claim grandly that he was on a "government-sponsored" peace mission. He funded himself by tapping an indulgent Lord Brocket for £200 and set off for Rome. With Halifax's signature on his official *laissez-passer*, he was able to meet the British Ambassador, whom he asked to arrange a meeting with Mussolini. Sir Percy Loraine reacted icily, making it very clear to London that he disapproved of the Foreign Secretary's decision to employ an amateur diplomat. "I found Mr Bryans' ideas very peculiar," he wrote to Halifax on 15 January, complaining that "he seemed to be running two hares which appeared to be hardly compatible with each other."[4]

Lonsdale Bryans's efforts to meet the Duce did not pay off, but Pirzio-Biroli arranged for him to meet his father-in-law. Posing as a "doctor" he travelled to Arosa in Switzerland, where von Hassel joined his wife, who was nursing their asthmatic son in a mountain sanatorium. After a pantomime of security precautions, in which he spent a day posing as a watercolourist in a snowstorm, Lonsdale

Bryans finally met von Hassel face to face on 22 February. They had three long walks through the bright snowfields below the ski station and an hour of discussion in the evening in the smoke-filled bar of the Post Hotel. The distinguished-looking German was able to confirm that an "important general" was involved in his anti-Hitler plot. But to set the coup in motion, von Hassel explained, his fellow conspirators needed "something tangible and solid and signed by Lord Halifax." If this was not possible they would accept "a coded message transmitted officially over the air."[5]

"I can only assure you that a statement from Halifax would get to the right people," von Hassel told his British contact. On the second day he handed him a seven-point "confidential" manifesto of intent written in his own hand but unsigned. When pressed, he added a separate signed letter pledging his commitment to working for a just peace. For Bryans these documents were proof of the success of his mission. He left next day for England, promising "to get a statement from Halifax." When he arrived in London, with von Hassel's documents securely folded in his pocket, the amateur diplomat was dismayed to find himself closed out by Foreign Office professionals. He was repeatedly told that Lord Halifax was too busy to see him, and this time another personal letter from Lord Brocket failed to open the Foreign Secretary's door. The evidence in the declassified British files shows that the permanent officials had grown weary of the Foreign Secretary's willingness to go on playing the peace game after receiving a further round of feelers from Göring. These had been relayed by a Shell-Mex oil executive named Baldwin Raper, who followed hard on the heels of the Bishop of Oslo's report of peace hints in his conversation with Göring. The permanent officials argued that neither approach would lead to "any useful result." Lord Halifax, however, "saw no harm" in encouraging Baldwin Raper, "provided that he is careful to give no sort of indication that he has any authority or message from H.M.G."[6]

When Bryans returned with the message from von Hassel, the channel to the German opposition via the Vatican had already opened up. To the permanent officials who were increasingly at odds with the Foreign Secretary over his handling of the peace feelers, Bryans's amateur mission seemed both pointless and potentially dangerous. Vansittart insisted that neither the generals "nor anybody else can or will deliver the goods of revolution." In support of his contention he cited the soundings taken by his intelligence agent Colonel Christie, who was in communication from Switzerland with members of the anti-Hitler opposition inside Germany. The Chief Diplomatic Adviser believed that it was a "doomed experiment" to negotiate with the Germans, "whether the will o' the wisp dances in the name of phantom Generals or of a fat field Marshal with a neutral go between."[7]

The Foreign Office view prevailed. After an initial meeting with Cadogan at which he handed over the memorandum, Bryans was summoned back and told that the British government could give none of the assurances requested. He was instructed to make a final trip to Switzerland to explain this to von Hassel, so as to "leave no frayed ends." This injunction was repeated by Cadogan when Bryans collected his travel documents on 11 April after receiving a coded cable from Pirzio-Biroli: "your return extremely urgent only way to save business."[8]

Two days later, when Bryans met von Hassel again in Arosa, he tried to put a positive construction on the British government's gratitude "for the very considerable risk" that the opposition leader had taken. The veteran diplomat was not deceived. "I gained the impression that Halifax and his group had no real faith in the possibility of attaining peace in this way, that is through a change in regime in Germany," he commented regretfully in his diary. Since the German invasion of Norway had begun, von Hassel knew it was even more urgent to get some sign of approval from London to convey to the military conspirators. The only concession Bryans could offer was that Cadogan had told him that some assurance had already been transmitted "by official channels." "Oh yes," von Hassel said, deducing that this was the message that Halifax had sent via the Pope. "We heard about it," he acknowledged, "but that is not the sort of thing we want." As they parted, they knew the peace initiative had collapsed.[9]

Bryans headed for Rome for desultory talks with Pirzio-Biroli, then returned to London with another lengthy memorandum. But even Cadogan declined to see him this time. The Permanent Secretary made a note on Lord Brocket's letter suggesting a £1,000 reimbursement for Bryans's expenses: "Reply that Ld H. does not want Mr. L.C. to do any further journeying, and that of course his financial commitments are entirely outside our scope, as he had never been commissioned by us to do anything, and we have asked nothing of him."[10]

This dismissive note serves as the epitaph on the British attempts to negotiate with the German opposition on the eve of the arrival of Roosevelt's envoy in Europe. As von Hassel dejectedly recorded in the secret diary he kept buried in a tea chest in his garden, "the visit of Sumner Welles was in the offing and this gave the generals the impression – wrongly, since it was not so intended – that the other side was ready to negotiate with Hitler and therefore dared not deprive him of his chance."[11]

APPENDIX 4

Soviet Penetration of the U.S. Embassy in Moscow

The investigation conducted by F.B.I. Special Agents Avery M. Warren and Lawrence C. Frank found that the G.P.U. (predecessor of the N.K.V.D.) maintained a round-the-clock watch on the U.S. Embassy. They discovered that when one of the prostitutes of the Nosion Hotel ring was seen in the company of an American Embassy attaché "no attempt is made to follow her." But "if a strange woman appears in such company she is followed until she leaves the company of her escort and is then taken into custody and questioned." Whenever a new man arrived in Moscow he would receive "numerous telephone calls from these girls," who were "assigned to individual men by the G.P.U." As a result they acquired an "amazing" knowledge of what went on in foreign diplomatic circles.

Many of the girls pretended not to know any English, and the diplomats would therefore talk among themselves, with complete indiscretion; the girls listened and reported back "all information that they obtain through their associations with the members of the Embassy staff." The F.B.I. agents were appalled to find that these women had "free access to the Embassy building and there was hardly a night when several of them were not there." The F.B.I. report strongly criticized the State Department policy of sending single members to Moscow, because if the lonely bachelors did not fall easy prey to the G.P.U. prostitutes, they were liable to become victims of "Sexual Perversion." The agents witnessed two male clerks engaged in "passionate embraces and kisses which could only lead to one conclusion." They uncovered at least one homosexual ring within the Moscow Embassy centred around the

Ambassador's private secretary; as they pointed out, this "could be used as a lever to pry confidential information" by the G.P.U.

Hoover's men also discovered that Ilovaiskaya's closest associate was a woman named Valentina who for three years had been the "paramour" of an employee of the Navy Department named Sylvester A—. He maintained a *dacha* for her and was living way beyond his pay of $100 dollars or less a month. The Navy employee had impressed the Ambassador by claiming to find a hidden microphone – although he never produced it – and had then claimed he had discovered a tap on the phone in the U.S. Embassy in Berlin while on a courier mission. Like Kent's friends, the Navy man had apparently supplemented his income by smuggling, using his diplomatic passport, while on courier runs for the Embassy. The F.B.I. investigation also learned that one of Kent's fellow code clerks, named Antheil, who had died while on a courier mission, had been extracting cables and ciphers from the U.S. Embassy in Tallin, the Estonian capital. He too had a Russian girlfriend. They had also been told that Alexander Kirk, the Chargé in Berlin, was on "dope" and that Soviets employed by the Embassy in Moscow hung around in the basement area to retrieve partially burned cables from the incinerator.

The F.B.I. report was a telling indictment of the lax security of the State Department in general and the Moscow Embassy in particular. It is little wonder that Hoover told the President that the report painted "such a surprising picture." The President was no doubt just as horrified as Hoover, but could take some comfort from the measures already taken as a result of the F.B.I. inspectors' report, including the replacement of code clerks and steps to improve security in the Code Room and the custody of confidential cables.[1]

APPENDIX 5

State Department Codes and Ciphers, May 1940

fter Tyler Kent's arrest, it was several weeks before the State Department was ready to fly out the necessary sets of replacement ciphers and code books. Until that was done, confidential messages from Washington to all its embassies could be trusted only to the slow diplomatic bag or the time-consuming U.S. Navy cipher machines to which Kent had never had access. This restricted immediate secure communications to the London, Paris, Rome and Tokyo embassies which were the only embassies where the naval attachés had the encrypting devices.[1]

What Kent had compromised was the M-138 strip cipher devices developed by the U.S. Army Signal Corps, which the State Department relied on for its most confidential communications. It was based on a flattened-out Bazeries cylinder encrypting device, which had first been developed during World War I. Each M-138 set had 100 strips of randomly arranged alphabets. Thirty were used at a time, and the message was enciphered by reading it letter for letter in groups of 15. The system afforded a high degree of security as long as the strips were changed often enough and their combinations of letter arrangements remained confidential. There were other non-machine ciphers, labelled from "A" to "D" in ascending degrees of security.[2]

Examination of the cables and documents found in Kent's room revealed that many were in the C-1 cipher and a considerable batch in D-1. This latter was the most secure code used for the secret messages; its code books, together with the carbon copies of all cables sent and received in D-1, were hand-delivered to the designated recipient and the carbons kept in the Code Room safe. The majority of the cables were in the so-called colour codes, named after the coloured cover of the enciphering books: Brown, which was used for low-grade confidential documents, and Grey for routine non-confidential communications. The colour codes, as Kent himself pointed out, were not considered secure.[3]

The legendary Colonel William F. Friedman (the U.S. Army crypt-analyst who broke the Japanese "Purple" machine cipher system) was one of the experts called in by the Secretary of State in the summer of 1940 to report on the security of the Department's code systems in the wake of the Kent affair. He confirmed Kent's assertion that the Grey Code was a "one-part alphabetical construction and its solution would be fairly simple for the good amateur, but this would not be necessary because any foreign nation which did not at least have a photographic copy of the Grey Code had a very unenterprising intelligence service." The Brown Code was more technical and less general in its vocabulary and was kept under a "lock and key when not in use." According to Lawrence Hiles it was "not authorized to be handled by foreign nationals."[4]

"The British have got the Brown Code," Kent recalled Kennedy warning the State Department after the Ambassador had been disconcerted to find that the Foreign Office appeared to know in advance what answers he was going to give at a conference on trade. The Grey Code was not even regarded as a secure system because foreign nationals were permitted access to the enciphering books. Over its twenty years of use, several code books had gone missing from U.S. embassies around the world. According to Kent the Department continued using Grey to condense messages and economize on cable charges and because "it kept things out of the newspapers."[5]

The military code expert Hiles emphasized that "the Grey Code possessed no security whatsoever." Indeed there were occasions when the President deliberately instructed the Secretary of State to use the Grey Code when he wanted American diplomatic traffic read, for example in 1935, after Italy had invaded Abyssinia, when Roosevelt, who "was very security conscious" and preferred to send really important messages in the Navy cipher, in this instance specified that his cable to the U.S. Ambassador in Rome was to be in Grey Code. By using a cipher he knew would be broken with ease, he managed to get his strongly worded opinions of Mussolini directly across to the Italians; at the same time he knew that they could make no diplomatic protest without admitting that they were breaking the U.S. code.[6]

Since all but two of the Roosevelt–Churchill exchanges for which Kent had taken copies were in the Grey Code – in both directions – the conclusion has to be drawn that the President not only did not regard them as confidential, but actually wanted Hitler and Mussolini to be aware of his direct communications with Churchill. Kent himself explained that the Germans could easily have tapped into telegraph and radio circuits to read the supposedly top secret President-Naval Person cables.

If Roosevelt knew that the Germans could read these telegrams, then so did Churchill. The British codebreakers at the Government Code and Cipher School had made the American traffic a prime target ever since World War I, and the Prime Minister's interest in security and intelligence was even more acute than the President's. Their knowledge that the Germans could read their exchanges puts a new dimension on the significance of their famous telegrams. Kent also pointed out that he had been instructed that their exchanges, despite the "secret and confidential" stamps, must be enciphered in the lowest grade code, "so that the British would not be helped in breaking the more confidential codes if they intercepted a message to which they knew the contents."[7]

APPENDIX 6

The Right Club Membership List

T he peers listed in the Right Club "Red Book" include Baron Redesdale, the father of the famous Mitford sisters, Lord Semphill the aviator and the Duke of Wellington. There were half-a-dozen large Scottish landowners and M.P.s who, like Ramsay, represented a Scottish constituency. The list of knights and hons read like a miniature *Who's Who*. Among them is Sir Alexander Walker, the millionaire chairman of Johnnie Walker whisky distillery. In the Commons there was a vice-chairman of the Conservative Party (Colonel Harold Mitchell) and two government whips (Colonel Charles Kerr – later Lord Teviot – and Sir Albert Edmondson). Other M.P.s included a member of the Church Assembly (Commander Peter Agnew) and Sir Ernest Bennett, the National Labour M.P. who was British delegate to the League of Nations.[1]

One of the most prominent peers, Lord Carnegie (later the Earl of Southesk), was a member of the Royal Family by marriage to Princess Maud, granddaughter of Queen Victoria. Fifty years later the Earl insisted that he "had never heard of the Right Club" but did admit to knowing Captain Ramsay "quite well." They had been at Eton and in the Guards together. "A very loyal patriotic man" was how the eighty-four-year-old Earl recalled his friend. "Churchill," he said, "was down on him because he was anti-semitic." Another of those listed was the future Duke of Montrose, who in the mid-sixties became a Minister of Defence in the breakaway Rhodesian government. He too denied being a member of the Right Club although he admitted knowing Ramsay.[2]

Not everyone appearing in the Red Book was necessarily an active member of Ramsay's anti-semitic Club, and it is still less likely that everyone listed had treasonous intents. But the sensitivity of the issue still disturbs the British establishment. So great was the "distress" caused to Sir Ernest Bennett's son, the former Conservative M.P. Sir Frederic Bennett, that he wrote to the *Daily Telegraph* fiercely repudiating what he described as a "hurtful slur" on his father's character. Since British law does not allow libel suits on behalf of the deceased, it was surprising that the newspaper printed a full apology, denying that there had been any intended allegation of "treachery or conspiracy against Winston Churchill." What cannot be denied, however, is that Sir Ernest Bennett's name appears in the Red Book and that he was one of those M.P.s on the Committee that called for a negotiated peace. The printed apology to Sir Frederic suggested that his father's name might have been included in the Right Club list "to encourage the others," an assertion that appears to fly in the face of Captain Ramsay's reputation as an "officer and gentleman."[3]

The one person named in the Right Club book who was tried and convicted of treason was William Joyce, better-known as Lord Haw Haw: this New York-born British subject was hanged in 1946.

APPENDIX 7

The Controversy over Hitler's "Halt Order"

The caution shown by Marshal von Rundstedt in his temporary "catch-up" order of 23 May 1940 was certainly employed by Hitler after the event to justify his "Halt Order" (Haltbefehl). But it cannot have been the decisive factor. Other explanations that have been offered include a supposed soft-spot for the Belgians, allegedly evident in the Führer's directive for the general conduct of operations, which set forth that "under no circumstances must the tanks be permitted to be entangled in endless confusion of rows of houses in Belgian towns." But this seems to have been directed at preserving German armour rather than Belgian lives. The account in the War Diary of Army Group A also records another justification that Hitler gave for the order: that "any further compression of the ring encircling the enemy could only have the highly undesirable result of restricting the activities of the Luftwaffe."[1]

Close examination of the available records and testimony shows that Göring played a less important role in the shaping of Hitler's decision than postwar myth has claimed. A memo of 23 May from the Führer's Army Adjutant records that Göring telephoned Hitler to demand that the "National Socialist" Luftwaffe be given the honour of destroying the British Army. But Göring's intelligence officer later insisted that the Führer did not agree to leave the sealing of the pocket to the Luftwaffe until *after* General Major Joseph Schmid had personally handed Göring the report that the German tanks were "closing on Dunkirk." This could only have been early on the afternoon of Friday, 24 May, before Guderian's leading tanks withdrew from the outskirts of Bergues. Schmid, who was considered a very reliable witness, was with Göring in his command train *Asia* in a specially prepared siding outside a mountain tunnel in the Eifel Forest.[2]

"I arrived at Göring's office, it was the afternoon at Polch" was how Schmid in 1954 recalled the moment. He was told that Göring was outside, and found him sunning himself at a table on a specially built outdoor podium. "The tanks are before Dunkirk," Schmid told him, at which "Göring slapped the desk and exclaimed: 'I must talk to the Führer immediately, this is a special job for the *Luftwaffe*.'" Schmid then listened in on Göring's phone conversation with Hitler. The course of the discussion, he said, made it unlikely that there had been any prearranged plan or agreement. Göring blustered and boasted how "the parts of the British Expeditionary Corps around Dunkirk would be beaten to pieces by his Luftwaffe." Thumping the table with his fist, he insisted that the mission should be designated the "most urgent special task" of the Luftwaffe, calling for the German armour to be withdrawn several kilometres to free the battlefield for his bombers.[3]

"Hitler acceded to Göring in the same way Göring had decided – without long consideration," Schmid recalled. "Göring was convinced, firm as a rock, that he would succeed in preventing a withdrawal of the British Expeditionary Force." Schmid was also present when General Jeschonnek, Göring's Chief of Staff, telephoned O.K.W. to arrange personally with General Jodl "the time of withdrawal of army forces and the point of time for the Luftwaffe attack." Jodl, who earlier that week had complained about Göring's "shooting his mouth off," was highly sceptical about the Luftwaffe's ability to deliver on a promise. So it appears that Göring's bombastic promise to finish off the British Expeditionary Force was just another in the battery of excuses that Hitler fell back on to justify his "Halt Order," the decision that had been greeted with angry amazement by the German military professionals as "preposterous." Major von Treskow of Rundstedt's staff declared it was "pure madness" and the O.K.H. consensus was that it would permit the British to build a "golden bridge so they can march straight off the beaches without getting their feet wet."[4]

Few dared to question the Führer's order, let alone ask for an explanation. Halder recorded that von Brauchitsch had a "very unpleasant interview with the Führer" that Friday evening and returned to O.K.H. that night under instructions to issue new orders, cancelling those sent out the previous day and calling only for the "encirclement" of the Allied enemies. "The left wing, consisting of Armour and mot[orized] forces, which has no enemy before it, will thus be stopped dead in its tracks upon the direct orders of the Führer," Halder grumbled, adding scornfully: "Finishing off the encircled enemy army is to be left to the Luftwaffe!!"[5]

The double exclamation-marks express Halder's contempt for such a ludicrous proposition. How could the Führer seriously believe that over forty divisions on the ground could be bottled up by the Luftwaffe at night-time or if bad weather grounded flying operations? The whole idea of leaving the Dunkirk perimeter to Göring was so ludicrous to O.K.H. that, in a bid to circumvent the Führer's order, von Brauchitsch authorized the sending of a signal that night instructing both Army Groups: "Further to O.K.H.'s instructions of 24 May, *the continuation of the attack* on to the line Dunkirk–Cassel–Estaires–Armentières–Ypres–Ostend *is permissible.* Accordingly the space reserved for Luftwaffe operations is reduced." This blatant invitation for the Army commanders to disregard the "Halt Order" was ignored by the cautious von Rundstedt. Hitler had left his headquarters that Friday afternoon assigning him full authority to decide how operations were to be conducted. Accordingly, the O.K.H. order was not passed on to the Panzer commanders. "There is no further possibility of any crisis – except of a purely local nature," von Rundstedt's war diary notes with astonishing complacency. "On the whole, therefore, the task of Army Group A can be regarded as having been fulfilled."[6]

At O.K.H. that night, the pedantic Halder was not nearly so sanguine about the military outcome. He was particularly disturbed when von Brauchitsch returned from Führer Headquarters with the news that Hitler had now "formed the fixed idea that the battle of decision must not be fought on Flemish soil, but rather in Northern France." There seemed no military justification whatever for this. Halder dismissed it as a flimsy excuse to conceal a decision taken by "political command," as he sarcastically referred to O.K.W. "To camouflage this *political move*," Halder noted, "the assertion is made that Flanders, crisscrossed by a multitude of waterways, is unsuited to tank warfare. Accordingly, all tanks and mot[orized] troops will have to be brought up short on reaching the line St. Omer–Béthune."[7]

Unsuitable terrain was the explanation given personally by Hitler to those generals who were bold enough to question his judgement. That was what Warlimont was told when he asked Jodl, who, he recalled, was "impatient about my enquiries." The deputy O.K.W. chief assured him that "the personal experience that not only Hitler but also Keitel [O.K.H. Chief] and himself had in Flanders during the First World War proved beyond any doubt that armour could not operate in the Flanders mud, or at any rate not without heavy losses." The same excuse was given to Panzer Group commander Kleist when he taxed the Führer about the "Halt Order" and asked why the British had been allowed to escape. "That may be so," Hitler had responded, "but I did not want to send the tanks into the Flanders marshes – and the British won't come back in this war."[8]

483

The Flanders mud "camouflage" blinded many postwar historians into believing that Hitler's experience in the World War I trenches was the deep-seated psychological reason behind his decision. Yet, like the other explanations, while this may have been a factor, it was not the whole answer. General Blumentritt, who is also regarded as a trustworthy source, suggested this was just an excuse, because Hitler must have known from the experience of the Polish campaign that the Panzer divisions had "coped with much more difficult ground" in the swamps and mud at the River San, Lemberg and Grodek.[9]

If Hitler really was so anxious that his Panzer divisions would bog down on 24 May, why did he agree to release them two days later to operate in the same terrain?

APPENDIX 8

Hitler's Plan for
a Strategic Alliance with Britain

Hitler's attempts to secure an alliance with Britain in 1940 can be shown from the documentary records to follow the plan he dictated to his fellow prisoner Rudolf Hess when they were both imprisoned in the Landberg fortress after the abortive Munich putsch of November 1923.

"In Europe there can be for Germany in the predictable future only two allies: England and Italy," Hitler wrote in *Mein Kampf*. Rambling, distorted by his anti-semitism though this programmatic essay is, it establishes the policy goals that he illuminated still more clearly in his so-called "Second Book." Published in 1928, its preface includes the deathless phrase that "politics is history in the making." As part of his exposition of how he was going to reshape global strategy, Hitler devoted a whole chapter to eulogizing the British Empire and explaining how Germany had first to bury the conflicts of the past and come to terms with Britain in order to become a world power. He proposed to do this by adopting a "fundamentally new political orientation which no longer contradicts England's sea and trade interests." In their turn, Hitler assumed that the British could be persuaded to abandon their two-century-old policy of interfering to destabilize the most powerful continental state in order to keep a balance of power in Europe.[1]

Naive though this expectation of Hitler's proved to be, it was an essential element in his blueprint for making Germany the dominant global power in two distinct phases. The first required establishing a great continental empire by first eliminating France as a rival, then destroying Bolshevism by a takeover of European Russia. In

485

the second stage, Hitler envisaged that Germany would become a colonial and naval power to rival the British Empire, Japan and the United States. The final struggle, he predicted, would be waged in the 1980s (after his own death) for world domination. Both stages of his strategic blueprint required that Germany should form an alliance with Britain, first against France and Russia, then against the United States.

"England does not want Germany to be a world power; but France wants no power that is named Germany," Hitler had written in *Mein Kampf*. So he did not underestimate the obstacles to making Germany the supreme European power. But he could only succeed by not getting into a fight with both the major continental powers, Russia and France, while at the same time being drawn into a running conflict with Britain. His solution was to buy off Britain by deferring German colonial ambitions in return for the British accepting German hegemony over Europe. When Britain repeatedly refused his offer of a formal détente in the thirties, Hitler, by a masterful combination of military bluff and diplomatic cunning, managed to pull off his step-by-step resurrection of German power. The remilitarization of Germany and the reoccupation of the Rhineland, followed by the annexation of Austria, were successfully achieved without provoking a European war.

At the same time Hitler had failed to achieve the "grand solution" of global compromise with Britain that Ambassador Ribbentrop promised to effect when he was posted to London in 1936. Appeasement was a poor substitute for the alliance with Britain that Hitler longed for. While it enabled him to dismember Czechoslovakia at Munich in 1938, it made war inevitable when Britain and France allied to deter German claims on Poland in the spring of 1939. To break the impasse, Ribbentrop was permitted to pursue his alternative strategy of forging alliances with Britain's potential enemies Italy, Japan and finally Russia. The alliance with the Soviet Union was for Hitler a temporary convenience. He agreed to it only to secure his eastern border while he set about smashing Poland and France in order to complete the first part of his plan to establish Germany as the monolithic continental power in Western Europe, in preparation for his crusade to the East.

"Everything that I undertake is directed against Russia," Hitler declared to Carl J. Burckhardt, the League of Nations Commissioner for Danzig on 11 August 1939. "If the West is too stupid and too blind to understand, then I will smash the West, and then turn all my concentrated strength on the Soviet Union." It is noteworthy that two weeks later he attempted to revive his elusive goal of an alliance with Britain by offering "generous terms" to London to stand aside over her guarantees to Poland. Even when his offer was spurned and Britain declared war, Hitler did not abandon hope that the enemy he had never wanted to fight would see the error of its ways and become Germany's friend and ally. So after demonstrating the military might of the Reich by gulping down Poland – whose army was as large as that of France – the Führer again offered Britain a "generous peace." When Chamberlain ungratefully refused again, Hitler decided that the only way of bringing Britain to her senses was to smash her continental ally France. When he gave his generals their marching orders he made it very clear that by smashing the West he did not mean destroying Britain.[2]

APPENDIX 9

Did Churchill Want Hitler to Eavesdrop on His Cables to Roosevelt?

It has long puzzled historians why two leaders who were both so meticulous about security and intelligence, Churchill and Roosevelt, should have conducted so much of their strategically important correspondence by an insecure channel.[1]

Part of the answer was provided by Tyler Kent himself, who confirmed that the Embassy Code Room had standing instructions that the "Former naval person–President" communications were to be encoded in the lowest grade of diplomatic cipher, so as to protect the more secure ciphers from British eavesdropping. If the Bletchley codebreakers had the original message, their crypt-analytic efforts would have been greatly facilitated. The Prime Minister's formerly secret files reveal too that Churchill knew about the insecurity of the Grey Code. It is therefore logical to infer that when he reverted to using the U.S. Embassy channel on 12 June 1940 he intended that his communications *should* be eavesdropped by the Axis powers, just as Roosevelt had done in 1935 when he specified the use of the Grey Code because he wanted to admonish Mussolini.

Corroboration for this appears on the duplicate Foreign Office copy of the cable the Prime Minister sent to Roosevelt via Kennedy on 13 June. A handwritten minute shows that John ("Jock") Balfour, head of the American Department, had confirmed this with the Cabinet Office, raising his concern that Kennedy's defeatism caused him to "hold forth to American journalists." But Balfour was assured that the Prime Minister was "fully aware that there were objections," including the security on telegrams passed to

488

Washington via the U.S. Embassy. Furthermore he was told that "there were special reasons & the message had to be sent in this way." As the minute by the head of the Foreign Office's American Department, J.V. Perowne, discloses, Churchill appears to have had another more cunning reason for his instruction.[2]

"This shows that Mr. Churchill is for reasons best known to himself determined to make use of the channel of the U.S. Embassy," Perowne minuted. "This may portend either (1) a desire to keep Kennedy in play or (2) *a hope that the Germans will get to know and understand how close our liaison with the Americans is.*"

Kennedy, as Halifax's diary confirms, had certainly become "distressed" that the messages to the President were not going through him. This was the "official" explanation Churchill asked should be given to Lord Lothian for simultaneously passing his messages to the President via the U.S. Embassy. But if the Prime Minister really had intended to keep these exchanges with the President so secret, he would have stuck to the secure British Embassy channel, even at the risk of Ambassador Kennedy "kicking up a row because he wasn't being taken sufficiently into our confidence." This was the view of Cadogan, who minuted that they should "lump that," because security was more important than the *amour propre* of the defeatist American Ambassador. Corroboration for Perowne's theory that Churchill wanted Hitler to learn from the exchanges just how closely the British were liaising with the President appears in the attached note from Churchill's private secretary, which suggests that the Prime Minister had a system for determining which channel was to be used depending on the sensitivity of the information to be communicated to the White House. The Foreign Office was instructed accordingly that "whenever a 'former naval person' message is despatched the question of *the method of transmission* should if possible be raised with the Prime Minister."[3]

Comparison of the two sets of messages, those that Churchill sent to Roosevelt via the U.S. Embassy and those relayed by the British Embassy in Washington, during the two crisis periods in May and June 1940 does indeed reveal differences of presentation, content and frequency. Messages reaching the President via Lord Lothian and the secure Foreign Office channel were regular, detailed and reflective of the diplomatic uncertainties of the United States' commitment to the Allies. By contrast, the telegrams sent via the U.S. Embassy – and presumably intended to reach Hitler – were "life-and-death" appeals for U.S. aid, which were significantly bunched in flurries before the military disasters of Dunkirk and the Fall of France. Furthermore they were emphatic in declaring Britain's determination to fight on regardless.[4]

It may be argued that this was precisely the message that Churchill wanted to reach the Germans in order to give Hitler pause. Moreover, those cables sent via the U.S. Embassy all assume that the United States not only can be relied on to supply the hundreds of fighter planes, thousands of tons of armament and scores of destroyers needed but will eventually become a belligerent. They also repeatedly remind the President of Hitler's designs on the British fleet and the danger that a Nazi take-over of Europe poses to the United States. Then there is the disparity in the number of exchanges, with eight strident appeals from Churchill in this period as against just three non-committal replies from Roosevelt. This again suggests that Perowne's assumption was correct and the Prime Minister was using the cables relayed via Kennedy to signal to Hitler that if he pressed Britain too hard the United States would come into the war.

Final proof could be provided by the German signal intercepts of the Grey Code. So far the only Churchill–Roosevelt intercept that has come to light in the German records is the translation of the Italian receipt of the one Anna Wolkoff passed to the Italian Military Attaché. The signal intercepts and codebreaks that survived the war have yet to be released to the Federal German archives by the British and American governments. But there is a growing presumption, if only because the *Forschungstelle* intercepted two of the Churchill–Roosevelt transatlantic telephone conversations, that the surviving and still secret *Forschungsampt* SIGINT records may contain more than just a single "Former naval person to President" message. Even without the final proof, it seems that both Roosevelt and Churchill were aware of the possibility of German eavesdropping. The Foreign Office file containing Balfour's letter is confirmatory evidence for contending that the "Former naval person" adopted the same stratagem involving the Grey Code that Roosevelt had used with Mussolini in 1935.[5]

APPENDIX 10

"An Unfortunate Skeleton":
The Butler/Prytz Affair

The controversy over the Prytz telegram erupted even before the war had ended, after the claim was made by Christian Günther himself. Still Sweden's Foreign Minister, he made the remarks that so upset the British government at a dinner of the Insititute of Foreign Affairs in Stockholm on 31 October 1944.

Günther was the guest of honour at the dinner, which was attended by over two hundred prominent politicians and journalists. Although it is clear from the records that the Foreign Minister's own decision in favour of the German transit rights was not influenced by the Prytz message, he did use it effectively at the Ministers' meeting and with the Foreign Affairs Committee. In 1944 it provided him with an alibi that he hinted at without mentioning Lord Halifax or Butler by name. According to the report of Sir Victor Mallet to the Foreign Office his audience "were left with the definite impression that the Swedish concession to Germany in the summer of 1940 had in fact been based on a broad hint from His Majesty's Government that Great Britain might come to terms with the Nazis." A report was leaked to the Swedish newspaper *Expressen*, which published the "remarkable revelations" on 17 November 1944.[1]

The Foreign Office immediately responded that the Swedish Foreign Minister's allusion to Prytz's conversation with Butler the day that France capitulated "was an excuse for Sweden's agreeing to the German military traffic." What Günther had actually said was that the Swedish government took its decision following "information received from London."

A major diplomatic row threatened to erupt when the British insisted that Günther "make amends." The Foreign Minister, who claimed he had been speaking off the record, issued a qualified public denial. Britain's Minister in Stockholm was incorrectly informed by the Secretary-General of the Swedish Foreign Ministry that the transit decision had actually been taken on 16 June, the day *before* the arrival of the Prytz telegram. This led to Mallet making an incorrect report to London that accounted for the strong position taken up by the Foreign Office. Mindful that Britain's "stouteheartedness when we stood alone is such a tremendous asset to our prestige in the world," the Foreign Office wanted to make a public statement to protect that reputation from a damaging misinterpretation. But British officials in Stockholm had strong reservations. They had been shown, for the first time, the full text of Prytz's "very detailed report" and concluded that there was "no doubt that Mr. Butler's remarks were not as strong as they might have been." Publishing what he was reported to have said four years earlier would, it was thought, sound "very fishy." The Foreign Office never realized the degree to which Mallet had been misled on this crucial point by Erik Boheman, the Secretary-General of the Swedish Foreign Ministry, who had apparently muddled his dates when he told the British Ambassador that "his decision was taken in principle on the day before the telegram from London was received i.e. on 16 June 1940." Dr. Munch-Petersen's extensive researches into the affair confirm that Boheman's memory in 1944 was "at fault." But the press stories died down and Mallet, who considered it "bad tactics to resurrect this ghost now," advised London that "we had better let sleeping dogs lie."[2]

This particular dog refused to remain lying down. The following year the issue came to the fore again when the Foreign Office declined permission for Prytz to include his 1940 telegram in an official Swedish White Book of diplomatic communications to explain the transit issue. The justification given for refusing publication was that the cable resulted from "a misunderstanding of what had been said by Mr. R.A. Butler." Prytz, however, was in no doubt that the motive was to preserve the Churchillian myth of British resolution in 1940 which, he wrote, would "doubtless be maintained for the benefit of future historians." When the White Book appeared in 1947, its preface referred to the British refusal to permit the publication of the 17 June telegram. This prompted a flurry of Swedish press stories and angry minutes in the Northern Department of the Foreign Office in London. "Our stand alone after the fall of France is a matter of outstanding importance which must not be impugned," one official minuted. But once again the British decided not to make any public statement because the "controversy is rather the personal reputations of Lord Halifax and R.A. Butler which are at stake."[3]

The Foreign Office once more resorted to the favourite aphorism of the British civil servant that it was "best to let sleeping dogs lie." Six years later the publication of wartime Swedish ministerial memoirs set the dog barking again as the Prytz telegram made headlines in the Swedish press. But the issue attracted no attention in Britain until September 1965, when Prytz took part in a Swedish Radio series about World War II. This time there were full reports of his statements in the British press. Butler, who had just retired from politics after failing to succeed Macmillan in the premiership, was about to become Master of Trinity College, Cambridge. With the self-righteous disdain of an elder statesman he brushed the issue aside, which led some journalists to speculate that the defeatist remarks Butler was alleged to have made in 1940 explained why Conservative insiders had referred to him as "the best Prime Minister Britain never had." "It was all so long ago," he proclaimed wearily. "I feel the whole thing is rather exaggerated. I rely on the confidence placed in me by Mr. Churchill." Prytz, on the other hand, vigorously disputed the charge that he had not reported Butler accurately on 17 June 1940. "I know I did not misunderstand him," he assured a British reporter. "I quoted him word for word."[4]

When compared with the documentary record, Lord Butler's lofty dismissal of the Prytz affair in his memoir *The Art of the Possible* amounts to a revealing lesson in the art of hypocrisy. He wrote that "to the best of my knowledge and belief no one with responsibility in the Foreign Office ever encouraged the view that we should depart from the path of honour." His patriotic euphemism appears intended to camouflage his own documented, but surreptitious, efforts at launching peace initiatives. As we have seen, these include his discussions with a German emissary in Lausanne in November 1939, his disparagement of Churchill to the Italian Ambassador four months later, and his defeatist talk with Pierrepoint Moffat in March 1940. As he was writing before the wartime records were released Butler was able laconically to dismiss the Prytz telegram by obfuscation and questioning Prytz's professional ability.

"I certainly do not recall," Butler wrote, "giving the amusing Swedish Minister, Björn Prytz, on the day that France capitulated grounds for supposing that any of us had become less bellicose." He maintained that he had gone "no further in responding to any peace sounding than the official line at the time which was that peace could not be considered prior to the complete withdrawal of German troops from all conquered territories." This was "common sense and not bravado," Butler wrote, accusing "certain interested parties in Sweden" of attempting to "cause mischief."[5]

Ripe with righteous indignation though Butler's protest was, he evaded all reference to actual statements he had made, including the ones that were labelled "fishy" by the Foreign Office. It seems surprising that he did not issue specific and outright rebuttals if he had been able to do so. Notwithstanding Butler's reputation in the Foreign Office for slipperiness, his official biographer contends somewhat apologetically that "there is nothing in Prytz's summary of their conversation that convicts him of anything more than . . . lukewarmness." This represents an immense watering down of the mildest of Foreign Office criticism, that "Mr Butler's remarks were not as strong as they might have been." Stronger words, including "defeatist," were used by the British Ambassador in Stockholm after seeing the full text of the Prytz cable. Butler had told Prytz that "no opportunity for reaching a compromise peace would be neglected," and these were the words of a dyed-in-the-wool appeaser, not a lukewarm one who, his biographer maintains, "was shaking off the habits of the appeasement school in which he had been trained."[6]

If Butler had not used the defeatist words that Prytz attributed to him, why did he not issue a line-by-line denial of the controversial telegram that had been dogging his career for thirty years? There is a "fishy" slipperiness too in his belittling of the "amusing Swedish Minister" who was "not a professional diplomat." How was it that Butler, who enjoyed a close – and presumably frank – working and social relationship with Prytz could write that the Swede "attributed to my interview with him a significance which was disputed not only by me but by Sir Alexander Cadogan." To suggest, as Butler does in his memoir, that the Permanent Secretary would have put it all in his diary if he had considered the meeting important, is yet another diversionary argument. Cadogan was not even present at the 17 June meeting with the Swedish Minister, of which Butler had found it convenient to keep no record. That Prytz would have put words in Butler's mouth is unlikely, since the Swedish archives show that he had not filed any previous reports advocating that Britain should make a compromise peace. In fact the reverse is the case. In April Prytz had been in favour of Sweden entering the war on the side of the Allies. On 14 June he cabled Stockholm that the British government's resolve was increasing rather than decreasing on the reports of German advances in France. Only in the City and among its associates in the Conservative Party had Prytz previously reported finding any British talk of a compromise peace.[7]

It would have been out of character for Prytz, whose mother was an English Jewess, to promote a British deal with the Nazis. This provided further grounds for believing that he would not have relayed the peace alert if he had not been given the strongest reasons by Butler for believing it to be a reflection of government thinking.

Nor is there any reason to suspect that his understanding of what Butler said was affected by his poor command of the language. Prytz had been educated at Dulwich College, an English public school, and had many British friends. The fact that he was a businessman by training and "not a professional diplomat" adds credibility to his report, which was transmitted straightforwardly without any diplomatic gloss. All the indications are that Prytz accurately reported what he was told, because the evidence does not support the contentions that he "misinterpreted," as the Foreign Office and Butler always maintained.

The Foreign Office records show that once they became aware of the full text of Prytz's telegram, they dropped any idea of publishing it. As one official minuted revealingly at the time, the Swedes "appear to have unearthed an *unfortunate skeleton*." Just how unfortunate the Foreign Office considered this skeleton to be is evident in the 1944 reports on it that are still being held by the Department.[8]

APPENDIX 11

Kenneth de Courcy

Kenneth de Courcy was born in 1909 of mixed Irish and French parents – from whom he derived the title Duc de Grantmesnil. De Courcy has had a life as remarkable as it is chequered, including service in the Coldstream Guards, several years as a well-regarded Conservative Party lobbyist, and a prison term served alongside Soviet spy George Blake. De Courcy's conviction, for fraudulent property transactions in Rhodesia, was, he has repeatedly maintained, on a technical charge trumped up by his establishment enemies, who wanted to discredit him because he knew about too many skeletons in British political closets.[1]

While it is impossible for the historian to judge his guilt or innocence, the voluminous folders of de Courcy's correspondence provide a fascinating insight into the political and diplomatic intrigues of the years immediately before and after World War II. They attest his prodigious efforts as a letter writer and collector of rumours. Among those with whom he regularly corresponded were the Duke of Windsor, whom he counted as a friend, Billy Graham, whom he assisted on his Christian crusades in Britain, and Lord Vansittart, who shared de Courcy's view of the danger of communist subversion. The fluency and frequency of the letters he exchanged with such prominent Tory politicians of the 1960s as Butler, Eden and Sir Alec Douglas-Home reflect his earlier role as gadfly, informant and go-between for senior Tories in the troubled inter-war years.

In 1934 de Courcy became the principal organizing force and secretary of a right-wing lobby of Conservative M.P.s, the Imperial

Policy Group. They set out to influence British government policy through the *Review of World Affairs*, a monthly journal of military and diplomatic information, which later became the *Intelligence Digest*. It was founded in 1938 at the time of the Munich Crisis with declared intention to "create a liaison between government and public opinion." The journal was opinionated, but unusually well-informed because de Courcy as editor succeeded in milking confidential details from his extensive network of military and political contacts in Europe and the United States. He turned the journal into a platform from which to interpret and criticize British policy, much to the annoyance of the Foreign Office, as the world lurched through the crises of 1939 and into war with Germany.

The files now missing from the Hoover Institution provide substantial corroboration for de Courcy's claim that he acted before the war as a freelance agent for British intelligence. He claims to have produced reports for Desmond Morton, later Churchill's intelligence adviser, as well as for Sir Stewart Menzies, the head of MI6. His pre-war and wartime trips took him to the United States, Germany, France, Italy and Bulgaria. In contemporary parlance de Courcy can best be described as a networker, with a knack for ingratiating himself into right-wing social, political and military circles. He had a keen ear for gossip, an astute pen and a capacity for intrigue that had brought him to the attention of Robert Bingham, the former American Ambassador in London. Under his sponsorship de Courcy developed extensive contacts in Washington. Shortly before the Munich Crisis in 1938 William Douglas-Home, the playwright and younger brother of Chamberlain's Parliamentary Private Secretary Lord Dunglass, became an assistant in the Imperial Policy Group. This appointment, de Courcy claims, was at the request and with the approval of the Prime Minister himself. At Chamberlain's express instruction, de Courcy claims, he provided independent intelligence assessments and reports to Downing Street.[2]

The Foreign Office evidently considered de Courcy important enough to keep open a file on his activities. This reveals that he was regarded as an increasing irritant when the *Intelligence Digest* was promoted in the United States as an accurate source of inside information because of its parliamentary and Whitehall connections. Resentful officials referred to de Courcy in spiteful minutes as "the evil genius" of the Imperial Policy Group, an organization criticized for being a "collection of busybodies." After war broke out, de Courcy was repeatedly branded a *"défaitiste"* by officials who reported him to MI5 with injunctions that appropriate steps should be taken to "discourage" his activities. It proved difficult to discourage the persistent de Courcy, who, when war broke out, stepped up the production of his memoranda, which he sent to sympathetic members of the government, including Lord Caldecote and Rab Butler. His line to Chamberlain through William Douglas-Home provided him with a certain amount of protection from irate officials like the one who acidly observed that Douglas-Home's "connection with No. 10 must make him valuable to Mr. de C." But the Foreign Office files and Butler's own papers show that it was the Under Secretary of State who was de Courcy's chief protector. It was Butler who minuted that there were "merits in the Group's work." He issued instructions to "take no action officially."[3]

"In January 1940 when I wanted to go to France there was very considerable hostility in the Foreign Office," de Courcy recalled, "but Halifax of course thought it would be a good thing to find out what was really happening." With the assistance of the Foreign Secretary and the Home Secretary, Sir John Anderson, de Courcy obtained the necessary travel permits for himself and William Douglas-Home. As the self-styled "Chief Observer of Foreign Affairs in Europe and America" of the Imperial Policy Group, de Courcy was already on first-name terms with many of the ambassadors in London. Doors were opened to him at the highest levels in Sofia, where he had consultations with King Boris of Bulgaria. In the Vatican he had an audience with Cardinal Maglione, the Secretary of State. In Paris, where he had family connections, he took high-level soundings from military and political leaders. On his fact-finding trip in the spring of 1940 de Courcy concluded that after six months of war the Allies still lacked the strategy, unity of purpose and cohesion to fight to a successful outcome with Germany. He did not state this openly, but he began hinting in his publications at the futility of continuing to fight Hitler because of a top-secret French military staff memorandum he had been shown in Paris by General Brécard, a staunch supporter of Pétain.

After de Courcy returned to England, he produced a series of veiled warnings that were published in the April edition of the Imperial Policy Group memoranda. By highlighting France's reaction to the Norwegian campaign, he sought to cast doubt on the strength of her civilian and military morale and her ability to stand up to the anticipated German offensive. He followed this report with a series of personal letters to his contacts in the government, including Butler.[4]

"We cannot hope to win this phase of the war unless we pull ourselves together," de Courcy warned the Under Secretary of State on 20 April, calling for an intensive propaganda campaign to bolster French civilian morale. The strategy that de Courcy believed Britain should adopt, but which he did not dare to call for openly, was for the Allies to use the Phoney War stalemate to reach an accommodation with Germany before the Führer launched his attack on the West. This would, he believed, allow Hitler to exhaust the Wehrmacht fighting Russia while Britain, with the aid of the United States, built up the military strength necessary for a successful showdown with Germany.[5]

"We *were* putting forward defeatist views," de Courcy reflected emphasizing the risks the Imperial Policy Group ran by calling for what he believed was the only sane military strategy for Britain. "When the Norwegian campaign began to go really seriously wrong, I believed that there was no choice, it was my duty," he said, explaining that he was well-informed about the Scandinavian operations because one of his closest friends was the Swedish Minister in London.

Björn Prytz, according to de Courcy, used to pass to him confidential information that Swedish intelligence obtained from Göring's chauffeur, who was one of their agents. He related how Prytz, after attending a dinner at the de Courcy home in Eaton Place, deliberately left behind on his desk a thirty-page Swedish intelligence brief on Luftwaffe strength and aircraft production. Carefully camouflaged sections of this report later appeared in the Imperial Policy Group's journal, astonishing R.A.F. Air Intelligence with its precision and detail. During the first week of May 1940 Prytz also made de Courcy aware of his government's growing anxiety at the Soviet move into the Baltic states. This raised the alarm in some quarters in Stockholm that Sweden might soon be left with no choice but to become part of a Russo-German *Lebensraum*. It therefore made strategic sense to de Courcy to promote the idea of Britain reaching an accommodation with Germany before it was too late to save France.

"Hitler will be absolute on the Continent, and we shall be absolute on the sea," de Courcy declared at fashionable London dinner parties. His defeatism was recalled by the Second Secretary of the British Embassy in Stockholm, who encountered de Courcy for the first time on 9 May when he was firmly asserting that Germany would attack the Balkans before France. While he was soon proved dramatically wrong over Hitler's intentions, de Courcy's warnings about France's ability to resist a massive onslaught by the Wehrmacht were quickly vindicated.[6]

DOCUMENTS

Совершенно секретно

НКВД СССР

ПЕРВОЕ УПРАВЛЕНИЕ

10 отдел

НА ТЕМАТИЧЕСКИЙ УЧЕТ
ВЗЯТО

ДЕЛО-ФОРМУЛЯР № 25344

ПОМОЩНИК

КЛИЧКА „ "

Начато „25" ХII 1942 г.

Окончено „4" 3. 194

Том № 1

В томах.

Арх. № 38856

Арх. 38856

Форма № 4

СОВЕРШЕННО СЕКРЕТНО

КОМИТЕТ ГОСУДАРСТВЕННОЙ БЕЗОПАСНОСТИ при СОВЕТЕ МИНИСТРОВ СССР

(отдел, управление)

ДЕЛО-ФОРМУЛЯР

№ 20566

" Чёрная Берта "

(кличка)

Начато „ " 195 г.

Закончено „ " 195 г.

Арх. № 28889

ТОМ № 1

Фонд

в томах

28889

Colonel Moraviec's report to the KGB *Rezident* in London, which reached Moscow Centre in cryptogram no. 450 of 21 October 1942, was considered so important by NKVD chief Lavrenty Beria that he ordered this report be made to Stalin and Molotov. Unknown to the British until this document was released to the author from the KGB Hess file codenamed "Black Bertha," the head of Czech military intelligence passed M16 information to the Soviets throughout the war in return for Russian assistance with the underground in occupied Czechoslovakia. Moraviec had learned from his British intelligence contacts that M16 had evidently laid a plot to lure Hess to Britain. (In accordance with Soviet bureaucratic procedure the signatory had not signed off by completing the day and year in the copy lodged in the file of the 1st Directorate. For a translation, see page 453, KGB archives, Moscow.)

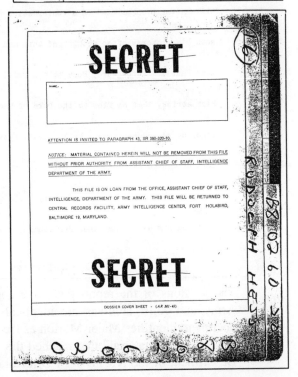

Cover page of the Hess file declassified by the U.S. National Archives in 1989. It encloses the report on Hess given to the U.S. military attaché in London in October 1941 by Churchill's intelligence aide, Major Desmond Morton.

"Hess landed and was captured just as the papers described. He was taken to a hospital and there told the doctor that "I am Rudolf Hess". The doctor laughed and said, "Yes, we have a fellow in the hospital here who thinks he's Solomon". But Hess persisted that he was Hess and demanded to see the Duke of Hamilton. The Duke appeared, talked with Hess and reported to authorities: "Yes, I think it's Hess, but don't take my word for it. I met him up on a platform during the Olympic Games and maybe shook his hand --- I can't really remember if I did or not --- but I didn't know him at all - never even carried on a conversation with him. I've seen his pictures often enough and this man certainly looks like Hess". (Afterward, Hess told a British official, Kirkpatrick, that he flew to the Duke of Hamilton because the Duke, he remembered, was a tall, Nordic type, obviously the sort of man to whom one could talk.") (Note: The Duke of Hamilton is not a tall man and it is quite possible that Hess confused him with some other Englishman. - R.E.L.)

The versions of the report that have come to light in the U.S. Army and KGB archives are identical—except that the Soviet document identifies Major Morton as the source of the 3 October 1941 "Agents material" that reached the 1st Section of the Third Department of the NKVD's 1st Directorate. (See page 447.)

От 3/X-41 г. *[рукописный текст]*
[рукописный текст]

Майор МОРТОН, личный помощник ЧЕРЧИЛЛЯ, за завтраком 26 октября сказал, что ГЕСС приземлился и был захвачен точно так, как это было описано в газетах. ГЕСС был доставлен в больницу, где он заявил доктору: "Я Рудольф ГЕСС."Доктор рассмеялся и сказал "Да в нашей больнице есть человек, который считает себя Соломоном". Но ГЕСС продолжал утверждать, что он ГЕСС и потребовал герцога Гамильтона. Пригласили Гамильтона, который поговорив с ГЕССОМ сообщил властям: "Я думаю, что это действительно ГЕСС, но поручиться за это не могу. Я видел его однажды на платформе во время олимпийских игр и кажется поздоровался с ним за руку:.. я не помню точно ..., но я совершенно его не знаю, никогда с ним даже не разговаривал. Я видел много фотографий ГЕССА, а данное лицо выглядит действительно, как ГЕСС". /Позднее ГЕСС сказал английскому чиновнику Кирхпатрику, что он направился к герцогу Гамильтону потому, что герцог, насколько он помнит "высокий, северного типа, человек, располагающий к себе"./.

Айвон Кирхпатрик, секретарь британского посольства в Берлине в течение длительного периода хорошо знавший ГЕССА, посетил его после Гамильтона. Кирхпатрик подтвердил, что это действительно ГЕСС.

ГЕСС заявил, что он прилетел к герцогу Гамильтону для того, чтобы сказать ему, что Германия собирается воевать с Россией ."Я знаю, что герцог сразу бы подумал, что для Англии было бы абсурдом продолжать борьбу против Германии Так как, если бы Англия продолжала борьбу на западе, мы бы вынуждены были уничтожить Англию, после уничтожения России".

Кирхпатрик:"Может быть Вы полагаете, что герцог мог бы что либо сделать для того, чтобы Англия заключила мир с Германией?"

ГЕСС:"Конечно. Кроме всего прочего он является герцогом. Он может пойти к королю и сказать ему о наших планах войны с большевиками, тогда король бы мог заключить с нами мир".

К."Что Вы скажете о правительстве?"

Г. "Это чепуха. Кто входит в правительство ЧЕРЧИЛЛЯ? Никто, кроме дураков, желающих уничтожить Германию и ставящих мир перед угрозой большевизма. Безусловно, король бы мог заключить с нами мир". Майор Мортон несколько раз был у ГЕССА. Однажды он разговаривал с ним относительно английских и немецких сводок о воздушных операциях. ГЕСС утверждал, что за прошлый год Англия потеряла 2000 самолетов, а Германия только 500. По заявлению Мортона в действительности имеется обратное соотношение.

СОВ. СЕКРЕТНО.

СПРАВКА

Вадим сообщил из Лондона, что:

1) по данным "Зенхен" ГЕСС прибыв в Англию заявил, что он намеревался прежде всего обратиться к ГАМИЛЬТОНУ знакомому ГЕССА по совместному участию в авиасоревнованиях 1934 года. ГАМИЛЬТОН принадлежит к так называемой кливденской клике. ГЕСС сделал свою посадку около имения ГАМИЛЬТОНА.

2) Кирк ПАТРИКУ, первому опознавшему ГЕССА чиновнику "Закоулка" ГЕСС заявил, что привез с собой мирные предложения. Сущность мирных предложений нам пока неизвестны. (Кирк Патрик - бывший советник английского посольства в Берлине).

14/У-1941 г.   № 376.

Резолюция тов. ЖУРАВЛЕВА - т. РЫБКИНОЙ - телеграфируйте в Берлин , Лондон, Стокгольм, Америку, Рим. Постарайтесь выяснить подробности предложений.

В е р н о: (ОСЕТРОВ)

Kim Philby kept Moscow Centre informed on what the Foreign Office had learned from Hess through "Vadim" (codename of the NKVD *Rezident* in London), who transmitted the Soviet agent's reports to Moscow in these two *Spravka*s, derived from cryptograms No. 376 and 338 received in Moscow Centre from London on 14 and 18 May 1941. Зεηχεη, Philby's cryptonym, was the German *Sonnchen*, "little sun." Закоυρκα was the cryptonym used when referring to the British Foreign Office. The handwritten notation on the second *Spravka* indicates that one copy was enclosed with the Hess file "Black Bertha" while another was put in Philby's *Sonnchen* file. (For translation, see page 442.)

СОВЕРШЕННО СЕКРЕТНО.

С П Р А В К А

Вадим из Лондона сообщает, что точных данных относительно целей прибытия ГЕССА в Англию еще не имеется.

По сведениям, полученным "Зенхеном", в личной беседе с его приятелем Томом ДЮПРИ (заместителем начальника отдела печати МИД"а) и еще не проверенным через

1. ГЕСС до вечера 14 мая какой-либо ценной информации англичанам не дал.

2. Во время бесед офицеров английской военной разведки с ГЕССОМ, ГЕСС утверждал, что он прибыл в Англию для заключения компромиссного мира, который должен приостановить увеличивающееся истощение обоих воюющих стран и предотвратить окончательное уничтожение Британской империи, как стабилизующей силы.

3. По заявлению Гесса, он продолжает оставаться лойяльным Гитлеру.

4. Бивербрук и Иден посетили Гесса, но официальными сообщениями это опровергается.

5. В беседе с Кирк Патриком, Гесс заявил, что война между двумя северными народами является преступлением. Гесс считает, что в Англии имеется

"Зенхен" считает, что сейчас время мирных переговоров еще не наступило, но в процессе дальнейшего развития войны, ГЕСС возможно станет центром интриг за заключение компромиссного мира и будет полезен для мирной партии в Англии и для Гитлера.

(по 18.5.41 г. К 338.)

ВЕРНС: Осетров   (ОСЕТРОВ)

The M15 record of Tyler Kent's interrogation in Ambassador Kennedy's office on 20 May 1940 was withdrawn from the U.S. National Archives on 6 November 1981 at the request of State (Department) G(reat) Br(itain) Intel(ligence). The cover for Kent's 1951 F.B.I. file shows "R" for Russian reclassification. The censor's pen has blacked out the source of the charge that Kent was collecting his handwritten copy of Churchill's 20 May 1940 cable to the President for the Soviets.

Present: The Ambassador, Captain Knight of the Military Intelligence Branch of Scotland Yard, Mr. Johnson, and Mr. Erhardt.

The Ambassador: This is quite a serious situation that you have got your country involved in. From the kind of family you come from – people who have fought for the United States – one would not expect you to let us all down.

Mr. Kent: In what way?

The Ambassador: You don't think you have? What did you think you were doing with our codes and telegrams?

Mr. Kent: It was only for my own information.

The Ambassador: Why did you have to have them?

Mr. Kent: Because I thought them very interesting.

Captain Knight: I am talking to you now by invitation of your Ambassador and not in any way in connection with matters which concern only Great Britain

on as I see it is this. I

should know you can be

ing with this woman, Anna

t.

position to prove that she

ion with Germany; that she

munication with Germany;

tile associations; that

she

ACCESS RESTRICTED

The item identified below has been withdrawn from this file:

File Designation   _Secret Codes, Kent_

Date   _20 May 40_

~~From~~

~~To~~   _Transcript_

In the review of this file this item was removed because access to it is restricted. Restrictions on records in the National Archives are stated in general and specific record group restriction statements which are available for examination. The item identified above has been withdrawn because it contains:

10 pgs / 5

☑ Security-Classified Information

☐ Otherwise Restricted Information

State / GBR / Intel
Authority

6 Nov 81
Date

GENERAL SERVICES ADMINISTRATION

GSA FORM 7117 (2-72)
GPO : 1973 O - 503-858

_R 1 R_

TAB # 1C

FEDER. BUREAU OF INVES. GATION

For's No.1
THIS CASE ORIGINATED AT ▮▮▮ Baito- ▮▮   F'L NO. 100-37;5

REPORT MADE AT	DATE WHEN MADE	PERIOD FOR WHICH MADE	REPORT MADE BY
▮▮▮	5-2-51	1-18;2-3,9;4-17,23,24-5.	6/▮▮▮▮

TITLE	CHARACTER OF CASE
TYLER GATEWOOD KENT	INTERNAL SECURITY - R

SYNOPSIS OF ▮▮▮▮

▮▮▮▮ readily fur-
nished background information concerning ▮▮▮▮ voluntarily
identified ▮▮▮▮ ANNA WOLKOFF, and her relationship
with TYLER GATEWOOD KENT; and furnished general information
relating to their conviction by the British court and
the activities upon which conviction based. ▮▮▮ expressed
belief subject was "working for both sides," based on his
expressions of enthusiasm for Moscow and Russia and his
apparent efforts to infiltrate "white Russian" circles
in London. ▮▮▮ could not further substantiate ▮▮▮ belief
in his connections with Soviet espionage activities.
▮▮▮ having been aware of ▮▮▮
in the anti-war campaign of the group headed by Sir
ARCHIBALD H. M. RAMSEY and claimed ▮▮▮▮ had been
"infatuated" with subject and completely under his influence. ▮▮▮ stated ANNA WOLKOFF is residing in London
at an unknown address ▮▮▮

1 Xerox Copy CIA
RUC 6/27/62-sse/bcb

COPIES DESTROYED
3991R AUG 30 1960

SEE REVERSE SIDE FOR
ADD. DISSEMINATION.

APPROVED AND FORWARDED ▮▮▮   SPECIAL AGENT IN CHARGE

DO NOT WRITE IN THESE SPACES

65- 27850   102

RECORDED - 120
INDEXED - 120
MAY 1 7 1951

COPIES OF THIS REPORT
5 - Bureau (65-27850)
4 - Baltimore (100-13801)
3 - Miami (65-2415)
3 - ▮▮▮

weeks. The battle in France
is very dangerous for both sides.
Although we are clearing down
two or three to one of their aircraft their numerical superiority is still very great. It
is vital for us to
have as soon as possible the
greatest possible number of Curtiss
P40 fighters now in course of
delivery to the ▮▮▮ army

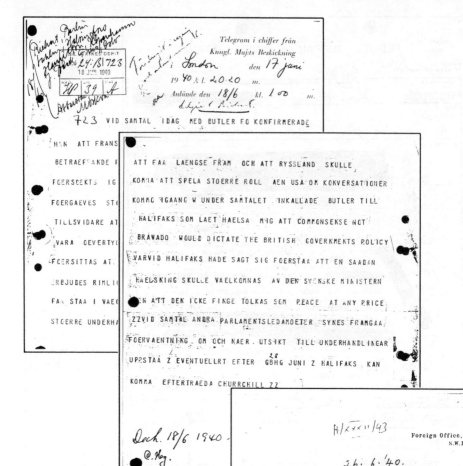

The telegram from the Swedish Minister in London, No. 723, shows the emphasis that Björn Prytz placed on Butler's meaning by leaving the words "commonsense not bravado," etc. in English. Churchill's letter to Halifax of 26 June 1940 drew attention to his "odd language," whose inference was as clear to the Prime Minister as it had been to Prytz. Butler's letter to the Foreign Secretary sidestepped the issue, but Kenneth de Courcy's account of his own role as an intermediary with Kennedy and Prytz is explicit—explaining perhaps why it has since disappeared from the Hoover Institution's archives. (See page 308.)

277

Quarto

10. Downing Street,
Whitehall.
June , 1940.

My dear Edward,

    It is quite clear to me from these
telegrams and others that Butler held odd language
to the Swedish Minister and certainly the Swede
derived a strong impression of defeatism. In these
circumstances would it not be well for you to find
out from Butler actually what he did say. I was
strongly pressed in the House of Commons in the
Secret Session to give assurances that the present
Government and all its Members were resolved to fight
on to the death, and I did so, taking personal
responsibility for the resolve of all. I saw a silly
rumour in a telegram from Belgrade or Bucharest and
how promptly you stamped upon it, but any suspicion
of lukewarmness in Butler will certainly subject us
all to further annoyance of this kind.

        Yours ever,

        Winston S. Churchill

... Lord Halifax
... to be
... Churchill.
... to persuade Hitler
(Halifax) were troubling
to get peace.
... once without the
... Hitler but would
... Eastern Europe to be
... to its former condition etc.
... Germany the mouth of the
... agree to that —
... Kennedy & put forward
the above that I said we only be possible if the two.
agreed to declare war if Hitler refused.
Kennedy agree — saw Halifax.
I saw Butler the next day at the Carlton Club.
He said both Halifax & Kennedy were delighted with
my views & W. I see Kennedy again to press him.
A few hours later Butler asked to see me again
for breakfast. About 4 hours later His War
Cancelled & I was asked to meet his Parliamentary
Private Secretary in St James's Park. I did so.
He asked me to destroy my whole file with Butler,
not see Kennedy again & retire to Scotland for a
few weeks. I agreed not to see Kennedy but refused
the two other requests. I said I would see Lordship.
Chairman asked me not to.

    The Swedish Minister (Pricks) confirmed to me
that Butler had said all the same proposals to
him — he so reported by official Telegram to
Stockholm (he did not is there now).

Bern

FROM Dated November 11, 1939

Rec'd 10:43 a.m.

Secretary of State,

Washington.

136, November 11, noon.

Reference my telegram No. 130.

~~VERY CONFIDENTIAL~~ FOR THE SECRETARY AND UNDER SECRETARY.

I have learned from my colleague, the Papal Nuncio,
that he was told in confidence by Motta that about a fortnight ago Butler, British Parliamentary Under Secretary of

---

PRESIDENCE DU CONSEIL
MINISTÈRE
DE LA
DÉFENSE NATIONALE
ET DE LA GUERRE.

Cabinet
du Ministre.

RÉPUBLIQUE FRANÇAISE.

7

Paris, le 20 Mai 1940

LD/

Offres éventuelles de paix de l'Allemagne

-o-

      M. NORDLING, Consul Général de Suède à Paris,
qui avait accompagné M. COULONDRE et le Général MITTELHAUSER
lors de la mission accomplie en Scahdinavie du 12 au 14 Avril,
est revenu quinze jours plus tard à Paris en traversant
l'Allemagne. Il s'est joint à une mission suédoise qui compre-
nait M. DAHLERUS, Industriel connu pour ses relations avec le
Maréchal GOERING, le Directeur des Affaires Economiques au
Ministère des Affaires Etrangères suédois et le Chef d'Etat-
Major des forces navales suédoises.

      Cette mission a proposé au gouvernement du Reich
un projet consistant essentiellement à assurer par des forces
navales suédoises la police des eaux norvégiennes et la
répartition équitable du minerai de fer entre l'Allemagne et
les Alliés. Ce projet a été repoussé par les Allemands.

      Le Maréchal GOERING a cependant tenu à voir
M. DAHLERUS qui, à plusieurs reprises, s'était fait l'intermé-
diaire d'offres de paix allemandes. Le Lieutenant du Führer a

    ....

State Department records show that Under secretary Butler secretly met Hitler's emissary Prince Max von Hohenlohe a month after the outbreak of war. French prime minister Reynaud, by contrast, rejected Göring's peace emissary Nordling at the height of the Battle for France. Churchill was no less resolute in resisting German peace feelers—but the British Minister in Berne continued to relay Vatican overtures to London despite his instructions to the contrary.

INDEXED

C F

7324/89/18

34

SPECIAL DISTRIBUTION AND WAR CABINET.

From SWITZERLAND.

Decypher.   Mr. Kelly (Berne).
                                1st July, 1940.

     D. 7.5 p.m.   1st July, 1940.
     R. 4.50 a.m.   2nd July, 1940.

No. 318.   rrrrrrrr

     Your telegram No. 198. C7324/59/18 No spares to attach

     Following from ~~Lemberg~~. Leigh Smith

     The Pope informed Osborne June 29th during one hours audience that he has been making indirect soundings (Osborne gathers in London, Berlin, Rome) as to chance of compromise. Osborne adds that Vatican have informed his colleagues that they would be very glad if a compromise could be reached but have tactfully avoided expressing themselves very strongly.

*They have expressed themselves clearly, if not strongly.
A straight answer to any papal intrigues
has been given in our tel No. 198.
(copy attached).
Southern Dept.
This has been dealt with —*

G. Warr. 3/7

N. Roberts 3/7

R. 3/7

*The Apostolic
Delegate made an approach 3/7
to the S. of S. on July 2. SD.
C7377/89/18. 3/7.*

C7377/89/18.   I will send —

E

C7324/89/18

10, Downing Street,
Whitehall. 33

Foreign Secretary.

     I hope it will be made clear to the

Nuncio that we do not desire to make any inquiries

as to terms of peace with Hitler, and that all our

agents are strictly forbidden to entertain any such

suggestions.

                    W.

          28.6.40.

BOX NO. 500,
PARLIAMENT STREET, B.O..
LONDON, S.W.1.

L.305.95.Dy.B   7th February 1940.

SECRET

PERSONAL & CONFIDENTIAL

Dear Johnson,

I think the following information may be of interest
to the State Department.

I have heard from an informant whose statements have
in other respects proved to be accurate, that at any rate
just prior to the war and possibly still, the German Secret
Service had been receiving from an American Embassy, reports,
at times two a day, which contained practically everything
from Ambassador Kennedy's despatches to President Roosevelt,
including reports of his interviews with British statesmen
and officials. The source from which the German Secret
Service got these documents is not definitely known, but is
someone who is referred to as "Doctor", and our informant
who is in a position to know, is of opinion that the
"Doctor" is employed in the American Embassy in Berlin.

The above information, as you will realise, is
extremely delicate and in any enquiries that you or the
State Department think fit to make, we should be grateful
if you would take every possible step to safeguard our
informant.

Yours sincerely,

Herschel Johnson,Esq.,
American Embassy.

The Secret M15 report naming the "Doctor" as a German source for the American Embassy was not shown to Ambassador Kennedy. His identity is one of the central enigmas of those critical months of 1940—as is the clear indication in Perowne's minute on the Prime Minister's cable, which strongly suggests Churchill wanted Hitler to know the contents of certain cables he sent to Roosevelt via the U.S. Embassy in London.

OUTWARD TELEGRAM

[This Document is the Property of His Britannic Majesty's Government, and should be
kept under Lock and Key.]

291

Cypher telegram to The Marquess of Lothian, (Washington).
        Foreign Office 13th June, 1940. 1.35 p.m.
No. 1090.
                        cccccccccccc
IMMEDIATE.

MOST SECRET AND PERSONAL.

        Following message from Prime Minister to President was
handed to American Counsellor this morning for transmission to
America.

        Begins.

        French have sent for me again, which means that crisis has
arrived.   Am just off.   Anything you can say or do to help the
now may make the difference.

        We are also worried about Ireland.   An American Squadron
at Berehaven would do no end of good I am sure.

        Ends.

FRANCE 1940

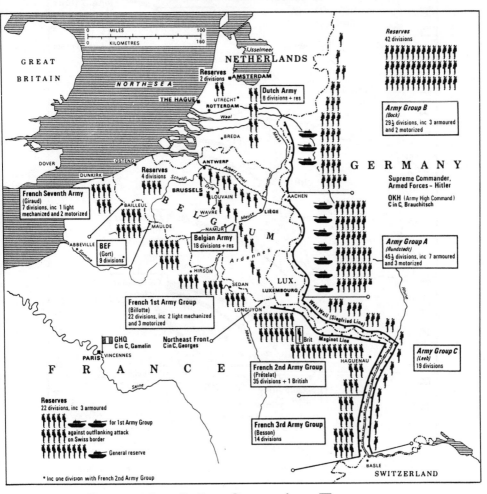

Strength of the Opposing Forces

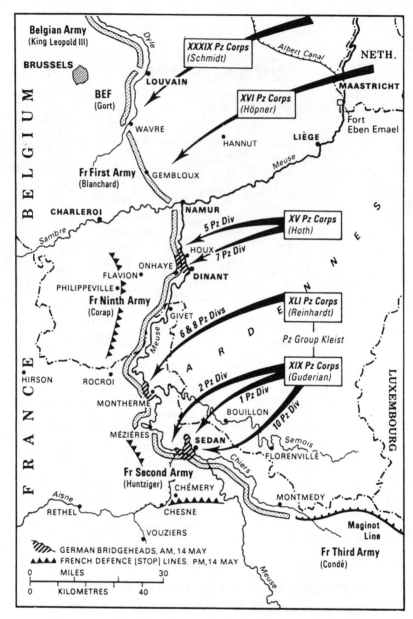

**Panzer Thrusts to and Bridgeheads
over the Meuse**

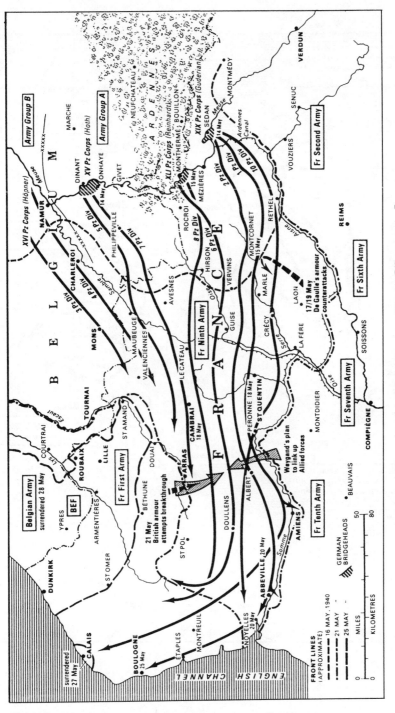

German Dash to the Channel

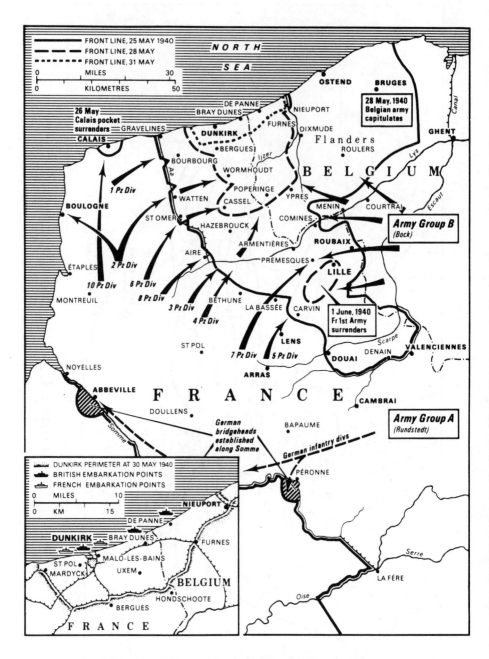

Squeezing the Allies' Perimeter

NOTES AND SOURCES

N.B. Emphases added by author unless otherwise indicated.

Abbreviations: principal archives, manuscripts and unpublished materials

1. UNITED KINGDOM

(i) *The Public Records Office, Kew, London:* PRO
Cabinet Records (CAB); Prime Minister's Papers (PREM); Foreign Office Records (FO); Home Office Records (HO); Admiralty Records (ADM); Army Records (WO); R.A.F. Records (AIR); Metropolitan Police Records (MEPO); Ministry of Information Records (INF)

(ii) *House of Lords Records Office:* HOL
Papers of Lord Beaverbrook; Papers of J. C. C. Davidson; Lloyd George Papers

(iii) *Cambridge University Library:* CUL
Papers of Earl Baldwin; Papers of Viscount Templewood (Sir Samuel Hoare)

(iv) *Churchill College Cambridge Archives:* CCA
Cadogan Manuscript Diaries; Christie Papers; Denniston Papers; Halifax Papers (Hickleton Collection); Vansittart Papers; the as

yet unreleased Churchill Papers, as cited by Martin Gilbert in the official biography

(v) *Trinity College Cambridge Archives:* TCCA
Papers of Lord Butler

(vi) *Bodleian Library, Oxford University:* BLO
Papers of Lord Simon; Earl Attlee Papers; Greenwood Papers

(vii) *Balliol College Library:* BCL
Nicolson Papers

(viii) *London School of Economics Library:* LSEL
Dalton Papers

(ix) *Borthwick Institute, Garrowby, Yorkshire:* BIG
Papers and Private Diary of Lord Halifax

(x) *Birmingham University Library:* BUL
Chamberlain Papers; Earl of Avon Papers

(xi) *Reading University, Edinburgh University*
Papers of Lord Lothian

(xii) *Centre for Military Studies, Kings College, University of London:* KUL
Liddell Hart Papers

2. UNITED STATES OF AMERICA

(i) *National Archives Washington D.C.:* NAW
State Department (RG 59); Chief of Staff Papers (RG 319); Captured German Documents (T-Series); Pearl Harbor Liaison Office (RG 84 PHLO); U.S. Army Intelligence G-2 Records IRR collection (RG 319)

(ii) *Franklin D. Roosevelt Memorial Library, Hyde Park, New York:* FDRL
President's Safe File Records (PSF); Berle Diaries; Morgenthau Diaries; Pell Collection; Toland Collection; Walton Moore Papers

(iii) *Library of Congress, Manuscripts:* LOC
Breckenridge Long Papers; Hull Papers; Ickes Papers; Frank Knox Papers; Landis Papers

(iv) *Stirling Library, Yale University:* SLY
Charles Parsons Collection; Stimson Papers; Sir William Wiseman Papers

(v) *Houghton Library, Harvard University:* HLH
J. Pierrepoint Moffat Papers

(vi) *Hoover Institution, Stanford University:* HISU
De Courcy Papers

(vii) *Georgetown University Library, Washington D.C.:* GUL
James D. Mooney Collection

(viii) *Boston University Library:* BUL
Cecil King Papers

(ix) *Federal Bureau of Investigation, Washington D.C.:* FBI/FOIA
(under personalities)

3. CANADA

National Archives of Canada: NAC
Mackenzie King Papers MG

4. FRANCE

(i) *Archives National:* AN
Reynaud Papers

(ii) *Archives of the Ministère des Affaires Etrangères:* MAE
Baudouin Papers; Charles-Roux Papers; Daladier Papers; Desjean
Papers; Reynaud Papers

5. ITALY

Foreign Ministry Archives, Rome: FMR

6. SWEDEN

Riksarkivet Swedish Foreign (Utrikes) Department Archive: UDA

7. GERMANY

(i) *Bundesarchiv, Koblenz:* BAK
(ii) *Auswärtiges Amt, Bonn:* AAB
(iii) *Institut für Zeitgeschichte, Munich:* IZM
(iv) *Nuremberg War Crimes Tribunal – The State Archive:* NSA

8. THE SOVIET UNION

The KGB Archive, Moscow: KAM

CHAPTER 1

(pp.1–20)

1. *Hansard,* 7 May 1941.

2. Harold Nicolson, *Diaries and Letters, 1939–45,* edited by Nigel Nicolson (London, 1967), 7 May 1941, pp. 164–5.

3. *Hansard,* 7 May 1941.

4. Ibid.; Nicolson, *Diary,* loc. cit.

5. Fighter Command War Room Log, AIR 16/698 PRO.

6. F.H. Hinsley *et al. British Intelligence in the Second World War,* Vol. 1 (Cambridge, 1979), pp. 315–28 and Appendix II.

7. Rudolf Hess, 1947, letters to his wife quoted by Ilse Hess, *Ein Schicksal in Briefen* (Leoni, 1971), pp. 82–7: "Der Flug"; interview with Felicity Ashby, April 1990.

8. Ibid.

9. "It appeared 90 miles E[ast] of Amble flying W[est]" is how Raid 42 was logged on to the main plot at 20.08 according to the 10 May 1941 entry of Fighter Command Headquarters War Diary. The radar contacts confirmed that the enemy intruder was moving at high speed on a south-by-west course that would take it south of Holy Island at under 9,000 feet. The resolving capability of the early radar sets left unclear how many planes actually made up the raid, so it was recorded as "1 plus" aircraft. Operational Record Book Fighter Command H.Q. AIR 24/538, 10 May 1941, annotated in red pencil to "R. Hess"; Log of R.A.F. Catterick, 10 May 1941, AIR 28/624; Fighter Command O.R.B. 19.48 entry for "Raid 42" AIR 24/539/PRO; Ashby interview and her article in *Aeroplane Monthly,* October 1987.

10. "Additional Notes on the Hess Incident by Group Captain the Duke of Hamilton," undated, 1945, INF 1/912 PRO.

11. James Douglas-Hamilton, *Motive for a Mission* (London, 1971).

12. "Report On Interview with Herr Hess by Wing Commander the Duke of Hamilton, Sunday 11th May 1941," PREM 3/219/7; Personal recollection by the Duke of Hamilton "taken from notes he made at the time" and quoted by Air Vice-Marshal Sandy Johnstone, C.B., D.F.C., in his book *Where No Angels Dwell,* foreword by the Duke of Hamilton (London, 1969), p. 90.

13. "Instruction 17," 21 March 1941, AIR 25/242 PRO.

14. "72 Blue left ground at 1959 to patrol FARNE ISLANDS to ST ABBS HEAD, looking for low flying aircraft. 72 Blue landed at 2110 hours." O.R.B. AIR 28/524 R.A.F. Station Ousten. R.A.F. logs reveal that two Spitfires had patrolled less than an hour earlier the sector through which the Me 110 flew unchallenged. These fighters from R.A.F. Ousten would have had the speed necessary to make an interception.

15. Cecil Bryant, D.F.M., interview and correspondence, November 1989.

16. Radar operators confirmed this report of "Raid 42," reflecting uncertainty over whether one of the Germans might have peeled off during the confusion with the echoes caused by the pair of Hurricanes over Holy Island. See Derek Wood, *Warning Red: The Royal Observer Corps and the Defence of Britain 1925 to 1975* (London, 1976), pp. 1–5; PRO AIR 27/624 O.R.B. of 72 Squadron, 10 May 1941, confirmed by Flight Sergeant Pocock, interviewed January 1990. Squadron Leader R. G. Woodman, also a wartime fighter pilot, believes from his own experience and his study of the records that 13 Group headquarters did not respond normally in the case of this particular German intruder. From what he learned from Al Deere, the New Zealand Battle of Britain ace, he concludes that the "door was left open" for Raid 42 to slip between the two Hurricanes on routine patrol to the north over the Farnes and the Spitfires on the ground at Aclington. Woodman, a wartime D.S.O. and D.F.C. who joined 13 Group that May, retraced Raid 42's flight in his Mosquito at the end of the war. He has still not been able to fathom why the Me 110 was tracked for all but fifteen minutes of the hour during which

it passed through the heavily patrolled and defended airspace.

17. "At 22.08 raid 42, 1 plus a/c at below 9,000 ft approached from SE. R.D.F. [Radio Direction Finding = Radar] plotted as travelling toward Holy Island and Turning E, fading. This may have arisen from plots 72 White who were detailed to raid and who plotted raid when searching off Farne and Holy Island. The time points were given by RDC proceeding Inland from Aclington toward north there jumping to Harwick & out sector, 72. Yellow One airborne 22.21 to 23.00 hours, was ordered to patrol Aclington and was then detailed to raid but plots jumped so far ahead of him, and he was unable to catch it. The raid was going at considerable speed and was reported by DOC as a Me 110. This, although surprising at the time, was afterwards found to be correct as the aircraft crashed and was found to have been piloted by Rudolf Hess," log book of R.A.F. Catterick, 10 May 1941, AIR 28/624 PRO; Hess, op. cit., p. 83.

18. Wood, op. cit., p. 2.

19. Hamilton, "Additional Notes," INF 1/192 PRO; Hamilton quoted by Johnstone, op. cit., p. 91.

20. The Boulton Paul Defiant had proved so ineffective against German fighters that the R.A.F. had relegated it to night-fighter duties against slow-moving bombers the previous year. The maximum speed of the DO 17 bomber was 255 m.p.h. (410 km/h) as against an Me 110's 336 m.p.h. (540 km/h). The Hurricane could reach 339 m.p.h. (545 km/h), the Spitfire 374 m.p.h. (602 km/h), against a Defiant's 303 m.p.h. (487 km/h). The Duty Controller at Prestwick did, however, recall that a "raid plaque appeared in the vicinity of Selkirk" flying west. He had immediately telephoned the controller at R.A.F. Ayr to suggest that if any of the slow Defiants were airborne, they could be taken up to 20,000 feet and vectored down at interception speed on to Raid 42. This according to the Duty Controller at Prestwick, Wing Comdr Hector MacLean, whose account, "Hess Lands in Scotland," appeared in Air Mail, Winter 1987.

21–2. Letter sent to commanding officer by Graham Donald on notepaper of Graham & Donald Ltd, Machine Tool Makers, Glasgow, dated 19.5.1941, in the Misc Collection of Imperial War Museum, London.

23. Hess, op. cit., p. 89. A passing freighter retrieved next day the tank installed to give the Me 110 the range needed for the mission. Hess also made reference to only a single fuel tank in the statements he made to Robert Gibson of the Home Guard, who arrested him, as reported in The Times, 14 May 1941: "He said he had fitted an extra petrol tank to his aeroplane before leaving and that when crossing the Scottish coast he had dropped his extra tank in the sea." Under good conditions the 1941 Mark D version Me 110 had a maximum range of 850 miles, just sufficient to have made the 830 miles from the Messerschmitt airfield outside Augsburg in Germany to Glasgow. But Hess's journey, as Woodman pointed out, included an hour (200 to 300 miles) of stooging out of range of British coastal radars waiting for dusk – and an additional 80 or so miles looping out and back over the west coast of Scotland. To cover the 1,200 miles of his actual flight he would have needed additional fuel reserves. But the jettisoned tank which would have resolved the mystery is not recorded with the wreckage of the Me 110 salvaged by No. 62 Maintenance Unit at Carluke, and no description of it has been found in R.A.F. records. If Hess's plane carried its additional reserve not in two wing tanks, but in a belly tank known as a Dachelbach ("dachshund belly"), this would explain why he only talked about having one extra petrol tank. It was not self-sealing and represented a potentially lethal hazard when empty and full of explosive vapour – which would explain why Hess made a point of ditching before attempting the dangerous final phase of the flight. Precisely what kind of additional fuel tank (or tanks) the Me 110 had fitted for the flight has caused much controversy.

Surviving photographs alleged by Hess's adjutant, the late Karlheinz Pintsch, to record the beginning of his mission certainly show an Me 110 not equipped with the two under-wing tanks but the much-reproduced picture's deep fuselage shadows could conceal the presence of a belly tank.

Hugh Thomas, the British surgeon and former military doctor who attended Hess in Spandau Prison, argues in his book *The Murder of Rudolf Hess* (London, 1979) and the revised edition *Hess: The Tale of Two Murders* (1988) that the apparent absence of wing tanks on the Me 110 that crashed in Scotland shows that it could not have been the one in which Hess took off from Augsburg. Thomas developed his controversial theory that the absence of wing tanks and X-rays taken of the prisoner that fail to show scarred lung tissue consistent with the severe bullet wounds Hess suffered in World War I argue that the Me 110 which crashed in Scotland was a second plane and that it was a double of the Deputy Führer who completed this mission.

24. Account of Major Graham Donald, Assistant Group Officer R.O.C. Glasgow, *The Journal of the Royal Observer Corps Club*, October 1942; Woods in *Warning Red* states that the Defiant had been dispatched from Prestwick to try and intercept the intruder. But the relevant O.R.B.s reveal that apart from the single Spitfire from 72 Squadron belatedly sent up from Aclington, no other aircraft was scrambled specifically to intercept Raid 42.

25. Hamilton quoted by Johnstone, op. cit., p. 92; Ilse Hess, op. cit., p. 88.

26. Hamilton quoted by Johnstone, op. cit., p. 91; Hamilton in his account contended this was because "this type of fighter aircraft had only once before been seen as far North." But what the Duke's vague report omits to mention is a second Me 110 appearance in broad daylight over Clydeside only two months earlier, which fighters under Turnhouse control had also failed to intercept. While Hamilton refers to the only previous appearance of an Me 110 so far north

on 10 August 1940, R.A.F. operational records note that on 14 March 1941 an Me 110 reconnaissance flight had photographed blazing oil tanks on Clydebank and was spotted by fighters, who failed to intercept it because of its superior speed. This Me 110 had flown up the Irish Sea from France, a much shorter distance than Hess's flight from Germany [Hamilton's report in PREM 3/219/7]; "Additional Notes," Hamilton, 1945, INF 1/912 PRO.

27. Radar detected two more German intruders heading into the airspace controlled by 13 Group during the small hours of the morning of 11 May. In marked contrast to Raid 42, the R.A.F. logs record "normal" action to intercept taken in each case when Sector Controllers promptly scrambled night fighters in good time to drive off the German raiders who had come in across the North Sea on very similar course to that taken by Raid 42. "A/c of 141 Squadron (Defiant) left ground at 0220 hours with orders to intercept raid 53 which was approaching sector coast from N.E. Raid did not make landfall in this sector, and turned away when approaching WHITBY." R.A.F. Ouston O.R.B. Air 28/624 PRO.

Then there is the curious way in which the Turnhouse Operations Record Book of 13 Group was written up. Its entry makes no specific mention of Raid 42, reading only that "2 Hostile and 2 unidentified raids were plotted between 1800 hrs & 2350 hrs. *22 a/c were detected in connection with these raids* but no contact was made." The decision to lump Raid 42 into a six-hour period appears inconsistent with standard practice and appears to have been done deliberately to give the impression that it was treated to a normal interception effort. Yet comparison with the individual logs of R.A.F. stations and squadrons in 13 Group suggests the opposite, because no fewer than 18 of the 22 aircraft were detailed to intercept the earlier raids. *Only four* planes (one pair of Hurricanes already up on patrol, a Spitfire and a Defiant) were therefore involved in any action against Raid 42 during the course of nearly an hour. In terms of actual fighters scrambled, this interception effort emerges as the puniest that entire evening. The Turnhouse controller felt it advisable – or was perhaps instructed – to telescope the whole evening's actions into the long entry to divert attention away from the fact that "1 Me 110 crash landed near Glasgow at 2306 hrs *not due to fighter action."* It is also significant that Fighter Command Headquarters *never* received a corrected report from Turnhouse, so its entry still records the fate of Raid 42 as *"shot down 2307"* [O.R.B. 13 Group R.A.F. AIR 25/233 PRO].

28. Hamilton quoted by Johnstone, op. cit., p. 91; Major Donald, op. cit.

29. Interview of Maclean, *New York Times*, 13 May 1941; *The Times*, 12 May 1941; "Report by Officer Commanding 3rd Battalion Renfrewshire Home Guard of the Incidents of the Nights of 10th/11th May 1941" WO 199/32881 PRO.

30. Major Donald, op. cit.

31. Major Donald, op. cit.; Lieutenant Clarke's report WO 190/3288A PRO.

32. Letter dated 14 May 1941 from Major Donald to Air Commodore Warrington Morris, reproduced in Woods, *Attack Warning Red*, op. cit., p. 263.

33–4. Major Donald, op. cit.

35. Hamilton quoted by Johnstone, op. cit., p. 91.

36. Hamilton, "Additional Notes," op. cit. INF 1/912 PRO; Hamilton quoted by Johnstone, op. cit., pp. 91–2.

37. The first edition of James Douglas-Hamilton's book *Motive for a Mission* (London, 1971) omits Major Donald's 1941 account: an omission that the Duke, who was then still alive, may have insisted upon because it conflicted with his own version of events. Yet when the same book was reprinted in 1979, after the publication of Dr. Thomas's *Murder of Rudolf Hess* and *after* the Duke's death, Donald's account is mentioned. The assertion that he especially asked the Turnhouse duty officer that the Duke should be informed of his identification

of Hess is categorically rejected: "the full message was not passed on in this form" (2nd edition, Edinburgh, 1979, pp. 172–3); Hamilton quoted by Johnstone, op. cit., p. 91; Captain White reported that "in spite of the lateness of the hour" he had telephoned R.A.F. Turnhouse sector command, only to be told that neither the Duke nor his intelligence officer, Flight Lieutenant Benson, was available. Turnhouse "Ops B" said "they had the story already from the Observer Corps and from Ayr." Benson had been "informed of the story and would leave for Glasgow at 0830 the following morning." Although White again emphasized that this was "not an ordinary case," his request for an immediate interrogation met with a rebuff because the duty officer said he "told him nothing new." Report of 15 May 1941 by Staff Captain Anthony White WO 199/3228A PRO. The B part of the War Office report, labelled HESS, remains a classified secret until 2017.

38. Report from Glasgow Area Command Colonel Firebrace 18.5.41 and 21.5.41 in Scottish Command Files WO 199/3288A PRO.

39. David Irving speculates in *Hess: the Missing Years 1941–1945* (London, 1987), p. 347, that the closed file (3288B) deals either with the letters that Hess brought with him or with the court martial proceeding against one of the army officers who was half-asleep and improperly dressed when the Home Guard unit arrived in Maryhill Barracks. It seems unlikely, however, that court martial proceedings (which are routinely closed) would be in this particular file. If a letter was found addressed to Hamilton (or possibly the King, as Irving suggests) then it seems likely that Colonel Firebrace would have used it as ammunition in his strongly worded complaint; O.R.B. R.A.F. Turnhouse AIR 28/864 Appendix PRO.

40. *New York Times*, 14 May 1941, quoting a United Press report of the previous day. The rivet holes were also noted by Major Donald in his report. The wartime R.A.F. operational logs contradict the impression created by Hamilton and

the Air Ministry at the time that Hess escaped shooting down only by the skin of his teeth. There is also clear evidence that Parliament was deliberately misled by an Air Ministry internal minute of 21 May 1941, claiming that Hess "might very likely have been shot down," which was justification for the tabling by a compliant Conservative M.P. of an "inspired" question "to clear the position of the Duke of Hamilton . . . if it were made clear that an attempt were [sic] made and was nearly successful." So the Air Minister assured the House of Commons (Memorandum to Secretary of the State for Air re Parliamentary Question 191/41 to be asked by Major Lloyd AIR 19/564 PRO).

41. Felicity Ashby interview; interview and correspondence with Sqn Ldr. R. G. Woodman; *The American Mercury*, Vol. LVI, no. 233 (New York, May 1943), pp. 519–28. (The Churchill article was a reprint of a piece he had written on the French World War I prime minister Clemenceau.) Neither Squadron Leader Woodman nor Cecil Bryant nor Felicity Ashby had ever heard of, let alone read, the *American Mercury* article until the author brought it to their attention. An article making very similar assertions appeared in Paul Merker, *Deutschland "Sein oder Nichtsein"* (Mexico, 1945), p. 254.

In view of its timing, "The Inside Story of the Hess Flight" appears to have been deliberately inspired by the same leaks of British secret service involvement that reached the N.K.V.D. from their sources in MI6. In 1943 the Russians were pressing Britain and the United States for more war supplies and the opening of a second front in Europe. The anonymous author betrayed both his motive and his source by stating that while Roosevelt and Churchill had consigned the Hess episode "to the limbo of hush-hush," his aim was to "place before the critics of Anglo-American policy toward the Soviet Russia the vital and silencing fact that at a difficult moment when he might have withdrawn his country from the war at Russia's expense, Churchill pledged Britain to continue fighting . . ." The

release by the K.G.B. of the French Military Intelligence reports about MI6 and the October 1942 report to Stalin that the British had lured Hess to Scotland adds weight to the argument.

42. It might be argued that the *American Mercury* piece also drew on British MI6 sources who were passing information, either directly or indirectly, to the Soviets. The "slant" of the article, as well as the details it gives of Hess's confinement and of negotiating terms that he discussed during his first interviews with Ivone Kirkpatrick, are too close to the record to be pure speculation. It is also worthy of note that a German-controlled Swedish newspaper had already made that claim the previous year: on 2 October 1942 *Dagposten* reported that a Berlin official had said that Hitler sent Hess to Britain "as his personal envoy" with generous peace terms "to propose a tie-up with the Tripartite Alliance against Soviet Russia" (as reported in the *New York Times*, 3 October 1942).

43. Robert E. Sherwood, *Roosevelt and Hopkins: An Intimate History* (New York, 1948), p. 194. Sherwood, who attended the dinner of close aides, noted that the President had expressed bafflement about the Hess flight some ten days after the flight.

44. Report of U.S. Military Attaché Robert E. Lee of 28 November 1941, "Rudolf Hess" B8026020 IRR Files Chief of Staff U.S. Army RG 319 NAW.

45. Quoted by Michael Foot, *Loyalists and Loners* (London, 1986), p. 174.

46. Winston S. Churchill, *The History of the Second World War* (6 vols., London, 1948–54), Vol. II, *Their Finest Hour*, p. 157.

CHAPTER 2
(pp. 21–51)

1. Claire Boothe, *New York Herald Tribune*, 16 May 1940.

2. Ibid.; J. Pierrepoint Moffat, *Diary*, 9 May 1940 HLH (hereafter Moffat, *Diary*).

3–4. Adolf Berle, *Diary*, 1940 FDRL (hereafter Berle, *Diary*).

5. Moffat, *Diary*; *New York Times*, 11 May 1940.

6. Paul Reynaud, *In the Thick of the Fight 1930–45*, translated by James D. Lambert (London, 1951), p. 293.

7. *New York Times*, 11 May 1940.

8. *The Diplomatic Diaries of Oliver Harvey 1937–1940*, edited by John Harvey (New York, 1970), 10 May 1940, p. 355.

9. The Private Diary of Lord Halifax, 10 May 1940, Halifax Papers BIG (hereafter Halifax, *Diary*).

10. Winston Churchill, *The History of the Second World War*, Vol. I, *The Gathering Storm* (London, 1948), pp. 596–7; War Cabinet (117) Conclusions, 10 May 1940, 8 a.m., CAB 67/7 PRO, and Martin Gilbert, *Churchill: Their Finest Hour* (London, 1983), p. 306.

11. *Hitler's Table Talk 1941–1944* (Oxford, 1988), p. 71.

12. The War *Journal* (*Kriegstagesbuch*) of General Franz Halder, English translation, RG 319 NAW (hereafter Halder, *Journal*); *Hitler's Table Talk*, op. cit., p. 71.

13. Reynaud, op. cit., p. 293.

14. Ibid., p. 297.

15. Elie J. Bois, *Truth on the Tragedy of France* (London, 1940); Harold Nicolson, *Diaries*, op. cit., p. 150.

16. *The Private Diaries of Paul Baudouin*, translated by Sir Charles Petrie (London, 1948), 9–10 May 1940, pp. 20–6.

17. Alistair Horne, *To Lose a Battle: France 1940* (London, 1979).

18. Telegram facsimile from O.K.W., reproduced in Claude Paillat, *Le Désastre de 1940*, Vol. 5, *La Guerre Eclair 10 Mai–24 June 1940* (Paris, 1985), p. 25.

19. Viscount Templewood (Sir Samuel Hoare), *Nine Troubled Years* (London, 1954), pp. 431–2; Military Coordination Committee Minutes No. 38, 10 May 1940, CAB 83/3 PRO.

20–21. *The Ironside Diaries 1937–1940*, edited by Roderick Macleon and Denis Kelly (London, 1966), 10 May 1940, p. 301.

22. War Cabinet (117) Conclusions, 10 May 1940, CAB 65/7 PRO.

23. The son of a Chicago businessman who naturalized and married into British society with the wealth of the Guinness brewing family, Channon "inherited" his father-in-law's safe Conservative seat. An ardent pro-Chamberlain supporter, his insatiable appetite for political and private gossip made Channon a shrewd, if waspishly partisan, diarist of the inside workings of the British ruling class. *Chips: The Diaries of Sir Henry Channon*, edited by Robert Rhodes James (London, 1967), 10 May 1940, p. 305.

24. Halifax, *Diary*, 14 March 1940; Churchill expressed his views a month later after the expeditions had been abandoned, War Cabinet (60) Conclusions, 5 March 1940, 65/6 PRO; for an authoritative account of Sweden's role in the "Winter War" settlement, see Professor Wilhelm Carlgren, *Swedish Foreign Policy in the Second World War*, translated by Arthur Spencer (London, 1977), pp. 16–22. This is an abridged English version of Professor Carlgren's *Svensk Utrikespolitik 1939–45* (Stockholm, 1973).

25. *The Empire at Bay: The Leo Amery Diaries*, Vol. II edited by John Barnes and David Nicholson (London, 1988), 4 April 1940, p. 585; Nicolson, *Diaries*, 3 April 1940, p. 66.

26. Even before Chamberlain's speech he had threatened the French with calling off the Norwegian operation, because Daladier feared German reprisals if the simultaneous mining of the Rhine went ahead. Churchill hurried off to Paris on 4 April to try to reconcile Reynaud's squabble with Daladier. He failed to persuade them to agree to Operation Royal Marine, but returned more determined than ever that the British should press on with Operation Wilfred to mine the Norwegian Leads. The on-off-on-again operation was accordingly rescheduled for 8 April. "I am so glad you stuck with Wilfred," Churchill wrote to Chamberlain after returning from Paris, "all is

moving." In contrast to two months of Allied dithering over a simple mining operation, the Wehrmacht took just six weeks to mount a major combined land, sea and air operation of considerable complexity. Hitler had ordered planning to begin on 21 February, just five days after Royal Navy destroyers, on Churchill's orders, defied Norwegian neutrality to rescue 300 British merchant seamen from the German raider supply ship *Altmark*. Hitler, suspecting from this incident and other intelligence that the British had designs on Norway, approved the operation on 1 April, the day before Chamberlain's taunt that he had "missed the bus," letter of 6 April 1940, Chamberlain Papers BUL.

27. Supreme War Council (7) Minutes 9 April 1940 CAB 99/3 PRO.

28. Ironside, *Diaries*, p. 247; 9–14 April 1940; 20 April, p. 272.

29. Ironside, *Diaries*, 23, 26, 27 April 1940, p. 287.

30. Amery, *Diaries*, 10 April 1940, p. 586.

31. Amery, *Diaries*, 29 April 1940, pp. 588–9; 1 May, p. 590; 23 April, p. 588; 1 May, p. 590.

32. John Colville, *The Fringes of Power: 10 Downing Street Diaries 1939–1945* (London, 1985), 27 April 1940, p. 112.

33. Halifax, *Diary*, 3 May 1940.

34. Channon, *Diaries*, 1 and 2 May 1940, p. 299; Nicolson, *Diaries*, 4 May 1940, pp. 74–5.

35. Halifax, *Diary*, 6 May 1940.

36. Channon, *Diaries*, 7 May 1940, p. 301.

37. Amery, *Diaries*, 7 May 1940, p. 592; *Hansard*, 7 May 1940.

38. Amery, *Diaries*, loc. cit.

39. Churchill, Vol. I, *The Gathering Storm*, p. 594.

40. Hugh Dalton, Manuscript Diary of 8 May 1940, Dalton Papers I/22 LSEL (hereafter Dalton *Diary*); *Hansard*, 9 May 1940.

41. Nicolson, *Diaries*, 8 May 1940, p. 79; *Hansard*, 7 May 1940.

42. Alistair Horne, *Macmillan*, Vol. 1 *1894–1956* (London, 1988), p. 138.

43. Channon, *Diaries*, p. 303; *Hansard*, 7 May 1940.

44. Ibid.

45. King George VI, 9 May 1940, Royal Archives Windsor, as quoted by John W. Wheeler Bennett, *King George VI; His Life and Reign* (New York, 1958), p. 446.

46. Nicolson, *Diaries*, 9 May 1940, p. 80; Amery, *Diaries*, 9 May 1940, p. 611.

47. Marginal note in proofs of Churchill's war memoirs, Churchill Papers 4/131, quoted by Gilbert in *Finest Hour*, op. cit., p. 287; Captain Edwards, Diary, 9 May 1940, quoted by David Irving, *Churchill's War: The Struggle for Power* (Australia, 1987), p. 260; Manuscript Diary of Alexander Cadogan, 9 May, Cadogan Papers ACAD/1 CCA (hereafter Cadogan, *Diary*).

48. Dalton, *Diary*, 8 and 9 May 1940; Amery, *Diaries*, 9 May, p. 612.

49–50. Halifax, *Diary*, 9 May 1940, BIG.

51. Diary note, 7 May 1940, G/13 Butler Papers TCCA; letter from Butler, 9 May 1940, quoted in Lord Birkenhead, *The Life of Lord Halifax* (London, 1965), p. 453.

52. Observations of a fellow member of All Souls, quoted by A. L. Rowse, *Friends and Contemporaries* (London, 1989), p. 200.

53. Halifax, *Diary*, 9 May 1940.

54. Earl of Avon, *The Eden Memoirs: The Reckoning* (London, 1965), p. 96.

55. Churchill, op. cit., Vol. I, p. 597; Chamberlain, *Diary*, 11 May 1940 (NC BUL, hereafter Chamberlain, *Diary*); according to Halifax's diary Chamberlain addressed the issue without beating around the bush: "At 4.30 I went across to No. 10 and the PM, Winston, David Margesson and I sat down to it. The PM recapitulated the position and said that he had made up his mind that he must go, and that it must be Winston

or me. He would serve under either. It would therefore be necessary to see the Labour people before they went to Bournemouth, and ask them whether they would on principle be prepared to join the government (a) under the present Prime Minister, or (b) under other leadership. David Margesson said that unity was essential and that he thought it was impossible to attain under the PM. He did not at that moment pronounce very definitely between Winston and myself and my stomach ache continued. I then said that for the reasons given the PM must probably go, but that I had no doubt at all in my mind that for me to take it would create a quite impossible position." (Halifax, *Diary*, 9 May 1940). Churchill's version, written from memory after the end of the war, is more dramatic, but it differs significantly: "Mr Chamberlain evidently had in his mind the stormy scene in the House of Commons two nights before when I had seemed to be in such heated controversy with the Labour Party. Although this had been in his support and defence, he nevertheless felt that this might be an obstacle to my obtaining their adherence at this juncture. His biographer, Mr Feihling, states definitely that he preferred Lord Halifax. As I remained silent a long pause ensued. It certainly seemed longer than the two minutes which one observes in the commemorations of Armistice Day. Then at length Lord Halifax spoke" (Churchill, Vol. I, p. 597).

56. Halifax, *Diary*, 9 May 1940, BIG.

57. Churchill, Vol. I, pp. 597–8.

58. Halifax, *Diary*, 9 May 1940; Cadogan, *Diary*, 9 May 1940.

59. Halifax, *Diary*, 9 May 1940.

60. Harris, *Attlee*, op. cit., p. 174; Clement Davies's account appears in Amery's diary for 9 May 1940: "Greenwood took up running and explained that the Prime Minister was entirely mistaken and that there was not the slightest prospect of the Opposition joining a government under him: they not only disliked him but regarded him as something evil"

(Amery, *Diaries*, 9 May 1940, p. 612); Harris, *Attlee*, p. 174.

61–2. Harris, *Attlee*, p. 174; Halifax, *Diary*, 9 May 1940.

63. Colville, *Diaries*, 9 May, p. 120; Robert Boothby, *Recollections of a Rebel* (London, 1978), p. 144; Ibid.; Dalton, *Diary* 8 and 9 May 1940.

64. Kennedy to Secretary of State, U.S. Confidential State Department Files Great Britain Internal Affairs, 1940–1944 841.0–841.3 RG 84 NAW.

65. Nicolson, *Diaries*, 10 May 1940, p. 82.

66. Dalton, *Diary*, 10 May 1940.

67. Churchill, Vol. I, p. 596; Earl of Avon, *The Eden Memoirs*, pp. 97–8.

68. Halifax, *Diary*, 10 May 1940.

69. Amery, *Diaries*, 10 May, p. 613.

70. Dalton, *Diary*, 10 May 1940; Colville, *Diaries*, 10 May, p. 121.

71. War Cabinet (119) Conclusions 4.30 p.m. 10 May CAB 65/7 PRO.

72. King George VI, Diary, 10 May 1940 cited by Wheeler Bennet, op. cit., p. 444.

73. Harold Nicolson, unpublished Manuscript Diary, 6 April 1955, Nicolson Papers BCL; Letter from Mrs Neville Chamberlain, 12 January 1954, to Sir Alan Lascelles commenting that the King failed to write on his resignation, NC 7/3/36 Chamberlain Papers BUL.

74. Although it was not until 1963 that a bill was passed enabling peers to renounce their titles, the King evidently believed that Parliament could have passed a special *ad nominem* in Halifax's case allowing him to sit in the House of Commons for the duration of the war.

75. Chamberlain's letter, 9 May 1940, NC 6/9/80 BUL.

76. Lord Birkenhead, *Halifax*, op. cit., p. 453.

77. Handwritten letter from Churchill to Chamberlain, 10 May 1940, NC 7/9/80; letters exchanged on 11 November 1940

between Churchill and Mrs Neville Chamberlain, NC 7/9/107 and NC 7/9/109 BUL.

78. *The Times*, 11 May 1940.

79. As quoted by A. L. Rowse, *Friends and Contemporaries*, op. cit., p. 198; "PM said that I was the man mentioned as most acceptable," Cadogan noted that Halifax had told him. This would have been in keeping with the impressions that the Foreign Secretary wanted to give to his Permanent head. That this version was hearsay is evident from the fact that Cadogan reverses the order of events, placing the discussion about the succession *after* the meeting with the Labour leaders (Cadogan, *Diary*, 9 May 1940 CCA).

80. Churchill, Vol. I, pp. 599–600.

81–2. Colville, *Diaries*, p. 122.

83. Joseph P. Kennedy unpublished memoirs, manuscript draft, pp. 297–8; James M. Landis Papers LOC. The untitled manuscript that was intended to be the Kennedy diplomatic memoirs was drafted by Landis, former Dean of the Harvard Law School, who worked on it in the early fifties, using Kennedy's diplomatic correspondence, notes and diary in addition to corresponding with the principal surviving State Department officials. Landis later told David E. Koskoff, author of *Joseph P. Kennedy: A Life and Times* (New Jersey, 1974, p. 514), that the project was abandoned because Kennedy concluded that publication of the memoir would cause embarrassment to the career of John F. Kennedy, who was then the junior Senator from Massachusetts. Two versions of the manuscript survive, a nearly complete early draft that Koskoff had access to and cites as "Landis MS", and the six fuller later draft chapters in the Landis Papers at the Library of Congress; General Raymond E. Lee, *The London Observer: The Journals of General Raymond E. Lee*, edited by James Luetze (London, 1972), p. 36.

84. Kennedy's Diary, quoted in Landis Ms p. 463; Halifax, *Diary*, 26 May 1940; Lord Reith, Chamberlain's Minister of Information, reported on a meeting with Kennedy that he attended with Lord

Halifax on 25 April in his autobiography *Into the Wind* (London, 1949), p. 371; Kennedy to Secretary of State, 26 April 1940, European War 1989 841.00/1464. RG 59 NAW; Moffat, *Diary*, 8 December 1939, HLH – he was probably referring to Churchill's friendship with financier Bernard Baruch; Kennedy quoted in Sumner Welles "Memorandum" of 12 March 1940; Report of Mission, 121.840 Welles, Summer RG 59 NAW.

85. W. H. Thompson, *Sixty Minutes with Churchill* (London, 1953), pp. 44–5.

CHAPTER 3

(pp. 52–75)

1. Butler diary note of 14 May 1940 G/13 Butler Papers TCCA (hereafter Butler, *Diary*).

2. Halifax, *Diary*, 11–13 May 1940; Churchill, probably in deference to Halifax, had kept his fellow appeaser from All Souls, Sir John Simon, in the government – by kicking him upstairs to the Lords as Chancellor. The leading arch appeaser Sir Samuel Hoare (architect of the Hoare–Lovat Pact) was exiled to Spain as Britain's Ambassador after vigorously protesting that he deserved to become Viceroy of India. Objections from Lord Salisbury's Tory rebels and Labour had forced Churchill to renege on his original intention to make Chamberlain Chancellor of the Exchequer. That influential position went to Kingsley Wood, with Chamberlain continuing to lead the Conservative Party in the House of Commons. Deciding who would sit at the long mahogany Cabinet table had involved a weekend of careful bargaining and balancing by Churchill and his parliamentary secretary Brenden Bracken. They had to weigh the demands of the anti-Chamberlain "gangsters" who had supported them against concessions to vested Tory Party power interests. The appointment of the leading Tory rebel Duff Cooper as Minister of Information angered the Party faithful. So did Churchill's decision to make Labour trade union leader Ernest Bevin Minister

of Labour and bring in Lord Beaverbrook, the Canadian newspaper magnate, as Minister of Aircraft Production. The Conservative Whip, David Margesson had significantly played a leading role in the political horse-trading, which kept twenty-one of the thirty-six ministerial posts in the hands of Chamberlain appointees.

3. With the exception of the Liberal leader Sir Archibald Sinclair, there was no lack of ministerial experience in the newcomers. The Labour members of the Cabinet, Clement Attlee, the Lord Privy Seal, Arthur Greenwood, the Minister without Portfolio, and A. V. Alexander, a former First Lord who succeeded Churchill at the Admiralty, had all served previously as ministers in the 1930 Labour government; Letter of George VI to Churchill, quoted by Sarah Bradford, *King George VI* (London, 1989), p. 313; Amery, *Diaries*, 12 May 1940, p. 616.

4. Boothby, *Recollections*, op. cit., p. 145; Neville Chamberlain to Ida, 11 May 1940, NC BUL; letter to Earl Baldwin from Viscount (J. C. C.) Davidson, formerly Conservative M.P. for Hemel Hempstead and confidant of former Tory Prime Minister Stanley Baldwin, dated 14 May 1940, Baldwin Papers CUL.

5. Butler to Hoare, 20 July 1940, Templewood Papers T/XIII/17 CUL; the warning was given by Nigel Roland, later British Ambassador to Portugal. It surprised Colville because Butler, who had been an intimate of Chamberlain as well as Halifax, had been held in high regard at Downing Street (Colville, *Diaries*, 11 May 1940, p. 124); Butler, *Diary*, 15 May 1940; Channon, *Diaries*, 15 May 1940, p. 310; Butler *Diary* note TCA.

6. Lord Sherfield (then Roger Makins), interview of April 1989; interview with Sir Frank Roberts, April 1990.

7. Birger Dahlerus had business with John Brown, who had built the great Cunard *Queen* liners. The Clydebank firm used him to handle its Polish interests in a Danzig shipyard. Dahlerus happened to know Hermann Göring, through Göring's deceased Swedish first wife, Baroness Karin von Kantzow. With the encouragement of Göring, Dahlerus spent the final weeks before war erupted in Europe shuttling between Stockholm, Berlin and London trying to break the deadlock in the Polish crisis precipitated by Hitler's demands on Danzig (Birger Dahlerus, *Last Attempt*, London, 1946).

8. Roberts interview.

9. Ibid.; *Summary of Principal Peace Feelers* September 1939–March 1941 (Foreign Office Digest prepared on 14 April 1941), PREM 4/100/8 PRO; *Documents on German Foreign Policy 1918–1945* (DGFP) Series D, Vol. 7 (Washington, 1954), pp. 140–3, "Memorandum of the Conversation Between the Führer and M. Dahlerus in the Presence of Field Marshal Göring." J.W. Brugel, *Dahlerus als Zwischenträger nach Kriegsausbruch in Historische Zeitschrift* (Munich, 1979), pp. 70 ff.

10. Nicolson, *Diaries*, 20 September 1939.

11. Chamberlain, *Diary*, 23 September 1939; Kennedy to Roosevelt, 30 September 1939, quoted by William L. Langer and S. Everett Gleason, *The Challenge of Isolation, 1937–1940* (New York, 1952), p. 252; Kennedy/Landis MS, p. 467; John M. Blum, *From the Morgenthau Diaries*, Vol II, *Years of Urgency 1938–1941* (Boston, 1965), p. 102. Roosevelt left it to his Secretary of State to slap down the Ambassador with the retort that he saw "no opportunity nor occasion for any peace move to be initiated by the United States." Kennedy to Hull, 11 September 1941 (FRUS), *Foreign Relations of the United States* (Washington, 1951), Vol. 1, p. 424.

12. FRUS, ibid.; Lothian to Halifax, 14 September 1939, FO 800/324/XXXVII/26; War Cabinet Conclusions, 19 September 1939, CAB 65/1 PRO.

13. Halifax to Lothian, 25 September 1939, FO 371/22816 PRO; Kennedy to Roosevelt, 20 September 1939, FDR Safe File "Kennedy" FDRL.

14. Statement by German Foreign Minister Ribbentrop and Soviet Foreign Minister Vyacheslav Molotov, *New York Times*, 29

September 1940. The Ribbentrop/Molotov statement was the signal for a flurry of semi-official German peace feelers. Franz von Papen, the former German Chancellor and ambassador to Turkey, suggested that Hitler would end the war if the Allies agreed to Germany retaining Danzig, the partitioning of Czechoslovakia, and a face-saving restoration of Germany's 1914 African colonies. *Summary Peace Feelers*, PREM 4/100/8 PRO and Franz von Papen, *Der Wahrheit eine Gasse* (Munich, 1952), pp. 516 ff.

15. Chamberlain, letter to Ida, 8 October 1939, quoted by Feihling, *The Life of Neville Chamberlain* (London, 1946), p. 426; Kennedy/Landis MS, pp. 466–77.

16. War Cabinet (39) Conclusions, 5 October 1939, CAB 65/1 PRO.

17. William L. Shirer, *The Rise and Fall of the Third Reich* (New York, 1960), p. 848.

18. Chamberlain quoted by Fähling, loc. cit.

19. Correspondence in FO 800/327 PRO: Rothermere to Lloyd George, 9 October 1939, Lloyd George Papers G/17/138 HOL.

20. Shirer, op. cit., DGFP VII, p. 248.

21. "Dahlerus cables" in FO 800/327 PRO; the Kennedy Interview with Halifax "a few days earlier" than 12 October 1939, according to Kennedy Landis MS, p. 469; minute by Halifax after conversation with the French Ambassador about Dahlerus, 12 October 1939, and another on 7 November, FO 800/327; *Summary Peace Feelers* PREM 4/100/8 PRO.

22. Nicolson, *Diaries*, 12 October 1939.

23. *Summary Peace Feelers*, PREM 4/100/8 PRO; the Foreign Secretary's "Peace Moves" Files contains no fewer than 28 entries under "Dahlerus" from September to December 1939; FO 800/327 PRO; Roberts interview.

24. Report of the U.S. Minister in Berne on a conversation with the Papal Nuncio in which he was told in confidence by Motta that "about a fortnight ago Butler, British Parliamentary Under Secretary of State for Foreign Affairs, had visited

Lausanne where he had met a German representative, Hohenlohe by name, with whom he had 'discussed the substitution of Goering for Hitler'" (Harrison to Secretary of State, 11 November 1939, 862.002 Hitler, Adolf/228 Confidential File RG 59 NAW); letter dated 20 June 1940, Hohenlohe to Hewel (Politisches Archiv AAB).

25. PREM 4/100/8 PRO; Berle, *Diary*, 12 October 1939; *Summary Peace Feelers*.

26. Unpublished autobiographical manuscript by James D. Mooney and W. B Wachtler, James D. Mooney Papers 55–63 ff. GUL.

27. Mooney followed Vansittart's instructions by sending a note to this effect back to Wolthart in Berlin by way of a trusted Belgian executive of General Motors. He waited ten days for the promised meeting with the Foreign Secretary because he was told not to cross lines with "another peace effort." The real reason was the Foreign Office's desire to stall Mooney before the upcoming House vote in the U.S. Congress to amend the Neutrality Act. Roosevelt's move to permit the United States to supply arms and equipment to the Allies on a cash-and-carry basis was backed by the Democrats, but opposed by the Republicans. Isolationists argued that changing the law to supply arms to belligerent nations would be the first step to war. Six days earlier, on 2 November 1939, the Senate had approved the amendment by a two-to-one margin (Mooney Ms, p. 69 GUL); *Summary Peace Feelers*.

28. Kennedy/Landis Ms, p. 467; p. 483.

29. *Summary Peace Feelers*; Mooney Ms, p. 74: Mooney records that it was quite specific, so that when he used the words "a form of government in Germany," Vansittart corrected him.

30. Mooney Ms, p. 83.

31. Broadcast of 19 November 1939, Churchill papers 9/138, cited by Gilbert, *Finest Hour*, p. 81; Birkenhead, *Halifax*, p. 450; Memorandum by Secretary of State Weizsäcker Annex 20 November 1939 DGFP VII, p. 427.

32. Interview with Lord Sherfield.

33. Halifax, Memorandum of Bonde conversation, 13 December 1939, FO 371/24495 PRO; ibid.; Cadogan, *Diary*, 23 December 1939.

34. Kennedy/Landis Ms, p. 547; Halifax, Memo, 23 January 1940, FO 371/44406 PRO; *Daily Telegraph*, 1 March 1940. See also Marquess of Tavistock (William Hastings S. Russell), *The Fate of a Peace Effort* (High Wycombe, 1940).

35. Translation of Bishop Eivind Bergrav's report of his interview with Lord Halifax in Moffat Papers HLH; Archbishop of York to Foreign Secretary, 10 January 1940, FO 371/24365 PRO.

36. Lord Halifax, *The Challenge to Liberty: Speech Delivered at the Sheldonian 27 February 1940* (Oxford, 1940), p. 12; A. L. Rowse, *Friends and Contemporaries*, op. cit., p. 197.

37. Ibid.

38. Sherfield interview; 4/100/8 PRO. Venlo incident was a carefully orchestrated plot organized by Walter Schellenberg. Captain Payne Best and Major Richard Stevens were lured to the Dutch border town of Venlo on 9 November on the pretext of meeting German generals who were plotting against Hitler. The two British MI6 officers were then seized and bundled across the frontier in an incident that German propaganda exploited to the full embarrassment of Britain's secret service. Schellenberg received an Iron Cross for its success. *Final Report on the Case of Walter Frederick Schellenberg* "The Venlo Incident" in SCHELLENBERG IRR RG 319 NAW. The Payne/Best German interrogation account, "Der Britische Nachrichtendienst," is quoted by Nigel West (Rupert Allason), *MI6: British Secret Intelligence Service Operation* (London, 1985), pp. 403–10; *Summary Peace Feelers*.

39–40. Osborne to Halifax, 9 January, FO 800/318. H/XV/363 PRO.

41. Vansittart, Docket minute, 13 February 1940, FO 371/24405 PRO; handwritten notes by Chamberlain cited by

Peter Ludlow, "Pabst Pius XIII, die Britische Regierung und die Deutsche Opposition in Winter 1939–40," *Vierteljahrhefte für Zeitgeschichte*, 1974, pp. 333 ff.

42. Halifax, *Diary*, 19 February 1940.

43. Chadwick, op. cit., p. 94.

44. "Germany: Peace approach to the Pope," notes and comments, 4 April 1940, FO 371/24407 PRO. Other approaches came from the exiled anti-Nazi German industrialist Fritz Thyssen and "the emissary in Holland and through Goerdeler in Switzerland." Sir Orme "Moley" Sargent of the Foreign Office was of the opinion that "the message received through the Pope is the most circumstantial and inspires the most confidence" and that the French should be alerted "soon" to avoid possible conflicts. His advice was not taken. Nor was Osborne told of the other approaches by the Foreign Office which took the collective view that "this was not the reason for the failure of the feeler passed on by the Vatican and Herr Thyssen." Minute by Sir Orme Sargent, dated 17 February 1940, FO 371/24405 PRO.

45. Vansittart, Minute, 9 February 1940, A 1309/131/45 FO/24238 PRO; Minutes on Docket FO 371/24418, dated 7 February 1940, PRO.

46. FDR to Kennedy, 3 November 1939, PSF "Kennedy" FDRL; Berle, *Diary*, 29 December FDRL; Sumner Welles, *A Time for Decision* (New York, 1944), p. 73; Breckinridge Long, Ms *Diary*, 12 March 1940, LOC.

47. Mooney Ms, p. 88 GUL; p. 91.

48. Vansittart, Memo, 16 February 1940, FO/371/24418 PRO.

49. Moffat, *Diary*, 17 February 1940.

50. Kirk, Memorandum, 11 March 1940, in Moffat Papers HLH.

51. Summary of conversation with Reich Chancellor Hitler, 4 March 1940, Mooney Papers GUL; Mooney's notes on meeting with Göring in company of Staatsrat Dr. Wolthart, and subsequent elaboration of various points by Wolthart, 7 March 1940. The Navy Department protested to the

White House that its vital communications channels and cipher staff were being overwhelmed with non-military business. "Addressee appreciates Mr. Mooney's Reports but hopes he will be able to compress current and future messages," Roosevelt cabled back to Mooney on 14 March. The President's displeasure might have been more marked if he had known that Alexander Kirk, the U.S. Chargé in Berlin, had learned that the General Motors executive had advised the Germans that "it was the President's personal idea that it was not necessary for peace for Hitler to be eliminated, as the British insisted" "Restricted" cable, 14 March 1940, Mooney Papers, GUL; Kirk, Memorandum, 11 March 1940, Moffat Papers HLH).

52. The Royal Navy blockade affected 80 per cent of Italian trade, operating from the British Mediterranean bases at Suez and Gibraltar. Since November 1939 the British had tightened the screws of "economic warfare" against Hitler by threatening to cut off Italy's seaborne imports of German coal as well as her exports of goods originating in the Reich. Since Mussolini did not have the hard currency to buy British coal, he was offered supplies of fuel in return for Italian armaments. When Hitler had denounced this as "blackmail" to keep Italy neutral, the Duce realized that he would soon have to face tough choices. As one of his ministers explained to the German Ambassador in Rome, Mussolini felt obliged "to dance as long as possible like an acrobat, keeping his balance toward both sides." Giovanni Venturi, Italian Minister of Communications, to Hans Mackensen, in Ambassador's report to Berlin No. 140 German Foreign Ministry Microfilms GFM (T-120 Series) 1571/380287 NAW). For a detailed analysis, see Macgregor Knox, *Mussolini Unleashed 1939–41: Politics and Strategy in Fascist Italy's Last War* (Cambridge, 1982), p. 70; Welles, Report of Mission, in 121.840, Welles, Sumner /132 RG 59 NAW.

53. Moffat, *Diary*, 28 and 29 February; the emissary is identified only as Mr. J. Y., who insisted that "the coup would come off before Easter." This convinced the American diplomat that the plotters "sounded like determined conspirators," although he told the emissary that he did not wish to know the names of the five leading members of the group.

54. Moffat, *Diary*, 1 March 1940; Welles, Report of Mission, op. cit.; Welles, Report of Hitler conversation, 2 May 1940, op. cit.; Welles, Report of Hess conversation, 3 March 1940; Göring conversation, 3 March 1940.

55. Welles, Report, 11 May 1940; Kennedy/Landis Ms, p. 569.

56. Welles, Report, 11 May 1940; Kennedy/Landis Ms, p. 570.

57. Welles, Report, 12 May 1940.

58. Minute of conversation with U.S. Military Attaché by A. Gage, 28 February 1940. It is interesting to note that despite two official recommendations that Churchill should be informed of the good impression he had made on Roosevelt's envoy, Cadogan vetoed it. "I feel some delicacy about asking the S of S (or the PM) to authorize our telling Mr Churchill that he made unique impression on Mr Welles" (C46564/89/18 371/24407 PRO); Welles, Report, 12 May 1940; Kennedy/Landis Ms, pp. 575–6.

59. Kennedy/Landis Ms, pp. 555–8; Moffat, *Diary*, 13 May 1940.

60. Kennedy/Landis Ms, ibid.

61. Kennedy/Landis Ms, pp. 572–4.

62. Welles, Report, 11 March 1940; the Minister of War, Oliver Stanley, insisted that "the British people demanded that the German people be taught a lesson." First Sea Lord Admiral Sir Dudley Pound declared "Berlin should be destroyed" and Germany occupied for fifty years. Lord Snell, speaking for the Labour Party, said that if Hitlerism went unchecked, men and women would "become no better than slaves."

63. Moffat, *Diary*, 11 March 1940.

64. Moffat, *Diary*, 13 March 1940; Butler, *Diary*, 13 March, cited in Gilbert, *Finest Hour*, p. 190: although there is no

Butler diary in Trinity College Archives, Dr. Gilbert assured the author that he was shown the diary by Lord Butler himself, and made notes of the passages he quotes.

65. Moffat, *Diary*, 13 March 1940.

66. Minute to the Secretary of State from Vansittart, 10 March 1940, FO 371/24407 PRO.

67. Welles, Report of Reynaud conversation, 14 March 1940.

68. Galeazzo Ciano, *Diario 1937–1943*, ed. De Felice (Milan, 1980), 4–10 March 1940; War Cabinet Conclusions, 9 March 1940, CAB 65/1 PRO.

69. Welles, Report, 16 March 1940; Philippino Anfuso, *Dal Palazzo Venezia al Lago di Garda* (Rome, 1949), p. 130.

70. Welles, Report 17 March 1940.

71. As quoted by Langer and Gleason, *The Challenge to Isolation*, op. cit., p. 375; Berle, *Diary*, 23 March 1940.

72. Mackensen to Berlin, No. 652, 9 April 1940, DGFP 582/241992 Vol. 7, op. cit.; for a lucid account of Mussolini's final moves to war, see Macgregor Knox, op. cit., pp. 89–90; *Documente Diplomatichi Italiani* (DDI), Series 9, Vol. IV (Rome, 1950), No. 642; Ciano, *Diario*, 10 April 1940.

CHAPTER 4

(pp. 76–99)

1. French Army Order of 12 May 1940, quoted by Alistair Horne, *To Lose a Battle: France 1940* (London, 1979), p. 303.

2. Account of Sergeant Prümers quoted by Horne, op. cit., p. 329.

3. Channon, *Diaries*, 13 May 1940.

4. Churchill echoed Giuseppe Garibaldi's famous rallying call to the Italian patriots of the Risorgimento: "Men, I'm getting out of Rome. Anyone who wants to carry on the war against outsiders, come with me. I can't offer you either honours or wages; I offer you hunger, thirst, forced marches, battle and

death. Anyone who loves his country, follow me"; unpublished note by Churchill intended for his war memoirs, Churchill Papers 4/194, Gilbert, *Finest Hour*, op. cit., p. 32.

5. Press statement reported by U.S. Embassy Berlin to State Department, 11 May 1940, RG 841.00/European War 1939–40 RG 59 NAW.

6. *Hansard*, 14 May 1940.

7. Channon, *Diaries*, 13 May 1940.

8. Hastings Ismay, *The Memoirs of General the Lord Ismay* (New York, 1960), p. 116; Editorial in the *New York Times*, 14 October 1940.

9–10. War Cabinet 120 Conclusions, 13 May 1940, CAB 65/7 PRO.

11. Cadogan, *Diary*, 13 May 1940; War Cabinet (120) Confidential Annex, 13 May 1943, CAB 65/13 PRO.

12. It was typical of Mussolini's bombast that he still refused to fix a precise date, telling Count Ciano only that Italy would come into the war within "ten to fourteen days and certainly by the end of the month." "He has decided to act," Ciano wrote in his diary that night, "and act he will" (*Diario*, 13 May 1940).

13. General André Beaufre, *Le Drame de 1940* (Paris, 1965), quoted by Horne, p. 359; Baudouin, *Diaries*, p. 28; French Order of the Day, quoted in Reynaud, *Thick of the Fight*, op. cit., p. 301.

14. General Edouard Ruby, *Sedan, Terre d'Epreuve* (Paris, 1948), quoted by Horne, op. cit., p. 348.

15. War Cabinet (121) Conclusions, 14 May 1940, CAB 65/7 PRO.

16. Baudouin, *Diaries*, 14 May 1940.

17–18. War Cabinet (122) Conclusions, 14 May 1940, CAB 65/7 PRO.

19. Churchill, Vol. II, op. cit., pp. 38–9; record of Reynaud telephone conversation, 15 May 1940, PREM 3/188/1 PRO; Churchill, Vol. II, p. 39; Baudouin, *Diaries*, 15 May 1940.

20. War Cabinet (123) Conclusions, 15 May 1940, CAB 65/7 PRO.

21. War Cabinet Confidential Annex, 15 May 1940, CAB 65/13 PRO.

22–3. Ibid.; the Bland Report and its accompanying minutes are in "Fifth Column Activities: Internment of all Enemy Aliens," 24 May 1940, 371/25189/424–447 PRO.

24. "Former naval person" telegram, 15 May 1940, PREM 3/468 PRO.

25. Memorandum for Secretary of State, 15 May 1940, *Berle Papers* FDRL.

26. Lieutenant-Colonel Guillaut's report, quoted by Horne, p. 430.

27. William C. Bullitt, quoted by Horne, p. 430.

28. Baudouin, *Diaries*, 10 May 1940.

29. Chiefs of Staff Committee No. 134, 15 May 1940, CAB 73/4 PRO; "My dear friend and colleague" letter to Reynaud, 16 May 1940, War Cabinet (124) Confidential Annex CAB 65/13 PRO.

30. War Cabinet (124) Conclusions, 16 May 1940, CAB 65/7 PRO.

31. Cadogan, *Diary*, 16 May 1940.

32. Reynaud's speech, quoted by Horne, p. 444.

33. Harvey, *Diaries*, p. 359.

34. Churchill, Vol. II, p. 42; Baudouin, *Diaries*, 16 May 1940.

35. Baudouin, *Diaries*, loc. cit.

36. Ibid.; Churchill, loc. cit.

37–8. Churchill, loc. cit.

39. Baudouin, *Diaries*, loc. cit.

40. Harvey, *Diaries*, 17 May 1940; Colville, *Diaries*, 17 May.

41. War Cabinet (126) Conclusions, 17 May 1940, CAB 65/7 PRO.

42. Ironside, *Diaries*, 17 May 1940, p. 314.

43. Roosevelt Telegram, 17 May 1940, PREM 3/468 PRO.

44. Cadogan, *Diary*, 17 May 1940.

45. Claire Boothe Luce, quoted by Horne, p. 523.

46. Baudouin, *Diaries*, 17 May 1940.

47. Halder, *Journal*, 16 May 1940; Field Marshal Erwin Rommel, cited in *The Rommel Papers*, edited by B. H. Liddell Hart (London, 1951).

48. Halder, *Journal*, 17 May 1940.

49. De Gaulle, *Call to Honour*, translated by Jonathan Griffin (London, 1955), pp. 44–5.

50. General Walter Warlimont, *Inside Hitler's Headquarters*, quoted by Horne, p. 54.

51. Halder, *Journal*, 18 May 1940.

52. Colville, *Diaries*, 18 May 1940.

53. Ironside, *Diary*, 17 May 1940, pp. 316–17; War Cabinet (127) Conclusions, 18 May 1940, CAB 65/7 PRO.

54–5. War Cabinet (128) Confidential Annex, 18 May 1940, CAB 65/13 PRO.

56. War Cabinet (128) Conclusions, 18 May 1940, CAB 65/7 PRO.

57. Minute of 18 May, Churchill Papers 20/13, cited by Gilbert, *Finest Hour*, p. 359.

58. Horne, p. 506; Antoine de Saint-Exupéry, *The Flight to Arras*, quoted by Horne, p. 499.

59–60. Reynaud, op. cit., pp. 339–40.

61. Halder, *Journal*, 19 May 1940.

62. Baudouin, *Diaries*, 19 May 1940.

63. Cadogan, *Diary*, 19 May 1940.

64. War Cabinet (129) Conclusions, 19 May 1940, CAB 65/7 PRO.

65. Mussolini to Churchill, 18 May 1940, quoted by Churchill, Vol. II, p. 108.

66. Halifax, *Diary*, 19 May 1940.

67. Cabinet Minutes (129) Conclusions, 19 May 1940.

68. Colville, *Diaries*, 19 May 1940, p. 135; Eden, *Diary*, 19 May 1940.

69. War Cabinet (129) Conclusions, 19 May 1940, CAB 65/7 PRO.

70–1. Gilbert, *Finest Hour*, pp. 364–5.

72. *Evening Standard*, 20 May 1940; Harvey, *Diaries*, 19 May 1940, p. 362.

73. Minute of 19 May 1940, Churchill Papers G4, cited by Gilbert, *Finest Hour*, p. 366.

74. "Former naval person" telegram, 20 May 1940, PREM 3/468 PRO; minute by David Scott of the Foreign Office American Departments, 20 May 1940, FO 371/24192 PRO.

75. Berle, *Diary*, 17 and 19 May 1940.

76. Kennedy to Hull, 15 May 1940, FRUS 1940 III pp. 224–5.

CHAPTER 5

(pp. 100–27)

1. Colville, *Diaries*, 19 May 1940.

2. Churchill seems to have had the MI5 operation against the Embassy code clerk in mind the previous day when he had a talk with his son which Randolph considered so historically significant that he made it the subject of a special memoir: "I think I can see my way through," Churchill announced as he shaved in the bathroom of Admiralty House early on Saturday morning. "Do you mean that we can avoid defeat or beat the bastards?" Randolph recalled asking his father as he finished hacking away at his stubborn beard. "Of course I mean we can beat them," Churchill shot back, flinging his razor into the basin. "Well, I'm all for it," Randolph responded, "but I don't see how you can do it." "I shall drag the United States in," Churchill declared with "great intensity" as he vigorously sponged his face (Randolph Churchill's recollections, dictated 13 February 1963, quoted by Gilbert, *Finest Hour*, op. cit., p. 338).

3. Confidential Files of U.S. Embassy London 1939–1940, 820.00 RG 59 NAW.

4. Kent, Tyler, Gatewood 123 Personnel Files /5–3040 RG 59 NAW. Copies were obtained from the Civil Records Division of the U.S. National Archives on 6 August 1980, two years before they were removed on 26 June 1982. The reason cited on the buff-coloured withdrawal cards that replaced these files was that their removal in 1982 was authorized under "Gr[eat] Br[itain] Intel[ligence]." Not only Johnson's sixteen-page report was reclassified, but also the subsidiary reports on the MI5 investigation of the activities of Kent, whose job as a code clerk allowed him access to some of the most secret reports and documents in the London Embassy. American bureaucracy, however, moved more slowly than the British government's determination to keep closed intelligence information shared under a secret and officially unacknowledged World War I intelligence-sharing agreement.

5ff. Knight disclosed to Johnson that Kent had been under observation by MI5 since he had arrived in England on 5 October 1939. Their interest in him resulted from his association with a "naturalized Swede of German extraction named Ludwig Ernst Matthias." Knight explained that they had been tipped off by the Stockholm police that Matthias was an undercover Gestapo agent. On 8 October Matthias had been followed to the Cumberland Hotel, where he met a man "subsequently identified as Tyler Kent, holder of United States Diplomatic Passport no. 405." Suspicions were aroused when he left the room with a "bulky envelope approximately 10" x 6." They "proceeded to spend an evening drinking and dining together"; Herschel V. Johnson Report dated 28 May 1940, US Emb Confidential Files 820.02 1939–1940 RG 59 NAW.

6. "Meeting with P. Game; Knight & Small at the Yard re BUF's etc." (Sir Philip Game was the Commissioner of the Metropolitan Police, who was technically the head of Special Branch; Small was Vera Small of MI5); handwritten day-diary of General Vernon Kell made available to the author.

7. Colville, *Diaries*, 19 May 1940.

8. The doorman had taken the envelope directly up to the Code Room before notifying Vice-Consul J. P. Palmer, the officer on night duty. He then telephoned Rudolf E. Schonfeld, the Secretary of the Embassy, who was at his home, to

come and deal with the matter. When Schonfeld arrived at 2 a.m., he was told that the message from the Prime Minister to the President was already partly encoded for transmission. Kent happened to be one of the code clerks on duty that night and he had opened it, although he had no authority to do so. Schonfeld reported that he had "scarcely finished" reading the "highly confidential" contents of the sealed envelope when he received a call from a Captain Elliot at the Admiralty, who said he wanted to come round and fetch the telegram. The only explanation given was that the Prime Minister "wished to have it back by six in the morning." Concerned about the "obviously dangerous implications" for security, Schonfeld telephoned the night duty officer at the Admiralty, who had "no inkling of what it was all about." He then rang Downing Street, only to be put through to the Admiralty. He spoke with Captain Pym, one of the Secretaries of the Committee of Imperial Defence, who confirmed that the Prime Minister did indeed require the return of his telegram "to consult further before sending the message." When Captain Elliot arrived at the Embassy a short time later, Schonfeld explained his concern and the precautions he had felt obliged to take. "In times like these one could not be too careful," Schonfeld wrote. "We naturally were obliged to safeguard the British Government as well as ourselves." According to Schonfeld, the Admiralty's emissary merely interjected with a nod, "Fifth Column Activities." The puzzled American official was surprised next day when the Churchill telegram came back to the Embassy for transmission to the White House at midday with no amendments at all (Schonfeld Report, 28 May 1940, US Emb Confidential File 820.1 RG 59 NAW.

9. Cadogan, *Diary*, 20 May 1940.

10. War Cabinet (131) Conclusions, 10 May 1940, CAB 65/7; Confidential Annex Minute 10, 20 May 1940, CAB 65/13 PRO.

11. Report submitted by Franklin C. Gowen, 28 May 1940, US Emb "Kent File." This thirteen-page document, like the Herschel Johnson report, was withdrawn as "Security Classified Information" by the State Department "GBR/Intel" in November 1981, RG 59 NAW.

12. Ibid.; interview with Mrs. Irene Danischewsky, June 1982.

13ff. Gowen report, op. cit.

14. Tyler Kent interviews, April 1982.

15. Kent, Tyler, Gatewood FBI File Bu 65–27850, 2 May 1951, "Internal Security R[ussia]" FOIA.

16. Kent FBI File; information from William C. Bullitt.

17. Bullitt's letter to Walton R. Moore, Assistant Secretary of State (one of those who had recommended Kent). In his communication of 14 June 1934 Bullitt states that after a "talking to . . . young Kent seems to have turned over a new leaf" and that he was therefore glad he did not "acquiesce in the universal recommendation of the officers of the Embassy and the Consulate that he should be fired." Kent became involved in what was referred to as the "Vulkmanic Rumpus," and in a letter from Moscow of 25 April 1935 Bullitt informed Moore that the row had died down but that "Kent is still keeping his nose firmly pointed to the North Star" (Walton Moore Papers FDRL).

18. Kent FBI File BU 65–27850 Internal Security R.; interview of Kent at Baltimore, 18 September 1951, FOIA.

19. The smuggling ring is revealed by a "Dear Pucia" letter written to Kent on 1 July 1937 by Clerk A. J. Barret (this revealing five-page letter was also removed by the State Department from the Kent File in 1982). It lists items of fur and jewelry which, as Barret reported from New York, were "appraised 200% per more than the cost of the things at the rate of 5 rubles equal $1.00." He wrote that if he pooled more money in Moscow he could have made "$1,500 clear profit." Kent admitted in his interview that Pucia was the nickname Barret used for him and that he had ignored his friend's injunction "you destroy this letter." The letter, dated 1 July 1937, from 661 West 180th Street New York, was one of the incriminating documents seized in the

raid on Kent's London flat on 20 May (US Emb Kent File RG 84 NAW); Kent had to make the long trip to London overland by way of Leningrad, Helsingfors and Oslo to Bergen, where he took a boat to Newcastle. It was on the train from Oslo that he said he struck up an acquaintance with Ernest Matthias. Kent said that the businessman was friendly and had bought a box of cigars; as a diplomat his bag was immune to search. "If he was a German agent as MI5 claimed, Matthias was travelling on a legitimate Swedish passport," Kent explained. "He made no secret that he had been in the German Army in the Great War and would probably be stopped and searched by the British." He was right. What Kent did not know was that the British had been tipped off by the Stockholm Police about Matthias. Tailed by Special Branch from Newcastle, he led them straight to Kent when he arrived to claim the package at the Cumberland Hotel on 5 October. Whether it really was cigars in the package, as Kent claimed, will never be known. He told the F.B.I. in 1951 that he had left the box in a taxi on the way to his hotel, emphatically denying that Matthias had ever met him at the Cumberland. Significantly, in view of later suspicions that Kent had Soviet links, his connection with a known Gestapo agent was never raised against him at his trial. Furthermore, a search of captured Gestapo and S.D. records failed to turn up any trace of the mysterious Matthias.

20. Kell Diary, 5 October 1940.

21. Interview with Dr. Georg Knupffer, August 1982; information in the MI5 report given to the U.S. Embassy the day Kent arrived in London that "just prior to the war and possibly still, the German Secret Service has been receiving from an American Embassy reports, at times two a day, which contained practically everything from Ambassador Kennedy's despatches to President Roosevelt" ("Secret" to Johnson from Liddell, 7 February 1940, 820.02 Confidential Files US Embassy London 1939–1940 RG 84 NAW).

22. Mrs. Irene Danischewsky, who was interviewed by the author in June 1982, was born in Russia the daughter of an Imperial Army Colonel who in 1916 came to London with his family on a posting to supervise the purchase of British munitions. She became a British citizen when she married Alexander Danischewsky, a naturalized former Russian citizen. Her husband was the eldest son of a family of Baltic Jewish traders based in St. Petersburg and Murmansk, who had set up a trading company before the Revolution to import turpentine, pitch and marine chandler's products. She admitted that she had started an affair with Kent shortly after meeting him, although she realized afterwards it was "very very wrong." She had visited Kent after his arrest and when he was sent to prison because she felt sorry for him. She tearfully said that she was "desperately sorry" that her name was revealed in the American records and begged that it should not be used in any way that would embarrass her family, threatening that she "didn't know what she would do" if it ever came out while she was alive. She is now deceased. She appears to have been only accidentally caught up in the Kent affair. It is, however, appropriate to add that there might be another Soviet connection, if not directly to Kent's paramour, then to the family firm of which her husband was managing director. Mrs. Danischewsky repeatedly insisted that her husband and his family were totally non-political – neither "pro nor anti" the Bolsheviks. This, she insisted, was true as far as she ever knew for her father-in-law, Israel Isaakovitch, and his brother Paul. Foreign Office files and British Naval Intelligence records for 1918, however, reveal that both Israel and Paul Danischewsky came under strong suspicion for being members of "a dangerous espionage operation" with links to the Bolsheviks (Report from British Legation, Christiana, 19 October 1918, FO 371/3374 PRO). After World War I the two brothers moved their base of operations to London, with headquarters in Great Tower Street and works in Managers Street, Poplar, near the West India Docks. In the records of Companies House their company was listed as "Tar,

539

pitch and turpentine importers." It is still in business, although at a different location, but during the interwar years, in common with many such firms which had continued dealings with the Soviets under favourable terms, MI5 suspected that it was operated by the N.K.V.D. as a convenient front for undercover operations and business transactions (information from Confidential MI5 source); Kent interview; Confirmation in the Transcript of "Rex v Tyler Gatewood Kent" *In camera* trials are not made public in Britain, but a copy of the transcript (hereafter "Kent Trial") was supplied to the U.S. Embassy in London and can be found in the State Department 123 File "Kent Tyler." Another version, which differs in some minor respects, was obtained by Kent himself in 1940 to prepare his appeal. He took it back to the U.S. in 1945 and it was later deposited in the Charles Parsons Collection in Sterling Library at Yale University.

23. Interview with Dr. Georg Knupffer, a White Russian exile who was President of the Monarchists' League. "They'll be nothing but talk of the Jews tonight," the commander of Knupffer's father's cruiser remarked when they spotted Captain Wolkoff's ship heading into port. According to British intelligence writer Nigel West, the Wolkoff security risk was not discovered and corrected until after the trial and conviction of the Admiral's daughter (Nigel West, *MI5* (London, 1981), p. 157).

24. Interview with the late Joan Miller (Mrs. Phipps), August 1982. Her ghostwritten autobiographical account of her role as Knight's assistant and undercover agent is given in *One Girl's War: Personal Exploits in MI's Most Secret Station* (Dingle, Co. Kerry, 1987). It is banned from publication in Britain.

25. Kent interview; Miller interview.

26. Kent interview.

27. Kent Trial. Transcript testimony of Marjorie Mackie (MI5 agent) that Wolkoff had mentioned Henlein and Hess as well as Frank. Her own written account of her trip to Germany in July 1939 mentioned only meeting Frank, whom she talked to for "two and a half hours," learning "of the forthcoming Germano-Soviet pact and all it would imply;" Kent Trial Transcript, p. 87; "Kent File" RG 84 NA.

28. Archibald H. Maule Ramsay, *The Nameless War* (Devon, 1952), pp. 1–48; 100–4.

29. Ramsay, pp. 100; 59; 83. "I had never heard of this Club until I met Jock in Brixton, but many distinguished people belonged to it and were perturbed when the police got hold of a list of members" (letter from Sir Barry Domville to Sir Charles Parsons, 5 December 1955, Parsons Collection SLY).

30. William Allen was the Solicitor General who prosecuted both Wolkoff and Kent. Elevated to the peerage as Earl Jowitt, he gave a personal and, it must be presumed, officially authorized account of both trials in *Some Were Spies* (London, 1954), p. 67.

31. Kent interview and Kent Trial, p. 58; Knufpper interview.

32. Kent interview; Kent was carefully vague about the precise date at the trial and in his F.B.I. interview. But his specific reference to "before Easter," which in 1940 was the third weekend in March, suggests that the crucial visit must have occurred sometime in the second week of March, a week after his first meeting with Ramsay.

33. Kent Trial, p. 151; p. 137; Ramsay, op. cit., p. 109.

34. Kent Trial, p. 138; Kent interview.

35. Kent Trial, pp. 138 and 83.

36. Knupffer interview; Gowen report, op. cit., Ramsay, op. cit., p. 103.

37. Kent interview; under the Official Secrets Act all the prosecution had to demonstrate was that Kent had been "obtaining and communicating documents which might be of use to the enemy for a purpose prejudicial to the safety and interests of the state" (Kent Trial, p. 200).

38. Interview with Malcolm Muggeridge, April 1985.

39. Miller, op. cit., p. 34; testimony of Marjorie Mackie (Mrs. Amor) and Helene de Muncke, Kent Trial, pp. 91–9; 97–109.

40. Kent Trial, p. 111.

41. Kent Trial, p. 142; p. 107; Mackensen to Berlin, 23 May 1940, No. 305 DGFP, op. cit. The translation appears on Film No. 9, Frames 371–3, of the cache of microfilmed records of the German Foreign Minister which former Foreign Ministry official Karl von Loesch had buried for safekeeping. Copies of the microfilms are in Bonn, London, Washington GFM 1/2 (Foreign Office Library) PRO; NA T-Series Roll 631 NAW. The list of cables found in Kent's possession makes no mention of the 16 May Roosevelt message, but Kennedy's cables Nos. 1598 and 1794 make it clear that it was in his possession (Memorandum for the Files, 3 March 1970, "TYLER KENT" FDRL). The U.S. files do not contain Kent's handwritten copy of this cable. "Where the Wolkoff copy is unknown at present," the First Secretary observed, noting that the copy "in Mrs Nicholson's possession remains in the hands of the police and has not been seen at the Embassy" (Johnson Memorandum, 28 May 1940, Kent File NAW; Ramsay, op. cit., p. 78).

42. State Department cable No. 872 was received in London at 1 p.m. on 16 May. Kent would therefore have had plenty of time to pencil a copy and pass it to Wolkoff for transmission to her Italian contact the same evening. Most likely it was in the letter Helene de Muncke put through the Duca del Monte's letterbox that same evening. Given MI5 standard operational procedure it would have been surprising if de Muncke had not first taken the latter to Knight to establish its contents before delivery. Therefore MI5 knew that Wolkoff's letter did not contain Norwegian invasion "plans" but the President's telegram refusing destroyers from the coding room of the U.S. Embassy.

43. Johnson Report and Index of the documents recovered from Kent's flat; "Kent File" RG 59 NAW.

44ff. Johnson Report. First General Interrogation of Kent after his arrest held in Ambassador Kennedy's Office, 20 May 1940; "Kent File," op. cit.

45. Kent interview; Ramsay, op. cit., p. 110.

46. Johnson Report, 20 May 1940; ibid.; Kent interview.

47ff. Johnson Report, op. cit.

48. Kent interview.

49. None of the Moscow report material has been released by the F.B.I. as part of Kent's file. The thirteen-page memorandum prepared by F.B.I. Special Agents Avery M. Warren and Lawrence C. Frank dated 13 March 1940 is Item 534, "Moscow," in the PSF "Hoover" FDRL.

50. Kent interview: Mrs. Kent was trying to raise $25,000 to purchase the cables, which were popularly believed to include one from Churchill to the President telling him "I am half American and the natural person to work with you. It is evident that we see eye to eye. Were I to become Prime Minister of Britain we could rule the world." The rumours gained such currency that Henry H. Klien, the attorney for Colonel Eugene Nelson Sanctuary, then being tried for sedition, threatened to call Mrs. Kent as a witness because the Churchill-Roosevelt cables included such supposedly damning evidence of a conspiracy to get the United States into the war in 1939–40 that Stalin "has held them as a whip over Roosevelt's head." The wild – and, as can now be seen, exaggerated – rumours of what the Churchill–Roosevelt cables really contained caused a mild uproar when the issue was aired in the Senate on 19 June 1944 and echoed in British parliamentary questions (Congressional Record, 19 June 1944, in F.B.I. Kent File together with the Memorandum letters and report to Roosevelt by J. Edgar Hoover). This was just three days after Kent's name had been raised in the House of Commons debate on the continued detention of Captain Ramsay and others under Defence of the Realm Regulation 18B.

To try to defuse the controversy over Kent, the State Department issued a press release confirming that he had been legitimately tried and imprisoned by the British for stealing U.S. government cables that "would have been useful to Germany." Their contents were not disclosed. Kennedy issued a statement denying that he had been "railroaded by Scotland Yard" while at the same time half-conceding the charge by stating that if "we had been at war he wouldn't have turned Kent over to the British, but would have sent him back to the United States" (Kennedy statement, *Washington Times Herald*, 5 September 1944).

51. At the time of his return, Kent insisted that he had to keep silent because a Federal Statute had made it an offence for government employees to disclose the contents of official cables. In 1982, however, he conceded that he "had nothing to say" about Roosevelt and Pearl Harbour and that the whole issue had been cooked up by his mother and her Republican friends. By 1962 the fifty-year-old Kent decided to give vent to his hatred of the Kennedys. His vehicle was the *Putnam County Sun*, a weekly Florida newspaper purchased, with his wife's money, to promote his anti-semitic right-wing diatribes. It was mastheaded as "Palatka's Only Independent Home-Owned Newspaper." Kent had used his position as proprietor to promote an unsuccessful campaign for Putnam county commissioner. The virulence of his anti-semitic, anti-liberal and anti-Black views transformed the formerly sleepy newspaper into a hate-sheet whose headlines screamed "Klan Needed in South Again." Kent declared the new President an "Essobbee" who was packing "Communist Front Members" into his Cabinet. Not surprising, least of all to Kent himself, were the attacks his views attracted. He claimed that the Jewish Anti Defamation League organized them, encouraging the *Miami Herald* and other Putnam County papers to launch libellous smears accusing him of being a traitor. He began fighting – and winning – lawsuits against those newspapers which too carelessly interpreted

the wartime reports to accuse him of being a criminal for betraying the country. He won on technicalities, because the Official Secrets Act for which he was imprisoned by the British did not make him a traitor or a spy to the U.S. When Joseph Kennedy was quoted by the *Miami Herald* as having made the same injudicious slip, Kent gleefully slapped a lawsuit on the President's father and the newspaper. But Kent was denied his day in court, and the public retribution he had so long planned, when Joseph Kennedy had a stroke in November 1962.

52. Memorandum of Mr. Ladd, Tyler G. Kent Internal Security (R), 4 April 1944, Kent File 65–2785 FBI FOIA; Handwriten note by Hoover on 19 April 1944; Memorandum for Mr. Tamm, "Tyler Kent Internal Security R." Kent File 65–27850 FBI FOIA; Report on Interrogation of Tyler Kent, 18 September 1951, No. 65–27850 FBI FOIA.

53. The interview was conducted by a Ernest J. Tsikerdanos of the State Department Office of Security; Interview with Kent, April 1982 (Memorandum C/C/Hiles from Kent, 30 July 1978, Toland Papers FDR), "Moscow's Moles on the Nazi Spy," Nigel West, *The Times*, 10 December 1983; West's MI5 source had confirmed that postwar "Mole" hunts had prompted a review of that case which revealed "that in fact Kent had been recruited by the Russians." Items discovered in Kent's flat by MI5, on re-examination, suggested a Soviet connection. There was a £50 ($200) note that he could not account for, since he was paid in U.S. currency and did not have a British bank account. The note was such an unusually high denomination for the time, equivalent to a $1,000 note today, that it attracted the attention of both the British and the F.B.I. Could it have been a Soviet payoff? In Kent's address book, among a large number of names, was that of the White Russian Anatoli V. Baikaloff, a journalist and head of the Russian League who was suspected of being an undercover Soviet. Among the first phone calls to be made to the

U.S. Embassy inquiring after Kent was one from the former Imperial Chargé E. Sabline – whose name did not appear in Kent's address book – but was known by both Knupffer and the British to have gone over to the Soviets. Then there was a mysterious phone call from P. Larsson & Sons, tailors in Great Pulteney Street, which turned out to be a false address. The mysterious Ernst Ludwig Matthias, the supposed Gestapo agent whose name does not show up on any of the captured records as a Gestapo agent, could have been an agent of Moscow. Most intriguing of all is the allegation made in 1942 by a Soviet employee at the U.S. Embassy in Moscow named Schifer who seems to have been put up to accuse Kent of trying to recruit him as a German spy. Inquiries to the K.G.B. archives have failed to disclose a "Kent" agent file.

54. Among the names listed were Ferdinand Kuhn of the London Bureau of the *New York Times*, and representative of INS and the Domei News, typed list of addresses and card found in black tin box (Kent File RG 59 NAW).

CHAPTER 6

(pp. 128–49)

1. Kennedy Press Statement, *Washington Daily News*, 5 September 1944.

2. Kennedy to Secretary of State, 20 May 1940; "Telegrams relating to case of Tyler Kent" US Emb London "CONFIDENTIAL" File 1940–1 RG 84 NAW; one of the phone calls was an "almost hysterical message" from Kent's mistress warning that Kent's flat had been raided. Another woman called to invite Kent round to cocktails that evening. Gowen, who passed the word to Scotland Yard, was told this was Enid Riddell, another Right Club member. She called again and left a message that Gowen picked up, telling Kent that he was expected for dinner at La Coquille restaurant that evening. He was later informed by Knight of MI5 that they had raided Riddell's house at 3

Chesham Street and established that she and the Italian Assistant Military Attaché had waited "until very late" at the West End restaurant, unaware that Kent was dining that night as a reluctant guest of His Majesty in a nearby police cell. Technically the code clerk's arrest that afternoon was illegal, because the official instruction from Washington stripping him of his diplomatic immunity did not arrive in London until well after midnight (Gowen Report).

3. "Upon receipt of your telegram Tyler Kent is dismissed from the government service as of this date" (Secretary of State to Kennedy 8 p.m. Washington time, "Kent Files;" Secretary of State to Kennedy, 20 May, and Kennedy to Secretary of State, 21 May, "Kent File" RG 59 NAW).

4. Kennedy Press Statement, loc. cit.

5. By 1942, all U.S. legations were equipped with the U.S. Navy's reconditioned enciphering machines which became the standard means of sending secure communications to and from the State Department (Secretary of State to Kennedy, 20 May 1940, "Kent File").

6. Peter Wright, *Spycatcher* (New York, 1987). A surviving MI5 officer involved with the Kent case who was interviewed by the author did not disagree with the deduction that the cables in Kent's apartment provided a windfall for British Intelligence.

7. Kennedy to Hull, 25 September 1939, FRUS 1939 Col 1, p. 500; Kennedy to President and Secretary of State, 15 May 1940, "Kennedy" PSF Safe File FDRL; Robert Murphy, *Diplomat Among Warriors* (New York, 1964), p. 38.

8. Diary of Harold Ickes, 10 March 1940 (microfilm version, which is more complete than the original, pages of which are now missing, presumably censored by the family) LOC (hereafter Ickes, *Diary*).

9. Lord Gladwyn (Gladwyn Jebb, who in 1940 was Cadogan's Private Secretary), *The Memoirs of Lord Gladwyn* (New York, 1972), p. 97.

10. The Marquess of Hartington was

later killed on active duty with the R.A.F. Although the informant was not named by Sir Berkeley Gage of the American Department of the Foreign Office, he was characterized as "a reliable friend" and is identifiable as Hartington because he was "in the Coldstream Guards" and "was on close terms through one or all of his [Kennedy's] daughters." Minute of 26 and 29 September 1939 by Sir Berkeley Gage in jacket "US Ambassador's views to the outcome of the war" FO 371/A6561/1090/45 PRO.

11. Minute by Sir John Balfour, 20 September 1939. Minute by JVP (Perowne) "More Kennediana" 18 January 1940 FO 371/24251 PRO. Although Balfour does not name the son, Gage's minute specifically referred to John F. Kennedy as the one who had shaped his father's negative attitude; Perowne Minute, 29 January 1940, FO 371/22827 PRO; Minute by Cadogan, 21 September 1939.

12. David Scott, Minute, 30 September 1939, docket "Baron Palmestierna's views on the US Ambassador" FO 371/6635/1090/45 PRO.

13. Minute by Victor Perowne, 30 September 1939, docket "Baron Palmestierna's view on the US Ambassador"; ibid.

14. David E. Koskoff, *Joseph P. Kennedy*, op. cit., p. 216; interview with David Koskoff.

15. American journalist, interviewed by David Koskoff, 26 July 1972, and quoted by him in *Kennedy*, p. 217; For an analysis of the stratagems that Kennedy and his Irish contemporary Ben Smith employed to manipulate the stock market, see Richard Whalen, *The Founding Father* (New York, 1964), pp. 103–11.

16. Note of letter and reply drafted by Secretary of Treasury, 16 April 1940, PSF "Kennedy" FDRL; Letter from Monnet B. Davis to Joseph Kennedy, 26 April 1941, citing "our conversation over the telephone" and enclosing extracts of 28 Statute 807; 22 USC Section 38 and the wording incorporated into the Foreign Service Regulations, in 123 Kennedy Joseph RG 84 NAW. It is also significant that Joseph P. Kennedy's surviving

papers in the Kennedy Memorial Library are closed to all researchers; nor are the financial files relating to how he amassed his fortune ever likely to be opened to public scrutiny. Koskoff, who investigated the rumours very thoroughly, believes that he came closest to establishing the truth about whether Kennedy had been illegally playing the financial markets when he interviewed Malcolm Macdonald, a minister in both Chamberlain's and Churchill's wartime administrations. Koskoff asked Macdonald specifically about the Foreign Office references to the American Ambassador's stock-market trading. "A lot of people heard it – at least in government circles," Macdonald said, adding knowingly: "Or perhaps even knew it" (Koskoff interview with Macdonald, 17 July 1972).

17. Signature of Cadogan and minute of Vansittart, 22 January 1940, FO 371/24251.

18. Von Dirksen to Weizsäcker, 13 October 1938, DGFP IV, p. 634; Dieckhoff to von Dirksen, 2 November 1938; ibid.

19. Mooney Manuscript, op. cit., p. 12; ibid.

20. Copy of a letter dated 2 May 1939 from Mooney to Puhl on Hotel Adlon stationery, Mooney Papers GUL.

21. Ibid.; Kennedy to Welles, 4 May 1939; Hull to Kennedy, 4 May 1939, State Department ("123 Kennedy, Joseph P," RG 84 NAW).

22. Summary in Mooney's hand, but the terms were evidently drawn up by a German (probably Wolthart), because the nouns are capitalized in the typescript headed "Further Requirements for the Meeting," Mooney Papers GUL.

23. Mooney Manuscript, op. cit.

24. *The Week*, 17 May 1940. A version of the story appears in the Ickes Diary, op. cit. LOC.

25–6. Liddell to Johnson, 7 March 1940, 820.02 US Emb London Confidential Files 1939–40 RG 59 NAW.

27. Johnson to Dunn, 8 Feb 1940, 820.02 London Embassy Confidential Files 1939–

40 RG 59 NAW; Only the London end of the "Doctor" correspondence survives, along with the two MI5 reports, in the U.S. Embassy London Confidential Files, because of the unique position of the State Department and the role James C. Dunn himself played before the war as the United States' only Foreign Intelligence operation. A former U.S. Ambassador to Rome, "Jimmy" Dunn returned to Washington to occupy a senior post in the European Section of the State Department. According to State Department records and the veterans of the U.S. Intelligence Community, he handled the information passed by MI5 to the Department under the secret 1918 agreement to share intelligence. Herschel V. Johnson, who enjoyed the total confidence of the British, managed the London end of this secret exchange. Although Dunn had the full trust and confidence of the President and the Secretary of State, once the United States was in the war, the military and the F.B.I. had exerted great pressure to eliminate the intelligence "knothole" controlled by Dunn. In the aftermath of the Kent affair in 1940, General Clayton Bissell, G-2 (Intelligence chief) of the U.S. Army, who as a former Military Attaché in London knew something of the importance of this channel of intelligence, called a meeting with Assistant Secretary Adolf Berle and J. Edgar Hoover to demand that armed military couriers take over the handling of all diplomatic traffic, particularly that which contained intelligence material. Available State Department records do not disclose precisely what was done as a direct result of Bissell's demands, but it appears that the security section was reorganized and steps taken to safeguard secret communications. When the United States entered the war after Pearl Harbour the following year, Jimmy Dunn's monopoly as gatekeeper of all the intelligence supplied by MI5 soon fell casualty to O.S.S. awareness that State's intelligence system was inadequate to meet the new demands. The records of his Department have not been released because they were absorbed after the war into the U.S. Intelligence Agencies, such as the C.I.A. and N.S.A., who pay more careful respect than State to the secrecy of the original 1918 agreement with the British.

28. "Personal and strictly confidential," Johnson to Dunn, 14 February 1940, 820.02 U.S. Emb London Confidential Files 1939–40 RG 84 NAW.

29. The informant had told the British that he happened to be in Jahnke's office when a stenographer-interpreter, who did the translation from English to German asked Jahnke if she could leave that afternoon as there had been nothing in from the American source. "No, the Doctor is not dictating this afternoon," Jahnke agreed. According to the British this was what led *their* informant to suppose that the American information was leaking from the Berlin Embassy. Jahnke's remark led MI6 or MI5 to conclude that "the Doctor" was "in constant contact and therefore presumably in Berlin." Just how current the Doctor's reports were could not be established. But for the period "June, July and August" of 1939, Johnson was told, "other information" they received was "at least a fortnight old."

30. "Personal & strictly confidential," Johnson to Dunn, 4 April 1940, 820.02 U.S. Emb London Confidential Files 1939–40 RG 84 NAW.

31. Letter from the Ministry of Economic Warfare to Cadogan, 26 March 1940, and another unheaded, dated 21 March 1940, sent in response to Cadogan's secret letter A 1945/G OF 371/24251 PRO; Sir Dick White, interviews, July 1984 and April 1989.

32. The German Foreign Ministry possessed a very extensive telephone monitoring and deciphering service which is known by 1940 to have penetrated some of the more secure State Department code systems. Precisely which ones were broken or when, cannot yet be established. The records of the *Pers Z* (the Z Section of the Personnel and Administrative Branch, the approximate equivalent of Britain's G.C.H.Q. at Bletchley Park) that were captured still remain classified – even from the German Foreign Ministry archive. Either because they

were destroyed or because such intercepts are kept secret at British insistence, there is no extensive body of records from Göring's Forschungsamt, or the O.K.W. Cipher Branch and the Reichssicherhauptampt (RHSA) Amt VI's Radio Observation Post, according to information provided by the Archives Section of the Auswärtiges Amt (German Foreign Ministry) in Bonn. David Kahn, relying on interviews, asserts that "in 1940 *Pers Z* began to break into one of the major US Department codes." But he was unable to confirm this because he found not a single "*Pers Z*" decrypt in the files of the Buro des Staatsekretärs in the Foreign Ministry Archives during the course of many years' study for his book, *Hitler's Spies: German Military Intelligence in World War II* (New York, 1978), pp. 185–6 and p. 576, n.

33. Johnson to Dunn, 14 February, op. cit., Kurt Jahnke F.B.I. File obtained under FOIA; "Final Report on the Case of Walter Schellenberg," IRR Records RG 319 pp. 16–17 NAW.

34. Schellenberg Report, Appendix XV, "Jahnke and the Jahnkeburo," op. cit.; I am grateful to Adrian Liddell Hart for this additional information from his extensive research and for drawing attention to the role of Markus, who he interviewed in 1989.

35. In addition to Jahnke's line to MI6, Schellenberg later uncovered a connection with the Japanese and Swiss intelligence services. Jahnke appears to have accumulated considerable wealth from the high fees he charged for his information before he disappeared in the spring of 1945 as the Red Army overran his estate in Pomerania in East Prussia. Schellenberg believed he had been killed, but Jahnke later turned up in East Germany after the war, when he would certainly have been working for the Soviets. According to Adrian Liddell Hart, Maurice Oldfield, the former MI6 chief, told journalist Philip Knightley that the head of Hess's Intelligence Service (presumably Jahnke) was a Soviet agent. On the evidence available, Jahnke appears to have been a triple agent all along.

Although he professed to be on the side of the British, Jahnke was really one of Moscow's more successful and sinister agents.

36. Johnson to Dunn, 4 April 1940, op. cit.

37. Kennedy to Hull, 24 August 1939, European War 1939–40. 760C.62/943 RG 84 NAW; Moffat, *Diary*, 25 August 1940; as Kennedy recounted it to James V. Forrestal, *The Forrestal Diaries*, edited by Walter Millis (New York, 1951), pp. 121–2.

38. This according to White House insiders Joseph Alsop and Robert Kinter, *American White Paper* (New York, 1940), p. 68; Kennedy/Landis MS, p. 191; Kennedy to Hull, 18 September 1939, FRUS 1939 Vol. p. 441.

39. Minute of conversation with Charles Hilliam, 12 October 1939, Louis Fischer, *Men and Politics* (New York, 1941), p. 625; FO 371/25251 PRO.

40. Landis interviewed by Koskoff: *Kennedy*, op. cit., p. 2.

41. Leeper to Perowne, 16 October 1939, FO 371/22817 PRO; *New York Daily News*, 10 December 1939.

42. Mooney had talked with Francis Rodd, a partner in the London merchant bank of Morgan, Grenfell. The city banker not only approved but advised "there has been a great deal of discussion on that subject from time to time in the City" (Notes on meeting with Mr. Francis Rodd, Mooney Papers GUL); Kennedy to Roosevelt, 20 July 1939; Roosevelt to Kennedy 22 July 1939, PSF "Kennedy" FDRL.

43. When Kennedy was appointed as Roosevelt's first Securities and Exchange Commissioner, he insisted on forgoing a professional government secretary to have Edward Moore by his side. His secretary therefore received token official pay of $1 a week, with his salary continuing to be paid by Kennedy. Moore also went along when his boss was made head of the Maritime Commission, and in 1938 when Kennedy became an ambassador, although departmental

concern was expressed at the propriety of Moore, a non-government employee, having access to the most confidential correspondence of the State Department. But during their time in London, nothing could have passed through the Ambassador's office that was not seen by Moore. He was implicitly trusted by Kennedy, who treated him and his wife Mary as part of his large family. This kept "Eddie" absolutely loyal and totally discreet, for which he was duly rewarded with a full salary paid from his retirement until he died in 1952 at the age of eighty. Richard Whalen, *The Founding Father*, op. cit.; Doris Kearns Goodwin, *The Fitzgeralds and the Kennedys* (New York, 1987); and Koskoff, op. cit.

44. 123, Kennedy, Joseph P., 1940, op. cit.

45. Kennedy to Hull, 17 April 1939; Hull to Kennedy, 18 April 1939; Kennedy to Hull, 20 April 1940.

46. Mooney notes that he landed at Southampton after crossing the Atlantic on the German liner *Europa*. This was itself an interesting coincidence, because F.B.I. records confirm that Nazi agents operated from this flagship of the Third Reich's merchant marine fleet. Although Mooney recorded no meeting with Kennedy, it would have been surprising if he did not at least make a courtesy telephone call while he was in London for two days before leaving for Berlin on 30 March (Itinerary European trip, 21 March – 11 May 1939 Mooney Papers GUL).

47. 123, Moore, Edward E. RG 59 NAW.

48. A. J. Sylvester, Lloyd George's long-time secretary and confidant, who supplied the former Prime Minister with a daily briefing from his inside sources in the government and Parliament. Memo to Lloyd George, 27 May 1940, G24 Lloyd George Papers HOL.

49. The docket is clearly marked "db" for diplomatic bag, 123 Kennedy, Joseph P. /289 RG 59 NAW.

50. Kent F.B.I. File 65-27850-134 (Baltimore Interrogation), 7 September 1951 FOIA.

51. Kent interview; Kent Trial, p. 147.

52. Kennedy to Rose Kennedy, quoted in Arthur J. Schlesinger, *Robert Kennedy and His Times* (Boston, 1978), p. 29.

53. *Boston Post* heading, 17 February 1940; *New York Times*, 17 December 1940.

54. *The Spectator*, 8 March 1940.

55. For an analysis of Kennedy's biased reporting, see Koskoff, op. cit., pp. 274–6.

56. Breckinridge Long, *Diary*, 24 June 1940, LOC; Hull to Kennedy, 22 June 1940; Hull to Kennedy, 24 June 1940; Kennedy to Hull, 27 June 1940; Hull to Kennedy 25 June 1040 RG59 NAW.

57. Kennedy to Hull, 22 June 1940, "Kent File" RG 59 NAW; Welles to Johnson, 20 November 1940, "Kent File" RG 59 NAW.

CHAPTER 7
(pp. 150–72)

1. Ironside, *Diaries*, 19 May 1940.

2. Heinz Guderian, *Mit den Panzer in Ost und West* (Stuttgart, 1942), p. 76; William Shirer, *Berlin Diary* (New York, 1941), p. 191; Halder, *Journal*, 21 May 1940.

3. Ironside, *Diaries*, 20 May 1940; Baudouin, *Diaries*, 20 May.

4. Cabinet (132) Conclusions, 21 May 1940, CAB 65/7 PRO; Ironside, Diaries, 20 May 1940.

5. War Cabinet (132) Conclusions, 21 May 1940.

6. Cadogan, *Diary*, 21 May 1940; War Cabinet (132) Conclusions, 21 May 1940.

7. Ironside, *Diaries*, 20 May 1940; von Rundstedt, interview by Basil Liddell Hart, *The German Generals Talk* (New York, 1948), p. 131.

8. Horne, *To Lose a Battle* op. cit., p. 576.

9. Harvey, *Diaries*, 21 May 1940; Reynaud, *Thick of the Fight*, op. cit., p. 322; Baudouin, *Diaries*, 21 May 1940.

10. Telegram No 246 from British Military Mission, 21 May 1940, PREM 3/1883/PRO; telegram to Reynaud of 21 May 1940, PREM 3/188/1 PRO; Colville, *Diaries*, 21 May 1940, p. 136.

11. Draft telegram to HM Ambassador Washington, 23 April 1940, PREM 3/475/1; "Most Secret and Urgent" First Lord to Prime Minister, 20 May 1940, PREM 3/475/1; Memo to A.V. Alexander, 21 May 1940, PREM 3/475/1 PRO.

12. Berle, *Diary*, 21 May 1940; Moffat, *Diary*, 21 May; Breckinridge Long, *Diary*, 21 May.

13. Bullitt to President, 16 May 1940; PSF "Bullitt" FDRL; 21 May; Breckinridge Long, *Diary*, 21 May.

14. Baudouin, *Diaries*, 22 May 1940.

15. Ismay, *Memoirs*, op. cit., p. 130.

16. Supreme War Council 12 Meeting, 22 May 1940, CAB 99/3 PRO.

17. Churchill, Vol II, p. 58; Baudouin, *Diaries*, 22 May 1940.

18. Cable as reproduced in Churchill, Vol. II, p. 58; Baudouin, *Diaries*, 22 May 1940.

19. War Cabinet (130) Conclusions, 19 May 1940, CAB 65/7 PRO.

20. Halifax, *Diary*, 23 May 1940.

21. Cabinet Confidential Annex (133) Conclusions, 22 May 1940, "Subversive Activities in London," CAB 65/13 PRO.

22. Mosley publicly declared that Britain must not become "The lackey of a foreign power" in 9 May issue of the BUF magazine *Nation*, which declared that "every member of the British Union would be at the disposal of the nation" to fight off an invasion. Robert Skidelski, *Sir Oswald Mosley* (London, 1977), pp. 446, 454.

23. War Cabinet (133) Conclusions, 22 May 1940, 10.30 a.m., CAB 65/7 PRO.

24. The right of appeal was to a Home Office Advisory Committee established under the Emergency Powers Act passed on 24 August 1939, when the Government had been empowered to make Regulations by Orders in Council for the Defence of the Realm. The so-called DORA Regulations did not need parliamentary assent and were published on 1 September 1939, the day Germany invaded Poland. The original Section 18B had permitted the Home Secretary to make a detention order only "if satisfied with respect to any particular person that with a view to preventing him acting in a manner prejudicial to the public safety or the Defence of the Realm, it is necessary to do so." After some 46 people had been detained by November 1939, Parliament objected that the law was too sweeping an incursion into the liberty of the citizen. The Home Office accordingly modified Regulation 18B so that detention orders could be made only against those of "hostile origin or associations" or in the case of "act" prejudicial to the public safety or the Defence of the Realm." This curtailed the Home Secretary's authority, since he could order preventive detention only if suspects were *already* committing acts that were unlawful.

25. Authorization by Sir Alexander Maxwell, Permanent Secretary of Home Office, 14 June 1940, MEPO 2/6433 PRO; Peter and Leni Gillman, *Collar the Lot: How Britain Interned and Expelled Its Wartime Refugees* (London, 1980), p. 128. The dramatic jump in the monthly pattern of detentions under Regulation 18B after May 1940 reflects the toughening of the law at the height of the Fifth Column scare after Churchill came to power: May *73*; June *826*; July *436*; August *153*; September *50*; October *33*; November *17* (MEPO 2/6433).

26. Sir Normal Kendal, MEPO 2/6433. *"Reasons for order made under Defence Regulation 18B in the case of Captain Archibald Maule Ramsay"*, Home Office Advisory Committee (Defence Regulation 18B), 24 June 1940 (reproduced in Ramsay, op. cit., p. 104). Lord Marley made the Gauleiter charge in the House of Lords. Ramsay threatened to sue him for libel if he repeated it outside, without the protection of parliamentary privilege. He did not.

27. A. J. Sylvester, *Life without Lloyd*

548

George: The Diary of A. J. Sylvester (New York, 1971), p. 63, 22 May 1940. Lloyd George was alerted four days after the new 18B regulation came into effect that the wave of detentions brought "a scandal of the first order" in the Home Office. "Either a member, or members of the Fifth Column have been doing good work inside this Department," Sylvester reported from the Whitehall gossip after the arrest of Kent and Wolkoff. He also relayed rumours that the "Buchmanite Moral Re-Armers," of the so-called "Oxford Movement" also were "associated with the Fifth Column." Sylvester had been Private Secretary to the Committee of Imperial Defence in the years 1914–21, then private secretary to Lloyd George and successive Prime Ministers. He therefore had informants in the ministries and in the government, whom he mined assiduously to keep his former master abreast of current developments. "If this is true, its effects may be far-reaching" Sylvester noted, "as it is clear that at least one very eminent civil servant is a member of the movement" (Sylvester to Lloyd George, 28 May 1940, Lloyd George Papers HOL).

28.   "Interview with Neville Chamberlain, Lord President of the Council," Kell, Diary, 24 May 1940; War Cabinet (133) Confidential Annex Conclusions, 22 May 1940, CAB 65/13 PRO; the case Ramsay v. New York Times and Others was heard before Mr Justice Atkinson in the King's Bench Division of the High Court on 3 July 1941 after the Sunday Edition of the New York Times had summarized four articles that had appeared that week written by Colonel Donovan, Roosevelt's emissary to London. They had been authorized for publication by Colonel Knox, the U.S. Secretary of War. None of the original stories on the Fifth Column in Britain had actually called Ramsay a traitor until the Sunday, as a result of over-zealous subbing in the editorial department in New York (Herschel Johnson to Secretary of State, 12 August 1941, and report in The Times, 1 August 1941; 123 Kent, Tyler RG 59 NAW).

29.   Ibid.; Colonel George Ramsay, interviewed by Eric Bailey for "Mysteries of the Red Book," article, Daily Telegraph, 22 May 1990.

30.   War Cabinet (133) Conclusions, Confidential Annex, 22 May 1940.

31.   Ramsay, op. cit., Kent interview.

32.   Interview with Dr Richard Griffiths, May 1980; Richard Griffiths, Fellow Travellers of the Right: British Enthusiasts for Nazi Germany 1933–39 (London, 1979); the author, who was programme consultant for Divided We Stand, broadcast on ITV Channel I on 23 May 1990, shares Dr. Griffiths' expressed belief that the Red Book is indeed the genuine article. Although technically it is part of Captain Ramsay's estate, his son, who would have the best claim to the Red Book, said he was unlikely to pursue it. "We just want to forget about the whole thing," Colonel George Ramsay told the press. Because of the sensitivity of the names of those members who are still alive, after Dr. Griffiths' research paper is completed he proposes to lodge the Red Book with the Weiner Library in London until such time as the full list of names can be made public.

33.   War Cabinet (134) Confidential Annex, 22 May 1940, Minute 1 CAB 65/13 PRO.

34.   Ibid.; Ironside, Diary, 22 May 1940.

35.   War Cabinet (134) Confidential Annex, 22 May 1940, Minute 1, Appendix II, "Note by the Secretary of State for War recording a conversation with Lord Munster (ADC to Lord Gort)," CAB 65/18 PRO.

36.   Chamberlain, Diary, 22 May 1940; War Cabinet (134) Conclusions, 22 May 1940, CAB 65/7 PRO.

37.   Colville, Diaries, 22 May 1940.

38.   Ironside, Diaries, 23 May 1940; Churchill, Vol. II, p. 62; 23 May Minute to CIGS, Churchill Papers, 20/13 cited by Gilbert, Finest Hour, op. cit., p. 383.

39–40.   War Cabinet (135) Conclusions, 23 May 1940, CAB 65/7 PRO.

41.   Ibid.; Major L. F. Ellis, The War in

France and Flanders 1939–40 (London, 1953), p. 139 and Supplement. Cadogan, *Diary*, 23 May 1940.

42. War Cabinet (134) Conclusions, 23 May 1940, CAB 65/7 PRO.

43. Ibid.; Cadogan, *Diary*, 23 May 1940.

44. War Cabinet (134) Confidential Annex, 23 May 1940, CAB 65/13 PRO.

45. Halifax, *Diary*, 23 May 1940. According to the Foreign Secretary they discussed reports of American correspondents in France. Kennedy to Hull, 24 May 1940, FRUS III pp. 31–2.

46. Joseph E. Davies to President, 23 May 1940, PSF 'Diaries' FDRL.

47. This point is made by Horne, op. cit., p. 589.

48. Supplement to the *London Gazette*, 10 October 1941; Dispatches of General Gort quoted by Horne, op. cit., p. 590.

49. Baudouin, *Diaries*, 23 May 1940.

50. *Hansard*, 23 May 1940; as quoted by Reynaud, op. cit., p. 369.

51. Reynaud, loc. cit.

52ff. Colville, interview with Martin Gilbert, quoted in Gilbert, *Finest Hour*, op. cit., p. 385; War Cabinet (134) Confidential Annex, 23 May 1940, CAB 65/13 PRO; Baudouin, *Diaries*, 23 May 1940.

53. Sir Arthur Bryant, *The Turn of the Tide: Based on the Diaries of Field Marshal Lord Alan Brooke* (New York, 1957), p. 59.

54. *Chief of Staff: The Diaries of Lieutenant General Air Henry Pownall*, edited by Brian Bond (London, 1972), 22 May 1940, p. 331.

55. Telegram, 23 May 1940, Churchill Papers 20/13, cited by Gilbert, *Finest Hour*, p. 383.

56. War Cabinet (135) Conclusions, 23 May 1940, CAB 65/7 PRO.

57. Ironside, *Diaries*, 23 May 1940.

58. Bryant, op. cit., *Diary*, 23 May 1940, p. 90.

59. George VI's diary entry for 23 May

1940, quoted by Wheeler Bennett, *George VI*, op. cit., p. 456.

60. Telegrams of 23 May 1940 received in Paris at 5 a.m., 24 May 1940, Churchill Papers 20/40, cited in Gilbert, *Finest Hour*.

CHAPTER 8

(pp. 173–96)

1. Colville, *Diaries*, 24 May 1940.

2. Cadogan, *Diary*, 24 May 1940.

3. War Cabinet (137) Conclusions, 24 May 1940, (137) CAB 65/7 PRO.

4–5. Baudouin, *Diaries*, 24 May 1940.

6. Reynaud, *Thick of the Fight*, op. cit., pp 370–1.

7–8. Churchill, Vol. II, p. 64.

9. Pownall, *Diaries*, 24 May 1940.

10. Hans Jacobsen and Jurgen Rohwer, *Dokumenten zum Westfeldzug* (Frankfurt, 1970), p. 120.

11. Pownall, *Diaries*, 24 May 1940.

12. Liddell Hart, *German Generals Talk*, op. cit., p. 133.

13. Guderian, *Mit den Panzer in Ost und West*, op. cit., p. 46.

14. Halder, *Journal*, 17 May 1940; Walter Warlimont, *Inside Hitler's Headquarters 1939–45* (New York, 1963), p. 95; p. 97.

15–17. Halder, *Journal*, 23 May 1940; letter from Blumentritt to Basil Liddell Hart, 17 May 1950, LH 9/24/218 Liddell Hart Papers KUL.

18. H. A. Jacobsen in Jurgen Rohwer (ed.), *Decisive Battles of World War II: The German View* (New York, 1965), p. 55; Warlimont, op. cit., p. 98; Halder, *Journal*, 23 May 1940; 24 May 1940.

19. Halder, *Journal*, 24 May 1940; Ellis, *War in France*, op. cit., appendix II, p. 383.

20. Jodl, *Diary*, 24 May 1940, Ms in IZM, also in *International Military Tribunal* 18900-PS; Telford Taylor, *The March*

of Conquest: German Victories in Western Europe 1940 (New York, 1958).

21. Jodl, *Diary*, 24 May 1940, cited by Liddell Hart LH 9/24/218 KUL. War Diary of Army Group A, as reproduced by Liddell Hart LH 9/24/218 KUL; Translation by Jacobsen, op. cit., p. 57; Churchill, Vol. II, pp. 76–8; the first and last part of the Haltbefehl does indeed lay down the outlines for the final stage of the battle: "On the Führer's order the attack to the east of Arras with VII and II Corps, in cooperation with the left wing of Army Group B, is to be continued towards the northwest. On the other hand, forces advancing northwest of Arras are not to go beyond the general line Béthune–Aire–St–Omer–Gavelines (Canal Line). On the west wing all mobile units are to close up and let the enemy throw himself against the above mentioned favourable defensive line" (translation in Jacobsen, op. cit., p. 57). Ellis, *The War in France*, p. 139 and Supplement, argues that the decision had been pressed on a willing Hitler by an even more cautious von Rundstedt, who "saw that if he was to get his own way when it differed from the ideas of O.K.H. he must make it appear that what he did was by the Führer's Orders." Ellis maintained that Hitler's responsibility had been "completely misrepresented" by the German generals and that it was von Rundstedt who iniated the order, "Hitler merely endorsed it" (p. 350). A leading American analyst, Telford Taylor, contended that "it is absurd to contend (as do the German generals in their postwar apologia) that Rundstedt had no responsibility for the stop-order as to argue as does Major Ellis that Rundtstedt had already acted on May 23 and that Hitler merely 'endorsed' Rundstedt's decision" (Taylor, *The March of Conquest*, p. 261).

22. Basil Liddell Hart, *History of the Second World War* (New York, 1971), pp. 81–2. "If Hitler had felt that his Halt Order was due to Rundstedt's influence, he would certainly have mentioned it, after the British escape, among the excuses he gave for his decision, for he was very apt to blame others for his mistakes. Yet in this case there is no trace of his ever having mentioned, in the course of his subsequent explanation, Rundstedt's opinion as a factor. *Such negative evidence is as significant as any*" (Liddell Hart, noted in *The German Generals Talk*, op. cit., p. 135).

23. Interview with Blumentritt, quoted by Liddell Hart, *The German Generals Talk*, op. cit., pp. 134–5; *History of the Second World War*, op. cit., p. 83.

24. Ibid.

25. Interview of von Sodenstern by Rear Admiral Walter Ansel, USN, on 22 March 1953, and letter from Sodenstern of 17 May 1940, LH 9/24/218 Liddell Hart Papers op. cit. (Walter Ansel, *Hitler Confronts England* (Durham N.C., 1960), p. 71). Admiral Ansel fails to do justice to his very extensive researchers as evidenced by the different versions given of the transcripts of notes and tapes that he had supplied to Liddell Hart, which survive in his papers headed "Further Evidence on the Dunkirk Halt Order." Ansel, for reasons unclear and unjustified, rolls Sodenstern's 17 May account of Hitler's "astonishing" conversation about England into Blumentritt's recollections which Liddell Hart (a more meticulous and reliable analyst) assigned to 24 May, *after* von Rundstedt's Halt Order.

26. Jodl, *Diary*, op. cit.; Liddell Hart, *World War II*, op. cit., pp. 82–3.

27. Liddell Hart, *World War II*, p. 83; letter from Blumentritt to Liddell Hart, 17 May 1950, LH 9/24/218 KUL. British historians contend that Liddell Hart had been misled by von Rundstedt, von Kleist and Guderian, who wanted to rehabilitate their own reputations by shifting the burden of blame onto the Führer. Guderian, in particular, too fawningly credited Liddell Hart's pre-war writings on armoured warfare with inspiring the Wehrmacht's tank tactics. Hans Adolf Jacobsen in *Dünkirchen* (Neckargememünd, 1958) meticulously details the German military decision-making process to conclude that Liddell Hart overplayed the political element in Hitler's decision. Telford Taylor, op. cit., pp. 262–4, also concludes that Liddell Hart

was too influenced by the efforts of the German generals to absolve themselves of responsibility for Dunkirk. So does Olaf Groeler's *Menetekel Dünkirchen* essay in *Zeitgeschichte für Geschichtswissenschaft*; (1961). Liddell Hart was certainly a close friend and adviser of Lloyd George, who drew up a long memorandum after the Battle of Britain setting out the reasons why the time had come to make a negotiated peace, according to his son, Adrian Liddell Hart. Typical of dismissive opinions of Liddell Hart's analysis is Nicholas Harman in his 1981 account *Dunkirk: The Necessary Myth* (revised edition, London, 1990), p. 36. This readable account, while debunking many of the cherished myths about the evacuation, labels as "fantastic" General Guderian's suggestion that Hitler let the B.E.F. escape on purpose. He suggests that Liddell Hart was taken in by an ingratiating Guderian. Harman apparently did not read Liddell Hart's analysis closely enough. Like other historians, he failed to appreciate that the argument was based on the postwar testimony not only of the Panzer Group commander, but also of other generals who had no such axe of admiration to grind.

Brian Bond – a former pupil – in *Liddell Hart: A Study of his Military Thought* (London, 1970, p. 227) also asserted that his mentor "made himself a leading champion of the captured German general," while John J. Mearscheimer, in *Liddell Hart and the Weight of History* (London, 1988), p. 185, makes the broadest frontal assault on the leading British military analyst and thinker of his generation. He suggests that Liddell Hart's rehabilitation of the German generals "as basically rational and decent men pitted against a madman" was too sympathetic and that they in turn flattered him by overemphasizing the contribution his writings had made to the Wehrmacht's doctrine of armoured warfare. This is the general view taken by Brian Bond in *France and Belgium 1939–1940* (London, 1975), p. 166. Alistair Horne, in his penetrating and evocative *To Lose a Battle* (op. cit.), p. 599, sidesteps the issue raised by Liddell Hart by opting for the conclusion of the British official

historian: that Hitler's anxiety took refuge in von Rundstedt's native caution.

Had these British writers given more weight to the primary sources in the Liddell Hart Archive – including interviews conducted by American military historians – they might not have been so hasty in their dismissals. Significantly the American historian George Lucacs is not nearly so dogmatic: in *The Duel: Hitler vs Churchill 10 May – 31 July 1940* (London, 1990), p. 91, he observes that "fifty years on, the source and the origins of that decision are not entirely clear."

28. Jacobsen argued that Hitler's "soft" attitude could not be squared with his "Directive 13," issued that same evening, which specifically stated that the "next object of our operation is to annihilate the French, English and Belgian forces." The Luftwaffe's task as designated by Hitler was "to break all enemy resistance on the part of the surrounded forces, to prevent the escape of the English forces across the Channel." Superficially the contradiction does appear startling, until it is appreciated that the Führer's Directives were not direct orders to commanders in the field. The Directives set the broad goals on which the Wehrmacht drew up their own operational orders. Moreover, apart from the first paragraph, Directive 13 is primarily concerned with defining the objectives for "Case Red," the next phase of the campaign against France. Since this was dependent on completion of the military encirclement already under way in Flanders, it is curious that Hitler should have chosen to describe this as the "next object." The Directive was also glaringly inconsistent with the halt he had imposed on immediate operations which would have achieved that object. Professor Jacobsen also asserted that treating the British "softly" was inconsistent with Hitler's approach to Britain – a point of view which can be challenged. If Hitler had a diplomatic agenda for interfering in order to cause a delay, he would hardly have advertised the fact to his generals. Furthermore, as the Chief of the Army had been to Führer Headquarters that Friday evening to find out why the final encirclement

was being delayed unnecessarily, the fact that the Directive was issued *after* von Brauchitsch's visit suggests Directive 13 could have been a sop to reassure the generals. How otherwise can it be explained that the declared objectives of the Directive are so inconsistent with the Führer's stonewalling of the efforts by O.K.H. over the next two days to have the Halt Order lifted? (Jacobsen, *Decisive Battles*, op. cit., p. 59). According to Adrian Liddell Hart, his father sustained a bitter argument with Jacobsen over the issue. It led to a falling out between them.

29. H. R. Trevor Roper (ed.), *Hitler's War Directive 1939–45* (London, 1964), pp. 26–9.

30. By the fiftieth anniversary of Dunkirk, the Liddell Hart theory had been dismissed by British writers as the invention of Panzer leaders sore that their Führer "should have intervened at that moment and robbed them of their final victory" (Philip Warner in *The Battle for France: Six Weeks That Changed The World* (London., 1990), p. 134). Then the American Norman Gelb, in *Dunkirk* (New York, 1989), did not discuss whether Hitler's desire for a compromise peace might have influenced his "Halt Order" decision other than to raise the fanciful possibility that it was influenced by astrologers' predictions "that the stars weren't right at that moment for a land operation by his tanks" (p. 131). Yet French historian Claude Paillet reviews all sides of the issue in his comprehensive and readable yet authoritative documentary compilation *Le Désastre de 1940: La Guerre Eclair* (Paris, 1985), pp. 384–7. Lucas, op. cit., pp. 91–5, examines Hitler's "moves and his rationalizations" and concludes he was not intending to offer the British a "golden bridge" to escape, crediting Göring's persuasiveness as the decisive factor.

31. The Duke of Buccleuch was one of the richest landowners in Britain, brother-in-law of the Duke of Gloucester and banking partner of the Queen's father, the Duke of Strathmore. An outspoken right-winger and champion of rapprochement with Hitler, the Duke was dismissed from his royal office as soon as Churchill became Prime Minister on 10 May 1940. Ironically it was the Duke of Hamilton who succeeded him as Lord Steward. The scandal was hushed up in the British press, but the *New York Times* carried a full report on 21 August 1940.

32. The French had sent a delegation to Stockholm in mid-April led by General Mittelhauser from the army and M. Coulondre from the Foreign Ministry. The plan, in which Dahlerus had played a leading part, would require the withdrawal of Allied and German forces from Norway in return for the Swedish Navy undertaking police operations and the division of its iron ore output equitably between the Germans and the Allies; Foreign Ministry Berlin to Stockholm, 30 April 1940, DGFP IX.

33. "Très Secret Offres éventuelles de paix de l'Allemagne – Cabinet Diplomatique" prepared for Président du Conseil, Ministère de la Défense Nationale et de la Guerre, 20 May 1940, (Reynaud Papers 1940 L-F-10 Vol. 5, MAE).

34. Paul Reynaud, *Mémoire envers et contre tous* (Paris, 1960), Vol. II, Annex XVI.

35. Ibid.; Offres éventuelles, 20 May 1940, op. cit.

36. "Possible Peace Moves" by Herr Hitler, 18 May 1940, FO 371/28407 PRO.

37. Minute by Frank Roberts, 18 May 1940, FO 371/28407 PRO.

38. Halder, *Journal*, 27 September, cited in Hildebrand, *The Foreign Policy of the Third Reich* op. cit., p. 55.

39. 7 November 1939 Büro Staatsekretär England, Politisches Archiv A.A.B.

40ff. The Führer Naval Conference, 21 May 1940, Wagner (ed.), *Langenvorträge des Oberfelshabers der Kriegsmarine von Hitler 1939–45* (Munich, 1972); Compare Hitler to Mussolini, 18 May 1940, No. 212, with Hitler to Mussolini, 18 May 1940, No. 272, DGFP op. cit.; Alfieri to Rome, No. 491, DDI 9 IV. As Professor Macgregor Knox has pointed out, it is significant that although Goebbels, Göring and even the State Secretary of the German Foreign Minister had urged belligerent action by Italy, "Hitler himself held back." Macgregor Knox, *Mussolini Unleashed*, p. 114; Mussolini to Hitler, 19 May 1940, No. 276, DGFP, op. cit.

41. Halder, *Journal*, 21 May 1940.

42. Blumentritt, interviewed by Liddell Hart, *World War II*, op. cit., p. 83.

43. Butler's memorandum of Bastianini meeting, 15 May 1940, FO 371/24943 PRO.

44. Reynaud, *In the Thick of the Fight*, op. cit., p. 404; Guariglia to Ciano, 17 May 1940, No. 458, DDI 9 IV.

45. Telephone call Guariglia to Ciano, 18 May 1940, No. 471, DDI 9 IV.

46. Bullitt to Hull, 20 May 1940, RG 59.7400011 European War 1939 NAW; Campbell to Foreign Office, 23 May 1940.

47–8. War Cabinet (135) Conclusions, 24 May 1940, CAB 65/13 PRO.

49. Cadogan, *Diary*, 24 May 1940. The published version omits Paresci's name which is marked to be omitted in the original manuscript version; Halifax's statement to the War Cabinet (138) Conclusions CAB 67/7 PRO.

50. Sir Llewellyn Woodward, *British Foreign Policy in the Second World War* (London, 1962), p. 50.

51. Stohrer to Berlin, 24 May 1940, No. 298 DGFP IX, op. cit.; Telegram Guariglia to Ciano, 14 May 1940, No. 565 DDI 9 IV; conversation which the Spanish Ambassador reported the previous day to the Foreign Minister in Madrid and which "on Franco's instructions" was relayed to the German Ambassador (Stohrer to Berlin, 25 May 1940, No. 315, DGPF XI).

52. Baudouin, *Diary*, 24 May 1940.

53. Testimony of Baudouin to the Special Committee, cited by Reynaud, *Thick of the Fight*, op. cit., p. 382; ibid.

54–5. Quoted by Reynaud, op. cit., pp. 370–1.

56. Minutes of Defence Committee, 24 May 1940, CAB 69/1 PRO.

57. Baudouin, *Diary*, 24 May 1940.

58. Reynaud, op. cit., p. 382.

CHAPTER 9

(pp. 197–225)

1. Pownall, *Diary*, 25 May 1940.

2. Dill to Churchill, quoted by Ellis, *War in France*, op. cit., p. 197; telegram Dill to Churchill, received at 2.25 p.m., 25 May 1940, PREM 3/188/3 PRO; Pownall, *Diary*, 25 May 1940.

3. Minute, 25 May 1940, Churchill Papers 4/150, cited by Gilbert, *Finest Hour*, op. cit., p. 394; Morton to Churchill, 25 May 1940, PREM 7/2 PRO; War Cabinet (138) Conclusions, 25 May 1940, CAB 65/7 PRO; Ironside, *Diary*, 25 May 1940.

4. Telegram, 25 May 1940, Churchill Papers 4/150, quoted by Gilbert, *Finest Hour*, p. 394.

5. War Cabinet (138) Conclusions, 25 May 1940, op. cit.

6. The information had come from Queen Ena's Chamberlain, via a Falangist officer with German contacts. According to the Spanish rumour, France would keep the present European frontier, but cede Tunis to Italy. Spain would also get Gibraltar after England had been invaded and conquered by Germany FO 371 PRO.

7. Major General Sir Edward Spears, *Assignment to Catastrophe*, Vol. 1, *Prelude to Dunkirk* (London, 1954), p. 189.

8. Spears, op. cit., pp. 190–2.

9. Ibid., pp. 200–1.

10. Baudouin, *Diary*, 25 May 1940.

11. German signal quoted in Ellis, op. cit., Appendix II, p. 385.

12. Hitler to Mussolini letter, 25 May 1940, No. 317 DGFP, op. cit.

13. Warlimont, *Inside Hitler's Headquarters*, op. cit., p. 99.

14. Halder, *Journal*, 25 May 1940.

15. General Hans Seidemann, von Richthofen's chief of staff, monitored the phone conversation and described the incident for Admiral Ansel in 1953, confirming it by letter a year later (Ansel, *Hitler Confronts England*, op. cit., p. 85).

16. Brooke, *Diary*, 25 May 1940; Bryant, *The Turn of the Tide*, op. cit., p. 96.

17. Colville, *Man of Valour*, op. cit., p. 216.

18. Berle, *Diary*, 18 May 1940.

19. Diary of W. L. Mackenzie King, 24 May 1940, Mackenzie King Papers MG 26; "Most secret and personal" Churchill to Menzies, Mackenzie King, Fraser and General Smuts, 24 May 1940, Mackenzie King Papers MG 26 J4 NAC.

20. Hugh L. Keenleyside, *Memoirs*, Vol. II (Toronto, 1982), pp. 34–5.

21. Memorandum for Prime Minister, "Report of a discussion of possible eventualities", prepared by Keenleyside on 26 May 1940. At Mackenzie King's suggestion he used codenames for those mentioned: Roosevelt became "Mr Roberts," Churchill "Mr Clark," Reynaud, "Mr Renard," Hull "Mr Hughes," Mackenzie King "Mr Kirk." As Keenleyside admitted in his memoir, "it was a bit foolish; because a blind man if interested in the subject could have seen through it" (Paper 281907 MG 26 J4 NAC).

22–3. Ibid.

24. Foreign Office to Lothian, 24 May 1940, CAB 65/13 PRO; "Entremise du Président Roosevelt, Ministère des Affaires Etrangères à Ambassadeur Français, Washington 25 May 1940." The next day when they compared notes in Washington the French Ambassador discovered a discrepancy with the British instruction. Term B in Lord Lothian's cable read "were prepared to consider reasonable Italian claims at the end of the war." The equivalent in Ambassador Saint-Quentins cable read only "all reasonable Italian claims." The two ambassadors therefore agreed to put forward to the President the more generous French version (Saint-Quentin to Ministère des Affaires Etrangères, 26 May 1940; Reynaud Papers, Vol. 5, MAE).

25–6. Report of the meeting with Bastianini given by Halifax to Sir Percy Loraine, 25 May 1940, War Cabinet (139) Conclusions, Confidential Annex, 26 May 1940, CAB/13 PRO.

27. Cadogan, *Diary*, 25 May 1940.

28. Jebb's conversation with Paresci as reported by David Dilkes in Cadogan, *Diary* note, p. 290. A search of the relevant files in the Italian Foreign Ministry Archives in Rome has so far failed to locate the Bastianini reports of 25 May 1940.

29. It adds to the suspicion about Halifax's motives to find that he makes no reference to his meeting with Bastianini in his private diary. Either he did not think it important, or he considered it so delicate that he deliberately omitted to mention it. The latter appears more likely, since the Foreign Secretary had raised the proposed Italian approach in the War Cabinet and it was certainly considered a major diplomatic issue by both Cadogan and Jebb. Cadogan records in his diary how Jebb called in to report at 11.15 p.m. that he had already had a further meeting with both Halifax and Bastianini. Presumably this was to relay Paresci's expectation that Gibraltar and the Mediterranean would be given as concessions to Italy. After meeting with the Foreign Secretary, Jebb then saw the Italian Press Attaché again – a meeting on which he promised Cadogan he would report in full "tomorrow morning."

30. Halifax, *Diary*, 25 May 1940.

31. Ibid., 26 May 1940.

32. Baudouin, *Diary*, 25 May 1940; Reynaud, *Thick of the Fight*, op. cit., p. 388.

33. It became a matter of bitter dispute with Weygand whether Reynaud had actually uttered the word "armistice" at this War Committee meeting. The draft minutes prepared by Baudouin had Reynaud saying in relation to the evacuation of Paris that "Taking this into account, it cannot be said that

our opponent will grant us an immediate armistice. It is not indispensable to avoid the capture of the Government if Paris falls." Although the Germans later published the draft, Reynaud had struck out the offending sentence; this was subsequently confirmed by Baudouin.

34. Reynaud, op. cit., pp. 390–2.

35. Ibid., p. 388.

36–7. Defence Committee Minute 9, 25 May 1940, CAB 69/1 PRO.

38. Berle, *Diary*, 26 May 1940.

39. Ironside, *Diary*, 25 May 1940.

40. Churchill, Vol. II, p. 65.

41. Colville, *Diaries*, 27 May 1940.

42. Churchill, Vol. II, p. 87.

43–5. War Cabinet (139) Conclusions Annex, 26 May 1940, CAB 65/13 PRO.

46. Chamberlain, *Diary*, 26 May 1940.

47. Cadogan, *Diary*, 26 May 1940.

48. Von Bock's *Diary*, quoted by Ansel, *Hitler Confronts England*, op. cit., p. 86.

49. Halder, *Journal*, 26 May 1940.

50. Reynaud, op. cit., p. 405.

51–2. War Cabinet Confidential Annex, 26 May 1940, op. cit.

53. Churchill, Vol. II, p. 109.

54. Reynaud, op. cit., p. 406.

55. Ibid., pp. 405–6.

56. The telegram on Downing Street notepaper signed Paul Reynaud records that it was telephoned to Weygand at 4.05 p.m., CAB 65/18 PRO; Ellis, *War in France* op. cit., p. 174.

57. Baudouin, *Diary*, 26 May 1940.

58. Baudouin, Note of 26 May, Baudouin Papers, Volume I, MAE; Baudouin, *Diary*, p. 58.

59. Churchill to British Ambassador in Paris for Reynaud FO 371/24382 PRO.

60. War Cabinet (140) Confidential Annex, 26 May 1940, CAB 65/13 PRO.

61. Halifax, *Diary*, 26 May 1940.

62. Chamberlain, *Diary*, 26 May 1940.

63. War Cabinet (140) Conclusions Confidential Annex, 26 May 1940, op. cit.

64. Ibid.; Chamberlain, *Diary*, 26 May 1940.

65. Ibid.; War Cabinet (140) Conclusions Confidential Annex, 26 May 1940; Chamberlain, *Diary*, 26 May 1940.

66. Cadogan, *Diary*, 26 May 1940.

67. Churchill, Vol. II, p. 73; Ellis, *War in France*, op. cit., p. 167.

68. Cadogan, *Diary*, 26 May 1940; "Possible Evacuation of the Royal Family, Government and Treasure," Minute by J. V. Perowne, 16 and 19 May 1940, opposing notes by P. Mason, FO 371/25793 PRO.

69. Secretary of State to Ambassador Phillips, 26 May 1940, FRUS Vol. IV.

70. Lothian to Foreign Office, No. 834, 26 May 1940, FO 371/25193 PRO; Bullitt for President Only No. 888, 26 May 1940, PSF "Bullitt" FDRL.

71. Lothian to FO, No. 834, 26 May 1940, FO 371/25193 PRO.

72. Mackenzie King, *Diary*, 26 May 1940 NAC.

CHAPTER 10

(pp. 226–55)

1. Colville, *Diaries*, 27 May 1940.

2. Halifax, *Diary*, 27 May 1940.

3–6. War Cabinet (141) Conclusions Confidential Annex, 27 May 1940, CAB 65/13 PRO.

7. Kennedy to Hull, 27 May 1940, FRUS 1940 p. 223.

8. Mackenzie King, *Diary*, 27 May 1940 NAC.

9. Phillips to State Department, 28 May 1940, FRUS 1940, p. 244.

10. Ciano, *Diario*, 27 May 1940; François-Poncet, however, omitted to tell Paris of his panicky offer when he reported Mussolini's negative response to Paris that evening.

11. Spears, *Assignment to Catastrophe,* op. cit., Vol. I, p. 239.

12. Baudouin, *Diary,* 27 May 1940.

13–14. Halder, *Journal,* 27 May 1940.

15. Baudouin, *Diary,* 27 May 1940; Spears, op. cit., p. 245.

16–22. War Cabinet (142) Conclusions Confidential Annex, 27 May 1940, 4.30 p.m., CAB 65/13 PRO.

23. Halifax, *Diary,* 27 May 1940.

24–26. War Cabinet (142) Confidential Annex Conclusions, 27 May 1940, 4.30 p.m., CAB 65/7 PRO.

27. Cadogan, *Diary,* 27 May 1940.

28. Halifax, *Diary,* 27 May 1940; Cadogan, *Diary,* 27 May 1940.

29. Churchill to Gort, 27 May 1940, Churchill, Vol. II, p. 80.

30. Churchill to Keyes, 27 May 1940; Churchill, Vol. II, p. 80.

31ff. War Cabinet (143) Confidential Annex, 27 May 1940, CAB 65/7 PRO.

32. Colville, *Diary,* 24 May 1940.

33. War Cabinet (144) Conclusions, 28 May 1940 CAB 65/13 PRO; Admiralty report of intercepted telephone conversation between the Head of the French Military Mission at Belgian HQ and Paris, 28 May 1940, PREM 3/69A PRO.

34. War Cabinet (144) Conclusions, 28 May 1940, CAB 65/13 PRO.

35. The King had ordered Belgian artillery to remain at their guns until the Germans reached them. There were also many instances where Belgian forces had sacrificed themselves to hold the front while permitting B.E.F. units to retreat. General Gort and his staff, who would never forgive King Leopold for refusing to allow Allied troops to move into Belgium before the Germans, "did not give credit where credit was due," according to leading British military historian Professor Bond, who contends (op. cit.) that Gort could and should have done more to assist the Belgian army in the final stage of the German offensive; Ellis, *War in France,* op. cit., pp. 146–9.

36–7. War Cabinet 144 Conclusions, 28 May 1940, CAB 65/13 PRO.

38. Churchill, Vol. II, p. 84.

39–40. Dalton, *Diary,* 27 May 1940.

41. Blanchard, cited by Colville in *Man of Valour* op. cit., p. 221.

42. Baudouin, *Diary,* 8 May 1940; Spears, op. cit., pp. 253–4.

43. The move had been made *after* François-Poncet's dispatch from Rome the previous evening reporting Mussolini's rebuff of the American President offer of mediation. In the early hours of the morning, at Daladier's behest, two assistants had drafted a telegram instructing the Ambassador in Rome to attempt a direct intervention, and the Secretary General of the Foreign Ministry was woken to give his approval for its dispatch. He was given the impression that the move had been agreed by the War Council meeting the previous evening. By 4 a.m. François Charles-Roux had "qualms of conscience" and blocked the telegram until he and Daladier had reviewed it with the Prime Minister. At their 9 a.m. meeting, Reynaud declared that he had never approved such a telegram and insisted that it should not be sent to Rome until an answer was received from the British (François Charles-Roux, *Cinq Mois Tragiques aux Affaires Etrangères (21 mai–1 novembre 1940),* quoted by Reynaud, op. cit., p. 413).

44. Roux, op. cit.; Ciano, *Diario,* p. 256.

45. Von Mackensen Berlin, Nos. 339–344, 29 May 1940, sent 1.20 a.m. DGFP pp. 461–5.

46. Churchill, Vol. II, p. 87.

47. *Hansard,* 28 May 1940; speeches by Hastings Lee-Smith, M.P., and Sir Percy Harris, M.P.

48. It appears that the Foreign Secretary deliberately misled the War Cabinet by implying that the meeting with the Italian Press Attaché had occurred *after* the previous day's discussion. Vansittart's meeting with Paresci had actually taken

place three days earlier, as had Halifax's second meeting with Bastianini. What the Foreign Secretary did not reveal was that he was so determined to get negotiations going with Italy that he had even toyed with the idea of bribing the Italian Foreign Minister. "I do not think we would ever have offered him enough to tempt him," Lord Halifax minuted after receiving the British Ambassador's report of the Duce's rebuff. "Loraine always disliked the idea of offering anything to Ciano. He never felt able to hand him £50,000 on the golf links." Cadogan, hoped "we shan't delude ourselves into thinking we shall do ourselves any good by making more 'offers' or 'approaches.'" The French accounts corroborate Halifax's independent overtures to Mussolini. It is evident that the Foreign Secretary was now having to reconstruct the sequence of events to avoid being hoisted on the petard of his own diplomatic intrigue (quoted by Dilkes in Cadogan, *Diaries*, p. 291; War Cabinet (145) Conclusions Confidential Annex, 28 May 1940, CAB 65/13 PRO).

49ff. War Cabinet (145) Conclusions Confidential Annex, 28 May 1940, CAB 65/13 PRO.

50. Chamberlain, *Diary*, 28 May 1940; War Cabinet (145) Conclusions Confidential Annex, 28 May 1940.

51–2. Dalton, *Diary*, 28 May 1940.

53. Churchill, Vol. II, p. 88.

54. Prime Minister for M. Reynaud, 28 May 1940, 11.40 a.m. in PRO, 28 May 1940, CAB 65/13 PRO.

55. War Cabinet (145) Conclusions Confidential Annex, 28 May 1940, CAB 65/13.

56. Letter from Lawford to Colville, 26 February 1941, PREM 3/468 PRO.

57. Kennedy to Hull, 24 May 1940, 740.0011, European War 1939/3005 7/10 RG 59 NAW.

58. Chamberlain, *Diary*, 15 May 1940; Sylvester, *Diary*, 28 May 1940.

59. Butler self-servingly claimed that they had been started by Hoare just before he left to become Ambassador

to Spain according to Channon, *Diaries*, 29 May 1940.

CHAPTER 11
(pp. 256–95)

1. War Cabinet (145) Conclusions Confidential Annex, 28 May 1940, CAB 65/13 PRO; Charles-Roux, *Cinq Mois*, quoted by Reynaud, *In the Thick of the Fight*, op. cit., p. 414.

2. Reynaud, op. cit., pp. 442–3.

3. War Cabinet (146) Conclusions, 29 May 1940, CAB 65/13 PRO; Cadogan, *Diary*, 29 May 1940; War Cabinet (146) Conclusions Confidential Annex, 29 May 1940, PREM 3/175 PRO.

4. War Cabinet (146) Conclusions, 29 May 1940, CAB 65/7 PRO.

5. Keenleyside, Memorandum for the Prime Minister, "Discussion of Possible Eventualities," Paper C281914, 29 May 1940, J4 NAC; Hugh L. Keenleyside, *Memoirs*, op. cit., Vol. 2, p. 38.

6ff. Keenleyside, Memorandum, 29 May 1940, op. cit.

7. Mackenzie King, *Diary*, 31 May 1940 NAC.

8. Cable from Purvis, 29 May 1940, CAB 115/83 PRO; Cable from Purvis, 30 May 1940, CAB 85/14 PRO.

9. Cable to Gort sent at 2 p.m., 30 May 1940, CAB 85/14 PRO.

10. Cable to Reynaud for General Georges sent 11.45 p.m., 29 May 1940, PREM 3/175 PRO; Spears, *Assignment to Catastrophe*, op. cit., p. 279.

11. Undated memorandum of the Australian High Commissioner with covering letter from Desmond Morton, 30 May 1930, PREM 7/2 PRO.

12. Letter from Lloyd George to Churchill, 29 May 1940; Churchill to Lloyd George, 30 May 1940, quoted by Sylvester, *Lloyd George*, op. cit., pp. 264–5.

13. War Cabinet (145) Conclusions, 30 May 1940, CAB 65/7 PRO; Sir Ronald

Campbell to Halifax, 30 May 1940, FO 800/312 PRO.

14. Defence Committee No. 12, 30 May 1940, CAB 69/1 PRO; Halder, *Journal*, 30 May 1940.

15. Spears, op. cit., p. 293.

16. Reynaud, op. cit., p. 450.

17. Spears, op. cit., p. 296; Reynaud, op. cit., p. 451.

18. Minutes of the 13th Supreme War Council Meeting, 31 May 1940, CAB 99/3 PRO.

19. Campbell to Halifax, 31 May 1940, FO 800/312 PRO; Minutes of the 13th Supreme War Council Meeting, 31 May 1940, CAB 99/3 PRO.

20. Spears, op. cit., p. 298.

21. Minutes of the 13th Supreme War Council Meeting, 31 May 1940, CAB 99/3 PRO.

22. Spears, op. cit., p. 319.

23ff. War Cabinet (151) Conclusions 11.30 a.m., 1 June 1940, CAB 65/7 PRO.

24. "My dear Joe" letter from Halifax to Kennedy, 1 June 1940, in PREM 3/462/2/3 PRO; Halifax, *Diary*, 3 June 1940.

25. Halifax, *Diary*, 31 May 1940; draft dated 29 May 1940, sent on 1 June, PREM 3.468 PRO.

26. Lothian to Foreign Office, No. 777,21 May 1940, FO 371/24192 PRO. The annotation by J. V. Perowne shows he was unaware on 23 May of the reason for Sumner Welles's suggestion; Colville, *Diaries*, 31 May 1940.

27. Mackenzie King to London, 31 May 1940, Mackenzie King, op. cit., Vol. 1, pp. 120–1; Minute, 31 May 1940, acknowledged by Cadogan and Halifax on 1 June, FO 371/24192; Minute by T. North Whitehead dated 30 May 1940, noted by Churchill 3 June, PREM, 3 476/10 PRO.

28. WSC minute on "Most secret" covering note letter dated 1 June of Desmond Morton attached to report of David Scott of the Foreign Office, PREM 7/2 PRO; Colville, *Diaries*, 1 June 1940.

29. War Cabinet (152) Conclusions, 2 June 1940, CAB 65/7; Chief of Staff Committee (163), 2 June 1940, CAB 79/4 PRO; Colville, *Diaries*, 2 June 1940; War Cabinet (152) PRO.

30. War Cabinet (152) Confidential Annex Conclusions, 2 June 1940, CAB 65/13 PRO.

31ff. War Cabinet (153) Confidential Annex Conclusions, 2 June 1940, CAB 65/13 PRO.

32. Ibid.; telegram from Churchill to Spears, 3 June 1940, PREM 3/175 PRO.

33. Churchill to Halifax, 6 June 1940, Churchill Papers 4/201, cited by Gilbert, *Finest Hour*, p. 459; Cadogan, *Diary*, 30 May 1940; Halifax, *Diary*, 30 May 1940.

34. War Cabinet (154) Conclusions Confidential Annex, 4 June 1940, CAB 65/13 PRO.

35. Minute from Sir Edward Bridges, 4 June 1940, PREM 3/468 PRO; Morgenthau *Diaries*, 5 June 1940, quoted by J. Morton Blum, *Roosevelt and Morgenthau: From the Morgenthau Diaries* (Boston, 1970), p. 326.

36. R. A. Butler, *The Art of the Possible* (London, 1971), pp. 85–6.

37ff. *Hansard*, 4 June 1940.

38. Letter of Vita Sackville West to Harold Nicolson, 4 June 1940, quoted in Nicolson *Diaries*, p. 93.

39. Ickes, *Diary*, 5 May 1940.

40. Churchill to Mackenzie King, 5 July 1940, PREM 4/43B/1, Professor Lindemann Minute of 5 June 1940, annotated by Churchill in PREM 3/475/1 PRO.

41. Reynaud, op. cit., p. 455.

42. Minutes of Meeting at 10 Downing Street, 11 a.m., 5 June 1940, CAB 127/13 PRO; Churchill to Reynaud 4.45 p.m., 5 June 1940, PREM 3/188/1 PRO; War Cabinet (156) Confidential Annex Conclusions, 6 June 1940, CAB 65/13 PRO.

43. Halifax, *Diary*, 6 June 1940.

44. Sylvester, *Lloyd George*, op. cit., p. 267.

45. Halder, *Journal*, 5 June 1940.

46ff. Baudouin, *Diary*, 6 June 1940.

47. War Cabinet (156) Conclusions, 6 June 1940, CAB 65/7 PRO.

48. War Cabinet (157) Conclusions, 7 June 1940, CAB 65/7 PRO.

49. Baudouin, *Diary*, 7 June 1940.

50. Baudouin, *Diary*, 8 June 1940.

51ff. Defence Committee (14), 8 June 1940, CAB 69/1 PRO.

52. Churchill to Reynaud, 8 June 1940, PREM 3/1888/1 PRO; Churchill to Smuts, 9 June 1940, PREM 4/43B/1 PRO.

53. Ibid.; Bullitt to Secretary of State, 9 June 1940, 740.0011 European War RG 59 NAW.

54–5. Baudouin, *Diary*, 9 June 1940.

56. War Cabinet (160) Conclusions, 10 June 1940, CAB 65/7 PRO; quoted by Dilkes, *The Diaries of Sir Alexander Cadogan*, op. cit., p. 296.

57. Colville, *Diaries*, 10 June 1940; Samuel I. Rosenmann (ed.), *The Public Papers and Addresses of Franklin D. Roosevelt*, Vol. 9 (New York, 1941), No. 58; *New York Times*, 11 June 1940.

58. Ibid.; Prime Minister to Lord Lothian for President, 11 June 1940, PREM 3/468 PRO.

59. Kennedy to Secretary of State, 10 June 1940, 740011 3487 5/10 RG 59 NAW.

60. *New York Times*, 10 June 1940; Bullitt to Secretary of State for the President, 10 June 1940, 740.0011 RG 59 NAW.

61. War Cabinet (161) Conclusions, 11 June 1940, CAB 65/7 PRO.

62. Spears, op. cit., Vol. 2, pp. 140–1.

63. Ibid., pp. 142–9.

64. Ibid.; Ismay, *Memoirs*, p. 140.

65. War Cabinet (163) Conclusions 5.30 p.m. 10 June 1940, CAB 65/7 PRO; Spears, op. cit., p. 142; quoted by Darlan in letter to Churchill on 4 December 1942, Churchill Papers 4/351; quoted by Gilbert, *Finest Hour*, p. 513.

66ff. Baudouin, *Diary*, 10 June 1940.

67. Ibid.; War Cabinet (163) Conclusions 5.30 p.m. 10 June 1940, CAB 65/7 PRO.

68. "Former naval person" to President (via US Embassy), 12 June 1940, PREM 3/468 PRO.

69. Colville, *Diaries*, 12 June 1940; Churchill, Vol. II, p. 129.

70. Kennedy to Secretary of State, 12 June 1940, 740.0011 3487 6/10 RG 59 NAW.

71ff. Halifax, *Diary*, 12 June 1940; Minute of J. V. Perowne dated 14 June 1940 on the copy of Churchill's 13 June cable sent to Lord Lothian, FO 371/24192 PRO; Churchill to Roosevelt, 13 June 1940, FO 371/24192 PRO.

72. Halifax, *Diary*, 13 June 1940; Spears, op. cit., p. 199.

73ff. Minutes of the meeting in Baudouin, *Diary*, 13 June 1940, pp. 101–4.

74. Supreme War Council 16th Meeting, 13 June 1940, CAB 99/3 PRO.

75. Spears, op. cit., p. 215.

76. Baudouin, *Diary*, 13 June 1940; Supreme Council War Minutes, 13 June 1940, CAB 99/3 PRO.

77. James Leasor, *War at the Top (based on the experiences of General Sir Leslie Holls K.C.B., K.B.E.)*, (London, 1959), p. 91.

78. Roosevelt to "Former naval person," 13 June 1940, Annex 1, CAB 65/7 PRO.

79ff. War Cabinet (165) Conclusions, 12 June 1940, 10.15 p.m., CAB 65/7 PRO.

80. Halifax, *Diary*, 13 June 1940.

81. Foreign Secretary to Sir Roland Campbell, 14 June, CAB 21/952 PRO; Ibid.

82. "Former naval person" to President, "Handed to Kennedy for dispatch," 1.15 a.m., 14 June 1940, PREM 3/468.

83ff. Kennedy to Hull, 14 June 1940, FRUS 1940, pp. 248–9.

84. Berle, *Diary*, 12 June 1940, pp. 223–4.

85. Bullitt to Secretary of State, 14 June 1940, FRS 1940, I, p. 250.

86. President for Kennedy, 13 June 1940, 740.0011 3487 7/10 RG 59 NAW; President to Former naval person, 14 June 1940, received 1.30 a.m. 15 June, U.S. Embassy London, PREM, 3/46 P.

87. War Cabinet (166) Conclusions 12.30 p.m. 14 June 1940, CAB 65/7 PRO.

88. Telegram, No. 239, 14 June 1940, CAB 69/1 PRO.

89. Halifax, *Diary*, 14 June 1940.

90. "British Strategy in a Certain Eventuality," dated 22 May 1940, CAB 65/7 PRO.

91. "Former naval person" to President, 15 June 1940, PREM 3/468/148 PRO.

92. President to Churchill, 14 June 1940, received 15 June 1.30 a.m. PREM 3/468/148 PRO.

93. Washington *Times Herald*, 14 June 1940. After the war Hitler's interpreter Dr. Paul K. Schmidt of the German Foreign Ministry revealed under interrogation that the "interview" had been cooked up by the German Foreign Ministry, which had used Karl von Weigand, chief foreign correspondent of the Hearst newspapers, to pass it off as his scoop (Rogge, *The Official German Report*, pp. 233–6, cited by Joseph P. Lash, *The Partnership that Saved the West* (London, 1971) p. 163); War Cabinet (167) Conclusions, 15 June 1940, CAB 65/7 PRO.

94. Telegram drafted 15 June, sent 16 June, to the Prime Ministers of Australia, New Zealand, Canada and South Africa, PREM 4/43B/1 PRO.

95. Baudouin, *Diary* 15 June 1940.

96. Telegram sent from Campbell in Bordeaux 10.45 p.m. 15 June 1940, PREM 3/468 PRO.

97. "Former naval person" to President, 10.45 p.m. 10 June 1940, PREM 3/3468 PRO.

98. Campbell to Foreign Office, 10 June 1940, PREM 3/468 PRO.

99. War Cabinet Minutes (168) Confidential Annex, 16 June 1940, CAB 65/13 PRO.

100ff. Baudouin, *Diary*, 16 June 1940.

101. War Cabinet (169) Conclusions, 16 June 1940, 3 p.m., CAB 65/7 PRO.

102. Colville, *Diaries*, 16 June 1940.

103. Baudouin, *Diary*, 16 June 1940.

104. Halifax, *Diary*, 16 June 1940.

CHAPTER 12

(pp. 296–323)

1. Halder, *Journal*, 17 May 1940.

2. Dowding, letter of 17 June 1940, Churchill Papers 2/393, quoted by Gilbert, *Finest Hour*, p. 564.

3. Report of Pétain broadcast in War Cabinet (170) Conclusions, 17 June 1940, CAB 65/7 PRO.

4. Churchill, op. cit., Vol. II, p. 191.

5. *Hansard*, 17 June 1940.

6. Ibid.; Churchill B.B.C. Broadcast, 17 June 1940, cited by Gilbert, *Finest Hour*, p. 556.

7. Kennedy to State Department, 17 June 1940, 740.00a European War 1939 38882/1/2 RG 59 NAW; "He went to see the PM about 6," Cadogan, *Diary*, 17 July 1940.

8. Halifax, *Diary*, 17 June 1940.

9. *Hansard*, 18 June 1940.

10–11. Churchill, Vol. II, p. 199.

12. Halifax, *Diary*, 18 and 19 June 1940.

13ff. Telegram 723, 17 June 1940, HP39A /XXXIII UDA (Swedish Foreign Ministry Archive, Riksarkivet, Stockholm). The difference in the unenciphered original was pointed out by Wilhelm M. Carlgren, *Svensk utrikespolitik 1939–45* (Stockholm, 1973, for the Royal Swedish Ministry for Foreign Affairs), p. 194. The "today" appears in the London Legation original.

14. Nine months into the war, Britain's blockade was biting into Sweden's overseas exports, making her economy ever more dependent on the Third Reich. From ball bearings to the exports of iron ore that fed the blast furnaces of the Ruhr, materials from Sweden helped sustain the wartime German armaments industry. This economic interdependence together with the Nazi occupation of Denmark and Norway left the Swedish government with little room to manoeuvre for fear that too independent a policy would encourage Hitler to order the takeover of their country. Public opinion in Sweden was firmly anti-Nazi, but while the government outwardly maintained its firmly neutral stance, the collapse of France following on the successsion of German military victories had eroded the resolve of the non-socialist ministers in the coalition government to oppose Berlin's pressure for transit rights.

15. See the condensed English version of Professor Carlgren's authoritative work *Swedish Foreign Policy during the Second World War* (London, 1977). I am indebted to Professor Carlgren for his generous assistance in examining and translating the relevant records, and for sharing his opinions with me.

16. No. 706, Report to Weizsäcker of meeting, 17 June 1940, DGFP IX; Richert report, op. cit.

17. Mallet to Foreign Office, 19 June 1940, FO 371/24859 PRO; Dr. Thomas Munch-Petersen makes a persuasive case that Prytz's telegram 703 influenced the decision of the three Social Democrat ministers of the national government in Sweden in his essay "Common Sense Not Bravado: the Butler-Prytz interview: 17 June 1940," *Scandia*, 1986.

18. Draft in Butler's handwriting of 20 June 1940 cable to Mallet, FO 371/24859 PRO.

19. Foreign Minister to Prytz, 19 June 1940, UDA HP39A/XXXIII; Prytz to Foreign Minister, 20 June 1940, UDA.

20. Mallet to Foreign Office, 20 June 1940, FO 371/24859 PRO.

21. Prytz to Foreign Ministry, 20 June 1940, UDA HP39A/XXXIII.

22. Butler to Mallet, 23 June 1940, FO 371/24859 PRO.

23. Interview with Professor Carlgren, 20 March 1989, and letter from Carlgren to the author, 22 March 1989.

24. Churchill to Halifax, 26 June 1940, FO 800/322 PRO.

25ff. Butler to Halifax, 26 June 1940, FO 800/322 PRO.

26. Halifax to Churchill, 27 June 1940, FO 800/322 PRO.

27. Copy of Prytz to Kabinettssekretär K. I. Westman, 28 August, 1946, UDA HP39A/XXXIII from the original in HP 1Ba LXXXIV UDA.

28ff. "Special Notes" written by de Courcy, 10 July 1961, which records: "I have only now felt it safe to record the facts as known to me," Box 3 File 10 de Courcy Papers HISU; author's correspondence with the Deputy Archivist of the Hoover Institution, August 1990.

29. De Courcy to Butler, 15 May 1940, RAB E3/4 55 TCCA; de Courcy to Butler, 21 May 1940, RAB E3/4 64 TCCA; Butler to de Courcy, 22 May 1940, RAB E 3/4 65 TCCA.

30. De Courcy to Butler, 30 and 31 May, RAB E3/4 66.67 TCCA; de Courcy to Butler, 2 June 1940 (2-V-40 on original letter is clearly a mistake), Butler RAB E3/5 71 TCCA.

31ff. De Courcy interview, July 1989; "Special Notes," 10 July 1961 HISU.

32. De Courcy to Butler, 24 June 1940, and Butler's acknowledgement, 26 June 1940, RAB 3/4 71 TCCA.

33. Butler to de Courcy, 23 September 1973, de Courcy Papers HISU; Butler Papers, TCCA; note by de Courcy on Butler letter, 24 September 1973, op. cit.; "Special Note," 10 July 1961, de Courcy Papers HISU.

34. De Courcy to Lord Caldecote, 28 June 1940, de Courcy Papers HISU; Lord Sherfield interview; Caldecote to

Cadogan, 26 June 1940, FO 371/25236 PRO.

35. Intercepted letter sent by de Courcy to M. Lemery and Madame Brécard, 17 June 1940, and minuted comment of 29 June 1940, FO 371/25236 PRO; note by William Strang, 8 July, and Butler's comment: "I think Mr. Strang has got about the right perspective for Mr. de Courcy," 15 July 1940, FO 371/25236 PRO.

36ff. Lord Sherfield interview.

37. Kennedy to State Department, 17 June 1940, PSF "Kennedy" FDRL; Halifax, *Diary*, 14 June 1940.

38. Chamberlain letter, 15 June 1940, NC 18/1116 BUL.

39. Prytz to Foreign Minister, 17 June 1940, UDA HP39A/XXXIII; after uncovering and assembling most of the pieces in de Courcy's intriguing historical jigsaw puzzle, Munch-Petersen concluded his "Common Sense Not Bravado" by deciding that Halifax and Butler *did not* intend to send a peace feeler to Berlin. He bases his conclusion on a) Halifax's apparent acceptance of Churchill's policy to fight on in his diary entry of 16 June; b) the "genuinely embarrassed and defensive" tone of Butler's 26 June letter to Halifax; and c) Prytz's 20 June cable advising Stockholm that Butler's message was not meant to be passed on. The evidence can now be interpreted the other way, with the record provided by de Courcy. Munch-Petersen acknowledged the importance of this connection but in 1986 was not able to substantiate the key connection arising from his reference to Prytz's 1946 statement about the decisive role played by the un-named Conservative publicist.

40. Ambassador Fransoni to Rome, 19 June 1940, No. 48, DDI, 9 V 47.

41. Professor Carlgren interview.

42. Richert to Foreign Ministry, 19 July 1940 HP39A/XXXIII UDA.

43. State Secretary to Foreign Minister, 19 June 1940, No. 487, DG FP X.

44. Weizsäcker memorandum of conversation, No. 474, 22 June 1940, DGFP IX D; Richert to Swedish Foreign Ministry, 22 June 1940, UDA HP39A/XXXIII; Weizsäcker memorandum of conversation, op. cit.

45. Richert to Swedish Foreign Ministry, op. cit.

46. The Swedish cables and reports that detail the seizure, protests and release of the destroyers are in UDA; I am grateful to Professor Carlgren for locating and translating the relevant sections. The British side of the affair is detailed in the War Cabinet Minutes of 18–24 June 1940, CAB 65/7 PRO and the Foreign Office Files.

47. Wallenberg Memorandum, 25 June 1940, HP39A/XXXIII UDA.

48. Mallet to Foreign Secretary, 25 June 1940, FO 371/24407 PRO.

49. It is the oft-stated policy of the Foreign Office to deny that British cryptanalysts of the Government Code and Cipher School were intercepting and routinely breaking the cipher of nations with whom HMG was technically at peace. But documentary evidence uncovered in recent years, including the private 1944 report of former GC & CS head Commander Denniston, confirms that this was one of the principal objectives of Bletchley Park (Denniston Papers CCA). The case of Soviet agent Anthony Blunt also reveals that his primary wartime activity for MI5 was supervising the interception and copying of dispatches in the diplomatic bags of neutral governments in London (Costello, *Mask of Treachery* op. cit.).

50. Memorandum of Mussolini/Hitler conversation, 18 June 1940, No. 479, DGFP IXC, pp. 608–10.

51. Ciano, *Diario*, 19 June 1940, p. 265.

52. *The Goebbels Diaries 1939–41*, edited by Fred Taylor (London, 1982), 16 June 1940, p. 122.

53. Quoted by Irving, *Hitler's War*, p. 298.

54ff. Joachim Ribbentrop, Interrogation by an unidentified British Army Officer,

5 August 1945 in IRR FILES XE00887 RG 319 NAW.

55. Undated interrogation of Foreign Ministry official, "The England Committee," IRR "Joachim von Ribbentrop" XE 000887 IRR Files RG 319 NAW.

56. Goebbels, *Diaries*, 25 June 1940.

CHAPTER 13

(pp. 324–51)

1. Keitel, quoted by Irving, *Hitler's War*, op. cit., p. 295.

2. Shirer, *Third Reich*, op. cit., pp. 976–7.

3. Armistice Negotiations, 22 June 1940, No. 522, DGFP IX, op. cit.

4. Shirer, op. cit., p. 981.

5. War Cabinet (176) Conclusions, 22 June 1940, 9.30 p.m. CAB 65/7 PRO.

6. Churchill speech notes, Charles Eade (ed.), *Secret Sessions by the Right Hon Winston S. Churchill O.M., C.H., M.P.* (London, 1949), pp. 8–16.

7. Memorandum FDR, 13 June 1940, in Matloff and Snell, *Strategic Planning for Coalition Warfare* (Washington, 1953), p. 14.

8. Lothian to Halifax, 17 June 1940, FO 371/24240 PRO; Churchill Minute, 24 June, FO 371/24240 PRO.

9. Halifax to Churchill, 28 June 1940, and Halifax to Lothian, 30 June, FO 371/24240 PRO; Churchill Minute of 30 June and preceding letters and exchanges in PREM 3/475/1.

10. Churchill to Canadian Prime Minister, 24 June 1940, PREM 4/43B/1 PRO.

11. Ibid.; Lothian to Prime Minister, 27 June 1940, PREM 4/43B/1 PRO.

12. Churchill to Lothian, 28 June 1940, PREM 3/3/476 PRO.

13. Ibid.; Report from British Ambassador, Tokyo, 27 June 1940, FO 371/24401 PRO; Minute of 27 June cable of British Ambassador, Tokyo, FO 371/24401 PRO.

14. British Ambassador, Belgrade to London, 22 June 1940, FO 371/24407 PRO; Cable from British Consulate, Athens, 27 June, FO 371/24407 PRO; Ambassador Berne to Foreign Office, 17 June, FO 371/24407 PRO.

15. Churchill minute, 23 June 1940, on jacket containing Cable from British Minister in Berne, 21 June 1940, FO 371/24407 PRO; Kelly to Foreign Office, 26 June, FO 371/24407 PRO.

16. Cadogan, *Diary*, op. cit.

17. Churchill Minute to Foreign Secretary, 28 June 1940, FO 371/24407 PRO; Foreign Office to Kelly, 29 June 1940, Special Distribution to the War Cabinet, FO 371/24407 PRO.

18. Memorandum by State Security, No. 65, DGFP X, op. cit.; Halder, *Journal*, 30 June 1940.

19. Chamberlain, *Diary*, 1 July 1940.

20. Minute, 26 June 1940, Churchill Papers 20/13, quoted by Gilbert, *Finest Hour*, p. 600.

21. Chiefs of Staff Report, 1 July 1940, PREM 3/416 PRO.

22. War Cabinet (179) Conclusions Confidential Annex, 22 June 1940, CAB 65/13 PRO.

23. Cabinet Minutes (184) Conclusions Confidential Annex, 27 June 1940, CAB 65/13 PRO.

24. Chiefs of Staff Paper, No. 510, "Implications of Action Contemplated in Respect of Certain French Ships," 30 June 1940, CAB 80/14 PRO.

25. Admiral North to Admiralty, 4 July 1940, ADM 1/19177 PRO. I am grateful to James Rusbridger for bringing these reports to my attention.

26. CinC Mediterranean to Admiralty, 3 July 1940, ADM 1/19177 PRO.

27. Admiralty to Flag Officer H, 2 July 1940, ADM 1/19178 PRO.

28. Signals, 2 July 1940, PREM 3/179/1 PRO.

29ff. Report of Proceeding Flag Office

Commanding Force H, 4 July 1940, ADM 199/826 PRO.

30. Quoted in Hervé Coutau-Bégarie and Claude Huan, *Darlan* (Paris, 1989), p. 271. The authors present a well-researched and objective account of the issues facing the French admirals on 3 July 1940 in a contemporary biography of Darlan that does much to redress the balance of earlier partisan British and French accounts. The old controversy still has the potential to burst into flame, as was evident from the critical salvos in the *U.S. Naval Institute Proceedings* (March 1990) of Captain Jack Bally (French Navy Retired), after Sir James Cable had given a partisan British review of the Coutau-Bégarie and Huan book.

31–2. Report of Proceeding Flag Office Commanding Force H, 4 July 1940, op. cit.; War Cabinet (146) Conclusions Annex, 3 July 1940, 11.30 a.m., CAB 65/14 PRO.

33. Signals, 3 July 1940, PREM 3/179/1 PRO.

34ff. Report of Proceeding Flag Office Commanding Force H, 4 July 1940, op. cit.; Baudouin, *Diary*, 3 July 1940.

35. Signals 3 July 1940, op. cit.

36. Captain Holland, "Narrative of the Third of June," ADM 205/6 PRO.

37. Report of Proceeding Flag Office Commanding Force H, 4 July 1940, op. cit.; Admiral Commanding North Atlantic to Secretary of the Admiralty, 4 July 1940, ADM 1/19177 PRO.

38. Admiralty to Flag Office North Atlantic, 17 July 1940, ADM 1/19177 PRO; Minute to First Lord of Admiralty, 20 July 1940, ADM 1/19177 PRO.

39. North to Secretary of the Admiralty, 6 August 1940, ADM 1/19178 PRO.

40. Baudouin, *Diary*, 3 July 1940.

41. Halifax, *Diary*, 3 July 1940.

42. Churchill, Vol. II, p. 211.

43ff. *Hansard*, 4 July 1940.

44. *The London Observer: The Journal of General Raymond E. Lee 1940–1* edited by James Lutze (London, 1971), 4 July 1940, p. 12; Sir John Colville in preface to Warren Tute, *The Deadly Stroke* (London, 1973).

45ff. Draft telegram from "Former naval person," 5 July 1940, PREM 3/462/2/3 PRO.

46. Halifax to Churchill, 5 July 1940, PREM 3/462/2/3 PRO.

47. Ibid.; Lothian to Prime Minister, 6 July 1940, PREM 3/426/2/3 PRO.

48. Jodl, *Diary*, 30 June 1940; Alfieri to Foreign Ministry Rome, 1 July 1940, DGFP p. 82; Führer Conferences on Naval Affairs, 1 July 1940, p. 61–2.

49. *Führer Directives*, op. cit., p. 45; Halder, *Journal*, 1 July 1940; ibid., 2 July 1940.

50. Halder, *Journal*, 8 July 1940; Führer Naval Conference, 11 July 1940.

51. Statistics compiled by Richard Hough and Dennis Richards, *The Battle of Britain: The Greatest Air Battle of World History* (London, 1989), Appendix 1.

52. Halder, *Journal*, 13 June 1940.

53. Führer Directive 16, 16 July 1940, DGFP X, pp. 226–9.

54. Special Distribution War Cabinet Kelly (Berne) to Foreign Secretary, 8 July 1940, FO 371/24407.

55. Kelly to Foreign Secretary, 14 July 1940, FO 371/24401 PRO.

56. Ibid.; Hewel letter, cited by Ulrich Schlie, *Western Powers and Peace*.

57. Minute by Frank Roberts on the Burckhardt and Hohenlohe telegrams, 16 July 1940, FO 371/24407 PRO; Minute by Roger Makins, 16 July, FO 371/24407 PRO.

58–9. Lothian to Foreign Secretary, 19 July 1940, FO 371/24408 PRO.

60. Halifax, note of a telephone conversation received at the Dorchester at 7 p.m. on 22 July 1940, FO 271/24407 PRO.

61. Lothian to Foreign Secretary, 24 July 1940, FO 371/24408 PRO.

62. Foreign Secretary to Lord Lothian, 24 July 1940, FO 371/24408 PRO.

63. Foreign Secretary to Lothian, 26 July 1940, FO 371.24408 PRO; interview with Malcolm R. Lovell. In connections with Pearl Harbour Inquiry, 31 October, 1944, *Pearl Harbor Liaison Office Files*, RG 80 NAW.

64. Diary note, 23 July 1940, in *Weizsäacker Erinnerungen* (Freiburg, 1950), p. 294; Thomsen to Weizsäcker, 23 July (Leonidas Hill (ed.), *Die Weizsäcker Papieren 1933–50* (Frankfurt-am-Main, 1974), p. 215).

65ff. Rosenmann, *Public Papers and Addresses of Franklin D. Roosevelt*, op. cit., p. 206.

66. Shirer, op. cit., p. 990.

67. Ciano, *Diario*, 8 July 1940.

68. Minute on a note of Vansittart cited by Colville, *Diaries*, 24 July 1940.

69. Halifax, *Diary*, 22 July 1940; Birkenhead, *Halifax*, op. cit., p. 460.

CHAPTER 14

(pp. 352–74)

1. Erich Kordt, *Nicht aus den Akten* (Stuttgart, 1950), p. 399.

2. Stohrer to Berlin, 23 June 1940, No. 2 DGFP X.

3. Foreign Minister to Stohrer, No. 6 DGFP X.

4. Churchill to British Ambassador in Spain, 22 June 1940, FO 800/327 PRO; Consul General, Barcelona, to Foreign Office, 21 June 1940, FO 800/326 PRO.

5. Hoare to Foreign Office, 20 June 1940, FO 800/327 PRO.

6. Interview with Sir Dudley Forwood, May 1988.

7. *New York Times*, 23 October 1937.

8. Report of Duke of Saxe-Coburg, 1936, No. 531, DGFP IV; Hoesch to Foreign Ministry, January 1936, No. 510 DGFP IV; Most Secret Memorandum of

J. C. C. Davidson, 14 February 1936; "Mrs. S. is very close to Hoesch and has, if she likes to read them, access to all Secret & Cabinet Papers!!!!!" (Davidson Papers HOL); FO 371/20274; PRO; Philip Ziegler, in *King Edward VII: The Official Biography* (London, 1990), pp. 267 ff., questions the reliability of the Duke of Saxe-Coburg, who he asserts was "notoriously unreliable as a witness." But even the official biographer concedes that "Whatever the scale of the King's pretensions, or the reality of his influence, there is no doubt that the German leadership took it seriously."

9. Ziegler, op. cit., p. 271. Notes on conversation between Ribbentrop and Prince Cyril, Regent of Bulgaria, 19 October 1943, 48/43 GRS, Büro Reichsausminister AA B.

10. Zech-Burchesroda to Weizsäcker, 27 January 1940, No. 580, DGFP, op. cit.

11. Ziegler, op. cit., p. 415, following Bloch, dismisses the significance of these cables, but accepts that they were serious breaches of security. As Charles Hingham established in *The Duchess of Windsor: The Secret Life* (New York, 1988), p. 272, the conversation referred to took place not at the Supreme Allied War Council but at a meeting of the British War Cabinet. This suggests that Churchill may have been far too trusting of the Duke's confidentiality.

12. Zech-Burchesroda to Weizsäcker, No. 621, 19 February 1940, DGFP VIII; Ziegler, op. cit., p. 416, points out that although technically the Duke may not have been officially released from the Military Mission, the British Ambassador in Paris had been advised on 20 May that Allied HQ "would prefer that HRH did not come back for the present." The Duke nevertheless did abandon his long-suffering aide Major E. D. (Fruity) Metcalfe without explanation or notification. Churchill evidently suspected that there was something odd in the Duke's sudden departure because in a later draft cable he pointedly directed the latter's attention to the fact that "there is a great deal of doubt as to the circumstances in wh[ich] your Royal Highness left Paris."

(Minute of 28 June on Duke of Windsor to Prime Minister cable, 27 June 1940, Churchill Papers 20/9, quoted by Gilbert, *Finest Hour*, p. 613).

13. Cadogan, *Diary*, 20 and 21 May 1940.

14. Stohrer to Foreign Ministry, 6 June 1940, No. 394 DGFP IX.

15. Stohrer to Ribbentrop, 12 July 1940, No. 160, DGFP X.

16. Hoare to Foreign Secretary, 11 June 1940 (reproduced in Viscount Templewood (Sir Samuel Hoare) *Ambassador on Special Mission* (London, 1946), p. 35); Stohrer to Berlin, 10 June 1940, No. 409 DGFP X, op. cit., Hoare to Foreign Office Special Distribution to War Cabinet FO 371/2414 PRO.

17. David Irving, in his controversial *Churchill's War* (op. cit.), pp. 332–3, inferred that closed items refer to the Prytz message. By truncating a sentence from Cadogan's diary entry of 18 June, "No reply from Generals," he mistook this reference to imply that the Foreign Office was awaiting a response from Berlin to the Prytz peace feeler. The line actually reads: "No reply from Germans: French situation still uncertain," a clear reference to the armistice terms, since the following sentence is "Can't get them absolutely tied up about their fleet . . ." Evidently following Irving's lead, Clive Ponting in *Myth and Reality 1940* (London, 1990), pp. 113–15, asserts that the "only possible explanation" for Cadogan's note "is that the Foreign Office were awaiting reply from the Germans to the initiatives, sent via Prytz to the British Embassy in Stockholm." Lucacs, in *Duel*, op. cit., also suggests, though more circumspectly, the possibility that the closed items relate to a peace discussion.

18. Item 6, War Cabinet Minutes (171), 18 June 1940, CAB 65/7 PRO, from the uncensored and still classified microfilm. The Gibraltar items on 18 June and 19 June follow items on the seizure of the Swedish destroyers (War Cabinet (170) Conclusions, 19 June 1940, CAB 65/7 PRO – *uncensored* microfilm).

19. Hoare to Lord Halifax, 26 June 1940, printed in *Special Mission*, op. cit., pp. 37–8.

20. Salazar to Portuguese Ambassador in London, 21 June 1940, *Dez anos de politica externa* (Lisbon, 1971), Vol. VII, No. 892.

21. "You know of course, Noël, that you can never be Dowager Duke of Kent," the Marquess of Carisbrooke had jokingly told Coward. Robert Bruce Lockhart, in his diary in 1933, noted "a scandal about George – letters to a young man in Paris. A large sum had to be paid for their recovery" (quoted without attribution by Christopher Warwick, *George and Marina* (London, 1988), pp. 70–1); interview notes of telephone conversation with Prince Wolfgang of Hesse, 24 November 1985, in *Sunday Times*.

22. Stohrer to Foreign Ministry, 2 July 1940, No. 86 DGFP IX.

23ff. Weddell to Secretary of State, 2 July 1940, FRUS III.

24. Hoare to Foreign Office, 30 June 1940, FO 371/24407 PRO; Hoare to Churchill, 27 June 1940, Templewood Papers XIII/16/29 CUL.

25. Index summaries of Windsor exchanges PD/XLI/15–21, "Closed until 2016," FO 800/327 PRO; Churchill to Duke of Windsor, 25 June 1940, FO 800/3261 PRO; Hoare to Prime Minister, 28 June 1940, Churchill Papers 20/9, quoted by Gilbert, *Finest Hour*, p. 698.

26. Forwood interview.

27. Stohrer to Berlin, 2 July 1940, No. 86 DGFP X.

28. Hoare to Foreign Office, 1 July 1940, FO 800/326 PRO; Viscount Templewood (Sir Samuel Hoare), *A Deep Laid Plot*, unpublished Ms in Templewood Papers XIIII-2 CUL.

29. "Secret and personal," Prime Minister to Duke of Windsor, 1 July 1940, Churchill Papers 20/9 cited by Gilbert, *Finest Hour*, p. 698. Text of cable closed until 2106 in FO 800/326 PRO; draft letter from Duke to Churchill, October

1940, Windsor Papers, Paris, quoted by Michael Bloch, *Operation Willi: The Nazi Plot to Kidnap the Duke of Windsor July 1940* (London, 1984), p. 74.

30. Churchill to the Duke of Windsor, Lisbon, 4 July 1940, Churchill Papers 20/9, quoted by Gilbert, *Finest Hour*, p. 699.

31. Diary of Sir Ronald Storrs, 14 July 1940, Churchill Papers 20/9, quoted by Gilbert, *Finest Hour*, p. 699.

32. Draft telegram with amendments, 3 July 1940, Churchill Papers 20/9, but Ziegler (op. cit., p. 434) now cites Lord Caldecote, the Dominion Secretary, as its author, telegram, 4 July, Churchill Papers 20/14, quoted by Gilbert, *Finest Hour*, pp. 700–1.

33. Stohrer to Berlin, 9 July 1940, B15/002545 DGFP X.

34. Ribbentrop to Stohrer, quoting in full Hoyningen-Huene to Berlin, 11 July 1940, No. 152 DGFP X.

35. Cited by Michael Bloch, op. cit., p. 96; interview described and cited by Bloch, p. 79.

36. Ibid.; Pell to Secretary of State, 20 July 1940, Pell Papers FDRL.

37. Lothian to Foreign Office, 18 July 1940, Churchill Papers 20/9; "Immediate – personal," Lothian to Prime Minister, 17 July 1940, Churchill Papers 9/20, quoted by Gilbert, *Finest Hour*, p. 702; Duke of Windsor to Churchill, 19 July 1940, Churchill Papers 20/9, quoted by Gilbert, *Finest Hour*, p. 702.

38. Prime Minister to Duke of Windsor, 23 July 1940, Churchill Papers 20/9, quoted by Gilbert, *Finest Hour*, p. 704.

39. Letter Churchill to Duke of Windsor, 27 July 1940, Churchill Papers 20/9, quoted by Gilbert, *Finest Hour*, p. 705.

40. Report by Marcus Cheke in FO 954/33/212 PRO.

41. Ziegler (pp. 434 ff.) acknowledges that the Duke's defeatist indiscretions were inexcusable, if exacerbated by wrongs he felt he had suffered. The official biographer concludes, "on the flimsy grounds of psychological speculation," from "what is known of the Duke's character" that he would "never have played the traitor's part."

42. Lord Beaverbrook's copies of the Cabinet discussion in 1945 and 1953, together with twenty-one of the German cables, were found in his papers, Box No. 13 G-25, Beaverbrook Collection HOL.

43. Churchill to Attlee, 26 August 1940; Attlee to Churchill, 25 August 1945; ibid., Beaverbrook Papers.

44. Evidence that the Germans were indeed penetrating the British diplomatic cipher appears in the 4 July telegram from the French Ambassador in Lisbon. This refers to information he was given by an "authoritative source" that the Germans had intercepted a cable from Churchill asking Dr Salazar for permission to establish three naval bases in Portugal. The source appears to have been the Spanish Ambassador in Lisbon, since La Baume refers to a copy of the telegram having been given by the Germans to General Franco who was able to effect a démarche by getting the Portuguese to refuse Britain's request (La Baume to Paris, No. 813, 4 juillet 1940, copy in Baudouin Papers, Vol. 8, MAE). Confirmation that the German diplomatic cipher was never broken was provided by the former wartime MI6 officer and historian Lord Dacre (Hugh Trevor Roper) to Michael Bloch in a letter published in the paperback editions of *The Duke of Windsor's War*.

45. Eisenhower to Churchill, 2 July 1953; memorandum by Prime Minister, 12 August 1953, Beaverbrook Papers HOL.

46. Ribbentrop to Stohrer, 11 July 1940, No. 152 DGFP X.

47. Stohrer to Ribbentrop, 12 July 1940, No. 159 DGFP X.

48. Stohrer to Ribbentrop, 23 July 1940, No. 211 DGFP X; Stohrer to Berlin, 25 July 1940, No. 224 DGFP.

49. Letter from Miguel Primo de Rivera to Duke of Windsor, 24 July 1940, reproduced in Bloch, *Willi*, op. cit., pp. 168–9.

50. Identified as "Viktor" and interviewed by Bloch, op. cit., p. 170.

51. Report of Walter Monckton, 8 August 1940, reproduced in Bloch, op. cit., p. 211; letter from Walter Monckton to Duchess of Windsor, 4 May 1956, reproduced by Bloch, op. cit., p. 176.

52. Schellenberg Log, 24 July–6 August 1940, R58/572 BA; Stohrer to Ribbentrop, 31 July 1940, No. 264 DGFP.

53. Stohrer to Ribbentrop, 30 July 1940, AA-B15/B002614 AAB; *Final Report on Schellenberg*, IRR RG 319 NAW; Schellenberg's report to Ribbentrop from Lisbon, 2 August 1940, No. 276 DGFP X.

54. Ribbentrop to Hoyningen-Huene, 31 July 1940, No. 265 DGFP X; Ribbentrop to Hoyningen-Huene, 31 July 1940, No. 265 DGFP X.

55. Report of Walter Monckton, 8 August 1940, as reproduced in Bloch, op. cit., p. 211.

56-7. Hoyningen-Huene to Ribbentrop, 15 August 1940, No. 884, DGFP X.

58. "Most Secret and personal: Decipher yourself" draft telegram, 3 July 1940, Churchill Papers 20/9, quoted by Gilbert, *Finest Hour*, p. 700.

CHAPTER 15

(*pp. 375–403*)

1. The U.S. Naval Attaché in Cuba reported in October 1941 that he had learned from a source in the German Legation in Havana that Hitler believed that "when the proper moment of destiny arrived he [the Duke of Windsor] will be the only person capable of directing the destiny of England" (Report of U.S. Naval Attaché, 14 October 1941, State Department 862.20241/56 RG 59 NAW); German sources attesting to Hitler's belief in the Duke include Goebbels's *Diary*, 2 May 1941, and Ulrich von Hassel's *Diary*, August 1941 (p. 225), which shows that the Duke was also regarded as a mediator by the monarchists in the underground opposition to Hitler.

2. Halder, *Journal*, citing report of Brauchitsch's meeting with the Führer, 22 July 1940.

3-4. Halder, *Journal*, 31 July 1940.

5. Führer Directive 17, 1 August 1940, DGFP X, pp. 390–1; Führer Conferences on Naval Affairs, op. cit., pp. 81–2.

6. Von Rundstedt Interrogation, cited by Shirer, op. cit., p. 100.

7. Cited in Hinsley, *British Intelligence* (op cit.), Vol. I, pp. 183–4; "Former naval person" to the President, 31 July 1940, PREM 3/426/2/3.

8. Ibid.

9. Kennedy to State Department, 31 July 1940, 740.0011 European War 1939 4923-3/4; Kennedy to State Department, 2 August 1940, 740.0011 EW/39 4929 3/4 RG 59 NAW.

10. Frank Knox to Mrs. Knox, 15 June 1940, Knox Papers Box 3 LOC.

11. State Department to Kennedy, 11 July 1940, RG 59 740.001 EW 1939/4570; Memorandum Welles to Roosevelt, 12 July 1940, Roosevelt to Knox, 13 July, PSF "Knox File" FDRL; Lee, *London Journal*, op. cit., 2 August 1940; Report by Admiral Godfroy of 2 May conversation with Donovan, ADM 199/1156 PRO.

12. Ickes, *Diary*, 3 August 1940; Roosevelt's record of cabinet meeting, Franklin D. Roosevelt, *FDR: His Personal Letters*, edited by Elliot Roosevelt (New York, 1950), Vol. IV, pp. 1050–1.

13. Lothian to Foreign Office, 4 August 1940, A 3670/131/45 PRO.

14. War Cabinet (220) Conclusions; Churchill to Halifax FO A 3670/131/45 PRO; Churchill, op cit., Vol. II, pp. 404–5.

15. Churchill, Minute to General Ismay, 1 August 1940, PREM 3/4751/1 PRO; Sidney Aster, *The Making of WWII*, op. cit., pp. 316–17; Churchill to Lothian, 7 August 1940; Churchill to Halifax, 8 August 1940 PREM 3/475/1 PRO.

16. Kennedy to State Department, 31 July 1940, US Embassy London Confidential File RG 59 NAW.

17. Draft of cable to be sent from King George VI to King Gustav, 3 August 1940, FO 371/24409 PRO.

18. Churchill, Vol. II, p. 286; *New York Times*, 15 August 1940.

19. *New York Times*, 11 May 1940; President to Prime Minister, 13 August 1940, PREM 3/468 PRO.

20. Ibid.; War Cabinet (227) Conclusions, 14 August 1940, CAB 65/8 PRO.

21ff. Colville, *Diaries*, 14 August 1940; "Former naval person" to President, 15 July 1940, PREM 3/462/2/3 PRO.

22. Morgenthau, *Diary*, 16 August 1940 FDRL; Moffat, *Diary*, 17 August 1940.

23. Memorandum, "Destroyer Deal," Stark to Secretary of Navy, 17 August 1940, CNO Files NAW.

24ff. *Hansard*, 20 August 1940.

25. Langer and Gleason, *World Crisis*, op. cit., Vol. I, pp. 763–4.

26. "Former naval person" to President, PREM 3/462/2 PRO.

27. A report drawn up in July for Treasury Secretary Morgenthau had put Britain's total gold reserves at just under $1.5 billion ($360 million), with her dollar holdings of £108 million (£27 million) and the estimated dollar value of British-held American securities estimated at a realizable value of $700 million (£156 million). Against this had to be set Britain's annual expenditure of $784 million (£186 million) in the United States. A quarter of her steel was imported from America at a cost of $400 million (£100 million); $200 million (£50 million) was spent on oil and raw materials; $84 million (£21 million) on tobacco and food; $100 million (£25 million) on manufactured goods. On top of this now had to be added $716 million (£179 million) for the aircraft on order and $340 million (£85 million) for munitions – a total of $1,056 million (£264 million) for war supplies. With British exports to America and income from the sterling area amounting to little more than $620 million (£156 million), the estimated adverse balance of payments to the United States from July 1940 to July 1941 was conservatively estimated by the U.S. Treasury at more than 1.5 billion dollars (undated Memorandum, *Dollar Requirements of The United Kingdom Exchange Control*, p. 618, Morgenthau Papers FDRL – dollar conversion 4:1, Bank of England records average for 1940); War Cabinet Confidential Annex (232), 20 August 1940, CAB 65/13 PRO.

28. Ibid.; Churchill, Vol. II, pp. 503–4.

29. Cadogan, *Diary*, 25 August 1940.

30. "Former naval person" to President, 25 August 1940, PREM 3/462/2/3 PRO.

31. Churchill, Vol. II, p. 302.

32. Halifax, *Diary*, 26 August 1940; Kennedy to State Department, 29 August 1940, FRUS 1940 III, pp. 73–4; Letter dated 29 August 1940 from Chamberlain, Churchill Papers 2/293, quoted by Gilbert, *Finest Hour*, VI, C.

33. Roosevelt to Churchill, 30 June 1940, PREM 3/462/2 PRO.

34. Air Historical Branch, *The Air Defence of Great Britain*, Vol. II, p. 215.

35. *Hansard*, 5 September 1940.

36. *New York Times*, 5 September 1940; Stimson, *Diary*, 7 September 1940.

37. Halder, *Journal*, 14 September 1940.

38. Churchill, Vol. II, pp. 297–8.

39. Führer Directive, 12 October 1940, DGFP X.

40. Roosevelt, Memorandum to Secretary of State, 28 August 1940, enclosing Kennedy letter and reply for approval PSF Hull File FDRL.

41. This was the second account he had given to Arthur Krock of the *New York Times*. Krock was a supporter and friend of Kennedy who had helped his son Jack rework his Harvard thesis into the best-selling *Why England Slept*. Arthur Krock, *Memoirs: Sixty Years on the Firing Line* (New York, 1968), p. 355; Welles to Kennedy, 10 October 1940, 123 Kennedy, Joseph P /300a RG 59 NAW.

42. Halifax to Lothian, 10 October 1940,

FO 371/24251/A4485/605/45 PRO; account given by Randolph Churchill in 1960 to C. L. Sulzberger on 15 January 1960 in his diary, published as *The Last of the Giants* (New York, 1970), p. 630.

43. Kent Trial Transcript, op. cit., p. 30.

44. Letter Roosevelt to Kennedy, 17 October 1940, 123 Kennedy, Joseph P., 304 2/3 RG 59 NAW.

45. As told to Arthur Krock, op. cit., p. 399.

46. Ibid., p. 335; private memorandum of Arthur Krock, quoted by Michael Beschloss, *Kennedy and Roosevelt: The Uneasy Alliance* (New York, 1980), pp. 217–19.

47. According to Randolph Churchill, MI5 had passed the sheaf of intercepted Kennedy cables and telephone calls to his father's private secretary, Brendan Bracken. With Churchill's approval, Bracken had shown them to Harry Hopkins, who was infuriated by Kennedy's critical opinions of Roosevelt; the President was even more angry (Randolph Churchill's conversation with C. L. Sulzberger in Paris on 14 January 1960: *The Last of the Giants*, op. cit., p. 630). In his acclaimed study *Kennedy and Roosevelt* (op. cit.), Beschloss concluded that the final reason why the Ambassador relented was not clear because there was a gap in the account of the dialogue that "remained a mystery." Beschloss, on the information available in 1980, discounted Randolph Churchill's account as "untypically heavy-handed." Evidence that has since come to light must lend credence to Randolph Churchill; and in any case Roosevelt would surely have handled any such damning information deftly in order not to reveal its British source to Kennedy.

48. See for example the Ambassador's Western Union Cable of 9 February 1940 to Jim Seymour FO 371/24251 PRO.

49. The Joseph P. Kennedy F.B.I. file obtained under the FOIA surprisingly contains no derogatory material other than crank letters and a 1942 report of "unknown reliability" about his being appointed Ambassador to Britain to handle his liquor interests. There is, however, a reference to the 1953 investigation by the Anti-Trust Division of the Justice Department into the Somerset Liquor Company that concluded that Kennedy "was never an officer" and only ever owned 2 per cent of the stock. A 1960 allegation that the father of the President-elect was a treasurer to the Vatican is also blacked out by the F.B.I. censor. The file is so full of glowing testimonial to Kennedy's "financial genius" and "intellectual honesty" that its squeaky-cleanness is surprising and unusual, given that F.B.I. files normally contain many unsolicited and unproven allegations. Also the Joseph Kennedy files do still contain references to his son Jack's wartime affair with Ingar Arvard, the Norwegian Ambassador's daughter, who was considered by the Bureau at the time to be a German agent. Kennedy's pristine official record may not have been unconnected with the fact that as soon as he returned to the United States he began flattering and cultivating J. Edgar Hoover. From 1943 to 1954 Kennedy was a "Special Service Contact" – or F.B.I. informant – passing on information on "pinkos"' (communists) to the Boston office. The fond regard Kennedy expressed for Hoover, which the Director reciprocated, included invitations to Kennedy family events and weddings. Nor can it be omitted that his son Robert became U.S. Attorney General and this may explain why his father's file does not now contain the details of the secret reports Hoover sent to Roosevelt in May 1941 asserting that "Joseph Kennedy, former Ambassador to England and Ben Smith, Wall Street Operator, had a meeting with Göring in Vichy France and thereafter had both donated considerable amount of money to German causes." These are cited in the index to the FDR PSF Hoover File, No. 758 5/3/41 FDRL – the actual report is missing. The F.B.I. file on Kennedy does, however, contain a curious testimonial obtained in 1956 from a State Department official "who was closely associated" with Kennedy

in London. Although his name has been removed by the censor's pen, it is probable that the informant was Herschel V. Johnson, who, while praising Kennedy's shrewdness, also said he was "easily excited to anger and during such a period of anger does not care what he says." If the informant was indeed Johnson, who had maintained a close relationship with MI5 and knew about "the Doctor" then a comment that he made assumes a special significance. The Bureau interviewer was told that he did not believe that Kennedy "was the type of man who would reveal information, classified or otherwise, which would be to the detriment of the United States" (F.B.I. Kennedy File interview with name-censored State Department Official, 14 January 1956).

50. Reuter's report of Kennedy statement, 3 December 1940, FO 371/24251 PRO.

51. Dalton, *Diary*, 15 October 1940.

52. Plesman Memorandum and 20 August covering letter from Air Attaché, British Legation in Stockholm, FO 371/24408 PRO; British Ambassador, Ankara, to Foreign Office, 21 August 1940, FO 371/24408 PRO.

53. I am very grateful to Adrian Liddell Hart for bringing his father's memorandum to Lloyd George to my attention in his letter of 19 August 1990.

54ff. British Ambassador in Stockholm to Foreign Office, 5 September 1940; letter from Mallet, 7 September 1940, Minutes and memoranda "on Peace Moves"; "Dr Ludwig Weissauer," FO 371/24408 PRO.

55. Hess's statement in his June 1941 meeting with Lord Simon (Simon Papers BLO); in 1939 Wiseman struck up a close friendship with Lord Lothian and he travelled down to Washington "every week to have dinner and talk things over with him" (W.B. Fowler, *British–American Relations 1917–18. The Role of Sir William Wiseman* (Princeton, 1969); Papers of Sir William Wiseman SLY).

56. Lothian to Churchill, 20 May 1940,

PREM 4/25/8; Minute to Bevin (Churchill Private Secretary) from GFD, 18 November 1940, PRO; Halifax, *Diary*, 6 June 1940.

57. Notes and Drafts of Mooney's meetings with Wiseman in Mooney Papers GUL.

58. Letters on the Hohenlohe–Wiedemann meetings and his "reports to Stephenson which he cabled to London at the time"; Wiseman to Sir Ronald Campbell British Embassy, 22 December 1942, Wiseman to Maj. Gen. John H. Hildring, War Department, 28 March 1947, World War II Wiseman Papers SLY; Wiedemann and Hohenlohe F.B.I. files FOIA F.B.I. Washington and the PSF "Hoover" Safe File FDRL; Rudolf Stoiber and Boris Celovsky, *Stephanie von Hohenlohe: Sie liebte die Mächtigen der Welt (Munich, 1988)*.

59. Wiseman report dated 3 October 1940, Wiseman WWII File Wiseman Papers SLY.

60. Covering letter and Memorandum from J. Edgar Hoover to President, 30 November 1940, PSF "Hoover" FDRL; F.B.I. records of the telephone exchanges between Hohenlohe and Wiseman, *Hohenlohe Espionage-G File*. The detailed verbatim record of the Hohenlohe–Wiseman–Wiedemann conversations at the Mark Hopkins Hotel, attributed to a "confidential source," can only have been obtained by bugging. *Hohenlohe Espionage G Files* FOIA; Wiseman report on 27 November meeting, 30 November 1940, Wiseman WWII Wiseman Papers SLY.

61ff. Hoover to Adolf Berle, 30 November 1940 741.6211/11-2940 RG 59 NAW; "The Substance of the attached was telephoned to the President on Saturday 30 November": note attached to "Memorandum of 30 November"; Meeting Mark Hopkins Hotel 7.30 – 1 p.m. [sic], 27 November 1940, Hohenlohe F.B.I. FOIA.

62. Letter to Lt. Gen. Sherman Miles G-2 U.S. Army, lodged with the F.B.I. 2 February 1941, Wiseman F.B.I. FOIA.

63ff. Notes and drafts of Mooney's meetings in "Wiseman" Mooney Papers GUL.

CHAPTER 16

(pp. 404–34)

1. Report in PREM 3/219/7 PRO.

2. Hamilton quoted by Johnstone, *Where No Angels Dwell*, op. cit., p. 92; Hamilton, 11 May 1941, PREM 3/219/7 PRO.

3–4. Ibid.

5–6. Hamilton as quoted in *Motive for a Mission*, op. cit., p. 176.

7. Hamilton, "Additional Notes," INF 1/912 PRO; Hamilton quoted by Johnstone, op. cit., p. 92; report in the *New York Times*, 29 August 1943, of the press conference in New York given by the Minister of Information the day before. "Herr Hess is a 'Nazi of very low mentality,' Mr. Bracken added, and stated the Duke, whom he had met once at the Olympic Games, was the right kind of man . . ." *The Times* of London, subject to wartime censorship, carefully omitted any reference to the Duke of Hamilton or his alleged meeting with Hess. Other British newspapers, such as the Liberal *News Chronicle*, were not so fastidious. (INF 1/912 PRO: the Cabinet minute regarding "information about Hess which had not been hitherto disclosed" and instruction to Cabinet members "to refrain from disclosing any of the information in their possession about Hess"). As a result of Bracken's remarks a parliamentary question was put down by Richard Stokes, the Labour M.P. who had been one of the prominent advocates of a negotiated peace with Germany; it was given a written answer. Bracken's own recollection is that he told the press in New York that Hess *claimed* to have once met the Duke of Hamilton.

8. Sinclair to Stokes, 30 September 1943, INF 1/912 PRO; "Hess once invited Honor and me to lunch in Berlin when we were there for the Olympic Games; we refused – but I remember that 'Duglo' Clydesdale, as he then was, *did go*, as did Pat Jersey. The world does not know that the Duke is thus concerned in the story" (Channon, *Diary*, 13 May 1941).

9. *The Times*, 14 August 1936: the occasion was the dinner given in honour of Sir Robert Vansittart, the Permanent Head of the Foreign Office, who had extended his visit to Berlin for exploratory talks with the Nazi leaders.

10. Quoted by Simon Haxey (pseudonym) in *Tory MP* (London, 1936), p. 198; among the diners can be found the name of "H. (Kim) Philby." The then unknown Cambridge graduate later became notorious as a Soviet spy who admitted he had served his apprenticeship as an undercover agent for Moscow, posing as a right-wing journalist to penetrate the pro-German faction of the British Establishment.

11. Hamilton, *Motive for a Mission*, op. cit., p. 69.

12. For a full discussion see Ursula Michel, *Albrecht Haushofer und der nationalsozialismus* (Stuttgart, 1974), and also Mansion Thielenhaus, *An Passung und Widerstand: Diplomaten 1938–41* (Paderborn, 1984).

13. Heinz Haushofer confirmed that in 1941 the Gestapo investigated rumours of alleged homosexual activities by his brother Albrecht. David Irving has also postulated that the affectionate tone of the correspondence suggests another, "more profound dimension to the relationship between the German diplomat and the Scottish peer (*Hess: The Missing Years 1941–5* (London, 1987), p. 76); information about Beaverbrook supplied from notes taken by Dr. Hugh Thomas in his 1974 interview with James Leasor, who told this author in 1990 "that he could not remember the homosexual story." But Leasor did confirm the role Beaverbrook played in encouraging his investigation. (interview with James Leasor, October 1990).

14. Joachim Ribbentrop, *The Ribbentrop Memoirs* (London, 1954), p. 67; *The Times*, 4 December 1937.

15. *The Times*, 6 October 1939.

16. Mrs. Violet Roberts was the daughter-in-law of the former British Viceroy of India, Lord Roberts. An old family friend of the Haushofers, she lived in Lisbon; full text of this letter is reprinted in

Hamilton, *Motive for a Mission*, pp. 160–1. A photostat of the "Terminal Mails" in the censor's longhand transcript of the second half of Haushofer's letter survives in INF 1/912 PRO.

17. Memo to the Director General of the B.B.C. from Herbert detailing the interception of the letter in 1/912. The "Secret" report on Hess declassified after forty-seven years by U.S. Army Intelligence reveals that the Military Attaché in London was informed that the Foreign Office official who was responsible for forwarding it on to the Duke "admitted that he had forgotten to send the letter to Hamilton after he had made copies of it." Lee report "Hess" IRR RG 319 NAW, op. cit.; the N.K.V.D. version of the Morton report also corroborates the story, 1st Sec 3rd Dept 1st div 3/10/41 "Black Bertha" File 20566 KAM; Hamilton (Undated 1945) INF 1/192 PRO.

18. Hamilton, *Motive for a Mission*, pp. 160–1.

19. Ibid., p. 48.

20. Ibid.; interview with T.A. Robertson, 24 April 1990.

21. Robertson interview; Hamilton, *Motive for a Mission*, pp. 163–4.

22. Hamilton, ibid.

23. Ibid., p. 173.

24. Hamilton, "Report," PREM 3//219/7/PRO.

25. "Additional Notes," Hamilton INF 1/912 PRO.

26. Hamilton quoted by Johnstone, op. cit., p. 92.

27. Churchill was weekending at Ditchley Park, Oxfordshire, and not Chequers, Cadogan, *Diary*, 11 May 1941.

28. Hamilton, "Additional Notes," op. cit.

29. *Flying Dream* by E. Phillips Oppenheim, in which the hero discovers that Hitler's plane has made a forced landing in England. Lest the dream might appear too contrived, Colville evidently honeyed the pot by adding his recollection of an Air Ministry Intelligence digest "that Göring was believed to fly over from time to time in a German bomber to gloat over the destruction which the Luftwaffe was wreaking over London," (John Colville, *Footprints in Time* (London, 1976), pp. 110–11).

30ff. Colville, *Diaries*, 11 May 1940, p. 387. In the more anecdotal earlier memoir Colville says that Lawford also said he "could only compare what had happened to an E. Phillips Oppenheim novel and that it had to do with the crashed Nazi plane" (Colville, *Footprints*, p. 112); interview with Nicholas Lawford, November 1989.

31. Lawford interview.

32. The broad gravel drives of Chequers were observed from the air, to make an arrow pointing directly at the house. Ditchley Park, by contrast, was not only further from the German bomber bases, but surrounded by a dense park full of trees off the Oxford to Stratford-on-Avon road. Ronald Tree, *When the Moon Was High: Memoirs of Peace and War 1897–1942"* (London, 1962), p. 130; Gilbert, *Finest Hour*, p. 841.

33. Tree, op. cit., p. 149; Robert F. Sherwood, *Roosevelt and Hopkins: An Intimate History* (New York, 1948), p. 177.

34. Colville, *Diaries*, and *Footprints*, op. cit., "Presently a secretary told me someone wanted to speak to me on the telephone *on behalf of the Duke of Hamilton*," Churchill wrote, stating that while the Duke was a "personal friend of mine," he "could not think of any business he might have that could not wait until morning." Since the unidentified caller had insisted "the matter was one of urgent Cabinet importance," the Prime Minister sent his private secretary, Brendan Bracken, to the telephone. "After a few minutes, Mr Bracken told me the Duke said he had an *amazing piece of information* to report," he wrote. "I therefore sent for him" (Churchill, Vol. II, p. 41; Cadogan, *Diary*, 11 May 1940).

35. Hamilton, "Additional Notes," op. cit., Hamilton, *Motive for a Mission*, p. 179; Hamilton quoted by Johnstone, op.

cit., p. 92; dinner was already over, because the Duke recalled that a pompous butler asked if he wished to join the gentlemen in the dining room for brandy and cigars or the ladies in the drawing room.

36. Hamilton, "Additional Notes," op. cit., Hamilton, *Motive for a Mission*," p. 180.

37. Hamilton, *Motive for a Mission*, ibid.; it is not explained precisely when Hamilton got a copy of Haushofer's September 1940 invitation; presumably he had been given it at his March meeting at the Air Ministry.

38. Hamilton, *Motive for a Mission*, p. 180.

39. Eden, *Memoirs*, Vol. II, p. 255; Hamilton, "Additional Notes," op. cit.; Irving, *Hess*, p. 348, citing "Churchill appointment diary, 12.5.41 in the possession of the author"; "The Duke repeated his story which was accepted with astonishment, or not accepted as the case may be"; Hamilton "Additional Notes," op. cit.; Cadogan "sent for C," according to his private diary. The head of S.I.S. (Special Intelligence Service, more popularly known as MI6) is the obvious candidate for the "someone" else whom Hamilton records in his 1945 account as present at this meeting besides Eden (Cadogan, *Diary*, 12 May 1940; Hamilton, "Additional Notes," op. cit.); in 1945 Hamilton states that "everybody seemed taken aback by the news." The Duke made no reference to the reaction "C," but one reason why Kirkpatrick was selected, according to a former member of the Foreign Office who liased with "C" during the war, was that Menzies may have already been suspicious about Hamilton's association with Haushofer (interview with Robert Cecil, February 1990).

40. Intercepted Deutschlandsender broadcast by German Home Stations, Monday 12 May, at 8 p.m., that DBST INF 1/912 PRO.

41. Citing interviews with Pintsch, Wulf Schwarzwäller, *Rudolf Hess: The Deputy* (London, 1988), pp. 170–1; quoted from a

1970 interview by Irving, *Hess*, p. 82; the Bodenschatz statement General Milch of the Luftwaffe is recorded in a conversation secretly monitored by the British on 20 May 1945, WO 208/4170 PRO; Schwarzwäller, op. cit., p. 148; Darlan, who was scheduled to meet Hitler, was subjected to a hurried conference with Ribbentrop (Coutau-Bégarie and Huan, *Darlan*, op. cit., p. 402); interrogation of von Ribbentrop, dated 25 August 1945, IRR RG 319 NAW.

42. General Halder, who as chief of O.K.H. was present at the Berghof, recorded in his diary: "Chronology of events: a Saturday: Führer received package containing documents and put aside, thinking it was some memorandum. Later opened it and found a letter informing him of the plan, and explaining the reasons. Glasgow was given as his destination. Wanted to visit Duke of Hamilton (President of the British Veterans Association)" (*The Halder War Diary 1939–42*, edited by Charles Burdick and Hans-Adolf Jacobsen (California, 1988), p. 388); Diary of Ambassador Walter Hewel, 13.5.41; Ilse Hess, *Schicksal*, op. cit., p. 78.

43. Hess, ibid.; interrogation of Gauleiter E.W. Bohle, quoted in Robert M.W. Kemper (ed.), *Das Dritte Reich um Kreuzverhör* (Munich, 1969), p. 103.

44. Schwarzwäller, op. cit., p. 157.

45. Hess, op. cit.; Halder, *Journal*, 12 May 1941, p. 388.

46. Von Ribbentrop IRR RG 319 NAW; Bodenschatz WO 208/4170 PRO.

47. Entry for 13 May (Tuesday) preceded by "Yesterday" from Goebbels, *Diaries*, p. 363.

48. Walter Stubbe, "In Memoriam Albrecht Haushofer," *Vierteljahrshefte für Zeitgeschichte*, July 1960, pp. 233–4.

49. The official announcement was made on 20 July 1941, but Butler records in his autobiography (op. cit., p. 87) that he had already been told of his move on 6 June 1941.

50. Hamilton, *Motive for a Mission*, p.

202; Haushofer was rearrested in December 1944, six months after the Stauffenberg plot of 9 July. He was shot by the SS on 23 April 1945, during the Battle for Berlin.

51.   Ivone Kirkpatrick, *Inner Circle* (London, 1959), p. 174.

52.   Eden and Cadogan diaries (op. cit.) for 12–13 May 1941. The original text of Churchill's draft statement read: "On the night of Saturday the 10th a Messerschmitt-110 was reported by our patrols to have crossed the coast of Scotland and to be flying in the direction of Glasgow. Since a Messerschmitt-110 would not have the fuel to return to Germany this report was at first disbelieved. However, later on a Messerschmitt-110 crashed near Glasgow with its guns unloaded. Shortly afterwards a German officer who had bailed out was found with a parachute in the neighbourhood, suffering from a broken ankle. He was taken to a hospital in Glasgow where he at first gave his name as Hort, but later on declared that he was Rudolf Hess and that he had come to England in the name of Humanity hoping that a peace might be made between Great Britain and Germany . . . Accordingly, an officer of the Foreign Office who was closely acquainted with Hess before the war was sent up by aeroplane to see him in hospital. He reports that the German officer is undoubtedly Rudolf Hess. As soon as he is recovered from his injury his statement will be carefully examined" (PREM 3/219/4 PRO).

53.   Eden and Cadogan diaries, ibid.

54.   *New York Times*, 13 May 1941.

55.   Kirkpatrick, op. cit., p. 174.

56.   Ibid.; Hamilton, *Motive for a Mission*, p. 182.

57.   Kirkpatrick, op. cit., p. 176.

58.   Memorandum dated 13/5/41 initialled "A(lexander) C(adogan)," commencing "MR. KIRKPATRICK has just (10.50 am) rung me up from Turnhouse Aerodrome to report shortly on his interview with Hess last night . . ." (PREM 3/219/17 p. 171 PRO).

59.   *The Times*, 12 May 1941; *Hansard*, 13 May 1941.

60.   Goebbels, *Diaries*, (Yesterday) entry for 14 May 1941, p. 354.

61.   Goebbels, *Diaries*, 15 May 1941; *The Secret Conferences of Dr. Goebbels: The Nazi Propaganda War 1939–43*, selected and edited by Willi A. Boelcke (New York, 1970), p. 163.

62.   Lord Halifax, speech given at Kansas City and reported in the *New York Times*, 13 May 1941; a "D" Notice banning the mentioning of Hamilton's name is cited in the unpublished diary of Cecil King, Editor of the *Daily Mirror*, 13 May 1941, King Papers BOUL; *New York Times*, 13 May 1941.

63.   Quoted in *New York Times*, 14 May 1941; "This is great news, Sir," said Sir Walter Monckton, Director General of the Ministry of Information, "Yes," replied Churchill, "the maggot seems to be in the apple"; Memorandum from the Press Relations Office to Director-General of Ministry of Information (Walter Monckton), 14 May 1941, INF 1/912 PRO.

64.   Goebbels, *Diaries*, 19 May 1941.

65.   *New York Times*, 13 May 1941.

66.   Ibid.; Rudolf Hess, Broadcast references to his activities during the period April 20–May 14 1941: Research Unit (Overseas) B.B.C., dated 15 May 1941, INF 1/912 PRO.

67.   Cadogan, *Diary*, 14 May 1941.

68.   Nicolson, *Diaries*, 16 May 1941 (Nicolson was then Parliamentary Secretary to the Ministry of Information); Cadogan, *Diary*, 14 May 1941; Eden, *Memoirs*, Vol. II, p. 256.

69.   Nicolson, *Diary*, 16 May 1941; *The Times*, 15 May 1941.

70.   *New York Times*, 15 May 1941.

71.   Cable of 14 May 1941, received 15 May, London, via US Embassy, PREM 3/469/409 PRO.

72.   P.M. Minute to Sir Alexander Cadogan, 16 May 1941, PREM 3/468/409 PRO.

73.   Memo by James H. Rowe, White

House administrative assistant to FDR, in "Missy" LeHand, the President's Secretary, dated 14 May 1941, Map Room Papers FDRL.

74. Cadogan, *Diary*, 15 May 1941; War Cabinet Conclusions, CAB 65/18 PRO.

75. Cecil Harmsworth King, *With Malice Toward None, The Diaries*, edited by William Armstrong (London, 1970), p. 129; the *Daily Mirror* was correct in claiming that Hamilton's role had been "disclosed" the previous day by official sources. Foreign Office approval had been given to the release, which stated: "It can now be disclosed that Hess made an attempt to communicate with the Duke by letters some months previously. The Duke immediately placed the letters in the hands of our Security authorities and Hess got no reply." This gaffe brought an 'angry protest from the Air Minister. The Ministry of Information official responded with a detailed reply pointing out that the offending release "deliberately skirts around the point" whether Hess wrote the letter himself. "It *admittedly departs from the truth*," he admitted. He said that the statement that the Duke had passed the letter to the authorities had been made to protect him. This was felt "less likely to give rise to suspicion of his conduct than saying that the letter had been intercepted" (INF 1/912 PRO).

76. Cadogan, *Diary*, 15 may 1941; what was discussed over lunch at Windsor has never been made public, and the Duke of Hamilton is not even rated worthy of mention by biographers who have been granted access to the Royal Archives. Wheeler Bennett, *King George VI* (op. cit.) makes no mention of either Hamilton or Hess; Hamilton, *Motive for a Mission*, pp. 194, 195.

77. Letter to Director General from E.H. Herbert, 26 May 1941, INF 1/912 PRO.

78. The correspondence and documents relating to the case and the behind-the-scenes legal wrangling are in AIR 19/864 PRO.

79. Prime Minister's Personal Minute, 18 May 1941, PREM 3/219/7 PRO.

80. Letter from J.G. Martin, the Prime Minister's private secretary, to W.I. Mallet at the Foreign Office, PREM 3/219/7 PRO.

81. Samples of censored mail opinion INF 1/912 PRO.

82. Goebbels, *Diaries*, 16–18 May 1941, pp. 368–71.

83. Cadogan, *Diary*, 19 May 1941; Cabinet Conclusions, 19 May 1941, CAB 65/18 PRO; *The Times* and the *New York Times*, 15 May 1941, citing "officials in Berlin yesterday."

84. "Former naval person" to President, 21 May 1941, PREM.

CHAPTER 17
(pp. 435–60)

1. According to N.K.V.D. operational procedure, "Vadim" (the London Resident's cryptonym) was not in inverted commas because he was a career officer of the N.K.V.D. On the other hand, Philby's "SONNCHEN" was, indicating that he was a controlled agent (Spravka No. 376, 14 May 1941, "Black Bertha" File 20566 KAM). The documentary evidence was not released for the TV programme *Cambridge Graduate*, a coproduction with an independent British television production company, Wallbury, made with the "cooperation" of the K.G.B. As a result, the programme's claim that Philby was the Kremlin's prime British source on the Hess flight was rejected by British commentators.

2. Reports from agents "GIT," "JUN," "FRANKFURTER," "EXTERN" (real names not supplied, for K.G.B. "operational reasons," from File No. 20566, "HESS – BLACK BERTHA" KAM. Mrs. Ribkyna, a veteran N.K.V.D. operative, later became celebrated as a writer of children's books.

3. *Rote Kapelle* was the codename given by the Germans to all the Soviet espionage networks in Europe that the Reichssichershauptampt (RSHA) began rolling up after the invasion of Russia in 1941. Extending from Germany to Belgium, France and Switzerland, the

underground Communist cells and tentacles of these networks of subversion and intelligence controlled by Moscow (both N.K.V.D. and G.R.U.) had since 1940 been increasingly focused on obtaining intelligence about the Nazis. For a factual analysis based on the German investigations, see *The Rote Kapelle – The CIA's History of Soviet Intelligence and Espionage Networks in Western Europe, 1936–1945* (Maryland, 1979). It is clear, however, from contacts in Moscow about the "Harnack" and "Schulze-Boysen" groups, broken by the Germans in 1942, that the full history of these networks can only be told with access to Soviet archives (filmed interview with Oleg Tsarev at K.G.B. headquarters, Moscow, February 1991).

4. Alexander Orlov, *Handbook of Intelligence and Guerilla Warfare* (Michigan, 1965), p. 10. Orlov, a.k.a. Leon Lazerevik Feldbin, had been at the O.G.P.U. N.K.V.D. headquarters in Moscow serving on the committee which evaluated secret reports for presentation to Stalin. He defected from Spain in 1936 after receiving a recall to Moscow that he feared would cost him his life. Reaching the United States, Orlov and his wife went to ground until after the dictator's death in 1953, when he surfaced to publish a sensational indictment of "Stalin's Crimes." One of the highest-ranking Soviet intelligence offers ever to defect, Orlov was considered a particularly reliable source of information by the N.K.V.D. Not until Oleg Tsarev was given access in 1990 to the Orlov File, which like all defector's records was kept sealed and separate in the K.G.B. Archives, was it generally known, even within Soviet Intelligence circles, that Orlor did not betray all the secrets he took with him to the United States. As Tsarev has revealed in "Flight into the Dark" (published in *Trud* on 20–21 December 1990), Orlov remained loyal to the service by not revealing the names of some sixty agents, including Philby and the Cambridge ring in Britain, which he had controlled before being posted to Spain.

5. Among the sources were neutral embassies, the Polish underground movement, and a source codenamed A-54, a senior Abwehr officer, Paul Thümmel, originally recruited before the war by the Czechs, who continued passing intelligence that was relayed to the British by Colonel Moravec (see p. 447). An unidentified senior member of the Nazi Party also supplied the U.S. Embassy in Berlin with sketchy details from Hitler's 18 December Barbarossa Directive. These were passed in general terms to the British Ambassador in Moscow, Sir Stafford Cripps, who relayed them to London in March 1941. Similar rumours reached the British Embassies in Sweden, Geneva and Ankara, and information also came in from Sweden. At the end of March the Polish underground reported that Germany would attack on 15 April, and during March A-54 (Thümmel) had confirmed that preparations for the attack were under way and provided information on objectives and the number of divisions. For a detailed analysis of the intelligence and conflicting evaluations made regarding Operation Barbarossa, see F.H. Hinsley *et al.*, *British Intelligence in the Second World War*, op. cit., Vol. I, pp. 429–83.

6. Churchill, op. cit., Vol. II, p. 300.

7. *Enigma* was the machine used to encrypt high-level military German signal traffic, which by 1941 was yielding up many – though by no means all – of its secrets to the round-the-clock efforts of British cryptanalysts at Bletchley Park. The stately cedar trees of this Bedfordshire estate north of London sheltered the wartime huts of the Government Code and Cipher School. The title was deliberately prosaic; the compound was one of the most closely guarded and secret facilities in wartime Britain. On 30 March 1941 the Bletchley analysts concluded that Luftwaffe *Enigma* messages reporting the diversion of three Panzer divisions from the Balkans to Poland suggested a major military operation against Russia "either for intimidation or for actual attack," GC & CS Report CX/JQ/S7 30 March 1941, cited by Hinsley, Vol. I, p. 452; this "sure information from a trusted agent" Churchill

wished to be passed on to Stalin with the hope that he would "readily appreciate the significance of these facts," Hinsley, Vol. I, p. 303; Gabriel Gorodetsky, "The Hess Affair and Anglo–Soviet Relations on the eve of Barbarossa," *English Historical Review*, April 1986, pp. 404–20.

8. MI appreciation, 1 April 1941, WO 190/893 PRO.

9. Most telling of the *Enigma* indicators that an attack was imminent was a 13 May Luftwaffe intercept that Fliegerkorps II, one of the units that had spearheaded the Blitz on Britain, was on its way to Poland; COS (41) 325 Résumé No. 89 in 22 May 1941 Conclusions, CAB 80/28 PRO.

10. Text from PREM 3/469 PRO; *The Diaries of Sir Robert Bruce Lockhart*, Vol. II, 1939–1945, edited by Kenneth Young (London, 1967), Tuesday, 13 May 1941, p. 99.

11–12. "Record of an interview with Herr Rudolf Hess (May 13)" Certified copy of a document in the files of HM Secretary of State for Foreign Affairs, 22 January 1946, Nuremberg Documents, State Archive Nuremberg M117 Hess.

13. Bruce Lockhart, *Diaries*, 28 May 1941, p. 101.

14. Kirkpatrick, *Inner Circle*, op. cit., p. 180.

15. "Hess" Nuremberg, op. cit., M117; M118; M119; Hamilton, "Additional Notes," op. cit.

16. "Secret" letter to G.E. Millard of the Foreign Office, dated 7 April 1945; Minute to Secretary of State for Air, "Foreign Secretary and Minister of Information to See," signed WSC, dated 7 April 1945, INF 1/912 PRO.

17–18. *Spravka* No. 338, 18 May 1941, report prepared by Ocetrov on 22 May 1941, "Black Bertha" File 20566, KAM.

19. Whether Hess was bisexual or simply enjoyed the company of Party homosexuals such as the S.A. leader Ernst Röhm, who was shot in the 1934 purge, is not clear from the Soviet agent's report in the "Black Bertha" file.

20. "I simply wrote in error," Eden explains ingenuously in the May ;1941 page referring to the February entries: Pocket Diary of Anthony Eden, 15 May 1941, Eden Papers BUL.

21. Cadogan, *Diary*, 15 May 1941.

22. Cadogan, report of conversation with Kirkpatrick, 13 May 1941, PREM 3 219/7 PRO.

23. Cadogan, *Diary* 19 May 1941; Bruce Lockhart, *Diaries*, 28 May 1941, p. 101.

24. "Most Secret," Eden to P.M., 27 May 1941, PRO; handwritten note from Cadogan to Secretary of State, "Prime Minister to see" in Eden's handwriting, 4 June 1941, PREM 3/2197 PRO.

25. Foley and Kendrick had run S.I.S. undercover operations in Berlin and Vienna under the standard MI6 guise of passport control officers.

26. Cadogan, *Diary*, 6 June 1941; Cadogan, "Most secret" memorandum, 6 June 1941, PREM 3/219/7 PRO.

27. Simon and Kirkpatrick were accompanied by a shorthand writer and Kurt Mass, a German consular official from an internments camp, whom Hess insisted on having as a witness; Document D 614, Copy of Foreign Office Transcript of "Most secret" interview with Rudolf Hess, Nuremberg State Archives. A copy is also to be found in the Simon Papers, BOL; Dutch television producer Karel Hille claims to have been given the "full version" of the Simon report in a file that former MI6 chief Sir Maurice Oldfield allegedly removed from the archives before he retired, entrusting it to the care of an emeritus professor of New College, Oxford. This file, he claims, contains a letter in which Lord Simon expresses doubts that the man he interviewed was Hess: interview with Karel Hille, October 1990, confirming article appearing in *The Independent on Sunday*, 28 October 1990.

28. Letter from Major Desmond Morton to H.L. d'A. Hopkinson, Foreign Office, 13 June 1941, Beaverbrook Papers HOL; Major Morton was a World War I veteran. With a special dispensation agreed to

by successive Prime Ministers, he had nurtured Churchill in his years out of office with secret information on Germany. This he obtained from the British intelligence services and other sources for the so-called "Industrial Intelligence Unit" he ran under Foreign Office auspices; Churchill, Vol. II, p. 302.

29–30. Morton, memo for the Prime Minister, dated 13 June 1941, PREM 3/219/7 PRO.

31. By 7 June the Bletchley Park analysts had worked out the German Order of Battle along the eastern front. This provided incontestable evidence that massive German armoured and infantry forces, supported by 2,000 aircraft, were poised to strike deep into the heart of Russia. GC & CS had also decrypted a message from the Italian Ambassador in Moscow reporting that his German colleague in the Soviet capital had just assured him that negotiations with Germany had come to a standstill. On 7 June the Swedish government warned the Foreign Office that Germany would resort to force against Russia on or about 15 June. On 10 June the decrypted message sent by Göring calling his Luftwaffe commanders on the eastern front to a conference on 15 June at his Karinhall estate made it clear that the invasion would not occur until after that date. On 12 June GC & CS decrypted a message from the Japanese Ambassador in Berlin reporting to Tokyo that Hitler had told him that the Russians were being obstructive and that he had decided that Communist Russia must be eliminated. See Hinsley, op. cit., Vol. I, pp. 470–8; Churchill, op. cit., Vol. III, p. 301.

32. Hinsley's reference to the missing appreciation is suspiciously equivocal: "There is no record of a JIC appreciation on that date but the JIC may have issued this view in a daily summary and the file of the JIC's daily summaries has not come to light" (op. cit., Vol. I, p. 477 footnote); ibid., p. 478.

33. Churchill, Vol. II, p. 46.

34. A thorough search of the G-2 incoming files for the period had failed to uncover the "Top Secret" cable from the Military Attaché in London – and, curiously, five whole days of traffic are missing from the records before 4 October, when it was sent; Rudolf Hess B8026020 IRR Files RG 319 NAW, Chief of Staff U.S. Army (hereafter Lee, "Hess").

35. The answer to both questions is to be found in the journal which Captain (later General) Raymond E. Lee kept while at his London posting. His entry for 31 October records how a *Time* magazine journalist named Laird arrived at his office after lunching with an intimate of Churchill who had provided him with "a complete and detailed exposition of the Hess case." Knowing he could not print the story, the journalist left a copy with the Military Attaché to check out its validity. After making several attempts to verify it, on 4 November Lee records that he showed the memoradum to the American Ambassador. *The London Journal of General Raymond E. Lee 1940–41*, op. cit., pp. 439–42.

36. The original report does not identify its source, only that it was "Agent's material that originated in the 1st Section of the 3rd Department of the 1st Directorate." It is dated X October 1941, but it refers to the Morton lunch of 26 October. On the fourth page is the handwritten notation "20/10/42?", a further indication that the officer who filed the report as folios 211–14 in the bound volume related it to page 230, the Colonel Moravec report dated 24 October 1942, File 205666 KAM; since March 1939, when Hitler annexed Czechoslovakia, Moravec and his staff had operated from two hotels near Victoria Station in London and were in frequent contact with their British counterparts in MI5 and MI6. File No. 25344 in the K.G.B. archives show Moravec to have been a valued and reliable Soviet source as long as the war lasted – a fact he omitted in his autobiographical account, *Master of Spies* (London, 1975).

37. Laird was "astounded by his good fortune and miserable as a newspaper man to think that he could not print this, for it would be the story of the year." He said he had brought the report for

580

Lee's opinion; the U.S. Military Attaché thought this had been done "because Churchill thought that *Life* and *Time* had been somewhat opposed to him and was now appealing for their support against the rising star of Beaverbrook, who is evidently about to join issue with Churchill over the question of an immediate offensive [the argument of the opening of a second Allied front to relieve the pressure on Russia]" (Lee's *Journal*, 31 October 1941, p. 437); Lee, "Hess," and "Agent's Material," p. 211, "Black Bertha" File 20566 KAM.

38. Ibid.

39. Lee, "Journal," 5 November 1941, p. 442.

40. Lee and N.K.V.D., "Hess," op. cit.

41. Ibid.; Major Morton described Hess's confrontation with the eminent psychiatrist, who spoke German. It had taken half an hour to discover the root of Hess's violent antipathy to those he called "Die Immigranten" who he claimed were a sinister threat to Hitler's power, but also trying to poison him. As Professor Robert Winks pointed out, Hess's use of the word *Immigranten* is curious, since it was a "foreignism" (*Einwanderer* is the usual German term for an immigrant). He suggests that the word had a contemporary implication to the Nazis. According to Morton, the psychiatrist suggested that "Die Immigranten" were either Jews or Communists. "No, we are obliterating the Jews," Hess declared, insisting also that "There are no communists in Germany." As he continued in the maniacal demonstration clutching at his own throat, it became evident that he was referring to the Bolshevik threat.

42–3. Lee and N.K.V.D., "Hess," op. cit.

44. Author's interview with Admiral Robert H. Weeks, June 1984. He was the U.S. Navy officer who went to Bletchley Park with the U.S. "Purple" Machine in March 1941; until the 7 December air-raid on Pearl Harbor, there was no certainty that a Japanese attack would bring the United States into the war. This was despite the personal assurances Roosevelt had given Churchill at their first summit that August aboard the battleship *Prince of Wales* in Newfoundland's Placentia Bay. For analysis and documentary evidence of the far-reaching defence agreements and the B-17 trade-off in the Far East which were reached at the so-called Atlantic Charter summit, see John Costello, *The Pacific War* (New York, 1981), pp. 94 ff., and Admiral Edwin T. Layton, Captain Roger Pineau and John Costello, *And I Was There: Pearl Harbor to Midway: Breaking the Secrets* (New York, 1985), pp. 131 ff.

45. Roberts interview, 1990.

46. Transcript of "Dr. Livingstone and Jonathan" conversation and the Hess memorandum *Germany–England from the Viewpoint of War Against the Soviet Union* handed to Lord Beaverbrook on 9 September 1941, Beaverbrook Papers HOL.

47. Note in the Beaverbrook Papers, op. cit.

48. Harriman note, quoted in its entirety in Robert E. Sherwood, *Roosevelt and Hopkins*, op. cit., p. 390.

49. Eden, *Diaries*, p. 257; Churchill, op. cit., Vol. III, p. 47.

50. Items 1–3 on "Affaire HESS," dated 5 September 1941, annotated in French and stamped by then "No 09764," were supplied from an N.K.V.D. file that remains unidentified "for operational reasons." Pages 51–6 include the French version of an article by Leopold Schwarzschild, "Capture Inattendue de Hess dans un piège tendu par le Secret Service," which appeared in the *Gazette de Montréal*, 4 August 1941. The final page is a letter summarizing the article sent by Eva Jean Tentry of Drury Lane, North Carolina, to a M. Gabriel Emmanueli, Carthage, Tunis, which was intercepted by the Vichy French censors on 15 September 1941. Schwarzschild's article is an extrapolation – largely speculative – which appears to be based on the same MI6 source who leaked the "Hess" story to the French military.

51. Report prepared by L. Beria on cryptogram received from London, No.

450, 21 October 1942, Folio 230, "Black Bertha" File 20566 KAM.

52. The original plan is set out as quoted by Hamilton in *Motive for a Mission*, p. 116. The Haushofer papers show that on 1 September Hess had a meeting with his former professor, who two days later asked his son Albrecht whether he could arrange a meeting to take peace soundings with either General Sir Ian Hamilton (a retired British military strategist who was outspokenly pro-German) or the Duke of Hamilton. As a result Haushofer held lengthy discussions at Hess's residence at Gallspach on 8 September on the best way of arranging for mediation with Britain. Already in the summer of 1940 Haushofer had sent a peace plan to Hoare using as a go-between one of his former pupils, Herbert Stahmer, a secretary at the German Embassy in Madrid. Albrecht believed that diplomats who had in the past expressed pro-German sympathies, such as Hoare or Lord Lothian, British Ambassador in Washington, would be the most effective in relaying the peace plan, but Hess leaned toward the Duke of Hamilton because of the direct connections he was believed to have with the King and the anti-Churchill faction in the House of Lords. Two days after these discussions, Hess wrote to Karl Haushofer that he believed the most promising channel was for Albrecht to write to take soundings of the Duke of Hamilton. Owing to postal delays this letter was not received by Haushofer *père* until 18 September. Five days later Haushofer *fils* wrote his letter to the Duke of Hamilton that was to be intercepted by the postal examiner and sent to MI5. For the censor's handwritten note of the letter, see INF 1/912 PRO. The full text of the letter is quoted in Hamilton, *Motive for a Mission*, pp. 146 ff.

53. Klaus Scholder (ed.) *Die Mittwochs-Gesellschaft. Protokolle aus dem geistigen Deutschland 1932 bis 1944* (Berlin, 1982); the von Hassel *Diaries*, 10 August 1940, p. 145, refers to peace feelers "between Kelly (British Minister in Berne) and Hohenlohe . . . at the beginning of July 1940"

54. Letter of 20 June 1940 Hohenlohe-Hewel, Hewel Papers AAB.

55. Felix Kersten, *The Kersten Memoirs 1940–1945* (London, 1956), pp. 208–9; Kelly to Foreign Office, 14 July 1940, FO 371/24407 PRO.

56. Kelly telegram re meeting with Hohenlohe, 9 December 1940, FO 371/24408; PREM 4/100/8 "Hohenlohe."

57. B.B.C. Broadcast Propaganda No. 29, "Rudolf Hess: Broadcast references to his Activities during the Period April 20–May 14 1941," dated 15 May 1941, INF 1/912 PRO. It is interesting to find that British military Intelligence raised the matter immediately with the Foreign Office, which in turn sought clarification from the British Ambassador in Madrid. "Rumoured visit of Herr Hess to Madrid," FO C41310, 4131 FO 371/26945 PRO.

58. As quoted by Hamilton in *Motive for a Mission* from Walter Stubbe, "In Memoriam Albrecht Haushofer," *Vierteljahrshefte für Zeitgeschichte*, July 1960, p. 253.

59. Entries for 3 and 5 May in Martha Haushofer, *Diary*, quoted by Jacobsen in *Karl Haushofer* (Boppard, 1979), p. 508.

60. Erika Mann, *"Also doch" Die Nation*, 20 February 1946; von Hassel, *Diaries*, p. 194; Ulrich Schlie, *The Western Powers, Germany and the Peace Issue in World War II 1939–41* (unpublished MS.).

61. Schlie, op. cit.

62. In a letter to *The Times*, 20 August 1987, James Leasor, author of *The Uninvited Envoy* (London, 1962), recalled his interview in 1960 with Lord Beaverbrook. A detailed presentation of Hess's wartime psychiatric history and medical records is to be found in Irving's very thorough *Hess: The Missing Years 1941–1945* (London, 1987).

Appendix 1
(*pp. 461–4*)

1. Colville, *Diaries*, p. 121.

2–3. Boothby, *Memoirs*, p. 144.

4. Chamberlain, *Diary*, 9 September 1940. The case that Chamberlain really intended Churchill to succeed him is argued by David Carlton in *Anthony Eden* (London, 1960), pp. 160–3. He does not, however, develop the rationale that Chamberlian had reason to suspect the Foreign Secretary of defeatism. I am grateful to Dr. Carlton for discussing his theory and my additional interpretation (interview, July 1989).

5. "Kingsley Wood. Question and Answer." The Woods memorandum was discovered amongst the papers of Lord Beaverbrook in a file of notes labelled "Italy to Readers Digest" by Paul Addison and interpreted in *The Road to 1945: British Politics and the Second World War*.

Appendix 2
(pp. 465–9)

1. For a general summary of the opposition, see Harold C. Deutsch, *The Conspiracy against Hitler in the Twilight War*. A fuller account is Lothar Kettenacker (ed.), *Das Andere in Deutschland in zweiten Weltkrieg: Emigration und Widerstand in Internationaler Perspektive* (Stuttgart, 1977). Professor Owen Chadwick's *Britain and the Vatican in the Second World War* (Cambridge, 1986) complements the original research by Peter Ludlow, "Pabst Pius XII, die britische Regierung und die deutsche Opposition im Winter 1939–40," *Vierteljahrshefte für Zeitgeschichte*, 1974.

2. Conwell-Evans is listed as a member and attender of functions of the Anglo-German Fellowship; see for example *The Times*, 15 July 1936. William L. Shirer, *The Rise and Fall of the Third Reich*, op. cit., p. 858, describes Conwell-Evans as "both an expert on Nazism and to some extent a sympathizer with it." Kordt, in a 1966 interview with Professor Deutsch, agreed, but said that Conwell-Evans later "underwent a considerable reversal" (Deutsch, op. cit., pp. 157–63, citing Erich Kordt, *Nicht aus den Acten* (Stuttgart, 1950), p. 338). Further information was supplied in conversations with Ulrich Schlie, resulting from his *The Western Powers, Germany and the Peace Issue in World War II, 1939–41* (unpublished MS.).

3. Messermith Memoranda, 20 November and 8 December 1939, in von Trott file 862.2011 RG 59 NAW; interview with Sir Frank Roberts. For a description of Von Trott's mission, see Giles MacDonagh, *A Good German: Adam Von Trott zu Solz* (New York, 1988), pp. 142 ff. The Jewish Supreme Court Justice Felix Frankfurter appears to have been responsible for Roosevelt's hostility to Von Trott. See also J. Edgar Hoover's negative reports on his activities in the PSF "Safe File" FDRL.

4. Interview with Sir Frank Roberts.

5. *The Von Hassel Diaries 1938–1944*, op. cit., p. xi. See also the enlarged edition, *Von anderen Deutschland, Die Hassel Tages-Bücher 1938–1944* (Berlin, 1988).

6. A fresh twist was added to the delicate secret negotiations by Vatican rumours that Hitler had fixed 14 January for launching his offensive against the West. The warning almost certainly originated from Hans Oster in the Abwehr and was leaked deliberately by the Pope, who had to protect his conscience and his *bona fides* if Holland or Belgium were attacked. According to Father Leiber there were seven exchanges from each side – a number that exceeds the records in Halifax's secret peace files. But both sources concur on the significance of the discussions that took place after the Pope had relayed Halifax's January response to his German contact.

7. Osborne to Halifax, "Personal and Secret," 7 February 1940, H/XV/370 FO 800/318 PRO; Leiber interview, quoted by Deutsch, op. cit., p. 148; this was a reference to the forced landing in Belgium by a German staff officer on 10 January who was found to be carrying part of the war plans for the O.K.W.'s offensive to the West.

8. George VI to Halifax, 18 February 1940, FO 371/24405 PRO.

9. Von Hassel, *Diary*, 16 and 18 March 1940.

Appendix 3

(pp. 470–3)

1. In the 1950s, Lonsdale Bryans wrote an overdramatized account, *Blind Victory*.

2. Folio 9, the first of three letters from Lord Brocket to Halifax, has been extracted from FO 800/326 H/XLIII/12 PRO, but it is in Brocket to Halifax, 25 February 1940, which was declassified.

3. Bryans, op. cit., p. 112; interview with Sir Frank Roberts.

4. Brocket to Halifax, 17 March 1940, H/XLIII/12 FO 800/326 PRO; Loraine to Foreign Office, 18 January 1940, H/XLIII 8FO 371/326 PRO.

5. Bryans, op. cit., pp. 63–7, elaborating on his undated typewritten report to Lord Halifax in FO 800/395 PRO.

6. Von Hassel, *Diary*, 22 February 1940; Peace Moves from Germany (Mr. Baldwin Raper) C3537, 22 February 1940, in FO 371/24406 PRO; cf. Halifax jacket note.

7. Memorandum to Secretary of State by Vansittart, 11 March 1940, FO 371/24406 PRO.

8. Bryans, op. cit., p. 74.

9. Von Hassel, *Diary*, 15 April 1940; Bryans, op. cit., p. 80.

10. Brocket to Cadogan, 17 March 1940, N/XLIII/40 PRO, FO 800/326 endorsed with minute signed A.C.

11. Von Hassel, *Diary*, 17–18 February.

Appendix 4

(pp. 474–5)

1. The full thirteen-page memorandum prepared by F.B.I. Special Agents Avery M. Warren and Lawrence C. Frank, dated 13 March 1940, is Item 534, "Moscow" in the Hoover File in the F.D.R. Library

Appendix 5

(pp. 476–8)

1. In 1942 all overseas legations were equipped with the U.S. Navy's reconditioned enciphering machines, which became the standard means of sending secure communications to and from the State Department. Information supplied by Lawrence Hiles, in Hiles letters to Harry Elmer Barnes, February 1964, "Toland Collection," FDRL.

2. David Kahn, *The Codebreakers* (New York, 1967), pp. 325 and 493; this according to Kent. He wrote on 16 February 1964 to Richard Whalen, biographer of Joseph P. Kennedy (*The Founding Father*, op. cit.), and sent a copy of his letter to Dr. Harry Elmer Barnes, the revisionist historian. Whalen relayed the information to Lawrence Hiles, who responded on 19 February 1964: Hiles/Barnes Correspondence, February 1964, "Toland Collection," FDRL.

3. "Secret and confidential" report on security at the U.S. Embassy, London, 22 March 1937: U.S. Emb London Confidential File 1937–8 RG 59 NAW; reports on breakdown by cipher and subject of the 1,500 telegrams found in Kent's flat: "Kent File," U.S. Emb London Confidential File 1939–40 RG 59 NAW.

4. Hiles correspondence, op. cit.

5. Kent letter to Whalen, 16 February 1964, op. cit.

6. Hiles correspondence, op. cit.; Hiles cites this among several examples to show that Roosevelt was well aware which cipher offered him secrecy and which did not.

7. Memorandum by Commander Alistair Denniston, former chief of GC & CS, dated 1944 (Den 1/4), Denniston Papers CCA; Kent interview.

Appendix 6

(pp. 479–80)

1. Identifiable as M.P.s in the Right Club membership list are: Peter Agnew, Conservative, Camborne, Sir Ernest Bennett, National Labour, Cardiff Central; Sir Samuel Chapman, Conservative & Unionist, South Edinburgh; Sir Albert Edmonson, Conservative & Unionist, Banbury Division of Oxford; Lt.-Col. Charles Kerr (later Lord Teviot), National Liberal, Montrose Burghs; John McKie, Conservative, North Galloway; Colonel Sir Harold Mitchell, Conservative, Clackmannanshire; Captain Archibald Ramsay, Conservative, Peebles; Hon. John Stourton (later Lord Mowbray), Conservative, Salford South; Mrs Mavis Constance Tate, Conservative, Frome. Identifiable as peers: Lord Carnegie (later the Earl of Inveresk); Marquess of Graham (later the Duke of Montrose); Earl of Galloway; Baron David Redesdale; Baron Semphill; the 5th Duke of Wellington. Information obtained from Dr. Griffiths.

2. Southesk and Montrose interviewed and quoted by James Hanning of the London *Evening Standard*, 12 May 1990.

3. Letter from Sir Frederic Bennett published in the *Daily Telegraph*, 22 May 1990; *Daily Telegraph*, 24 May 1990.

Appendix 7

(pp. 481–4)

1. Directive for the Conduct of the War in the West, 9 October 1939, in Ellis, *War in France*, op. cit., p. 351; cited in Liddell Hart, LH 9/24/218 KUL.

2. Lieutenant General Gerhard Engel, who was Army Adjutant seconded to Hitler, 23 May 1940, copy of the memorandum in the Munich Institut für Zeitgeschichte. See Hans Meier-Welcker, "Der Entschluss zum Anhalten der deutschen Panzertruppen in Flandern 1940," *Vierteljahrshefte für Zeitgeschichte* II, July 1954, p. 288. Engel is cited by Jacobsen, op. cit., p. 56, and David Irving, *Göring* (New York, 1989), p. 290. Irving additionally cites the 254-page memo by Nicolaus

von Below. However, the published version of the account of Hitler's Luftwaffe adjutant does not specify whether Göring's bragging telephone call was made on Thursday or the Friday. Nicolaus von Below, *Als Hitlers Adjutant 1935–45* (Mainz, 1970), p. 232; transcript of tape made by Schmid in 1954 and transcribed by Walter Ansel for Liddell Hart 9/24/218 Liddell Hart Papers KUL. Ansel's published account assigns the conversation to 23 May. It is possible that Schmid's usually reliable memory was at fault, but since his recollection was so vivid, it is more likely that the final decision *was* taken on the 24th, as his account implies. This is also corroborated by his recollection of Jesshonnek's call to Jodl to agree on the orders to be cut. If this had been done the day before, as Ansel claims, then it would not have been a surprise to von Brauchitsch to find that the Luftwaffe were given the assignment of containing the B.E.F. on the evening of the 24th. While Göring may well have been pressing the Luftwaffe's right to share in the final victory, interestingly the Engel account (above) suggests that even Hitler's adjutant was uncertain until he arrived at von Rundstedt's headquarters that Friday morning. The balance of the factors as they are now known suggests that Hitler endorsed the plan until after he had given the Halt Order. If it had been decided the day before, he would surely have issued the orders to O.K.H. on 23 May, and not, as actually happened, on 24 May.

3. Schmid tape, op. cit.; diaries, notes and records of General Adolf Heusinger, a staff officer at O.K.H. cited by Pierre Galante, *Hitler Lives* (London, 1981), p. 91. See also Kurt Assman, *Deutsche Schicksalsjahre* (Wiesbaden, 1950), p. 167.

4. Ibid.

5. Halder, *Journal*, 24 May 1940.

6–7. Reproduced by Jacobsen and Röhwer in *Dokumente zum Westfeldzug*, op. cit., p. 127.

8. Interview with Warlimont, quoted by Basil Liddell Hart, *World War II*, op. cit., p. 82; interview with von Kleist, quoted

by Liddell Hart, *The German Generals Talk*, op. cit., p. 134.

9. Blumentritt to Liddell Hart, 17 May 1950, LH 9/24/218 KUL.

Appendix 8
(pp. 485–7)

1. Adolf Hitler, *Mein Kampf* (New York, 1939), p. 980; *Adolf Hitler's Secret Book*, introduction by Telford Taylor (New York, 1965), p. 157. See the seminal conclusions of the late Professor Andreas Hilgruber, especially *Germany and the Two World Wars* (Harvard, 1981), *Hitlers Strategie, Politik und Kriegführung 1940–41* (Frankfurt-am-Main, 1965); *Kontinuität und Diskintinuität in der deutschen Aussenpolitik von Bismarck bis Hitler* (Düsseldorf, 1971); the works of Professor Klaus Hildebrand further develop the theme of the underlying unity of Hitler's global strategy and diplomatic aims: *The Foreign Policy of the Third Reich* (Berkeley, 1971) and *The Third Reich* (London, 1984). See also Professor Eberhard Jäckel, *Hitler's World View: a Blueprint for Power* (Connecticut, 1972) and *Hitler in History* (New England, 1984), and Hans-Adolf Jacobsen, *Nationalsozialistische Aussenpolik, 1933–1938* (Frankfurt-am-Main, 1968), *Der Weg zur Teilung der Welt: Politik und Strategie 1939 bis 1945* (Coblenz, 1977). These works reinforce the arguments in support of the interpretation given in the works of Hilgruber and Hidebrand. An opposing view is taken by Gerhard Weinberg in *The Foreign Policy of Hitler's Germany* (Chicago, 1980) and "Hitler and England 1933–1945: Pretence and Reality," *German Studies Review*, Vol. 8, 1985, pp. 299 ff. The question of whether Hitler was aiming at world domination or only at domination of Europe is still highly controversial for historians. For a discussion of the principal arguments see Milan Hauner, "Did Hitler Want a World Domination?" *Journal of Contemporary History*, Vol. 13, 1978, pp. 15 ff.; Jochen Thies, *Architekt der Weltherrrschaft* (Düsseldorf, 1980) and Norman Rich, *Hitler's War Aims* (New York, 1974).

2. Hitler, *Mein Kampf*, ed. cit., p. 899; Carl J. Burckhardt, *Meine Danziger Mission, 1937–1939* (Munich, 1960), p. 348.

Appendix 9
(pp. 488–90)

1. See Warren P. Kimball, *Churchill and Roosevelt: The Complete Correspondence* (Princeton, 1984), pp. xx–xxi.

2. Minutes of J.V. Perowne and J. Balfour dated 14 June 1940 on the copy of Churchill's 13 June cable sent to Lord Lothian FO 371/24192 PRO.

3. See letter from Eric Seal (P.M. Private Secretary) to Foreign Office, 17 June 1940, FO 371/24192; Peck to Mallet, 3 July 1940, FO 371/24192, folio 239; minute by Cadogan, 14 June 1940, FO 371/24192, folio 243, PRO.

4. I am grateful to Jasper Wight for making available to me the results of his research for *A Matter of Life and Death: A Study of Churchill and Roosevelt's private correspondence during the crucial period between Dunkirk and the Fall of France.*

5. These telephone conversations of 4 July 1943 and 5 February 1944 and the German records that have surfaced showed that the transatlantic radio circuits were monitored from a converted youth hostel on the Dutch coast by the Research Institute of the Deutsche Reichspost known as the *Forschungsstelle*. An authoritative analysis of what is known about German SIGINT is given by David Kahn, *Hitler's Spies*, pp. 172–9; Perowne minute, 14 June op. cit.

Appendix 10
(pp. 491–5)

1ff. Minute, 13 December 1944, FO 371/43509 PRO; Mallet to Foreign Office, 18 November 1944, following cable of 6 November 1944, FO 371/43509 PRO.

2. Minute by Labourchere and marginal note by Mallet FO 188/488 PRO;

Munch-Petersen, "Common Sense and Not Bravado," op. cit.; Chief of Foreign Office Northern Department to Mallet, 28 December 1944, FO 371/4368 PRO.

3. Miss D.A. Bingley, Foreign Office Librarian's Department, to Prytz, 30 August 1946, FO 370/1321 PRO; Prytz report to Swedish Foreign Ministry, 28 August 1946, HP 39A/XXXIII; Swedish Foreign Ministry, *Transiteringsfrgen juni–december 1940 (Akstycken utgivina av Kungl. Utrikesdepartementet*, Stockholm, 1947), p. V; *Aftonbladet*, 18 February 1947; Minutes of 29 November and 15 December 1947 FO 371/66493 PRO.

4. Minute of 3 February 1948 FO 188/609 PRO; *Daily Telegraph*, 10 September 1965; *Daily Express*, 10 September 1940; Lord Butler of Saffron Walden, *The Art of the Possible*, op. cit., p. 100.

5. Butler, ibid.

6. Anthony Howard, *RAB: The Life of R.A. Butler* (London, 1987), p. 100; Mallet to Foreign Office, 6 November 1944, FO 371/43509 PRO; Howard, ibid.

7. Prytz to Foreign Ministry, 14 June 1940, UDA HP39a/XXV.

8. Minute of 8 November on "Anglo–Swedish Relations," jacket N 698/865/42 FO 371/43509 PRO; Folio 29 of N 7102/685/42 is "retained in the Department of origin," FO 371/43509 PRO.

Appendix 11

(pp. 496–9)

1. The conviction of de Courcy at the Central Criminal Court in December 1963 was on a charge of "inducing a person to enter an agreement by dishonest concealment of material facts" and it involved eight forgery and two perjury counts relating to a property development scheme in Southern Rhodesia in which it was alleged investors had been defrauded. The prosecution resulted in a two-month court case that hinged on ante-dating of documents by de Courcy in a complex web of overseas land and development companies. The case finally turned on the affidavit of a Swiss national, Baron Peter von Dumreicher, the principal Crown witness, whose testimony de Courcy challenged as unreliable. Although he lost a subsequent appeal, escaping from custody in the process to draw attention to his case, de Courcy has resolutely continued his legal efforts to have the conviction overturned on the grounds that the testimony on which he was convicted was false (papers relating to the case of *R. v. Courcy*, Hoover Institution).

2. Still an energetic correspondent, de Courcy sets great store by the importance of his freelance reporting to MI6. That he certainly contributed to MI6 is evident from the series of report in Box 1, files 13–14, de Courcy Papers. But he was only one of a large network of unpaid young men with good political connections at home and overseas whom Menzies relied on to feed him with gossip and intelligence. But the number of Foreign Office entries on de Courcy attests to the wide circulation of the *Intelligence Digest* and the resentment of professional officials at the editor's assertions that the information and opinion the journal disseminated was authoritative and semi-official. Their irritation with de Courcy became acute after the war began; interview with de Courcy, July 1989.

3. Minute on "Activities of the Imperial Policy Group in United States" by J. Balfour, 15 February 1939, FO 371/2287 PRO.

4. De Courcy interview; De Courcy to Butler, 20 April 1940, RAB E3/4 TCCA.

5. *Memorandum of Information on Foreign Affairs*, April Issue, 28 April 1940, "The Northern Crisis" and "Reaction in France," copy in Butler Papers RAB E3/4 TCCA.

6. Roger Hinds, *The Gymnasium of the Mind* (Salisbury, 1984), p. 701.

Index

590

594

597

598

599